Brief Contents

UNIT 1 Entrepreneurial Pathways 23

Chapter 1 Entrepreneurs Recognize Opportunities 24

Chapter 2 Franchising 56

Chapter 3 Finding Opportunity in an Existing Business 78

Chapter 4 The Business Plan: Road Map to Success 96

Honest Tea Business Plan 127

Unit 1 **Entrepreneurial Pathways: SPANX—Idea to Entrepreneurial Opportunity 154**

UNIT 2 Who Are Your Customers? 159

Chapter 5 Creating Business from Opportunity 160

Chapter 6 Exploring Your Market 190

Unit 2 **Opportunity Assessment: Kitchen Arts & Letters, Inc.— An Independent Bookstore Defies Industry Odds 217**

UNIT 3 Integrated Marketing 221

Chapter 7 Developing the Right Marketing Mix and Plan 222

Chapter 8 Pricing and Credit Strategies 246

Chapter 9 Integrated Marketing Communications 270

Chapter 10 Marketing Globally 310

Chapter 11 Smart Selling and Effective Customer Service 344

Unit 3 **Integrated Marketing: Empact—Making an Impact for Entrepreneurs 368**

UNIT 4 Show Me the Money: Finding, Securing, and Managing It 371

Chapter 12 Understanding and Managing Start-Up, Fixed, and Variable Costs 372

Chapter 13 Using Financial Statements to Guide a Business 396

Chapter 14 Cash Flow and Taxes 432

Chapter 15 Financing Strategy: Debt, Equity, or Both? 462

Unit 4 **Show Me the Money: Finding, Securing, and Managing It— Lee's Ice Cream 492**

UNIT 5 Operating a Small Business Effectively 497

Chapter 16 Addressing Legal Issues and Managing Risk 498

Chapter 17 Operating for Success 530

Chapter 18 Location, Facilities, and Layout 558

Chapter 19 Human Resources and Management 582

Unit 5 **Operating a Small Business Effectively: ONLC Training Centers—Virtual IT Training in a Classroom 613**

UNIT 6 Leadership, Ethics, and Exits 617

Chapter 20 Leadership and Ethical Practices 618

Chapter 21 Franchising, Licensing, and Harvesting: Cashing in Your Brand 636

Unit 6 **Cashing in the Brand: Honest Tea— From Start-Up to Harvest 655**

Appendix 1 Sample Student Business Plan 661
Appendix 2 BizBuilder Business Plan 689
Appendix 3 Resources for Entrepreneurs 696
Appendix 4 Useful Formulas and Equations 702
Glossary 703
Index 711

Contents

UNIT 1 Entrepreneurial Pathways 23

Chapter 1

Entrepreneurs Recognize Opportunities 24

Entrepreneurship Defined 25
    What Is an Entrepreneur? 25
    The Economic Questions 26
    Voluntary Exchange 27
    Benefits and Challenges of Free Enterprise 27
    What Is a Small Business? 28

Why Become an Entrepreneur? 28
    The Desire to Make Money Is Not the Only Reason to Start a Business 30
    Definitions of Success—Monetary and Other 30
    Taking the Long View 31

Benefits and Costs of Becoming an Entrepreneur 31
    Cost/Benefit Analysis 32
    Opportunity Cost 33
    Seeking Advice and Information to Succeed 33

Entrepreneurial Options 35

How Do Entrepreneurs Find Opportunities to Start New Businesses? 37
    Entrepreneurs Creatively Exploit Changes in Our World 37
    Where Others See Problems, Entrepreneurs Recognize Opportunities 38
    Train Your Mind to Recognize Business Opportunities 38
    Entrepreneurs Use Their Imaginations 39

An Idea Is Not Necessarily an Opportunity 39
    Opportunity Is Situational 40
    The Five Roots of Opportunity in the Marketplace 40
    Integrating Internal and External Opportunities 40
    Establishing Strategies 41

Paths to Small Business Ownership 42
    Securing Franchise Rights 42
    Buying an Existing Business 42
    Licensing Technology 43
    Do Not Take Unfair Advantage of Someone Else's Creativity 43
    The Many Faces of Entrepreneurship 44

Making the Business Work Personally and Professionally 45
    A Business Must Make a Profit to Stay in Business 45
    Profit Is the Sign That the Entrepreneur Is Adding Value 45
    Profit Results from the Entrepreneur's Choices 45
    Seven Rules for Building a Successful Business 46
    The Team Approach 46

Chapter 2

Franchising 56

Defining Franchising 57
    What Are the Types of Franchises? 57

Positive Aspects of Franchises 59
    Start-Up Assistance 59
    Instant Recognition 60
    Purchasing Power 60
    Advertising and Promotional Support 60
    Operating Guidelines and Assistance 61
    Record of Success 62

Drawbacks of Buying a Franchise 62
    Constraints on Creativity and Freedom 62
    Costs 63
    Standards and Termination 64

The Structure of the Franchise Industry 64

Franchising and the Law 65

Steps for Franchise Selection 67

Exploring Global Franchising Opportunities 69

Chapter 3

Finding Opportunity in an Existing Business 78

Reasons to Buy an Existing Business 80
    Quicker, Easier Start-Up 80
    Reduced Risk 80
    Bargain Potential 81
    Your Knowledge Can Be Beneficial 81

Potential Pitfalls of Buying an Existing Business 81
    Investment Requirements 82
    Buying Someone Else's Problems 82
    Business Is Not a Good Fit 83

Finding and Evaluating Available Businesses 83

Sources of Existing Businesses   83

Due Diligence—Reality versus the Story   84

Determining the Value of a Business   86

Negotiating and Closing a Purchase   88

Buying into a Business over Time   88

Family Business as an Entrepreneurial Opportunity   88

Chapter 4   The Business Plan: Road Map to Success   96

Feasibility Analysis: Does My Idea Work?   97

Analyzing Product and/or Service Feasibility   98

Analyzing Market and Industry Feasibility   99

Analyzing Financial Feasibility   101

Creating a Business Model Canvas   102

What Is a Business Plan?   105

Why Do You Need a Business Plan?   106

Writing a Business Plan Early Will Save You Time and Money   106

Your Business Plan Is the Key to Raising Capital   107

The Business Plan Is an Operations Guide   107

Business Plan Components   107

Cover Page and Table of Contents   108

Executive Summary: A Snapshot of Your Business   108

Mission, Vision and Culture   109

Company Description: Background and Track Record   110

Opportunity Analysis and Research: Testing Ideas   110

Marketing Strategy and Plan: Reaching Customers   111

Management and Operations: Making the Plan Happen   112

Financial Analysis and Projections: Translating Action into Money   113

Funding Request and Exit Strategy: The Ask and the Return   117

Appendices: Making the Case in Greater Detail   118

Business Plan Suggestions   118

Presenting Your Business Plan   119

Business Plan and Venture Competitions   120

Honest Tea Business Plan   127

Unit 1   **Entrepreneurial Pathways: SPANX—Idea to Entrepreneurial Opportunity   154**

UNIT 2   Who Are Your Customers?   159

Chapter 5   Creating Business from Opportunity   160

Apple and the Personal Computer   161

Business Definition   162

What Sort of Organization Do You Want?   163

Your Company's Core Values   163

Your Company's Mission Is to Satisfy Customers   164

Your Company's Vision Is the Broader Perspective   165

Your Company's Culture Defines the Work Environment   165

The Decision Process   166

Your Competitive Advantage   167

Find Your Competitive Advantage by Determining What Consumers Need and Want   168

You Have Unique Knowledge of Your Market   168

The Six Factors of Competitive Advantage   169

Is Your Competitive Advantage Strong Enough?   169

Checking Out the Competition   170

The Most Chocolate Cake Company   171

Competitive Strategy: Business Definition and Competitive Advantage   173

Feasibility Revisited: The Economics of One Unit as a Litmus Test   174

Defining the Unit of Sale   175

Cost of Goods Sold and Gross Profit   175

Your Business and the Economics of One Unit   176

The Cost of Direct Labor in the EOU— An Example   178

Hiring Others to Make the Unit of Sale   178

Going for Volume   179

Chapter 6   Exploring Your Market   190

Markets and Marketing Defined   191

A Business That Markets versus a Market-Driven Business   192

ENTRSHIP
& SM
MAN

Second Edition
Global Edition

Steve Mariotti • Caroline Glackin

PEARSON

Boston   Columbus   Indianapolis   New York   San Francisco   Upper Saddle River
Amsterdam   Cape Town   Dubai   London   Madrid   Milan   Munich   Paris   Montréal   Toronto
Delhi   Mexico City   São Paulo   Sydney   Hong Kong   Seoul   Singapore   Taipei   Tokyo

Special thanks to Shelby Cullom Davis.
Also thanks to Kathryn Davis, Shelby M. C. Davis,
Kimberly La Manna, Abby Moffat, and
Diana Davis Spencer.

—Steve Mariotti

To my children, Elise and Spencer, whose support and love
are essential parts of this book.
To my parents, Howard and Maria Wiedenman,
who truly understood the importance
of education. My love and gratitude.

—Caroline Glackin

Editor in Chief: Stephanie Wall
Head of Learning Asset Acquisition, Global Editions: Laura Dent
Acquisitions Editor: Dan Tylman
Program Management Lead: Ashley Santora
Program Manager: Claudia Fernandes
Editorial Assistant: Linda Albelli
Senior Acquisitions Editor, Global Editions: Sandhya Ghoshal
Senior Project Editor, Global Editions: Vaijyanti Ghose
Marketing Manager: Lenny Ann Raper
Project Management Lead: Judy Leale
Project Manager: Ilene Kahn

Senior Manufacturing Production Controller, Global Editions: Trudy Kimber
Media Production Manager, Global Editions: M Vikram Kumar
Procurement Specialist: Michelle Klein
Art Director: Janet Slowik
Text Designer: S4Carlisle Publishing Services
Cover Designer: Lumina Datamatics
Cover Art: Francesca Yorke © Dorling Kindersley
Full-Service Project Management: Christian Holdener; S4Carlisle Publishing Services
Composition: S4Carlisle Publishing Services

Pearson Education Limited
Edinburgh Gate Harlow
Essex CM20 2JE
England

and Associated Companies throughout the world
Visit us on the World Wide Web at:
www.pearsonglobaleditions.com

© 2015 by National Foundation for Teaching Entrepreneurship published by Pearson Education

British Library Cataloguing-in-Publication Data
A catalogue record for this book is available from the British Library

ARP impression 98

ISBN 10:   1-292-07867-7
ISBN 13: 978-1-292-07867-0

Typeset in New Aster LT Std by S4Carlisle Publishing Services

Printed and Bound in Great Britain by Ashford Colour Press Ltd

Market and Marketing Research Support
Success 192

Research Your Market *Before* You Open
Your Business 192

Types and Methods of Research 193

Getting Information Directly from the Source:
Primary Research 193

Getting Information Indirectly:
Secondary Research 194

Market Research Helps You Know
Your Customer 195

Customer Research 197

Industry Research: The 50,000-Foot
Perspective 199

Make Market Research an Integral
Part of Your Business 200

How Customers Decide to Buy 201

Owning a Perception in the Customer's
Mind 201

Features Create Benefits 202

Home Depot: Teaching Customers So
They Will Return 202

Which Segment of the Market
Will You Target? 203

Successful Segmenting: The Body Shop 203

Applying Market Segmentation Methods 204

The Product Life Cycle 206

Is Your Market Saturated? 207

Market Positioning: Drive Home
Your Competitive Advantage 207

Developing a Marketing Plan 208

**Unit 2 Opportunity Assessment:
Kitchen Arts & Letters, Inc.—
An Independent Bookstore Defies
Industry Odds 217**

UNIT 3   Integrated Marketing   221

Chapter 7   **Developing the Right Marketing
Mix and Plan 222**

The Four Marketing Factors 223

Product: What Are You Selling? 224

Create Your Total Product or Service
Concept 224

Focus Your Brand 225

Ford's Costly Failure: The Edsel 225

Ford's Focus on Success: The Mustang 225

How to Build Your Brand 226

Price: What It Says about Your
Product 228

Place: Location, Location, Location! 228

Promotion: Advertising + Publicity 229

The Fifth P: Philanthropy 229

Cause-Related Marketing 230

Gaining Goodwill 230

Not-for-Profit Organizations 231

Teach for America and Upromise 231

What Entrepreneurs Have Built 232

You Have Something to Contribute 232

Developing a Marketing Plan 232

Marketing Analysis 233

Marketing as a Fixed Cost 234

Calculate Your Breakeven Point 234

Chapter 8   **Pricing and Credit Strategies 246**

Pricing: Image, Value, and Competition
Together 247

Strategies and Tactics for Effective
Pricing 248

Pricing Varies by the Type of Firm 251

Pricing Techniques for Manufacturers 251

Pricing Techniques for Wholesalers 252

Pricing Techniques for Retailers 252

Keystoning—The Retailer's Rule
of Thumb 253

Pricing Techniques for Service
Businesses 254

Pricing Principles 255

Extending Credit to Customers 255

The Costs and Benefits of Credit 255

Types of Credit 255

Credit's Impact on Pricing 257

Managing the Credit Process 258

Sources of Credit Information 259

Aging of Receivables 259

Credit Regulation 259

Discounts, Incentives, and Other
Price Adjustments 260

Chapter 9   **Integrated Marketing
Communications 270**

Use Integrated Marketing Communications
for Success 271

Reinforce the Company's Unique Selling
Proposition 271

Promotional Planning 272

Create a Promotional Strategy Using
Promotions Opportunity Analysis 272

Determine a Promotional Budget 274

The Advertising Advantage   275
   Advertising Agencies and Freelancers   276
   Types of Advertising   277
   Media Planning and Buying:
   Focus on Your Customer   278
   The Media   278
   Broadcast Media   279
   Print Media   280
   Outdoor Advertising (Out-of-Home
   Advertising)   282
   Advertising Measurement: Beyond Reach
   and Frequency   284
   Marketing Materials Should Reinforce
   Your Competitive Advantage   286
   Collateral Materials: Print and
   Multimedia   286

Sales-Promotion Solutions   287
   When to Use Promotional Tools   287
   Advertising Specialties   287
   Trade Show Exhibits   288
   Mall Carts or Kiosks   288

Alternative Marketing   289
   Other Media Venues   290

Database and Direct-Response
Marketing   291
   Data Collection, Coding, and Mining   291
   Marketing Communications Driven
   by Databases   292

E-Active Marketing   293

Publicity Potential   296
   Generating Publicity   296
   Telling the Story   297
   Sample Press Release   298
   Follow Up a Press Release   298
   Public Relations   298

Chapter 10   **Marketing Globally   310**
Reasons to Market Globally   311
   Market Expansion   312
   Access to Resources   314
   Cost Reduction   315
   Location-Specific Advantages   315
   Improving Quality Levels   316

Strategy Options for Global Ventures   316
   Importing   316
   Exporting   317
   Strategic Alliances   321
   International Licensing   322
   International Franchising   323
   International Facilities   323

Challenges to International Trade   324
   Economic Risk   324
   Political Risk   325
   Organizational Capacity   325
   Legal and Regulatory Barriers   327
   Cultural and Ethnic Considerations   328

Support for Global Ventures   329
   Market Research, Analysis, Planning,
   and Readiness   329
   Customer and Partner Identification
   and Relationship Building   330
   Financing   331

Trade Agreements Influence Global
Marketing   334

Chapter 11   **Smart Selling and Effective
Customer Service   344**
Selling Skills Are Essential to Business
Success   345
   Selling Is a Great Source of Market
   Research   346
   The Essence of Selling Is Teaching   346
   The Principles of Selling   346

The Sales Call   348
   Electronic Mail, Blogs, and Social
   Networks   348
   Prequalify Your Sales Calls   349
   Focus on the Customer   349
   The Eight-Step Sales Call   350
   Three Call Behaviors of Successful
   Salespeople   351
   Analyze Your Sales Calls to Become
   a Star Salesperson   351
   Turning Objections into Advantages   352
   Use Technology to Sell   352

Successful Businesses Need Customers
Who Return   354
   Customer Service Is Keeping Customers
   Happy   354
   The Costs of Losing a Customer   354
   Customer Complaints Are Valuable   355

Customer Relationship Management
Systems   356
   Why Does CRM Matter?   357
   Components of CRM for the Small
   Business   358
   How Technology Supports CRM   359

Unit 3   **Integrated Marketing:
Empact—Making an Impact
for Entrepreneurs   368**

UNIT 4   Show Me the Money: Finding, Securing, and Managing It   371

Chapter 12   **Understanding and Managing Start-Up, Fixed, and Variable Costs   372**

What Does It Cost to Operate a Business?   373

Start-Up Investment   374

Brainstorm to Avoid Start-Up Surprises   374

Keep a Reserve Equal to One-Half the Start-Up Investment   375

Predict the Payback Period   376

Estimate Value   377

Fixed and Variable Costs: Essential Building Blocks   378

Calculating Critical Costs   378

Calculating Total Gross Profit (Contribution Margin)   379

Calculating EOU When You Sell Multiple Products   379

Fixed Operating Costs   381

Fixed Operating Costs Can Change Over Time   381

Allocate Fixed Operating Costs Where Possible   382

The Dangers of Fixed Costs   383

Using Accounting Records to Track Fixed and Variable Costs   383

Three Reasons to Keep Good Records Every Day   383

Cash versus Accrual Accounting Methods   386

Recognizing Categories of Costs   386

Chapter 13   **Using Financial Statements to Guide a Business   396**

Scorecards for the Entrepreneur: What Do Financial Statements Show?   397

Income Statements: Showing Profit and Loss Over Time   398

Parts of an Income Statement   398

A Basic Income Statement   399

The Double Bottom Line   400

An Income Statement for a More Complex Business   400

The Balance Sheet: A Snapshot of Assets, Liabilities, and Equity at a Point in Time   402

Short- and Long-Term Assets   404

Current and Long-Term Liabilities   404

The Balance Sheet Equation   404

The Balance Sheet Shows Assets and Liabilities Obtained through Financing   404

The Balance Sheet Shows How a Business Is Financed   405

Analyzing a Balance Sheet   406

Depreciation   408

Financial Ratio Analysis: What Is It and What Does It Mean to You?   408

Income Statement Ratios   408

Balance-Sheet Analysis   411

Chapter 14   **Cash Flow and Taxes   432**

Cash Flow: The Lifeblood of a Business   433

The Income Statement Does Not Show Available Cash   433

Rules to Keep Cash Flowing   435

Noncash Expenses Can Distort the Financial Picture   435

The Working Capital Cycle   435

The Cyclical and Seasonal Nature of Cash Flow   435

Reading a Cash Flow Statement   438

The Cash Flow Equation   438

Forecasting Cash Flow: The Cash Budget   438

Creating a Healthy Cash Flow   441

Managing Inventory to Manage Cash   441

Managing Receivables to Manage Cash   443

The Cash Effects of Accounts Receivable   443

The Life Cycle of Accounts Receivable   443

The Financing of Accounts Receivable   444

Managing Accounts Payable to Manage Cash   444

Negotiating Payment   444

Timing Payables   445

Capital Budgeting and Cash Flow   445

The Burn Rate   446

The Value of Money Changes Over Time   447

The Future Value of Money   447

The Present Value of Money   448

Taxes   450

Cash Flow and Taxes   450

Filing Tax Returns   450

Collecting Sales Tax   451

Tax Issues for Different Legal
Structures   451

Make Tax Time Easier by Keeping
Good Records   451

**Chapter 15   Financing Strategy: Debt, Equity,
or Both?   462**

Going It Alone versus Securing
Financing   463

How Often Do Small Businesses Really
Fail?   464

What Is the Best Type of Financing
for You and Your Business?   464

Gifts and Grants   465

Debt Financing   466

Debt Financing: Pros and Cons   466

Equity Financing   468

Equity Financing: Pros and Cons   468

Where and How to Find Capital That
Works for You   469

Having an Excellent Business Plan Goes
a Long Way   472

How Capital Sources Read Your Business
Plan   472

Family and Friends   472

Financial Institutions and Dimensions
of Credit   472

Community Development Financial
Institutions (CDFIs)   474

Venture Capitalists   475

Angels   476

Insurance Companies   477

Vendor Financing   477

Federally Supported Investment
Companies   477

Financing for Rural/Agricultural
Businesses   477

Self-Funding: Bootstrap Financing   478

Accessing Sources Through Online
Networking   478

Investors Want Their Money to Grow:
Can You Make It Happen?   479

How Stocks Work   479

How Bonds Work   480

**Unit 4   Show Me the Money: Finding,
Securing, and Managing It—
Lee's Ice Cream   492**

**UNIT 5   Operating a Small Business
Effectively   497**

**Chapter 16   Addressing Legal Issues
and Managing Risk   498**

Business Legal Structures   499

Sole Proprietorship   499

Partnership   501

Corporation   502

Tips for Entrepreneurs Who Want to Start
a Nonprofit Organization   504

Contracts: The Building Blocks
of Business   507

Working with an Attorney   507

Drafting a Contract   508

A Successful Contract Should Achieve
the Four A's   508

Letter of Agreement   509

Breach of Contract   509

Small Claims Court   509

Arbitration   509

A Contract Is No Substitute
for Trust   509

The Uniform Commercial Code (UCC)   510

The Law of Agency   510

Bankruptcy   511

Protecting Intangible Assets:
Intellectual Property   513

Trademarks and Service Marks   513

Copyright   515

Electronic Rights   515

Patents   516

Protecting Tangible Assets:
Risk Management   517

Insurance Protects Your Business
from Disaster   517

Basic Coverage for Small Business   517

How Insurance Companies Make
Money   518

Protect Your Computer and Data   519

Disaster Recovery Plans   519

Licenses, Permits, and Certificates   520

Chapter 17   Operating for Success   530

Operations Permit Businesses to Deliver
on Their Promises   531

The Production-Distribution Chain   532

Supply Chain Management   533
  Finding Suppliers   534
  Managing Inventory   534
  Creating a Purchasing Plan   536
  Managing the Chain: Analyzing and Selecting Vendors   536
  Legal Considerations   537
The Idea-To-Product Process   537
  Why Manufacturing Is Unique   538
Job Shops   538
Manufacturing Tips   539
  Just-in-Time Manufacturing   539
  Product Design and Costs   540
  Making versus Buying   541
  Facilities Location and Design   542
Defining Quality: It Is a Matter of Market Positioning   542
  Profits Follow Quality   542
Organization-Wide Quality Initiatives   542
  Benchmarking   543
  ISO 9000   544
  Six Sigma   544
  Total Quality Management   545
  Malcolm Baldrige Award   545
Using Technology to Your Advantage   546
  Computer Access Is Essential   546
  Capture the Potential of the Telephone   546
  Identify Market-Specific Software and Technology   547
  Electronic Storefront (Web Site)   547

Chapter 18   Location, Facilities, and Layout   558
The Importance of Physical Location   559
Key Factors in Deciding on a Location   560
Different Types of Businesses Have Different Location Needs   561
  Options and Criteria for Manufacturing Facilities   561
  Options and Criteria for Wholesale Businesses   562
  Options and Criteria for Retail Businesses   562
  Options and Criteria for Service and Professional Businesses   563
  Evaluating Location Alternatives   564
  Facilities Design and Layout   569
  Special Considerations for Home-Based Businesses   572
  Special Considerations for Web-Based Businesses   573

Chapter 19   Human Resources and Management   582
Business Management: Building a Team   583
  What Do Managers Do?   583
Adding Employees to Your Business   584
  Growing Your Team   591
  Creating and Managing Organizational Culture   592
  Determining Organizational Structure   593
  Getting the Best Out of Your Employees   595
  Communicating Effectively   595
Human Resources Fundamentals   596
  Compensation and Payroll   597
  Benefits   597
  Organizational Development   597
  Education and Development   598
  Labor Law and HR Compliance   598
  Performance Management   599
  Human Resources Strategy   602
  Firing and Laying Off Employees   602

Unit 5   Operating a Small Business Effectively: ONLC Training Centers—Virtual IT Training in a Classroom   613

UNIT 6   Leadership, Ethics, and Exits   617

Chapter 20   Leadership and Ethical Practices   618
The Entrepreneur as Leader   619
  Leadership Styles That Work   619
  How Entrepreneurs Pay Themselves   620
  Manage Your Time Wisely   621
Ethical Leadership and Ethical Organizations   622
  An Ethical Perspective   623
  Establishing Ethical Standards   623
  Corporate Ethical Scandals   625
  Integrity and Entrepreneurial Opportunities   626
  What Is Integrity?   626
  Doing the Right Thing in Addition to Doing Things Right   626
  Balancing the Needs of Owners, Customers, and Employees   627
  Complying with the Law   627

Social Responsibility and Ethics 628

   Leading with Integrity and Examples 628

   Encourage Your Employees to Be Socially Responsible 628

Chapter 21 **Franchising, Licensing, and Harvesting: Cashing in Your Brand 636**

What Do You Want from Your Business? 637

   Continuing the Business for the Family 637

   Growth through Diversification 638

Growth through Licensing and Franchising 638

   Focus Your Brand 639

   When Licensing Can Be Effective 639

   Franchising Revisited from the Franchisor Perspective 639

   How a McDonald's Franchise Works 640

   Do Your Research before You Franchise 640

Harvesting and Exiting Options 641

   When to Harvest Your Business 641

   How to Value a Business 641

   The Science of Valuation 642

Creating Wealth by Selling a Profitable Business 643

   Harvesting Options 644

Exit Strategy Options 646

   Investors Will Care about Your Exit Strategy 647

Unit 6 Cashing in the Brand: Honest Tea—From Start-Up to Harvest 655

Appendix 1 Sample Student Business Plan— University Parent 661

Appendix 2 BizBuilder Business Plan 689

Appendix 3 Resources for Entrepreneurs 696

Appendix 4 Useful Formulas and Equations 702

   Glossary 703

   Index 711

Preface

Helping Students Own Their Future

Entrepreneurship and Small Business Management (ESBM), Second Edition, is the newest textbook in a line of entrepreneurship textbooks written by Steve Mariotti, founder of the Network for Teaching Entrepreneurship (NFTE). This is the second written with professor and entrepreneur Caroline Glackin, and it promotes entrepreneurship as a career option for college students. It is built on the success of *Entrepreneurship: Starting and Operating a Small Business,* Third Edition, with greatly expanded coverage of the details of managing and growing a small business.

Business students, as well as those from other disciplines, can benefit from *ESBM.* For business students, it recasts their prior learning from a typical corporate context and focuses it on small and entrepreneurial enterprises. For students in such fields as hospitality, the arts, engineering, and fashion merchandising, the text introduces key business concepts and provides examples from a broad range of careers. Cases from hospitality, technology, retail, manufacturing, distribution, real estate, finance, and not-for-profit organizations bring a wealth of learning opportunities. Most importantly, *ESBM 2e* is a balanced mix of the academic and applied components of entrepreneurship education. Students are introduced to the theories, methods, and requisite knowledge and skills required of entrepreneurs and are immediately given practical examples and discussion opportunities. Using the Application Exercises and Exploring Online features at the end of each chapter, they are encouraged to take this new knowledge and apply it in their own lives, so that the course materials are reinforced and internalized.

Highlights of New Content and Changes

Entrepreneurship and Small Business Management, Second Edition, contains new content and some changes, including the following:

- *Eight new Chapter Openers.* These feature more small and entrepreneurial enterprises. New cases are: Bridgecreek Development, Mercedes, Virgin Group Ltd., University Parent, Aravind Eye Care System, Chilly Dilly, inDinero, and Paula Jagemann.
- *Eleven new short End-of-Chapter Case Studies.* Urban Decay, SarahCare of Snellville, Happy Belly Curbside Kitchen, BNI, MooBella, Gentle Rest Slumber, Holterholm Farms, Gelato Fiasco, The Bun Company, Khan Academy, and Anago Cleaning Systems.
- *Seven new longer End-of-Chapter Case Studies.* Foursquare, Wahoo's Fish Tacos, Rosi and Brian Amador, Chilly Dilly's Ice Cream, Airbnb, AYZH, and iContact.

- *All New Unit Cases.* These are more current and relatable for students and include: Spanx, Kitchen Arts & Letters, Inc., Empact, Lee's Ice Cream, ONLC Training Centers, and Honest Tea.
- *Step into the Shoes, Entrepreneurial Wisdom, BizFacts, and Global Impact Features.* These have been updated and expanded with 29 new featured items, including 22 Step into the Shoes, 1 Entrepreneurial Wisdom, 2 BizFacts, and 4 Global Impact Features. These features connect chapter content to business facts and examples to reinforce learning.
- *New Honest Tea Featured Business Plan.* From its early stage funding search, this example provides students with an interesting start-up plan for a company that is also featured in the Unit 6 case.
- *BizBuilder Business Plan Questions.* These have been added to chapters to connect the content to student work using the business plan templates.

Combining Street Smarts and Academic Smarts

Entrepreneurship and Small Business Management, Second Edition, is an extension of the academic programs developed by Steve Mariotti under the auspices of NFTE. Since 1987, NFTE has reached over 500,000 graduates and trained more than 5,000 teachers in 15 countries to impart its innovative entrepreneurship curriculum through its 18 U.S. and 11 international program sites. NFTE is widely viewed as a world leader in promoting entrepreneurial literacy and has a proven track record of helping young people start a great variety of successful ventures.

This textbook unites Steve Mariotti's experience as an entrepreneur with relevant academic theory and practice, supported by a rich variety of examples and stories that include experiences from NFTE program graduates who have started their own businesses. Caroline Glackin brings years of experience in the university classroom, as a lender to small and microbusinesses, and as an entrepreneur and small business owner. Together, these two authors have produced a text that is practical, useful, and academically solid.

Organization

Entrepreneurship and Small Business Management, Second Edition, is organized to follow the life cycle of an entrepreneurial venture from concept through implementation into harvesting or replication. It is a comprehensive text written in light of the reality that college students often take only one course in entrepreneurship and the topic is covered in a multitude of ways. For instructors who will teach the course as a "business plan," *ESBM 2e* offers step-by-step content to build a plan over a semester or a quarter. For those who focus on the management of small and entrepreneurial ventures, there is an abundance of high-quality material on the critical topics of management, human resources, marketing, and operations for such ventures. For those charged with teaching a comprehensive introductory course, all of the components are provided.

Chapter Learning System

Chapter Openers Set the Stage

Each chapter starts with an inspirational quote, Learning Objectives that provide a "road map" so readers know where they are headed, and then an opening case study. The reader connects with a story of a real business in the opening vignette that sets the stage for upcoming material.

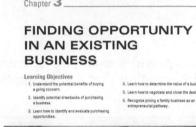

"Step into the Shoes" of the Experts

Step into the Shoes appears in each chapter and gives insight into the business practices of entrepreneurs and an opportunity to discuss the brief example. It brings the content to life with real-world application.

Step into the Shoes . . .
Maritza Gonzalez and Noel Cruz—Kumon Math and Reading Center

Kumon Math and Reading Centers, a successful franchisor, had been providing supplemental academic support to students in Newark (New Jersey) Public Schools for four years, through the No Child Left Behind program, when Maritza Gonzalez and Noel Cruz opened a new center there. Maritza is a Kumon parent (that is, a parent of a child in the Kumon system), a product of Newark Public Schools, and a graduate of Montclair State University. For her, the opportunity to direct a Kumon Math and Reading Center is a chance to give back to the community. Noel Cruz headed up the No Child Left Behind program with Kumon and was an assistant principal at a charter school in Newark. Kumon is a 54-year-old after-school math and reading program with 26,000 centers in 47 countries (more than 1,500 in the United States) that totals more than four million students globally.[3]

[3]Kumon, accessed June 23, 2009, and July 1, 2013, http://www.kumon.com/AboutUs.

Stockbyte/Thinkstock

BizFacts

BizFacts impart useful information regarding entrepreneurship statistics, company practices, or business applications.

BizFacts

Entrepreneurship has proven to be an effective way for minorities and women to enter the business world.

- More than 6.1 million businesses were minority-owned in 2007, and they generated $871 billion in revenues.
- There were more than 12.4 million non-farm businesses owned by women (or co-owned equally with men), accounting for 45.4 percent of all U.S. companies.

Source: U.S. Small Business Administration, accessed June 29, 2013, http://www.sba.gov.

Entrepreneurial Wisdom

Entrepreneurial Wisdom contains insights or advice that will help students in the preparation of a business plan or management of an enterprise.

Entrepreneurial Wisdom . . .

A new business usually will require time before it can turn a profit. Federal Express, in fact, suffered initial losses of a million dollars a month! But if you are not making enough money to stay in business, that is the market speaking. It is telling you that your business is not satisfying consumer needs well enough. Do not take it personally. Many famous entrepreneurs opened and closed a number of businesses during their lifetime.

Henry Ford failed in business twice before the Ford Motor Company was a success. If you want to be a successful entrepreneur, start growing a thick skin and decide right now that you intend to learn from failures and disappointments. Do not let them get you down. Learn, so that you do not make the same mistakes again.

Global Impact

Global Impact, featured in each chapter, provides examples of entrepreneurial ventures around the world or information that can be applied in global trade.

Global Impact . . .

Raw Material Prices Challenge Manufacturers

When the price of crude oil rises, much of the world feels the pain. Manufacturers using crude oil in their production are affected. When copper prices rise, the effects are also felt worldwide. Volatile raw-material costs in one area can have huge ripple effects on prices around the world. Whereas labor costs frequently are perceived to be a primary driver of manufacturing costs, the impact of changing raw materials prices may also be quite significant, particularly when they are volatile. Manufacturers must control raw material costs to create sustainable profits.

Manufacturers have to buy smarter, explore alternate materials, and evaluate their ability to increase prices to their customers. Manufacturers source potential materials for purchase globally to attain the most favorable pricing, making any changes an international issue. Thus, a price increase in crude oil in Saudi Arabia has ripple effects on Main Street U.S.A.

Source: Jill Jusko, "Rethinking Raw Materials," *IndustryWeek.com*, August 1, 2006, accessed March 29, 2009, http://www.industryweek.com.

New! Honest Tea Business Plan

This is the plan developed by founders Seth Goldman and Barry Nalebuff during Honest Tea's first year of operations. It appears following Chapter 4 and includes a comprehensive market analysis and detailed historical financials. The business raised over $1 million at a time when sales were less than $250,000 and the company had operating losses. The Honest Tea plan is an excellent example for students and one that many of them will intuitively understand as customers of bottled tea.

Business Plan for 1999
December 1998
4905 Del Ray Avenue, Suite 304
Bethesda, Maryland 20814
Phone: 301-652-3556
Fax: 301-652-3557

E-mail: sethandbarry@honesttea.com

Table of Contents

Mission Statement 110
Executive Summary 111
Company Story 111
The Product 112
  The Taste 112
  Low in Calories 112
  Health Benefits of Brewed Tea 113
  Cultural Experience of Tea 113
  Flagship Line of Flavors 114
Production and Manufacturing 114
Market Opportunity 115
  Beyond Snapple—The Emerging Market for Quality Bottled Tea .. 115
  Profile of Target Customer 116
  Market Research 117
  Market Response 117
Marketing and Distribution 119
  National Natural/Specialty Foods Channels 120
  Higher End Food Service 120
  Promotion 120
  Packaging and Pricing 120
  International Markets 121
  Product Development and Future Products 121
Management 121
  President & TeaEO 121
  Chairman of the Board 122
  Brewmaster 122
  National Sales Director 122
  Retail Sales Manager 122
  Consultants and Advisors 122
Statement and Aspirations for Social Responsibility .. 123
Financial Statements—Year-to-Date and Projections .. 123
The Investment Opportunity 130
  The Offering 130
  Financing History 130
  Exit Strategies 130
  Investment Risks 130
  Competitive Advantage 130
A Parting Thought 131

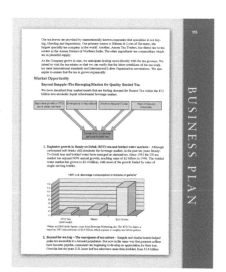

End-of-Chapter Learning Portfolio

End-of-chapter materials help students demonstrate a working understanding of key concepts and develop critical-thinking skills.

All chapters include the following:

- **Key Terms** list.
- **Critical Thinking Exercises** that require students to consider important issues and support thoughtful responses.
- **Key Concept Questions** that review core topics.
- **Application Exercises** that give students a structured opportunity to reinforce chapter topics through experience.
- **Exploring Your Community and Exploring Online** assignments that invite students to go into their business communities or search online for information.
- **BizBuilder Business Plan Questions** guide students through the development of business plan components as they learn new information throughout the book.
- **Cases for Analysis** include one short case and one longer case with analytical questions. Cases cover a variety of issues and draw on real business scenarios. Examples of businesses that may be familiar to students include eHarmony, Krispy Kreme, and Khan Academy. Other organizations that may be less familiar include Happy Belly Curbside Kitchen, 23andme, MIDA Trade Ventures, iContact, and Enablemart. These cases reflect a diverse set of entrepreneurs, industries, and geographic locations.

Entrepreneurship Portfolio

Critical Thinking Exercises

2-1. What are four positive aspects of franchising for a business start-up? Why are they important?

2-2. What are some challenges faced by franchisees?

2-3. Describe the type of franchise you might want to open.

2-4. Franchisees agree to pay a variety of fees to franchisors, initially and ongoing. Describe these fees, and discuss why understanding their impact on profitability and cash flow is important to franchisees.

Key Concept Questions

2-5. Compare and contrast product and trade-name franchising with business-format franchising.

2-6. Explain why the FDD is critical to analyzing a franchise opportunity.

2-7. What, if any, trends in franchising suggest continued expansion of the industry? Contraction? Cite your sources.

Application Exercise

2-8. Identify an industry or type of business that interests you. Select a community where you would like to locate such an organization (select a business that would have a physical presence). Find two competitors already in that market space and one franchisor that is not. Would it or would it not make sense to open a franchise in the community?

Exploring Online

2-9. Visit the Wahoo Fish Taco Web site at http://www.wahoos.com. What are the advantages of a Wahoo Fish Taco franchise according to the site? What franchise opportunities are available?

2-10. Visit the International Franchise Association Web site at http://www.franchise.org. Find a franchise organization that is unfamiliar to you. Find the following information about the franchisor:
   a. When did it begin offering franchises?
   b. How many company-owned units does it have?
   c. What are its initial financial requirements (start-up fee, net worth, liquid resources)?
   d. What type of franchisor is it (product or trade-name or business-format)?

If the information is not available on the International Franchise Association (IFA) Web site, try others from the list in **Exhibit 2-3**.

Entrepreneurship Portfolio

Critical Thinking Exercises

5-1. Use the following charts to define a business you would like to start, and analyze your competitive advantage.

Business Definition Question	Response
The Offer. What products and services will be sold by the business?	
Target Market. Which consumer segments will the business focus on?	
Production Capability. How will that offer be produced and delivered to those customers?	
Problem Solving. What problem does the business solve for its customers?	

Competitive Advantage Question	Competitive Difference (USP)
The Offer. What will be better and different about the products and services that will be sold?	
Target Market. Which segments of consumers should be the focus of the business to make it as successful as possible?	
Production and Delivery Capability. What will be better or different about the way the offer is produced and delivered to those customers?	

Attributes Important to Customers	Weight (a)	Your Company Rating (b)	Your Company Weighted Rating (c = a × b)	Competitor Number 1 Rating (d)	Competitor Number 1 Weighted Rating (e = a × d)	Competitor Number 2 Rating (f)	Competitor Number 2 Weighted Rating (g = a × f)	Competitor Number 3 Rating (h)	Competitor Number 3 Weighted Rating (i = a × h)
Quality									
Price									
Location									
Selection									
Service									
Speed/ Turnaround									
Specialization									
Personalization									
Total	1.00								

Additional Resources

Instructor Resources

At the Instructor Resource Center, www.pearsonglobaleditions.com/mariotti, instructors can access a variety of print, digital, and presentation resources available with this text in downloadable format. Registration is simple and gives instructors immediate access to new titles and new editions. As a registered faculty member, you can download resource files and receive immediate access to and instructions for installing course management content on your campus server. In case you ever need assistance, our dedicated technical support team is ready to help with the media supplements that accompany this text. Visit http://247.pearsoned.com for answers to frequently asked questions and toll-free user support phone numbers.

The following supplements are available for download to adopting instructors:

- Instructor's Resource Manual
- Test Bank
- TestGen® Computerized Test Bank
- PowerPoint Presentations

Student Resources

BizBuilder Business Plan Worksheets and Templates Online

Go to www.pearsonglobaleditions.com/mariotti to download business plan and presentation templates that will help students write a plan and present it.

- *BizBuilder Business Plan Worksheets* provide step-by-step instructions on building a business plan. The MS Word document contains a comprehensive set of questions and tables organized by business plan section. The Excel document includes Start-Up Costs, Sales Projections, Income Statement, Balance Sheet, Cash Flow, and Ratio Analysis worksheets.
- *BizBuilder Business Plan Template* provides a professional-looking format for a business plan that ties in with assignments in the text.
- *BizBuilder Business Plan Presentation Template* guides the student through the process of creating a PowerPoint presentation deck for a business plan.

Students can build their business plans using the BizBuilder worksheets. Appendix 2 provides students with instructions on how to use the worksheets that mirror the planning process in the book and contains more questions in some areas than are found in commercially available planning software. Once they have created a plan using the worksheets, students can generate a professional-looking document using the BizBuilder Business Plan Template.

CourseSmart eTextbook

CourseSmart eTextbooks were developed for students looking to save on required or recommended textbooks. Students simply select their eText by title or author and purchase immediate access to the content for the duration of the course using any major credit card. With a CourseSmart eText, students can search for specific keywords or page numbers, take notes online, print out reading assignments that incorporate lecture notes, and bookmark important passages for later review.

---

*This product may not be available in all markets. For more details, please visit www.coursesmart.co.uk or contact your local Pearson representative.

About the Authors

STEVE MARIOTTI, founder of the Network for Teaching Entrepreneurship (NFTE), is considered one of today's leading experts in education for at-risk youth. He has been helping young people develop marketable skills through learning about entrepreneurship for 30 years.

Starting his career as a treasury analyst for the Ford Motor Company, Mariotti changed career paths in 1982 when he gave up operating his own import-export firm to become a special education teacher in the New York City school system, where he remained for five and a half years. His first assignments were in the East New York and Bedford-Stuyvesant neighborhoods of Brooklyn; he also taught in what was, at the time, the notorious "Fort Apache" neighborhood of the South Bronx.

While teaching in these demanding environments, Mariotti gained a breakthrough insight for successfully motivating his economically at-risk students—it was showing them that entrepreneurship, learning how to start and operate their own small businesses, was a way to financial independence. This perception, combined with his solid business background, inspired Mariotti to create a program to bring entrepreneurial education to at-risk young people.

In 1987, the Network for Teaching Entrepreneurship was formed and received nonprofit 501(c)(3) status from the IRS the following year. Now, 25 years later, NFTE continues its mission of bringing entrepreneurship-education programs to youth from low-income communities on a global basis. The organization has reached over half a million young people since its founding and currently has programs and licensees in 18 states, as well as in Belgium, Chile, China, Colombia, Germany, India, Ireland, Israel, and New Zealand.

Steve Mariotti received a B.B.A. and M.B.A. from the University of Michigan, Ann Arbor. He also studied at Harvard University, Stanford University, and Brooklyn College. He has been the subject of many national media profiles, including *ABC Evening News* and *20/20+*. In addition, he is the coauthor of some 20 books and manuals on entrepreneurship that together have sold over one million copies. Mariotti is an active member of the Council on Foreign Relations and has presented papers at the World Economic Forum in Davos.

Among the many honors awarded to Steve Mariotti are Best Teacher of the Year, National Federation of Independent Businesses, 1988; Honorary Doctorate in Business and Entrepreneurship, Johnson and Wales University, 1990; Social Entrepreneur of the Year, the Chief Executive Officer's Club; *Inc.* Magazine's Social Entrepreneur of the Year Award; Ernst & Young Entrepreneur of the Year Award, 1992; Award from the Minority Business Development Agency of the U.S. Department of Commerce; University of Michigan Business School Entrepreneur of the Year Award; Association of Educational Publishers' Award for Best Math Curriculum, 2010; the Bernard A. Goldhirsh Social Entrepreneur of the Year Award; the New York Enterprise Report's 2012 Founder's Award for Social Entrepreneurship; and 2012 inductee into the Entrepreneurship Hall of Fame.

CAROLINE GLACKIN, Ph.D., is a "pracademic" who has succeeded as a microenterprise and small business owner and manager, as an executive director of a community-development financial institution, and as an academic in areas of community-development finance, entrepreneurship, and management. She is the Edward L. Snyder Endowed Chair for Business Administration at Shepherd University in West Virginia. She has been assisting entrepreneurs in achieving their dreams for over 30 years.

Glackin earned a doctorate from the University of Delaware, where her research emphasis was on microfinance. She received an M.B.A. from The Wharton School at the University of Pennsylvania and a B.A. from Bryn Mawr College. Her professional career began with the DuPont Company, American Bell, Bell Atlantic, and American Management Systems. She has consulted for businesses and not-for-profit agencies in turnaround and high-growth situations. After exiting a family business, she became the executive director of a Community-Development Financial Institution serving businesses and not-for-profits.

Dr. Glackin has succeeded in leading change in the practical fields of her research and has received numerous honors and awards. These include the first Gloeckner Business Plan Award at The Wharton School, the Minority Business Advocate of the Year for Delaware from the U.S. Small Business Administration, and the She Knows Where She's Going Award from Girls Inc. Dr. Glackin co-chaired the Delaware Governor's Task Force for Financial Independence. She has participated in the Cornell University Emerging Markets Think Tank Series and has presented her research and pedagogy at numerous professional conferences.

ENTREPRENEURIAL PATHWAYS

Chapter 1
ENTREPRENEURS RECOGNIZE OPPORTUNITIES

Chapter 2
FRANCHISING

Chapter 3
FINDING OPPORTUNITY IN AN EXISTING BUSINESS

Chapter 4
THE BUSINESS PLAN: ROAD MAP TO SUCCESS

© Kurhan/Fotolia

ENTREPRENEURS RECOGNIZE OPPORTUNITIES

Learning Objectives

1. Explain what entrepreneurs do.

2. Describe how free-enterprise economies work and how entrepreneurs fit into them.

3. Find and evaluate opportunities to start your own business.

4. Explain how profit works as a signal to the entrepreneur.

Tom Szaky of Terracycle, Inc.
(Paul Zimmerman/Getty Images)

I would like to thank my coauthor, Caroline Glackin, without whose talent and expertise this text would not have been possible, and Tony Towle, who from NFTE's inception has helped me organize my thoughts and experiences. I must single out the help of two outstanding educators: John Harris and Peter Patch. I would also like to acknowledge the significant contributions of NFTE executives Amy Rosen, Michael J. Caslin, III, J. David Nelson, Julie Silard Kantor, Leslie Pechman Koch, Jane Walsh, Neelam Patel, Daniel Rabuzzi, Victor Salama, Del Daniels, Jonathan Weininger, Deirdre Lee, Rupa Mohan, Christine Poorman, Joel Warren, and Essye Klempner.

Special thanks as well to Stephanie Wall, Daniel Tylman, Claudia Fernandes, Ilene Kahn, and the rest of the team at Pearson for their professionalism and editorial assistance.

Thanks also to Tom Goodrow of the Springfield Enterprise Center and the National Association of Community College Entrepreneurship (NACCE) and to John Christesen of SUNY Westchester Community College.

Additionally, I am grateful to Howard Stevenson, William Bygrave, Bob Pritzker, the late Jeffry Timmons, and NFTE Board Member Stephen Spinelli for imparting their wisdom, and to Richard Fink of Koch Industries, Carl Schramm of the Ewing Marion Kauffman Foundation, and Mike Hennessy and John Hughes of the Coleman Foundation. Special thanks to Eddy Bayardelle and Melanie Mortimer of Merrill Lynch Global Philanthropy, and Kim Davis of the JPMorganChase Foundation.

In addition, I would like to recognize the efforts and contributions of members of NFTE's National Board of Directors, and I would like to acknowledge the inspired guidance provided by our National Executive Committee. I am deeply grateful to the many philanthropists who have supported our work, including the Scaife Family Foundation, the Newark Boys' and Girls' Clubs, the William Zimmerman Foundation, the Goldman Sachs Foundation, The Shelby Cullom Davis Foundation, the Microsoft Corporation, The Nasdaq Educational Foundation, and Ronald McDonald House Children's Charities.

Further, I would like to acknowledge Steve Alcock, Harsh and Aruna Bhargava, Lena Bondue, Dawn Bowlus, Shelly Chenoweth, Janet McKinstry Cort, Erik Dauwen, Clara Del Villar, Christine Chambers Gilfillan, Andrew Hahn, Kathleen Kirkwood, Michael Simmons, Sheena Lindahl, Cynthia Miree, Henry To, Carol Tully, Dilia Wood, and Elizabeth Wright, as well as Peter Cowie, Joseph Dominic, Paul DeF. Hicks, Jr., Ann Mahoney, David Roodberg, Phyllis Ross Schless, and Remi Vermeir, who have all provided countless insights into providing entrepreneurial opportunities to young people.

In addition, I would like to thank my brother, Jack, the best CPA I know, and my father, John, for financing much of NFTE's early work, and for their continuing love and guidance. Thanks are due to all the other teachers, students, experts, and friends who were kind enough to look over my work and help me improve it. Finally, I want to thank my mother, Nancy, a wonderful special education instructor who showed me that one great teacher can affect eternity.

Steve Mariotti

To my coauthor Steve Mariotti, who brought hope, opportunity, and change out of adversity to create the Network for Teaching Entrepreneurship and started this journey—many thanks. Also thanks to Tony Towle, who has provided numerous insights to make this text sing. As Steve noted, the team at Pearson has been wonderful to work with again. Faculty reviewers and faculty members who have contacted me directly regarding earlier materials are always a valued source of insights.

Most importantly, I appreciate the terrific entrepreneurs who shared their stories with me, including the good, the bad, and the downright ugly! Their interest in sharing their experiences with students and willingness to carve out time to tell their tales demonstrates the kind of energy and enthusiasm we associate with successful entrepreneurs. They have made this endeavor interesting and engaging.

On a more personal note, I would like to thank my "family" at Shepherd University for their support and encouragement as I worked on *Entrepreneurship and Small Business Management, 2e*. Special thanks to Jay Azriel, Cynthia deLeon, Gordon DeMeritt, Meg Galligan, Heidi Golding, Terri Hasson, Ann Marie Legreid, Kathy Reid, Cindy Vance, and Sheila Vertino. Finally, to Elise and Spencer for being the best cheering section a mother could ever have—thanks and love to you both.

Caroline Glackin

Pearson would like to thank and acknowledge the following people for their work on the Global Edition. For her contribution: Hinna Pathak, Faculty, Xavier Institute of Management and Entrepreneurship, Bengaluru. And for their reviews: Anushia Chelvarayan, Faculty of Business, Multimedia University, Malaysia; Bhavani Ravi, HR Consultant; Sandeep Puri, Faculty, IMT Ghaziabad.

Acknowledgments

First, sincere thanks to the team of reviewers and consultants who provided insightful feedback during the development of our books:

Harvey Lon Addams, *Weber State University, Ogden, UT*

Elaine Allen, *CPA, Vice Chair, Not-for-Profit Sector, Mitchell & Titus, LLP*

Larry Bennett, *President, Benland Innovations, LLC*

Sunne Brandmeyer, *Retired Lecturer/Advisor, Center for Economic Education, University of South Florida, Tampa, FL*

Stanlee Brimberg, *Teacher, Bank Street School for Children, New York, NY*

Howard W. Buffett, Jr.

John R. Callister, *Cornell University, Ithaca, NY*

John D. Christesen, *SUNY Westchester Community College, Valhalla, NY*

Steve Colyer, *Miami Dade College, Miami, FL*

Alan J. Dlugash, *CPA, Partner, Marks Paneth & Shron LLP*

Alex Dontoh, *New York University, New York, NY*

Thomas Emrick, *Ed.D.*

Joyce Ezrow, *Anne Arundel Community College, Arnold, MD*

Rita Friberg, *Pueblo Community College, Pueblo, CO*

George Gannage, Jr., *West Georgia Technical College, Carrollton, GA*

Thomas Goodrow, *Springfield Technical Community College, Springfield, MA*

Janet P. Graham, *Coastal Carolina University, Conway, SC*

Vada Grantham, *Des Moines Area Community College, Ankeny, IA*

John Harris, *Eastern High School, Bristol, CT*

Deborah Hoffman, *CPA, Director of Finance, Math for America*

Donald Hoy, *Benedictine College, Atchison, KS*

Samira Hussein, *Johnson County Community College, Overland Park, KS*

Eileen M. Kearney, *Montgomery County Community College, Blue Bell, PA*

Sanford Krieger, *Esq., General Counsel & Managing Director, AEA Investors LP*

Jawanza Kunjufu, *D.B.A. President, African-American Images*

Corey Kupfer, *Esq., Partner, Hamburger Law Firm, LLC*

Walter Lara, *Florida Community College, Jacksonville, FL*

Emily H. Martin, *Faulkner State College, Bay Minette, AL*

Alaire Mitchell, *Former Assistant Director of Curriculum Research, New York City Board of Education*

Timothy R. Mittan, *Southeast Community College, Lincoln, NE*

Eric Mulkowsky, *Engagement Manager, McKinsey and Company, Inc.*

Raffiq Nathoo, *Senior Managing Director, The Blackstone Group, LLP*

Ray E. Newton, III, *Senior Managing Director, Evercore Partners Inc.*

Arnold Ng, *Pepperdine University, Rancho Palos Verdes, CA*

William H. Painter, *Retired Professor of Law, George Washington University*

Peter Patch, *Patch and Associates*

Alan Patricof, *Founder, Apax Partners and Greycroft Partners*

Carolyn J. Christensen Perricone, *CPA, SUNY, Westchester Community College, Valhalla, NY*

Robert Plain, *Guilford Technical Community College, Jamestown, NC*

Laura Portolese-Dias, *Shoreline Community College, Seattle, WA*

Christopher P. Puto, *University of St. Thomas, Minneapolis, MN*

Richard Relyea, *President, NY Private Equity Network (NYPEN)*

Linda Ross, *Rowan University, Glassboro, NJ*

Ira Sacks, *Esq., Partner, Law Offices of Ira S. Sacks LLP*

William Sahlman, *Harvard Business School, Cambridge, MA*

Arnold Scheibel, *MD, Professor of Neurobiology, University of California at Los Angeles*

William Searle, *Asnuntuck Community College, Enfield, CT*

LaVerne Tilley, *Gwinnett Technical College, Lawrenceville, GA*

Marsha Wender Timmerman, *LaSalle University, Philadelphia, PA*

Liza Vertinsky, *Emory University, Atlanta, GA*

Peter B. Walker, *Managing Director, McKinsey and Company, Inc.*

Larry Weaver, *Navarro College, Corsicana, TX*

Donald A. Wells, *University of Arizona, Tucson, AZ*

Dennis R. Williams, *Pennsylvania College of Technology, Penn State, Williamsport, PA*

ENTREPRENEURIAL PATHWAYS

Chapter 1
ENTREPRENEURS RECOGNIZE OPPORTUNITIES

Chapter 2
FRANCHISING

Chapter 3
FINDING OPPORTUNITY IN AN EXISTING BUSINESS

Chapter 4
THE BUSINESS PLAN: ROAD MAP TO SUCCESS

© Kurhan/Fotolia

ENTREPRENEURS RECOGNIZE OPPORTUNITIES

Learning Objectives

1. Explain what entrepreneurs do.

2. Describe how free-enterprise economies work and how entrepreneurs fit into them.

3. Find and evaluate opportunities to start your own business.

4. Explain how profit works as a signal to the entrepreneur.

Tom Szaky of Terracycle, Inc.
(Paul Zimmerman/Getty Images)

Tom Szaky was a 19-year-old college student in need of inspiration for a business plan competition, when he happened to visit friends who were using red worms to compost waste that they then used as plant fertilizer. The idea captured his imagination, and he created a business plan for an environmentally friendly company that would convert trash into fertilizer. Although he finished in fifth place in the competition, Szaky moved ahead to make the company a viable venture.[1]

TerraCycle Inc. has expanded its product lines to encompass a wide range of recycling and upcycling, including branded products for Target and Kraft Foods. The company is the producer of the world's first product made from and packed in recycled waste: fertilizer generated from waste. Szaky sells to some of the world's largest retailers, including Wal-Mart, Target, and Home Depot, and oversees programs that involve entire communities in recycling projects. Sales exceed $20 million per year, and the company has collected literally billions of discarded items. TerraCycle plant food was twice named the most eco-friendly product in Home Depot. Tom Szaky and TerraCycle have turned trash into treasure.

Entrepreneurship Defined

Have you ever eaten a Subway sandwich? Used an Apple device? Listened to music with Skullcandy headphones? The entrepreneurs that founded these companies brought these products into your world. Entrepreneurship is all around us.

What Is an Entrepreneur?

Most Americans earn money by working in *business*. They are somehow engaged in the buying and selling of products or services in order to make money.

product something tangible that exists in nature or is made by people.

- A **product** is something that exists in nature or is made by human beings. It is *tangible*, meaning that it can be physically touched.
- A **service** is labor or expertise (rather than a tangible commodity) exchanged for money. It is *intangible*. It cannot actually be touched.

service intangible work that provides time, skills, or expertise in exchange for money.

Someone who earns a living by working directly for someone else's business is an *employee* of that business. There are many roles for employees. At Ford Motor Company, for instance, some employees build the cars, some sell the cars, and some manage the company. But employees have one thing in common—they do not *own* the business; they work for others who do. They know how much money they can earn, and that amount is limited to salary or wages, plus bonuses and any stock options they may receive.

entrepreneur a person who recognizes an opportunity and organizes and manages a business, assuming the risk for the sake of potential return.

People who have their own businesses work for themselves and are called small business owners, or **entrepreneurs**. Entrepreneurs are often both owners and employees. For an entrepreneur, the sky is the limit as far as earnings are concerned. Unlike an employee, an entrepreneur owns the profit that his or her business earns, and may choose to reinvest it in the business or take it as payment.

Learning Objective 1 ▶

Explain what entrepreneurs do.

An entrepreneur is someone who recognizes an opportunity to start a business that other people may not have noticed, and jumps on it. As economist Jeffry A. Timmons writes in the preface of *New Venture*

---

[1]TerraCycle Inc., accessed June 23, 2013, http://www.terracycle.net.

Creation: Entrepreneurship for the 21st Century, "A skillful entrepreneur can shape and create an opportunity where others see little or nothing—or see it too early or too late."

The French word *entrepreneur* began to take on its present-day meaning in the seventeenth century. It was used to describe someone who undertook any project that entailed risk—military, legal, or political, as well as economic. Eventually, it came to mean someone who started a new business venture—often of a new kind or a new (or improved) way of doing business. French economist Jean-Baptiste Say wrote at the turn of the nineteenth century:

> An entrepreneur is an economic agent who unites all means of production—the land of one, the labor of another and the capital of yet another, and thus produces a product. By selling the product in the market he pays rent on land, wages to labor, interest on capital and what remains is his profit. He shifts economic resources out of an area of lower and into an area of higher productivity and greater yield.[2]

Say argued that entrepreneurs "added value to scarce resources." Coal is a resource because it is used as fuel. Wood is a resource because it can be used to build a house or a table, to make paper, or to burn as fuel. Economists consider *scarce* all resources that are worth money, regardless of their relative availability.

Debbi Fields, founder of Mrs. Fields Cookies, took resources—eggs, butter, flour, sugar, chocolate chips—and turned them into cookies. People liked what she did with those resources so much that they were willing to pay her more for the cookies than it cost her to buy the resources to make them. She *added value* to the resources she purchased by what she did with them and created a multimillion-dollar business in the process.

Entrepreneurs may have different reasons to start and continue their businesses, but they share the common focus of creating sustained value. Entrepreneurs seek opportunities that they envision as generators of incremental income, or *wealth*. Whether the business is intended to meet short-term household cash needs or to grow into a publicly traded company, viability is critical. Each activity of the firm should be driven by this need.

The Economic Questions

Since the beginnings of human society, people have had to answer the same basic questions:

- What should be produced?
- When will it be produced?
- How will it be produced?
- Who will produce it?
- Who gets to have what is produced?

Families and individuals, as well as businesspeople, charitable organizations, corporations, and governments, all have had to answer these questions. The system created by making these decisions is called an *economy*. The study of how different groups answer the questions is called *economics*.

An economy is the wealth and resources of a country or region, including its financial structure. The economy of the United States is a **free-enterprise system** because it is characterized by private (rather than governmental) ownership of capital assets and goods; anyone is free to start

free-enterprise system
economic system in which businesses are privately owned and operate relatively free of government interference.

[2]Jean-Baptiste Say, *A treatise on political economy; or the production distribution and consumption of wealth* (*Traité d'économie politique ou simple exposition de la manière dont se forment, se distribuent et se composent les richesse.*), C. R. Prinsep, trans. [slightly modified] and Clement C. Biddle., ed. (Philadelphia: Lippincott, Grambo & Co., 1855). Library of Economics and Liberty, accessed June 26, 2013, http://www.econlib.org/library/Say/sayT.html.

a business. Americans do not have to get permission from the government to go into business, although they are expected to obey laws and regulations.

The free-market system, which is also called **capitalism**, typifies the following attributes:

- Individuals and companies may compete for their own economic gains.
- Private wealth and property ownership are permissible.
- Free-market forces primarily determine prices.

Cash or goods invested to generate income and wealth is called **capital**; in a free-enterprise system anyone who can raise the necessary capital may start a business.

Voluntary Exchange

The free-enterprise system is also sometimes referred to as a private enterprise free-trade system because it is based on **voluntary exchange**. Voluntary exchange is a transaction between two parties who agree to trade money for a product or service. Each wishes to take advantage of what the trade offers. The parties agree to the exchange because each will benefit.

For example, José has a construction business, and his neighbors hire him to renovate their kitchen. He wants to earn money and is willing to use his skills and time to do so. The neighbors are willing to give him money to get the renovation done. They each have something the other wants, so they are willing to trade. A satisfactory exchange only takes place when both parties believe they will benefit. Robbery, in contrast, is an *involuntary* exchange.

Benefits and Challenges of Free Enterprise

The public benefits from living in a free-enterprise system, because it discourages entrepreneurs who waste resources by driving them out of business. It encourages entrepreneurs who use resources to satisfy consumer needs efficiently by rewarding them with profit.

◀ **Learning Objective 2**
Describe how free-enterprise economies work and how entrepreneurs fit into them.

capitalism the free-market system, characterized by individuals and companies competing for economic gains, ownership of private property and wealth, and price determination through free-market forces.

capital money or property owned or used in business.

voluntary exchange a transaction between two parties who agree to trade money for a product or service.

Global Impact . . .

Free Trade

For much of recorded history, international trade was difficult and hazardous. To sell products in another country often required long and dangerous journeys overland or by ship. Many countries were closed to outside trade. Governments also used their power to give their own businesspeople a competitive advantage over those from other countries by establishing trade barriers, such as imposing taxes (tariffs) on foreign goods that made them very expensive. Governments could also enforce restrictions on how many imports or exports could cross their borders.

Today, trade barriers have fallen in many parts of the world. The North American Free Trade Agreement (NAFTA) of 1994 eliminated trade barriers between the United States, Mexico, and Canada. This turned the entire continent into a free-trade zone. The General Agreement on Tariffs and Trade (GATT) cut or eliminated tariffs between 117 countries. This evolved into the World Trade Organization, which now has 159 members.

Where entrepreneurs are free to trade voluntarily, to as large a market as possible, their ability to find customers to buy their goods or services increases, as well as their overall ability to meet consumer needs. Meanwhile, the Internet has made it much easier for businesses to sell to clients all over the world. Shipping, too, has become much faster and less expensive.

Society in general benefits because free enterprise encourages competition between entrepreneurs. Someone who could make cookies that taste as good as Mrs. Fields Original Cookies and sell them at a lower price would eventually attract Mrs. Fields's customers. This would force Mrs. Fields to lower prices to stay competitive or the company would go out of business. Consumers would benefit because they would get to buy the same-quality cookie at a lower price.

On the flip side, free enterprise has some disadvantages. If a company fails, the employees are out of work. Owners who have invested their financial resources in the business lose money. Other companies or individuals that depended on the products and services of the failed business themselves lose customers or suppliers.

What Is a Small Business?

The public often thinks of business only in terms of "big" business—companies such as Apple, Wal-Mart, Microsoft, McDonald's, and Berkshire Hathaway. However, the vast majority of the world's businesses are small businesses. A small business is defined by the U.S. Small Business Administration's Office of Advocacy as having fewer than 500 employees and selling less than $5 million worth of products or services annually. A neighborhood restaurant, a mattress manufacturer, and a clothing boutique are examples of a small business; even a leading local employer may be classified as "small" under this definition.

Surprisingly, the principles involved in running a large company—like Microsoft—and a corner deli are the same. However, the operations of a small business are not the same as those of a large one. Most multimillion-dollar businesses in this country started out as small, entrepreneurial ventures. This is why entrepreneurship is often called the engine of our economy. It drives our economic creativity, giving rise to wealth and jobs and improving our standard of living.

Why Become an Entrepreneur?

Entrepreneurs put a great deal of time and effort into launching their own businesses. While establishing a business, an entrepreneur may also pour all of his or her money into it. An entrepreneur may not be able to buy new clothes or a fancy car, go on vacation, or spend much time with family—until the business becomes profitable and starts generating cash.

If so much work and sacrifice are involved, why become an entrepreneur? The entrepreneur is working for the following rewards:

1. *Control over time.* Do you work better at midnight than at 8 A.M.? If you start your own business, you will have control over how you spend your time by the type of business it is. Are you the kind of person who would rather work really hard for two weeks, nonstop, and then take a break? If you are an entrepreneur, you can structure your schedule to make this possible. You can also choose to hire others to perform tasks that you do not like to do or are not good at, so you can stay focused on what you do best. Bill Gates liked to spend his time designing software. He hired people to manage Microsoft's operations and to market and sell its products. Many eBay entrepreneurs have carved out flexible schedules for responding to orders, packaging, and shipping. Bricks-and-mortar retail stores, on the other hand, do not often afford such flexibility.

2. *Fulfillment.* Successful entrepreneurs are passionate about their businesses. They are excited and fulfilled by their work. Entrepreneurs who are working to reach their full potential are rarely bored, because there is always plenty to do. If one facet of running the business is uninteresting, and they have the income to support it, they can hire someone else for that task.

   Social entrepreneurs who want to contribute to societal improvement find ways to do this while also earning profits. Founders of not-for-profit organizations create enterprises to address public issues that are personally important. Other entrepreneurs start lifestyle businesses that allow them to earn money while following a passion. For example, avid pilots may operate aviation-oriented businesses in which they can fly often, such as specialty delivery companies or flight instruction. Art lovers may open galleries, create art-rental firms, or operate art tours.

Exhibit 1-1 *"Do You Have What It Takes?" Quiz*
12 Points or More: You are a natural risk-taker and can handle a lot of stress. These are important characteristics for an entrepreneur to have to be successful. You are willing to work hard but have a tendency to throw caution to the wind a little too easily. Save yourself from that tendency by using cost/benefit analysis to carefully evaluate your business (and personal!) decisions. In your enthusiasm, do not forget to look at the opportunity costs of any decision you make.
6 to 12 Points: You strike an excellent balance between being a risk-taker and someone who carefully evaluates decisions. An entrepreneur needs to be both. You are also not overly motivated by the desire to make money. You understand that a successful business requires hard work and sacrifice before you can reap the rewards. To make sure that you are applying your natural drive and discipline to the best possible business opportunity, use the cost/benefit analysis to evaluate the different businesses you are interested in starting.
6 Points or Fewer: You are a little too cautious for an entrepreneur, but that will probably change as you learn more about how to run a business. You are concerned with financial security and may not be eager to put in the long hours required to get a business off the ground. This does not mean that you cannot succeed as an entrepreneur; just make sure that whatever business you decide to start is the business of your dreams, so that you will be motivated to make it a success. Use cost/benefit analysis to evaluate your business opportunities. Choose a business that you believe has the best shot at providing you with both the financial security and the motivation you require.

In addition to your paid professional advisors, such as attorneys and accountants, individual advisors or an advisory board can be the difference between success and failure. Even if you are forming a venture with a full slate of experienced technical and managerial professionals, the guidance of a carefully composed advisory board can provide valuable counsel and connections. Such a board might meet only once or twice a year to listen to your problems, share experiences, and help you avoid mistakes. During the times between meetings, advisors may also be able to offer substantial assistance.

Of course, taking advantage of available courses in entrepreneurship, whether brief workshops, individual college courses, an entrepreneurial certificate program, or a degree program, can offer considerable benefits. The opportunity to learn from the experiences of others and to systematically explore entrepreneurial options and build skills will be important. There are numerous Internet resources for nascent entrepreneurs, too.

A well-prepared entrepreneur is more likely to stay on the path to success.

Entrepreneurial Options

Entrepreneurship extends beyond the fast-growing technology enterprises that are most commonly associated with it. There are many variations on entrepreneurship, and the opportunities are innumerable. Entrepreneurship may include for-profit enterprises that support the missions of not-for-profit organizations, businesses designed for social impact, and ventures that are environmentally oriented.

Social entrepreneurship has multiple definitions and forms, but in general it is commonly thought of as a for-profit enterprise that has the dual goals of achieving profitability and attaining beneficial returns for society. Another view is that of taking an entrepreneurial perspective toward social problems.[5] Gregory Dees has created the following definition:

social entrepreneurship
a for-profit enterprise with the dual goals of achieving profitability and attaining social returns.

> Social entrepreneurs play the role of change agents in the social sector by:
>
> - adopting a mission to create and sustain social value (not just private value),
> - recognizing and relentlessly pursuing new opportunities to serve that mission,
> - engaging in a process of continuous innovation, adaptation, and learning,

---

[5]Gregory Dees, "The Meaning of 'Social Entrepreneurship,'" May 30, 2001, accessed July 9, 2013, http://www.fuqua.duke.edu/centers/case/documents/dees_SE.pdf.

- acting boldly without being limited by resources currently in hand, and
- exhibiting heightened accountability to the constituencies served and for the outcomes created.

In this view, social entrepreneurship is less about profit than it is about social impact.

In addition to the broadly defined "social entrepreneurship," there is the more recent concept of the **social business**, "a non-loss, non-dividend company designed to address a social objective within the highly regulated marketplace of today. It is distinct from a non-profit because the business should seek to generate a modest profit but this will be used to expand the company's reach, improve the product or service or in other ways to subsidize the social mission."[6] In his book *Creating a World without Poverty—Social Business and the Future of Capitalism*, Mohammad Yunus suggests two kinds of social business:

- Type I provides a product and/or service with a particular environmental, social, or ethical purpose. Grameen Danone does this by providing food for the poor in Bangladesh.
- Type II is profit-oriented business with ownership consisting of underprivileged people who have the opportunity to benefit directly or indirectly.

In addition, **venture philanthropy** is a subset or segment of social entrepreneurship. Financial and human capital is invested in not-for-profits by individuals and for-profit enterprises with the intention of generating social rather than financial returns. In some cases, venture philanthropy may involve the investment of capital in the for-profit, commercial part of a not-for-profit. In others, it may mean investing in not-for-profits directly, to encourage entrepreneurial approaches to achieve social impact.

Green entrepreneurship is another form of social entrepreneurship and can be defined as: "Enterprise activities that avoid harm to the environment or help to protect the environment in some way."[7] TerraCycle is an excellent example of green entrepreneurship. According to the Corporation for Enterprise Development (CFED), green entrepreneurship can:

- create jobs and offer entrepreneurship opportunities,
- increase energy efficiency, thus conserving natural resources and saving money,
- decrease harm to workers' health,
- enable businesses to tap into new sources of local, state, and federal funding,
- take advantage of consumer preference for environmentally friendly goods, and
- preserve limited natural assets on which businesses and communities depend for business and quality of life.

Each of these alternative approaches offers opportunities for innovation and growth for the right entrepreneur.

---

social business a company created to achieve a social objective while generating a modest profit to expand its reach, improve the product or service, and subsidize the social mission.

venture philanthropy a subset or segment of social entrepreneurship wherein financial and human capital is invested in not-for-profits by individuals and for-profit enterprises, with the intention of generating social rather than financial returns on their investments.

green entrepreneurship business activities that avoid harm to the environment or help to protect it in some way.

Organically grown produce
(Ulrich Willmunder/Shutterstock)

---

[6]Muhammad Yunus, *Creating a World without Poverty: Social Business and the Future of Capitalism*, New York: PublicAffairs, 2009, p. 320.

[7]"Green Entrepreneurship," *Corporation for Enterprise Development: Effective State Policy and Practice*, Volume 5, Number 2, April 2004, http://www.cfed.org.

How Do Entrepreneurs Find Opportunities to Start New Businesses?

In the twentieth century, Joseph Schumpeter expanded on Say's definition of entrepreneurship by adding that entrepreneurs create value "by exploiting an invention or, more generally, an untried technological possibility for producing a new commodity or producing an old one in a new way, by opening up a new source of supply of materials or a new outlet for products, by reorganizing an industry and so on."[8] This view emphasizes innovation as the key to entrepreneurship. Management expert Peter Drucker simplified this view to the essential core of creating a new business, taking on risk, and persevering in light of uncertainty.[9]

Schumpeter's definition describes five basic ways that entrepreneurs find opportunities to create new businesses:

◄ **Learning Objective 3**
Find and evaluate opportunities to start your own business.

1. Using a new technology to produce a new product
2. Using an existing technology to produce a new product
3. Using an existing technology to produce an old product in a new way
4. Finding a new supply of resources (that might enable the entrepreneur to produce a product more economically)
5. Developing a new market for an existing product

Entrepreneurs Creatively Exploit Changes in Our World

Today's economists and business experts have defined entrepreneurship even more specifically. Drucker pointed out that, for a business to be considered entrepreneurial, it should exploit changes in the world. This is in alignment with Schumpeter's definition of entrepreneurship but explicitly takes it a step further—to take advantage of circumstances. These changes can be technological, like the explosion in computer technology that led Bill Gates and Paul Allen to start Microsoft, or cultural, like the collapse of Communism, which led to a great many new business opportunities in Eastern Europe. Babson professor Daniel Isenberg narrows the definition of entrepreneurship to "the contrarian creation and capture of extraordinary value."[10]

Nothing changes faster than technology. Not so many years ago, there were no bar codes and no electronic scanners, hardly anyone used e-mail, and "smart phones" didn't exist. Today, even the smallest of organizations needs to use current technologies to be competitive. Sharp entrepreneurs increase their efficiency by taking advantage of the latest breakthroughs in business equipment. To learn about what's new in technology, read current business and trade magazines and visit such Web sites as:

- TechCrunch, *http://www.techcrunch.com*.
- Start-up Digest, *http://www.start-updigest.com*.

Peter Drucker defined an entrepreneur as someone who "always searches for change, responds to it, and exploits it as an opportunity." Entrepreneurs are always on the lookout for ways to create businesses from the opportunity of change.

---

[8]Joseph A. Schumpeter, *Capitalism, Socialism and Democracy*, New York: Harper & Row, 1942.

[9]Peter Drucker, *Innovation and Entrepreneurship: Practice and Principles*, New York: Harper Collins, 1985.

[10]Daniel Isenberg, *Worthless, Impossible and Stupid: How Contrarian Entrepreneurs Create and Capture Extraordinary Value*, Cambridge, Massachusetts: Harvard Business Press, 2013.

How Do Entrepreneurs Create Business Ideas?

1. *They listen.* By listening to others, entrepreneurs get ideas about improving a business or creating a new one. Create one business idea by listening. Describe how you got the idea.
2. *They observe.* By constantly keeping their eyes and ears open, entrepreneurs get ideas about how to help society, about what kind of businesses they could start, and about what consumers need. Create a business idea by observing. Describe how you got the idea.
3. *They analyze.* When entrepreneurs analyze a problem, they think about what product or service could solve it. Create a business idea by thinking up a solution to a problem. Describe how you arrived at the idea.

Where Others See Problems, Entrepreneurs Recognize Opportunities

Here is a simple working description of an entrepreneur that captures the essentials: An entrepreneur recognizes opportunities where other people see only problems or the status quo.

Many famous companies were started because an entrepreneur turned a problem into a successful business. An entrepreneur recognized that the problem was actually an opportunity. Where there are dissatisfied consumers, there are likely opportunities for entrepreneurs.

Anita Roddick was an excellent example of an entrepreneur who started off as a dissatisfied consumer. She started The Body Shop International because she was tired of paying for unnecessary perfume and fancy packaging when she bought makeup, and she thought other women might feel the same way.

Train Your Mind to Recognize Business Opportunities

An important step in becoming an entrepreneur is to train your mind to recognize business opportunities. A further step is to let your creativity fly. Consider developing your entrepreneurial instincts by asking yourself:

- What frustrates me the most when I try to buy something?
- What product or service would really make my life better?
- What makes me annoyed or angry?
- What product or service would take away my aggravation?

BizFacts

Entrepreneurship has proven to be an effective way for minorities and women to enter the business world.

- More than 6.1 million businesses were minority-owned in 2007, and they generated $871 billion in revenues.
- There were more than 12.4 million non-farm businesses owned by women (or co-owned equally with men), accounting for 45.4 percent of all U.S. companies.

Source: U.S. Small Business Administration, accessed June 29, 2013, http://www.sba.gov.

Entrepreneurs Use Their Imaginations

Businesses are also formed when entrepreneurs not only fume about products or services that annoy them but fantasize about products or services they would like to have in their lives. Jump-start your imagination by asking yourself such questions as:

- What is the one thing I would like to have more than anything else?
- What would it look like? What would it taste like?
- What would it do?
- What innovative product or service idea have I been mulling over in my mind?
- What problem have I encountered in everyday life and thought: "There has to be a better way to do this?"

Consider posing these questions to friends and family members as well. You might hear about an opportunity you had not yet recognized.

An Idea Is Not Necessarily an Opportunity

Not every business idea you may have or invention you may explore is an opportunity. In fact, most ideas are not viable business possibilities. An *opportunity* has a unique characteristic that distinguishes it from an ordinary idea. An opportunity is *an idea that is based on what consumers need or want and are willing to buy sufficiently often at a high enough price to sustain a business*. A successful business sells products or services that customers need, at prices they are willing to pay. Many a small business has failed because the entrepreneur did not understand this. It is critical that an idea has "legs" for it to succeed.

In addition, according to Jeffry Timmons, "An opportunity has the qualities of being attractive, durable, and timely and is anchored in a product or service which creates or adds value for its buyer or end user."[11]

Timmons's definition of a business opportunity includes these four characteristics:

1. It is attractive to customers because it creates or adds value for its customers.
2. It will work in the business environment.
3. It can be executed in a defined window of opportunity.
4. It can be implemented with the right team to make it durable.

Larry Lilac/Alamy

The window of opportunity is the length of time available to get the business idea to market before the market either diminishes due to lessening demand or is dominated by a competitor. You might have a great idea, but if other entrepreneurs have it too, and have already brought it to the marketplace, that window of opportunity is probably closed.

Remember, not every idea is an opportunity. For an idea to be a genuine opportunity, it must lead to the development of a product or service that is of value to the consumer and is profitable for the business.

---

[11] Jeffry Timmons, *New Venture Creation: Entrepreneurship for the 21st Century*, 5th ed., New York: Irwin/McGraw-Hill, 1999, p. 7.

Entrepreneurial Wisdom . . .

A useful way to evaluate a business idea is to look at its strengths, weaknesses, opportunities, and threats (SWOT). This is called **SWOT analysis**.

- **Strengths**—All the capabilities and positive points the entrepreneur has, from experience to contacts. These are internal to the organization.
- **Weaknesses**—All of the negatives the entrepreneur faces, such as lack of capital or training or failure to set up a workable accounting system. These are internal to the organization.
- **Opportunities**—Any positive external event or circumstance (including lucky breaks) that can help the entrepreneur get ahead of the competition.
- **Threats**—Any external factor, event, or circumstance that can harm the business, such as competitors, legal issues, or declining economies.

SWOT analysis consideration of the internal strengths and weaknesses of an organization and the external opportunities and threats which it may face.

Opportunity Is Situational

A problem is one example of an opportunity that entrepreneurs need to be able to recognize. A changing situation or a trend is another. Opportunity is *situational*, meaning it is dependent on variable circumstances. There are no rules about when or where an opportunity might appear. Change and flux create opportunities.

Think about recent changes in computer technology. In the early 1990s, the conventional wisdom was that only the biggest telecommunications companies were in a position to exploit the Internet and all the opportunities it had to offer. How could entrepreneurs compete with established, resource-laden companies? The opposite has been true, however. Entrepreneurs penetrated and, indeed, have dominated the market for Internet-based services. Think of Facebook, Google, and Foursquare. Each was an entrepreneurial venture that left industry giants scrambling to catch up.

It can take a huge corporation (think dinosaur) multiple years to develop and implement a new business strategy, while entrepreneurs can be nimble and enter and exit the market like roadrunners. Successful entrepreneurs can "turn on a dime rather than a dollar bill."

The Five Roots of Opportunity in the Marketplace

Entrepreneurs can exploit "five roots of opportunity."[12] Notice how similar these are to Schumpeter's definition of entrepreneurship.

1. **Problems** your business can solve
2. **Changes** in laws, situations, or trends
3. **Inventions** of new products or services
4. **Competitive advantage** in price, location, quality, reputation, reliability, speed, or other attributes of importance to customers
5. **Technological advances** that entrepreneurs take from the laboratory to the marketplace

Integrating Internal and External Opportunities

It is helpful not only to be aware of the five roots of opportunity in the marketplace but to think also about how we perceive opportunities ourselves. Opportunities fall into two classes: internal and external. An internal opportunity is one that comes from inside you—from a personal hobby,

---

[12] Adapted from John Clow (ed.), *Master Curriculum Guide: Economics and Entrepreneurship*, New York: Joint Council on Economic Education, 1991.

Step into the Shoes . . .

Russell Simmons Makes Rap Happen

ssell Simmons
Everett Collection
./Alamy)

In the late 1970s, Russell Simmons was promoting rap concerts at the City University of New York. At the time, rap was considered a passing fad, but Simmons really loved it. Even though most record executives thought rap would be over in a year or two, Simmons truly believed it was a business opportunity. He formed Def Jam Records with fellow student Rick Rubin for $5,000. Within a year, they produced hit records by Run DMC and LL Cool J, and Simmons went on to become a multimedia mogul.

Simmons took a chance on this opportunity because he felt that, if you personally know 10 people who are eager to buy your product or service, 10 *million* would be willing to buy it if they knew about it. Luckily, he was right about rap's popular potential, but he could have been wrong. That can be a problem with perceived opportunities: You may be passionate about something, but there may not be enough consumer interest to sustain an actual business venture.

Simmons loved rap and hoped that other people would, too. That was the internal factor—he had the passion to sustain himself as he worked 24/7 to make his dream come true. As it turned out, music fans were a little bored with rock at that time and looking for a fresh sound. Rap filled the bill. This was an external opportunity that happened to coincide with Simmons's internal commitment.

interest, or even a passion—or inside your organization. These can come in the form of the resolution of a problem, such as creating a viable product from scrap material, or the potential for a new product line.

An external opportunity, in contrast, is generated by an outside circumstance. External opportunities are conditions you notice that make you say to yourself, "Hey! I could start a great business from that!" For example, you see that people in your neighborhood are complaining about the lack of available day care, so you start a day care center after confirming the market need. But what if you find out very quickly that two-year-olds get on your nerves? That can be a major drawback for external opportunities. Your idea may fill a market need, but you may not have the skills or interest to make it a successful business.

The best business opportunities usually combine both internal and external factors. Ideally, a business that you are passionate about will fill a sustainable need in the marketplace.

Establishing Strategies

Business success hinges on the creation and application of profitable strategies to the work at hand. A **strategy** is a plan for how a business intends to go about its own performance and outdo that of its competition. Michael Porter created a "strategy framework" that delineates cost leadership and differentiation as low-cost and product-uniqueness strategies.[13] It also layers in the concept of focus strategies, which work in narrow market segments rather than broad ones. The illustration in Figure 1-1 shows how each of Porter's Generic Strategies relates to the other.

A firm using a product-uniqueness strategy bases its competitive advantage on its ability to differentiate the firm's products and/or services from others in its competitive market space. Such factors as quality, availability, customer service, and the like are critical to differentiation, as will be discussed in greater detail in the marketing chapters of this text.

If you choose to emphasize a low-cost approach, you will be using a "cost-leadership" strategy. This means that you are finding ways to reduce

strategy a plan for how an organization or individual plans to proceed with business operations and outperform that of its competitors.

[13]Michael Porter, *Competitive Strategy: Techniques for Analyzing Industries and Competitors*, New York: Free Press, 1998.

Figure 1-1 *Porter's Generic Strategies*

Scope of Target Market	Strategic Advantage	
	Product Uniqueness	**Low Cost**
Industry-Wide (Broad)	Differentiation Strategy	Cost Leadership Strategy
Market Segment (Narrow)	Focus Strategy (Differentiation)	Focus Strategy (Low Cost)

Source: Adapted from Michael Porter, *Competitive Strategy: Techniques for Analyzing Industries and Competitors* (Free Press, 1998).

the costs of operations and management sufficiently to be able to undercut the pricing of your competition and to sustain that price advantage.

Another component of the Porter framework is that of a focus strategy. This line of attack narrows in and creates a laserlike focus on a particular market segment or group. Rather than strategically targeting an entire industry, you locate a niche or subset of the customer base and focus your marketing efforts on it. If you can find a sufficiently large niche to sustain your business, you can set the company apart from the competition and maintain the advantage. A focus strategy can work with differentiation and cost leadership.

Paths to Small Business Ownership

Not all business owners start their ventures from the ground up. Although the emphasis of this book is on starting and growing your own enterprise, the paths to business ownership are varied. You could buy an existing company, secure franchise rights, license or purchase critical technology or methods, inherit a company, or be hired as a manager.[14] There are pros and cons to each approach, and it will be worthwhile to give thought to each option. Note the possibilities in **Exhibit 1-2**.

Securing Franchise Rights

> **franchise** is a legal and commercial relationship between the owner of a trademark, service mark, trade name or advertising symbol and an individual or group seeking to use that identification in a business.

"A **franchise** is a legal and commercial relationship between the owner of a trademark, service mark, trade name or advertising symbol and an individual or group seeking to use that identification in a business."[15] For many people who want to own and operate a business, it is worthwhile to consider franchising as a path to business ownership. (See Chapter 2 for a discussion of franchising as an entrepreneurial opportunity.)

Buying an Existing Business

> **acquisition** a business purchase.

The purchase of a business, or **acquisition**, can be a good way to jump-start entry into small business ownership. There is both an art and a science to buying an existing business.

The challenge is to do a complete, in-depth analysis of the opportunity, just as you would for a start-up, with the added dimension of taking into account an existing history, whether for better or worse. Be wary of owners whose businesses seem to be too good to be true or who are overly eager to sell. Be thorough, whether you are buying an entire firm, a customer list, or some or all assets and especially if you are taking on some or all debt. Done well, buying a business can be the starting point for success.

---

[14]Jerome A. Katz and Richard P. Green, *Entrepreneurial Small Business*, New York: McGraw-Hill/Irwin, 2008.

[15]U.S. Small Business Administration Workshop, "Is Franchising for Me?" accessed December 2007, http://www.sba.gov/idc/groups/public/documents/sba_homepage/serv_sbp_isfforme.pdf.

Exhibit 1-2 *Selected Business Entry Options*

Business Aspects	Start a Business	Buy an Existing Business	Secure a Franchise or License	License Technology
Customers	None	Established	None—but may have name recognition	None
Location	Needed	In place	Assistance possible	Needed
Management Control	Owner	Owner	Owner within terms of license	Owner within terms of license
Operational Control	Owner	Owner	Owner within terms of license	Owner
Marketing	Needed	In place (+/−)	Assistance possible. Rules absolutely.	Needed
Reputation	None	In place (+/−)	Should be. If not, why license?	Possible
Royalties/Fees	Not usual	Maybe	Ongoing	Likely
Financing	Needed	Prior owner may provide	Assistance possible	Needed
Disclosures	None	Buyer beware	UFOC and contracts	Agreement

Done poorly, buying a business can be more challenging and problematic than starting a new venture. (See Chapter 3 for a more in-depth discussion.)

Licensing Technology

One way to potentially shorten the product-development cycle and to access innovative technology is to identify and *license* that technology—that is, to enter into a contract to use it without purchasing the rights to own it. Whether you acquire such rights through a university, state economic development office, federal agency such as NASA, or an individual scientist/inventor, you can create a business based on technology transfer. Or, you may find that it makes more sense to purchase the rights outright, or over time.

The MBA team of Bruce Black and Matt Ferris, from the University of Georgia, developed a business plan that garnered numerous competitive awards for the KidSmart Vocal Smoke Detector, someone else's creation that they arranged to bring to market. The product is now available in major retail stores and on the Internet, through Signal One, the successor company.

Before securing franchise rights, purchasing a business, or licensing technology, be certain to do your research thoroughly to understand what you are and are not buying, and what your ongoing obligations—financial, operational, legal, and reporting—will be. Because these transactions are complex and can have significant financial and personal implications, it is important to invest in qualified legal and financial counsel before signing any agreements of this kind.

Do Not Take Unfair Advantage of Someone Else's Creativity

You would be upset if someone made money from your invention or artistic creation, so resist the urge to base your business on someone else's creative work. Be sure that any business you start respects the intellectual property of others.

- Do not sell counterfeit knockoffs of popular brands.
- Do not take graphics, music, or content from the Web without permission and/or payment.
- Always know the source of the goods you buy from suppliers to avoid the risk of receiving stolen property.

The Many Faces of Entrepreneurship

Entrepreneurs are as diverse as the composition of the economy. They are of all ethnicities, races, and religions and come from every socioeconomic status. They enter into self-employment for a wide range of reasons and choose to continue as entrepreneurs or return to outside employment for just as many. There are women and minority entrepreneurs and young entrepreneurs in record numbers. Continuing an American tradition, there are also refugee and immigrant entrepreneurs.

This diverse and ever-changing pool of entrepreneurs does not produce a single path to entrepreneurial success. Rather, the types of businesses formed reflect the diversity of the founders. In addition to full-time ventures founded to maximize growth and wealth, some are started as part-time and microenterprises, "gazelles," artisanal and opportunistic businesses, and others.

Gazelles

gazelle a company that achieves an annual growth rate of 20 percent or greater, typically measured by the increase of sales revenue.

A classic entrepreneurial story is that of a pair of inventors who develop a new, innovative technology or product in a garage, basement, or dormitory; lift themselves up by their bootstraps into a wildly successful business venture in virtually no time; take the company public; and become incredibly wealthy in the process. This stereotype describes the founders of a high-potential venture with the potential to become a **gazelle**, a company that achieves an annual growth rate of 20 percent or greater, typically measured by the growth of sales revenue.

Gazelles tend to be the exception rather than the rule for entrepreneurial enterprises but are a significant type of firm. Gazelles are financed by a combination of found resources with significant outside assistance. They rely heavily on external financial support and counsel.

Microenterprises

microenterprise a firm with five or fewer employees, initial capitalization requirements of under $50,000, and the regular operational involvement of the owner.

Most businesses are founded as **microenterprises**, which are defined as businesses with five or fewer employees, initial capitalization requirements of less than $50,000, and the habitual operational involvement of the owner. In fact, more than 60 percent of all U.S. firms have four or fewer employees, according to the U.S. Small Business Administration.[16] The Association for Enterprise Opportunity (AEO) estimates that the more than 25.1 million microenterprises in the United States account for 88.2 percent of all businesses and 22 percent of all private employment.[17]

Microenterprises are founded for a variety of reasons and are often more fluid than other types of businesses. These firms may be founded to provide only part-time employment for their owners. They may not be intended as long-term enterprises and may not have the goal of growing larger. They may be planned as only temporary ventures to provide income during periods of unemployment or to supplement household finances for a particular purpose. **Lifestyle businesses** are microenterprises that permit their owners to follow a desired pattern of living, such as supporting college costs or taking vacations. On the other hand, a microenterprise could make the difference between a family living in poverty and achieving economic stability.

lifestyle business a microenterprise that permits its owners to follow a desired pattern of living, such as supporting college costs or taking vacations.

Mainstream Small Firms

These constitute the bulk of the small businesses in the public perception, in the press, and in community visibility. They provide, or have the

---

[16]U.S. Small Business Administration, Office of Advocacy, 2013.

[17]Association for Enterprise Opportunity, accessed June 30, 2013, http://www.microenterpriseworks.org.

potential to provide, substantial profits to their owners. Mainstream small firms can be operated by founder-entrepreneurs, subsequent generations of family members, successor owners, or franchisees. They create many of the jobs included in statistics from the U.S. Small Business Administration and employ the majority of American workers. Unlike many micro-enterprises, they are established with continuity and permanent wealth building in mind and are more often registered with local, state, and federal agencies.

Making the Business Work Personally and Professionally

What makes a business work is not only profitability and cash flow, although they are necessary. Each entrepreneur has his own goals and objectives for the business. As an entrepreneur, it will be up to you to determine how you want your business to be and to make it happen.

A Business Must Make a Profit to Stay in Business

No matter how big or small, a business must make a **profit**—that is, show a positive gain from operations after all expenses are subtracted. Most businesses lose money initially because entrepreneurs have to spend money to set up operations and advertise to attract customers. If the business cannot make a profit and generate cash, eventually the entrepreneur will be unable to pay the bills and will have to close.

> **profit** amount of money remaining after all costs are deducted from the income of a business.

Closing a business is nothing to be ashamed of, if you operate ethically and learn from the experience. In fact, many successful entrepreneurs open and close more than one business during their lives. If your venture is not making a profit after you have gotten it up and running, that is a signal you may be in the wrong business. Closing it may be the best decision.

An entrepreneur may change businesses many times over a lifetime in response to changing competition and consumer needs.

Profit Is the Sign That the Entrepreneur Is Adding Value

Profit is the sign that an entrepreneur has added value to the resources he or she is using. Debbi Fields added value to scarce resources by creating something that people were willing to buy for a price that gave her a profit. In contrast, not making a profit is a sign that the entrepreneur is not using resources well and is not adding value to them.

> ◄ **Learning Objective 4**
> Explain how profit works as a signal to the entrepreneur.

Profit Results from the Entrepreneur's Choices

An entrepreneur's choices directly affect how much profit the business makes. For example, suppose, like Debbi Fields, you have a business selling homemade cookies. You might decide one week to buy margarine instead of butter because it is cheaper, even though the cookies may not taste as good made with margarine. This type of choice is called a **trade-off**. You are giving up one thing (taste) for another (money).

> **trade-off** the act of giving up one thing for another.

If your customers do not notice the change and continue to buy your cookies, you have made a good choice. You have conserved a resource (money) and increased your profit by lowering your costs. The increase in profit confirms that you have made the right choice.

If your customers notice the change and stop buying your cookies, your profit will decrease. The decrease in profit signals that you have made a bad choice. Next week you should probably go back to butter. The profit signal taught you that your customers were dissatisfied and the trade-off was not worth it. Every choice an entrepreneur makes is a trade-off.

Seven Rules for Building a Successful Business

Russell Simmons and Rick Rubin were successful in creating Def Jam because they instinctively applied the seven basic rules of building a successful business:

1. ***Recognize an opportunity.*** Simmons believed that rap music was an untapped business opportunity.
2. ***Evaluate it with critical thinking.*** He tested his idea by promoting concerts and observing consumer reaction.
3. ***Build a team.*** Simmons formed a partnership with Rubin.
4. ***Write.*** Simmons and Rubin created a realistic business plan.
5. ***Gather resources.*** Simmons and Rubin pooled their $5,000.
6. ***Decide ownership.*** Simmons and Rubin formed a legal partnership.
7. ***Create wealth.***

The Team Approach

While most businesses do not hire employees, successful entrepreneurial ventures grow well beyond their initial founder. Some have multiple co-founders while others grow their teams along with their businesses. The team approach can make or break a business. For example, alone, neither Simmons nor Rubin had enough skills or money to launch a record label, but together they were able to do it. Their business was also helped by the fact that each knew different artists and had different contacts in the recording industry.

Potential team members are all around you. Some might be in your immediate circles of friends and family members who have skills, equipment, or contacts that would make them valuable business partners. At the same time, you may reach across the globe to find other team members. Perhaps you very much want to start a Web site design business, because you know of companies in your community that want to put up Web sites.

Entrepreneurial Wisdom . . .

Build Your Brain

Becoming a successful entrepreneur is all about making connections, those "Aha!" moments when you realize what your business opportunity is or when you figure out how to do something better than the competition. Research indicates that mental exercise will help your brain become better at making such connections. Even the most erudite scientists recognize the value of activities that encourage brain cells to make new connections. Robotics engineer Hugo de Garis, who has worked on such projects as building an artificial brain for an artificial cat, plays classical piano every day before he sits down at the computer. "This helps to build my own brain," he told *The New York Times.*[18] Arnold Scheibel, head of the University of California–Los Angeles Brain Research Institute, suggests the following brain-builders:

- Solving puzzles
- Playing a musical instrument
- Fixing something; learn to repair cars or electrical equipment
- Creating art, writing poetry, painting, or sculpting
- Dancing
- Making friends with people who like to have interesting conversations

[18]Nicholas D. Kristof, "Robokitty," *The New York Times*, August 1, 1999.

You are a graphic artist, but you do not know how to use Web site development programs. If you have a friend who has that knowledge, you might start a business together. Or maybe you would like to start a DJ venture, but you only have one turntable or laptop computer. If you form the business with a friend, you can pool equipment. (When forming a business team, organize the enterprise so that everyone involved shares in the ownership and profits. People work better when they are working for themselves.) Just be careful of jumping into business relationships with undue haste.

Now carry this idea a step further. Everyone you meet is a potential contact for your business, just as you may be a valuable contact for theirs. Thinking this way will encourage you to *network*, or exchange valuable information and contacts with other businesspeople. Keep your business cards with you at all times and truly view every individual you encounter as an opportunity for your business. Remember, though, that networking is a two-way street. See how you can help those that you meet rather than always focusing on how they can help you. The results can be nothing short of amazing.

Chapter Summary

Now that you have studied this chapter, you can do the following:

1. Explain what entrepreneurs do.
   - Entrepreneurs start their own businesses and work for themselves.
   - Entrepreneurs recognize opportunities to start businesses that other people may not have noticed.
   - Entrepreneurs shift economic resources from an area of lower productivity into an area of higher productivity and greater yield. By doing this, they add value to scarce resources.
2. Describe how free-enterprise economies work and how entrepreneurs fit into them.
   - The free-enterprise system is based on voluntary exchange. Voluntary exchange is a trade between two parties who agree to trade money for a product or service. Both parties agree to the trade because each benefits from the exchange.
   - The free-enterprise system encourages entrepreneurs who use resources efficiently to satisfy consumer needs by rewarding them with profit.
3. Find and evaluate opportunities to start your own business.
   - The five roots of opportunity are:
     i. problems that your business can solve;
     ii. changes in laws, situations, or trends;
     iii. inventions of totally new products or services;
     iv. competition (if you can find a way to beat the competition on price, location, quality, reputation, reliability, or speed, you can create a very successful business with an existing product or service); and
     v. technological advances (scientists may invent new technology, but entrepreneurs figure out how to sell it).
4. Explain how profit works as a signal to the entrepreneur.
   - Profit is the sign that an entrepreneur has added value to the scarce resources he or she is using.
   - Not making a profit is a sign that the entrepreneur is not using resources well and is not adding value to them.

5. A business opportunity is an idea plus these three characteristics:
   - It is attractive to customers.
   - It will work in your business environment.
   - It can be executed in the defined window of opportunity.
6. Use cost/benefit analysis to make decisions.
   - Cost/benefit analysis is the process of comparing costs and benefits in order to make a good decision.
   - Cost/benefit analysis can be inaccurate without including opportunity cost. This is the cost of missing your next-best investment.
7. Use **SWOT** analysis to evaluate a business opportunity.
   - Strengths: all of the capabilities and positive points that the entrepreneur has, from experience to contacts. These are internal to the organization.
   - Weaknesses: all of the negatives the entrepreneur faces, such as lack of capital or training or failure to set up a workable accounting system. These are internal to the organization.
   - Opportunities: any positive external events or circumstances (including lucky breaks) that can help the entrepreneur get ahead of the competition.
   - Threats: any external factors, events, or circumstances that can harm the business, such as competitors, legal issues, or declining economies.

Key Terms

acquisition, 42
capital, 27
capitalism, 27
commission, 29
cost/benefit analysis, 32
dividend, 29
entrepreneur, 25
franchise, 42
free-enterprise system, 26
gazelle, 44
green entrepreneurship, 36
lifestyle business, 44
mentor, 33
microenterprise, 44

opportunity cost, 33
product, 25
profit, 45
salary, 29
service, 25
social business, 36
social entrepreneurship, 35
strategy, 41
SWOT analysis, 40
trade-off, 45
venture philanthropy, 36
voluntary exchange, 27
wage, 29

Entrepreneurship Portfolio

Critical Thinking Exercises

1-1. Are creativity and entrepreneurship two sides of the same coin? Illustrate the argument with an example.

1-2. Is being able to make a profit important for the success of a business? If yes, how does profit indicate the worth of a business?

1-3. If you were to start a business, what would be your opportunity cost? In other words, what is the next-best use of your time? How much money could you make working at a job, instead? The answer to this last question will give you a rough idea of how to value your time when you start a business and figure out how much to pay yourself.

1-4. Describe an idea that you have for a business. Explain how it could satisfy a consumer need.

1-5. What are the steps to convert a business idea into a successful business? Illustrate with an example from your country.

1-6. Is money the only motivator for a person to become an entrepreneur? Substantiate your response with suitable reasons.

1-7. List five business opportunities in your environment and the need(s) each would satisfy. Note whether the opportunity you describe is internal, external, or a mix.

Key Concepts Questions

1-8. Define small business.

1-9. Does everyone live by selling something? If yes, illustrate with examples.

1-10. What are the unethical or unfair practices to watch out for when venturing into a new business?

1-11. How important is cost/benefit analysis in entrepreneurship?

1-12. Identify a few successful small or medium business enterprises in your country. Visit their Web sites and write a summary of how the business started (200 words or fewer). Remember to create a proper citation for the article.

Application Exercises

1-13. Have a conversation with a friend or relative. Ask this person to tell you about which things he or she finds frustrating in the area/neighborhood. Write down these comments.

Step 1: Generate at least three business opportunities from this conversation.

Step 2: Use the checklists below to evaluate your three business ideas as opportunities.

Step 3: Choose the best of the business opportunities and write a SWOT analysis for it.

Step 4: Create a cost/benefit analysis for starting this business. Use the analysis to explain why you would or would not actually start it.

Business Idea 1 _____	Critical Evaluation	
Would it be attractive to potential customers?	Yes _____	No _____
Would it work in your business environment?	Yes _____	No _____
Is there a sufficient window of opportunity?	Yes _____	No _____
Do you have the skills and resources to create this business?	Yes _____	No _____
If you do not have the skills and resources to create this business, do you know someone who does and might want to create the business with you? (Consider how you might determine this.)	Yes _____	No _____
Business Idea 2 _____	**Critical Evaluation**	
Would it be attractive to potential customers?	Yes _____	No _____
Would it work in your business environment?	Yes _____	No _____
Is there a sufficient window of opportunity?	Yes _____	No _____
Do you have the skills and resources to create this business?	Yes _____	No _____
If you do not have the skills and resources to create this business, do you know someone who does and might want to create the business with you?	Yes _____	No _____
Business Idea 3 _____	**Critical Evaluation**	
Would it be attractive to potential customers?	Yes _____	No _____
Would it work in your business environment?	Yes _____	No _____
Is there a sufficient window of opportunity?	Yes _____	No _____
Do you have the skills and resources to create this business?	Yes _____	No _____
If you do not have the skills and resources to create this business, do you know someone who does and might want to create the business with you?	Yes _____	No _____

Exploring Your Community

1-14. Interview an entrepreneur, preferably in person. Entrepreneurs are busy people, but many are willing to spend time speaking with someone who is interested in what they are doing. Meeting over a light meal might be the most efficient use of the entrepreneur's time. Before the interview, brainstorm 10 questions in the following four categories. After the interview, be sure to write a thank-you note.

a. *Information gathering.* Open the interview with questions about the entrepreneur's family (any other entrepreneurs in it?) and educational and work background.

b. *About the business.* Next, ask questions about how the business was started. How did the entrepreneur recognize an opportunity and develop it?

c. *Running the business.* Ask about which challenges arose as the business got underway and how they were solved.

d. *Reflection.* Ask the entrepreneur to reflect. What advice would he or she give to an aspiring entrepreneur? Has running a business been rewarding?

Exploring Online

Visit an Internet search engine such as Google, Yahoo, or Bing. Search for one of the following terms: *entrepreneurship ideas*, *businesses for sale*, *franchise opportunities*. For the search that you selected, answer:

1-15. Which search engine and term was used and

1-16. What were the number of matches ("hits").

Next, find a site that looks promising and answer these questions:

1-17. What is the Web site (URL and name)?

1-18. Who is sponsoring the Web site?

1-19. Is the Web site selling a product or information (as a primary function, not through banner ads)? If so, what products or information?

1-20. Identify three businesses/ideas/opportunities from the site, and state why they might or might not be viable opportunities for you.

Alamy

Sandy Lerner cofounded Cisco Systems in 1984 with her former husband, Leonard Bosack. It became a world leader in sales of computer routers. When she was ousted from the company in 1990, Lerner had the time and financial resources to focus on charitable activities and other business possibilities. By 1995, she was ready to start another company that would fill a market void.

Lerner believed that there was an opportunity in the beauty market for quality, nontraditional products. According to the Urban Decay Web site, "Our story opens 15 years ago, when pink, red and beige enslaved the prestige beauty market. Heaven forbid you wanted purple or green nails, because you'd either have to whip out a marker, or risk life and limb with that back alley drugstore junk." She had seen a Chanel polish that was a deep red color, nearly black, but found little else in high-end products that met the need she identified.

Lerner's business manager introduced her to a creative businesswoman and self-described makeup addict, Wende Zomnir, and the business began to take shape. "Over high tea, the two forged a pact that led to renegade nail polish mixing sessions in Wende's Laguna Beach bungalow." Urban Decay launched in 1996 with 12 nail enamels and 10 lipsticks. "Inspired by seedier facets of the urban landscape, they bore groundbreaking names like Roach, Smog, Rust, Oil Slick and Acid Rain. The first magazine ad queried 'Does Pink Make You Puke?,' fueling the revolution as cosmetics industry executives scrambled to keep up." Today, the company describes itself as, "Urban Decay is beauty with an edge. It is feminine, dangerous and fun . . . appealing to anyone who relishes her individuality and dares to express it."

Even after the '90s grunge style faded, Urban Decay thrived. The company became a global organization; it is a popular full cosmetic line at major retailers such as Sephora, Macy's, and Ulta and is found on the Internet through Beauty.com. Urban Decay is sold by retailers in the Middle East, the United Kingdom, Italy, Canada, France, Singapore, and Spain. After several transitions, it is currently owned by L'Oreal Cosmetics, and Zomnir continues to work at the company.

Urban Decay notes factors contributing to its success: "And although UD fans around the world might approach our products in wildly different ways, we've noticed they share an independent spirit that unites them. Maybe this hunger for something unique explains the passionate support we've received over the years."

Clearly, Lerner and her cofounders saw opportunity in beauty.

Case Study Analysis

1-21. What unmet needs of the consumer contributed to the success of Urban Decay?

1-22. Was founding Urban Decay an expected next step after leaving Cisco Systems for Sandy Lerner? Why or why not?

1-23. What characteristics made Urban Decay an opportunity rather than simply an idea? Which of the five roots of opportunity apply here?

1-24. Is there a future for Urban Decay? What might that future look like?

Case Sources

"Sandy Lerner," *Encyclopedia of World Biography*, accessed June 29, 2013, http://www.notablebiographies.com/newsmakers2/2005-La-Pr/Lerner-Sandy.html.

Urban Decay, accessed June 28, 2013, http://www.urbandecay.com.

Foursquare is the ubiquitous location-based social network that creatively incorporates gaming elements and marketing. It is the brainchild of Dennis Crowley and Naveen Selvadurai.

The Founders

Crowley and Selvadurai met in New York City in 2007. They worked for different technology companies (AreaCode and Socialight, respectively), but in the same office space. Crowley is a graduate of Syracuse University. He has a degree in advertising and holds a master's from New York University's Interactive Telecommunications Program. Selvadurai, a software engineer, holds computer science degrees from King's College (London) and Worcester Polytechnic Institute (Worcester, Massachusetts).

Dennis Crowley and Naveen Selvaduri
(Scott McDermott/Getty Images)

Both founders had prior experience in the technology field. Crowley worked at Jupiter Communications directly out of college, and Vindego after that. He cofounded Dodgeball in 2003 and sold it to Google in 2005; he worked for Google after the acquisition. Then, he joined AreaCode as its director of product development. Selvadurai worked at Sun Microsystems, Lucent, RunTunes, and Sony Music. He later joined Socialight as its Vice President of Engineering.

The companies where the founders worked were related to the business that Foursquare is today. Vindego created mobile applications, including city guides. Dodgeball was based on Crowley's graduate thesis, which he partnered with Alex Rainert (currently head of product at Foursquare) in order to commercialize the concept. Dodgeball was a location-based social networking option for mobile devices that was available in a number of U.S. cities. Google acquired and operated Dodgeball until 2009, when Dodgeball was shut down and replaced with Google Latitude. AreaCode was a software start-up in the area of game play when Crowley worked there.

RunTunes was a company, started by some friends of Selvadurai, that aimed to bring music to phones. It was bought by Sony Music. Finally, Socialight is a company that creates and promotes local content with social interaction and user-content contributions.

According to Christopher Nomes, "Partnership between Naveen and Dennis was a perfect match. Both young and brilliant, both with already hefty working experience from working in cool and innovative companies, and both with ability to take everything they learned and forge it into something new and special that will overshadow everything they did before."

Creating at the Kitchen Table

About a year after they met, Crowley and Selvadurai began building the first version of Foursquare at Crowley's kitchen table in the East Village. In March 2009, Foursquare launched at South by Southwest Interactive. Most recent numbers suggest that Foursquare has over 30 million users and is growing at a rate of 25,000 new users per day. Daily check-ins exceed 3 billion.

© NetPhotos/Alamy

The App

Foursquare is widely popular and becomes an even more useful mobile app with its increasing numbers of users. As users check in on their mobile devices at various locations, such as restaurants, retail stores, and museums, they can

The same study projects economic contributions of a significant multiple of this base.

The industry is led by several mammoth franchisors, accounting for thousands of franchisees worldwide. At the same time, there are numerous smaller franchisors with local and regional franchisees. *Entrepreneur* magazine publishes an annual issue devoted to franchising that provides insight into the industry. It is informative to compare the *Entrepreneur* rankings from year to year to understand the trends affecting industries and specific companies.

In addition to the types of franchises described earlier, several other kinds have emerged and are growing in popularity. **Internet franchises**, such as We Simplify the Internet (WSI; http://www.wsimarketing.com) have taken hold as the World Wide Web has become ubiquitous. Internet franchises are franchise companies that do not depend upon physical location for the delivery of their products or services; rather, they are virtual businesses. Also, **conversion franchising** has gained popularity, wherein an existing stand-alone business or local chain becomes part of a franchise operation. Another trend is **piggybacking**, or **co-branding**, in which two franchises share locations and resources. Examples of this include Baskin-Robbins and Dunkin' Donuts. The franchising industry continues to expand and reach new entrepreneurs.

Internet franchise a type of franchise company that does not depend on physical location for the delivery of its products or services; rather, it is a "virtual" business.

conversion franchising a stand-alone business or local chain becoming part of a franchise operation.

piggybacking or **co-branding** occurs when two franchises share locations and resources.

Franchising and the Law

Franchises are governed by state and federal laws and regulations. The Federal Trade Commission (FTC) is the primary government agency involved in oversight. The FTC primarily serves to protect the interests of franchisees by directing the disclosure rules for franchisors. The process and specific requirements have evolved significantly over the past century, with the most recent changes occurring in 2008.

◀ **Learning Objective 4**
Recognize the legal aspects of franchising.

Step into the Shoes . . .

Buying a Franchise: College Hunks Hauling Junk—Miami

Ronald Rick III and Christopher Poore, students in an entrepreneurial consulting class at the University of Miami, were assigned to assist a company in finding a U of M franchisee. They chose a junk-removal company called College Hunks Hauling Junk, a company cofounded by an U of M alumnus nearly a decade earlier.

Rick and Poore investigated the College Hunks system and ultimately saw the potential of the company for themselves. The business duo met cofounder Omar Soliman when he spoke about entrepreneurship at U of M. Meeting with Soliman gave them the confidence—both in themselves and in the system—to apply for a franchise.

Less than a year later, Rick and Poore launched their College Hunks location in Miami. Now, these two twenty-somethings appear to be retracing the steps of CEO Soliman and his cofounder, President Nick Friedman, who were in their early twenties when they started the company.

Soliman and Friedman launched College Hunks Hauling Junk in 2005 and by 2007 had become the youngest franchisors in America. They later added College Hunks Moving to increase

revenue through synergy and the dual brand has since grown exponentially. Now, their franchise system includes 46 locations covering 25 states and counting.

The HUNKS (Honest, Uniformed, Nice, Knowledgeable Students) for the most part still are students from local colleges and universities.

Soliman and Friedman seek franchise owners from all walks of life. The company is adamant that the most important attribute for a potential franchisee to possess is the passion to grow a business through a client-focused approach.

Christopher Poore and Ron Rick (Chris Poore, College Hunks Hauling Junks Inc.)

Source: College Hunks Hauling Junk, accessed July 1, 2013, http://www .collegehunkshaulingjunk.com. Alexandra Leon, "From students to start-ups: Local college grads open businesses," *Miami Herald,* January 7, 2013, accessed May 7, 2013, http://www.miamiherald.com/2013/01/07/3171513/from-students-to-start-ups-local.html#storylink=cpy.

The **Franchise Disclosure Document (FDD)** has replaced the Uniform Franchise Offering Circular (UFOC) as the primary source of information for prospective franchisees regarding franchisors. It is registered with the FTC and must be organized into a common format so that prospective franchisees may more readily compare franchise opportunities. The FDD which discloses the terms of the franchise relationship and any pertinent financial and legal issues affecting the franchisor, must be provided by the franchisor a minimum of 14 days before the signing of a franchise agreement. As a practical matter, as a prospective franchisee, you should secure this document as early in the exploration and negotiation process as possible. The FDD includes such information as:

- *Overview and background.* Company review and offer, background information on key personnel and directors, and disclosures of current and past litigation or bankruptcy.
- *Fees and costs.* All initial fees, all anticipated operating fees, and a table of the potential cost ranges for every part of the initial investment.
- *Contractual obligations.* Table of franchisee responsibilities with specific reference to the franchise agreement and the FDD, and an extensive list of franchisor obligations, from pre-opening through ongoing operations. Also included are details about training programs and any required point of sale, advertising, or other required franchise systems, along with a list of personal obligations of the franchisee.
- *Territory.* Terms regarding the limits of the protected territory that the franchisee will receive. This could be a very large or very small area. Or, there could be no protected territory. This has huge significance for the franchisee because franchisors have often put franchisees so close together that they compete with one another for business.
- *Financial performance.* Franchisor discloses the performance of franchisee units by providing statistical information with clearly stated assumptions and explanations of limitations. Prospective franchisees are best served by taking this data and carefully analyzing it to secure a better understanding of what is and is not stated and to use it as a launching point for further research.
- *Data regarding existing units.* Table data regarding the existing units in the franchise system and the units that have closed or transferred ownership can assist in understanding both the franchisor's success rates and "churn."
- *Financial statements and contracts.* Past three years of the franchisor's audited financial statements and all contracts the franchisee is required to execute. Contracts include the franchise agreement and those for advertising co-op rules and conditions, real estate, personal guarantees, and territory development. Prospective franchisees should acquire legal and accounting review for these.
- *Termination, renewal, transfer, and dispute resolution procedures.* Policies regarding exit strategies, including fees and restrictions, as well as rules regarding mediation and/or negotiation versus legal action are the best ways to understand the reality of costs, fees, requirements, and other conditions set by the franchisor. The refusal of a prospective franchisor to provide this information should be a red flag for any franchisee. Regardless of what a salesperson or franchise broker says to you, the FDD conveys the pertinent information.

In addition to the FDD, each franchisor and franchisee must enter into a **franchise agreement**, which is the legal document governing the specific franchise. Included in the franchise agreement are the following:

© Roberto Herrett/Alamy

- the term of the agreement—length of time the franchisor and franchisee agree to work together;
- standards of quality and performance;
- an agreement on royalties—usually a percentage of the franchisee's sales paid to the franchisor;
- a noncompete clause stating that, for instance, if you are licensing a McDonald's franchise, you cannot also own a Blimpie's;
- a "hold harmless" clause that may release the franchisor from specific actions or violations of state laws;
- integration clauses that may block the franchisee from suing the franchisor for misrepresentation or deception that occurred prior to the signing of the agreement;
- choice of venue or other provisions that require the franchisee to settle disputes with the franchisor in the franchisor's state;
- clauses regarding termination, renewal, and transfer of the franchise;
- territories—franchisors usually assign a territory in which an individual franchisee can do business; within the assigned area, no other franchisee from that company will be allowed to compete.

franchise agreement contract that determines the specific parameters of the relationship between the parties in a franchise.

As with any legal agreement, professional legal counsel skilled in this type of contract should be hired and engaged to explore fully the contents prior to signing it, or paying any money to the franchisor. In addition, prospective franchisees may want to hire an accounting professional to provide a review of the franchise agreement and proposed business plan.

Steps for Franchise Selection

Deciding to purchase a unit franchise, or a master or area franchise, is a major decision that is best undertaken after complete due diligence. Numerous steps are involved in becoming a franchisee and it is important to pursue each. Skipping any one step, or not fully completing it, may create short-term and/or long-term barriers to success.

 **Learning Objective 5**
Learn how to research franchise opportunities.

- ***Self-reflection and engagement of core supporters.*** Franchising is not for everyone who wants to enter into self-employment. Taking the time to reflect on individual goals and objectives, as well as lifestyle and financial considerations, is vital. The FTC provides a readiness assessment tool for franchise ownership in its *Buying a Franchise: A Consumer Guide* (http://business.ftc.gov/documents/inv05-buying-franchise-consumer-guide). It should take about five minutes to complete and may provide valuable insights for prospective franchisees. Also, having the genuine, enthusiastic support of a core group of friends and family is critical to achieving and maintaining desired personal factors when deciding whether to buy a franchise.

- *Industry, type, geography, or brand selection, brand name, or business-format franchising.* If the outcomes of the reflection and analysis suggest franchising would be an excellent option for you, choosing the franchise will be the next step. Some individuals have a desire to be associated with a particular industry. Others would prefer a retail firm, a service company, a home-based organization, or the like. Still others have more interest in the geographic location of the franchise operation than the particular industry or type of business. Another set of prospective franchisees might have a franchise in mind with the geographic location more flexible, such as Insomnia Cookies. For certain people, the greater flexibility of brand-name franchising is more desirable than business-format franchising. You can weigh these and other factors (such as the start-up franchise fee) to arrive at a set of guidelines for selection.

- *Research.* The decision-making process above will require some research, but it will be more focused on internal factors. With the results of this effort in hand, you can conduct further research to narrow the list of franchise choices to a manageable level before conducting in-depth analysis. The research need not be costly or complex, but it should be thorough enough to avoid traps and missteps at this early stage. A number of resources are listed in **Exhibit 2-3**.

- *Narrow the list of options.* The research should provide enough information to narrow the list of potential franchises down to a few. Now it is time to conduct in-depth research and hone in on the individual companies.

franchise broker an individual acting as an intermediary between the franchisor and prospective franchisee.

- *Make the broker decision.* Prospective franchisees can decide at any point whether or not to use a **franchise broker**, which is a

Exhibit **2-3** *Resources for Franchise Research*	
Documents	
Franchise Opportunities Guide	http://www.franchise.org
A Consumer Guide to Buying a Franchise	http://business.ftc.gov/documents/inv05-buying-franchise-consumer-guide
Web Sites	
http://www.entrepreneur.com/franchises.html	*Entrepreneur* magazine
http://www.franchisetimes.com	*Franchise Times* magazine
http://www.inc.com	*Inc.* magazine
http://www.money.cnn.com	*Money* and *Fortune* magazines
http://www.worldfranchising.com	*World Franchising* magazine
http://www.internationalfranchisedirectory.net/	International franchising opportunities
http://www.franchising.com	Franchising opportunities
http://www.franchisehandbook.com	Franchise database
http://www.bison.com	Franchise information
http://www.FRANdata.com	Franchise information services
http://www.ifa-university.com	IFA University
Trade Associations	
International Franchise Association	http://www.franchise.org
American Association of Franchisees and Dealers	http://www.aafd.org
Trade Shows	
International Franchise Expo	http://www.mfvexpo.com
National Franchise and Business Opportunities	http://www.franchiseshowinfo.com

third-party consulting company that prescreens prospective franchisees and matches them with franchisors. Broker and consultant fees are generally paid by the franchisors.

- *Visit franchise operator(s).* Before contacting the short list of franchise companies directly, those who are considering franchises with physical sites open to the public can strategically visit one or more units to observe them. Such visits are for information gathering and to observe such aspects as traffic flow, environment, quality of franchise décor and materials, management, and so forth. This is more akin to acting as a secret shopper than a formal visit. Try not to visit locations in your neighborhood or in the immediate area where you would be operating.

- *Contact the franchisor.* You should request basic preliminary information from each franchise company. Typically, this information is available through a Web site or franchise development staff. The basic information will permit the screening of the small pool of franchise possibilities and narrowing it to one or two finalists. The steps from this point on will become intense and time consuming.

- *Perform due diligence on a specific franchise.* A franchise company will probably require completion of a qualification questionnaire, which will enumerate your experience and financial qualifications. Once this is accepted, the franchise company will share its FDD, and you should analyze and understand it completely before moving forward. Calls to existing franchisees, possibly including a visit to the franchise company headquarters, will be important next steps. Internet research and Web buzz about a franchisor can also be taken into consideration, although these are best considered with a healthy dose of skepticism. Have people who are familiar with FDDs review them and other documents to check what you are looking at before agreeing to anything.

- *Explore financing options.* Each prospective franchisee will have a different personal financial situation. It is essential to know what your personal resources will be—from friends and family, financial institutions, private investors, and the franchisor. Identifying financial capacity can and should begin in the early-research phase.

- *Make a decision, negotiate the franchise agreement, and engage professional counsel.* The timing of this will depend upon the individual franchisee but is an essential step. The FDD and franchise agreement will be sufficiently complex that even the most sophisticated franchisee should engage legal and financial advisors.

- *Make it work!* The franchisor can provide the brand, the products, and even the system, but the franchisee has to make the business work. Astute franchisees will take advantage of all the training and assistance they have received and will reap the benefits of being part of a successful franchise.

Exploring Global Franchising Opportunities

Franchising is a global phenomenon and opportunities abound in all areas of the world. It is common for franchisors to strategically identify countries or regions in which they plan to expand and to seek out franchisees in those areas. Some franchisors require the franchisees to be citizens of the countries in which they are developing franchises. Most franchisors prefer to expand through master franchises or area franchises rather than single units, selling franchise rights to large geographic areas or to entire countries. It is also common for franchisors to create joint ventures with existing firms in the markets they are entering.

◀ **Learning Objective 6**
Explore international franchising.

© david pearson/Alamy

Franchisors such as McDonald's and Intercontinental Hotels have been selling international franchises for decades. As of 2013, they have 15,365 and 1,408 international franchises, respectively.[10] Subway has 13,549 foreign franchises, and The UPS Store has 331 Canadian units, according to *Entrepreneur.com*. Other franchisors have just begun to reach out beyond the borders of the United States. At the same time, franchisors from overseas have extended their reach beyond national borders to span the globe.

The decision to franchise globally is far more complex than addressing local and regional variations. Ethnic, cultural, and religious diversity compels variations in the business format and operations. For example, menus must be adjusted for dietary preferences and restrictions, uniforms may have to vary, advertising and promotion will be different, as will hours and cost structures. In addition, human resources issues and policies must be altered for governing law and custom. However, there are many lucrative and rewarding franchising opportunities around the world.

Chapter Summary

Now that you have studied this chapter you can do the following:

1. Define and describe franchising.
    - A franchise is a business that markets a product or service developed by the franchisor, typically in the manner specified by the franchisor.
    - Product and trade-name franchising is the licensing of a product or the production of a product, and the use of the trademark, logo, or other identifying feature of the franchise.
    - Business-format franchising takes place when the franchisee secures the product and trade-name benefits, and the operating, quality assurance, accounting, marketing methods, and support of the franchisor.

---

[10]Entrepreneur 2013 Franchise 500, *Entrepreneur* magazine. Accessed July 1, 2013, http://www.entrepreneur.com/franchises/mcdonalds/282570-0.html and http://www.entrepreneur.com/franchises/subway/282839-0.html.

2. Identify the positive and negative aspects of franchising.
   - Start-up assistance (+)
   - Advertising and promotional support (+)
   - Operating guidelines and assistance (+)
   - Record of success (+)
   - Constraints on creativity and freedom (−)
   - Costs (−)
   - Standards and termination (−)
3. Understand the structure of the franchise industry.
   - Large franchisors control most of the industry.
   - Types include Internet franchises, conversion franchising, and co-branding.
4. Recognize the legal aspects of franchising.
   - Franchise Disclosure Document (FDD) is essential.
   - State and federal regulations govern franchising.
   - A franchise agreement and other legal documents will be involved.
   - Use good legal counsel.
5. Learn how to research franchise opportunities.
   - Self-reflect and engage core support people.
   - Explore industry, type, geography, or brand selection and brand name, or business-format choice.
   - Research using available resources.
   - Narrow the list of options.
   - Make the broker decision.
   - Visit franchise operator(s).
   - Contact the franchisor.
   - Perform due diligence on the specific franchise.
   - Explore financing options.
   - Make a decision and negotiate the franchise agreement, engaging professional counsel.
   - Make it work!
6. Explore international franchising.
   - Opportunities are available worldwide.
   - Decision is more complex than domestic franchising.

Key Terms

area franchise, 58
business-format franchising, 58
co-branding, 65
conversion franchising, 65
cooperative advertising fee, 60
franchise, 57
franchise agreement, 67
franchise broker, 68
Franchise Disclosure Document (FDD), 66

franchisee, 57
franchising, 57
franchisor, 57
Internet franchise, 65
master franchise, 58
multiple-unit franchise, 58
piggybacking, 65
product and trade-name franchising, 58

Entrepreneurship Portfolio

Critical Thinking Exercises

2-1. Does franchising limit an entrepreneur's freedom and creativity? Illustrate your arguments with examples.

2-2. What factors should one consider before taking up a franchise?

2-3. Would you like to become the franchisee of an international organization? Why or why not?

2-4. If one wants to be successful, not only does one have to be in the right place at the right time but also do something about it. Describe and discuss two instances that illustrate this.

Key Concept Questions

2-5. Define franchise. What are the different types of franchises? Choose any franchise and discuss its type.

2-6. Which franchising format do you think is more prone to legal complications?

2-7. What, if any, trends in franchising suggest continued expansion of the industry? Contraction? Cite your sources.

Application Exercise

2-8. Identify an industry or type of business that interests you. Select a community where you would like to locate such an organization (select a business that would have a physical presence). Find two competitors already in that market space and one franchisor that is not. Would it or would it not make sense to open a franchise in the community?

Exploring Online

2-9. Visit the Wahoo Fish Taco Web site at http://www.wahoos. com. What are the advantages of a Wahoo Fish Taco franchise according to the site? What franchise opportunities are available?

2-10. Visit the International Franchise Association Web site at http:// www.franchise.org. Find a franchise organization that is unfamiliar to you. Find the following information about the franchisor:

a. When did it begin offering franchises?

b. How many company-owned units does it have?

c. What are its initial financial requirements (start-up fee, net worth, liquid resources)?

d. What type of franchisor is it (product or trade-name or business-format)?

If the information is not available on the International Franchise Association (IFA) Web site, try others from the list in **Exhibit 2-3**.

SarahCare of Snellville—A Franchise Opportunity in Adult Day Care

Aysha Treadwell Cooper transitioned from her role in advertising sales in Tampa, Florida, to the ownership of a SarahCare franchise in the Atlanta area in 2010. For Cooper, an Indiana native, this was a return to her professional roots and personal passion. Cooper has a degree in public health and worked in a children's hospital prior to leaving Indiana. She also has strong feelings for her community of Snellville, Georgia. She became active in the community prior to opening her franchise, saying, "I knew that to open the business, I needed to learn about the community. . . . It taught me about how to make a difference as an individual and a community advocate." Today, she is the owner and Executive Director of SarahCare of Snellville.

SarahCare of Snellville is a franchisee of SARAH Adult Day Service, Inc., a Canton, Ohio-based franchisor that has franchisees in 18 states. The company "offers a franchising opportunity that meets the two criteria for a successful and socially responsible business: a booming demographic market with even more potential for growth, and excellent senior care. The SarahCare Adult Day Care Services franchise allows entrepreneurs to become part of this expanding industry, while enriching their lives as they help seniors age in place." Currently, the company is adding locations through the existing network, rather than through new franchisees.

Specifically, Cooper describes her SarahCare facility as "a place that provides a stimulating environment and a place for entertainment and relaxation for those whose lives are impaired by cognitive impairment, such as Alzheimer's disease and dementia. It aims to keep communities strong and families together."

According to the SarahCare Web site, the Complete SarahCare® Franchise Package includes:

- State of the Art Operational System
- Site Selection Assistance
- Space Design
- Adult Day Care Business Plan Template
- SarahCare Marketing System
- Advertising and Promotional Materials
- 5-Day Operations Training
- Ongoing Support and Training by Experienced Professionals

The company was founded in 1985 by Dr. Merle Griff, a gerontologist, when she opened her first center. She opened a second center in nearby Massillon, Ohio, after a few years. In 2004, the second center was relocated for growth and named SarahCare of Belden Village. That same year, SARAH Adult Services began offering franchises. The company now recommends that there should be a defined driving radius that includes about 10,000 adults aged 60 and above for each facility that opens.

SarahCare works with franchisees and their real estate brokers to find sites and make them ready for a SarahCare Adult Day Care facility. The franchisor provides guidelines, checklists, and answers to frequently asked questions. It also offers prototype centers and will create an initial space plan as part of the franchise fee. The décor has been designed for the SarahCare centers with two color palettes and a preferred vendor who offers equipment and furnishings. The centers are meant to "offer [a] warm and home-like environment and are designed to accommodate the varied needs of our participants." A final site inspection is performed by SarahCare personnel.

SarahCare of Snellville is managed by Cooper, who has a background in healthcare. However, this is not required. Some centers are managed by executive directors who are not the owners. In these instances, the franchisor assists in the hiring process. One benefit that the franchisor promotes is that center hours are from 7:00 a.m. to 6:00 p.m. on Monday through Friday, leaving time for family. For Cooper, the mother of a young child, this is quite appealing.

SarahCare of Snellville is Cooper's opportunity to combine her interests in healthcare, the elderly, and her community into her profession through franchising.

Case Study Analysis

2-11. What type of franchise is SarahCare?

2-12. Using the Web sites listed under Case Sources or others that you can find, identify each of the following for a SarahCare franchise: franchise fee, net worth requirement, total initial investment, and ongoing royalty fee.

2-13. What are some of the distinctive advantages that would lead a franchisee to select a SarahCare franchise?

2-14. What might be some potential concerns about buying a SarahCare franchise?

Case Sources

"Aysha (Treadwell) Cooper profile," LinkedIn, accessed July 2, 2013, http://www.LinkedIn.com/profile/view?id=42351744&locale=en_US&trk=tyah.

Samantha Graham, "Wednesday's Woman: Aysha Cooper," *Snellville Patch*, accessed May 7, 2013, http://snellville.patch.com/articles/wednesdays-woman-aysha-cooper.

"SARAH Adult Day Services Franchise Information," Franchise *Gator*, accessed July 2, 2013, http://www.franchisegator.com/sarahcare-franchise/.

"SarahCare," *SARAH Adult Day Services, Inc.*, accessed May 7, 2013, http://www.sarahcare.com.

Case Study | Pietsch Siblings: Wahoo's Fish Taco® Franchisees

How Wahoo's Began

Before it became a successful franchise chain, Wahoo's was a small, Californian restaurant born from three brothers' craving for fish tacos. Growing up in Brazil and California, Wing Lam, Ed Lee, and Mingo Lee learned a lot about running a business by helping out in their family's Chinese restaurant. After discovering fish tacos while surfing in Mexico, the three brothers combined their knowledge of surfing culture and the restaurant industry into an entrepreneurial venture of their own.

When the first Wahoo's Fish Taco was opened in 1988, it was decorated with donated products from local surf businesses. The food was a combination of the Brazilian, Mexican, and Asian flavors and ingredients the brothers loved. The restaurant quickly became popular because of its unique, fresh, and healthy food. Today, there are more than 50 Wahoo's franchise locations in California, Nevada, Colorado, Nebraska, New York, Texas, and Hawaii. One of these restaurants was started by three other siblings from the Pietsch family.

Wahoo's Comes to Hawaii

Wahoo's first Hawaiian franchise came about in a roundabout way. While working in Los Angeles for the Angels baseball team, Stephanie Pietsch Gambetta met Wing Lam by chance, and a business friendship developed. Stephanie's brother Mike and sister Noel also liked the Wahoo's franchise concept. Born and raised in Honolulu, all three siblings thought a Wahoo's restaurant would do well in Hawaii's surfing-oriented culture.

To make a long story short, the Pietsches invited Wing and his brothers to Hawaii for a surfing trip and asked to be considered as franchisees. Even though the Pietsches' restaurant experience was limited, their knowledge of the local area, and Stephanie's extensive sports-marketing background, gave them an edge. The Pietsches opened their Wahoo's restaurant in 2006.

Wahoo's uses a hands-on approach with its franchisees. The company provides mandatory training for approximately one month. Thereafter, communications continue via telephone and visits from Wing. Wahoo's open-door policy allows for plenty of give-and-take discussions between franchisor and franchisee. According to Mike Pietsch, "Franchising is a good way to get into business because there are systems already in place." Stephanie adds, "The franchise provides a support system so there's a resource for asking questions, training, and growing the business."[1]

Learning Valuable Lessons

The Pietsch-owned franchise was an immediate success, with customers lining up clear around the restaurant. "The first six months were a blur," Noel recalls. "We were doing better than we ever expected, but at a frantic pace."[2] After only five months, the Honolulu-based franchise became one of the top sales leaders for Wahoo's Fish Taco.

In the process, the owners learned many valuable lessons as they gained more experience. For example, keeping the restaurant staffed with quality employees was difficult in Hawaii's tight labor market. During the first year and a half, almost the entire staff turned over about three times.

"Now," Noel says, "we are rarely hiring because we have a solid team of people who really want to be here and work hard at what they do." Stephanie adds, "We really learned to work on our efficiency. We're setting goals and controlling what we can, be it labor or food costs."[3]

Learning to improve their communication was another important lesson. Although they admit to having made mistakes, the Pietsches also feel they have learned how to make their business run smoother based on those experiences. They also schedule time to get together away from the restaurant to discuss how the business is working.

Marketing the Business

The Wahoo's franchise chain targets a particular customer mindset. This customer focus includes individuals who actually participate in extreme

---

[1]Susan Sunderland, *"Something's Fishy @ Wahoo's,"* Midweek Kau'i, accessed July 2, 2013, http://www.midweek.com/content/story/theweekend_coverstory/somethings_fishy_wahoos.

[2]Ibid.

[3]Jacy L. Youn, *"Lessons Learned - Wahoos Fish Tacos,"* Hawaii Business, January 2009, accessed July 2, 2013, http://www.hawaiibusiness.com/SmallBiz/January-2009/Lessons-Learned-Wahoos-Fish-Tacos/index.php.

sports, such as surfing, skateboarding, and snow-boarding. However, a much larger market segment is made up of those who simply want to live vicariously through others who are living a sports lifestyle.

Wahoo's encourages their franchisees to use regional sports and charity events, as well as other types of local grassroots opportunities, to help market their businesses. For example, the Pietsches' restaurant sponsors many surfing and body-boarding events. Noel remarks, "We support the youth a lot because if we get them eating at Wahoo's, they'll do it the rest of their lives."[4]

To help grow their business, the Pietsch team opened a catering division. One promotional method they use involves taking food samples to the offices of local companies. The Pietsches also came up with an idea, endorsed by Wahoo's, for placing a lunch wagon at one of the local beaches. These two additional arms of the business help generate revenue but have lower overhead costs than adding an additional restaurant.

Wahoo's Franchise Information

Wahoo's Fish Taco is looking for franchise candidates who have restaurant experience (in particular, multi-unit restaurant experience). However, as with the Pietsch siblings, applicants with other types of business backgrounds may be considered.

Wahoo's also prefers applicants with the financial means to potentially own and operate at least three restaurants in a particular geographical area. More than one restaurant provides the franchisee with a greater economy of scale. Because of Wahoo's national contracts with various vendors, larger volumes of ingredients can be purchased at a lower cost. In essence, the more fish tacos that are produced, the less expensive each one becomes, and so profits increase.

The initial franchise fee is $35,000 for the first restaurant and $27,500 for each additional one. The ongoing royalty fee is 5 percent of gross sales, paid weekly. Also, each franchisee must allocate 2 percent of gross sales for marketing and advertising. Wahoo's estimates that the cost of building a brand new restaurant will range between $425,000 and $715,000, depending on store location and size, materials used, and other local factors.

[4]Ibid.

© Christina Kennedy/Alamy

On advice from Wahoo's, a franchisee should provide his or her own start-up money, rather than borrow it. In the restaurant business there are seasonal ups and downs that affect cash flow. So, it is always best to have some available working capital to help avoid getting caught in a financial crunch.

In the end, however, money and experience are only part of a successful equation. To be a peak performer in the restaurant business, owners have to love the work they do and know how to have fun doing it. That's the bottom line.

Case Study Analysis

2-15. Why did the Pietsches decide to purchase a Wahoo's Fish Taco franchise rather than start a restaurant on their own?

2-16. Name something the Pietsches could have done better to make their business start-up go more smoothly.

2-17. What does the Pietsch-owned franchise do on an ongoing basis to maintain and grow success?

2-18. What type of a franchise is Wahoo's Fish Taco? What makes this true?

Case Sources

Allison Schaefers, "Yahoo for Wahoo's," *Honolulu Star-Bulletin*, June 11, 2006, accessed July 2, 2013, http://archives.starbulletin.com/2006/06/11/business/story01.html.

Jacy L. Youn, "New Business Lessons," *Hawaii Business*, January 2009, accessed July 2, 2013, http://www.hawaiibusiness.com/SmallBiz/January-2009/Lessons-Learned-Wahoos-Fish-Tacos/index.php.

Kurtis Takamine, "Wahoo!" *AsianLife*, April 14, 2008, accessed July 2, 2013, http://www.asianlife.com/magazine/view/articles/id/645838631.

Susan Kang Sunderland, "Something's Fishy @ Wahoo's," *MidWeek* Kaua'i, March 2, 2007, accessed July 2, 2013, http://www.midweek.com/content/story/theweekend_coverstory/somethings_fishy_wahoos

Wahoo's Fish Taco, Accessed July 1, 2013, http://www.wahoos.com.

Chapter 3

FINDING OPPORTUNITY IN AN EXISTING BUSINESS

Learning Objectives

1. Understand the potential benefits of buying a going concern.

2. Identify potential drawbacks of purchasing a business.

3. Learn how to identify and evaluate purchasing opportunities.

4. Learn how to determine the value of a business.

5. Learn how to negotiate and close the deal.

6. Recognize joining a family business as an entrepreneurial pathway.

Siri Stafford/Thinkstock

Many businesses succeed through the entrepreneurial effort of owners who were not the founders. Charles R. Walgreen, Sr., became a store owner in 1901 when he purchased a pharmacy from Isaac Blood in Chicago for $6,000.[1] Walgreen had worked at the store as a pharmacist and was not satisfied with the quality or customer service there or at pharmacies in general. (He had worked in drugstores since he was a teenager.) However, he saw value in taking over a business that was already in existence, and started with one that he knew well. Walgreen saw that the neighborhood was thriving, but the store was struggling. It did not take long for Walgreen's innovative approach to store layout and merchandising to reap rewards. He opened a second store in 1909 and by 1919, he had incorporated 20 stores as Walgreen's Inc.

Not content to rest on this success, Walgreen's "shook up" the soda fountain portion of the pharmacy business in 1922 with the invention of the malted milkshake by Ivar "Pop" Coulson, which was a revolutionary product and boosted sales phenomenally. By 1926, Walgreen had opened his 100th store in Chicago, and the company went public the following year. In 1939, upon its founder's death, Walgreen's transitioned the presidency to his son, Charles Walgreen, Jr., illustrating business growth through acquisition, a public stock offering, and generational transfer. This leadership change was followed by continued expansion that resulted in Walgreen's becoming the nation's largest self-service retailer by 1953.

Walgreen's continued to grow and successfully transferred the presidency to the third generation in 1969. The company reached the $1 billion sales mark in 1975 and opened its 1,000th store in 1984. Charles Walgreen III retired in 1999 but remained on the board of directors. Walgreen's continued its rapid growth trajectory through acquisition, including the acquisition of New York's Duane Read chain and Take Care Health Systems, adding clinics to its business mix.

Walgreen's is a classic example of entrepreneurial success through acquisition and internal growth.

Many entrepreneurs, like Charles Walgreen, Sr., elect to purchase a going concern rather than starting a business "from scratch." Others decide to apply their entrepreneurial talents to existing family-owned businesses they buy.

Lightworks Media/Alamy

[1] *Source: Walgreen's.* Accessed March 17, 2009 and July 3, 2013, http://www.walgreens.com/marketing/about/history.

Exhibit 3-1 *Entrances and Exits of U.S. Establishments, 2007–2011*					
	2007	**2008**	**2009**	**2010**	**2011**
Entrants	819,375	712,836	609,303	662,975	682,171
Exits	713,588	704,795	805,677	705,659	659,452
Net Job Creation	1,368,177	863,022	−5,931,824	−1,715,301	1,777,680

Source: U.S. Dept of Commerce, Bureau of the Census, "Business Dynamics Statistics," accessed July 3, 2013, http://www .census.gov/ces/dataproducts/bds/data_firm.html.

Both approaches are potential pathways to success through opportunities found in already existing businesses. Approximately 750,000 businesses change ownership each year, demonstrating the popularity of this option. **Exhibit 3-1** provides insights into the number of business starts and closures per year, which illustrates that the number of businesses changing ownership is greater than the number started de novo.

Reasons to Buy an Existing Business

Learning Objective 1

Understand the potential benefits of buying a going concern.

Becoming a successful entrepreneur is a process that can be simplified and accelerated by purchasing an operating business. Entrepreneurial risk can be reduced and potential bargains may be available. However, buying an existing business can also be a route to ownership that is fraught with pitfalls. This is truly a case of *caveat emptor*—let the buyer beware. However, the well-prepared shopper can find the right business to buy.

Quicker, Easier Start-Up

A successful existing business has already leapt over many of the hurdles that would be encountered by a start-up venture. The issues of location, customer development, product or service delivery, and supplier relationships, among others, have been addressed. By acquiring existing relationships and operations, you can save much of the time and effort required to put these into place. Employees can be a particularly valuable part of an acquisition, as they bring institutional memory and relationships to the new owner. In many cases, the seller will also agree to remain in the business for a predetermined length of time to assist in the transition.

Of course, the full benefits of these assets will be realized only if they are truly represented. For example, employees will have to stay with the firm and cooperate with the new owner to provide the value expected. Customer, supplier, and financial-institution relationships need to be positive and healthy. If these conditions are met, you may be many steps ahead of the game by purchasing the right business.

Reduced Risk

Entrepreneurs who carefully consider the best fit for themselves and perform a thorough search and careful research can significantly decrease the risk of failure through an acquisition. The majority of small businesses that change owners are still in business five years later, about double the rate of start-up survival.

Stepping into an existing business can reduce risks associated with uncertainties and unknowns. Start-up businesses face multiple risks, primarily those of not finding a sufficient market and not being able to operate profitably. By buying a going concern, you can take advantage of the established customer base and the systems that are in place to generate cash flows and profits. Whereas past success does not ensure future success, it does increase the likelihood that a business will be profitable.

Bargain Potential

Whereas bargain hunting is not likely to be your primary motivation in purchasing an existing business, it is possible to buy a going concern for less than it would cost to start a similar company. In some cases, a business may be losing money according to its books and records but reveal a solid cash-flow opportunity when examined closely. Or, there may be waste and poor management that can be improved upon to gain value. By the same token, an overly eager seller or a price that sounds too good to be true may be a sign that the opportunity actually *is* too good to be true. This is another example of why solid research and due diligence is so critical to a purchasing decision.

Your Knowledge Can Be Beneficial

If you find a business for sale that you already understand, it can jump-start the ownership process. It may be that you work in the same industry or type of firm. Or perhaps this type of company is a supplier to or a customer of your current company. Maybe you have transferable skills from prior experience that fit.

You can have an understanding of a business from skills attained in your volunteer activities, or as a stay-at-home parent or caregiver, rather than through employment experience. Or, you can seek out employment in the type of company you want to purchase so that you will have operating experience in advance. For example, buying a restaurant without ever having managed one is often a recipe for disaster.

Of course, if you have an opportunity to buy the business where you work, you may have an advantage. In this case, you may already know the positive and negative aspects of the business and can make a more informed decision. Be careful, though, because your perspective as an employee may be limited or biased.

In any event, if you have or can build an understanding of the type of business you are buying, you will make a more informed purchase decision and reduce your learning curve.

Potential Pitfalls of Buying an Existing Business

Whereas an existing business can provide a hedge against entrepreneurial risk, there are numerous hazards in purchasing a going concern. Typically, you will have to secure more capital to buy a business than to start one up because you are paying for the established customer base, supplier relationships, and skilled employees. Another pitfall that can be fatal is the potential for being misled, whether intentionally or not, regarding the true condition and viability of the firm. Yet another is electing to take ownership of a company built in the mold of the previous owner and finding that it is not a good fit for you. Still another frequent issue is that a company's existing customers often are no longer customers after the sale. The customers of a company before it is sold do not necessarily remain so afterwards, in which case revenues will be lower than anticipated. These dangers can be avoided, or at least minimized, by carefully researching every aspect of the organization, its customers, suppliers, and employees, as well as the financial

◄ **Learning Objective 2**
Identify potential drawbacks of purchasing a business.

Zhu Difeng/Shutterstock

Global Impact . . .

Buying Ownership in a Business You Understand—Globally and Locally

Theresa Rogers has had a lifelong passion for wine. She has taken that passion, and her extensive knowledge of the industry, and applied it to running Horseneck Wines and Liquors since she purchased the company in 1989. Rogers began studying Hugh Johnson's *Pocket Encyclopedia of Wine* at the age of 19 and secured a job as a salesperson in the Fine Wine division of Heublein, covering the five boroughs of New York; from working on commission, she rose to managing a sales force. From there, Rogers worked with a small company to build a brand called Bollini Chardonnay, the first Italian Chardonnay to be marketed across the United States that sold for less than $10 per bottle. Rogers built the brand to 30,000 cases in the major American markets over a three-year period. She then went to work for the Empson Company, one of the first Italian exporters of the finest Italian

wines, such as Gaja from the Piedmont region. Rogers works with Angelo Gaja to bring his brand to the forefront of the Barbarescos and Barolos.

Rogers bought her first store in 1986 and sold it in 2005. She purchased Horseneck, located in Greenwich, Connecticut, as her second store. Horseneck Wines and Liquors has grown from a $500,000 wine shop into a firm with $5 million in annual sales and one of the largest collections of fine and rare wines in the state. Rogers took an existing business and built on its potential by plowing her profits back into the company and creating market opportunities. She established her networks and customer base through contributions to charity events, holding wine-tasting parties, and building relationships with local retailers and restaurateurs. As with any wine store, Horseneck sells a range of international wines and spirits, but went one step further—collecting rare wines and carrying the largest collection of Bordeaux, Burgundies, and Italian wines in Connecticut. Rogers started with an existing business and made it truly her own.

Source: Courtesy of Horseneck Wine and Liquors.

reports and tax returns. Outside counsel regarding the accounting and legal issues involved is strongly recommended. Again, due diligence and thoughtful deliberation are essential ingredients to a business purchase.

Investment Requirements

Buying an existing business will require gathering the financial resources needed to complete the transaction and operate successfully. When you start a business from scratch, you will have to build your own customer base, create your brand, hire employees, and develop a supply chain. When you buy a business, this work has been done for you, but the individual who did all that—the owner—will need to be compensated for it, raising the financing requirements.

Buying Someone Else's Problems

Whereas buying a business has many advantages that may translate into market benefits, you will also take over its challenges and problems. Some of these challenges may be obvious and are among the reasons that you saw value in buying the business in the first place. Others may be well hidden and need digging to discover. Undisclosed issues might include:

- dissatisfied customers, suppliers, employees, or creditors;
- plant and equipment that is obsolete, inefficient, or in need of costly repairs;
- lack of innovation or failure to keep up with market trends;
- obsolete or overvalued inventory and/or accounts receivable; and
- patents no longer valid and in force (this can be discovered through the U.S. Patent and Trademark Office).

These types of issues can catch you off guard, cost you your investment, and bring a lot of heartache. Be deliberately diligent in understanding exactly what you are getting and not getting.

Business Is Not a Good Fit

Whereas it is important to find a business that meets the prospective buyer's financial, industry, and other criteria, none of those factors will matter if it does not fit well with personality, lifestyle, and work-environment requirements. It is easy to get caught up in the excitement of the purchase, but a business that is a poor fit at the owner level will soon become a burden, no matter how outwardly successful it may be or become. You need to "keep your eyes on the prize" and remember that the prize includes lifestyle factors that are important to you.

Examples of poor fits abound. For example, if you are hands off as a manager and you buy a business that requires you to get out on to a production floor and roll up your sleeves whenever someone is out, or you have to be "chief cook and bottle washer," you may rapidly come to resent the business. If you like to work late at night but need to be present during traditional retail store hours, you will be exhausted and unhappy, at least until you can afford to comfortably adapt your schedule.

Finding and Evaluating Available Businesses

The process of finding and evaluating available businesses is similar to that of identifying a business to start or franchise to buy. The first step is to carefully evaluate your personal goals and objectives and the support of those closest to you. Through an iterative process, you can determine your focus and gather data accordingly. Once you have identified one or a few prospective sellers, the critical stage will be due diligence followed by negotiation and closing the deal.

◀ **Learning Objective 3**
Learn how to identify and evaluate purchasing opportunities.

Sources of Existing Businesses

Sources of leads to available businesses abound. The challenge is identifying the sources most suited to your individual goals and objectives and sifting through the potentially overwhelming amount of data to find the pertinent information for decision making. At first, your search may be extremely broad, much as it could be for a franchise opportunity. After thoughtful evaluation of your decision-making criteria and priorities, it should be possible to narrow the search to businesses meeting your industry, geography, size, life-cycle, profitability, and other criteria. **Exhibit 3-2** lists a number of sources for leads regarding businesses for sale.

In addition to the do-it-yourself sources noted in the exhibit, **business brokers** buy and sell businesses for a fee, in essence serving as a matchmaker. These brokers may have a small portfolio of businesses they are selling, or they may be part of a regional, national, or international network of brokers. Their income is based on their ability to close a sale, so be wary of any broker who seems overly aggressive. The International Business Brokers Association, Inc., is the largest association in the industry, so check to see if a broker is a member. You may also want to check with your local Better Business Bureau and with the broker's references before paying any fees or entering into an agreement. As with any contractual relationship, proceed with due caution and understand what you realistically can gain through the process.

business broker a company or individual that buys and sells businesses for a fee.

Type/Source	Resource/Opportunity
Exhibit 3-2 *Sources of Leads on Businesses for Sale*	
Direct Inquiry/Networking	
Current employer	Opportunity to purchase the business or referral to available businesses
Current commercial customers and suppliers	Opportunity to purchase the business or referral to available businesses
Competitors	Opportunity to purchase the business or referral to available businesses
Friends and family	Networks with leads to businesses for sale
Solicitation	
Direct mail	Using a limited mailing to targeted companies and/or individuals seeking leads
Advertising—local and regional publications, business magazines and newspapers, trade publications. (See *SRDS Business Publications* for a list of trade journals.)	Advertisements of businesses for sale and/or placing an advertisement for a purchase. Trade publications can be particularly useful when searching for a particular type of company.
Internet	
BizBuySell—http://www.bizbuysell.com	Sends registered users e-mail alerts regarding businesses for sale
Craigslist—http://www.craigslist.org	Free listing service for sellers and buyers
Business Broker Net—http://www.businessbroker.net	Classified advertising for buyers and sellers
BizQuest—http://www.bizquest.com	Searchable paid listings of businesses for sale
Merger Network—http://www.mergernetwork.com	Matching qualified-buyer members with sellers

However you identify a business to buy, it is crucial to have others on your team (or at least, on your side) who know what they are doing with respect to the business you are considering. It is even better if they have done this before. Having access to resource people that have also started and operated a business can help.

Due Diligence—Reality versus the Story

The process of searching for and identifying a business to buy can be an exhilarating and emotional time. It is also a time when rational thought and clear, well-developed research and analysis will be critical to success. It is easy to fall in love with the idea of owning a business and overlook the

Step into the Shoes . . .

ThompsonGas—Acquiring Opportunities

J. Randall (Randy) Thompson grew up with ThompsonGas as a presence in his life. His grandparents, Lloyd and Dortha Thompson, founded the company in 1946 and his father, Jim, took the reins in 1969. Randy took over operations of the Boonsboro, Maryland, business in 1996 at the age of 27 and began to grow it slowly.

After making the decision to grow strategically and rapidly through acquisitions, the ThompsonGas team began to acquire other family-operated suppliers of appliances and propane gas for commercial and residential customers. They purchased 27 companies between 1996 and 2012 and became the 18th largest distributor in the United States in 2012.

Initially, ThompsonGas identified potential acquisition candidates and pursued them. More recently, owners wishing to sell have begun to court ThompsonGas. This process has yielded a market footprint across the Eastern United States.

The third generation of the Thompson family created an entrepreneurial opportunity from an existing business.

Source: Courtesy of Thompson's Gas & Electric Service, Inc.

pitfalls and problems. Thus, **due diligence**, which is the exercise of reasonable care in the evaluation of a business opportunity, is vital. You have to sift through the story the seller and/or broker is telling you to discover the reality of the situation. Whether there is unintentional failure to disclose the full and true nature of conditions or a deliberate fabrication of information, the burden is on the buyer to identify the issues. Unlike the Franchise Disclosure Document, no standard, federally regulated disclosure is required, so discovery is up to the buyer and his or her attorney and accountant.

due diligence the exercise of reasonable care in the evaluation of a business opportunity.

Due diligence requires that the buyer acquire a broad range of information about the business, starting with the background information from the seller and through personal observation. Today, a quick scan of the Internet for information on the company and/or owner can provide ready access to information such as customer satisfaction/dissatisfaction, press coverage, and legal issues. Outside parties can provide a more complete picture of the firm. For example, bankers, suppliers, employees, and customers may provide realistic assessments and data. However, inconsistent or conflicting information, refusal to provide contact names, or hesitancy to open up to questions are all signs of potential problems and should be heeded.

If you want to truly understand a potential acquisition, information from stakeholders can prove invaluable. Internal documents, financial audits, and other information from the owners are critical to the process, but input from suppliers, customers, and employees helps to create a complete picture. It is perfectly appropriate to request lists of current and former suppliers, customers, and employees, both satisfied and dissatisfied, to interview. You are likely to get more of the truth about the business from its stakeholders. However, take care to avoid disclosing the potential sale if the current owner is protecting that information.

Part of the due diligence process should be to identify the real reason the owner is selling. Whereas people may offer such explanations as retirement, illness, relocation, or change of heart, the real answer may be something less benign. Common undisclosed reasons to sell a business are:

- lack of sufficient cash flow,
- unprofitability,
- difficulty in finding and retaining necessary staff,
- loss of exclusive franchise rights,
- pending changes in zoning or traffic patterns,
- changing industry or market conditions that will limit growth potential,
- entrance of new competitors,
- desire to start a new, competitive business in a better location, and
- pending or active litigation.

By completing the due diligence process, a prospective buyer may find that none of these negative circumstances exists and will feel comfortable making the purchase. However, it is better to find out about any potential pitfalls in advance and to address them than to receive unpleasant surprises after the purchase is final.

You can expect to receive information from a business broker and are well within your rights to request whatever information you require to make your decision. Sellers may be hesitant to disclose too much information to potential buyers because of concerns about competitive issues or the potential damage of disclosure should the sale not go through. They may require a signed **nondisclosure agreement**, a legal document enumerating the type of information that is to remain confidential.

nondisclosure agreement a legal document enumerating the type of information that is to remain confidential.

The prospective buyer can and should request full disclosure of all aspects of the business that pertain to its potential success. **Exhibit 3-3** lists

Exhibit 3-3 *Records and Information for a Prospective Buyer to Review*

- Financial statements, audited if available, for the previous three to five years
- Tax returns for the previous three to five years
- Bank deposit tickets for the past two years
- Employee records and turnover history for five years
- Ownership/shareholder structure and agreements, with any changes, for five years
- Statements of the business capital structure and assets, including nature of ownership
- Description of the products/services offered, with pricing and promotional materials
- Statements of condition of machinery, equipment, and physical plant, including any appraisals (followed by physical inspection)
- Inventory records (followed by physical inspection)
- Contracts, liens, leases, and other legal agreements
- Patents and records of patent-protection maintenance
- Other intellectual property protection, such as trademarks, copyrights, and sales marks
- Description of the technology in use, including computer software and dates of upgrades
- Disclosure of pending and active litigation, zoning, and regulations, as well as recently completed litigation
- Customer lists and sales records
- References from both satisfied and dissatisfied customers
- Supplier lists and references
- Credit and collections history in summary form and by account
- Statement of anticipated material changes
- Noncompete agreements

the records of information a buyer should request and review during due diligence. These are highly sensitive data for a business owner and may not be made readily available. Recognize that you have to be able to access any organizational documents, contracts and leases, financial statements, and tax returns to even consider purchasing a business. The more of the other items you can review, the better, particularly if you sense or observe something that may be problematic.

With this information in hand, you can work with skilled professionals, such as attorneys and accountants, to piece together a more realistic view of the business opportunity.

Determining the Value of a Business

The valuation of a business is a combination of art and science, ultimately a matter of arriving at a price and set of terms that both the buyer and seller find acceptable. For a public company, valuation is the worth of the stockholders' equity. For a going concern with audited financials, the determination can be based on projected earnings and cash flows. For other going concerns, the process is more complex because the quality and reliability of the financial information is less certain. The primary methods of valuation are asset valuation, earnings valuation, and cash flow valuation.

Asset valuation is a method that analyzes the underlying value of the firm's assets as a basis for negotiating the price. The four most common standards are

1. ***Book value.*** Starting with the value of assets reported in the books and records of the firm as a reference point, the actual value will depend on its accounting practices, such as allowances for losses and depreciation.

Learning Objective 4 ➤

Learn how to determine the value of a business.

asset valuation a method that analyzes the underlying value of the firm's assets as a basis for negotiating the price.

2. *Adjusted book value.* This takes into account any of the discrepancies identified in the calculation of book value and looks at the actual market value versus the stated book value. Intangible assets are often excluded in this method.

3. *Liquidation value.* This is a determination of the net cash that could be obtained through disposing of assets via a quick sale, with liabilities either paid off or negotiated away. It also includes the cost of liquidating. Neither buyers nor sellers are particularly interested in establishing a price based on liquidation, but it does establish a "floor," or minimum value, for the firm.

4. *Replacement value.* This is the determination of the cost of newly purchasing the assets, as would be required to start up the firm. This is also used more as a point of reference than as a pricing option.

Earnings valuation is a method that assesses the value of the firm based on a stream of earnings that is multiplied either by an agreed-upon factor (the capitalization factor) or by the price/earnings ratio (for a publicly traded company). As with any methodology of this nature, the challenge is how to determine the variables. Three ways of looking at earnings are

> **earnings valuation** a method that assesses the value of the firm based on a stream of earnings that is multiplied either by an agreed-upon factor (the capitalization factor) or by the Price/ Earnings ratio (for a publicly traded company).

1. *Historical earnings.* Start with the value of earnings reported in the books and records of the firm over multiple years. This can then be adjusted for items that will distort earnings, such as salaries of family members or depreciation. Historical earnings can be valid if future earnings can be reasonably projected as a result.

2. *Future earnings under current ownership.* This considers additional information that is available above and beyond historical earnings, such as economic changes, the competitive environment, and new products and services that have been introduced.

3. *Future earnings under new ownership.* This is a determination of the projections you make according to the changes you plan to implement. This may be the upper limit of what you are willing to consider.

In addition to determining which type of earnings to use, valuation will depend on which measure of earnings is selected. Will it be before or after taxes? Will it be earnings before interest and taxes (EBIT) or operating income? Which one is selected may make a significant difference in the valuation. It is traditional to use the after-tax earnings value without extraordinary items. However, if the new owner will have a different financing structure, using EBIT may be best. Ultimately, a price must be negotiated to the satisfaction of both the buyer and seller.

Another method of arriving at the worth of a business is to calculate the **cash flow valuation**, using projected future cash flows and the time value of money to arrive at a figure. This requires assessing the future expectations of cash flows from the business and applying financial calculations to arrive at the current value. It is less likely to be used for an entrepreneurial venture, but may be considered as an option.

> **cash flow valuation** a method of calculating the worth of a business by using projected future cash flows and the time value of money.

Whatever value is calculated through quantitative methods, the final price should also reflect nonfinancial variables. While performing due diligence, you gathered information regarding the market space, the competitive environment, the legal and regulatory status of the firm, and any pending changes in the physical environment or labor situation, or need for investment in plant, property, or equipment. The value of customer goodwill must be factored into the price, and the competitive and legal environments also have an impact on pricing. The offer price and the maximum amount you are willing to pay should encompass all of the factors you have identified. This price will have to be tempered by what you can afford.

Negotiating and Closing a Purchase

Learning Objective 5

Learn how to negotiate and close the deal.

Once you complete your research, perform due diligence, and decide that you would like to purchase a particular business, it is time to negotiate the final price and terms of the sale and close the transaction. Whereas it is the objective of both parties in the negotiation to reach an agreement, their respective goals are very different. As the buyer, you are working to secure the best price possible, to reduce your initial investment capital costs and maximize returns. The seller is working to recoup as much money as possible through the sale. Remember, the price you pay should be no greater than you determined in advance. It is better to have invested the time and resources and then walk away from a deal that is not the right fit than to pursue it and find that you cannot reach your goals.

When determining the price and terms of the sale, it is essential to clearly establish what is being purchased—assets only or the business as a whole. An asset sale reduces the buyer's liability because the outstanding debts and any undisclosed or unknown liabilities remain the seller's responsibility. In a whole business sale, the buyer acquires all the assets and liabilities of the company, known or unknown. You may also complete a purchase of the whole business and address the liability issue through an indemnification clause in the sales contract.

In addition to the stated price of the business, the terms of the sale will be a major factor. Will the previous owner hold a note payable on all or part of the purchase price? Under what repayment terms? Does a noncompete agreement restrict when and where the seller can open the same kind of business? Is the seller remaining with the business for a specified amount of time to perform particular duties? Sometimes a seller may want a quick sale and wish to cut all ties. In other situations, there may be tax advantages to having a different structure. This needs to be clearly spelled out in the sales contract.

All of the terms and conditions should be agreed on, with appropriate professional counsel for all parties, prior to the formal closing date. You should clearly understand all legal agreements and have them either drawn up or reviewed by your legal counsel. The investment in professional advice prior to the sale can be crucial. Once the closing is complete, you will have signed a number of important legal documents, including a bill of sale, any financing contracts, and other agreements. You will now be the owner of an operating business!

Buying into a Business over Time

One option that may permit a current owner to separate from a company gradually, receive a stream of payments, and support customer loyalty is purchasing a business over time. You may create such an arrangement in a variety of ways. Typically, the future owner joins the existing company with gradually increased responsibility and equity. This permits time to more fully understand the existing operation while the owner is still present and active and allows for a smoother transition. As with any purchase agreement, it must be carefully structured to protect all parties.

Family Business as an Entrepreneurial Opportunity

family business a firm that has two or more members of the same family managing and/or working in it and that is owned and operated for the benefit of that family's members.

Much has been written about start-ups, franchises, and business acquisitions as entrepreneurial paths. Joining a **family business**, a firm that has two or more members of the same family managing and/or working in it and that is owned and operated for the benefit of that family's members, can present an opportunity for entre-preneurial success as well.

Whether it is the second generation or the tenth, there may be significant room for innovation, growth, and wealth building. For example, when Alan Levin became president and CEO of Happy Harry's Discount Drugs in the late 1980s to fill a void left by the unexpected death of his father, Harry, he began an adven-ture that led to expansion from a handful of stores to 76 outlets 20 years later, when he sold the firm to Walgreen's. Clearly, Alan had found entrepreneurial oppor-tunity in a family business. There was ample opportunity for fostering entrepre-neurial energy and talent.

Alamy Images

With a family business, much like the acquisition of any going concern, there is a chance to build on its strengths and to turn around problematic aspects. The greatest differ-ence is that the changes will benefit the family and not only the buyer. A sound core business can provide a solid foundation for growth and expansion. If you join a family business in which your insights and en-ergy are appreciated and supported, you can be part of the team that has built upon prior success. If the family business is floundering, perhaps suffering from sales decline, cash flow challenges, or other factors that threaten its viability, you can bring a fresh perspective and an additional skill set to the firm.

As with participating in any venture, and perhaps even more so because of the family aspect, you should proceed with your eyes wide open when joining a family business. Your role and the roles of others in the company should be clearly defined, as should your compensation and participation in profits and ownership. How you will work with one another should be discussed frankly to prevent miscommunications that can lead to permanent breakdowns in family relationships. To the extent that it is viable, conduct your due diligence as if you were purchasing a business from an unrelated party, but recognize that the very process of exploring the opportunity must be carried out with family relationships in mind.

◀ Learning Objective 6
Recognize joining a family business as an entrepreneurial pathway.

Step into the Shoes . . .
Putting Spring into a Third-Generation Business

Brothers Tom and David Walker grew up at the Oregon Mattress Company in Newburg. Their grandfather, Cecil Austin Walker, founded the company in 1932, and their father, Richard, oper-ated it into the 1990s. Tom and David worked with their father for a number of years to expand the business and enhance its overall viability. They moved from producing under the Lady Americana label to Restonic, a well-respected national brand, and Sleep EZ, their own brand.

Since 2009, Oregon Mattress opened five national brand factory outlet stores featuring mattresses produced in its Portland-area factory. The BedCo Mattress Superstores are located in Newburg, Lake Oswego, Cedar Hills, Tigard, and Happy Valley. The Walkers saw an opportunity to increase their share of the local market through direct retail sales of locally produced mattresses, including hard-to-find custom sizes and shapes, and their signature round beds. Now, as the fourth generation of Walkers (TJ Walker is the Director of Operations) joins Oregon Mattress Company, the firm is bouncing back in a weak economy.

Oregon Mattress Co.

Source: Courtesy of Oregon Mattress Company.

Perhaps the notion of joining a family business has been appealing from a very young age. Perhaps it is best to experience working in other businesses or fields of endeavor and turning to the family business later. Perhaps you will be drawn into the business because of a family emergency or tragedy. Regardless of the point of entry or reason, your best entrepreneurial opportunity may lie within the family business.

Chapter Summary

Now that you have studied this chapter you can do the following:

1. Understand the potential benefits of buying a going concern.
   - Start-up can be quicker and easier.
   - Reduced risk results from the established business structure and relationships.
   - The potential to identify and purchase a business at a bargain price exists.
2. Identify potential drawbacks of purchasing a business.
   - The current owner may fail to disclose negative information regarding the firm's condition.
   - The business may be a poor fit for the buyer.
   - Pitfalls may be avoided through a thorough due diligence process and use of qualified professional counsel.
3. Learn how to identify and evaluate purchase opportunities.
   - Identify personal goals and objectives to create the best match.
   - Use the many resources available to identify prospective purchases.
   - Perform due diligence to secure the most complete and accurate information.
4. Learn how to determine the value of a business.
   - Use asset, earnings, and/or cash flow valuation methodologies to arrive at a range of potential prices.
   - Consider the spectrum of nonfinancial factors in the price.
   - Arrive at offer and maximum price before entering the negotiations.
5. Learn how to negotiate and close the deal.
   - Recognize the mutual goal of making the transaction happen, despite differing individual goals.
   - Negotiate a price and set of terms that is satisfactory to all parties.
   - Hold a formal closing and complete all legal documents with the support of qualified legal and accounting counsel.
6. Recognize the joining of a family business as an entrepreneurial pathway.
   - A family business may have the potential to foster entrepreneurial energy and talent.
   - A sound core business provides a solid foundation for future success.
   - A floundering family business offers a chance to turn around the company and benefit the entire family.
   - Sometimes an entrepreneurial opportunity is right in front of us; we just have to recognize it.

Key Terms

asset valuation, 86
business broker, 83
cash flow valuation, 87
due diligence, 85

earnings valuation, 87
family business, 88
nondisclosure agreement, 85

Entrepreneurship Portfolio

Critical Thinking Exercises

3-1. Is joining a family business better than establishing a new one? Why or why not?

3-2. What are the major factors to be determined in the negotiations to buy a business?

3-3. What factors ought to be considered while buying a business?

3-4. What are the potential opportunities and pitfalls of buying an existing business?

Key Concept Questions

3-5. In determining the value of a business distinguish between asset valuation, earnings valuation, and cash flow valuation.

3-6. Explain three ways businesses can be valued.

3-7. Describe the potential problems in buying a business.

Application Exercise

You have been considering going into business for three years and have saved $10,000 toward this dream. Since graduating from college two years ago, you have worked full time at a bank as a credit analyst and part time at a bookstore. These jobs have given you some perspective on financial services and retail trade. Now, you are ready to dig in and find a business to buy or start.

3-8. How will you decide what type of business to own (industry, geography, lifestyle, technology, etc.)?

3-9. Why would you (or would you not) weigh the option of buying a business?

3-10. Identify three possible sources of information on businesses for sale and find two possibilities from each. List the information that is provided on these six businesses.

3-11. Select one of the businesses and explain why it interests you as a possible investment.

Exploring Online

3-12. Perform a search of business brokers through an Internet search engine of your choice. What are the first five listings (excluding the sponsored links)?

3-13. Visit one of the Internet resources listed in **Exhibit 3-1**. Search for businesses for sale. Look at convenience stores, auto repair shops, or restaurants. Answer the following:

a. Which site and business type did you select?

b. How many businesses were listed for sale in your category?

c. Were there categories of businesses under the main search category? If so, what were they?

d. Examine one of the businesses for sale and record the information provided.

Case Study | A Family Affair

bikeriderlondon/Shutterstock

From as long as Deanna could remember, she had helped her mother in The Pantry, a small but successful bakery and restaurant that was known for unique desserts and pastries. When she was young, she helped clean tables in the small area for customer seating. As she grew older, she helped take phone orders and worked at the bakery counter.

Although succession plans were never discussed, Deanna had always planned to work full time in the business after college and eventually take over the company management when her mother retired. Deanna's mother and father had divorced when Deanna was very young, and because she was an only child, there were no other siblings to take control of the company. If Deanna did not assume ownership, the business would have to be closed or sold to an outsider.

In 1999, Deanna went off to college to study restaurant management. She enjoyed being away from home more than she had anticipated and did very well in her courses. She also became aware of other career opportunities in the food industry that she had never before considered. She realized she would gain valuable experience by working for other companies before she returned to her mother's business.

At about the same time, however, Deanna's mother remarried. Her new husband had two daughters of his own, aged 16 and 17. Because employee turnover at The Pantry was always a concern, Deanna's mother was more than happy to have his daughters work in the business part time while they were in high school.

To Deanna, though, this was a cause for concern. Now that she had stepsisters, the ownership of The Pantry was not necessarily hers when her mother retired. She was concerned that, if she accepted a position with another company after college, her mother might interpret that as a lack of interest in The Pantry. Once, when she was home during a spring break, she tried to initiate a conversation about the future of the business. Her mother's response was, "I'm only 45 now, and I'm not going to retire for a long time. So don't worry about it."

Deanna also realized that, in the future, if her mother and stepfather gave equal ownership to all three daughters, this would result in her owning one-third, whereas the two stepsisters together would own two-thirds. If the relationship did not work well, she would always be outvoted. She would not have control of the business, and even under the best of circumstances, this was not appealing.

Case Study Analysis

3-14. If you were in Deanna's position, what would you do?

3-15. Identify options that Deanna's mother and stepfather could consider rather than dividing business ownership equally among the children.

3-16. How could this business serve to provide entrepreneurial opportunities for Deanna?

Case Source

Peggy A. Lambing and Charles R. Kuehl, *Entrepreneurship*, 4th ed. (Upper Saddle River, NJ: Pearson Education, Inc., 2007), p. 263.

Krispy Kreme Doughnuts®

Prospects and Risks in Buying a Business

The history of Krispy Kreme Doughnuts® illustrates some of the potential opportunities and pitfalls that can result from buying an existing business. Since its beginning, Krispy Kreme has been bought and sold several times, with both successful and disastrous outcomes.

Alamy Images

Building on a Secret Formula

The ongoing success of Krispy Kreme started with a unique formula, still in use today. In 1933, Ishmael Armstrong bought a doughnut shop, a special recipe for yeast-raised doughnuts, and the name "Krispy Kreme" from Joe LeBeau, a French chef originally from New Orleans. Armstrong started producing doughnuts using that secret formula in his shop in Paducah, Kentucky. He also hired his nephew, Vernon Rudolph, to help with the production process and to sell the doughnuts to businesses.

Because of the difficult economic times during the Great Depression, Armstrong didn't sell enough doughnuts from the shop in Paducah to be profitable. So he and Rudolph left Kentucky and went to the larger city of Nashville, Tennessee. There, they opened another doughnut shop, hoping that the new location would produce greater sales.

Not much later, in 1935, Armstrong sold his doughnut shop in Nashville to Vernon Rudolph's father, Plumie Rudolph, and moved back to Kentucky. With the help of his sons, Vernon and Lewis, Plumie Rudolph ran not only the Nashville store but opened two others—one in Charleston, West Virginia, and another in Atlanta, Georgia.

Continued Growth and Success

Even though the family doughnut shops were successful, Vernon Rudolph still wanted his own store. In 1937, he and two of his friends left Nashville to start their own venture. They had $200, some doughnut-making equipment, and the special recipe. They had difficulty finding the right location. Finally, they settled on Winston-Salem, North Carolina, because it had the headquarters of a nationally advertised brand (cigarettes). They used their last $25 to rent a site on Main Street. They got the ingredients needed to make their first batch of doughnuts on credit and sold them through a walk-up window for 25 cents per dozen. Although the main portion of his sales continued to be wholesale customers, Rudolph did not ignore the retail trade.

Over the next 10 years, Rudolph opened a shop in Charlotte, North Carolina, and bought five more, including the Charleston, West Virginia, store owned by a relative. Krispy Kreme was trademarked in 1946 and incorporated in 1947. Also in 1947, the company licensed its name to franchisees it called "associates." Agreeing to buy the special doughnut mix from Krispy Kreme and to follow its operating standards, these associates opened their own doughnut stores.

By 1960, Krispy Kreme had become more standardized and was recognized by its red, green, and white logo and the shops' green-tiled roofs. A coffee bar also became a standard feature at all Krispy Kreme outlets. Most shops had a small glass window that allowed customers to look inside the kitchen and get a partial glimpse of the doughnuts being made.

The Wrong Fit

Krispy Kreme continued to prosper, growing to more than 60 stores in the southeastern United States by 1973, when Vernon Rudolph died at the age of 58. The company endured a terrifically difficult time following his death; the bank held Krispy Kreme in trust and the company had to be sold. In 1976, it was sold to Beatrice Foods of Chicago, a large conglomerate that included dairy, meat, grocery, candy, and other food-related companies.

Krispy Kreme's family-oriented business model did not fit with Beatrice Food's big-business approach. The new owner focused primarily on raising profits and decided that the way to do so was to make major changes. For example, Krispy Kreme's logo was redesigned in an attempt to modernize it. In an effort to bring in new customers at slow times during the day, other foods were added to the menu, including soups, sandwiches, and biscuits. But this increased shops' operating costs without increasing customer numbers.

Perhaps worst of all, the popular Krispy Kreme doughnut recipe was altered in an effort to cut costs and improve revenue margins. Those decisions almost ruined Krispy Kreme. The customer's experience and the unique taste of the doughnuts were no longer the focus.

Getting Back on Track

In 1982, a group of frustrated Krispy Kreme franchisees, led by Joseph A. McAleer, Sr., pooled their resources to buy back Krispy Kreme from Beatrice Foods. What they didn't have in savings, they borrowed, and they purchased the company for almost $22 million. They restored the doughnut formula and business model used in former years. However, the leveraged buyout created a large debt that kept the company from growing much over the next 10 years and it created a structure that required consensus for major decisions.

In the late 1980s and early 1990s, Krispy Kreme's new owners studied consumer research, both past and present, to help identify the heart of the Krispy Kreme brand. Although some of the research was formal, a lot of information was gathered through spontaneous discussions with customers. Over and over, the business's owners heard stories about happy memories eating hot doughnuts with friends and family.

As a result, Krispy Kreme expanded the idea of allowing customers to peek inside the kitchen by developing a theater-like atmosphere in many of the stores. Instead of a small window, glass walls were built around the production area. Customers were now able to see the entire doughnut-making process. When the "Hot Doughnuts Now" neon sign was turned on outside, it signaled to customers that fresh doughnuts were being made, so they could come in to watch.

Going Public: Transferring Ownership Again

Krispy Kreme, Inc., became a publicly traded company in 2000 by joining the NASDAQ (ticker KREM) at $21 per share and raising about $60 million. It joined the New York Stock Exchange (NYSE: KKD) in 2001. The infusion of capital was largely used for rapid expansion. The value of the stock reached almost $50 per share by August 2003.

However, the company failed to meet its quarterly projections and reported its first loss as a public company in May of the following year. The Securities and Exchange Commission (SEC) made informal and formal inquiries into several Krispy Kreme practices that led to restatement of most of their financials for 2004. In 2005, the long-time CEO was replaced by a turnaround specialist. A substantial number of stores were closed. Observers were concerned about management struggles, accounting issues, and franchisee problems. By 2009, the stock value had dropped to just over $1.00 per share.

As of July 8, 2013, shares traded at $19.72 per share with a market capitalization of $1.29 billion.

Earning a Place in History

By the early years of the new century, Krispy Kreme had nearly 300 retail stores that together produced more than 2 billion doughnuts annually. Today, the company has rebounded from the challenges of the last decade. It continues to grow, with about 773 locations in 22 countries, including the United States, Canada, Mexico, the United Kingdom, China, Qatar, Australia, and India, to name a few.

Krispy Kreme executives have learned from mistakes made in the past by their predecessors. Instead of rushing to implement new plans before the time is right, each potential new geographic location is carefully studied to make sure its market will support a full-scale doughnut operation. Krispy Kreme's management also spends time checking out sites for the individual stores. In addition, potential franchisees and employees are thoroughly screened. Those selected are required to maintain meticulous standards in order to ensure consistent product quality.

Even though these business strategies are time consuming, Krispy Kreme's successful comeback has proved that this approach works well. In fact, the company is now an official part of American history. In 1997, after 60 years in business, Krispy Kreme was inducted into the Smithsonian Institute's National Museum of American History.

Case Study Analysis

3-17. How many times has the company been sold? When and by whom to whom?

3-18. What mistakes did Beatrice Foods make after purchasing Krispy Kreme? Why wasn't Krispy Kreme a good fit for Beatrice Foods?

3-19. What opportunity did the franchisees see in buying back Krispy Kreme rather than starting a new company from scratch?

3-20. Describe several business lessons that can be drawn from Krispy Kreme's history.

3-21. Krispy Kreme started as a family business. How has that influenced the operation of the company?

3-22. Identify three questions you would have asked Ishmael Armstrong while performing due diligence for the potential purchase of Krispy Kreme Doughnuts. List three questions you would ask today if you were considering becoming a Krispy Kreme franchisee.

Case Sources

Juliette Arai (October 1998), Wendy Shay and Franklin A. Robinson, Jr. (January 2004), "Krispy Kreme Doughnut Corporation Records, ca. 1937–1997," *Smithsonian Institute National Museum of American History, Archives Center*, accessed July 3, 2013, http://americanhistory .si.edu/archives/d7594.htm.

Kate O'Sullivan, "Kremed!" *CFO Magazine*, June 1, 2005, accessed July 8, 2013, http://www .cfo.com/printable/article.cfm/4007436.

Kirk Kazanjian and Amy Joyner, *Making Dough: The 12 Secret Ingredients of Krispy Kreme's Sweet Success.* Hoboken, NJ: John Wiley & Sons, Inc., 2004.

Krispy Kreme Doughnuts. Accessed July 3, 2013, http://www.krispykreme.com.

Mark Tosczak, "Slim down or melt down? Issues loom at Krispy Kreme," *The Business Journal*, January 2, 2006, accessed July 8, 2013, http:// www.bizjournals.com/triad/stories/2006/01/02/ story1.html.

electronically to interested parties. With proper technology, you can also include audio to accompany the presentation. Whereas it is always preferable to make a presentation in person, this can be an effective way to submit your business plan to investors at their convenience. Remember, though, that proper nondisclosure agreements are an absolute necessity, because business plans are the valued property of their developers.

Your Business Plan Is the Key to Raising Capital

As mentioned, bankers and other potential investors will refuse to consider funding an entrepreneur without a business plan (unless the loan or investment you are seeking is very small). You may have a brilliant idea, but if it is not written out, people will be extremely unlikely to invest in your business or loan you money.

George Doyle/Getty Images

A well-written plan will show investors that you have carefully thought through how you intend to make your business profitable. The more detail you offer investors about how their money will be used, the more willing they will be to invest. The financial projections should be realistic and attainable. Your plan should be so thoughtful and well written that the only question it raises in an investor's mind is: "How much can I invest?"

The Business Plan Is an Operations Guide

Whether or not you need to raise capital, a business plan will be a vital tool for guiding the internal operations of your enterprise. Business owners and managers increase the probability of success by taking the plan in their heads and committing it to paper. The transition may be bumpy, because the process of writing a coherent plan will require answering difficult questions. However, in addition to guiding you as the entrepreneur, developing the plan will generate an increased clarity of vision, mission, and goals for your entire team. With your business plan as your benchmarking tool, you can compare your company's progress to your stated plan. You can also use the business plan as a point of reference when it seems you are going off track or becoming distracted from your goals. The presence of financial and operational goals and measures, as well as mission and vision statements, can feed a drive for success and motivate a team to excellence.

Business Plan Components

As you begin a new enterprise, you can find a seemingly endless variety of problems to address and questions to answer. Such a situation could quickly overwhelm you if you don't have a plan. However, by the time you have worked through all the steps of a business plan, you will have answers. You will develop a love *for* the business, rather than being in love with the *idea* of the business and having unrealistic expectations. The order of the components of a plan can vary somewhat, but there are elements common to all. An outline of one kind of business plan is illustrated in **Exhibit 4-1**.

◀ **Learning Objective 5**
Understand the components of a business plan.

Exhibit 4-1 *Business Plan Outline*

Cover Page
Table of Contents
1.0   Executive Summary
2.0   Mission, Vision, and Culture
3.0   Company Description
4.0   Opportunity Analysis and Research
    4.1 Industry Analysis
    4.2 Environmental Analysis
    4.3 Competitive Analysis
5.0   Marketing Strategy and Plan
    5.1 Products/Services
    5.2 Pricing
    5.3 Promotion
    5.4 Place
6.0   Management and Operations
    6.1 Management Team
    6.2 Research and Development
    6.3 Physical Location
    6.4 Facilities
    6.5 Inventory, Production, and Quality Assurance
7.0   Financial Analysis and Projections
    7.1 Sources and Uses of Capital
    7.2 Cash Flow Projections
    7.3 Balance Sheet Projections
    7.4 Income Statement Projections
    7.5 Breakeven Analysis
    7.6 Ratio Analysis
    7.7 Risks and Assumptions
8.0   Funding Request and Exit Strategy
    8.1 Amount and Type of Funds Requested
    8.2 Exit Plan
    8.3 Milestones
Appendices
    Resumes
    Sample Promotional Materials
    Product Illustrations/Diagrams
    Detailed Financial Projections

Cover Page and Table of Contents

Begin the plan as you intend to continue it. The cover page should be professional, neat, and attractive. It should provide the name of the business and the principals, the date, contact information, and any confidentiality statement. The table of contents should be sufficiently detailed so an investor or manager can easily find a section, but not so detailed that it takes up multiple pages of the plan.

Executive Summary: A Snapshot of Your Business

The executive summary has to be compelling and comprehensive. It may be the only part that many people will read. It will be the hook that either catches potential investors or loses their attention. If a reader doesn't fully understand the business concept and the purpose of the plan from the executive summary, the rest of the plan is likely to remain unread. The executive summary must encapsulate the story of the business clearly and concisely, propose the funding request, and inspire enthusiasm for the possibility of its success.

This section should be written last and limited to one or two pages. It should answer the *who, what, when, why,* and *how* questions for the business. Who will manage the business? What will it do, and what is the owner asking for in the plan? When will the proposed plan be implemented? How will the business succeed? Done well, the reader will have a "light-bulb" moment and be eager to read the rest of the plan.

Mission, Vision and Culture

Each company has the opportunity to create its own unique mission, vision, and culture. The founding team can determine how to strategically use the company's competitive advantage to satisfy customers. Culture that the owners model and support can be shaped according to the environment and the manner of treating employees, customers, and other stakeholders. The **mission** of your business, expressed in a mission statement, is a concise communication of strategy, including your *business definition* and *competitive advantage*. The function of a **mission statement** is to clarify what you are trying to do, and it can provide direction and motivation to those who are involved in the business.

A clearly stated mission statement not only tells your customers and employees what your business is about, but can also be a guide for every decision you make. It should capture your passion for the business and your commitment to satisfying your customers. The mission statement should be clear and concise, no more than 40 or 50 words.

The **vision** for your business will be broader and more comprehensive, painting the big picture of what you want your organization to become. It is built on the core values and belief system of the organization. It is typically shorter than the mission statement, with a loftier perspective.

The **culture** of an organization, whether intentionally or unintentionally created, is largely defined by its leadership. You can build a culture for your company by making beliefs, values, and behavioral norms explicit and intentional. A business's culture has many components, including attitudes toward risk-tolerance and innovation and its orientation with respect to people, team formation and outcomes, attention to detail, and communication. Whether you want a free-thinking, aggressive company with informal communications or a structured, formal organization with more "official" interactions, you will set the standards and be the role model for your business's culture.

mission a concise communication of strategy, including a business definition and explanation of competitive advantage.

mission statement a brief, written statement that informs customers and employees what an organization's goal is, and describes the strategy and tactics to meet it.

vision a broader and more comprehensive perspective on an organization than its mission; built on the core values and belief systems of the organization.

culture the beliefs, values, and behavioral norms of an organization.

Global Impact . . .

Upcycling Waste Internationally—TerraCycle, Inc.

Wu Kaixiang/Corbis Images

In 2003, John Szaky's TerraCycle won a business plan contest from Carrot Capital for $1 million in seed funding. But the venture capital firm wanted TerraCycle to drop its environmental focus, and Szaky turned down the offer. It was a critical decision that later helped the business achieve its competitive advantage.

TerraCycle converts unrecyclable packaging waste to upcycled products. An early inspiration was implemented when TerraCycle ran out of money to buy bottles in which to sell fertilizer derived from worm waste. It was decided to pack it in recycled soda bottles. This concept expanded into the production of other green products. Pencil holders made from Kool-Aid packets, tote bags made from Capri Sun-drink pouches, and backpacks made from Clif Bar wrappers are just a few examples of the more than one hundred TerraCycle products sold in large retail chains—including Home Depot, Whole Foods, Wal-Mart, and Target. The concept has spread to the United Kingdom, Brazil, Mexico, Israel, Canada among others. By working with concerned groups in each country, TerraCycle has the potential of becoming an iconic representative of upcycled waste. TerraCycle calls this process turning "branded" waste into "sponsored" waste.

Source: TerraCycle, Inc., accessed July 10, 2013, http://www.terracycle.com.

Company Description—Background and Track Record

If the company is already established, is a franchise, or is the reincarnation of a previous business, there will be a history to share with the reader of the plan. The business description does not need to be long. It should simply provide the background for understanding the rest of the plan. It should include summary information about the company's founding, its progress, and its financial success.

If this is a start-up venture, this section should describe briefly the background story of the company, explaining what you have done thus far and why you have done it. The legal form of the business (sole proprietorship, corporation, LLC, partnership) should also be noted.

Opportunity Analysis and Research: Testing Ideas

The opportunity-analysis and research section will provide the credible data and information to determine and demonstrate the market viability of your proposed business on paper, and perhaps in the field, before you start. It should be a clear description of why the business presents an excellent opportunity, based on sound research and logic. Entrepreneurs often either put little time and attention into this section or ignore data that contradict their optimistic view of the opportunity. This can prove to be a fatal flaw in business planning. A well-researched opportunity analysis can help to move your business to the head of the line for financing.

industry analysis a critical view of industry definition, industry size and growth (or decline), product and industry life cycle, and any current or anticipated legal or regulatory concerns.

The **industry analysis** will provide the broad context for your business plan. It will deal with such factors as industry definition, industry size and growth (or decline), product and industry life cycle, and any current or anticipated legal or regulatory concerns. Determining industry structure, including geographic distribution, business size of member firms, concentration of power, and rates of failure, is also important. For example, the failure rate of restaurants is notoriously high and should be addressed in a business plan for a dining establishment. This is also the place to discuss how you will track industry developments on an ongoing basis.

environmental analysis a review that addresses the roles of the community, region, nation, or the rest of the world, as they relate to a business.

The **environmental analysis** addresses the roles of the community, region, nation, and/or the rest of the world as they relate to your business. Whether or not demographic and family changes are working in your favor could mean adjustments for the business. Changes in technologies and economic conditions might radically alter your plans. Examples could include the aging of the baby boomer generation or the prevalence of computer technology.

proof of market an investigation that provides evidence of a market opportunity.

The opportunity analysis should include a **proof of market** investigation that will provide evidence of a market opportunity for your organization. This should identify market size, both in terms of dollars and units. There have to be enough customers who will purchase your product or service in sufficient quantity at a high enough price and often enough for your business to be sustainable.

target market groups defined by common factors such as demographics, psychographics, age, or geography that are of primary interest to a business.

Next, this analysis should describe your **target market** segments, which are groups of people defined by common factors, such as demographics, psychographics, age, or geography. For example, your target market segment for a gospel club may be African-American Christians between 18 and 25 years of age living in the Detroit metropolitan area. Discuss the size of your target market and the market share that would be attainable.

competitive analysis research that compares an organization with several direct and indirect competitors by name in a manner that is meaningful to targeted customers.

A **competitive analysis** is the next important component of the opportunity analysis. This should compare your organization with several direct and indirect competitors by name and include comparisons that would be meaningful to customers. The format of a competitive analysis can vary significantly, but it must make clear where your competitive strengths and weaknesses are and where there are holes in the competitors' businesses. Factors to compare may include, but would not be limited to, location, product selection, market share, product or service quality, experience, advertising, pricing, finances, capacity, hours, size and skill of workforce, and reputation.

Marketing Strategy and Plan: Reaching Customers

A description of how you will reach your customers and your anticipated sales volume brings the opportunity and research discussion to the bottom line of sales. Your **marketing mix** will be the combination of the four factors (the "Four Ps") that form your competitive advantage—also known as *core competency*—product, price, promotion, and place. As you choose the elements of your **marketing plan**, always keep your vision in mind. What benefit is your product or service providing to customers?

- *Products/Services.* The product or service should meet or create a customer need. The distinctive features and benefits of the product or service must be clearly stated. Remember, the packaging is also part of the product. If you are introducing an innovative technology, the value of the innovation to customers warrants explanation here.

- *Pricing.* The product or service has to be priced so that your target customers will buy it and the business will make a profit. Price should reflect your vision, strategy, and policy. It has to be right. For example, if you are marketing a luxury item, a relatively low price might not send the right message to your target customer. Highlight competitive advantages—such as quality, credit terms, warranty type and length, service, and innovativeness—that support the pricing.

- *Promotion.* Promotion consists of advertising, publicity, and other promotional methods, such as discount coupons or giveaways. Publicity is free, whereas advertising is purchased. The description of your promotional plans should be specific with respect to the methods used, the time line for implementation, and the budget. Often this section is further divided into advertising, public relations and publicity, and direct marketing. **Advertising** consists of paid promotion through media outlets, such as broadcast or cable television, the Internet, radio, magazines, and newspapers. **Public relations** consists of community activities that are designed to enhance your organization's image. **Publicity** is free notice in the media presented as news. **Direct marketing** includes telemarketing, direct mail, in-person selling, and other personalized efforts.

- *Place.* This is the venue from which you will sell and distribute your product. Your selling location should be where consumers in your target market do their shopping. Where should you go to bring your product or service to the attention of your market? If you are selling a luxury item, you will need to place it in stores or on Web sites that are visited by customers who can afford it. Included in *place* is your selection of a type of sales force (i.e., independent, company, single line, or multiline), any geographic definition of your market, and all channels of distribution. Are you going to sell directly to consumers, work through wholesale distributors, be Web-based, or sell at retail?

marketing mix the combination of the four factors—product, price, place, and promotion—that communicates a marketing vision.

marketing plan a statement of the marketing goals and objectives for a business and the intended strategies and tactics to attain them.

advertising paid promotion through media outlets.

public relations community activities that are designed to enhance an organization's image.

publicity free promotion.

direct marketing includes telemarketing, direct mail, in-person selling, and other personalized promotional efforts.

Management and Operations: Making the Plan Happen

The people you hire and the processes you plan to implement will be an essential part of your business plan. This is where the rubber meets the road in the planning process.

The management team is often the deciding factor for a potential investor's decision to financially support a business. Moreover, with all other factors being equal, a strong management team will be successful in a business and a weak one will fail. The team must be composed of an effective balance of members with technical expertise (e.g., engineering, marketing, accounting, and operations), experience in the field, and life experience. Briefly discuss the current and proposed management team and reference their resumes in the appendices.

It can also be worthwhile to add an organizational chart representing the company as it is proposed in the near term and with growth. In addition, descriptions of key roles and responsibilities, and the compensation rates and structures for each, will need to be included.

If your business will be involved in research and development, this section should describe it. Include the state of development, such as prototype, testing, or commercialization. Any patents, patents pending, or other intellectual property should be discussed, with the limits or law (not losing protection) and the stage of commercial readiness.

The description of the physical location is similar to the discussion of *place* in the marketing mix but with the emphasis on logistics and workforce readiness. Describe the desired physical location(s) of the organization and the rationale. For example, if you require a concentration of highly skilled scientists, you might want to locate near a university with a strong science orientation or near other firms with similar labor-pool requirements. Local wage rates and community support are other factors to mention. In addition, geographic proximity to customers and/or suppliers or distributors may be a critical site factor. Other aspects to consider are business-friendly laws and courts, tax rates and structures, school systems, overall quality of life, and environment.

The facilities required for the success of your enterprise should be discussed in detail. You should describe the building according to its type and size, and equipment should be specified and "costed out" (details can be included in the appendices). If you know that you require production, warehousing, showroom, or office space, you can describe each. This is where you should discuss your plans to lease or purchase property and equipment and a tipping point for going from lease to purchase. Remember that it isn't financially prudent to buy a building when you only need a small "incubator" space to get started. Often, nascent entrepreneurs immediately want to buy their own facilities and brand-new equipment. In reality, leasing space and equipment reduces required start-up capital and can provide greater flexibility.

The production methods and inventory-control systems that you plan to use will be critical to your success. Even if you are in a service enterprise, you will have supply issues to address in terms of staffing, logistics, and materials. The business plan is an opportunity to set inventory control systems, production processes, and quality-assurance methods. You can highlight any technological innovations that will enhance the company's competitive position. What to include will vary considerably, but the identification of your choices and methods of measurement is essential.

The facilities and equipment for your business should be discussed in detail with the entire management team (© Blend Images/Alamy)

Step into the Shoes . . .

JackThreads, Planning for Success

Jason Ross, JackThreads founder
(Bloomberg/Getty Images)

After Jason Ross graduated from Ohio State University in 2003 with a degree in finance, he and a friend founded a sports marketing company. In 2005, they sold SMI Ventures after realizing that they weren't passionate about it and wanted to do something with greater potential for growth.

Jason decided he wanted to start an entrepreneurial venture that he could be passionate about and that had viable prospects for growth. He had a passion for street wear and was a bargain shopper. He identified the opportunity to create a pure-play e-commerce-flash-sale site that met his criteria. This time, he recognized the value of creating a business plan. Jason comments, "Everybody stresses, 'Write a business plan before you start a company!' but we were young and naïve and didn't do it. Now I definitely recommend it. While I wrote the business plan for JackThreads in 2006, I was working at bars, working anywhere I could find part-time money that would allow me to keep pursuing this dream. And I was always bouncing ideas off my friends and local VCs in Columbus."[4]

JackThreads launched in July 2008 as a members-only boutique e-commerce site offering private, limited-time sales events. Products include contemporary fashion apparel for surfing, skating, and street wear, as well as sneakers and accessories. The lines are strictly menswear and are priced 40 to 80 percent off retail. Five to seven new sales are posted daily and run for between 48 and 72 hours.

In 2011, Jason teamed up with Adam Rich and Ben Lerner and became part of Thrillist. The Thrillist.com site provides a digital lifestyle publication for men. As of early 2013, JackThreads had over three million members. The time Jason devoted to researching and planning JackThreads has paid off handsomely.

Sources: Lauren Drell, "JackThreads' Jason Ross: How a Kid from Ohio Took the Fashion World by Storm," *AOL Small Business*, February 8, 2011, accessed May 8, 2013, http://smallbusiness.aol.com/2011/02/08/jackthreads-jason-ross-how-a-kid-from-ohio-took-the-fashion-wo/. *JackThreads.* Accessed July 9, 2013, https://www.jackthreads.com.

Financial Analysis and Projections: Translating Action into Money

The financial section of the business plan will be the numerical representation of all that you wrote previously. This section should demonstrate organizational viability in financial terms. Commercial lenders in particular will often go directly from the executive summary to the financials before reading anything else. If the numbers make sense, they may look at the rest of the plan. If not, your plan may well land in the trash basket. Your financial estimates should be as realistic as you can make them. Don't pad the numbers. It is not in your best interest to create unrealistic expectations, to delude yourself and your business associates, or to have potential investors or lenders reject your projections as pie-in-the-sky. You are likely to show initial losses, and you should be up front about this. The financials should match both the general market and the other information you provided throughout the business plan. Investors can sense overblown numbers and will react accordingly.

- *Sources and uses of capital.* This section is the numeric representation of the start-up costs plus a verbal description of capital requirements. It states where you expect to obtain your financial support and how you will use the funds. When securing bank or community development financing, your lender may require you to "draw down" (take in incremental amounts) funds in accordance with your list of costs. It is essential to make the list as complete and accurate as possible. It is a sad day for everyone when an entrepreneur's credit and cash are completely exhausted just short of the start-up point. A sample start-up cost list is shown in **Exhibit 4-2**.

---

[4]Lauren Drell, "JackThreads' Jason Ross: How a Kid from Ohio Took the Fashion World by Storm," *AOL Small Business*, February 8, 2011, accessed May 8, 2013, http://smallbusiness.aol.com/2011/02/08/jackthreads-jason-ross-how-a-kid-from-ohio-took-the-fashion-wo/.

Exhibit 4-2 Start-Up Costs		
Item	**Cost**	**Estimate/Actual**
Start-Up Expenses		
Accountant Fees	$300	Estimate
Expensed Equipment	900	Actual
Financial Institution Fees	350	Estimate
Identity Set/Stationery	750	Estimate
Insurance	2,200	Estimate
Legal Fees	3,000	Estimate
Licenses/Certificates/Permits	550	Actual
Marketing Materials	4,400	Estimate
Payroll (with taxes)	5,500	Estimate
Professional Fees—Other	300	Estimate
Rent	1,200	Actual
Research and Development	200	Estimate
Travel	3,200	Estimate
Utilities	200	Estimate
Web Fees	8,000	Estimate
Other	1,500	Estimate
Total Start-Up Expenses	**$32,550**	
Start-Up Assets		
Cash Balance for Starting Date	$10,000	Actual
Equipment	41,800	Actual
Furniture and Fixtures	21,975	Actual
Leasehold Improvements	5,200	Estimate
Machinery	3,700	Actual
Rent Deposit	1,200	Actual
Signage	6,000	Estimate
Utility Deposit	400	Actual
Other	1,500	Estimate
Total Start-Up Assets	**$91,775**	
Total Start-Up Requirements	**$124,325**	

cash flow statement
a financial statement showing cash receipts less cash disbursements for a business over a period of time.

- *Cash flow projections.* The **cash flow statement** shows cash receipts less cash disbursements over a period of time. Creating your cash flow projections for three years will bring financial potential and risks into clear focus both for you and your stakeholders. Don't be alarmed to see negative numbers on your first couple of efforts at this. However, if the numbers truly do not work, it might be time to reconsider your business approach, or the basic concept, rather than simply manipulating the figures to achieve satisfactory results on paper.

   In a start-up business, cash flow is likely to be negative at various points, such as the early months or in certain seasons. A business cannot survive long with negative cash flow, so it must increase cash coming in (revenues, loans, equity investments, and the like) and/or reduce the amount of cash going out (expenses, equipment purchases, debt repayment, for example). Remember, be realistic about these projections. Be careful of significantly increasing your revenue projections solely to improve the numbers. If you add debt, account for its interest and principal repayment in future periods. When you have finished your business plan, it should never show a negative cash balance at the end of a period, because negative cash means you are overdrawn in your accounts, and projecting overdrawn accounts in a business plan, or operating that way, is hardly a best practice. You may very well have suffered losses that are reflected on your income statement, but the ending cash balance cannot be negative. **Exhibit 4-3** shows how cash balances are calculated.

- *Balance sheet projections.* Your three years of projected **balance sheets** will provide snapshots of your business at specific points in time, such as the last day of a month, quarter, or year. Balance sheets show the business's **assets** (what you own), **liabilities** (what you owe), and **net worth**, or **owner's equity**. These statements provide insights into your financing strategy and overall business health. **Exhibit 4-4** shows a rudimentary balance-sheet format.

balance sheet a financial statement summarizing the assets, liabilities, and net worth of a business.

asset any item of value.

liability a business debt.

net worth the difference between assets and liabilities.

owner's equity net worth.

$$\text{Assets} = \text{Liabilities} + \text{Owner's Equity}$$

Exhibit 4-3 *Cash Flow Calculations*	
Starting Cash	(+)
Cash In from Operations [Sales]	(+)
Cash Out from Operations [Cost of Goods Sold, Expenses, Taxes]	(−)
Cash In from Investing [Equity Infusions, Earnings on Investments]	(+)
Cash Out from Investing [Equipment Purchases, Repaying Investors]	(−)
Cash In from Financing [Loans]	(+)
Cash Out for Financing [Repayment of Debt]	(−)
Ending Cash Balance [Starting Balance for Next Period]	(=)

Exhibit 4-4 *Balance Sheet Summary Format*

Balance Sheet for XYZ Company As of (Month) (Day), Year			
Assets	**Year 1**	**Year 2**	**Year 3**
Cash	$_____	$_____	$_____
Accounts Receivable	_____	_____	_____
Inventory	_____	_____	_____
Capital Equipment	_____	_____	_____
Other Assets	_____	_____	_____
Total Assets	**$xxxxx**	**$yyyyy**	**$zzzzz**
Liabilities			
Short-Term Liabilities	$_____	$_____	$_____
Long-Term Liabilities	_____	_____	_____
Owner's Equity	$_____	$_____	$_____
Total Liabilities & Owner's Equity	**$xxxxx**	**$yyyyy**	**$zzzzz**

income statement a financial document that summarizes income and expense activity over a specified period and shows net profit or loss.

profit and loss statement (P&L) an income statement.

breakeven point when the volume of sales exactly covers the fixed costs.

- *Income statements for three years.* An **income statement** (or **profit and loss statement—P&L**) summarizes income and expense activity over a specified period, such as a month, quarter, or year, and shows *net profit* or *net loss*. Generally, start-up enterprises suffer losses for several months, or even a few years, depending on the type of business. You can show initial losses in your statements, but they must be comparable to industry norms, and you must have cash to cover any shortfalls. The projections you provide should clearly be your best estimate and based on the detailed breakdown of sales, pricing, cost, and other data contained in your plan. It is helpful to show best-case, worst-case, and expected scenarios for income. Be careful to avoid ski-slope projections, which add projections linearly, with profitability occurring suddenly in either year three or five. A simple example of an income statement is shown in **Exhibit 4-5**.

- *Breakeven analysis.* This calculation will determine your organization's **breakeven point**—that is, when the volume of sales exactly covers the fixed costs. Calculating the breakeven point will help demonstrate whether there is a viable market for your business. For example, if there are 1,500 students in a school and you must sell 2,500 yearbooks to reach breakeven, you know that it is time to reconsider your plan. Breakeven is calculated as

$$\frac{\text{Fixed Cost (\$)}}{\text{Gross Profit per Unit (\$)}} = \text{Breakeven Units}$$

- *Ratio analysis.* To understand your business performance relative to your industry peers, you can use ratio analysis. A business plan should include standard ratios: gross profit, quick, current, debt, collection period, receivable turnover, inventory turnover, net profit on sales, net profit to assets, and net profit to equity. One of the best ways to interpret your calculated ratios is to compare them with others in your industry via the Risk Management Association (RMA) Annual Statement Studies, which you may access at a library or purchase online for specific industries (http://www.rmahq.org). If you use Business Plan Pro, industry ratios will be available when you

Exhibit 4-5 *Income Statement Summary Format*

Income Statement for XYZ Company For the Year Ending December 31			
	Year 1	**Year 2**	**Year 3**
Net Sales Revenue (+)	$_____	$_____	$_____
Cost of Goods Sold (−)	_____	_____	_____
Gross Profit (=)	$_____	$_____	$_____
Operating Expenses (−)	$_____	$_____	$_____
General Expenses (−)			
Other Expenses (−)	_____	_____	_____
Net Income before Taxes	$_____	$_____	$_____
Taxes	$_____	$_____	$_____
Net Income	$_____	$_____	$_____

calculate them for your business plan. By comparing your business from one period to another and looking at the industry norms, you can adjust the way you will operate, or you can explain why you are outperforming your industry through your competitive advantages or underperforming because of specific circumstances.

- *Risks and assumptions.* All businesses take risks and make their projections based on assumptions. To present a realistic plan, you will need to state your assumptions and known risks explicitly. You will have done some of this in your SWOT analysis; this section pertains to the financial projections. For example, you can include the per-unit costs and volume projections, anticipated tax and benefits rates, and other calculated and projected values. You can also articulate the risks of implementation delays, cost overruns, lower-than-expected sales, industry price wars, and so forth. As with the other sections in your plan, this should be balanced and realistic, not overstated or underplayed.

Funding Request and Exit Strategy: The Ask and the Return

Your business plan should explicitly state the amount of funds you will need in accordance with the financial projections you provide. Whether the need is $500 or $50 million, the reasoning for the request will have to be clear and compelling. Then you should identify the type of financing you require or are requesting and include your own financial contribution and that of any partners or co-owners, the amount of debt (loans) you will need to take on, and the percentage of equity (ownership) you want to retain. This is where you state the financing terms that you would like, including rates and repayment periods. Recognize that this is part of a negotiation process and that the request should be carefully structured. If you intend to sell shares of stock in a corporation or are forming a business partnership, legal counsel will be essential so that you do not violate federal regulations and laws or create an improper agreement. The importance of your "ask" cannot be overemphasized. Business plan readers need to know what you want.

The exit strategy is the way in which you and/or your investors expect to leave the company someday in a planned and orderly way. For investors, this might mean a buyout plan for their equity, or an **initial public offering (IPO)** when the company goes public—that is, puts itself on the stock exchange. It could mean the sale of the business when certain benchmarks are met or at a predetermined point in time. It could mean having you give up day-to-day operations according to a succession plan. Lenders and investors will want to know how they will recoup their investment and earn enough profit to warrant the risk they are taking.

initial public offering (IPO) first offering of corporate stock to investors on the open (public) market.

Any business plan is only as strong as its implementation schedule. Therefore, the schedule—timetable—of *milestones* (goals) that you include will be important to your business and your stakeholders. By establishing realistic deadlines for the completion of activities, you demonstrate knowledge and understanding of the necessary tasks. You can use PERT or GANTT charts, techniques that will be described in the final unit of this book, or any structured method that details the starting and ending dates of tasks and enumerates the resources needed and the responsibility of personnel. Using a software tool such as Microsoft Project or Excel can make this process easier to manage.

Step into the Shoes . . .

Turning Play into Profits

P'Kolino, LLC, 2004 MOOT Corp Competitor

What happens when you pair up two Babson MBA students with an idea and a group of students from the Rhode Island School of Design (RISD)? In 2004, the answer was P'Kolino, a creative company focused on "better" play.

Antonio Turco-Rivas and J. B. Schneider worked together to create a winning business plan that succeeded in being selected for the prestigious international business plan competition called MOOT Corp in 2004. Their initial product was an innovative play table designed by the RISD team.

Since then, Turco-Rivas and Schneider have combined their interests as fathers with a desire to have well-designed

products for children to create a successful company. P'Kolino products are sold in such upscale locations in New York as the Metropolitan Museum of Art, the Guggenheim Museum, the Museum of Modern Art, the Strand Book Store, and Saks Fifth Avenue. National mass-market retailers Toys R Us and Buy Buy Baby feature P'Kolino products in selected stores.

For P'Kolino's founders, the business plan was an exercise that let them play in the children's market.

Source: P'Kolino, accessed July 9, 2013, http://www.pkolino.com.

Appendices: Making the Case in Greater Detail

The appendices will provide you with an opportunity to strengthen your business plan with examples and details that are not critical for inclusion in the main portions. This is the place to add management resumes, sample promotional materials, and illustrations or diagrams of products and packaging. In some cases, the detailed financial projections will appear in the appendices. Each appendix should be numbered and placed in the plan according to the order of reference in the text. The appendices should be listed in your table of contents.

Business Plan Suggestions

As you put together your business plan, a number of guidelines and suggestions can help you get the most value for your time and effort. These will make the plan look more professional, easier to read, and more likely to be thoughtfully considered. In fact, you will find it easier to refer back to your business plan if it is clear, concise, visually appealing, and well organized. With this in mind, you should:

Learning Objective 6

Be able to demonstrate proper development and formatting of a business plan.

- *Write for your audience.* Whether the plan is for an internal (you and your team) or an external (lenders and investors) audience, it will need to address issues and concerns in language your readers will understand. They need to see that this business is something they want to be on board with (if company personnel) or that it satisfies a market need (if potential investors).

- *Show that you are assuming personal risk.* No matter who the audience is, they will want to know that you are emotionally, intellectually, and financially invested in the business.

- *Be clear and concise.* Simple, direct language written without too many adjectives or unnecessarily complex terminology is best. Even for highly technical sections, the business plan should avoid jargon and repeated references made through acronyms and initials. This includes writing in a pompous (self-important) way. Keep it simple. Readers know that explaining a complex subject in a clear, concise manner requires a thorough understanding of the subject. Depending on your audience and the type of business, your plan should be from 15 to 40 pages long, including appendices.

- *Use current data and reports for your industry.* This is important to validate that you are being realistic and have truly done your research. If you are out of step with current or anticipated conditions, the assumptions that you make for your financial and market performance are likely to be inaccurate and unrealistic.

- *Choose a voice and stick with it.* It is best to write your business plan in the third person (not the first-person—"I" or "we") to give it an objective tone. Be careful not to switch back and forth between voices.

- *Use a consistent, easy-to-read format.* Choose a format and use it consistently throughout the plan. For example, using 1-inch margins, double spacing, and a serif font (such as Times New Roman) will make the document easy to read.

- *Number and label.* Number pages, figures (drawings, illustrations, photos), and tables, and refer to each in the text by title and number to make it easy for the reader to understand and find sections of the plan. Each figure or table should be numbered sequentially and should be given a heading.

- *Present it professionally.* A professional business plan on high-quality paper with a neat, attractive cover, cover page, and professional binding will go a long way to impressing the reader. A dirty, dog-eared, or unbound business plan will probably not even be read. An overly fancy, elaborate plan, bound like a book, with four-color glossy illustrations, may cause the reader to wonder why you have gone to such unnecessary expense, suspecting that you are either being wasteful or are perhaps camouflaging an unsound plan with bells and whistles.

It is a good idea to have others look at your business plan before you circulate it to potential investors. If you can get relatively objective friends, colleagues, or family members to read the plan as early as the first draft, you can probably get valuable feedback and ideas for improvement. If you need assistance with spelling and grammar, or any other aspect of the format, this is the time to get it. It is also a good time to use any community resources that may be available to you, such as a Small Business Development Center (SBDC) or Rural Entrepreneurship Center.

Presenting Your Business Plan

A written business plan is only one component of the business-planning process. It may open the door for a presentation to potential investors (stakeholders), or it may be the leave-behind document that is meant to remind the investors of your conversation. In either case, the presentation of the road map for your venture, whether live, Web-based, or in some other form, is your opportunity to convey your business concept to a particular audience and then to have an interactive discussion regarding your proposal.

Business plan presentations may be formal or informal, and you may have anywhere from a few minutes to a couple of hours for the complete presentation and discussion. Presentations to venture capitalists may be limited to as little as 5 to 20 minutes. Regardless of the setting or audience, your presentation should be articulate, well thought out, organized, rehearsed, polished, and professional. As you work on plans for your

Exhibit 4-6 *Venture Presentation Tips*	
Timing	• Be prompt and ready to start on time. • Use the entire time allocated and use it productively.
Audience	• Know your audience and tailor the presentation accordingly. • Establish rapport with the audience.
Presentation Style	• Dress appropriately and maintain a professional demeanor. • Be enthusiastic, but not artificial or arrogant. • Use proper pronunciation and language.
Presentation Contents	• Create a "hook" to capture the audience quickly. • Hit the highlights without going into excessive detail. • Keep it simple by emphasizing key points and avoiding technical jargon and acronyms that will lose your audience's interest. • Use visual aids, such as slides and sample or prototype products, to reinforce your message without distracting from it. • Emphasize the benefits of the opportunity so that they are absolutely clear to the audience. • Conclude with a "Thank You."
Follow-Up	• Expect and prepare for questions. Be thoughtful and positive in your responses. • Contact each audience member to move toward your goals.

Source: Adapted from Thomas W. Zimmerer and Norman M. Scarborough, *Essentials* of *Entrepreneurship and Small Business Management*, 5th ed. (Upper Saddle River, NJ: Prentice Hall, 2007).

elevator pitch a 15-second to 2-minute presentation that conveys in an engaging way what a business is proposing and why the listener should be interested.

enterprise, it is a good idea to work on an **elevator pitch** that quickly conveys to the listener in an engaging way what you are proposing and why he or she should be interested. This quick spiel should take 15 seconds to a maximum of 2 minutes (the duration of an elevator ride). It is often more challenging to boil the business plan down to its essentials than to make a full exposition. For a formal presentation, an attractive multimedia presentation, free from errors, excessive animation, and other distractions is advisable. Some venture presentation tips are given in **Exhibit 4-6**.

Business Plan and Venture Competitions

Numerous business plan and venture-funding competitions are held each year for young people, undergraduate students, graduate students (primarily MBAs), and nonstudent professionals. Many business schools and classes hold internal competitions and then advance winners to regional, national, and even international events. Prizes may range from $500 to financing and professional-services packages worth millions. A list of selected regional, national, and international competitions for undergraduate and graduate students can be found in **Exhibit 4-7**. Business plan and pitch competitions provide advantages and disadvantages. Certainly, the preparation for competition is an excellent opportunity to put a deadline on the creation of a plan, and the presentations are opportunities to hone a variety of skills, as well as strengthen the concept. Also, competitions may provide significant cash prizes and access to venture capital. However, business plan competitions are time consuming and can prove a distraction from making progress on the actual business. Some competitions will likely have team guidelines that do not conform to your actual business team, so the competitors on the team will have varying levels of interest

Exhibit 4-7 *Business Plan and Venture Competitions for Undergraduate and Graduate Students*

Competition	Host/Sponsor	Web Site
Audacia International Business Plan Competition	Great Lakes Institute of Management, Chennai, India	http://greatlakes.edu.in/events/conferences/Entrepreneurship-Conference.html
Brown-Forman Cardinal Challenge	University of Louisville	http://business.louisville.edu/cardinalchallenge/
Camino Real Venture Competition	University of Texas at El Paso	http://caminorealcompetition.org
Cardinal Challenge Business Plan Competition	University of Louisville	http://business.louisville.edu
CEO Best Elevator Pitch Competition	Collegiate Entrepreneurs, Organization	http://www.c-e-o.org
CU Cleantech New Venture Challenge	University of Colorado at Boulder	http://nvc.cucleantech.org
Cornell Venture Challenge	Cornell University	http://www.brventurefund.com/cornell-venture-challenge
Dell Social Innovation Challenge	Dell/University of Texas at Austin	http://www.dellchallenge.org
Emerging Business Leaders Summit (EBLS) Business Plan Competition	Minority Business Development Agency	http://www.medweek.gov
FLoW Business Plan Competition	California Institute of Technology	http://flow.caltech.edu
Giants Entrepreneurship Challenge	University of North Dakota	http://business.und.edu/entrepreneurship/entrepreneurshipchallenge.cfm
Global Social Entrepreneurship Competition	University of Washington	http://www.foster.washington.edu
Global Social Venture Competition	University of California at Berkeley, London Business School, Columbia University, Indian School of Business, Thammasat University	http://www.gsvc.org
Global Venture Labs Investment Competition	University of Texas at Austin	http://www.mccombs.utexas.edu/Centers/Venture-Labs-Investment-Competition.aspx
Harvard New Venture Competition	Harvard Business School	http://www.hbs.edu/entrepreneurship/new-venture-competition/overview.html
HATCH Startup Pitch Competition at SXSW	Houston Technology Center	http://www.hatchpitch.com/hatch-startup-pitch-competition-at-SXSW
IBK Capital Ivey Business Plan Competition	University of Western Ontario	http://www.iveybpc.com
Idea to Product Competition (I2P)	University of Texas at Austin	http://www.ideatoproduct.org
MIT Clean Energy	MIT, U.S. Department of Energy, NSTAR	http://cep.mit.edu
MIT $100K Entrepreneurship Competition	MIT	http://wordpress.mit100k.org
McGinnis Venture Competition	Carnegie Mellon University	http://www.mcginnisventurecompetition.com
New Venture Championship	University of Oregon	http://www.oregonnvc.com
NYC Next Idea Competition	Columbia University	http://www.nycedc.com/program/nyc-next-idea
OFC Venture Challenge	Clark Atlanta University	http://www.ofcvc.org
Oh-Penn for Business: College Business Plan Competition	Grove City College	http://gccentrepreneurship.com/events/oh-penn-for-business-college-business-plan-competition/
Rhode Island Business Plan Competition	University of Rhode Island	http://ri-bizplan.com

(Continued)

Exhibit 4-7 *Business Plan and Venture Competitions for Undergraduate and Graduate Students (continued)*

Competition	Host/Sponsor	Web Site
Rice Business Plan Competition	Rice University	http://www.alliance.rice.edu/alliance/RBPC.asp
Spirit of Enterprise MBA Business Plan Competition	University of Cincinnati	http://www.uc.edu/ecenter/
Student Venture Open	University of San Diego	http://www.wbtshowcase.com/wbt/web.nsf/pages/bizplan.html
TiE International Business Plan Competition	The Indus Entrepreneurs	https://www.tie.org/initiative/TiE-International-Business-plan-competition
Utah Entrepreneur Challenge	University of Utah	http://www.uec.utah.edu
Wake Forest Elevator Corp.	Wake Forest University	http://www.mba.wfu.edu
West Virginia Statewide Collegiate Business Plan Competition	West Virginia University	http://www.be.wvu.edu/bpc/

Sources: Compiled and updated from www.Mootcorp.org and Mark Cannice, "Getting in on the University Business Plan Competition Circuit," Entrepreneur, October 19, 2009.

and commitment, which may create tension and conflict. Even if you win a competition, you may not want to accept the prize if the terms and conditions are not acceptable. Your time might be better spent elsewhere. Weigh the pros and cons before investing the time and effort.

Chapter Summary

Now that you have studied this chapter, you can do the following:

1. Know what a business plan is and describe it:
   - a road map to success,
   - a history and a plan for an organization, and
   - a plan meeting the needs of various audiences.
2. Create a Business Model Canvas:
   - Make a visual representation of the nine facets
   - Key Partners
   - Key Activities
   - Key Resources
   - Value Propositions
   - Customer Relationships
   - Channels
   - Customer Segments
   - Cost Structure
   - Revenue Streams
3. Explain the various purposes of a business plan and the audiences for it.
   - A business plan is used by entrepreneurs to organize their thoughts before starting a business and to determine business viability.
   - It can be used to raise money from investors and lenders. Almost always, bankers and other potential investors will refuse to consider funding an entrepreneur who does not have a business plan.
   - It can help guide the operation of the business.

4. Understand the components of a business plan.

   The parts of a business plan include a cover page; table of contents; executive summary; mission, vision, and culture; company description; opportunity analysis; marketing strategy and plan; management and operations; financial analysis and projections; funding request; exit strategy.

5. Be able to demonstrate proper development and formatting.

   A solid, viable business plan that is sloppy and filled with errors may be rejected on that basis alone. The business plan should be well organized, neatly presented, and written in correct English.

Key Terms

advertising, 111
asset, 115
balance sheet, 115
breakeven point, 116
business model, 102
business plan, 105
cash flow statement, 114
competitive analysis, 110
culture, 109
direct marketing, 111
elevator pitch, 120
environmental analysis, 110
feasibility analysis, 98
income statement, 116
industry analysis, 110

initial public offering (IPO), 117
liability, 115
marketing mix, 111
marketing plan, 111
mission, 109
mission statement, 109
net worth, 115
owner's equity, 115
profit and loss statement (P&L), 116
proof of market, 110
public relations, 111
publicity, 111
target market, 110
vision, 109

Entrepreneurship Portfolio

Critical Thinking Exercises

4-1. Shawn is creating a business that provides advertising on public restroom stall doors. He is funding the project from his personal savings of $5,000 and does not expect to use any outside financing. Should he create a business plan? Why or why not?

4-2. Charity and Debra are planning to license technology from NASA that would make it impossible to accidentally lock a child in a car. The technology is complex, and the market analysis and financial assumptions take up a lot of pages. The two women have written an 80-page business plan. Explain your concerns about the length of the plan in light of the chapter text.

4-3. Why is it important to have a detailed plan before one embarks on a business?

4-4. Envision a product/service of your choice. Check for its feasibility in the current market. Discuss whether or not the product/service has any market opportunities. Substantiate with details of your research.

4-5. How do the five industry forces identified by Porter come into play in a feasibility analysis? Illustrate with an example.

Key Concept Questions

4-6. What are the factors to be considered in a feasibility analysis? How does it help in making a business plan?

4-7. What are the components of a business plan? Although often ignored by entrepreneurs, why is opportunity analysis and research important?

4-8. What is the difference between "analyzing market and industry feasibility" and "opportunity analysis and research"? Illustrate with an example.

4-9. Is a business model the same as a business plan? If not, what are the differences in the approach and the expected benefits of the two?

4-10. Name three categories of investors/lenders that might have an interest in your business plan.

4-11. Will you present the same business plan to both internal and external audiences? Why or why not? If not, what aspects of the plan will differ?

4-12. What is an elevator pitch? What makes it more challenging than other presentations?

Application Exercises

4-13. Create a Business Model Canvas for Honest Tea based on the business plan in the Appendices.

4-14. Call and visit an entrepreneur in your community to discuss business plans.

    a. Ask whether he or she wrote a business plan before starting the business. Since then?

    b. If the owner did write a plan, for what has it been used?

    c. If the owner did not write a plan, why not?

    d. Did the owner have any assistance in writing or reviewing the plan?

    e. If so, what was the source of assistance?

Exploring Online

4-15. Find a business plan on the Internet. Examine it to see whether it follows the guidelines provided in this text. Use a highlighter to mark the sections of the plan that are present. Then, make a list of missing or incomplete sections. Indicate how it does/does not follow the rules for formatting and content. Is the plan viable? Why or why not? Would you invest in it? Why or why not?

In Your Opinion

4-16. If an entrepreneur presents a business plan that an investor believes is deliberately vague and has provided inflated financial statements, what should that investor do?

Honest Tea
Business Plan

Business Plan for 1999
December 1998
4905 Del Ray Avenue, Suite 304
Bethesda, Maryland 20814
Phone: 301-652-3556
Fax: 301-652-3557

E-mail: sethandbarry@honesttea.com

Table of Contents

Mission Statement. 110

Executive Summary 111

Company Story 111

The Product. 112

    The Taste 112

    Low in Calories 112

    Health Benefits of Brewed Tea 113

    Cultural Experience of Tea 113

    Flagship Line of Flavors 114

Production and Manufacturing 114

Market Opportunity 115

    Beyond Snapple—The Emerging Market for Quality Bottled Tea. 115

    Profile of Target Customer 116

    Market Research 117

    Market Response 117

Marketing and Distribution. 119

    National Natural/Specialty Foods Channels 120

    Higher End Food Service. 120

    Promotion 120

    Packaging and Pricing 120

    International Markets. 121

    Product Development and Future Products 121

Management 121

    President & TeaEO 121

    Chairman of the Board. 122

    Brewmaster 122

    National Sales Director 122

    Retail Sales Manager. 122

    Consultants and Advisors 122

Statement and Aspirations for Social Responsibility .123

Financial Statements—Year-to-Date and Projections 123

The Investment Opportunity. 130

    The Offering 130

    Financing History 130

    Exit Strategies 130

    Investment Risks 130

    Competitive Advantage 130

A Parting Thought. 131

Mission Statement

Honest Tea seeks to provide bottled tea that tastes like tea—a world of flavor freshly brewed and barely sweetened. We seek to provide better-tasting, healthier teas the way nature and their cultures of origin intended them to be. We strive for relationships with our customers, employees, suppliers and stakeholders which are as healthy and honest as the tea we brew.

Executive Summary

Honest Tea, a bottled iced tea company, has completed a strong summer of sales in the mid-Atlantic region and is now raising capital to fund the brand's expansion across the United States as well as overseas. Since the all-natural tea first hit the mid-Atlantic market in June of 1998, Honest Tea has developed a loyal following of customers who have made the product the best-selling tea in its largest account, Fresh Fields/Whole Food Markets, significantly outselling Snapple and the Whole Foods 365 brand. In addition to success in retail channels, Honest Tea has also been warmly received in food service channels.

Unlike the sweetened tea drinks made from concentrate or powder which currently dominate the $2 billion bottled tea market, Honest Tea is brewed with loose leaf tea and then barely sweetened with pure cane sugar or honey. The product is poised to take advantage of the rapid growth in the bottled tea, bottled water, and natural food markets, as well as the developing "tea culture" in the United States. It also has potential to tap into the large market of health-conscious diet soda drinkers. The target audience is an emerging subset of the population, which seeks out authentic products and is attuned to global and environmental issues.

Toward the end of the summer and through the fall the company continued to penetrate large supermarket chains and is in the process of finalizing a national network of brokers and distributors for 1999. In September 1998 the company hired two sales managers, each of whom brings more than 15 years of experience and contacts to the business.

Although there was an often painful and occasionally costly product development phase, the company has now perfected the brewing and production process to the point where it can produce several thousand cases in one shift with the desired consistency. In early 1999 the company will add a West Coast site to its current East Coast production site. In addition, the company will be implementing steps to consolidate its packaging operation which will widen the per case profit margin.

The company has demonstrated an ability to gain free media coverage, including stories in the *Washington Post*, the *Wall Street Journal*, and *Fitness Magazine*. It has also cultivated a loyal customer base among some of the country's most influential celebrities which it intends to publicize at the appropriate time. It has just entered into a contract with a well-recognized public relations firm, which has demonstrated its success with several early-stage companies. Finally, the company has finalized a partnership with a Native American tribe that will position Honest Tea to emerge as a leader in the socially responsible business movement.

Honest Tea is looking to raise up to $1.2 million in equity capital to finance the national distribution of the product as well as the introduction of two new flavors and international sales.

Company Story

Honest Tea is a company brewed in the classic entrepreneurial tradition. After a parching run through Central Park in 1997, Seth Goldman teamed up with his Yale School of Management professor, Barry Nalebuff, to reignite their three-year old conversation on the beverage industry. While at Yale Goldman and Nalebuff had converged on the opportunity in the beverage market between the supersweet drinks and the flavorless waters. The energy they share around the idea of a less-sweet beverage leads to several marathon tea-brewing sessions. Their conversation is fueled in part by their extensive travels through tea-drinking cultures such as India, China and Russia. As ideas and investors for the company gather critical mass, Seth takes the dive. He leaves his marketing and sales post at Calvert Group, the nation's largest family of socially and environmentally responsible mutual funds, and launches Honest Tea out of the guest room in his house. Using five large thermoses and label mock-ups, he sells the product to the eighteen Fresh Fields stores of the Whole Foods Market chain. Once the tea has been manufactured, the company moves into a small office and distributes tea out of U-Hauls until other distributors start carrying the product. By the end of the summer, Honest Tea has become the best-selling tea throughout the Fresh Fields chain and has been accepted by several national supermarket chains and distributors.

The Product

The Taste:

Bottled tea that tastes like tea, freshly brewed and barely sweetened.

Somewhere between the pumped-up, sugar-saturated drinks and the tasteless waters, there is a need for a healthier beverage which provides genuine natural taste without the artificially concocted sweeteners and preservatives designed to compensate for lack of taste.

Honest Tea allows people to enjoy the world's second most popular drink the way hundreds of civilizations and nature intended it to be. Tea that tastes like tea—A world of flavor freshly brewed and barely sweetened. The concept of Honest Tea is as direct and clear as the tea we brew—we start with select tea leaves from around the world, then we brew the tea in spring water and add a hint of honey or pure cane sugar. Finally, we filter the tea to produce a pure genuine taste that doesn't need a disguise.

Unlike most of the bottled teas in the marketplace, Honest Tea is not made with bricks of tea dust, tea concentrate, or other artificial sweeteners or acids. The tea has no bitter aftertaste or sugar kick, and does not leave a syrupy film on the drinker's teeth. To make a comparison with wine, today's leading iced teas are like jug wine and Honest Tea is like Robert Mondavi Opus One. But unlike fine wine, premium bottled tea is quite affordable, usually priced under $1.50 for 16 ounces.

Although taste is the primary benefit of drinking Honest Tea, the product has three other benefits which enhance its acceptance and marketability:

Low in calories:

A 12-ounce serving of Honest Tea has 17 calories, dramatically less than other bottled teas or comparable beverages. We have found that the low-calorie profile of Honest Tea makes the drink attractive to three key audiences – 1) Disenchanted bottled tea drinkers who think the drinks are too sweet, 2) Bottled water drinkers who long for taste and variety and 3) diet soda drinkers who are interested in a low-calorie beverage that doesn't contain artificial sweeteners such as Nutrasweet. The following table illustrates the difference between Honest Tea and the rest of the beverage market:

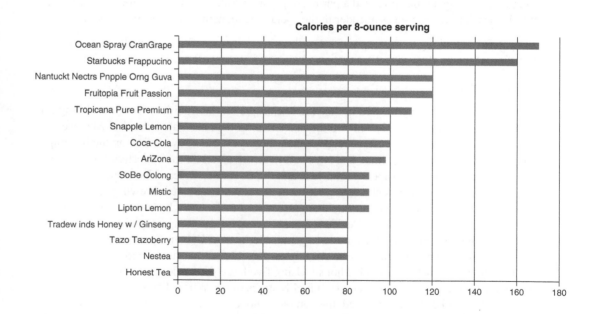

Calories per 8-ounce serving

There are three other players in the less-sweetened bottled tea market that can be considered among the competition for Honest Tea: TeJava, Malibu Teaz and The Republic of Tea. All three brands are currently based and primarily focused on the West Coast. We are heartened by their existence because it confirms our belief that there are untapped opportunities in the beverage market, particularly on the East Coast, where none of the new entrants has any significant presence. TeJava, which is enjoying a warm reception in California, is a mild-tasting, zero-calorie unsweetened tea produced by Crystal Geyser that comes in only one flavor. We believe this product, which has been described by a beverage consultant as "water with a tea aftertaste," would be more flavorful if it were barely sweetened. While TeJava clearly competes with our product, we believe there is room for more than one product in the low-calorie tea marketplace. We also believe that Honest Tea has an edge over TeJava because our drinks are more flavorful and come in a wider variety of flavors.

Malibu Teaz is a company focused on lightly sweetened herbal tea, 35 calories for an 8 ounce serving. The products seem to have limited distribution and the label, which features a topless mermaid, seems designed to cater to a different clientele than Honest Tea.

The Republic of Tea is a well-established producer of loose leaf teas which has recently begun selling unsweetened bottled tea exclusively through its catalogue and premium restaurants. The cost of a four-pack in the catalogue is $15.00, or $3.75 for a 17 ounce bottle. We believe that this price is not viable in retail channels and have spoken with several disillusioned distributors whose experience confirms that assumption. Even if the Republic of Tea changed its sales strategy, we still see room for more than one player in the low-calorie tea market. We also think the modest amount of natural sweetener in Honest Tea helps create a superior flavor.

One other brand that can be considered competition is Tazo, which presents itself as "The reincarnation of Tea." While Tazo is enjoying some success in natural foods channels, we feel that Honest Tea is different from Tazo in three important ways: first Honest Tea is genuine tea whereas Tazo is usually tea mixed with juice or other sweeteners, (usually 80 calories for an 8-ounce serving). Secondly, Tazo's packaging, with its mysterious symbols and discussion of "the mumbled chantings of a certified tea shaman" is designed to reach a New Age audience. In contrast, the colorful art on the Honest Tea labels are accessible to a wider audience, offering a more genuine tea experience. Finally, Tazo's price point is significantly higher than Honest Tea in supermarket channels, selling for $1.69 versus Honest Tea's price of $1.19. Where the two brands have competed head-to-head, Honest Tea has significantly outsold, and in many cases, eliminated Tazo from the shelf. Our response to Tazo's "reincarnation of tea" is that tea doesn't need to be reincarnated if it is made right the first time.

Health benefits of brewed tea:

The curative properties of tea have been known for thousands of years. Because Honest Tea is brewed from genuine tea leaves it imparts many health benefits not found in tea-flavored drinks. In addition to serving as a digestive aid, tea has powerful antioxidants, which impair the development of free radicals which contribute to cancer and heart disease. The antioxidants in green tea are believed to be at least 100 times more effective than Vitamin C and twenty-five times better than Vitamin E at protecting cells and DNA from damage believed to be linked to cancer, heart disease and other potentially life-threatening illnesses.

Cultural experience of tea:

Each Honest Tea flavor is brewed based on a recipe perfected over generations in a specific region of the world. As a result, drinking Honest Tea becomes a cultural experience, from the genuine tastes to the distinctive international art and information on the label. While some bottled teas seek to cloak themselves in a cosmopolitan mantle by including exotic-looking drawings on the label, the front of each Honest Tea label features authentic art from the culture of origin.

Flagship line of flavors

Our flagship line of teas come from four different continents:

Kashmiri Chai – The people of Kashmir have mixed spices into their chai for generations. Our recipe is made with spring water, premium tea leaves, crushed cardamom, cinnamon, orange peel, cloves, pepper, ginger, malic acid and a touch of sucanat evaporated sugar cane juice. Approximately one third the caffeine of coffee.

Black Forest Berry – Our Black Forest Berry tea is a fruit infusion made with spring water, hibiscus, currants, strawberries, raspberries, brambleberries, elderberries, and a touch of unrefined organic cane sugar. Caffeine-free.

Moroccan Mint – Our Moroccan Mint is a tightly rolled green tea from China blended with a generous amount of peppermint, brewed in spring water with citric acid and a touch of white clover honey. Approximately one fourth the caffeine of coffee.

Gold Rush – Our Gold Rush tea is an herbal infusion made with spring water, rooibush, rose-hips, chamomile, cinnamon, peppermint, ginger, orange peel, malic acid, and a touch of raw cane sugar, and natural flavors. Caffeine-free.

Assam – These golden-tipped flowery leaves from the Sonarie Estate gain their distinctive taste from being picked as tender leaf buds at the height of the season. Brewed in spring water with Vitamin C, malic acid, unrefined organic cane sugar, and a hint of maple syrup. Approximately one half the caffeine of coffee.

In early 1999 we will be introducing two new teas:

Decaf Ceylon – In response to feedback from more than 500 sampling events where we continually heard requests for a decaffeinated black tea, we will be introducing a Decaf Ceylon with lemon grass. The label for this tea features original art which captures the cultural and relaxing attributes of the tea.

First Nation's Peppermint – After months of negotiation and a consultation with the tribal elders, we have developed an organic herbal tea in conjunction with a woman-owned company based on the Crow Reservation in Montana. This tea is exciting not only for its flavor but also for the partnership we have developed with the tribe. In addition to licensing the flavor and artwork from the tribe, we are also buying the tea from our partner on the reservation with the understanding that over time the community will develop the capacity to grow all the ingredients on the reservation. This unprecedented relationship should prove to be a valuable public relations tool.

Production and Manufacturing

Though we had our share of "learning experiences" along the way, we have developed several proprietary brewing tools and techniques which enable us to manufacture several thousand cases of tea a day on both coasts with the desired consistency. In addition, since we have a full-time brewmaster on staff, the company retains the knowledge of manufacturing the product, instead of relying on a co-packer for that information.

The tea is brewed at a brewing and bottling facility located within driving range of the target market. The site was selected based on numerous criteria including capacity, reputation, quality control, production efficiency and willingness to invest in a long-term partnership with Honest Tea. All partners involved in the production process meet United States Department of Agriculture Hazard Analysis Critical Control Plant (HACCP) standards. We are in the process of obtaining Kosher certification from the Orthodox Union ("Circle U").

In early 1999 we will be making a change in our manufacturing process that will not affect the quality of the product but will have important ramifications for our profitability. Instead of a two-step packaging process, we will consolidate the brewing and labeling under one roof. This consolidation will save Honest Tea more than two dollars a case.

Our tea leaves are provided by internationally known companies that specialize in tea buying, blending and importation. Our primary source is Hälssen & Lyon of Germany, the largest specialty tea company in the world. Another, Assam Tea Traders, has direct ties to tea estates in the Assam District of Northern India. The other ingredients are commodities which are in plentiful supply.

As the Company grows in size, we anticipate dealing more directly with the tea growers. We intend to visit the tea estates so that we can verify that the labor conditions of the tea workers meet international standards and International Labor Organization conventions. We also aspire to ensure that the tea is grown organically.

Market Opportunity

Beyond Snapple–The Emerging Market for Quality Bottled Tea

We have identified four market trends that are fueling demand for Honest Tea within the $72 billion non-alcoholic liquid refreshment beverage market.

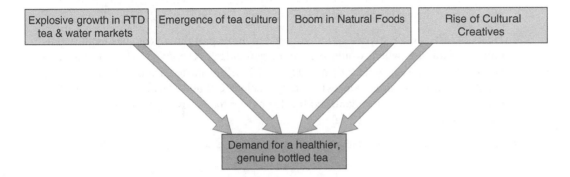

1. **Explosive growth in Ready-to-Drink (RTD) tea and bottled water markets** – Although carbonated soft drinks still dominate the beverage market, in the past ten years Ready-To-Drink teas and bottled water have emerged as alternatives. Since 1992 the US tea market has enjoyed 60% annual growth, reaching sales of $2 billion in 1996. The bottled water market has grown to $2.4 billion, with most of the growth fueled by sales of single-serving bottles.

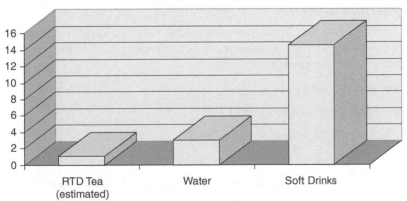

1997 U.S. Beverage consumption in billions of gallons*

*Water and Soft drink figures come from Beverage Marketing, Inc. The RTD Tea figure is based on 1997 sales estimate of $2.5 billion, which equates to roughly one billion gallons.

2. **Beyond the tea bag – The emergence of tea culture** – Snapple and similar brands helped make tea accessible to a broader population. But now in the same way that gourmet coffees have become popular, consumers are beginning to develop an appreciation for finer teas. Over the last six years U.S. loose leaf tea sales have more than doubled, from $1.8 billion

	February 28	March 31	April 30	May 31	June 30	July 31	August 31	September 30	October 31	November 30
LIABILITIES & EQUITY										
Liabilities										
Current Liabilities										
Accounts Payable	$ -	-	-	-	-	-	(16)	-	-	-
Total Accounts Payable	$ -	-	-	-	-	-	(16)	-	-	-
Credit Cards										
First USA		$ 231	826	968	604	2,694	188	1,679	5,239	1,471
Halssen and Lyon		(5,000)	(2,560)	(2,560)	(2,438)	538	-			
Mayer Bros.		(5,000)	(5,000)	(500)	7,585	7,295	6,298	-	-	-
Slate Packaging			(30,800)	(12,914)	436	7,295	14,000	-	-	-
Staples					170	181	-	66	219	-
Strasburger and Siegel, Inc.		(1,000)	356	$356	356	-	-	-	-	-
Total Credit Cards	$ -	(10,770)	(37,179)	(14,651)	6,713	18,003	20,486	1,745	5,458	1,471
Total Current Liabilities	$ -	(10,770)	(37,179)	(14,651)	6,713	18,003	20,471	1,745	5,458	1,471
Total Liabilities	$ -	(10,770)	(37,179)	(14,651)	6,713	18,003	20,471	1,745	5,458	1,471
Equity										
Capital Investment @ 0.01 PAR	$ 20,000	300,001	505,001	507,501	517,501	517,501	517,501	517,501	517,501	517,501
Net Income	(3,125)	(23,898)	(77,929)	(113,668)	(182,992)	(214,813)	(232,186)	(249,833)	(349,231)	(369,248)
Total Equity	$ 16,875	276,103	427,072	393,833	334,509	302,688	285,315	267,668	168,270	148,253
TOTAL LIABILITIES & EQUITY	$ 16,875	265,334	389,893	379,182	341,222	320,691	305,786	269,413	173,728	149,725

BUSINESS PLAN

Exhibit E Honest Tea Income Statement 1998

	Feb	Mar	Apr	May	June	Jul	Aug	Sep	Oct	Nov
Ordinary Income/Expense										
Income										
Sales - Glass Bottles				14,035	9,396	26,806	55,988	49,221	31,633	31,003
Sales Discounts Off Invoice Glass Bottles				(21)	(22)	(101)	(2,878)	(1,985)	-	(181)
Total Income	-	-	-	14,014	9,374	26,705	53,109	47,236	31,633	30,822
Cost of Goods Sold										
Contract Labeling			23,831	5,461	3,169	6,859	6,277	15,121	12,901	8,420
Bottles & Caps		5,000	(5,000)		19,656	8,017	6,552		17,633	
Label Printing				12,425	10,182				6,485	
Spring Water			33	1,250	2,025	675	1,660	1,350	1,104	675
Sweeteners				2,694		2,784	2,520	3,346		
Tea			7,480	2,700	445	1,877		5,155	3,180	3,594
Freight - Glass Bottles				1,891	2,833	1,480	3,033	6,741	5,953	2,400
Brewmaster Fees - Glass				4,500	10,962	4,710	6,775	5,214	15,146	2,415
Broker Fees					144					
Tea Supplies		381	112	13						23
Total Cost of Goods Sold	-	5,381	26,456	30,934	49,415	26,402	26,817	36,927	62,403	17,527
Gross Profit	-	(5,381)	(26,456)	(16,920)	(40,041)	302	26,293	10,308	(30,769)	13,295
Expense										
Broker Commissions								100	1,638	-
Consultants & Interns										
Consultants	1,323	13,000	3,000	7,244	6,000	6,600	3,915	7,290	11,337	6,390
Total Consultants & Interns	1,323	13,000	3,000	7,244	6,000	6,600	3,915	7,290	11,337	6,390
G & A Expenses										
Bank Fee		15	10	120			44		9	60
Payroll Fee			86	46	49	47	91	49	137	94
Other Licensing		20								
Legal						490			18,991	
Miscellaneous	50					400				(178)
Computer Supplies/Software		236	486		110				(10)	45
G & A Expenses - Other					30	241				
Insurance - Business						1,751				(5)
Memberships		300				290	300	73	30	
Office Supplies		252	106	3	642	513	971	1,185	367	
Photocopies			30	3			61	292		
Recruitment						26	362			
Rent				1,833			3,666	917	917	917
Postage and Delivery		65	330	263	234	1,377	687	552	813	943
Telephone	90	149	166	161	505	756	665	623	626	520
Total G & A Expenses	140	1,036	1,214	2,428	1,568	5,891	6,848	3,691	21,880	2,395

	Feb	Mar	Apr	May	June	Jul	Aug	Sep	Oct	Nov
Marketing Expenses										
Marketing & Promotions					14	2,544	3,257	4,640	4,096	84
Wearables				1,550	1,394	675			7,571	2,126
Corp. Samplers, Demos						831	1,641	344	486	-
Independent Samplers, Demos						164				-
Packaging Supplies for Samples				105				377	140	213
Public Relations							10,000		5,586	
Donations										-
Sampling Wages				30		115	521	555		
Trade Show Fees & Other Exp.					45	64			500	300
Website Fees			35	35	35	135	35	35	35	35
Total Marketing Expenses	-	-	35	1,720	1,488	4,528	15,454	5,950	18,414	2,758
Payroll Taxes & Benefits										
Medical Insurance										796
Payroll Taxes			1,208	493	1,188	1,184	1,405	843	1,251	1,532
Total Payroll Taxes & Benefits	-	-	1,208	493	1,188	1,184	1,405	843	1,251	2,328
R&D										
Product Development			4,461	1,161		410			146	
Market Research					6,398		-	-	-	-
Graphic Development	100	112	5,000				-	-	-	-
Total R&D	100	112	9,461	1,161	6,398	410	-	-	146	-
Payroll Wages										
Salaries and Wages			12,500	5,792	12,250	12,250	14,917	10,040	11,566	17,066
Total Payroll Wages			12,500	5,792	12,250	12,250	14,917	10,040	11,566	17,066
State/Federal Taxes										
State Franchise Tax	50	-	-						-	
Licenses & Fees		970	79						245	250
Total State/Federal Taxes	50	970	79						245	250
Travel & Entertainment										
Travel and Lodging		252	55	375	446	918	1,336	642	2,127	214
Mileage				62	724	1,462	330	30	164	1,925
Meals		22	23	63	134	73	370	12	195	102
Total Travel & Entertainment	-	274	78	500	1,303	2,453	2,036	683	2,485	2,241
Total Expense	1,612	15,392	27,575	19,340	30,196	33,316	44,574	28,598	68,960	33,427
Net Ordinary Income	(1,612)	(20,773)	(54,032)	(36,259)	(70,237)	(33,014)	(18,282)	(18,289)	(99,729)	(20,133)
Other Income/Expense										
Other Expense										
Interest/Dividend Income										
Interest Income	-	-	-	(520)	(914)	(1,193)	(909)	(642)	(331)	(116)
Total Interest/Dividend Income	-	-	-	(520)	(914)	(1,193)	(909)	(642)	(331)	(116)
Total Other Expense	-	-	-	(520)	(914)	(1,193)	(909)	(642)	(331)	(116)
Net Other Income	-	-	-	520	914	1,193	909	642	331	116
Net Income	(1,612)	(20,773)	(54,032)	(35,739)	(69,324)	(31,821)	(17,373)	(17,647)	(99,398)	(20,017)

BUSINESS PLAN

BUSINESS PLAN

Exhibit F
Honest Tea Cash Flow Projections 1999

	Jan	Feb	Mar	Apr	May	Jun	Jul	Aug	Sep	Oct	Nov	Dec	1999
Starting Cash	$ 100,000	$ 1,046,136	$ 941,078	$ 863,133	$ 848,706	$ 908,967	$ 971,072	$ 1,047,802	$ 1,346,907	$ 1,488,037	$ 1,635,398	$ 1,776,446	$ 100,000
Cash in from Operations (Sales)	$ 80,219	$ 96,525	$ 162,338	$ 266,906	$ 347,344	$ 363,188	$ 377,813	$ 402,188	$ 377,813	$ 337,594	$ 281,531	$ 201,094	$ 3,294,553
Cash out from Operations (COGS, Expenses, Taxes)	$ 134,083	$ 201,583	$ 240,283	$ 281,333	$ 287,083	$ 301,083	$ 301,083	$ 303,083	$ 236,683	$ 190,233	$ 140,483	$ 137,233	$ 2,754,246
Cash in from Investing (equity infusions, earnings on investments)	$ 1,000,000	$ -	$ -	$ -	$ -	$ -	$ -	$ 200,000	$ -	$ -	$ -	$ -	$ 1,200,000
Cash out from Investing (equipment purchases, repaying investors)	$ -	$ -	$ -	$ -	$ -	$ -	$ -	$ -	$ -	$ -	$ -	$ -	$ -
Cash in from Financing (loans)	$ -	$ -	$ -	$ -	$ -	$ -	$ -	$ -	$ -	$ -	$ -	$ -	$ -
Cash out for Financing (repayment of debt)	$ -	$ -	$ -	$ -	$ -	$ -	$ -	$ -	$ -	$ -	$ -	$ -	$ -
Ending Cash Balance (= starting balance for next period)	$ 1,046,136	$ 941,078	$ 863,133	$ 848,706	$ 908,967	$ 971,072	$ 1,047,802	$ 1,346,907	$ 1,488,037	$ 1,635,398	$ 1,776,446	$ 1,840,307	$ 1,840,307

ASSUMPTIONS

Collections = Net 45 day

Purchases = Prepaid 30 days

Equity raised in January and August totaling $1.2 million

Debt not required for financing

Other assumptions per Profit and Loss Projection for 1999

Exhibit F Honest Tea Income Statement Projections 1999

	Jan	Feb	Mar	Apr	May	Jun	Jul	Aug	Sep	Oct	Nov	Dec	Total
Ordinary Income/Expense													
Income													
Sales	$ 80,000	$ 112,000	$ 240,000	$ 320,000	$ 400,000	$ 400,000	$ 400,000	$ 400,000	$ 400,000	$ 320,000	$ 240,000	$ 160,000	$ 3,472,000
Sales Discounts and Damage	$ 800	$ 1,120	$ 31,200	$ 3,200	$ 4,000	$ 52,000	$ 4,000	$ 4,000	$ 52,000	$ 3,200	$ 2,400	$ 1,600	$ 159,520
Total Income	$ 79,200	$ 110,880	$ 208,800	$ 316,800	$ 396,000	$ 348,000	$ 396,000	$ 396,000	$ 348,000	$ 316,800	$ 237,600	$ 158,400	$ 3,312,480
Cost of Goods Sold													
Total Cost of Goods Sold	$ 72,800	$ 156,000	$ 160,000	$ 200,000	$ 200,000	$ 200,000	$ 200,000	$ 200,000	$ 160,000	$ 120,000	$ 125,000	$ 80,000	$ 1,873,800
Gross Profit	$ 6,400	$ (45,120)	$ 48,800	$ 116,800	$ 196,000	$ 148,000	$ 196,000	$ 196,000	$ 188,000	$ 196,800	$ 112,600	$ 78,400	$ 1,438,680
Expense													
Broker Commissions	$ 3,200	$ 4,480	$ 9,600	$ 12,800	$ 16,000	$ 16,000	$ 16,000	$ 16,000	$ 16,000	$ 12,800	$ 9,600	$ 6,400	$ 138,880
Consultants & Interns	$ -	$ -	$ -	$ -	$ 4,500	$ 4,500	$ 4,500	$ 7,500	$ -	$ -	$ -	$ -	$ 21,000
G & A Expenses	$ 31,420	$ 31,420	$ 31,420	$ 31,420	$ 31,420	$ 31,420	$ 31,420	$ 31,420	$ 31,420	$ 31,420	$ 31,420	$ 31,420	$ 377,040
International					$ 875	$ 875	$ 875	$ 875	$ 875	$ 875	$ 875	$ 875	$ 7,000
Marketing & Promotion	$ 7,000	$ 8,000	$ 12,500	$ 15,300	$ 16,300	$ 30,300	$ 30,300	$ 29,300	$ 15,400	$ 12,200	$ 5,700	$ 5,700	$ 188,000
Miscellaneous	$ 1,736	$ 1,736	$ 1,736	$ 1,736	$ 1,736	$ 1,736	$ 1,736	$ 1,736	$ 1,736	$ 1,736	$ 1,736	$ 1,736	$ 20,832
Research & Development	$ 15,000	$ 3,000	$ 2,000	$ 2,000	$ -	$ -	$ -	$ -	$ -	$ -	$ -	$ -	$ 22,000
Sales Support	$ 8,750	$ 8,750	$ 8,750	$ 8,750	$ 8,750	$ 8,750	$ 8,750	$ 8,750	$ 8,750	$ 8,750	$ 8,750	$ 8,750	$ 105,000
Total Expense	$ 67,106	$ 57,386	$ 66,006	$ 72,006	$ 79,581	$ 93,581	$ 93,581	$ 95,581	$ 74,181	$ 67,781	$ 58,081	$ 54,881	$ 879,752
Net Ordinary Income	$ (60,706)	$ (102,506)	$ (17,206)	$ 44,794	$ 116,419	$ 54,419	$ 102,419	$ 100,419	$ 113,819	$ 129,019	$ 54,519	$ 23,519	$ 558,928
Other Income/Expense													
Other Expense													
Interest/Dividend Income													
Interest Income	$ 200	$ 941	$ 863	$ 848	$ 908	$ 971	$ 1,047	$ 1,146	$ 1,288	$ 1,435	$ 1,576	$ 1,640	$ 12,863
Total Interest/Div. Inc.	$ 200	$ 941	$ 863	$ 848	$ 908	$ 971	$ 1,047	$ 1,146	$ 1,288	$ 1,435	$ 1,576	$ 1,640	$ 12,863
Total Other Expense	$ 200	$ 941	$ 863	$ 848	$ 908	$ 971	$ 1,047	$ 1,146	$ 1,288	$ 1,435	$ 1,576	$ 1,640	$ 12,863
Net Other Income	$ 200	$ 941	$ 863	$ 848	$ 908	$ 971	$ 1,047	$ 1,146	$ 1,288	$ 1,435	$ 1,576	$ 1,640	$ 12,863
Net Income	$ (60,506)	$ (101,565)	$ (16,343)	$ 45,642	$ 117,327	$ 55,390	$ 103,466	$ 101,565	$ 115,107	$ 130,454	$ 56,095	$ 25,159	$ 571,791

ASSUMPTIONS

Effective invoice price (case)	$ 16.00
Cost per case on 4/99	$ 8.00
Cost per case until 4/99	$ 10.40
Percent of brokered sales	80%

International Marketing

R&D	$ 7,000
Total	$ 7,000

Overhead & GNA Monthly

Salaries	$ 24,000
Insurance	220
Office rent	2,300
Legal expenses	1,000
Accounting	400
Benefits/staff support	1,500
Phone/computer	1,000
Travel	1,000
Total	$ 31,420

Marketing & Promotion

Trade shows	$ 10,000
PR agency & ex	50,000
Sales sheets &	8,000
Sampling	70,000
Shirts & promo	12,000
Postage/shipping	6,000
Reg. radio ads	30,000
Website	2,000
Total	$ 188,000

Sales Support

Slotting/intros	$ 80,000
Coolers	25,000
Total	$ 105,000

Finished Inventory

12/31/98 inventory	$ 120,000
12/31/99 inventory	$ 125,000

1999 Totals

Gross income	$3,312,480
Total COGS	$1,873,800
Gross profit	$1,438,680
Gross Profit Margin	43.4%
Expenses	$ 879,752
Pretax net	$ 571,791
Profit Margin	17.3%

BUSINESS PLAN

The Investment Opportunity[4]

Honest Tea is seeking equity investments totaling $1.2 million in equity capital to finance the national distribution of the product as well as the introduction of two new flavors and international sales.

The Offering

(Excluded from the Plan)

Financing History

Initial financing for Honest Tea came from the founders, Seth Goldman and Barry Nalebuff, and their friends and family. This equity funding of approximately $500,000 was used to start the business and to generate the first production run.

Exit Strategies

Investors in Honest Tea would be able to realize a return on the appreciation of their investments under any of the following scenarios:

Investment by a strategic partner—As Ocean Spray's recent purchase of a significant share of Nantucket Nectars demonstrates, there may be opportunities for investors to realize their gains through the sale of their Honest Tea shares to a strategic investor who can help the company expand its production and distribution.

Acquisition—There are numerous precedents of companies that might be interested in leveraging the integrity and purity of Honest Tea's brand. Some recent examples are the acquisition of Mistic and Snapple by Triarc. Honest Tea has already been approached by some well-known beverage companies to discuss possible acquisition opportunities.

Initial Public Offering—If Honest Tea meets our expectations for growth, the Company might consider some form of public offering to raise capital for expansion in the future.

Investment Risks

In addition to the economic and business factors which pose risks for most early-stage companies, an investment in Honest Tea carries several other risks:

Product Risk—Although we are insured for product liability, a health-related incident such as the one Odwalla experienced several years ago could do significant damage to the Honest Tea brand name. Of course, since our product is pasteurized twice, there is less of a risk that the same types of bacteria could emerge.

Competitive Risk—Republic of Tea, a company that has a well-established brand name among tea lovers, might decide to enter the retail market with a more competitively priced product. Such a move could dampen the uniqueness of our message. Crystal Geyser, a company which has deep pockets and preexisting distribution relationships, might decide to introduce additional products beyond TeJava and spread its distribution more aggressively beyond the West Coast.

Management Risk—At this point, the development of the company has been concentrated largely in the hands of Seth Goldman and Barry Nalebuff. If either of them were unable to continue to play a role in the Company's progress, the growth of Honest Tea might be impaired.

Competitive Advantage

The results of this past summer clearly indicate that Honest Tea has tapped into a market opportunity. When we were planning the company's strategy last year we entertained the idea

[4]The Investment Opportunity section, including the offering and financing history is not included in the business plan as available on the Honest Tea Web site. The comments included here are based upon multiple sources and are meant to be a fair representation of the original information.

of spending several years building up a strong presence in a local market before expanding nationally. We have chosen to grow in a more aggressive manner for several reasons:

Market Niche—We have created a new beverage category and are currently the only company filling that category. If we hesitate, other companies are likely to move in.

Compelling brand image and story—The packaging, presentation and profile of the Honest Tea brand fit together extremely well with the product. Although we may improve on the bottle design in the future, this is a package that comes close to selling itself. It is also a brand and a story, which has successfully gained free media coverage, and should continue to do so.

Management Team—We have developed a team with the right combination of sales experience and market creativity that is capable of growing the company on a national, and even international, scale.

A Parting Thought

Prospective investors in Honest Tea are advised to keep in mind the words of Sung Dynasty poet Li Chi Lai who cited the three great evils that might beset the land:

> the spoiling of gallant youths through bad education; the degradation of good art through incompetent criticism; and the waste of fine tea through careless making.

While we may not be able to have much direct influence over education and the arts, Honest Tea stands poised to restore integrity to a beverage that has brought people together for hundreds of generations and throughout dozens of civilizations. There has never been a time when consumers have been so overwhelmed with choices. And yet there has never been a time when integrity and authenticity are as cherished as they are scarce. There has never been a better time for Honest Tea.

SPANX—Idea to Entrepreneurial Opportunity

Getty Images

Sara Blakely
(Evan Agostini/AP Images)

White pants. Pantyhose. Scissors. How do these become the opportunity for a highly successful business? When you add Sara Blakely to the equation. She was a woman facing the problem of panty lines showing under white pants, so she took a pair of scissors and cut the feet off the pantyhose. Certainly, Sara wasn't the first woman to do so. However, she was the first to see an entrepreneurial opportunity and create a successful venture as a result. Spanx was born out of this "ah-hah!" moment for Sara.

SEEING OPPORTUNITY IN A PROBLEM

Blakely recognized that women (and men, too) are often bothered by underwear lines and lumps and bumps in their body shapes. She looked at the types of body-shaping garments on the market in the late 1990s and was not satisfied, finding them uncomfortable and ugly. She wanted to make products that were more comfortable and attractive.

Since the introduction of the original Spanx line, Blakely has spotted other opportunities. Her desire for a bra that doesn't show "back fat" resulted in the creation of "Bra-llelujah." Her identification of an opportunity for control-top fishnet tights yielded "Tight-end Tights." In 2010, Spanx added a product line for men, recognizing that many men also had problems that could be solved by shape wear.

Going from idea to product is not always easy. For Blakely and her team, the manufacturer is frequently the naysayer.[5] She has to push the boundaries as a contrarian who creates value.

THE WOMAN BEHIND THE BRAND

Sara Blakely was recognized as the world's youngest self-made billionaire (at the age of 41) by *Forbes* in 2012. She was also selected as one of *Time*'s 100 Most Influential People. And, in 2013, she pledged one-half of her fortune to charity through the Giving Challenge. The success of her entrepreneurial venture has enabled her to be a major philanthropist.

[5]David S. Kidder, *The Startup Playbook*, San Francisco: Chronicle Books, 2012, p. 37.

Blakely was raised in an upper-middle-income household where her father, an attorney, routinely challenged the children with the question, "What did you fail at today?"[6] This suggested that the kids should have tried to accomplish something, for without trying there is no failure—or success. After college, Blakely sold fax machines door-to-door for seven years. She developed sales and organizational skills during this time.

At a particularly difficult time in her life, Blakely's father gave her Dr. Wayne Dyer's *How to Be a No-Limits Person*, which she credits as a life-changing influence. She learned to see opportunity in adversity and impediments. Blakely became very clear about spending time thinking, to create new ideas. When she cut the feet off the pantyhose, she was poised to spot an opportunity and move forward with it.

RESOURCES

Spanx emerged through a lot of ingenuity, hard work, and limited financial resources. Blakely kept her sales job for a year while she pursued her goal. She didn't share what she was doing with anyone, wanting to establish her plan first. She shared it with hosiery mills and potential investors, but not with her family and friends. She used her time and the $5,000 she had saved to create a prototype and promote it. In fact, Blakely did much of the initial patent filing herself, hiring a patent attorney to do only a minimal portion. She understood that the patent was more for marketing purposes than as protection from competition.

Blakely used "guerilla" marketing techniques to introduce Spanx to the market. She stood in stores with a laminated set of photos showing a woman (herself) wearing white pants with and without Spanx. She exemplified and articulated the value proposition—thinner appearance, no lines, no restriction on style of shoe.

She also gave considerable thought to naming and packaging. For example, from her work as a stand-up comic, Blakely knew that words with the "k" sound can elicit laughs. However, for a brand name, the letter "X" gives the impression of strength. Blakely wanted her product names to be memorable. Hence, the originality of Spanx, and subsequent names of Assets, Red Hot Label by Spanx, and Eur-sleek-A were created. Her packaging was inspired by looking at what was on high-end store displays and making the Spanx packaging more attractive and eye-catching.

In addition to acting as chief salesperson when she started out, Blakely did her own publicity. She also engaged friends who were passionate about the product to assist her. These shoestring efforts yielded fantastic results in 2000, when Oprah Winfrey named Spanx one of her "favorite things." This publicity catapulted Spanx into the marketplace.

[6]Ibid., p 32.

Laurie Ann Goldman
(Ben Rose/Getty Images)

TEAM

At the beginning, Blakely had to fulfill all of the company roles herself, rely on friends, or hire contractors to complete tasks. She had a product concept, but it needed to be produced, tested, marketed, and delivered, in return for payment. She realized that the product's technical specifications and production were best left to manufacturers of pantyhose, for whom this would be a use of excess capacity. Blakely relied on their feedback.

Getting the sort of team that she needed was often challenging. For example, hosiery mills repeatedly turned her away, often rudely. Her eventual manufacturer initially turned her down. However, after he discussed the idea of footless pantyhose with his daughters, he understood the opportunity and worked with Sara.

Two years after starting Spanx, Blakely was able to begin hiring employees. She focused on finding people who had strengths in her areas of weakness. She recognized that she was more creative than consistent and not well-suited for day-to-day management. She hired a CEO, Laurie Ann Goldman, who has been with Spanx since 2000. Goldman created Spanx's first business plan. Blakely also worked to move from tasks she did not enjoy to those she did.

SPANX EXPANDS INTO SHAPE WEAR, SWIMWEAR, AND HOSIERY

Since its launch in 2000, Spanx has experienced phenomenal growth. Its product line has grown from a single style of footless tights to over 200 products, including shape wear, swimwear, and hosiery. The original Spanx line continues to be sold at many high-end retailers, such as Nordstrom's, Neiman Marcus, and Saks Fifth Avenue. A line of products for Target has been introduced under the ASSETS by Sara Blakely brand, and for Kohl's as ASSETS Red Hot Label by Spanx. In addition, the SPANX for Men line was introduced in 2010.

Spanx products are mentioned in a variety of media on a frequent basis. Just about any guide to looking good will suggest Spanx shape wear. Stars such as Joan Rivers and Kelly Osborne have mentioned Spanx when critiquing runway fashions. Sara herself has graced the cover of *Forbes* magazine.

As of 2012, Spanx, based in Atlanta, Georgia, was estimated to generate $250 million per year in revenue with a 20-percent return. Because Sara Blakely continues to be the 100-percent owner, this private company does not have to disclose its financial information to the public. Spanx has customers in more than 50 nations and is opening retail stores and in-store boutiques across the United States. With all of this success, the mission of Spanx remains, "To help women feel great about themselves and their potential."

TURNING PROFITS INTO PHILANTHROPY

From the start, Blakely has always been a staunch supporter of empowering women, a focus that was built into the Spanx mission. Her parents recall that she was always concerned about constraints on opportunities for women, both in the United States and abroad.[7] As the company grew, so did her opportunities to make an impact in this area.

In 2004, Blakely was a competitor on the Fox TV reality show *The Rebel Billionaire: Richard Branson's Quest for the Best*. Sara took three months away from Spanx and traveled with Sir Richard and her fellow competitors, accomplishing various business-related tasks along the way. Sir Richard surprised Blakely by giving her the $750,000 that he had earned from the show so that she could start her own charitable foundation. In 2006, he was part of the launch of the Sara Blakely Foundation. The foundation focuses on education and entrepreneurship for women around the globe.

The Sara Blakely Foundation's mission is: "Dedicated to changing women's lives through support of awareness education in four primary areas: Self, Social, Entrepreneurial/Financial and Environmental."[8] Oprah Winfrey was a key to Sara's early success with Spanx and in 2007 the Sara Blakely Foundation made a $1 million contribution to the Oprah Winfrey Leadership Academy Foundation in South Africa.

Sara Blakely has created value for men and women worldwide, captured value for herself, and been able to share her wealth—all by recognizing an opportunity and realizing its worth.

Case Study Analysis

U1-1. What benefits of entrepreneurship does Sara Blakely appear to have attained?

U1-2. Is the desire to earn an income a key motivator for Blakely? Explain your answer.

U1-3. What was Blakely's opportunity cost when she started Spanx?

U1-4. Which of Schumpeter's five basic ways to find opportunity applies to Spanx, both at its start and today? What was the opportunity?

U1-5. Which of Porter's generic strategies best fits Spanx?

U1-6. If Blakely had wanted to buy an existing business to create Spanx, what sort of company would have been logical? Why? Would an acquisition have been feasible? Why or why not?

U1-7. If you were writing a business plan for the Spanx start-up, what knowledge, skills, and abilities would you attribute to Blakely? What expertise would you suggest was needed?

U1-8. Create a business model canvas for Spanx at its start-up in 2000. How would it differ today?

---

[7]Ibid, p. 37.

[8]"Spanx Gives Back," Spanx, Inc., accessed July 9, 2013, http://pages.email.spanx.com/sarablakelyfoundation/.

Case Sources

Clare O'Connor, "Undercover Billionaire: Sara Blakely Joins the Rich List Thanks to Spanx," *Forbes*, March 7, 2012. Accessed July 7, 2013, http://www.forbes.com/sites/clareoconnor/2012/03/07/undercover-billionaire-sara-blakely-joins-the-rich-list-thanks-to-spanx/4/.

Clare O'Connor, "How Sara Blakely of Spanx Turned $5,000 into $1 billion," *Forbes*, March 14, 2012. Accessed July 7, 2013, http://www.forbes.com/global/2012/0326/billionaires-12-feature-united-states-spanx-sara-blakely-american-booty.html.

David S. Kidder, *The Startup Playbook,* San Francisco: Chronicle Books, 2012. *Spanx, Inc*. Accessed July 10, 2013, http://www.spanx.com.

WHO ARE YOUR CUSTOMERS?

Chapter 5
CREATING BUSINESS FROM OPPORTUNITY

Chapter 6
EXPLORING YOUR MARKET

© michaeljung/Fotolia

CREATING BUSINESS FROM OPPORTUNITY

Learning Objectives

1. Define your business.

2. Articulate your core beliefs, mission, and vision.

3. Analyze your competitive advantage.

4. Perform viability testing using "the economics of one unit."

Tony Hsieh, Zappos.com
(Getty Images)

Entrepreneurs find and take advantage of opportunities that others don't recognize or cannot access the resources to exploit. When Zappos.com founder Nick Swinmurn became frustrated by looking for shoes in a San Francisco mall and online, he saw an opportunity to create an online pure-play e-commerce megastore that would carry a multitude of sizes, styles, and colors. Swinmurn was three years out of college when he launched ShoeSite.com, with $150,000, in 1999. Within a month, he relaunched as Zappos.com. In 2000, Tony Hsieh of Venture Frog Incubators saw the opportunity in Zappos, investing $1.1 million and joining Swinmurn. The company has thrived on providing the best selection and service, with a focus on the "wow" factor and delivering happiness. Zappos.com carries more than 1,000 brands, employs 3,800 people, and has annual revenues in excess of $1 billion.[1] In November 2009, Amazon.com acquired Zappos.com Inc. in a deal valued at $1.2 billion. Zappos.com has since expanded its product offerings to include handbags, clothing, and other items and was restructured into 10 separate companies.

Apple and the Personal Computer

market a group of people or organizations that may be interested in buying a given product or service, has the resources to purchase it, and is permitted by law and regulation to do so.

In 1943, IBM's founder Thomas Watson commented, "I think there is a world market for about five computers." A **market** is a group of people or organizations that may be interested in buying a given product or service, has the resources to purchase it, and is permitted by law and regulation to do so. When Watson made his statement, computers were forbiddingly large and expensive machines that only the government, universities, and a few giant corporations could afford. That was the perceived *market* for computers at the time.

By the 1970s, however, a few people were talking about creating "personal" computers. These enthusiasts were outside of mainstream thinking. One such visionary was Steve Wozniak, who had landed his first job at Hewlett-Packard, then as now a major company. He was also attending meetings of the Homebrew Club, a Palo Alto–based group of electronics hobbyists. Wozniak was determined to build a small personal computer to show the club members, using existing technology. He believed that there was a much larger market for hobbyist computers than IBM and Hewlett-Packard thought. Hewlett-Packard, IBM, and Tandy all had personal computers on the market, but not of the sort Wozniak envisioned.

Steve Wozniak, Apple cofounder
(Getty Images)

Wozniak offered Hewlett-Packard a chance to codevelop his small computer. The company was not focused on desktop computing, and the technology did not fit within its computer or calculator strategies, so it turned him down. Wozniak's friend Steve Jobs also was interested in the technology and set out to sell some hobbyist computers. After some time and considerable effort, Jobs sold 100 circuit boards to a local start-up computer shop, and then Wozniak, Jobs, and three helpers soldered together the components in the garage of Jobs's home in Cupertino, California.

[1]Zappos.com Inc., accessed July 21, 2013, http://www.zappos.com.

Wozniak worked on his design concepts until he created the Apple II, which could display pictures and text. It is now considered one of the great achievements in computer history. Jobs, meanwhile, searched for an investor. Finally, after being turned down by friends and family, he found Mike Markkula, who also saw the possibilities of Apple. Markkula agreed to invest $80,000 in the company in return for a significant share of equity. He also put together Apple's business plan and worked to secure additional investors. This is a classic demonstration of entrepreneurs recognizing opportunities others do not see.

By 1984, Apple had sales of $1.5 billion, and sales topped $155 billion in fiscal year 2012. Wozniak and Jobs recognized an opportunity that led to a product that satisfied the needs of an enormous market the giants of the industry did not recognize.

Business Definition

Learning Objective 1

Define your business.

Before you can start a business, you should define it along several dimensions. This *business definition* includes the offer, target market, and product and delivery capability—answering the questions of who, what, and how. A solid business definition has three elements:

1. ***The offer.*** What will you sell to your customers? That is called your *offer* and includes the complete bundle of products and services you will be bringing to the marketplace. This should address not only the tangible product or intangible service but its benefits. For example, you will provide online and telephone fitness-consulting service for an initial four-week period at $25 per week, or eight weeks at $20 per week.

2. ***Target market.*** Which segment of the consumer market are you aiming to serve? As discussed in Chapter 4, this will be your *target market*. Defining your target market in a way that will help you identify qualified potential customers is an important factor in achieving success. This definition must be precise enough so that you can identify a viable market for the business and focus your marketing efforts. A target market of every adult in the United States is clearly too broad and unfocused. A market of every member of Congress from the state of Rhode Island (three individuals) would be too narrow.

3. ***Production and delivery capability.*** How will you provide your offer to your targeted customers? This includes how to perform the key activities required to produce the product or service, deliver it to your customers, and ensure they are satisfied. This part of the business definition includes the primary activities of

   - buying, developing, or manufacturing the product;
   - identifying its potential qualified customers and selling the product to them;
   - producing and delivering the product or service; and
   - receiving payment.

manufacturing making or producing a tangible product.

wholesale buying in bulk from manufacturers and selling smaller quantities to retailers.

retail selling individual items to consumers.

Apple began as a manufacturing business, making a product. There are three basic types of product businesses:

1. **Manufacturing** is producing a tangible product and selling it, either through distributors or directly to end customers.

2. **Wholesale** is buying in bulk from manufacturers and selling smaller quantities to retailers.

3. **Retail** is selling individual items to consumers.

Step into the Shoes . . .

Zhang Xin—Building a Real Estate Empire from Opportunity

Real estate developer Zhang Xin has built a fortune by identifying economic opportunities in China. She is the cofounder and CEO of SOHO China. As of March 2013, she and her family had an estimated net worth of $3.6 billion.[2]

This is a very different life from her early days of living in poverty in Henan province and in Hong Kong. She left China for an education in England at the University of Sussex and then Cambridge. Her work history includes investment banking in New York and Hong Kong. Yet, she always maintained ties to the land of her birth.

Zhang and her husband, Pan Shiyi, created Beijing Redstone Industries Co. Ltd., a property development firm they later renamed SOHO China, in 1995. SOHO China is the nation's largest commercial real estate developer, with 56-million square feet of developments and is a public company, trading on the Stock Exchange of Hong Kong. Zhang and Pan saw opportunities for modern, high-style properties in Beijing and Shanghai when others did not.

Zhang is a prominent woman in China, with over 5 million Sina Weibo (similar to Twitter) followers. She is recognized for her business acumen, her role in urbanizing China, and the staunch belief that democracy will come to China.

Sources: Caroline Howard, "The World's Most Powerful Women, Zhang Xin & Family (#50)," *Forbes*, May 22, 2013, accessed on July 20, 2013, http://www.forbes.com/profile/zhang-xin/2013. "Company Profile," SOHO China, accessed July 19, 2013, http://www.sohochina.com/en/about.

Zhang Xin, SOHO China (Bloomberg/ Getty Images)

What Sort of Organization Do You Want?

Each organization has the opportunity to create a unique mission, vision, and culture that will be supported by its core values. The management team can determine how to use the company's competitive advantage to satisfy customers. The organization's culture can be shaped according to the business environment and by the way employees, customers, and other stakeholders are treated—an example that is set by the founding entrepreneur (owner).

Your Company's Core Values

When you start your own company, what beliefs will you use to guide it? These are the **core values** of your business. Core values include the fundamental ethical and moral philosophy and beliefs that form the foundation of the organization and provide broad guidance for all decision making. Examples of the core values of a business might be:

- "At Superior Printing, we engage in business practices that affect the environment as little as possible."
- "At Sheila's Restaurant, we believe in supporting local organic farmers."

◀ **Learning Objective 2**
Articulate your core beliefs, mission, and vision.

core values the fundamental, ethical, and moral philosophy and beliefs that form the foundation of the organization and provide broad guidance for all decision making.

Exercise

Imagine you are Nick Swinmurn or Tony Hsieh of Zappos.com. On a separate sheet of paper, define your business:

1. Who will the business serve?
2. What will the business offer? What products or services will it sell?
3. How will the business provide the products or services it offers? What are the primary actions and activities required to conduct this business?

---

[2]Caroline Howard, "The World's Most Powerful Women, Zhang Xin & Family (#50)," *Forbes*, May 22, 2013, accessed on July 20, 2013, http://www.forbes.com/profile/zhang-xin/2013.

Core values will affect business decisions. The owner of Superior Printing, for example, will choose ink that is less harmful to the environment over a cheaper ink that is more harmful. Superior Printing may also have a paper-recycling program to minimize its paper consumption. The owner of Sheila's Restaurant will buy fruits and vegetables from local organic farmers. Your core beliefs will affect everything, from the cost of materials to the prices you charge and how you treat customers. For additional examples of core values, see **Exhibit 5-1**.

Your Company's Mission Is to Satisfy Customers

The mission of your business, expressed in a *mission statement*, is a concise communication of your purpose, business definition, and values. The function of a mission statement is to clarify what the business is trying to do in the present, but it can provide direction and motivation for future action through a clear and compelling message.

As noted in Chapter 4, a well-crafted mission statement will not only tell your customers and employees what your business is about, but can (and should) be a guide for every decision you make. It should capture your passion for the business and your commitment to satisfying your customers. A mission statement should be limited to 40 or 50 words to induce clarity in concept and expression. The mission statement should address the following topics: target customers; products and services; markets served; use of

---

Exhibit 5-1 *Core Values*

Zappos.com

1. *Deliver WOW through service*
2. *Embrace and drive change*
3. *Create fun and a little weirdness*
4. *Be adventurous, creative, and open-minded*
5. *Pursue growth and learning*
6. *Build open and honest relationships with communications*
7. *Build a positive team and family spirit*
8. *Do more with less*
9. *Be passionate and determined*
10. *Be humble*

Dow AgroSciences

To ensure the prosperity and well-being of Dow AgroSciences employees, customers, and shareholders, cumulative long-term profit growth is essential. How we achieve this objective is as important as the objective itself. Fundamental to our success are the core values we believe in and practice.

- *Employees are the source of Dow AgroSciences success. We communicate openly, treat each other with respect, promote teamwork, and encourage personal initiative and growth. Excellence in performance is rewarded.*

- *Customers receive our strongest commitment to meet their needs with high quality products and superior service.*

- *Products are based on innovative technology, continuous improvement, and added value for our customers and end users.*

- *Our conduct demonstrates a deep concern for human safety and environmental stewardship, while embracing the highest standards of ethics and citizenship.*

DuPont Company

Safety, concern, and care for people, protection of the environment, and personal and corporate integrity, are this company's highest values, and we will not compromise them.

technology; importance of public issues and employees; and focus on survival, profitability, and growth.

Here is an example of a mission statement for the Most Chocolate Cake Company:

> To create the richest, tastiest, most chocolaty cakes in our area. The cakes will be made from the finest, freshest ingredients according to our secret recipes and decorated with our extraordinary frostings and fillings. They will make any event as special as our cakes!

The Most Chocolate Cake Company's mission statement defines the business and its competitive advantage, the core of its strategy. Examples of mission statements from a range of organizations appear in **Exhibit 5-2**.

Your Company's Vision Is the Broader Perspective

The *vision* for your business is broader and more comprehensive than its mission, painting a picture of the overall view of what you want your organization to become in the future, not what it is at the moment. It is built on the core values of the organization. It should energize your people, and they should embrace it with enthusiasm and passion. This means that the vision has to be compelling across the organization. It has to matter. Employees need to be empowered to fulfill the vision. Examples of vision statements for various organizations appear in **Exhibit 5-3**.

Your Company's Culture Defines the Work Environment

The culture of an organization is largely shaped by its leadership. *Culture* is composed of the core values in action. Leaders of a company build a particular culture by making the beliefs, values, and behavioral norms

---

Exhibit 5-2 *Mission Statements*

The Dow Chemical Company—To constantly improve what is essential to human progress by mastering sciences and technology.
Google—To organize the world's information and make it universally accessible and useful.
The Hershey Company—Undisputed Market Leadership.
Krispy Kreme Doughnuts—To touch and enhance lives through the joy that is Krispy Kreme.
Nike—To bring inspiration and innovation to every athlete in the world.
Teach for America—is growing the movement of leaders who work to ensure that kids growing up in poverty get an excellent education.
Walt Disney Company—To be one of the world's leading producers and providers of entertainment and information, using its portfolio of brands to differentiate its content, services and consumer products.
Wounded Warrior Project—To honor and empower wounded warriors.

Exhibit 5-3 *Vision Statements*

Amazon—Our vision is to be earth's most customer centric company; to build a place where people can come to find and discover anything they might want to buy online.
Bimbo Bakeries USA—We strive to be a highly productive and deeply humane company.
DuPont Company—Our vision is to be the world's most dynamic science company, creating sustainable solutions essential to a better, safer, healthier life for people everywhere.
General Motors—To design, build and sell the world's best vehicles.
Kiva—We envision a world where all people – even in the most remote areas of the globe— hold the power to create opportunities for themselves and others.
Krispy Kreme Doughnuts—To be the worldwide leader in sharing delicious taste and creating joyful memories.

explicit and intentional. Culture includes factors such as risk tolerance and innovation; orientation with respect to people, teams, and outcomes; attention to detail; and communications norms. Organizational culture is learned by members of the team in a number of ways, including anecdotes, ceremonies and events, material symbols, and particular use of language. For example, at General Electric, stories of Jack Welch are legendary. At Hewlett-Packard there was the "Hewlett-Packard Way," based on anecdotes passed down from one generation of employees to the next. Those who work in small enterprises often see the top management daily and take their cues directly, because there are very few or no layers between them. As enterprises become larger, the firm's leaders may not often be on view to most employees and frequently take on larger-than-life roles through stories.

Ceremonies can make a significant difference in a company's culture. Are there periodic recognition events for innovation? Does the company invite family members to appropriate occasions throughout the year? Is there a birthday celebration for each employee? Are years of service recognized? Material symbols come in many shapes and forms. At the Wilmington, Delaware, headquarters of Legacy MBNA America, the values of the company appear on every archway, and handprints of the employees make colorful wall art in some buildings. At any business, reserved parking spots and special privileges for certain employees send a message to everyone. Are these spaces for top executives? Expectant mothers? Are office sizes determined by pay grade? Finally, language tells a lot about the culture. Is everyone on a first-name basis with everyone else? Are some people addressed formally and others not? Is the language around the company in general formal or informal? Is communication respectful?

These and many other factors are all part of the culture of an organization. Culture should be crafted to follow core beliefs and support the mission and vision of the business.

The Decision Process

Translating opportunity into success can and has happened in literally millions of different ways. Each business has a different story. However, there are three primary routes in the deliberate-search process to identify opportunities:

- The entrepreneur looks for business opportunities through a process of identification and selection, beginning with self-developed (or group-developed) ideas.
- The entrepreneur uses essentially the same process but starts with research on hot businesses, trends, or growth areas.
- The entrepreneur has an idea for a product or service and searches for a market.

These processes are illustrated in **Figure 5-1**.

In each case, a decision is made based on personal values and thinking. Whereas each ultimately funnels the procedure down to a business concept, the processes are repeated—often with many ideas being considered—before a viable picture emerges. The first two options are market driven; the third is product driven. Entrepreneurs do better looking to the market(s) of interest, rather than creating a product and then trying to find a customer base. You can do all this alone, but it is best to work with others who will provide honest, constructive feedback.

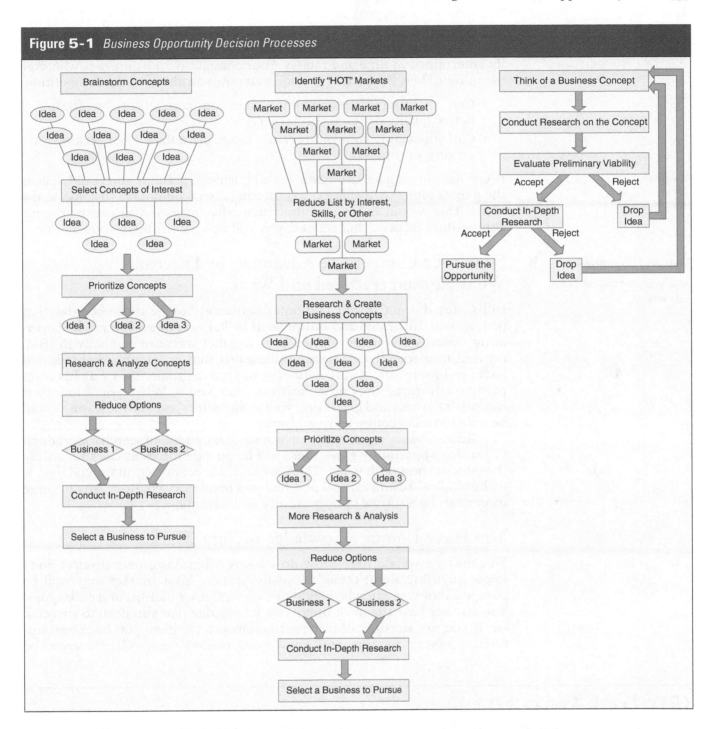

Figure 5-1 *Business Opportunity Decision Processes*

Your Competitive Advantage

For your business to be successful and to fulfill your mission and vision, you will need a strategy for beating the competition. This will be your *competitive advantage,* or core competency. It is whatever you can do better than the competition that will attract a sufficient number of customers to your business so it can succeed. The competitive advantage must be *sustainable* in order to create long-term viability. Your competition is defined by your target market and can be *direct* (selling the same or similar products to the same market) or *indirect* (selling different products that compete for the same share of customer spending). For example, a children's museum will indirectly compete with rental movies/movie theaters, indoor/outdoor play areas, sports and recreation, and other leisure-time activities for family entertainment time and money. Your competitive advantage is whatever meaningful benefit you can provide that puts you ahead of the competition.

- Can you attract more customers than your competitors by offering better quality or some special service?
- Can you supply your product at a lower price than other businesses serving your market?

If you are running a video game rental business, perhaps you could deliver the games along with snacks, so customers would not have to come to the store. That would be your competitive advantage. If you can beat your competitors on price *and* service, you will be very strong in your market.

Learning Objective 3

Analyze your competitive advantage.

> ## Find Your Competitive Advantage by Determining What Consumers Need and Want

Bill Gates did not invent computer software, but he did recognize that people were frustrated and intimidated by it. From there, he supplied operating systems that he purchased from another software company to IBM, created user-friendly software applications that consumers wanted, and packaged them attractively with easy-to-read manuals. That was his competitive advantage over other software companies. When you know your customers' wants and needs and your competitors' capabilities, you should be able to find a competitive advantage.

Remember, as you identify environmental trends and search for product- or service-opportunity gaps, there will be outside forces at work regarding the effectiveness of the idea. These will include economic and social forces, technological advances, and political and regulatory changes. Any of these forces can be a source of opportunity and advantage.

You Have Unique Knowledge of Your Market

You may be wondering: "How do I figure what customers need? I don't know anything about them." Actually, you do. Your market may well be composed of your friends, neighbors, classmates, relatives, and colleagues. You already have the most important knowledge that you need to succeed. Or, if you are starting a business to address a problem you have encountered, chances are that you know your market very well. However, be

Global Impact . . .

SOFTtribe Founders See That Tropical Tolerance Is Needed for Software in Ghana

Herman Kojo Chinery-Hesse and Joe Jackson saw an opportunity in the need for adapting software for tropical climates when they founded SOFTtribe in 1991. Their company develops software, taking into consideration the unique requirements of the West African social and business environment. According to their partner, Microsoft, "The SOFTtribe software is practical and resilient, functional under conditions of intermittent connectivity, power fluctuations, low bandwidth, and operators who, as a rule, are less familiar with computing than in some other parts of the world."[3]

Chinery-Hesse has been called the Bill Gates of Ghana for his success in building SOFTtribe. It is the largest software company in Ghana and is a Microsoft partner to permit its expansion.

---

[3]"Taking African Business Global," Microsoft Unlimited Potential, May 27, 2009, accessed January 13, 2010, http://www.microsoft.com/unlimitedpotential/.

careful to make the distinction between what you are assuming and what is true, so that you will make good decisions.

Sir Richard Branson, the CEO of Virgin Corporation, chose "Virgin" because it reflected his total inexperience in business. His empire, which includes Virgin Megastores, Virgin Atlantic Airways, and Virgin Mobile, began as a tiny discount mail-order record company, which he started at age 19 after he had dropped out of high school. Branson knew his market—other young people who were into music—very well. Then, he learned about the other markets before he entered them.

How will you know if a business idea is going to be successful? You cannot have a guarantee, but your market will tell you a lot about your chances. The answer will come in the form of the signal called *profit*. You can learn a lot about the potential for success well ahead of starting your enterprise, through customer and market research, in addition to competitive analysis.

The Six Factors of Competitive Advantage

Competitive advantage comes from one (or a combination) of six factors:

1. *Quality.* Can you provide higher quality than competing businesses?
2. *Price.* Can you offer a lower price on a sustained basis than your competition, or does your higher price reflect quality and/or uniqueness?
3. *Location.* Can you find a more convenient location for customers?
4. *Selection.* Can you provide a wider range of choices than your competitors can?
5. *Service.* Can you provide better, more personalized customer service?
6. *Speed/turnaround.* Can you deliver your product/service more quickly than the competition?

The importance of each factor will depend on the wants and needs of target customers. More isn't always better, if customers aren't interested.

Is Your Competitive Advantage Strong Enough?

When deciding whether your business concept is viable, it will be essential to determine your competitive advantage and whether it is strong enough. According to Jeffry Timmons's *New Venture Creation*, a successful company needs to do one of the following.

- *Sell to a market that is large and growing.* The market for smart phones is a good example. New products are being marketed to meet the demand, such as printers that turn digital photos into prints with digital-photo frames.
- *Sell to a market where the competition is able to make a profit.* It will be interesting to observe what happens in the market for hybrid cars. The jury is out as to whether the companies manufacturing them can make a profit, so most automakers are not yet entering the field. There still may not be a sufficiently large market to make entry worthwhile.
- *Sell to a market where the competition is succeeding but is not so powerful as to make it impossible for a new entrepreneur to enter.* Microsoft has been taken to court several times by competitors who argue that it is so big that new software companies cannot enter the market. **Barriers to entry** are the factors that contribute to the ease or difficulty of a new competitor joining an established market, and they cannot be so high that market entry and success are not possible.

barriers to entry the factors that contribute to the ease or difficulty of a new competitor joining an established market.

Entrepreneurial Wisdom . . .

A new business usually will require time before it can turn a profit. Federal Express, in fact, suffered initial losses of a million dollars a month! But if you are not making enough money to stay in business, that is the market speaking. It is telling you that your business is not satisfying consumer needs well enough. Do not take it personally. Many famous entrepreneurs opened and closed a number of businesses during their lifetime.

Henry Ford failed in business twice before the Ford Motor Company was a success. If you want to be a successful entrepreneur, start growing a thick skin and decide right now that you intend to learn from failures and disappointments. Do not let them get you down. Learn, so that you do not make the same mistakes again.

- *Sell a product or service that solves problems consumers may have with the competition.* Problems can include poor quality or slow delivery. FedEx beat its competition—the Flying Tigers, the U.S. Postal Service, and United Parcel Service (UPS)—when it entered the package-delivery market with guaranteed overnight service.
- *Sell a product or service at a competitive price that will attract customers.* UPS fought back by offering a less-expensive overnight delivery service than FedEx's.

In addition to the above, it is also necessary to:

- understand the needs of your customers;
- have a sustainable competitive advantage or multiple, evolving advantages; and
- deliver a product or service that meets your customers' needs at the right price.

Checking Out the Competition

One useful exercise is to learn everything you can about particular competitors, especially those that have earned the respect of the marketplace. Try to identify the sources of their competitive advantage. Examine their Web sites. Conduct Internet searches. Track their advertising and promotion, including print, broadcast, Internet, and sponsorships. If they are retailers, shop their stores or have your friends and family do so. Get to know them (but do not do anything unethical or illegal to obtain information). You will also need to keep an eye on your competition after you have started your business, because new factors might undermine your competitive advantage.

Today's entrepreneurs, even those starting microenterprises and lifestyle businesses, may face competition from far beyond their neighborhoods, because customers can go shopping on the Web. Optimism is a trait that frequently goes with entrepreneurship, so beginning entrepreneurs tend to get excited about the Web's huge customer base. What they often do not consider is that the competition is already selling to their potential customers through the Web. Therefore, get online and conduct a thorough search of your industry. You may find that there is literally a world of opportunity or, conversely, that the world is full of competitors.

To determine whether you have a competitive advantage that will enable you to outperform your closest and strongest competitors, ask these questions:

unique selling proposition (USP) the distinctive feature and benefit that sets a company apart from its competition.

- *Competitive offers.* How does your offer compare with those of your leading competitors? What are the key features of each?
- *Unique selling proposition.* Based on that comparison, what is your **unique selling proposition (USP)**, the distinctive feature and benefit

that sets you apart from your competition? This will require a comparison of offers and identifying what is unique about yours. What is it about your offer that your competitors cannot or will not match?

- **Cost structure.** What is different about your business activities and the cost of doing business, compared to the competition? Overall, are you at a cost advantage or disadvantage?

To be successful, you must have a USP that will attract customers to buy from you. Second, you must have a cost structure that is sufficiently advantageous so that, when all of your costs are deducted from your revenue, you will have sufficient profit left over. If you can achieve a cost advantage or at least minimize any cost disadvantage, this will help you achieve a profit. This profit is your reward for operating a successful business.

The Most Chocolate Cake Company

There are a number of ways to highlight your competitive advantage and to identify opportunities. In this example, Amy makes and sells specialty chocolate cakes. She chose this product because she loves chocolate and she enjoys baking cakes. She decided to make the *most chocolate* cakes possible. From this decision, she developed the concept for her product and the name of her business, The Most Chocolate Cake Company, LLC.

Amy's target market was the segment of the public in Springfield that loved chocolate cakes but did not have the time or interest in baking them. Because cakes are usually purchased for special occasions, Amy believed she could charge a premium price, at least as much as a bakery store cake.

She decided she would make the cakes special by:

- using the finest ingredients and a secret recipe (quality);
- personalizing each cake through expert custom-decorating (selection); and
- baking the cakes to order, so they would be fresh for the event (quality).

Amy bakes her cakes at home in her specially designed commercial kitchen, which makes them literally homemade, and thus reduces the cost of producing them—she is not renting commercial space or paying a staff. Of course, the flip side of baking at home is that her production is relatively limited. Also, she may have to take time to deliver each cake, depending on local zoning regulations regarding retail trade. **Exhibit 5-4** shows her business definition in tabular form.

Amy expects, after careful analysis, that her more chocolaty cake with its special frosting and decoration, as well as its freshly homemade quality, will be successful in the marketplace. This is her USP. She intends for it to be a source of competitive advantage, along with the cost advantage of baking the cakes at home. Based on this analysis, she has determined how she wants to make her offering better and different from those of her competitors.

Sergio33/Shutterstock

Competitive Analysis

Another approach to the analysis is to compare your business concept with the competitors that you have identified through your research. A simple comparative table is a good way to display this.

Exhibit 5-4 *Business Definition*

Business Definition Question	The Most Chocolate Cake Company
1. *The Offer.* What products and services will be sold?	Chocolate cakes with various fillings and decorations for special events at premium prices.
2. *Target Market.* Which consumer segment will the business focus on?	People who love chocolate and want a special cake for a special event. Dual income households with greater than median income.
3. *Production Capability.* How will that offer be produced and delivered to those customers?	Homemade and baked to order to ensure freshness, using high-quality ingredients and a secret recipe.
4. *Problem Solving.* What problem does the business solve for its customers?	Great appearance and flavor without the work or mess for special occasions.

Exhibit 5-5 *Comparative Analysis—Qualitative—The Most Chocolate Cake Company*

	Most Chocolate Cake Company	Mega Super Market, Inc.	Average Bakery Co.	Fancy Bakery, LLC
Quality	Excellent	Fair	Fair	Excellent
Price	Fair	Good	Moderate	Poor
Location	Moderate	Excellent	Moderate	Good
Selection	Fair	Moderate	Good	Moderate
Service	Excellent	Fair	Moderate	Fair
Speed/Turnaround	Good	Excellent	Moderate	Fair
Specialization	Excellent	Poor	Fair	Moderate
Personalization	Excellent	Moderate	Good	Excellent

The table should include each of the six factors of competitive advantage. Plus, if there are particular features that you want to highlight, or specific aspects of the six factors, adding them to the table will make them more prominent. These ratings can be done solely by you—your team—through market research techniques, or however you think you can get the most unbiased responses.

There are many ways to construct this type of competitive analysis table. **Exhibit 5-5** includes a simple qualitative competitive analysis which shows ratings of excellent, good, moderate, fair, and poor for each factor with each competitor. The entrepreneur (or prospective customers) can establish this information by using their knowledge of each competitor. It should take into account those factors that are of greatest importance to the target market. Such a table will make competitive advantages and weaknesses readily apparent.

The chart in **Exhibit 5-6** is an example of a more quantitative approach to competitive analysis. First, based on industry data or quality customer research, each factor is assigned a weight according to its importance to the company's target customers, with the total of all factors equaling 1.00 (or 100%). For example, *quality* could be weighted 0.20, *location* weighted 0.10, with other factors adding up to 0.70, if customers are very concerned about the quality of the product and whether they can buy it on the Internet. Second, each competitor should be rated on an odd-numbered scale, such as 1 to 5, with 1 being lowest and 5 being highest, on each factor. For example, the Most Chocolate Cake Company could rate a 5 on quality and 2 on selection, whereas the supermarket could rate 2 on quality and 5 on location.

Exhibit 5-6 *Comparative Analysis—Quantitative—The Most Chocolate Cake Company*

Attributes Important to Customers	Weight (a)	Most Chocolate Cake Company Rating (b)	Most Chocolate Cake Company Weighted Rating (c = a * b)	Mega Super Market Rating (d)	Mega Super Market Weighted Rating (e = a * d)	Average Bakery Co. Rating (f)	Average Bakery Co. Weighted Rating (g = a * f)	Fancy Bakery, LLC Rating (h)	Fancy Bakery, LLC Weighted Rating (i = a * h)
Quality	0.20	5	1.00	2	0.40	2	0.40	5	1.00
Price	0.10	2	0.20	4	0.40	3	0.30	1	0.10
Location	0.10	3	0.30	5	0.50	3	0.30	4	0.40
Selection	0.15	2	0.30	3	0.45	4	0.60	3	0.45
Service	0.10	5	0.50	2	0.20	3	0.30	2	0.20
Speed/Turnaround	0.05	4	0.20	5	0.25	3	0.15	2	0.10
Specialization	0.20	5	1.00	1	0.20	2	0.40	3	0.60
Personalization	0.10	5	0.50	3	0.30	4	0.40	5	0.50
Total	1.00		4.00		2.70		2.85		3.35

Third, to calculate a weighted score, each rating should be *multiplied* by the associated weight to obtain a total. For example, if quality is rated 0.20 and Most Chocolate's quality is rated 5, the weighted value is 1.00. Looking across the competitors' scores on individual factors can yield insights into areas of strength or vulnerability. Finally, all the weighted values for each company should be totaled and an overall rating calculated. By looking at the ratings, it becomes apparent who the strongest and weakest competitors are, and a company can address the results of the analysis.

Competitive Strategy: Business Definition and Competitive Advantage

Your business will only succeed if you can offer the customers in your market something more, better, and/or different from what the competition is doing. Your competitive advantage (core competency) is essential and, once you establish it, your business decisions will start to fall into place. Every advertisement, every promotion, even the price of your product and the location of your business should be designed to get customers excited about your competitive advantage.

Your **competitive strategy** combines your business definition with your competitive advantage. A competitive advantage must be *sustainable*, meaning that you can keep it going. If you decide to beat the competition by selling your product at a lower price, your advantage will not last long if you cannot afford to continue at that price. Small business owners should realize that price alone is not likely to work as an advantage in the long run. A larger business can almost always beat you on price, because it can buy larger quantities than you can, and therefore probably receive a greater discount from suppliers.

Being able to temporarily undercut the competition's prices is not a competitive advantage. Being able to *permanently* sell at a lower price because you have discovered a cheaper supplier *is* a competitive advantage. Being able to develop and maintain proprietary product or service features and benefits is another approach to finding a sustainable advantage.

competitive strategy the combination of the business definition with its competitive advantage.

strategy a plan for how an organization or individual intends to outdo competitors.

tactics the specific ways in which a business carries out its strategy.

Strategy versus Tactics

Your **strategy** is the plan for outperforming the competition. Your **tactics** are the ways in which you will carry out your strategy.

If you plan to open a bookstore, how will you compete with the chain outlet in the neighborhood? This competitor buys many more books than you do and will receive higher discounts from wholesalers, so you will not be able to compete on price. How else could you attract customers? Perhaps you could make your bookstore a kind of community center, so people will want to gather there. What tactics could you use to carry out this strategy?

- Hold poetry readings and one-performer concerts to promote local poets and musicians.
- Create special-interest book-discussion groups.
- Offer free tea and coffee.
- Provide comfortable seating areas for conversation and reading, to encourage customers to spend time in your store.
- Set up a binder of personal ads as a dating service.

If your tactics attract enough customers to make a profit, you will have found a strategy for achieving a competitive advantage. Remember, you will also have to create a strategy that considers online bookstores and e-books.

To find a competitive advantage, think about everything your business will offer. Examine your location, product/service, design, and price. What can you do to be different—and better in some way that matters significantly to your customer base—from the competition?

Feasibility Revisited: The Economics of One Unit as a Litmus Test

Once you have chosen a business idea and determined your competitive advantage, you should make a preliminary analysis to determine whether the idea would be financially viable. In other words, can you provide your product or service at a price that will cover your costs and provide you with a profit? Wozniak and Jobs were able to set up business in an office

Step into the Shoes. . .

Mental Floss, LLC—Cooler Conversations

Logan Mock-Bunting/
Getty Images

Will Pearson and Mangesh Hatti-kudur, students at Duke University, were interested in learning and in trivia and started an educational campus newsletter in 2000. By the following year, it had been named *Mental Floss* and, with funding, soon had a national following. These former history and anthropology majors, respectively, created a company that now has a print publication, online materials, books, games, and retail products—based upon the opportunity they identified and pursued.

Mental Floss magazine has sections such as Right Brain, Left Brain, Scatter Brain, and Spin the Globe. The company sends daily e-mails, called "Water Cooler Ammo," for unpaid subscribers. They also sell products such as "MBA in a Box" and creative T-shirts via the Web site.

Mental Floss was purchased by Dennis Publishing in 2011, but Will and Mangesh continue to be active in the business.

Source: Mental Floss, LLC, accessed July 18, 2013, http://www.mentalfloss.com.

once they secured Markkula's investment in Apple. This gave them a better environment in which to develop and introduce the Apple II, and that gave them operating profits. Before investing a great deal of time, effort, and money on your business concept, you can use what you learned from your competitive analysis to make a preliminary assessment of the financial opportunity. There will be considerably more financial analysis to be done before opening your doors, but this is a good point at which to do a preliminary evaluation.

◀ **Learning Objective 4**
Perform viability testing using "the economics of one unit."

Entrepreneurs use profits to pay themselves, to expand their businesses, and to start or invest in other businesses. Therefore, every entrepreneur needs to know how much **gross profit** (price minus cost of goods sold) the business will earn on each item it sells. To do this, entrepreneurs can calculate the **economics of one unit of sale (EOU)**, which will reveal how much gross profit is being earned on each unit of the product or service that is sold.

gross profit total sales revenue minus total cost of goods sold.

economics of one unit of sale (EOU) the amount of gross profit that is earned on each unit of the product or service a business sells.

Defining the Unit of Sale

Begin with the **unit of sale**, which is the basic unit of the product or service sold by the business. Entrepreneurs usually define their unit of sale according to the type of business. For example:

unit of sale the basic unit of the product or service sold by the business.

- *Manufacturing.* One order (any quantity; e.g., 100 watches).
- *Wholesale.* A dozen of an item (e.g., 12 watches).
- *Retail.* One item (e.g., 1 watch).
- *Service.* One hour of service time (e.g., one hour of lawn-mowing service) or a standard block of time devoted to a task (e.g., one mowed lawn).

If the business sells a combination of differently priced items (such as in a restaurant), the unit of sale is more complicated. The entrepreneur can use the average sale per customer minus the average cost of goods sold per customer to find the economics of one unit of sale. The formula would be as follows:

> Average Sale per Customer − Average Cost of Sale per Customer = Average Gross Profit per Customer

A business that sells a variety of items may choose to express one unit of sale as an average sale per customer (see **Exhibit 5-7**).

Cost of Goods Sold and Gross Profit

To get a closer look at one unit of sale, entrepreneurs analyze the **cost of goods sold (COGS)** of one unit. These are:

cost of goods sold (COGS) the cost of selling one additional unit of a tangible item.

- the cost of materials used to make the product (or deliver the service) and
- the cost of labor directly used to make the product (or deliver the service).

For a product, the cost of direct labor used to make the product plus the cost of materials used are the COGS. The equivalent for a service business, the **cost of services sold (COSS)**, are the cost of the direct labor used to produce the service plus the cost of the delivery of the service.

cost of services sold (COSS) the cost of selling one additional unit of a service.

The cost of goods sold can be thought of as the cost of selling "one additional unit." If you buy watches and then resell them, your COGS per unit is the price you paid for one watch. Once you know your COGS, you can calculate gross profit by subtracting COGS from revenue (see **Exhibit 5-8**).

Exhibit 5-7 *Unit of Sale as a Combination of Different Items*

UNIT OF SALE AND ECONOMICS OF ONE UNIT OF SALE

Type of Business	Unit of Sale	Economics of One Unit of Sale	Gross Profit per Unit
1. Retail & Manufacturing	One item (e.g., one tie)	$7 − $3 = $4	$4
2. Service	One hour (e.g., one hour of mowing a lawn)	$20 − $10 = $10	$10
3. Wholesale	Multiple of same item (e.g., one dozen roses)	$240 − $120 = $120	$120
4. Combination	Average sale per customer minus average cost of goods sold per customer (e.g., restaurant meals)	$20 − $10 = $10	$10 average gross profit

Exhibit 5-8 *Economics of One Unit of Sale versus Total Gross Profit*

	Economics of One Unit (EOU)	Total Gross Profit for 12 Units (@ $10 per Unit Sold)
Price Sold/Revenue	$20	$240 (12 × $20)
−Cost of Goods Sold	−$12	−$144 (12 × $12)
Gross Profit	$8	$96 (12 × $8)

Your Business and the Economics of One Unit

The economics of one unit of sale is a method for seeing whether your business idea could be profitable. If one unit of sale is profitable, the whole business may be. On the other hand, if one unit of sale is *not* profitable, then no matter how many units you sell, the business will never be successful. The EOU is best for determining what will not be profitable, because the total opportunity analysis will consider all the other costs of doing business. The EOU is a quick and easy method to determine whether profitability is unlikely. Let's use **Exhibit 5-8** as an example.

Say you have a business selling decorative hand-blown wineglasses that you buy from a local artist wholesale for $12 each and resell to friends for $20 each. The cost of goods sold for each wineglass is the wholesale price of $12 (gross profit = $8).

You buy a dozen glasses for $12 each wholesale. Your unit of sale is one glass. Your cost of goods sold is $12 per unit, assuming you have no direct labor cost.

You sell all the glasses at $20 each. Here is how you would calculate your gross profit.

Total revenue = 12 glasses × $20 selling price = $240
Total cost of goods sold = 12 glasses × $12 purchase price = $144
Total gross profit (contribution margin) = $96
$240 revenue − $144 COGS = $96 total gross profit

Total Revenue − Total Cost of Goods Sold = Total Gross Profit

You made a gross profit of $96.

For a manufacturing business, one unit might be one pair of sneakers. The costs would include **direct labor**, the money paid to the people who made the product (sneakers, in this example), and the supplies, such as fabric, rubber, and leather (see **Exhibit 5-9**).

The manufacturer makes a gross profit of $3 for every pair of sneakers sold. That may not seem like much, but manufacturers sell in *bulk*. In other words, a manufacturer might sell several million pairs of sneakers per year.

direct labor Employees that actively produce or deliver a product or service.

Exhibit 5-9 *Economics of One Unit, Manufacturing*

ECONOMICS OF ONE UNIT (EOU)			
Manufacturing Business: Unit = 1 Pair of Sneakers			
Selling Price per Unit:			$15.00
Labor Cost per Hour:	$4.00		
No. of Hours per Unit:	2 hours	$ 8.00	
Materials per Unit:		4.00	
Cost of Goods Sold per Unit:		$12.00	12.00
Gross Profit per Unit:			$ 3.00

Exhibit 5-10 *Economics of One Unit, Wholesale*

ECONOMICS OF ONE UNIT (EOU)	
Wholesale Business: Unit = 1 Dozen Pairs of Sneakers	
Selling Price per Unit:	$240.00
Cost of Goods Sold per Unit:	180.00
Gross Profit per Unit:	$ 60.00

Exhibit 5-11 *Economics of One Unit, Retail*

ECONOMICS OF ONE UNIT (EOU)	
Retail Business: Unit = 1 Pair of Sneakers	
Selling Price per Unit:	$60.00
Cost of Goods Sold per Unit:	20.00
Gross Profit per Unit:	$40.00

Exhibit 5-12 *Economics of One Unit, Service*

ECONOMICS OF ONE UNIT (EOU)		
Service Business: Unit = 1 Hour		
Selling Price per Unit:		$50.00
Supplies per Unit (hair gel, etc.):	$ 2.00	
Labor Costs per Hour:	25.00	
Cost of Goods Sold per Unit:	$27.00	27.00
Gross Profit per Unit:		$23.00

The economics of one unit also applies to wholesale, retail, and service businesses. Assume the wholesaler buys a set of one dozen pairs of sneakers from the manufacturer for $180 and sells them to a retailer for $240 (see **Exhibit 5-10**).

The retailer pays the wholesaler $240 for one dozen pairs of sneakers. The retailer's COGS, therefore, is $20 ($240/12 for the shoes only; the retailer does not add direct labor). The store sells one pair at a time to customers for $60 (see **Exhibit 5-11**).

Here is the economics of one unit for a hair stylist who charges $50 per cut (see **Exhibit 5-12**).

The Cost of Direct Labor in the EOU—An Example

Janet has a business designing handmade bookmarkers. Her unit of sale is one bookmarker. Below is additional information about Janet's business:

- She sells 40 bookmarkers per week to a bookstore in her neighborhood.
- Her selling price is $4.50 each, including an envelope.
- Her costs are 80¢ per card for materials (construction paper, glue, and paint) and 20¢ each for the envelopes, for a total of $1.00 each.
- On average, it takes her one hour to make six bookmarkers.
- Janet pays herself $9 an hour.

The direct labor for each bookmarker is $1.50 ($9/6). Janet wisely realizes that she must include the cost of her labor in the EOU. See how she did this in **Exhibit 5-13**.

Janet's gross profit is $2 per bookmarker sold. Assuming no other expenses, such as taxes, she will keep this as owner of the business. She also earns $1.50 per bookmarker by supplying the labor, thus ending up with a profit of $3.50 per bookmarker.

Now, think back to Amy of the Most Chocolate Cake Company and perform a similar analysis.

- Amy takes an average of two hours to bake a cake.
- It costs $5 for the ingredients for an average cake.
- Amy pays herself $15 an hour.
- The price of an average cake is $40.

This cost structure ($5 materials and $30 direct labor) yields a gross profit of $5 per cake on a $40 cake. With the gross profit of $5 and the $30 she paid herself, Amy ends up with $35 per cake. Assuming she does not have to deliver the cakes, this may be sufficient for her. If she needs to earn more, she will have to charge more, work faster, work more hours, or decrease the costs. These may or may not be realistic options.

Hiring Others to Make the Unit of Sale

Janet realizes that if the bookstore wants to order more bookmarkers, or if she can sell them to additional bookstores, she will not have enough time to make them all herself. To solve this issue, she hires a friend to make the bookmarkers for $9 per hour. Although the EOU will stay the same, Janet will have more time to look for new opportunities for her business. Her income from the business will now come solely from the gross profit, which is currently $2 per unit.

Exhibit 5-13 *EOU Example, Janet's Company*

ECONOMICS OF ONE UNIT (EOU)		
Manufacturing Business: Unit = 1 Bookmarker		
Selling Price per Unit:		$4.50
Materials:	$1.00	
Labor:	1.50	
Cost of Goods Sold per Unit:	$2.50	2.50
Gross Profit per Unit:		$2.00

Amy from the Most Chocolate Cake Company can produce about 20 cakes during a 40-hour workweek and 30 cakes in 60 hours. That means she can earn $600 to $750 per week, or between $31,200 and $39,000 per year before taxes, without allowing for vacation or sick days. There would be an additional $100 to $150 in gross profit per week before other expenses are figured. Assuming Amy can sell 20 to 30 cakes per week at $40 each, she will have a maximum income of about $46,800.

Amy knows that she will have other expenses, so $40,000 is more realistic. Like Janet, Amy would like to earn more than that per year, so she too could add employees if the market would support greater volume. If she paid her employees $15 per hour (assumed for this example as the minimum living wage), she would need to sell 8,000 cakes per year to make her $40,000. That is 154 cakes per week, requiring perhaps seven full-time bakers. This would not be possible in her home kitchen. The EOU analysis helps to identify this challenge.

However, we have to be sure that Amy is not comparing apples to oranges when making the analysis. With more people, the tasks could be delegated, so that it takes only one hour per cake, bringing the gross profit to $20 each. If Amy could also get better pricing on ingredients because of increased volume, the gross profit would be even higher. At $20 per unit gross profit, Amy would need to sell only 2,000 cakes per year, or 39 per week. That could be accomplished with two full-time bakers. As a home-based business, that would be more realistic.

Amy, like any entrepreneur, has to decide what is achievable and what her goals are.

Going for Volume

Janet meets a bookstore-supply wholesaler. He offers to buy 2,000 book-markers if Janet can deliver them in one month and sell them for $3.50 each, $1 less than she had been getting. This would reduce her gross profit but offer higher revenue. Three questions immediately came to her mind:

1. *Can I produce the 2,000-unit order in the required time frame?* After doing some calculations, Janet realizes that if she hires 10 people each to work 35 hours a month, she could deliver the order in time. Janet convinces 10 people to take on the one-month commitment by offering $12 per hour.

2. *If I lower the price to $3.50 for each bookmarker (instead of $4.50), will I still make an acceptable gross profit per unit?* To answer this question, Janet creates a chart (see **Exhibit 5-14**) and realizes that her new gross profit per unit would be $1. Let us look at the EOU if she factors in her labor at $12 per hour, or $2 per bookmarker.

3. *How much in total gross profit will I make from the order?* To answer this question, Janet creates another chart (see **Exhibit 5-15**) and realizes that her total gross profit would be $1,000.

Janet concludes that $1,000 in gross profit is much better than earning $80 a week in gross profit, plus $60 a week for her labor (what she earned making the bookmarkers herself each week at a selling price of $4.50). Even though the wholesaler is asking for a lower selling price, her total revenue, and therefore her total gross profit, would be much higher. When Janet realizes that she could deliver the order in the required time and make $1,000, she accepts the offer.

Exhibit 5-14 *EOU Example, Janet's Company with Employees*

ECONOMICS OF ONE UNIT (EOU)		
Manufacturing Business: Unit = 1 Bookmarker		
Selling Price per Unit:		$3.50
Materials:	$1.00	
Labor:	1.50	
Cost of Goods Sold per Unit:	$2.50	2.50
Gross Profit per Unit:		$1.00

Exhibit 5-15 *Gross Profit Projection, Janet's Company with Employees*

GROSS PROFIT PROJECTION (BASED ON EOU)		
Janet's Total Gross Profit		
Revenue ($3.50 × 2,000 bookmarkers):		$7,000.00
Materials ($1 × 2,000):	$2,000.00	
Labor ($2.00 × 2,000):	4,000.00	
Cost of Goods Sold:	$6,000.00	6,000.00
Gross Profit:		$1,000.00

Five breakthrough steps entrepreneurs can take to understand preliminary feasibility are:

1. calculating the unit of sale,
2. determining the economics of one unit of sale,
3. substituting someone else's labor,
4. selling in volume, and
5. creating jobs and operating at a profit.

At first, an entrepreneur can be part of his own economics of one unit. If you start making (manufacturing) computers in your garage, like Steve Jobs and Stephen Wozniak did when they started Apple, you should include your labor on the EOU worksheet.

Over time, though, Jobs and Wozniak made enough profit to hire others to manufacture the computers. Jobs and Wozniak took themselves out of the economics of one unit so they could be the creative leaders of the company. And, by lowering prices, they were able to sell millions of units.

currency a term for money when it is exchanged internationally.

foreign exchange (FX) rate the relative value of one currency to another.

Global Impact . . .

Selling Your Product around the World

Through the Internet, even a very small business run by one person can reach customers internationally. What if a customer from Germany contacts you through your Web site and wants to pay for your product in euros, the currency of much of Europe? **Currency** is a term for money when it is exchanged internationally. In the United States, the currency is the dollar. In Japan, it is the yen. In Mexico, it is the peso.

The **foreign exchange (FX) rate** is the relative value of one currency to another. It describes the buying power of a currency. The FX rate is expressed as a ratio. If one dollar is worth 1.25 euros, to calculate how many euros a certain number of dollars is worth, multiply that number by 1.25.

$$\$5 = \$5 \times €1.25 = €6.25$$

How would you figure out how many dollars €6.25 is worth? Simply divide €6.25 by 1.25 to get $5.

Tip: There are currency converters available online, such as at http://finance.yahoo.com/currency?u.

Chapter Summary

Now that you have studied this chapter, you can do the following:

1. Define your business.
   - Identify the three basic types of "product" businesses.
     - Manufacturing is the making of a tangible product.
     - Wholesale is the buying in quantity from a manufacturer and selling to a retailer.
     - Retail is selling to individual consumers.
2. Articulate your core beliefs, your mission, and your vision.
3. Analyze your competitive advantage.
   - Your competitive advantage is whatever you can do better than the competition that will attract customers to your business.
   - Find your competitive advantage by analyzing what consumers in your market need.
4. Perform feasibility analysis by calculating the economics of one unit of sale.
   - The EOU is the basis of business profit.
   - Entrepreneurs use profits to pay themselves, expand the business, and start or invest in new businesses.
   - The entrepreneur chooses how the unit is defined:
     - One item (unit)
     - One hour of service time (if the business is a service business)
     - For businesses that sell differently priced items, the average sale per customer, or total sales divided by the number of customers:

   Total Sales/Number of Customers = Average Unit of Sale

   - To get a closer look at the costs involved in figuring one unit, entrepreneurs analyze the cost of goods or services sold (COGS or COSS) of a unit.
     - The cost of materials used to make the product (or deliver the service)
     - The cost of labor used to make the product (or deliver the service)
   - Once you know your cost of goods sold, you can calculate gross profit. Subtract total COGS from your total revenue to get your gross profit.

   Revenue − COGS = Gross Profit

Key Terms

barriers to entry, 169
competitive strategy, 173
core values, 163
cost of goods sold (COGS), 175
cost of services sold (COSS), 175
currency, 180
direct labor, 176
economics of one unit
   of sale (EOU), 175
foreign exchange (FX) rate, 180

gross profit, 175
manufacturing, 162
market, 161
retail, 162
strategy, 174
tactics, 174
unique selling proposition
   (USP), 170
unit of sale, 175
wholesale, 162

Entrepreneurship Portfolio

Critical Thinking Exercises

5-1. Use the following charts to define a business you would like to start, and analyze your competitive advantage.

Business Definition Question	Response
The Offer. What products and services will be sold by the business?	
Target Market. Which consumer segments will the business focus on?	
Production Capability. How will that offer be produced and delivered to those customers?	
Problem Solving. What problem does the business solve for its customers?	
Competitive Advantage Question	**Competitive Difference (USP)**
The Offer. What will be better and different about the products and services that will be sold?	
Target Market. Which segments of consumers should be the focus of the business to make it as successful as possible?	
Production and Delivery Capability. What will be better or different about the way the offer is produced and delivered to those customers?	

Attributes Important to Customers	Weight (a)	Your Company Rating (b)	Your Company Weighted Rating (c = a * b)	Competitor Number 1 Rating (d)	Competitor Number 1 Weighted Rating (e = a * d)	Competitor Number 2 Rating (f)	Competitor Number 2 Weighted Rating (g = a * f)	Competitor Number 3 Rating (h)	Competitor Number 3 Weighted Rating (i = a * h)
Quality									
Price									
Location									
Selection									
Service									
Speed/ Turnaround									
Specialization									
Personalization									
Total	1.00		_____		_____		_____		_____

5-2. What are the different business opportunity decision processes? Which one would you prefer for a product driven opportunity, and why?

5-3. Explain how this statement applies to becoming a successful entrepreneur: Spotting opportunities consists of looking at the same thing as everyone else and thinking something different.

5-4. What strategies will you use to compete with your rivals? Illustrate with examples.

5-5. Identify a global company of your choice. Discuss its core values, vision and mission statements.

5-6. Suppose your new venture was a souvenir shop at a tourist destination, what would be the competitive strategy and tactics that you will employ to gain a sustainable advantage?

Key Concept Questions

5-7. How would you determine the core values of your envisioned business?

5-8. What is the average unit of sale for the following businesses?
- Business 1: A restaurant that serves $2,100 in meals to 115 customers per day.
- Business 2: A record store that sells $1,500 worth of CDs to 75 customers per day.

5-9. Sue, of Sue's Sandwiches, sells sandwiches and soda from a sidewalk cart in a popular park near her house. She sets up her cart in the summers to earn money for college tuition. Last month she sold $1,240 worth of product (sandwiches and sodas) to 100 customers. She spent $210 on the sandwich ingredients and buying the sodas wholesale. Her unit is one sandwich ($4) plus one soda ($1). Define the unit of sale and calculate the economics of one unit for Sue's Sandwiches.

5-10. How can one determine whether one's advantage is strong enough or sustainable? Illustrate with a real-life example.

5-11. Is there a service presently available to only a few consumers, or one that is not available yet all? Write about a service that you can imagine eventually becoming very popular and the need(s) it will meet.

5-12. How does analyzing the cost of goods sold (COGS) or cost of services sold (COSS) of one unit help an entrepreneur gauge the viability of their business?

5-13. If the FX rate between the Japanese yen and the euro is 189.35:1, how many yen will equal 10 euros?

Application Exercises

5-14. You own a small record label. You sell CDs through your Web site for $15, including shipping and handling. You get an offer from someone who owns a record store in Germany who wants to buy your CDs at $10 each and sell them for €30. He says his profit from each sale would be €12 and he will split it with you. Assuming the exchange rate between the dollar and the euro is $1 = €2:
- a. How much profit would you get from the sale of each CD in the German store?
- b. How much is that profit in dollars?

c. Is this a good business opportunity for you? Why or why not?

d. If the FX rate between the dollar and the euro falls to $1 = €1, would this still be a good business idea for you? Why or why not?

Exploring Online

5-15. Use the Internet to research suppliers for a business you would like to start or can envision. Describe the business and list the URL, e-mail, phone and fax, and street address for five suppliers you located via the Internet.

5-16. Visit *http://www.download.cnet.com/windows* and find three shareware programs that would be of value to you as an entrepreneur. List them.

BizBuilder Business Plan Questions

After studying this chapter, you should be able to answer the following Business Plan Questions. The entire outline for the Business Plan is found in Appendix 2.

1.0 Executive Summary

    A. What is the full legal name of your organization?

    B. What products or services will you offer?

2.0 Mission, Vision, and Culture

    A. Write a mission statement for your organization of 50 or fewer words that clearly states your competitive advantage, strategy, and tactics.

    B. Create a vision statement for your organization.

    C. Describe the core beliefs you will use to run your organization and how they will be reflected in its culture.

    D. Identify the ways you plan to run a socially responsible organization.

Case Study | Happy Belly Curbside Kitchen—Finding Opportunity in Healthy Food

Owners Terry and Dawn Hall created Happy Belly Curbside Kitchen out of their experiences, knowledge, skills, and interests. The founders had 30 years of experience in the hospitality business. They traveled extensively across the United States to meet the requirements of their careers in hospitality. They were the children of small business owners and have restaurant experience combined with formal hospitality education.

Terry and Dawn recognized several patterns in their travels:

1. The availability of fresh, natural food is far less than the need for it.
2. Declines in small-business viability.
3. The inverse relationship between the availability of healthy food and the level of obesity.

When their daughter, Mayer, was born, Terry and Dawn decided that they wanted her to eat only healthy, fresh foods. They were frustrated by how difficult it was to find the food they wanted when they ate in restaurants. And, they wanted flexibility in work schedules and the opportunity to support their community. This led to the idea of creating a mobile restaurant serving the fresh, healthy foods they desired.

After the initial frustration of being turned down repeatedly by mainstream banks, even though they had related work experience, savings, excellent credit, and no debt, the Halls learned of a financing resource in their community that had different parameters. They secured their initial financing from Access to Capital for Entrepreneurs (ACE Capital), a Cleveland, Georgia-based community development financial institution. ACE had a combination of its own resources and funds from Create Jobs for USA available and was looking for borrowers like the Halls. The loan process took seven days for approval. With the funding from ACE, Happy Belly was able to get rolling. The Halls remodeled their commercial kitchen, purchased a food truck, and hired some dozen people.

Happy Belly Curbside Kitchen is part of the highly competitive Atlanta food-truck market but has some distinctive twists. The Halls don't call their business a food truck, rather a "curbside kitchen." They have a corporate sponsor, the Big Green Egg, producers of the high-end grill that is pictured on the vehicles. The menu changes frequently, depending on what is fresh and local. Orders are taken on iPads by staff in front of the kitchens, rather than from windows in the truck itself. Also, the company has a full commercial kitchen in nearby Smyrna, Georgia, that they use for catering. These factors combine to permit their providing a great variety of fresh, healthy food.

It was the Halls' intention to keep the money earned in the local community. They donated 5 percent of profits to the local Boys and Girls Club and purchased locally whenever possible.

Happy Belly targets customers in Fulton and Cobb Counties and focuses on its core value of healthy eating. The Halls partnered with Adam Verner, a local farmer. This is part of what they termed "farm to street," a play on the farm-to-table movement. They were named one of the 10 Healthiest Food Trucks in America in *Shape* magazine and expanded to two trucks serving the Atlanta area, along with an increasingly successful catering business.

Happy Belly Curbside Kitchen is locally based with a global view.

Case Study Analysis

5-17. How did Terry and Dawn Hall identify the market for Happy Belly Curbside Kitchen? What process did they follow to analyze opportunities?

5-18. What knowledge, skills, and abilities did the Halls have before starting their company?

5-19. Why might *Shape* magazine have named Happy Belly Curbside Kitchen as one of the 10 Healthiest Food Trucks in America? How would they be healthier than most food trucks?

5-20. How is this business tied to a social mission? What do the owners do to demonstrate their commitment?

5-21. Identify four critical resources for Happy Belly and how the owners secured them.

Case Sources

Happy Belly Curbside Kitchen, accessed July 18, 2013, http://www.happybellytruck.com.

Nicole McDermott, "The 10 Healthiest Food Trucks in America," *Shape*, accessed July 22, 2013, http://www.shape.com/healthy-eating/meal-ideas/10-healthiest-food-trucks-america?page=6.

Terry Hall, "Cooking Up Healthy Food and Job Creation in Atlanta," *Huffington Post*, January 28, 2013, accessed July 22, 2013, http://www.huffingtonpost.com/create-jobs-for-usa/ace-happy-belly_b_2551021.html.

Case Study | Translating Talent in Three Businesses

Ken Durden/Shutterstock

Rosi and Brian Amador apply their talents to three businesses. Sol y Canto (Sun and Song) is a six-member Latin-roots musical group led by Rosi and Brian. MusicAmador Productions is an independently owned record label that produces Sol y Canto's recordings. Amador Bilingual Voice-Overs involves the family in professional voice-over work in English and Spanish. The common thread in the businesses is voice and communication. The Amadors have leveraged their finely honed professional musical talents, and native English and Spanish-speaking skills, to create business opportunities.

Rosemarie Straijer Amador was born in San Juan, Puerto Rico, to an Argentine father and Puerto Rican mother. Rosi was raised by performer parents, who passed on to her their love of Latin American rhythms and musical styles. Her mother, Josefina (Josephine) Del Mar—her stage name—was a dancer, singer, and actress who appeared in the United States and Europe with Bob Hope, Dean Martin, Jerry Lewis, and other famous performers, and in Mexico with comic actor Cantínflas (Mario Moreno). Her father, Jaime Straijer (Jaime Andrada was his stage name) started out in radio in Buenos Aires and later became an actor, touring all over Latin America. When they settled down to have a family, Rosi's parents opened their own publishing company in San Juan to service the horse-racing community. Rosi moved to the United States for the last two years of high school and graduated with a degree in Spanish and French from Bryn Mawr College. She briefly worked in retail and

administrative roles and served as the manager of the socially conscious actor theater company Underground Railway Theater for five years, where she learned how to manage, fund-raise, and book a performing arts ensemble nationally. With her husband Brian, she cofounded their first Latin band, Flor de Caña (1984–1994) which she also managed and booked. In 1992 she founded MusicAmador, initially a Latin music booking agency representing eight Latin music and dance ensembles. In 2005 she merged her agency with two other booking agencies to become the Vice President of the Roots Agency and its Latin Division Director until 2007. In 1994 Rosi and Brian founded Sol y Canto, once again taking on managing and booking duties.

Brian Amador is a self-described "Chicano-Gringo mongrel" from Albuquerque, New Mexico. He graduated from the New England Conservatory of Music, having studied classical guitar, composition, and improvisation. He also studied flamenco guitar in Albuquerque and Madrid. In 1995 he received a highly competitive grant for musical composition awarded to "exceptional artists" by the Massachusetts Cultural Council. For five years, he was principal guitarist for the Ramón de los Reyes Spanish Dance Theater. As musical director and guitarist for Sol y Canto, he has produced several CDs, arranged and composed in styles from all over Latin America and the Caribbean, and developed a unique guitar style that incorporates Latin American, flamenco, and African elements. He has written and arranged music for different permutations of Sol y Canto, as well as for that ensemble with string quartet and orchestra. In 2009, the nation's oldest and most prestigious artists' colony, the MacDowell Artist Colony, granted Brian a fellowship, where he composed the bulk of his latest major work, "Sabor y Memoria: A Musical Feast in Seven Courses" for Sol y Canto and string quartet.

Sol y Canto

Rosi explains, "Sol y Canto was founded as a result of an experience: in 1984 my husband and I met through a three-week cultural exchange tour to Nicaragua. We created our first band, *Flor de Caña*, out of that life-changing event, committed to singing about the reality in Central America and opening the eyes of the North American people as to the role of our government

Many kinds of statistics are available from the U.S. Government Printing Office. The latest edition of *The Statistical Abstract of the United States* is available online and provides 1,400 statistical tables.

Industry Research: The 50,000-Foot Perspective

Industry research focuses not on individual consumers, but on a segment of business as a whole. It provides a broader perspective and shows trends, new and emerging opportunities, and industry norms. If you want to start a record label, you will need to know how the recording industry is doing. Is it growing? Are people buying more CDs this year, or fewer? Who are the major consumers of CDs? Which age group buys the most recordings? What kind of music is selling?

To make the best use of industry data, you will have to identify your industry correctly and examine it. The codes of the North American Industry Classification System (NAICS) are generally used as industry identifiers. Once you have the NAICS code (six digits), you can readily search many sources of data. You can find NAICS codes in the *North American Industrial Classification System: United States, 2007*, or online at the U.S. Census Web site (http://www.census.gov/epcd/naics02/) in which you will enter a keyword and then narrow your selections until you find the best fit for your organization.

Once you have identified your industry, you can perform data searches to find relevant statistics and reports. Some places to look include the Standard and Poor's *Industry Surveys*, the U.S. Census Web site (http://www.census .gov), Wetfeet.com (http://www.wetfeet.com/asp/industries_atoz.asp), and BizMiner (http://www.bizminer.com). A local college or university may subscribe to services such as IBISWorld or Dun and Bradstreet, which offer an abundance of information. The Census data will include the number of firms, revenues, number of paid employees, and more. In many cases, industry reports are available on the Census site. There are numerous other sources as well. Once you identify them, you can answer such questions as

- What is the scale (size) of the industry, in units and dollars?
- What is the scope (geographic range) of the industry? Is it local (city or neighborhood only), regional (covering a metropolitan area or state), national, international (present in two or more countries), or global (everywhere)?
- Is it a niche industry, or does it reach a mass market?
- What does industry and individual company profitability look like?
- What trends are occurring in the industry? Is it growing? Declining? Stagnating?
- What is the structure of the industry? Is it highly concentrated, with a few companies in control? Is it highly fragmented, with a lot of competition?
- What competition is in the market space, and what are they doing? Perform an industry SWOT analysis to visualize this.

The methods to use for industry research overlap with those for customer research to some extent, but they reach further. Some methods to try include:

- *Interviews.* Perhaps you can find people in the industry (staff) or who study the industry (stock analysts, professors, economic-development professionals) who will share insights and data.
- *Observation.* This might include taking public tours of industry facilities, visiting trade meetings, and so forth.

- *Tracking.* Keeping track of industry advertisements and reports could help. For example, you may want to start a financial services company, so tracking interest rates will be vital.
- *Written sources for statistical data.* A variety of sources in printed form were suggested previously in this chapter. Check out the Internet Public Library at http://www.ipl.org/div/subject/browse/bus82.00.00/. For industry and firm profitability, try online services for a fee, such as Risk Management Association (RMA) or BizMiner. Or use free library resources, such as *RMA Annual Statement Studies: Financial Ratio Benchmarks*.
- *Books and articles.* Books and articles are available about almost any business topic that you can imagine. If your library doesn't have what you need, you might be able to acquire it for free through inter-library loan.
- *Competitor Web sites.* As noted previously, annual reports often include excellent descriptions of companies within an industry and their respective operating environments.
- *Trade associations and chambers of commerce.* Virtually every industry has at least one professional or trade association. You can search online by industry plus the word *association* to find them. Or, you can look in Gale Publishing's *Directory of Associations* at a library. The American Society of Association Executives gateway (http://www.asaecenter.org) has an online list of members, and you can find association magazines and journals at http://www.mediafinder.com.

By taking the time to research and understand your industry, you can be more successful in your own business. Plus, you will learn a lot more about your field!

Ford and Chrysler each spent millions on market research before producing, respectively, the Mustang and the minivan. It was worth millions of dollars to these companies to determine if the public wanted these automobiles because it was going to cost tens of millions to produce them.

Make Market Research an Integral Part of Your Business

Market research is not something you only do once. Make it an ongoing part of your operations. Just as your tastes and desires change as you learn about new ideas and products, so do those of your customers. By continuing to survey your customers as your business develops, you will stay

Global Impact . . .

College Degrees for the Military

Active-duty members of the U.S. military and their families tend to relocate frequently, often internationally. This job-related relocation makes completing a college degree at a single traditional bricks and mortar, four-year college difficult at best.

American Military University is a wholly online, private, for-profit, degree-granting program with students across the United States and in more than 100 other countries. Established by a retired Marine Corps officer, James P. Etter, the university has a well-defined target market: the military and their families.

Course delivery, subjects, and content are designed with the military in mind. As long as they have Internet access, military students can enroll and take courses. Also, military personnel earn education benefits from the government and can use them at American Military University.

American Military University has served its global target market profitably for over 20 years.

Source: American Military University website, accessed July 24, 2013, http://www.apus.edu.

current with their needs and their feelings about your product. You can provide customers with prepaid response cards and conduct in-store or telephone surveys, depending on your business. By carefully reviewing your customer purchasing and contact history, you can target your surveys for maximum effectiveness.

How Customers Decide to Buy

How will you figure out who the potential customers are for *your* business? It is critical to understand not only which customers are in your target market, but how they will purchase your product (or service).

Step 1. If you have developed a product or service, ask yourself what consumer need it will serve. Arm & Hammer turned this marketing question into a gold mine by developing its simple baking-soda powder into toothpaste, laundry detergent, air and carpet fresheners, and deodorants.

Step 2. Think about who might actually buy your product. Remember that the people who use a product are not always the purchasers. Mothers generally buy children's clothes; if you are making children's playsuits, they should offer features/benefits that appeal to mothers. They could be marketed as easy to clean, for example.

Step 3. Analyze the buying process that will lead customers to your product.

1. *Awareness.* The customer realizes a need. Advertising is designed to make consumers and business customers aware of potential needs, for everything from dandruff shampoo to office supplies to automobiles.

2. *Information search.* The customer seeks information about products that could fulfill a need. Someone looking for a multivitamin might pick up a brochure on the counter of the local health food store or simply look on the shelves of a supermarket or drug store. A retailer might search online for sign companies.

3. *Evaluate alternatives.* Once information is gathered on a single product, the customer may want to examine alternatives before making a purchasing decision. The individual looking for a multivitamin might check out what's available in the health food store, and compare the price and content with the more commercial brands found in the local supermarket or drug store. The business owner might get several quotations on the needed business signs.

4. *Decide to purchase.* The first purchase is really a test; the customer is trying a product to see how well it performs (or testing the quality of the service).

5. *Evaluate the purchase.* If your product or service is satisfactory, the customer may begin to develop loyalty to your business and tell others about it, as well. Now, how can you keep that customer for life?

Owning a Perception in the Customer's Mind

More valuable to McDonald's than all the Big Macs it sells every year is the perception it owns in the minds of its customers—that every time they patronize a McDonald's, they will eat food that tastes exactly the same as at every other McDonald's, that the prices will be reasonable, and that the service will be friendly and fast.

For Burger King to compete with McDonald's, it had to fight for a mind share of the fast-food customer. Burger King opened its attack with "Have It Your Way," which targeted McDonald's mass-manufacturing approach to making hamburgers. It followed up with "Broiled, not Fried" and "The Whopper Beats the Big Mac."

It is almost impossible to topple an established leading brand in a market. Burger King's executives wisely decided that their goal was to be a strong number two. As number two, you try to create a new category (broiled instead of fried hamburgers, for instance) rather than attempting to take over the competitive advantage of the number one company in the market. Avis lost money for 15 years while trying to overtake Hertz. The company finally accepted its number two position and turned it into a competitive and profitable advantage through its "We Try Harder!" advertising campaign.

You do not have to be number one to be successful; discover a competitive advantage and attack the market by creating a new category in the customer's mind. Domino's Pizza found a competitive advantage by delivering orders in less than 30 minutes. That one marketing insight helped create a hugely successful company.

Features Create Benefits

There is a subtle, but important, difference between the benefits and the features of a product. The features are facts. The features of a drill might include its hardness and sharpness, but the benefit is that it makes a hole. The feature of a Teflon coating on a pan creates the benefit of easy cleaning. The essence of selling is showing how and why the outstanding features of a product or service will benefit customers. Smart marketers always emphasize benefits, not features, because consumers will buy what solves their problems or makes their lives more pleasant.

Home Depot: Teaching Customers So They Will Return

Home Depot's marketing vision is not just to sell tools and materials but to teach people how to use them to improve their homes and lives. The company's marketing vision focuses on what its customers need Home Depot products to do.

Successful companies are not built on one-time sales but on repeat business. The owners of Home Depot have calculated that a satisfied customer is worth more than $35,000 in sales over the customer's lifetime. They found that the slogan "More saving. More doing." works for their customer base.

Home Depot's multimillion-dollar insight was that its customers not only needed the products it sold but also help in using them.

BizFacts

Minority business owners (often defined to include women) should contact local corporate offices and ask about minority purchasing programs or find the local office of the National Minority Supplier Development Council (http://www.nmsdcus.org) or government diversity agency. Many companies and most government agencies are committed to buying up to 25 percent of their supplies and services from minority-owned businesses.

The most successful companies pay close attention to consumer demands. They constantly observe their customers, survey them, and analyze their wants and needs. They hire people to look for customer needs that might be going unfulfilled. This is all part of customer analysis, one step in developing a marketing plan.

Which Segment of the Market Will You Target?

Marketing strategies are focused on the customer, and a business has to choose which customers to target. Your product will not be needed by everyone. You will have to figure out which segments of the market to pursue.

There is a huge market for home repair, including professional carpenters and builders. Home Depot's competitive advantage would not be strong in the market segment composed of professionals, in which the distribution channels are strong and well established. A **market segment** is composed of customers who have a similar response to a certain type of marketing. Home Depot chose to market primarily to the nonprofessional, private individual.

market segment a group of consumers or businesses that have a similar response to a particular type of product or service.

In the cosmetics industry, one segment reacts positively to luxuriously packaged, expensive brands. Another is most responsive to products that claim to reduce signs of aging. Another's primary concern is (reasonable) price. A company that recognizes these market segments and chooses one to concentrate on will do better than a business that tries to sell its cosmetics to every adult female in the country.

It is difficult to target very different segments of a market simultaneously. Volvo, for example, has established a reputation as a safe, family car. It targets parents with young children. Volvo would have a difficult time also trying to market a two-seat convertible sports car to young adults who are concerned more with style and speed than safety.

Successful Segmenting: The Body Shop

The Body Shop is a good example of the success that can result from choosing the right market segment. Founder Anita Roddick disliked paying for expensive packaging and perfuming when she bought cosmetics. She was also annoyed by the extravagant claims made by many cosmetics companies and by the high prices of their perfumes and lotions. Price became an integral part of the image for many products. A brand called Joy, for example, was marketed as the most expensive perfume in the world.

Roddick saw an opportunity to create a different line of cosmetics. She would use natural products that would be packaged inexpensively and marketed without extravagant claims. As she writes in her book, "It is immoral to deceive a customer by making miracle claims for a product. It is immoral to use a photograph of a glowing sixteen-year-old to sell a cream aimed at preventing wrinkles in a forty-year-old."[1]

Roddick tapped into a segment of the cosmetics market that had been neglected, and her business grew explosively as a result. Her success proves that selling an honest product honestly can be the best marketing strategy of all.

But what if Roddick had found that there were very few women interested in natural cosmetics? If she had determined this before starting, then she could have changed her segmentation strategy. If not, her business would not have survived, because even though the cosmetics market is

---

[1]Anita Roddick, *Body & Soul, Anita Roddick Tells the Story of the Body Shop, Inc.*, New York: Crown Publishers, 1991.

large, her segment would have been too small to support her venture. It is possible to go after a small, niche segment, but then your price would have to be high enough to make a profit, and the customers would have to buy often enough to keep your business going. Jaguar and Rolls-Royce each sell far fewer cars than Honda or Ford, but at much higher prices. Jaguar and Rolls target the luxury segment of the car market.

Applying Market Segmentation Methods

Marketers have developed four basic ways to segment:

- *Geographic.* Dividing a population by location.
- *Demographic.* Dividing a population based on a variable such as age, gender, income, or education. For business customers, variables such as sales volume and number of employees could matter.
- *Psychographic.* Dividing a population by psychological differences, such as values (conservative, liberal, open-minded, traditional), lifestyle (sedentary, active), personality traits (worrier, Type A, shy, extroverted), and social group (white collar, blue collar).
- *Behavioral.* Dividing the market by purchase behaviors that have been observed, such as brand loyalty or responsiveness to price.

Say you want to make and sell hacky sacks on your college campus. Twenty thousand students attend the college. If 50 of the 200 students surveyed are interested in buying your hacky sack, you might expect that approximately 5,000 students of the 20,000 would represent your total potential market. Which segments of that market should you target?

If your company has limited resources, you might choose to target only one segment. A large company might decide to appeal to the entire market by designing a product tailored for each segment. Gap Inc., for example, has three product lines—Old Navy, Gap, and Banana Republic— each priced for and tailored to a segment of the sportswear market.

You could use any of the four segmentation methods listed previously for your hacky sack business, as shown in **Exhibit 6-2**.

Step into the Shoes . . .

How Thomas Burrell Became a Leader in Marketing to African Americans

Thomas Burrell, founder of Burrell Advertising
(Michael L. Abramson/Getty Images)

To market a product or service to a specific market segment, you must research what the people who comprise it want. In the late 1960s, major corporations became more conscious of the potential clout of African-American consumers but were unsure how to market to them.

In 1971, Thomas Burrell and Emmett McBain opened one of the first black-owned advertising agencies in the United States. By the following year, Burrell had convinced McDonald's that Burrell Advertising could help the huge company expand into the African-American market. Burrell came to be the fastest-growing and largest black-owned advertising agency in the country and continues to be one of the largest multicultural global marketing firms.

Burrell Advertising has created more than 100 commercials for McDonald's. Other Burrell clients have included Coca-Cola, Ford Motor, Johnson Products, Schlitz Brewing, Blockbuster Entertainment, Procter & Gamble, Jack Daniel Distillery, Polaroid, Stroh Brewing, and First National Bank of Chicago.

While no longer involved in the marketing firm, Burrell himself could probably quote the demographics of the African-American market off the top of his head. He has combined his company's thorough market research with his own personal experience as an African-American male to create powerful appeals to the targeted market.

Exhibit 6-2 *Hacky Sack Segmentation**		
Segmentation Method	**Description**	**Estimated Size of Segment**
Geographic	Residents within 2 miles of Mid-Size University	600,000
Demographic	Age 18–24 Full-time students	60,000 45,000
Psychographic	Active lifestyle	15,000
Behavioral	Extroverted Fun-loving Play hacky sack	10,000 18,000 500

*Research would be needed to identify these values.

One way to gauge your market would be to interview a sample of 200 students with a survey while showing them the product and asking such questions as:

- Do you play a sport, whether competitive or not?
  - If so, how often do you play?
  - What, if any cocurricular activities do you participate in?
- Do you own a hacky sack?
  - If so, how much did you pay for it?
  - Where did you buy it?
  - How long have you had it?
  - How often do you use it?
- Would you be interested in purchasing this hacky sack, if it were available?
- How much would you pay for this hacky sack?
- How many of these hacky sacks would you buy per year?
- What suggestions do you have to improve this hacky sack?

Once you have chosen your market segment, you can really fine-tune your market research, because you now have to focus only on these customers—not on every potential customer in your market. Collecting data from the people in your market segment can be fun as well as financially rewarding. Here are a few questions you can adapt to your own product or service:

1. Do you currently use this type of product?
2. What brand of this product do you currently use?
3. Where do you buy it? Please be specific about the source, such as the name and location of the store, the direct-marketing representative, or Web site.
4. How much do you pay for it? (Probe for size and price, if appropriate.)
5. How often do you buy it?
6. Would you buy our product/service?
7. How much would you be willing to pay for it?
8. Where would you shop for it?
9. How would you improve it?
10. Now that you have seen/tasted/felt/smelled this product, what do you consider to be its closest competitor?
11. Is our product/service worse or better than those of our competitors? Please explain.

The Product Life Cycle

product life cycle (PLC)
the four stages that a product
or service goes through as
it matures in the market—
introduction, growth, maturity,
and decline.

You will also need to analyze where your market is in its **product life cycle (PLC)**. The PLC is the set of four stages that a product or market goes through from its beginning until its end. **Figure 6-1** illustrates two product life cycles.

1. *Introduction.* Your product or service is in the invention and initial-development stages. It is new to the market and is essentially unknown, so you will need to introduce it to potential customers who may be curious about your product but not familiar with it. Marketing at this stage will require education and testing with price and presentation. Modification of the design or technology may be required. When the personal home computer was first introduced, Apple's marketing was focused on convincing consumers how easy it would be to use. Apple used the same strategy in the introduction of subsequent products.

2. *Growth.* Once you achieve success in introducing your product or service to the marketplace, your organization will grow and inevitably invite attention from competition, as well as perhaps attract new entrants in the field. Perceiving your growth in sales, competitors now start entering your market, or more strongly defend their own market spaces, so efforts at this stage will have to focus on communicating your competitive advantage to consumers. Customer purchases increase dramatically; you have reached the limits of your current market.

3. *Maturity.* At this stage, consumers have become knowledgeable about both you and your competitors. The market has become relatively crowded, and there is no more growth as your product or service is currently offered. Marketing will need to focus on promoting brand loyalty. Stability of profits now depends more on cost strategies as demand has become relatively flat.

4. *Decline.* At this point, your competitive advantage has eroded, and sales and profits are declining. New developments will be necessary to revive the market's interest.

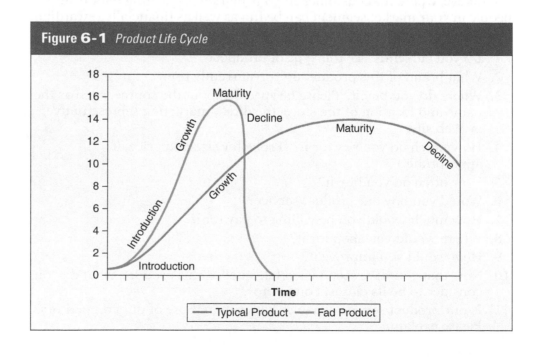

Figure 6-1 *Product Life Cycle*

Product life cycles are applicable in different ways. For example, the Pet Rock, essentially a small stone that people were to pretend was a pet, had a very short life cycle. Such fad items attain popularity quickly and mature and decline equally rapidly. Other products, such as prescription drugs, will have longer life cycles because of patent protection, high market-entry costs, and their medical necessity for certain population groups. Ideally, you will look at the overall life cycle of a market to determine where your product or service will fit.

It is important for you to understand where each product or service is in the PLC. See **Figure 6-1** for an illustration of the PLC of a typical product and for a fad item. It is important to have a continuous flow of new products, so that your organization as a whole is sustainable. For example, if you owned a pharmaceutical company, you would want to introduce new medicines well before the existing ones reached maturity/decline, so that there would be continuity in revenue. You would also want to find new uses for existing drugs, to extend their life cycles. For example, AstraZeneca's Seroquel was initially approved for schizophrenia and was used off-label for bipolar disorder. To extend Seroquel's life cycle, AstraZeneca sought U.S. Food and Drug Administration (FDA) approval for the additional use. This is far less costly and quicker than developing a new brand-name drug.

For services, the life cycle is essentially the same as for products. However, extending the life cycle can be easier for a service than for a product. Starting a new cycle could be as simple as modifying the delivery process.

In addition, if you are considering acquiring an existing business, it is critical to understand where in the PLC its products and services are. Are they all toward the end of their life cycles? Mixed? At the beginning? This will dramatically affect the future value of the company.

Is Your Market Saturated?

Figuring out where your product is in the PLC will tell you whether your market is close to saturation. In other words, have all 3 million people in your market already bought a competitor's product? Nokia, for example, had a 39 percent share of the global market of $1.1 billion in mobile phones.[2] But that market was nowhere near saturation. Meanwhile, Nokia introduced its Short Message Service (SMS), which allows e-mail messages to be sent between mobile phones in Finland. SMS quickly became Finnish teenagers' favorite way to communicate. Observing how quickly the technology spread among Finnish teenagers gave the Nokia management ideas about how they would market SMS in the 140 countries where they sold cell phones.

Market Positioning: Drive Home Your Competitive Advantage

After deciding which market segments to target, an entrepreneur will need to figure out what position the company should try to occupy in those segments. The *position* of a product is its relative place in the customer's mind compared with its competitors. The goal of market **positioning**, therefore, is to distinguish your product or service from others being offered to the market segments you have targeted. You can do that by focusing on your competitive advantage. "Have It Your Way," Burger King promised, driving

◀ **Learning Objective 4**
Position your product or service within your market.

positioning distinguishing a product or service from similar products or services being offered to the same market.

[2]Mark Landler, "Nokia Pushes to Regain U.S. Sales in Spite of Apple and Google," *The New York Times*, December 10, 2007.

home its competitive advantage—that at Burger King you can specify exactly how you want your hamburger prepared and garnished.

As you can see from the Burger King example, positioning involves clearly communicating your competitive advantage to the consumer and demonstrating how your product/service is different. Your goal is to position your product/service clearly in the mind of your target market as the brand that provides that difference. Use the following format to develop a positioning statement for your business:

> **(Your business name/brand) is the (competitive industry/category) that (provides these benefits, or points of difference) to (audience/ target market).**

Here is an example: *Microsoft is the leading global software producer that provides affordable computer solutions to businesses.*

By the time you have completed the four steps of your marketing plan, you will know your potential customers, your competitors, and your market intimately. It is a lot of work but well worth it. Make a commitment to let marketing drive your business decisions, and you will greatly increase the odds that your business will be successful.

Developing a Marketing Plan

After you understand how customer-focused marketing should permeate your business, you will be ready to develop a plan for introducing your product to your market. The marketing plan can serve as a stand-alone document or be part of an overall business plan. Either way, it should be a functioning, evolving part of your business. We began with customer analysis because before you can develop a marketing vision, you will need to know who your customers are and what they want.

Q: Why does a customer go to a hardware store to buy a drill?

A: Because she needs to make a hole.

The *hole* is what the customer needs, not the drill. If the hole could be purchased at the store, the customer would not bother with the drill. If you are marketing drills, therefore, you should explain to the customer what good holes they make. If someone invents a better hole-maker, drill manufacturers will soon be out of business.

Your marketing plan must include an understanding of prospective customers and their wants, needs, and demands. It should also identify and analyze market segments. The plan should incorporate industry research and trend analysis. It will state your market-positioning approach. In short, a marketing plan looks at all aspects of the market space for your enterprise, from the broadest perspective to the narrowest.

Chapter Summary

Now that you have studied this chapter you can do the following:

1. Explain how marketing differs from selling.
   - Marketing is the business function that identifies your customers and their needs and wants.
   - Through marketing, your business will come to mean something clear and concrete in the customer's mind. Above all, marketing is the way a business communicates its competitive advantage to its market.

2. Understand how market research prepares you for success. Market research is the process of finding out who your potential customers are, where you can reach them, and what they want and need.
   - Getting the information directly from the subject: primary research.
     - Personal interviews
     - Telephone surveys
     - Written surveys
     - Focus groups
     - Observation
     - Tracking
   - Getting information indirectly: secondary research.
     - Online searches
     - Books and articles
     - Trade associations, chambers of commerce, public agencies
     - Review of books and records
     - Researching customers and industries
3. Choose your market segment and research it.
   - Before you can develop a marketing vision for your business, you will need to know who your customers are and what they want.
     1. A market segment is composed of consumers who have a similar response to a certain type of marketing.
     2. Segmentation methods:
        a. *Geographic.* Dividing a population by location.
        b. *Demographic.* Dividing a population based on a variable like age, gender, income, or education.
        c. *Psychographic.* Dividing a population by psychological differences such as political opinion (conservative, liberal) or lifestyle.
        d. *Behavioral.* Dividing the market by observable purchase behaviors such as brand loyalty or responsiveness to price.
4. Position your product or service within your market.
   - The goal of market positioning is to distinguish your product or service from others being offered to the same market segments. You can do that by focusing on your competitive advantage.
   - Use the following format to develop a positioning statement for your business: (Your business name/brand) is the (competitive industry/category) that (provides these benefits, or points of difference) to (audience/target market).

Key Terms

demographics, 198
market research, 195
market segment, 203
marketing, 192

positioning, 207
primary research, 193
product life cycle (PLC), 206
secondary research, 193

Entrepreneurship Portfolio

Critical Thinking Exercises

6-1. Step One: Customer Analysis

Describe the typical consumer your business plans to target.

Segment/Attribute	My Customer
Geographic 1. 2. 3.	
Demographic 1. 2. 3.	
Psychographic 1. 2. 3.	
Behavioral 1. 2. 3.	

What need(s) do you plan to satisfy for this customer?

6-2. Step Two: Market Analysis
- How large is the total market for your product or service? How did you arrive at this figure?
- Which segment of this market do you intend to target? Why? How large is the segment?
- Describe your segmentation method. Why did you choose this method?

6-3. Choose five people from your market segment to research with a survey. Write 10 questions in a scaled format and ask the survey participants to frame their responses on a scale of 1 to 5, or design your own range. Also ask five open-ended questions (questions that cannot be answered with a yes or no, or scaled response).

Key Concept Questions

6-4. Which research technique would best suit your envisioned product or service, and why?

6-5. How do customers decide to buy a product? For example, how would you make the decision to buy organic vegetables?

6-6. Analyze where the market is in its PLC with reference to smart phones. Analyze the positions of iPhone and Android One in their PLC.

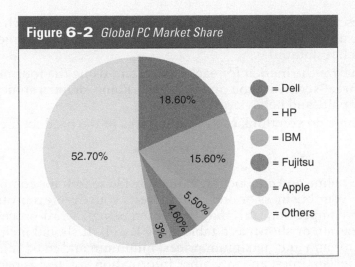

Figure 6-2 *Global PC Market Share*

6-7. Read and interpret the chart in **Figure 6–2**.
 a. Which single provider has the largest market share? What is the percentage?
 b. What share do the two largest suppliers enjoy together?
 c. How much bigger is IBM's share than Apple's?
 d. If there are approximately 100 other smaller makers of personal computers, about how much market share would each have on average?
6-8. Research can give you a great deal of information, but you will have to use your math skills to make it more useful. For example, imagine you are interested in opening a dog-care service and you have gathered the following facts:
 • In 2000, the U.S. Census Bureau estimated that there were 2.67 people per household.
 • According to your city's public records, the population of your community is 80,000.
 • The *U.S. Pet Ownership & Demographics Sourcebook*[3] estimates that the number of dog-owning households in a community equals 0.361 multiplied by the total number of households.
 • The *Sourcebook*[4] also estimates that the number of dogs in a community equals 0.578 multiplied by the total number of households—or 1.6 multiplied by the number of dog-owning households.

Determine:
 a. The number of dog-owning households in your community.
 b. The number of dogs in your community. Round your answers off to the nearest whole number.

Application Exercises

Order food at three different restaurants/vendors; then answer the following:
 6-9. Did you observe any differences in how the employees handled your order? Describe them.

---

[3]2007 American Veterinary Medical Association, Schaumburg, IL.
[4]Ibid.

6-10. Describe what you believe to be the marketing vision of each restaurant based on what you observed. Write a positioning statement for each restaurant.

6-11. Analyze the market for each restaurant, using the four methods of market-segmentation analysis: geographic, demographic, psychographic, and behavioral.

6-12. Where do you think each restaurant is in the product life cycle?

Exploring Online

6-13. Go online and conduct an industry-wide search for competition for your business or one that interests you. Create a profile of the competition (this may be written using a word-processing program or shown as a table using Excel). It should include minimum and maximum prices, minimum and maximum ordering times, and any other information you feel is pertinent.

BizBuilder Business Plan Questions

After studying this chapter, you should be able to answer the following Business Plan Questions. The entire outline for the Business Plan is found in Appendix 2.

4.0 Opportunity Analysis and Research

A. Describe your target customers along as many dimensions as you have defined (demographic, geographic, psychographic, and behavioral, along with trends and decision-making process).

B. Describe the research methods you used to develop this section (surveys, focus groups, general research, and statistical research).

4.1 Industry Analysis

A. What is the industry or set of industries within which your organization operates? Include any applicable NAICS codes.

B. What factors influence the demand for your product or service?

C. What factors influence the supply of your product or service?

D. How large is your total industry (historic, current, projected size)? How do you know?

E. What are the current and anticipated characteristics and trends in the industry? Be specific and use valid and reliable sources.

F. What are the major customer groups for the industry (consumers, governments, businesses)? Describe them in detail.

G. How large is your specific target market (number of customers, size of purchases, frequency of purchases, trends)? Quantify it.

4.2 Environmental Analysis

A. Perform a SWOT (strengths, weaknesses, opportunities, and threats) analysis of your organization. Remember that strengths and weaknesses are "internal to your organization" and opportunities and threats are external.

B. What external/environmental factors are likely to impact your business? How? When?

C. Are there customers for your business in other countries? How do you plan to reach them?

4.3 *Competitive Analysis*

  A. How do you define/describe your competition, both direct and indirect?

  B. Describe your competitive advantage(s) along the dimensions of quality, price, location, selection, service, and speed/turnaround as they apply.

  C. Find three specific competitors and describe them using either a qualitative assessment or a quantitative one. Be certain to include the most critical factors from a customer perspective.

  D. Describe any international competitors you have found who may be able to access your customers. How do you intend to compete with them?

  E. Describe your strategy for outperforming the competition.

  F. What tactics will you use to carry out this strategy?

  G. What, if any, barriers to entry can you create or use to block out competitors? How will you do so?

American Electrical: Understanding the Market Sparks a New Venture

Tom McCormick, American Electrical, Inc.

Entrepreneur Tom McCormick was the vice president of sales for an $800-million global manufacturer of electrical components when he proposed an idea for expansion to his boss. By creating another company to sell accessory items to the 50 percent of the market not being supplied through their existing company because of distribution restrictions, the business could generate considerable additional profits. McCormick led the skunk works project that created a business plan and proposals. The projections were extremely favorable, but due to other pressing issues within the organization, it was ultimately decided that the concept did not fit the company's strategy.

McCormick always wanted to have his own business: "I talked about it constantly to the point where some close friends made fun of me!" In college, he had sold T-shirts, met with business brokers, and networked. When his present employer rejected his expansion proposal, McCormick decided it was time to take the business plan and

run with it. "I knew where my first 100 sales were going to be and I had already researched who and how." He found suppliers, starting with one in Germany, and hired a graphic designer to produce two short product catalogs. In July 1997, he took $60,000 from his retirement fund and founded American Electrical, Inc. It wasn't an easy start, even knowing who to talk to and how to sell; it was still an uphill battle to get people to change. Offering a 20 percent discount to market pricing was one good reason for the potential customer to take a look. In the end, it was persistence that prevailed—never giving up—as well as making it as easy as possible for the customer to make a seamless change in the specifications, while improving margins.

Today, McCormick's company generates approximately $4 million per year in sales and has five full-time employees. It operates out of a 5,000-square-foot office/warehouse in Richmond, Virginia. American Electrical imports electrical and electronic-control components from 12 companies, primarily in Europe, for the industrial-controls marketplace in the United States. Tom McCormick took his business plan and turned it into a successful venture.

Courtesy of American Electrical, Inc.

Case Study Analysis

6-14. In what areas of the market did McCormick do research before starting his business?

6-15. What research methods would you recommend for American Electrical today? Name three specific sources of information.

6-16. How did McCormick identify American Electrical's market? Name the segmentation method and the segment he chose.

6-17. What is the role of marketing in McCormick's business?

Russell Simmons, Hip-Hop Entrepreneur

Russell Simmons, media mogul
(Ray Tamarra/Getty Images)

Russell Simmons turned off his cell phone and took a rare moment to admire the view from his fourteenth-floor office in midtown Manhattan. At 47, Simmons knew he had a lot going for him. As the president of Rush Communications, he sat at the helm of a constellation of successful enterprises, including a record label, a clothing line, a philanthropic arts foundation, and a multimedia production company. Lately, he had been thinking about how to leverage his influence as a hip-hop mogul to inspire young people to get involved in social issues, such as voter registration and education reform. Yet, when he was growing up in Hollis, Queens, in the 1960s and 1970s, Simmons never could have imagined that his life would have turned out like this.

Window of Opportunity

Early on, Simmons decided that he wanted to make his own way in the world. His father had been a teacher, and his mother worked as a recreation coordinator. Both enjoyed stable jobs, but Simmons was not driven by a need for security. He wanted to live a fast-paced life and call his own

shots. In 1977, Simmons, who never liked school very much, enrolled at the City College of New York as a sociology major. That year, something happened that permanently changed the course of his life. He went to hear a rap artist named Eddie Cheeba perform and was amazed to see how the rapper had cast a spell over the audience with his freestyle rhymes. In Simmons's own words:

> *Just like that, I saw how I could turn my life in another, better way. . . . All the street entrepreneurship I'd learned, I decided to put into promoting music.*[5]

At that time, rap and hip-hop were underground musical styles, but Simmons set out to change this. He believed that rap music had the potential to reach a larger audience, and so he teamed up with another aspiring rap producer, Rick Rubin. Rubin had built a recording studio for rap artists in his New York University dorm room. Together, they decided to transform Rick's studio into a viable record label. By 1985, Def Jam Records was officially underway.

Def Jam experienced its first surge of success when it scored a hit with Run DMC's remake of the Aerosmith classic, "Walk This Way." Bridging the worlds of rock and rap music turned out to be a stroke of genius. Simmons and Rubin single-handedly introduced a whole new market of mostly white, suburban, heavy-metal music fans to hip-hop. Suddenly, Run DMC was being featured on MTV, and rap was no longer an underground fad.

Marketing Insight: Authenticity Matters

Simmons learned an important lesson from Run DMC's success. He realized that these artists had gone to the top of the charts because they had remained true to their street style and musical origins. Whereas Run DMC may have popularized wearing gold chains, branded sneakers, and nameplate belts among suburban teenagers, these were the fashions that its core audience of urban youth had already embraced. Simmons understood that

[5]Russell Simmons, *Life and Def: Sex, Drugs, Money + God,* New York: Crown Publishing, 2002.

The selection of your product or service and its branding will be a critical part of your marketing mix.

Focus Your Brand

The key to building a successful brand is to focus tightly on the primary benefit you want customers to associate with your business. Marketing expert Al Ries explains that the most successful businesses *focus* their marketing, so that they come to own a category in the customer's mind.[1] You want to own a benefit the way Volvo owns safety or Federal Express owns guaranteed overnight delivery.

Even entertainers can become a brand. Oprah Winfrey is among the most recognized and wealthiest celebrities in the world today. She is the head of a global media empire and a philanthropist.[2] From her roots in Nashville radio, Winfrey became a media mogul, with such well-recognized names as *The Oprah Winfrey Show*; *O, The Oprah Magazine*; *O at Home*; *OWN—the Oprah Winfrey Network*; *Oprah & Friends Radio*; Harpo Films; and Oprah.com.[3]

Oprah Winfrey, philanthropist and media mogul (MARK J. TERRILL/ AP Images)

Ford's Costly Failure: The Edsel

One of the most notorious examples of a product whose failure was caused by lack of focus is the car Ford introduced in 1958, the Edsel.

Ford tried to include every kind of gadget and design element the company thought consumers might possibly want in a car. They also manufactured multiple models at varying prices that overlapped some Mercury models, thus confusing the public as to which brand was a step up from which. The goal seemed to be to try to appeal to everyone, but Ford soon learned that trying to appeal to everyone resulted in appealing to almost no one. The Edsel had no outstanding benefit that could be clearly marketed. In addition, consumers didn't really like the way the car looked. In the first year, some 63,000 Edsels were produced when sales had been estimated at 200,000 cars.

Even millions of dollars of promotion will not make consumers buy a product they do not want. Ford spent more money on advertising the Edsel than had ever been spent on one line of cars. Three years and $350 million later, Ford pulled the plug on the Edsel.

Ford's Focus on Success: The Mustang

Ford learned from the Edsel mistake, however. When it introduced the Mustang in 1964, it focused very clearly on a target market of people from 20 to 30 years old who wanted a powerful car. Everything about the Mustang, from its design to the colors it came in, was focused on appealing to young drivers. The marketing described the Mustang as "For the young at heart." Only one model was offered. The Mustang was a huge success.

Interestingly, Ford tried to offer some luxury and four-door versions of the Mustang a few years later. Sales dropped, probably because the brand had started to lose focus. The Mustang remains one of Ford's stronger sellers.

---

[1]Al Ries, *Focus: The Future of Your Company Depends on It*, New York: HarperCollins, 2005.

[2]Oprah.com, accessed July 9, 2009, http://www.oprah.com.

[3]*The Oprah Winfrey Show* and *Oprah & Friends* are registered trademarks of Harpo, Inc. *O, The Oprah Magazine* and *O at Home* are registered trademarks of Harpo Print LLC.

Global Impact . . .

One for One

Blake Mycoskie, TOMS Shoes founder
(Kennell Krista/AP Images)

Blake Mycoskie, Founder and Chief Shoe Giver of TOMS Shoes, conceived of his global for-profit enterprise using cause-related marketing while taking a vacation from another entrepreneurial venture. He was in Argentina when he happened to connect with an American woman who was involved in a shoe drive. She told him about the need for shoes on a consistent and reliable basis. He saw the traditional *alparagata*, a ubiquitous casual canvas shoe, as an opportunity, and developed the concept of "one for one"—or donating one pair of shoes for every pair sold. Blake worked with his polo instructor,

Alejo Nitti, to modify the traditional designs of the alparagata for the U.S. market.

During the first year of sales, Blake, his family, and friends personally distributed 10,000 pairs of shoes in Argentina. By September 2010 TOMS had given its one millionth pair. Today, TOMS Shoes are distributed in over 60 countries through some 100 Giving Partners.

TOMS Shoes are made in Argentina, China, and Ethiopia with expansion into India, Kenya, and Haiti planned. The company is working to ensure that by 2015 one-third of its Giving shoes will be produced in the same regions where they will be distributed.

Source: TOMS Shoes, accessed July 30, 2013, http://www.TOMS.com. Blake Mycoskie, *Start Something That Matters,* New York: Spiegel & Grau, 2011.

How to Build Your Brand

You can build your own brand by following these steps:

- *Choose a business name that is easy to remember, describes your business, and helps establish mindshare,* which refers to the degree to which your business will come to mind when a consumer needs something your product or service could provide.

- *Create a logo that symbolizes your business to the customer.* A **logo** (short for *logotype*) is an identifying symbol for a product or business. A logo is printed on the business's stationery, business

logo short for logotype, a company trademark or sign.

Some of the world's best known trademarks
(© Anatolii Babii/Alamy)

cards, and flyers. When a logo has been registered with the U.S. Patent and Trademark Office to protect it from being used by others, it is called a **trademark**—defined as any word, name, symbol, or device used by a manufacturer or merchant to distinguish a product. The Nike "swoosh" is an example of a logo. So are McDonald's "golden arches."

trademark any word, name, symbol, or device used by an organization to distinguish its product.

A company uses a trademark so that people will recognize its product instantly, without having to read the company name or even having to think about it. Rights to a trademark are reserved exclusively for its owner. To infringe on a trademark is illegal.

- *Develop a good reputation.* Make sure your product or service is of the quality you promise. Always treat your customers well. You want people to feel good when they think of your brand or hear it mentioned.

- *Create a brand personality.* Is your brand's personality youthful and casual, like the Gap's? Safe and serious, like Volvo's? Customers will respond to brand personality and develop a relationship with it. Personality will reinforce your name and logo.

- *Communicate your brand personality to your target market.* What type of advertising will best reach your target market? Where should you put flyers? Which newspapers, magazines, or blogs does your target market read?

Always present yourself and your business in such a way that people will have confidence in your product or service. Anything that harms your reputation will damage your sales and profits. Anything that boosts

Step into the Shoes . . .

Context Media: Health

Shradha Agarwal and Rishi Shah were undergraduate students and entrepreneurs at Northwestern University when a late-night discussion led to the idea for "hyper-local health content delivery." In 2006, they cofounded ContextMedia, Inc., in Chicago.

Shradha describes the company's role as follows: "We empower the doctor to educate and inspire patients to live healthier. Everything we do, we measure up to that mission."[4] In fact, the firm brands itself as a "for-benefit" company, meaning that is a for-profit enterprise that exists for social benefit.

ContextMedia owns and manages digital healthcare networks that deliver programming at the point of care. The content is developed by experts in their fields and vetted by medical advisors. ContextMedia: Health places complimentary television systems in the patient waiting rooms of medical professionals that provide programming on diabetes, cardiovascular health, and rheumatology. The patient-education playlist is dynamic and targets videos most suitable to each demographic and practice by means of adaptive learning algorithms (similar to that of Pandora, for music). Physicians can customize the content of the playlists and add their own; they do not need to worry about maintenance. The more than 20,000 participating

Rishi Shah
(ContextMedia, Inc.)

Shrada Agarwal

healthcare providers agree to play the programming during office hours.

Revenue comes from commercials placed between patient-education segments. There are no infomercials or advertorials, and health care providers can have specific commercials removed from their video. Advertisers include firms such as nutrition and fitness companies, pharmaceutical firms, and medical-device manufacturers. Advertising rates are based on a complex formula determined by the time of ad exposure, quality of ad exposure, and strength of call-to-action follow-on from patients.

ContextMedia has found a way to deliver targeted advertising for its clients while offering important health information where it is likely to have impact.

---

4 ContextMedia, "Team – Shradha Agarwal," accessed July 30, 2013, http://www.contextmediainc.com.

your reputation, on the other hand, will have a positive impact on your business. Toward that end:

- Provide a high-quality product or service.
- Maintain the highest ethical standards.
- Define your product or service clearly. *Focus*.
- Treat your employees well.
- Make all your advertisements positive and informative.
- Associate your company with a charity.
- Become actively involved in your community.

Price: What It Says about Your Product

As reported by author Jay Conrad Levinson, a study of consumers in the furniture industry found that price came ninth when they were asked to list factors affecting their decision to make a purchase.[5] Confidence in the product was the number one influence on buying patterns, and quality was number two. Service was third.

Although your customers may not think exactly like those who buy furniture, the lesson here is that simply undercutting your competitors' prices will not necessarily win you the largest market share. For one thing, consumers tend to infer things about the quality or specialness of a product or service based on its price. It is important, therefore, for entrepreneurs to consider not only the economics but also the psychology of pricing. Studying the pricing strategies of your competitors will tell you a lot about the importance of psychological pricing in your market. A detailed discussion of pricing and credit policies appears in Chapter 8.

Place: Location, Location, Location!

Regarding place, the type of business you are running will influence your choice of location and your distribution system for reaching out from that place to your customers. For a retail business, site location is the key to attracting customers. Ideally, you will want your store or business to be where your target market is. This is why you did the work of consumer and market analysis to figure out who your customers were. You should know where they shop. Your goal is to find a location you can afford that is also convenient for your potential customers.

Wal-Mart has done an efficient job of choosing locations that are ideal for attracting potential customers who are underserved by similar retailers. Wal-Mart was the first mass-merchandise store to choose locations in rural and semirural markets. This strategy has been so successful that other stores now seek to be located near a Wal-Mart.

Of course, the Internet has made it possible for an entrepreneur to start a retail business out of her home and reach customers all over the world. This has led to the belief that online stores can forgo the expense of renting a location that caters to foot traffic. As the old saying goes, however, you can lead a horse to water, but you can't make him drink. How do you get your customers to your site and then induce them to buy? If you are planning to start a retail business online, you must figure out how you will attract customers to your Web site—that is, how you will *market* the site.

---

[5]Jay Conrad Levinson, *Guerrilla Marketing Attack*, Boston: Houghton Mifflin, 1989.

For nonretail businesses, the key to location might be cost or convenience rather than proximity to the market. Wholesale businesses that require a great deal of storage space do best in areas where rent or property costs are low, where there is space for large commercial buildings, and where their trucks and vans have easy access to roads and highways.

The Internet is making it easier for people who provide services—such as graphic or Web-site design, writing/editing, or accounting—to start businesses at home. Communication with clients is easy via e-mail, and the overhead costs are certainly minimal. On the other hand, working at home requires discipline and a tolerance for isolation. If you are the sort of person who would not be happy spending your workdays by yourself, it is probably not for you.

Promotion: Advertising · Publicity

Promotion is the use of advertising and publicity to get your marketing message out to your customers. Advertising, as discussed in Chapter 4, is paid promotion that is intended to generate increased sales of your product or service. Examples of advertising include television commercials, billboards, and magazine ads. Publicity is free mention of a company, person, event, product, or service in media outlets, such as newspapers and magazines or on radio or television. Chapter 9 will go into the topics of advertising and promotion in more detail, including the categories listed in **Exhibit 7-1**.

The Fifth P: Philanthropy

There is a long, proud connection in the United States between entrepreneurs and **philanthropy**, a concern for human and social welfare that is expressed by giving money through charities and foundations. A **foundation** is a **not-for-profit organization** that manages donated funds, which it distributes through grants to individuals or to other nonprofit organizations that help people and social causes.

Many philanthropic organizations in the United States were established by entrepreneurs. As a business owner, you have a responsibility to help the communities you serve. The people and causes you choose to support should be those that matter to you. Your philanthropy may also generate positive publicity because you can choose to promote your giving. For this reason, marketing experts sometimes consider philanthropy as the fifth marketing P.

◀ Learning Objective 3
Determine the mix of promotion to use for your business.

philanthropy a concern for human and social welfare that is expressed by giving money through charities and foundations.

foundation a not-for-profit organization that manages donated funds, which it distributes through grants to individuals or to other nonprofit organizations that help people and social causes.

not-for-profit organization an entity formed with the intention of addressing social or other issues, with any profits going back into the organization to support its mission.

Exhibit 7-1 *Advertising and Promotion Options*

Promotion Methods		
Advertising specialties	Coupons	Public speaking
Banner ads	Direct mail	Samples or demonstrations
Billboards	Directories	Signs
Blogs	Flyers	Social media
Broadcast media	Networking	Special events
Brochures	Newsletters	Sponsorships
Business cards	Print media	Telemarketing
Catalogs	Promotional clothing	Web sites

The Bill and Melinda Gates Foundation is one of the world's largest charitable organizations, with $36.4 billion in capital. This money comes from the personal wealth they earn from Microsoft and other contributions. As a private foundation, it is required by the federal government to give away a minimum of 5 percent of the fair market value of its assets every year (this is usually less than the earnings on the fund's investments). The Gates Foundation provides a great deal of money annually, $3.4 billion in 2012, to other charities. These in turn use the money for social and community programs that the Gates Foundation supports, such as those relating to education and health care.

Learning Objective 4
Find a way to add the fifth P, philanthropy, to your business.

You can be philanthropic even if you have very little money to donate. You can give your time in volunteer work for an organization you believe in. If you know how to paint a house, for example, or if you have some carpentry skills, you could contribute your efforts to help build homes for an organization such as Habitat for Humanity, which provides affordable housing for low-income families. If you love animals, volunteer at your local animal shelter.

Cause-Related Marketing

cause-related marketing promotional efforts inspired by a commitment to a social, environmental, or political cause.

Cause-related marketing—marketing inspired by a commitment to a social, environmental, or political cause—is an easy way to work philanthropy into your business. You could donate a fixed percentage of your profits (perhaps 1 or 2 percent) to a particular charity and then publicize that fact in your marketing materials. Or you could donate something from your business. If you own a sporting goods store, you could donate uniforms to the local Little League team.

Encourage your employees to participate in charitable work, too. Volunteerism is a great way to improve morale and make a difference. AT&T pays its employees to devote one day a month to community service.

Gaining Goodwill

Many entrepreneurs try to make a difference in their communities by giving money and time to organizations that help people. Microsoft, for example, made it possible for the National Foundation for Teaching Entrepreneurship (NFTE—now the Network for Teaching Entrepreneurship) to develop an Internet-based entrepreneurial curriculum, BizTech. Microsoft has donated both money and computer-programming expertise to this project.

Why would Microsoft do this?

- First, Bill and Melinda Gates and other Microsoft executives believed in NFTE's mission and wanted to help young people learn about business. The Internet-based program has made it easier to teach entrepreneurship to youth around the world.

goodwill an intangible asset generated when a company does something positive that has value.

- Second, Microsoft gained publicity and **goodwill**, which is composed of intangible assets, such as reputation, name recognition, and customer relations. Goodwill can give a company an advantage over its competitors.

Entrepreneurial Wisdom . . .

Be sure to obtain videotapes of any mention you receive on television. There is no more powerful sales tool than a video that includes a story, however brief, on your business.

Not-for-Profit Organizations

Not-for-profit organizations are those whose purpose is to serve a public cause rather than to accrue profits for investors. The Internal Revenue Service classifies nonprofits under section 501(c)(3) in the tax code. These corporations are tax-exempt. This means they do not have to pay federal or state income taxes, and they are neither privately nor publicly owned. Essentially, a board of directors controls the operations of a 501(c)(3) nonprofit.

Such well-known institutions as the Boys and Girls Clubs of America, the YMCA, the Girl Scouts, the Red Cross, and Big Brothers/Big Sisters are all examples of nonprofits. Their founders were social entrepreneurs and, although they did not earn large sums of money personally and could not have sold their organizations at a profit, they received great satisfaction and made a difference. Wendy Kopp of Teach for America and Michael Bronner of Upromise, described in the following section, are two examples of social entrepreneurs who founded innovative and successful nonprofit organizations.

Teach for America and Upromise

Founded in 1990 by Wendy Kopp, Teach for America recruits recent college graduates to become public school teachers. The organization has trained some 28,000 young teachers and placed them in two-year teaching positions in under-resourced schools, where they impact about 750,000 students annually.

Upromise was founded in 2001 by Michael Bronner, a former marketing executive who became a social entrepreneur. Bronner felt strongly that the cost of sending a child to college had become much too expensive for most families. He believed that there needed to be an effective way of helping families save money for higher education.

Bronner developed the idea that a portion of the money families already spent on popular goods and services, such as groceries and toys, could go into a college savings account for their children. Upromise works with thousands of organizations, such as Sprint, Dell, Century 21, and Expedia.com. Every time a member of Upromise makes a qualified purchase from one of these companies, a percentage of the sale automatically goes into a special college account. By 2013, over $700 million has been saved in this way.

Step into the Shoes . . .

The Body Shop's Campaigns

One of the strongest examples of cause-related marketing by an entrepreneur is the late Anita Roddick's The Body Shop, a chain of cosmetic and skin-care products stores. The company ran media campaigns on causes ranging from saving whales to preserving rain forests, and each campaign had the same result: It attracted customers in droves. In 1990, The Body Shop Foundation was set up to fund projects in areas such as education, environmental conservation, and domestic violence.

Roddick (who died in 2007) once estimated that The Body Shop gained about $4 million per year in publicity from its various campaigns for solving social and environmental problems.

Anita Roddick, founder of The Body Shop
(Chris Buck/Corbis)

What Entrepreneurs Have Built

Many philanthropic organizations in this country were created by entrepreneurs who wanted to do good works with some of the wealth they had earned. Entrepreneurs have financed great museums, libraries, universities, and other important institutions. Some foundations created by famous entrepreneurs (in addition to the Gates Foundation) include the Rockefeller Foundation, the Coleman Foundation, the Charles G. Koch Foundation, the Ford Foundation, and the Goldman Sachs Foundation.

Some of the most aggressive entrepreneurs in American history, such as Andrew Carnegie, have also been the most generous. In 1901, after a long and sometimes ruthless business career, Carnegie sold his steel company to J. P. Morgan for $420 million. Overnight, Carnegie became one of the richest men in the world. On retiring, he spent most of his time giving away his wealth to libraries, colleges, museums, and other worthwhile institutions that still benefit people today. By the time of his death in 1919, Carnegie had given away over $350 million to philanthropic causes.

You Have Something to Contribute

You may not have millions of dollars to give to your community—yet. But there are many ways you can be philanthropic that will help others, get your employees excited, and create goodwill in your community:

- Pledge a percentage of your profits to a nonprofit organization you have researched, believe in, and respect. Send out press releases announcing your pledge.
- Become a mentor to a younger entrepreneur. Help that individual by sharing your contacts and expertise.
- Volunteer for an organization that helps your community. Find out how you can serve on its board of directors or fill another vital role.
- Sell your product to a charity that you support at a discount. The charity can then resell it at full price to raise money.
- After reflection, you will realize that you have a lot to give. Remember, making a contribution does not necessarily mean donating money. You can provide time, advice, and moral support.

These days, customers have access to a lot of information about what companies do with their money. Make sure you are always proud of your business. Choose to support causes that are important to you and that make business sense, too. Philanthropy will strengthen your relationship with your customers because it goes beyond the sale and into what is truly important in people's lives.

Developing a Marketing Plan

Learning Objective 5

Understand the importance of a marketing plan.

The marketing plan can be a stand-alone document or the section of a business plan that identifies the organization's marketing strategy and tactics and presents a comprehensive statement of how it will secure and retain its customers. The plan will include a clear discussion of the product or service, price, promotion, and channels of distribution for the company, and a detailed description of the competition and target market. The marketing plan clarifies how you will sell your products or services and where you fit into the competitive landscape. The primary roles of the marketing plan include:

- demonstrating to potential investors that your company can grow and offer returns,
- identifying the most beneficial target markets for the organization,

- evaluating the competitive and industry environments,
- illustrating the pricing strategy, and
- detailing the promotional plan and budget.

Either a stand-alone marketing plan or one incorporated into a business plan will include the same market-analysis information. The stand-alone plan should also include a *situation analysis*; financial projections and information; an implementation time line or outline; and methods for evaluating success and assuring it, as well as any supplemental supporting materials. **Exhibit 7-2** shows the components of each type of plan. As with business plans as a whole, marketing plans should be organic documents that are reviewed and revised on a regular basis to keep them timely and useful.

◄ **Learning Objective 6**

Identify the critical components of a marketing plan.

Marketing Analysis

The analysis of the market is the heart of the marketing plan. This brings together the various strategic and tactical components of the marketing efforts into a single comprehensive section. It is essential that the template for the sales plan include the five Ps of marketing. The product, price, promotion, place, and philanthropy are detailed here. Wrapped around the core marketing strategy and selling plan are the descriptions of the overall market and the specific target market for the company, the marketing goals and objectives, and any future and contingency plans. Future plans could include a discussion of planned research and development as well as any growth designs, whether through product line expansion, additional channels of distribution, or other means. Contingency plans show how your organization will react to moves by your competitors or other changes in the marketplace. They will diagram strategies and options you will use to address these changes and demonstrate your understanding of the need to be prepared for change in a competitive landscape.

Exhibit **7-2** *Marketing Plan Components*		
Component	**Stand-Alone Plan**	**Business Plan Section**
OPPORTUNITY ANALYSIS	✓	
Industry Analysis	✓	
SWOT Analysis	✓	
Environmental Analysis	✓	
Competitive Analysis	✓	
MARKETING ANALYSIS		
Overall Market and Target		
Goals and Objectives	✓	✓
Marketing Strategy	✓	✓
Product/Service	✓	✓
Pricing Strategy	✓	✓
Promotion Strategy/Plan	✓	✓
Place/Distribution	✓	✓
Philanthropic Plan	✓	✓
Future and Contingency Plans	✓	✓
FINANCIAL PROJECTIONS	✓	
IMPLEMENTATION TIME LINE	✓	
MEASUREMENT	✓	
SUPPLEMENTAL MATERIALS	✓	

Marketing as a Fixed Cost

Let's say you want to launch a new software program. You have researched the consumer environment, pinpointed your market segment, and determined your marketing mix. You are now ready to implement a marketing plan that will get your vision out there. There is one more question: Can you afford to carry out your plan?

Marketing is part of your business's fixed costs. Marketing should not be budgeted as a percentage of sales but rather as money that is needed to drive sales. As you remember, fixed costs are those that do not vary with sales; they include utilities, salaries, advertising, insurance, interest, rent, and depreciation. There are also variable costs, such as commissions, that fluctuate with sales. For a business to survive, though, it must be able to cover its fixed costs. Most fixed costs, such as rent, insurance, and utilities, are hard to cut back if your sales are slow.

Marketing costs are more flexible. They fall into the category of advertising, but may also show up under salaries, if you hire a marketing consultant or full-time marketing staff. They will be a critical component in determining your company's breakeven point and its viability.

Calculate Your Breakeven Point

Learning Objective 7

Use breakeven analysis to evaluate your marketing plan.

The question is this: Can you sell enough units to pay for your marketing plan? The breakeven point, as discussed in Chapter 4, is the moment at which a business has sold enough units to equal its fixed costs. If you estimate that your market is approximately 3 million people, but you have to sell 5 million units just to cover the cost of your marketing, the plan is not viable.

This is why calculating the breakeven point will tell you if your marketing plan can work. It shows whether you will cover your fixed costs with the number of units you plan to sell. If not, the one place you can cut costs is your marketing plan. However, you should do this with care.

Breakeven Analysis for an Artist

Josh is an artist who supports his painting career by creating unique tank tops with airbrushed designs. The shirts are popular with young women in Manhattan's East Village, and Josh sells the shirts each weekend at a flea market on East 4th Street. Let's say he buys eight dozen (96) tank tops for $576. He airbrushes them and sells them all at the weekend flea market for $1,152. Josh considers one tank top his unit of sale. The cost of goods sold (COGS)—without labor—would be calculated as $576/96 = $6, with selling price per unit $1,152/96 = $12.

- How much did each tank top cost Josh? This is his cost of goods sold (COGS).
- How much did he charge for each tank top? This is his selling price per unit.
- Josh's unit of sale is one tank top.
- Josh's cost of goods sold is $6.
- Josh's selling price is $12.

$$\$12 \text{ (Selling Price per Unit)} - \$6 \text{ (Cost of Goods Sold per Unit)}$$
$$= \$6 \text{ (Gross Profit per Unit)}$$

- Josh's gross profit per unit is $6 per tank top.

Next, Josh needs to take a look at his fixed costs. Let's say he spends $150 a month on renting his space at the flea market and $30 monthly on flyers (advertising). The balance of his marketing is free—on Twitter and Facebook and through word of mouth. His monthly fixed costs are $150 + $30 = $180. How many tank tops does he have to sell to cover his fixed costs each month? Use the following formula:

$$\frac{\text{Fixed Cost}}{\text{Gross Profit per Unit}} = \text{Breakeven Units}$$

$$\frac{\text{Fixed Cost: \$180}}{\text{Gross Profit per Unit: \$6}} = 30 \text{ Breakeven Units}$$

Josh needs to sell 30 tank tops to cover his fixed costs. Josh typically sells about 20 tank tops each weekend, so in one month he can expect to sell

$$20 \text{ Units} \times 4 \text{ Weekends} = 80 \text{ Units}$$

Josh can spend $30 per month on flyers. He could even afford to add another expense to his marketing plan, such as getting business cards printed or setting up a Web site, from which customers could order shirts and also find out where he would be selling on particular a weekend, as his location varies.

We do need to recognize that Josh did not include any labor cost, because he paid himself from the profits. If Josh were to add in $3 per shirt of labor costs, his COGS would rise to $9, and his gross profit per unit would drop to $3. His new breakeven point would be 60 units. Additionally, any payment for the time it took to sell the shirts would come out of the profits.

Breakeven Analysis of a Restaurant

Here is a breakeven analysis from a chicken restaurant in Florida called Mary Ann's.

Typically, a customer at Mary Ann's buys a bucket of chicken for $8 and a drink for $2, so the average sale per customer is $10. Therefore, a business unit is defined as a $10 sale. The cost of goods sold for each unit is $3.50 for the chicken and $0.50 for the drink, so the cost of goods sold is $4.00 per unit.

Mary Ann's fixed costs for a month are

Utilities	$1,000
Salaries	$3,000
Ads	$1,000
Interest	0
Insurance	$1,000
Rent	$2,000
Total	$8,000

The restaurant is open on average 30 days per month.

To figure out how many units Mary Ann's has to sell each month to break even, divide the gross profit per unit into the monthly fixed costs.

$$\text{Gross Profit per Unit} = \text{Unit Price (\$10)} - \text{COGS (\$4)} = \$6$$

$$\text{Breakeven Units} = \frac{\text{Monthly Fixed Costs (\$8,000)}}{\text{Gross Profit per Unit (\$6)}} = 1{,}333 \text{ Units}$$

Because the store is open 30 days per month, to break even Mary Ann's has to make 45 average sales per day:

$$\frac{1,333 \text{ Units}}{30 \text{ Days}} = 44.43 \text{ (45 Units per Day)}$$

Breakeven is the point at which fixed costs are recovered by sales, but variable costs are not included and no profit has yet been made. Once you have determined your breakeven point, the next question in the analysis is, "Can my business reach breakeven in its relevant market?" In the previous example, can Mary Ann's reasonably expect to break even and sell 45 buckets of chicken a day? The answer to this question for your business venture will be in the market research you have conducted to get to this, the last step in creating a marketing plan. You should know the answer. If not, you must conduct further research until you can confidently gauge the viability.

Breakeven analysis is a good tool for examining all your costs and should be performed frequently. It is especially important after you have completed your marketing plan and before you open your business, to see if your plan is realistic.

Chapter Summary

Now that you have studied this chapter, you can do the following:

1. Combine the four Ps—product, price, place, and promotion—into a marketing mix.
2. Determine the attributes of your product or service.
3. Choose where and how to advertise your business.
   - Promotion is the use of advertising and publicity to get your marketing message to your potential customers.
   - Publicity is free mention of your business—in newspapers or magazines or on radio or television.
   - An advertisement is a paid announcement that a product or service is for sale. Examples of advertising include television commercials, billboards, and magazine ads.
4. Decide how your business will help your community philanthropically.
   - Philanthropy is the giving of money, time, or advice to charities in an effort to help solve a social or environmental problem, such as homelessness, pollution, or cruelty to animals.
   - You can be philanthropic even if you have very little or no money to offer. You can donate your time by volunteering for an organization that has aims you want to support.
5. Understand the importance of a marketing plan:
   - demonstrating to potential investors that your company can grow and offer returns,
   - identifying the most profitable target markets for the organization,
   - evaluating the competitive and industry environments,
   - illustrating the pricing strategy,
   - detailing the promotional plan and budget.

6. Identify the critical components of a marketing plan:
   - opportunity analysis,
   - marketing analysis,
   - financial projections,
   - implementation time line,
   - measurement, and
   - supplemental information.
7. Use breakeven analysis to evaluate your marketing plan.
   - Breakeven is the point at which a business sells enough units to cover its fixed costs.
   - Breakeven analysis tells you if your marketing plan is viable. It shows whether you can cover your fixed costs with the number of units you plan to sell.

Key Terms

cause-related marketing, 230
foundation, 229
goodwill, 230
logo, 226

not-for-profit organization, 229
philanthropy, 229
trademark, 227

Entrepreneurship Portfolio

Critical Thinking Exercises

7-1. What are the factors to keep in mind while designing a logo? What do you have in mind for the logo of your envisioned business, and why?

7-2. Explain how pricing tells a story about your product.

7-3. Where do you plan to locate your business? Explain.

7-4. How do you plan to include philanthropy in your marketing mix?

7-5. Use the following chart to describe your marketing mix.

	Your Business
Product	
Place	
Price	
Promotion	
Philanthropy	

7-6. What is the 4th "P" (Place) more relevant to, service or product? Illustrate your argument with examples.

Key Concept Questions

7-7. Brainstorm five creative ways for a small business with a low budget to advertise and promote its products or services using the latest developments in communications and Internet technology.

7-8. How are the four Ps of a marketing mix interrelated? How does tweaking one affect the other? Illustrate with an example.

7-9. Can the fifth P, philanthropy, be incorporated in every marketing mix? Illustrate with examples from two different industries.

Application Exercise

7-10. Visit a library (public or university) and locate its reference section. What resources can help you to open a business like Honest Tea? Identify at least six.

7-11. Use the following chart to describe the basics of your marketing plan section.

Component	What Will You Include?
OPPORTUNITY ANALYSIS	
Industry Analysis	
SWOT Analysis	
Environmental Analysis	
Competitive Analysis	

Component	What Will You Include?
MARKETING ANALYSIS	
Overall Market and Target	
Goals and Objectives	
Marketing Strategy	
Product/Service	
Pricing Strategy	
Promotion Strategy/Plan	
Place/Distribution	
Philanthropic Plan	
Future and Contingency Plans	
FINANCIAL PROJECTIONS	
IMPLEMENTATION TIME LINE	
MEASUREMENT	
SUPPLEMENTAL MATERIALS	

7-12. Visit three independently owned businesses (in the same industry) in person. Identify the target market for each (demographic, geographic, psychographic, and behavioral). Note the various advertising and promotional methods in use for each location. Search online for company Web sites. Ask the store owner or manager where the business advertises and whether it creates press releases. Report back on the results.

Exploring Online

7-13. Find out and list how much it would cost to run a banner ad on three Web sites. What are the pricing options? Are they listed on the companies' Web sites? Where did you find the information?

BizBuilder Business Plan Questions

After studying this chapter, you should be able to answer the following Business Plan Questions. The entire outline for the Business Plan is found in Appendix 2.

5.0 Marketing Strategy and Plan

    A. Explain how your marketing plan targets your market segment.

    B. What percentage of the market do you feel you need to capture for your business to be profitable? Explain this.

    C. Write a positioning statement for your business.

    D. How do you plan to grow the organization (self-generated, franchising, acquisition)?

5.1 Products/Services

    A. What products/services do you intend to market?

    B. Explain how your product will satisfy customer needs and wants.

C. Where is your product/service in the product life cycle and where in its industry?

F. How will your organization help others? List all the organizations to which you plan to contribute. (Your contribution may be time, money, your product, or something else.)

G. Do you intend to publicize your philanthropy? Why or why not? If you do, explain how you will work your philanthropy into your marketing.

5.2 Pricing

A. Describe your pricing strategy (value, prestige, cost-plus, penetration, skimming, meet-or-beat, follow-the-leader, personalized, variable, or price lining) and structure and the gross margins you expect to generate.

B. What will your discount structure, if any, be? How will it impact your average price (your pocket price)?

C. Will you extend credit to customers? On what terms? If doing retail sales, what forms of payment will you accept?

5.3 Promotion

C. What is your business slogan?

D. Do you have a logo for your business? How do you intend to protect it?

E. Where do you intend to advertise? (be specific, including identifying reach and frequency)

F. How do you plan to get publicity for your organization?

5.4 Place

A. Where do you intend to sell your product (physical and/or virtual locations)? Describe the advantages and disadvantages of your location(s). If you have a specific site, provide detailed information about it.

Case Study | 23andMe

Anne Wojcicki and Linda Avey, founders of 23andMe
(Donald Bowers/Getty Images)

Recent years have seen an explosion in genetic research and the use of DNA technology. 23andMe, founded in 2006 by Anne Wojcicki and Linda Avey, helps customers understand their unique genomes, which are made up of 23 pairs of chromosomes. 23andMe's Personal Genome Service, winner of *Time* magazine's 2008 Invention of the Year award, gives people data about their ancestry and possible predispositions for health conditions. Individuals are also given the chance to help advance health research.

The basic service may be purchased on the company's Web site for a one-time fee of $99. A collection kit is shipped to the customer, who sends a saliva sample to 23andMe. Several weeks later, the customer can view the results online. By participating in this service and in other follow-up surveys, 23andMe's customers can provide data for genetic-research initiatives through 23andWe, the research arm of 23andMe.

In the fall of 2008, 23andMe dropped its basic price from $999 to $399 to help increase customer demand. At that time, Avey indicated that lower costs for mechanisms used to scan genomes helped to make the price reduction feasible. 23andMe's primary competition, Navigenics,

and deCODE genetics, charged about $2,500 and $1,000, respectively, for similar services. Avey explained:

> *It's really more about getting the price down to a point that is more affordable. If that was what was holding [customers] back, this will be a better price for them to get involved.*[1]

When 23andMe reduced its price, the chief executive of Navigenics, Mari Baker, commented that cheaper does not always mean better. Baker admitted that her company's costs were much greater than 23andMe's new price. Avey pointed out that the lower price not only makes genetic information accessible to more individuals, it simultaneously helps to find more answers to genetic-risk problems.

In December 2012, 23andMe again reduced its price. Anne Wojcicki explained:

> *23andMe has raised more than $50 million in new financing with the goal of reaching one million customers. To help us reach our goal, we are happy to announce today, that we are dropping our price to $99. One million customers can be the tipping point that moves medicine into the molecular era. Hundreds of you have written to us about how genetic information changed your lives and, in some cases, saved your lives. We believe genetics should be an integral part of health care and we will work hard in the coming year to help genetics become part of everyone's health and wellness.*[2]

23andMe is located in the Silicon Valley, a region in the San Francisco Bay area known for its technological firms. 23andMe now stands alongside many other high-tech businesses, such as Microsoft, Apple, and Intel, as part of Silicon Valley's history of entrepreneurial innovation. 23andMe is funded in part through prominent

[1]Andrew Pollack, *DNA Profile Provider Is Cutting Its Prices*, accessed August 2, 2013, http://www.nytimes.com/2008/09/09/business/09gene.html.

[2]Anne Wojcicki, "One Million Strong: A Note from 23andMe's Anne Wojcicki," 23andMe Blog, accessed August 1, 2013, http://blog.23andme.com/news/one-million-strong-a-note-from-23andmes-anne-wojcicki/.

health-science and technology companies, angel investors, and venture capital firms, listing Google, Inc., Genentech, Inc., and New Enterprise Associates on its promotional information. In short, 23andMe brings medical technology to individual consumers at a price designed to encourage purchase and thereby increase genetic data.

Case Study Analysis

7-14. What is the product/service offered by 23andMe?

7-15. What could 23andMe's new pricing structure suggest about its brand? In other words, what risk(s) did 23andMe take when it cut its basic price in half? To $99?

7-16. What role does company location likely play in 23andMe's marketing strategy?

7-17. List factors to include in a breakeven analysis for 23andMe. Suggest the company's strategy for achieving a breakeven point.

7-18. How has 23andMe woven philanthropic attitudes into its business? Name some specific ways in which the company could incorporate philanthropy further into its marketing mix.

Case Sources

23andMe, Inc. Web site, accessed August 1, 2013, https://www.23andme.com.

New York Times Web site article, DNA Profile Provider Is Cutting Its Prices, http://www.nytimes.com/2008/09/09/business/09gene.html.

Malia Mills:
Love Thy Differences

When 25-year-old Malia Mills decided to launch her own swimwear company, she set out to do much more than just sell high-end bathing suits. Mills wanted to inspire a beauty revolution that would fundamentally change the way women felt about themselves. A graduate of Cornell University with a degree in apparel design, with studies at La Chambre Syndicale de la Couture Parisienne in Paris, Mills at first worked in the fashion world as a designer for established apparel companies. But Mills (a native of Hawaii) saved the money for the start-up investment in her own business by working as a waitress in New York City. She started Malia Mills Swimwear in 1991 and began working full time at the company in 1994.

The slogan of Mills's business is "Love Thy Differences," and Mills is serious about

Arnaldo Magnani/Getty Image

encouraging all women, regardless of age, weight, or body type, to feel good about themselves and to celebrate their uniqueness. In Mills's world, if a woman does not like the way she looks in a swimsuit, it is the suit that has to change, not the woman. As she explains, "We are passionate about inspiring women to look in the mirror and see what is right instead of what is wrong."

The Polaroid Project

If you walk past the Malia Mills Swimwear flagship store in New York's SoHo, the first things you will notice are the photographs in the window. Instead of showcasing fashion models, the window display features a collage of Polaroid pictures of actual customers wearing her signature swimwear. These Polaroids draw customers into the store, as it is so unusual to see "real" women wearing a company's swimsuits. This Polaroid project began as an offbeat idea thought up by a summer intern on a particularly slow sales day. Mills liked the idea of using photographs of her customers because it resonated with the core mission of her business.

Place Matters: Setting the Right Tone

To create a comfortable environment for her customers, Mills has constructed her stores to look and feel like cozy lounges. She herself always hated trying on bathing suits in department stores under the glare of unflattering fluorescent lights. In her boutiques, the lighting is soft, and dressing rooms are located in the back so that the customers will not feel exposed to other shoppers. She provides free bottled water so that they can feel relaxed and at home. Sales associates are always on hand to assist with finding the appropriate suits. Mills does not believe in a one-size-fits-all design philosophy. People's bodies do not come in packages of small, medium, and large. Accordingly, her tops are sized like lingerie, and bottoms come in sizes 2 to 16. All pieces are sold as separates, which allows customers to mix and match across different style and fabric options, as well as size. Malia Mills introduced the concept of selling separate tops and bottoms before this was common retail practice.

The Price/Production Connection

Malia Mills's suits are priced at the high end of the swimwear market. A bikini top or bottom will cost somewhere between $145 and $175, and one-piece suits run an average of $325. This pricing scheme reflects some of the choices Mills has made as an entrepreneur about how her suits are produced. For example, she chooses to manufacture in New York City instead of outsourcing production to Asia or elsewhere, where labor costs are lower. According to Mills, "It costs us much more per unit to sew our suits locally but supporting our community is worth it. The women (mostly) who sew our suits do so with extra care—we visit them often and they know how important quality is to us."

Mills chooses to import the fabrics she uses from Europe, and she typically buys them in small quantities, which is more costly, so that her designs stay fresh. Mills also pays a premium to the fabric mills that custom-dye her materials in unique colors, and this also contributes to the bottom line of her manufacturing costs. Her suits are so well made that she sometimes worries about undercutting herself in the marketplace. If the average woman owns two or three bathing suits, and a Malia Mills suit can last several years, it could take a long time for a customer to seek a replacement.

Smart Selling Requires Trial and Error

Early on, Mills sold her suits wholesale to department stores, but she found that this strategy did not fit well with her core mission. Mills's suits got lost on the racks next to other brand-name apparel, and the salespeople did not understand how to answer customers' questions about the unique features of her product, such as how they are sized differently from other swimsuits. Eventually Mills decided to sell directly to the consumer. Maintaining control over the sales process has allowed Mills to stay true to her mission of providing women with an enjoyable and empowering experience, purchasing swimwear that fits in a relaxed environment.

Promotions: Getting the Word Out

Over the years, Mills has been successful in generating PR. Her company has been profiled in major publications such as *The New York Times*, *Sports Illustrated*, and *Harper's Bazaar*. It has helped to have celebrities such as Madonna wearing her suits, especially when they are photographed in public. Recently, Mills began purchasing advertising for the first time in local print media. She is doing this as an experiment to see if it has a noticeable impact on generating new customers. In the meantime, the growth of Malia Mills Swimwear continues to be propelled by word of mouth and customer loyalty. Each day, the business connects with passersby who are lured into the store by the Polaroid photographs of ordinary women wearing her bathing suits. Once these women walk in off the street, there is a pretty good chance that they will walk out as customers.

Case Study Analysis

7-19. Describe the unique features of Malia Mills's product.

7-20. Malia Mills Swimwear is not inexpensive. Why do you think customers are willing to pay a premium for her suits?

7-21. The case mentions that Malia Mills Swimwear is currently experimenting with paid advertising. If you were in charge of marketing for the company, how would you assess whether it was cost-effective enough to continue purchasing advertising?

7-22. What kind of environment is Malia Mills trying to create in her stores? Why is this important?

7-23. Besides her own boutiques, specialty stores, and the Internet, what might be some additional sales venues for Malia Mills Swimwear to consider exploring?

Installment Credit

Some small businesses directly extend **installment credit**—loans to be paid back in installments over time—to their customers. Typically, the customers are purchasing large-ticket items—such as used cars, bedding, or furniture—that they want or need to finance over time. Some firms build business relationships with finance companies and/or banks for this purpose.

installment credit loans that are to be paid back in installments over time.

If a company has sufficient capital to provide its own installment payment programs and can assume the risk, it may earn significant revenues on the interest from financing. Customers who receive such credit must pay principal and interest over the life of the loan. The business retains an ownership interest in the purchased item as collateral on the loan (e.g., the car title), so it can reclaim (repossess) the merchandise if the customer fails to adhere to the loan terms. Many smaller used car dealers who promise credit to all customers (no matter how questionable their credit) use this type of financing as a primary source of revenue, sometimes selling the same vehicles to a succession of owners and repeatedly repossessing them. You should determine how this type of credit arrangement fits within your ethics, and the laws in your area, before pursuing such a strategy. The decision to extend installment credit is a business decision, the risks and rewards of which need to be weighed.

Trade Credit

Providing credit directly to business customers is customary practice for manufacturers and wholesalers. Orders may be released with a range of different credit terms. For example, if the product is custom-made or the credit risk is high, it may be sold on cash-in-advance (CIA) terms, requiring prepayment from the customer before either production or shipping. If the customer is new or has credit issues, the product may be shipped with a cash-on-delivery (COD) arrangement, requiring the delivering party to collect payment in full, perhaps in the form of a cashier's check or the like, prior to completing the delivery. Other credit is extended through the agreement on the day payment will be due—such as 30, 60, or 90 days. If you want to add an incentive for early payment, a discount can be included; for example, the customary *2/10, net 30* is shorthand for a 2 percent discount offered for payment within 10 days; full payment is expected within 30 days.

Credit's Impact on Pricing

Any type of credit offered to a customer reduces the amount of funds received and/or delays their receipt. In order to price objectively, the costs of extending credit must be fully incorporated into the pricing decision. For example, the credit-card processing fees can reduce the amount received from an individual sale by about 10 percent. Customers, of course, do not view the cost of the credit card usage for a business as a discount and usually are unwilling to pay extra for it. (However, some universities do charge a fee for tuition payments made by credit card.) So, the credit card costs are reductions in earnings for the firm. The same is true for any prompt or early payment discounts offered to trade customers. Installment credit may either increase or decrease, depending on its structure and the quality of the credit. Also, payment terms mean waiting longer for your funds, so that you may need to incur borrowing costs of your own or face negative cash-flow impact.

◀ **Learning Objective 4**
Explore the role of trade credit in pricing.

Managing the Credit Process

The decision to extend credit is part of the pricing decision and financial analysis of the business. If the decision is for the firm to retain the credit-granting process rather than transferring the risk to a third party for a fee, a procedure should be established well ahead of granting credit. This process should make an objective analysis of whether the buyer can and will repay the debt and when he will do so. The analysis also should determine how, if at all, to compel repayment in the case of delinquency or default.

A credit application is an excellent starting point for consumer- and trade-credit analysis. A well-designed credit application will request the following information for trade credit:

- Contact name, telephone numbers, fax, and e-mail
- Full business name and aliases (DBA)
- Complete street address (a P.O. Box is not sufficient)
- Date and state of incorporation, if applicable
- Date founded
- Employer identification number (EIN) or Social Security number
- DUNS number (from Dun and Bradstreet), if applicable
- Full legal name and complete contact information for any owners of 10 percent or more, with ownership percentage noted
- Names and contact information of three or four supplier references
- Name and contact information of commercial bank reference
- Financial resources, revenues, debt position, and other pertinent information
- Amount of credit and payment terms requested
- Estimated annual purchasing volume
- Financial statements or tax returns as appropriate to the amount of credit requested
- Signature line, giving legal permission to acquire credit information

For consumer credit, similar information is needed, including full information on any cosigners and a listing of other creditors (such as credit card companies, auto loans, home mortgages).

Global Impact . . .

Raw Material Prices Challenge Manufacturers

When the price of crude oil rises, much of the world feels the pain. Manufacturers using crude oil in their production are affected. When copper prices rise, the effects are also felt worldwide. Volatile raw-material costs in one area can have huge ripple effects on prices around the world. Whereas labor costs frequently are perceived to be a primary driver of manufacturing costs, the impact of changing raw materials prices may also be quite significant, particularly when they are volatile. Manufacturers must control raw material costs to create sustainable profits.

Manufacturers have to buy smarter, explore alternate materials, and evaluate their ability to increase prices to their customers. Manufacturers source potential materials for purchase globally to attain the most favorable pricing, making any changes an international issue. Thus, a price increase in crude oil in Saudi Arabia has ripple effects on Main Street U.S.A.

Source: Jill Jusko, "Rethinking Raw Materials," *IndustryWeek.com*, August 1, 2006, accessed March 29, 2009, http://www.industryweek.com.

Depending on the nature of your business and the amount of credit requested, you may require business financial statements, audits, and/or tax filings. Similar documents can be requested from consumers. However, remember that the credit process is part of your sales and marketing and customer-service efforts. There is a fine line between requesting the information you need to make a credit decision and overburdening and annoying the customers to the point of losing them. Ask only for what you need and will use in making the credit determination, rather than everything that might be "good to know."

Sources of Credit Information

The best indicator of future performance is past performance. This truism is particularly applicable with respect to credit. The first and best source of credit information is your customer's credit history and an explanation of any irregularities in it. Credit applicants with poor credit history should be given an opportunity to provide a letter of explanation, and you can decide whether they have taken responsibility for the problems or are denying responsibility and blaming others. Bankers and other lenders know that customers who have taken responsibility for credit issues make far better customers than those who refuse to do so. This is sometimes called taking a stand of responsibility versus the stand of a victim. If you decide to take a risk on people and/or companies with less than perfect credit, it is vital to understand your risk.

Consumer credit histories are available through consumer credit agencies, particularly Experian, TransUnion, and Equifax. Business credit information may be available through Dun and Bradstreet (D&B; http://www.dnb.com), customer financial statements, and other suppliers and industry professionals. Bankers may also be a resource. The fees associated with securing credit information should be considered in your costs of doing business. Remember to be objective about the information you obtain and to filter out biased or subjective data from objective analysis. At the same time, proceed with caution when red flags begin to appear.

Aging of Receivables

If you decide to extend credit to customers, you will need to track and manage repayment of the *accounts receivable* you generate. The most critical element of this process is to get into the habit of timely billing and consistent, effective collections. As your firm grows, these procedures will need to be formalized and carried through to maximize cash flow. As will be discussed in Chapter 15, setting up a receivables aging schedule and carefully monitoring your carrying costs are important in calculating prices and to safeguard your company's overall financial health.

Credit Regulation

State and federal laws govern the process of securing credit information and disclosing credit terms and conditions. These protections have been created for the benefit of consumers to shield them from unscrupulous lenders. Before you create your credit policies, application forms, and processes, obtain the appropriate legal information. It will be beneficial to have your credit documents and procedures reviewed by legal and accounting professionals to ensure that you are starting off correctly.

Discounts, Incentives, and Other Price Adjustments

Learning Objective 5
Consider discounts, incentives, and other price adjustments.

The final price customers pay for a product or service can be reduced by discounts from list prices. Some price adjustments, in addition to cash discounts and accounts receivable carrying costs, are

- order size (quantity) discounts,
- annual/quarterly/monthly volume discounts or bonuses,
- dealer and distributor discounts,
- promotion discounts and bonuses,
- merchandising discounts,
- cooperative advertising and marketing allowances,
- product or product-line rebates,
- exception discounts, and
- freight/shipping allowances.[4]

pocket price the portion of the total price that remains after all pricing factors are deducted.

These price adjustments could come through any number of areas of the company and can vary widely from customer to customer, not necessarily according to a particular strategy, such as volume. The same product could have a broad range of prices—you might be surprised to see the differences. Michael Marn and Robert Rosiello have created methods for understanding pricing structures within a firm.[5] The **pocket price** is what remains after all pricing factors, such as discounts and allowances, are deducted from lists or invoices to reach the final price. The "pocket price waterfall" is a visual representation of this concept. **Figure 8-3** illustrates the concept of a pocket price waterfall for a manufacturer.

In addition to looking at the pocket price waterfall, managers may explore the range of prices at which the same product or service is sold to different customers. The pocket-price band shows the range of prices for a given unit volume of a particular item at a given point in time.[6] **Figure 8-4** illustrates a pocket-price band.

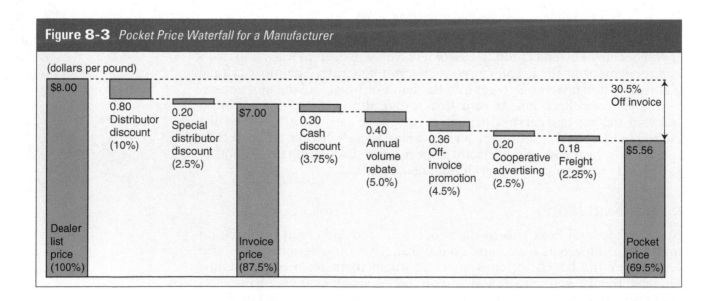

Figure 8-3 *Pocket Price Waterfall for a Manufacturer*

(dollars per pound)

$8.00 — Dealer list price (100%)
0.80 Distributor discount (10%)
0.20 Special distributor discount (2.5%)
$7.00 — Invoice price (87.5%)
0.30 Cash discount (3.75%)
0.40 Annual volume rebate (5.0%)
0.36 Off-invoice promotion (4.5%)
0.20 Cooperative advertising (2.5%)
0.18 Freight (2.25%)
30.5% Off invoice
$5.56 — Pocket price (69.5%)

---

[4]Michael V. Marn and Robert L. Rosiello, "Managing Price, Gaining Profit," *Harvard Business Review*, September–October 1992.
[5]Ibid.
[6]Ibid.

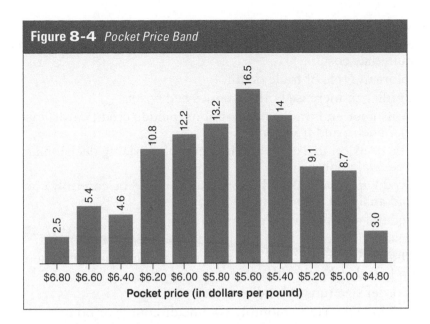

Figure 8-4 *Pocket Price Band*

Pocket price (in dollars per pound)

Values by pocket price:
- $6.80 — 2.5
- $6.60 — 5.4
- $6.40 — 4.6
- $6.20 — 10.8
- $6.00 — 12.2
- $5.80 — 13.2
- $5.60 — 16.5
- $5.40 — 14
- $5.20 — 9.1
- $5.00 — 8.7
- $4.80 — 3.0

If you are establishing pricing for new products or markets, you can keep tighter control by looking at the price more holistically, with a view toward the list, intermediate, and pocket prices. Regardless of the age or maturity of the firm, understanding where prices can be eroded and establishing and maintaining policies and procedures to ensure that prices are well managed are best practices. Remember to make changes or establish adjustments to pricing based on the factors that matter most to your customers. Get the most from your investment.

Chapter Summary

Now that you have studied this chapter you can do the following:

1. Understand the relationship between price and overall strategy.
   - Pricing positions the product or service.
   - Pricing strategy should match company strategy.
   - Following a logical process can lead to better pricing.
2. Multiple pricing strategies are available to businesses.
   - Value pricing—offering more for less.
   - Prestige pricing—setting a high price to convey high quality or uniqueness.
   - Cost-plus pricing—applying a factor to calculated costs.
   - Penetration pricing—charging lower initial prices to capture market share.
   - Skimming pricing—charging higher initial prices.
   - Meet-or-beat-the-competition pricing—just what it says.
   - Follow-the-leader pricing—using one competitor as a model for your pricing.
   - Personalized (dynamic) pricing—charging different prices according to what the market will bear.
   - Price lining—setting a range of pricing levels.
3. Determine markups.
   - Manufacturers and retailers often double their cost—called keystoning.

- Wholesalers often add 20 percent.
- Service firms may use cost plus a markup based on hourly and materials costs.

4. Explore the role of trade credit.
   - Credit can increase both revenues and costs.
   - Consumer and trade-credit options include credit cards, installment debt, and trade credit.
   - The decision to extend credit is part of a pricing decision and financial analysis.
   - Credit applications and information should be carefully compiled and analyzed from a variety of sources.
   - Federal and state regulations apply.

5. Consider discounts, incentives, and other price adjustments.
   - These adjustments will reduce the final price that customers pay and need to be considered:
     - order size (quantity) discounts,
     - annual/quarterly/monthly volume discounts or bonuses,
     - dealer and distributor discounts,
     - promotion discounts and bonuses,
     - merchandising discounts,
     - cooperative advertising and marketing allowances,
     - product or product-line rebates,
     - exception discounts, and
     - freight/shipping allowances.[7]
   - The pocket price waterfall and pocket-price band assist in analysis.

Key Terms

cost-plus pricing, 249
elastic demand, 255
follow-the-leader pricing, 250
inelastic demand, 255
installment credit, 257
market clearing price, 255
markup pricing, 249
merchant card services, 256
meet-or-beat-the-competition
  pricing, 249

penetration pricing, 249
personalized pricing, 250
pocket price, 260
prestige pricing, 249
price, 247
price lining, 250
skimming prices strategy, 249
value pricing, 249
variable pricing strategy, 250

---

[7]Michael V. Marn and Robert L. Rosiello, "Managing Price, Gaining Profit," *Harvard Business Review*, September–October 1992.

Entrepreneurship Portfolio

Critical Thinking Exercises

8-1. Meet with a partner and discuss the pros and cons of the following pricing strategies: value pricing, keystoning, cost-plus, penetration strategy, skimming strategy, and meet or beat the competition—for each of your respective businesses. Present your recommendations for each other to the class.

8-2. Identify two retailers—a world-renowned one and one well known in your country. Find out their pricing strategy and explain why you think they chose the strategy and what benefits they might have derived from it.

8-3. How does pricing affect the strategy and value of a brand? Discuss with an example of your choice.

Key Concept Questions

8-4. Define cost-plus pricing. Why is it used so frequently? What are the drawbacks associated with using it?

8-5. What pricing principles should be considered by an organization before deciding a pricing strategy? Illustrate with examples.

8-6. Which pricing strategy would be best for a new firm in an industry with large, dominant firms? Give three reasons to justify your choice and illustrate with a real-world example.

8-7. What is the basis on which the price of the same product varies from firm to firm? For example, how do you expect a particular product to be priced by a manufacturer and a retailer?

8-8. Analyze the pros and cons of using keystoning alone as a pricing strategy. Illustrate your argument with an example.

Application Exercises

8-9. Using the markups described in the chapter, calculate the price at each link in the distribution chain for a blouse that cost the manufacturer $4.75 to make:

Manufacturer's cost: $_____
Manufacturer's price: $_____
Wholesaler's cost: $_____
Wholesaler's price: $_____
Retailer's cost: $_____
Retailer's price: $_____

8-10. Create a pocket price waterfall for an electric yo-yo by Creative Toy Manufacturing (CTM). The list price is $5.50 each with a minimum order of 12 dozen. The standard dealer discount (off invoice) is 50%, and the order discount is 3% for orders of more than 20 dozen. There is a special promotion of $0.10 each off of invoice. The payment terms are 2/10 net 30. Because CTM is encouraging customers to advertise the electric yo-yo, there is a 5% cooperative advertising allowance for dealers. Customers are being offered a rebate of $0.50. What is the pocket price for CTM?

Exploring Online

8-11. Perform an Internet search on either a product or service comparable to what you plan to market or one that you personally own. Attempt to find at least three sites that sell it.

a. List the applicable price point, including all discounts, allowances, and promotions, plus any shipping and handling required.

b. Are the prices different on each? Why do you suppose this is?

c. Explain any challenges you had in performing the steps in this exercise. What do they tell you about the product or service? The companies selling them?

8-12. Visit the PayPal Web site (http://www.paypal.com) and one of the following: Intuit Payment Services (http://www.intuit-gopayment .com), Square (http://www.squareup.com), E-Commerce Exchange (http://www.ecenow.com, TransFirst (http://www.transfirst.com), or Charge.com. Make a chart comparing the charges and requirements for merchants with each.

BizBuilder Business Plan Questions

After studying this chapter, you should be able to answer the following Business Plan Questions. The entire outline for the Business Plan is found in Appendix 2.

5.2 *Pricing*

A. Describe your pricing strategy (value, prestige, cost-plus, penetration, skimming, meet-or-beat, follow-the-leader, personalized, variable, or price lining), structure, and the gross margins you expect to generate.

B. What will your discount structure, if any, be? How will it impact your average price (your pocket price)?

C. Will you extend credit to customers? On what terms? If doing retail sales, what forms of payment will you accept?

If you like to cook, have ever purchased a gourmet cooking item, or ever shopped in a gourmet kitchen store, chances are you have a Harold Import Company (HIC) product in your kitchen. Since its start in 1957, HIC has sold over 20 million pieces of porcelain dinnerware worldwide.

When Harold Laub launched HIC, it became the first company to import the 10.25-inch white coupe dinner plate into the United States from Japan. But that was only the beginning. Soon, HIC was importing a wide range of white porcelain items that included bakeware as well as dinnerware. When Harold's wife, Mildred, joined the company in 1962, she helped expand the business further, with imports of kitchen gadgets.

Today, HIC distributes more than 3,500 houseware, gourmet food, and kitchen products from 25 different countries, including the original 10.25-inch white coupe dinner plate. HIC is still run by members of the Laub family, who continue to diversify the product lines while maintaining high quality.

As a standard procedure, HIC asks each new business customer to fill out a form containing basic company information. Items on this form include mailing, shipping, and e-mail addresses; contact names and telephone numbers; the type of business and its resale tax identification number; and the customer's desired method of payment.

If the customer wishes to establish an account with terms of net 30 days, a credit application must also be completed. This form requires the contact information for three vendors from whom the customer has previously purchased goods.

Harold Import Company calls each of the provided trade references to find out the customer's payment history. If responses are positive, an HIC account with credit is set up. The credit limit is determined by a combination of factors. HIC staff look at the amount of credit the customer is requesting and the amount of credit its references currently provide to determine their level of comfort. If feedback indicates late payments, HIC asks the customer to provide banking information. In these questionable cases, the customer may pay with a credit card or send a prepayment, which is almost always a company check. By using this process, HIC is able to provide multiple

Harold Import Company Inc.

payment options to potential buyers, while keeping risk at a minimum.

For established customers, the credit limit is typically 40 percent of their yearly sales volume. The reason for this level is that if HIC's customer fails to pay its obligation, on average, HIC's loss is limited to its expected profit. If an established customer needs credit beyond the 40 percent, the HIC staff examines the situation on an individual basis and makes the determination based on factors that include payment history, frequency of ordering, length of time as a customer, and general creditworthiness within the industry.

Case Study Analysis

8-13. What types of credit does HIC offer?

8-14. What types of general information does HIC ask all new customers to provide?

8-15. Describe the process used by HIC to evaluate credit risk and to determine an acceptable means of payment.

8-16. In general, what are the pros and cons for HIC to offer credit options?

Case Source

Harold Import Company Web site, accessed August 6, 2013, http://www.haroldimport.com.

Texas Jet—Premium Pricing for Premium Service[8]

Lead with Service and Turn Time into an Asset

Texas Jet is a gas station for airplanes. However, owner Reed Pigman, Jr., doesn't use today's gas station as a model for thinking about his business. He uses the Ritz Carlton Hotel chain as his guide. Reed says, "The people who fly and ride in private planes are the same people who stay at a Ritz Carlton or other luxury hotels. That means they don't compare us to the corner gas station, they compare us to the luxury service they get when they travel."

Reed's business operates 13 hangars totaling more than 225,000 square feet and supplies two-thirds of the fuel at Meacham Field, located in Fort Worth. Private aircraft depend on a network of fueling stations called fixed-base operations (FBOs), and Texas Jet is one of the best in the world, according to *Professional Pilot* magazine and *Aviation International News*.

In 2009 and 2010, Texas Jet was named the number one FBO by the pilots surveyed. *Professional Pilot* based its judgment on the fact that Texas Jet is a place the pilots enjoy while they are waiting for their customers to return. More significantly, the pilot's customer is given the red-carpet treatment.

Reed Pigman, Jr., Texas Jet
(Small Business School)

There is a very demanding supply chain within these operations, with high levels of expectations regarding customer service. The pilot is the customer of Texas Jet, and the passengers are the customers of the pilot. Although a few pilots own their planes, most are the full-time employees of the companies that own them, and often the passengers are key executives of those companies. The passengers could also be individuals who have a fractional ownership in a private airplane, who have chartered an airplane, or who are just paying for an empty leg. Everyone is a choice customer, and all expect top-quality care and attention to detail.

Texas Jet sells jet fuel and support services to the private airplanes. When the pilots prepare a flight plan, the destination FBO is part of the plan. They will need to buy fuel, but there are choices with respect to which FBO they will select. Whereas the pilots may spend extended time at the FBO's facility, the passengers generally spend very little time there. However, the few minutes the passengers do spend there are critical to the pilot's success.

Texas Jet employees literally throw out a red carpet for passengers to step on. This is going on while the pilot is checking gauges and shutting things down. The pilot chose Texas Jet and gets the credit for the red-carpet treatment, while taking care of matters in the cockpit. It is a special touch. Reed says, "The pilots want to know when they pull up on our ramp that we will take care of the boss in the back of the airplane. We will handle every request with a smile."

Texas Jet arranges for the ground transportation to pick passengers up right at plane-side and, if they need food on the airplane, that is handled too. While the passengers are taking care of business or social obligations in Fort Worth, the pilots have a place at Texas Jet to sleep, work out, eat, relax, visit with other pilots, watch TV, send e-mails, check the weather, and work on flight plans.

[8]Case prepared by Hattie Bryant of the Small Business School.

For example, a daily newspaper may reach 500,000 people one time. A directory may reach two million people 12 times a year. In addition to reach and frequency, businesses can consider gross ratings points, based on "opportunities to see." **Opportunities to see (OTS)** is the cumulative number of exposures in a given time period, usually four weeks. For example, if you place four ads on a TV show that is televised twice a week, you will get 32 OTS in a four-week period (four ads per show × two shows per week × four weeks). **Gross ratings points (GRP)** are calculated by multiplying the media vehicle's rating (reach) by the OTS, or number of insertions, to measure the intensity or impact of a media plan.

An important consideration in advertising is the "waste." If you wanted to reach 25- to 35-year-old working women with children in San Francisco, you would consider advertising in the *San Francisco Chronicle*. There would be a lot of waste, but it might be the best choice available. When you calculate the cost-per-impression (cost of the advertising divided by the number of times people see it), you will know if it makes sense. Sometimes it might be more logical to purchase advertising in smaller, more targeted publications.

The process of purchasing media may include multiple parties. The **media planner** is the person that creates a media plan with a particular advertising schedule. A **media buyer** purchases time/space and negotiates pricing and scheduling details. This individual works with the media sales representatives. In a small advertising firm, the same individual may do both planning and buying. Or, you may do this yourself. Remember, regardless of how it is done, advertising should not be random or infrequent. It needs to be regular and well planned.

Broadcast Media

Communication outlets that use "air space," including radio and television, make up the broadcast media. Advertising often can be purchased, or publicity garnered, for your business from local as well as national media outlets.

- *Television.* Even though TV advertising rates are comparatively high, television can be an effective media option. An entrepreneur with a new business can sometimes negotiate discounted rates or get free mention (publicity) if he or she has a good story. If you have a product or service that would benefit from TV or radio advertising, consider going with a media-buying service instead of purchasing it yourself. Media-buying services are granted the same 15-percent discount as

opportunities to see (OTS) the cumulative number of exposures in a given time period—usually four weeks.

gross ratings points (GRP) calculated by multiplying the media vehicle's rating (reach) by the OTS, or number of insertions, to measure the intensity (impact) of a media plan.

media planner an individual who creates a media plan, including a detailed advertising schedule.

media buyer an individual who purchases advertising time/space and negotiates pricing and scheduling details.

Dobiey/Alamy

advertising agencies, but they often return 10 percent of the savings to you, the advertiser, keeping 5 percent as their fee. You can find media buyers in the *Yellow Pages*.

The nature of TV advertising has changed significantly from the medium's early days, when there were only three channels and limited programming. The number of channels has grown tremendously, and the availability of TiVo, DirecTV, videos, and other options has changed the impact of television advertising. With the targeted audiences for cable channels, advertising can be more focused. At the same time, the sheer number of viewing options, and the capability of the viewer to skip over advertisements, means that effectiveness can be hard to measure.

- *Radio.* Radio advertising is sold in a variety of ways, with prices based on the length of your ad, the time of day it will run, and its duration and frequency. Radio stations can provide you with sophisticated data regarding their listeners, so that you can more readily determine whether there is a good fit with your target market. University and local community radio stations often do not carry advertising but might be willing to mention a new business venture that has an interesting or unusual angle. As with TV, radio advertising has changed over the years. The recent advent of satellite radio—and the ability to hear music without ads—has had an impact as well but, according to the annual RADAR report from the Radio Advertising Bureau (RAB), the weekly audience for radio was over 242 million in 2012, which totaled some 93% of the U.S. population over 12 years of age.[5]

Print Media

Newspapers, magazines, and directories are examples of print media. The best print media for your business is not always the largest, most well-recognized newspaper or magazine. In fact, you may find that community newspapers or lifestyle publications are better targeted, more economical, and more effective. A year-long study of newspaper advertising determined that a potential customer needs to see an ad at least nine times before the marketing message penetrates.[6] In addition, the study found that, for every three times a consumer sees an advertisement, he ignores it twice. This indicates that a consumer will have to see your ad 27 times before actually buying something.

If you take out a newspaper ad that will appear three times a week, therefore, commit to running it for nine weeks at the very least. The most common advertising mistake entrepreneurs make is to give up too soon. One gauge of how effective a particular advertising medium will be for your business is to observe it for a while and see whether your competitors use it regularly. If they do, they are probably seeing a good return on their investment, so you could, too. Remember, print media has suffered as electronic media has grown exponentially. Be certain to request independent confirmation of subscriber and readership data provided by media representatives, to confirm the accuracy of their claims.

It is important to use effective design for all of your print advertising and to reinforce your brand each and every time. **Figure 9-3** is an example of a print advertisement that incorporates the five main parts of a print ad: headline, deck (subhead), copy (text), graphics (photos or drawings), and your company logo with any tagline.

---

[5]"Radio's Audience Continues to Remain Strong," *RADAR June 2012 Report*, Arbitron, Inc., June 12, 2012, accessed August 3, 2013, http://arbitron.mediaroom.com/index.php?s=43&item=822.

[6]Conrad Levinson, *Guerrilla Marketing*, Boston: Houghton Mifflin, 1994.

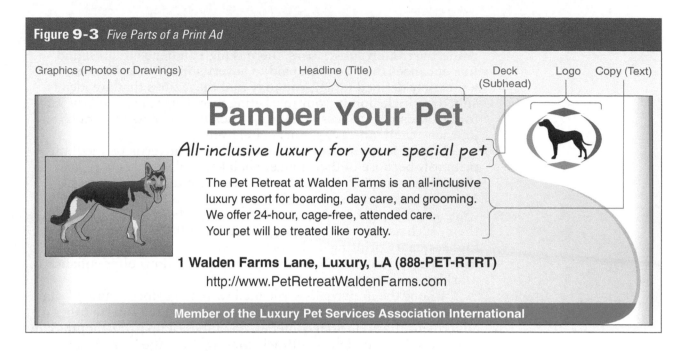

Figure 9-3 *Five Parts of a Print Ad*

- *Newspapers.* Newspapers may be published daily, weekly, or even less frequently. They can be community-based, local, regional, national, or international, and focus on news, finance, or any other topic. For a retail store serving a radius of five miles or fewer, a weekly community newspaper could be ideal. For a major investment bank, *The Wall Street Journal* would possibly be the best choice. A Catholic bookstore may find the best fit in the local diocesan weekly. In addition to and related to geographic scope, circulation can range from several hundred to millions. With the widespread use of the Internet, many newspapers also have online editions.

    The number of advertising options in newspapers is large and changes frequently. Classified advertising and display advertising are common features of newspapers. However, what varies is how they can be placed. Many newspapers now create special editions or special-interest advertising sections, to be inserted in the newspaper or distributed separately. For example, Gannett publications have periodic inserts such as "Prime Life," "Celebrations," parenting, camp programs, home sections, and the like. Each of these is directly targeted to a particular demographic, lifestyle, or other segment of the public, and includes pertinent advertising and editorial content.

    There is an entire category of nonsubscription publications made available at targeted distribution points. These publications, often in newspaper format, include parenting publications, entertainment guides, home and real estate advertising, ethnic publications, natural foods and nutrition publications, and so forth. Some of them include stories about their advertisers or invite advertisers to submit stories.

    Newspapers have the advantage of being highly flexible with significant credibility. You can place ads so that they change frequently. Readers pay attention to the articles they read and have sufficient interest in the ads that advertisers can put detailed information in them. The disadvantages of newspapers include difficulties in targeting, as well as a short shelf life. Also, if you want to run a national campaign, the buying process is costly and cumbersome.

- *Magazines.* Publications classified as "magazines" offer highly segmented markets and are targeted by those interests. Because readers are often subscribers, there is high audience interest and this enhances the attention paid to advertising. If your business has a precisely defined target, you may find magazines that are ideally suited for inclusion in your marketing mix. This is particularly true for business-to-business marketing, because business and trade journals reach target customers effectively.

  Magazines differ from newspapers as an advertising medium primarily because of their longer shelf life. Subscribers may read through a magazine several times, yielding multiple exposures. Moreover, magazines may be passed along to others, such as with trade journals, or be left in a common area where people can read them, such as a doctor's waiting room. In addition, magazines have higher-quality printing and more options. Scratch-and-sniff ads, fold-outs, cut-outs, and other unusual presentations offer enhanced marketing advantages.

  Among the drawbacks associated with magazines, "clutter" can be problematic, particularly with magazines that have more pages of advertising than editorial content. Lead times of up to six months can make it difficult to deliver a timely message, and the long shelf life can mean that the ads may survive beyond the advertisers' intentions—especially in the case of volatile or highly competitive industries.

- *Directories.* Telephone books and directories with membership lists from professional associations or chambers of commerce are examples of directories. They can be an excellent source of customer leads and good advertising venues. They tend to have a long shelf life and may be referred to repeatedly. You may use professional directories, in particular, if you can clearly identify professional associations or organizations that have members in your target audience. Advertisements and listings in directories should focus more on institutional advertising, due to the longer-term nature of the medium.

Outdoor Advertising (Out-of-Home Advertising)

Billboards are the most commonly recognized type of outdoor advertising. They are almost always in highly visible locations and use short, punchy copy that motorists can grasp at a glance. There are other forms of outdoor advertising, such as signs on park benches, stadium-fence ads, and the like. The nature of outdoor advertising has changed with the advent of technological innovations. For example, animated videos are projected in Times Square in New York through the use of LED technology. The pie chart in **Figure 9-4** shows the distribution of outdoor advertising revenue for its providers, according to the major product categories of billboards, transit, and street seating.

Billboard advertisements have the advantage of long life (contracts are generally one month or more), and the ads can be quite spectacular because of their scale. Commuters are exposed to the ad multiple times as they travel past it, twice a day. However, billboards have short exposure time unless traffic is particularly heavy and slow, or there is a traffic signal or stop sign that causes motorists to pause.

Mobile billboards (a truck covered with advertising) will travel specified routes or park in desired locations to provide highly targeted advertising on a relatively grand scale. These are being banned in some cities

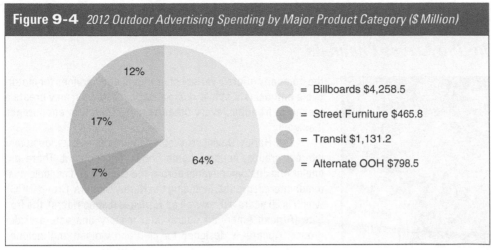

Figure 9-4 *2012 Outdoor Advertising Spending by Major Product Category ($ Million)*

- = Billboards $4,258.5
- = Street Furniture $465.8
- = Transit $1,131.2
- = Alternate OOH $798.5

Source: "OOH Revenue by Format," Outdoor Advertising Association of America, accessed August 3, 2013, http://www.oaaa.org/ResourceCenter/MarketingSales/Factsamp;Figures/Revenue/OOHRevenuebyFormat.aspx#.

and challenged on the basis of environmental impact and risk of distracting drivers.

Billboards are most commonly used to advertise for local services and amusements (e.g., eating places, insurance agencies, banks, recreational facilities, hotels and motels, resorts, and grocery stores), real estate, communications, public transportation, and media advertising. According to the Outdoor Advertising Association of America Web site (http://www.oaaaa.org), outdoor advertising expenditure is 4 percent of the U.S. media total. Depending on your business type, marketing objectives, and budget, outdoor advertising could be a viable option.

Billboard advertisement
(© Jeff Morgan 01/Alamy)

Step into the Shoes . . .

Harley Davidson—Marketing Across Channels

© Carl DeAbreu/Alamy

Harley-Davidson Motorcycles were introduced in 1903 by founders William S. Harley and Arthur, Walter, and William A. Davidson. Little did they know how strong a brand they had brought into being! Today, the bar-and-shield logo is one of the most widely recognized trademarks.

Harley-Davidson's stated purpose is, "We fulfill dreams of personal freedom." The company does this through its products and its integrated marketing efforts. Along with its motorcycles,

the company offers a variety of products and services for motorcycle enthusiasts. While *riding* a Harley-Davidson may create a feeling of freedom, every other aspect of the firm encourages it as well.

The Harley-Davidson Web site features events, customer interest groups, apparel, home goods, and content. There are dealer and customer events across the country and multiple customer interest groups, including the Harley Owners' Group (HOG), which is 30 years old, as well as *Harlistas* (Latino riders), the Iron Elite (African-American riders), and military and veteran rider groups. Apparel is designed for men and women and includes motorcycle gear and branded fashions. Home goods include barware, mugs, coolers, signs, collectibles, and the like. In addition, the company earns significant revenues from licensing its brand.

Motorcycle enthusiasts are encouraged to contribute content to the Harley-Davidson Web site. For example, during the 110th anniversary celebration, customers could create pictures to post on the "Graphic Wall." They could also contribute stories to an area called "My Epic Ride."

To round out their marketing efforts, there is also a Harley-Davidson Museum in Milwaukee, where the company was founded and has its headquarters.

Source: Harley-Davidson, accessed August 3, 2013, http://www.harley-davidson.com.

Advertising Measurement: Beyond Reach and Frequency

Measuring the impact of your advertising will be based on results, but it is often difficult to assess this directly, because of the many factors that influence the purchasing decision. Consider the various media options carefully. **Exhibit 9-2** shows the pros and cons of some of them. Once the selections are weighed, the effectiveness of each should be measured. Factors should include cost and projected results.

In order to effectively compare the outlay involved with different media, calculate the **cost per thousand (CPM)**, which is what you will pay to reach 1,000 members of the medium's audience (not the purchaser's). CPM is calculated as:

cost per thousand (CPM) the cost of reaching 1,000 of the media vehicle's audience.

$$CPM = (Cost\ of\ Media\ Buy\ (\$)/Total\ Audience) \times 1,000$$

For example, if the cost of a four-color, full-page ad in *Sports Illustrated* is $950,000, and its total readership is 15,000,000, its CPM is $63.33 ([$950,000/15,000,000] × 1,000).

The CPM calculation makes it possible to compare media vehicles, but it does not consider the advertiser's target market explicitly, and that target market might be significantly smaller than the total readership. The **cost per rating point (CPRP)** is an additional measure of the efficiency of a media vehicle to a company's target market. It is calculated by dividing the cost of the media purchase by the vehicle's **rating** (the percentage of the company's target market exposed to a TV show or print ad):

cost per rating point (CPRP) a measure of the efficiency of a media vehicle in a company's target market, calculated by dividing the media buy's cost by the vehicle's rating.

rating the percentage of a company's target market exposed to a TV show or print ad.

$$CPRP = Cost\ of\ Media\ Buy\ (\$)/Vehicle's\ Rating$$

Exhibit 9-2 *Pros and Cons of Selected Advertising Media*

	Pros (Advantages)	Cons (Disadvantages)
Television	Low CPM Highly targeted with cable High intrusion value High reach and frequency potential Message is immediate	High cost for ad campaign Clutter Short life of advertising message High production costs Long lead time
Radio	Relatively low cost Short-term commitment Short lead time Message is immediate Promotes recall Mobility (radios travel with people)	Auditory only Clutter—information overload Short life of advertising message Low attention Local nature
Newspapers	Geographic targeting Short lead time Flexibility and credibility More copy potential Direct response possible	Expense may be high Demographic targeting is limited Short shelf life Declining readership Waste Poor-quality production
Magazines	Targeted reader interest High color/production quality Direct response possible Long shelf life	Lack of immediacy Exposure dispersed over time Longer lead times High cost
Internet	Targeting potential Moderate cost Global reach Relatively short lead time	Not ubiquitous Banner ads feed-click through to full ads
Outdoor Media	Repeat exposures Geographic selectivity Moderate CPM High-impact, dramatic ads possible	Limited message size Limited demographic selectivity Initial design and production costs Short exposure time

It is important to recognize that a media vehicle may have a low CPRP but also only reach a small part of the company's target market. In order to address whether an ad in a specific media vehicle will effectively reach a company's target market, the "weighted" (demographic) CPM can be calculated as

> Weighted CPM = (Ad Cost ($) × 1,000)/Actual Audience Reached

For example, *Sports Illustrated* has a standard CPM of $63.33, and you want to reach the professional athletes who read it; your research shows 10,000 of *Sports Illustrated*'s readers are in this category. The weighted CPM would be ($950,000 × 1,000)/10,000, or $95,000), which would not seem to be the most efficient expenditure of funds to reach professional athletes. Once the weighted CPM is calculated, you can compare it to other potential media choices to make a buying decision.

All of this information can be valuable in deciding which media to select. When combined with your advertising message and design, you can create a complete program. The key is to outlay funds just sufficient to reach the target audience as frequently as needed to achieve your advertising objectives.

Business cards carry your message and image
(Don Farrall/Photodisc/Getty Images)

Marketing Materials Should Reinforce Your Competitive Advantage

All promotional items for your business should reflect and reinforce your marketing vision, which in turn will reinforce your competitive advantage. They should include the name of your business, your logo, and a slogan, if you have one.

In fact, you will have a much stronger impact if all your business materials are tied together with a strong, coordinated image. This should extend beyond your logo into the format, font style, colors, and look of your materials. As you create your stationery and business cards (identity set), advertisements, publicity pieces, and brochures, the consistency of your image will help to convey your competitive advantage. If it is done well, your image will be in alignment with your strengths, and you will be positioned for success. If this is done poorly, you will lack credibility, which can then harm, if not destroy, your chances of success.

Good marketing materials serve three functions:

1. Creating them will organize your business thinking.
2. They will enable you to teach others in your company about the business.
3. They will enable you to go into the marketplace and sell your product or service with confidence.

Collateral Materials: Print and Multimedia

Advertising can get people interested in your business but, before they buy, prospects will often want more information. Depending on your business, brochures will enable you to provide that information and turn interest into a sale.

At the bottom of every print ad you run, offer to send a brochure or provide a link to your Web site. When you mail the brochure, include a personal letter thanking the prospective customer for requesting it. If you do not hear back in a few weeks, send a follow-up note. You are establishing

Global Impact . . .

Naked Communications

The first British Invasion may have been the arrival of the Beatles in 1964, but the second seems to have come in the form of a global communications firm, Naked Communications, which arrived in the United States with considerable attention and interest. Naked Communications is a global organization with offices in London, New York, and 14 other cities. Clients include Johnson & Johnson, Coca-Cola, American Express, Nokia, Lugz, Kimberly-Clark, and ad agencies such as BBDO, Lowe, and Leo Burnett. Naked Communications is neither an advertising agency nor a traditional media planning firm, and it chose a name that conveyed the company's approach to integrated marketing: stripping a concept bare and then working to find the best promotional path.

The team at Naked believes that the right approach to advertising is to gather all the people who have brand responsibility together and work toward an answer to the question, "What's the right message communicated in the right way through the right channel in order to effectively reach the right consumer?"[7] Global business requires global communications, and organizations to support them. Naked Communications does just that.

---

[7]Danielle Sacks, "Is Mad. Ave. Ready to Go Naked," *Fast Company*, October, 1999, accessed August 3, 2013, http://www.fastcompany.com/magazine/99/naked.html.

one-on-one contact with someone you did not know before, the kind of personal connection that can lead to a sale. The brochure could actually close the sale itself, by providing a toll-free number to call.

Whether you use print, audio, or video brochures will depend on your budget and your business.

Sales-Promotion Solutions

Sales promotions provide another set of tools to add to the mix. Various efforts to increase sales volume by specified levels, which either reward purchases or provide discounts, can be effective for both consumer and business-to-business marketing. Sales-promotion solutions do not have to be complex or sophisticated to work. In fact, it is best if they are simple and easily understood. If an incentive program is difficult to figure out, customers may simply not bother to participate, because it won't be worth the trouble. **Exhibit 9-3** identifies some common types of sales-promotion methods.

◀ **Learning Objective 5**
Discuss sales promotion.

When to Use Promotional Tools

Promotional tools are best used when the strategy calls for a highly targeted, time-limited boost in response. They can be excellent ways to encourage new-product trials and for raising seasonal performance. They should always be part of the overall marketing strategy and budget. Contests and sweepstakes are a way of securing product engagement and, potentially, repeat sales (e.g., for a game that includes purchases to collect game pieces). Coupons require the customer to actively seek out your product on the shelves or to contact you for the product or service. *Sampling* brings the product or service message to life for the customer through experience. Bonus packs and tie-ins lead to a trial of additional products.

Advertising Specialties

The strategic inclusion of specialty items can be an effective sales-promotion tool. Freebies are always a draw with customers, but do not disappoint them with gifts that look and feel cheap. The best giveaways are those that are useful, such as pens, on which prospective customers will see your business name and contact information. Visit wholesalers, or search online to investigate discount prices on quantities of calculators, watches, pens, or other appropriate items.

Exhibit 9-3 *Sales-Promotional Tools*

Consumer	Business-to-Business
Coupons	Incentives
Contests and Sweepstakes	Contests
Refunds and Rebates	Refunds and Rebates
Sampling	Sampling
Premiums	Allowances
Tie-ins	Trade Shows
Bonus Packs	

Trade Show Exhibits

The use of trade show exhibits is a proven promotional strategy for business-to-business companies and can also succeed for certain types of consumer marketing. This is one of the best forms of experiential marketing, because it lends itself to having prospective customers try out your products, or having services demonstrated. Whereas the cost of trade-show space, a professionally designed booth, transportation, and other related expenses can be relatively high, the opportunity to have impact can make it worthwhile. This is particularly true for business-to-business marketing that can be accomplished at targeted professional conferences, providing an efficient means to reach many potential customers with a consistent message. Tsnn.com reports that there are 15,000 trade shows, exhibitions, public events, and conferences each year. The keys to successful trade show promotion include preparation, booth training for all staff, quality exhibits, careful goal setting, and consistent efforts to reap the benefits of the investment.

Mall Carts or Kiosks

For many seasonal businesses, or businesses that are working to create full-scale retail operations, mall carts or kiosks may prove effective. Signing a multiyear lease for a retail store is not likely to make sense for a seasonal business such as a Christmas or Halloween operation. Sometimes such businesses can find vacant retail spaces to rent for just a season, or they can partner with others to rotate in and out of a store. In other situations, they can create a business model of changing seasonal inventory and focus. However, for many business owners, these options are not practical or desirable, and having a temporary retail location is preferable. Also, if you are working on a retail concept and want to try out the idea—products, prices, and so forth—a temporary location is a good opportunity to "test-drive" your business before investing in longer-term, more costly retail space. Such a trial run may also provide sales and marketing data that will

Trade show exhibits for business-to-business promotion
(© Andrew Holt/Alamy)

assist you in attracting financing. For an investment of $1,500 to $10,000, plus inventory and rental fees, you could be up and running.

Alternative Marketing

The marketing approaches described thus far have been practiced for many, many years and are considered to be tried-and-true methods. However, marketing has evolved with changing times and technology to include more recent forms. The following is a discussion of some of the alternative types of marketing in use today.

◀ Learning Objective 6
Explore alternative marketing options.

Guerilla Marketing

J. Conrad Levinson coined this term in 1984 with his book of the same name, meaning original, unconventional, and inexpensive small-business strategies. Since then, **guerilla marketing** has expanded to encompass other kinds of unconventional categories, such as viral marketing, buzz marketing, word-of-mouth advertising, and grassroots marketing. The notion is to find creative, surprising ways to get your message to your target market without spending a fortune.

guerilla marketing original, unconventional, and inexpensive small-business promotional strategies.

Buzz Marketing

Buzz marketing is another name for word-of-mouth marketing. It can occur naturally (*organic buzz marketing*) or can be jump-started by the organization (*amplified buzz marketing*). It is one of the most effective forms of promotion available, because people are sharing their excitement and enthusiasm about a product or service with others who trust and value the advice. By giving your customers an outstanding experience, you are encouraging organic buzz marketing. If you can create *amplified* buzz marketing, it will boost recognition and marketing still further.

buzz marketing another name for word-of-mouth marketing.

Product Placement/Branded Entertainment

The use of product placement in television, movies, and other scenarios is another good promotional tool. Such positioning reaches consumers on a more subconscious level and doesn't contain an overt sales pitch. When the movie *E.T.* hit the theaters, Reese's Pieces were included as a product placement, and they continue to be associated with the movie decades later. The duration of in-show brand appearances during an average hour of prime-time network television programming was just short of 8 minutes during the fourth quarter of 2008, with an average of almost 14 minutes during unscripted reality programming, and just about 6 minutes per hour during scripted programs.[8] Today, there are firms that focus on locating and negotiating product placements. Two such companies are Creative Entertainment Services (http://acreativegroup.com) and GameShowPlacements.com (for game and cable shows). Depending on your product, it might be worthwhile to pursue placement possibilities.

Lifestyle Marketing

In order to successfully market their brands, companies are striving to align them with consumer needs, interests, desires, and values and to apply lifestyle marketing with knowledge of consumer behavior. This form of marketing reaches beyond the traditional demographic approaches to engage customers based on how they live.

---

[8]TNS Media Intelligence press release, May 4, 2009.

In-Store Marketing

There are numerous options for carrying out in-store marketing, whether in your own space or in businesses where your product is sold. For example, signage, shelf placement, sampling, and "edutainment" can all play roles. Which ones are best will depend on your marketing strategy.

- *Samples or demonstrations.* Offer samples of your product to potential customers who pass by your business. Or take samples to a high-density location, such as a park or town square. If you are selling a service, consider demonstrating it outdoors or in a mall (get permission first). When you open your business, you can give away samples of your product to encourage potential customers to tell their friends about it. Many large businesses, such as BJ's Wholesale Club and Sam's Club, make extensive use of sampling and edutainment to encourage purchases. **Edutainment** is the combining of education and entertainment to make a more lasting impression on an audience. You might use this method to show the originality of your product and engage the interest of prospective customers.

- *Point-of-purchase and shelf placement.* These opportunities include the complete visual component of your in-store placement, such as packaging, any couponing with shelf placement, and special-display units. By putting products where prospective customers will be drawn to them visually, you are increasing the chances of purchase. Well-designed point-of-purchase materials can make a huge difference in sales.

- *Back of receipt marketing.* Customers can receive coupons for the current store or for ones that are targeting a similar base.

edutainment a promotion that combines education and entertainment to make a more lasting impression upon an audience.

Other Media Venues

In addition to the methods and media described above, a number of other venues are worth noting. These options should also be considered in your planning. See **Exhibit 9-4** for examples of other media venues.

Rack of brochures for tourists
(Dorling Kindersley/Alamy)

Exhibit **9-4** *Other Media Venues*		
Ambient Advertising	**Indoor Advertising**	**Other Advertising**
Parking Lots	Movie Theaters	Carryout Menus
Tunnels	Video Games	Shopping Bags
Escalators	Bathroom Stalls	Advertising on Clothing
Benches (Bus Stops)	Commercial Trucks	Brochure Racks
	Airline In-Flight	

Database and Direct-Response Marketing

The use of databases is integral to the previous advertising and promotion discussion, with respect to data research and analysis, but its value can far exceed those applications. Through the use of selected databases, you can create communications that are highly targeted and customized, thereby increasing your impact and effectiveness. At the same time, marketing efforts that engage your customers and have direct-response mechanisms can build your customer base and foster customer loyalty. It is less costly to maintain repeat customers than to generate new ones. Thus, the emphasis of database marketing is to identify customers and build loyalty. The primary focus is on relationship-building rather than sales.

◀ **Learning Objective 7**
Analyze database and direct-response marketing opportunities.

Data Collection, Coding, and Mining

In order to be successful in data marketing, you must have quality data, such as

- Customer names and mailing addresses
- E-mail addresses
- Any customer profile or preference data
- Purchasing and returns history
- Web-site visiting information (from cookies on company site)
- Customer survey results
- History of contacts, including calls and correspondence
- History of promotional contacts and responses
- Additional data and data analysis from external sources

Data should be collected at each point of interaction, without being intrusive or annoying to the customer. Remember to update addresses through the U.S. Postal Service or another service provider at least once a year, because 20 percent of the U.S. population moves each year. Updating e-mail addresses is important for the same reason.

Coding the data you have collected is an essential step toward analyzing and using it to its maximum effectiveness. With proper coding, you can create marketing campaigns and personalize communications programs. You can calculate the profit earned from a particular customer or customer segment, which is known as **lifetime value**. The calculation of lifetime value is generally figured in one-year increments over, say, three or five years. Another measure is **RFM analysis**, which is the creation of a three-digit score for each customer based on *recency* (date of most recent purchase), *frequency* (number of purchases over a specific time period), and *monetary value* (dollars spent on company products within a given period). The method you use can be one of these, or a different coding method that you design and find meaningful.

lifetime value the total profit earned from a particular customer or customer segment.

RFM analysis the creation of a three-digit score for each customer based on recency, frequency, and monetary values.

data mining a computer program that analyzes and sorts data, in order to identify a business's best existing customers and model those who might become even better.

Once data is collected and coded, you can use **data mining**—a computer program to analyze and sort data—to identify your existing clientele and model those who might become particularly excellent customers.

Marketing Communications Driven by Databases

Database information and analysis can fuel your market-driven communications to cross-sell customers, tailor promotions, and to project future purchases. By making effective use of these database options, you can personalize your approach to customers, create greater engagement and loyalty, and build sales and repeat purchases. Typically, such programs take the form of e-mail, telemarketing, or direct mail—more often with customer permission rather than unsolicited offers—or through loyalty/ frequency programs. Related to your database marketing will be direct-response marketing, which promotes products directly to customers and prospects through direct mail, catalogs, the Internet, and other media.

E-mail Marketing

Targeted customers may opt in to e-mail marketing programs for reasons such as a chance to win a sweepstakes or access specific content or because they are existing customers and want e-mail offers and updates. Kohl's department stores solicit customer e-mail addresses with the promise of advance notice of sales and a $5 coupon. Once you secure the permission to e-mail, ensure that the program is successful both for you and your customers by having a plan that reinforces the incentive to participate. Also, remember to provide your customers with an opt-out choice, and keep track of what does and does not work.

Direct Mail

Consumers and business-to-business customers can be targeted with direct mail, and you can use this method with internally generated or purchased lists. It is vital to target the mailing according to the customers on the list— understanding whether list members have a previous purchase history and keeping in mind that what is of interest to them can make a world of difference. Direct mail can be targeted, and results can be measured through response rates. Direct mail is an excellent method of getting customers to your Web site. However, direct mail suffers from the clutter created by the volume of direct-mail offers received by consumers and by the potentially high cost of producing and mailing materials. **Exhibit 9-5** lists reasons for the use of direct mail.

Catalogs

Even with the growth of online shopping, catalogs represent a viable direct-response marketing option. They are low pressure and can direct readers to Web sites for purchases. When you have built a list of 10,000 names, it might be time to pay for a color catalog, because then the price of printing per catalog will be sufficiently low. You can produce a two-color catalog economically with even fewer names.

Coupons

Another form of direct mail that you might want to consider is coupons. You can send out discount (price break) coupons as an incentive to first-time customers or offer discounts for a limited time. This will encourage people to try your product or service. There are businesses that package coupons (card packs) from multiple companies into a mailer and send it to a targeted audience. You can save money by piggy-backing on their targeting.

Exhibit 9-5 *Direct-Mail Opportunities: When You Think of Your Use of Mail Advertising, What Applications Come to Mind?*

New customer acquisition	53.8%
Customer communication	53.2%
Building brand awareness	51.2%
Generating sales	50.7%
Generating leads	43.2%
Building customer loyalty	40.1%
Driving store traffic	31.1%
Building customer confidence	26.6%
Other	6.7%

Source: "Recent Research—2009 Marketing in a Down Economy," from Advertising Age Custom Publishing, March 30, 2009. Copyright 2009 Advertising Age. Used by permission.

Infomercials and Direct-Response Commercials

Both of these methods use paid television advertising to prompt direct purchases. Infomercials are typically one-half hour in length and play on cable television late at night. Direct-response commercials may be found on any channel. They are often 60-second spots that encourage viewers to "Call now!" with prompts of a toll-free number or Web site, or both.

Telemarketing

Companies use in-bound and out-bound telemarketing to support their sales and marketing efforts. Once you have compiled an extensive database of customers, you can use it to invite them to events or sales. You can also purchase lists. Be careful that you adhere to rules and guidelines with regard to telemarketing and that you respect "Do not call" requests. Sometimes it is worthwhile to hire professional telemarketers. In-bound telemarketing can be highly effective. You can cross-sell or up-sell customers that have called you.

E-Active Marketing

Internet advertising has grown with the expansion and adoption of Internet technology. Not only have entrepreneurs and major corporations come to include online advertising and promotion as a regular part of the media mix, entire industry segments have evolved to serve the interactive media field. The number of advertising opportunities is seemingly infinite, ranging from Google to little-known sites. Businesses can elect to use display advertising in the form of banner ads, pay to raise their visibility within search engines, or partner with other online companies to obtain mention and have customers directed to them. They can use social media, blogs, and e-mail. These options continue to expand and evolve at a rapid pace. When the two major components of Internet marketing—e-commerce and interactive marketing—combine, **e-active marketing** results. You can make the best use of e-active marketing approaches by marrying them with your offline efforts to create a unified approach to marketing. **Figure 9-5** shows the level of interest in adults and young people in various types of information from businesses.

◀ Learning Objective 8
Incorporate e-active marketing.

e-active marketing when the two major components of Internet marketing—e-commerce and interactive marketing—combine.

E-Commerce

The provision of an electronic storefront and/or other forms of electronic commerce is one way of implementing your marketing strategy, as discussed in Chapter 6.

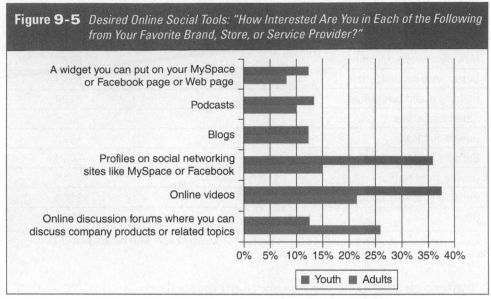

Figure 9-5 *Desired Online Social Tools: "How Interested Are You in Each of the Following from Your Favorite Brand, Store, or Service Provider?"*

Base: U.S. online adults, age 18 and older, and U.S. online youths, ages 12 to 17.

Source: North American Technographics Media and Marketing Online Survey, Q2 2008; North American Technographics Youth Online Survey, Q2 2008; Forrester Research, Inc., *The Social Tools Consumers Want from Their Favorite Brands,* report prepared by Josh Bernoff, April 16, 2009, http://blogs.forrester.com/a/6a00d8341c50bf53ef01156f827e11970c-pi (accessed May 21, 2009).

Interactive Marketing

Interactive marketing means addressing customers, absorbing their input, and reaching out to them again to make it clear you have paid attention. Whereas interactive marketing is not necessarily online marketing, the collection of customer information and subsequent communication is facilitated by the Internet. An excellent example of the use of interactive marketing is Amazon.com, which collects user information to make purchase recommendations.

Online Advertising

This typically takes the form of banner advertisements on Web sites. These can be highly targeted, based on the online habits and interests of consumers. Such ads can be purchased directly from the owners of the Web sites on which you wish to advertise, or through brokers who purchase online advertising for specific target markets. For small, local businesses with a Web site, it may be possible to work in partnership with other companies that sell complementary products to create "click-through" opportunities for their customers to visit your site, and vice versa. This type of advertising includes pay-per-click (PPC), wherein firms bid on keywords that they would expect their potential customers to use to search for their type of goods and services, so that they can appear in the search return results as "sponsored ads" and thus become considerably more visible. With this type of advertising, you only pay when someone clicks on your ad.

Brand Spiraling

brand spiraling integrating a company's conventional offline branding strategy with its Internet strategy by using conventional approaches to drive traffic to its online sites.

Integrating a company's conventional offline branding strategy with its Internet strategy can be accomplished through **brand spiraling**, which is the term for businesses using conventional approaches through print and broadcast media to drive traffic to their online sites. Once customers are guided to those sites, the companies take advantage of Internet interactivity and learn more about them. This knowledge is used to further refine sales and marketing tactics. They also can use e-mail addresses and other information to reach customers in additional ways. The brand spiral is a continuous learning and changing process for a firm that assists in reaching and influencing customers through both online and offline tactics.

Blogs

A **blog** (short for "Web log") is a journal that appears on the Internet periodically (perhaps daily) and is intended for the public. **Blogosphere** is the collective term used for all the blogs on the Internet. Businesses provide blogs, often written by their owners, to create a personal connection with customers. These are only effective if the information is kept interesting and timely, and customers are led to the sites by other promotions. Some blog-hosting services include:

Blogger	http://www.blogger.com
LiveJournal	http://www.livejournal.com
Twitter	http://www.twitter.com (microblogging)
TypePad	http://www.typepad.com
WordPress	http://www.wordpress.com
Xanga	http://www.xanga.com

blog (short for Web log) a journal that appears on the Internet periodically (perhaps daily) and is intended for the public.

blogosphere the collective term used for all the blogs on the Internet.

Online Social Networks

The number and variety of online social networks has grown phenomenally in recent years and is expected to continue to do so. Social networks such as Facebook, MySpace, and LinkedIn, as well as those for interest-specific niches (e.g., Flickr, imeem, BlackPlanet, Classmates.com, Goodreads, and MyHeritage), continue to evolve, as new uses emerge. Advertising opportunities on these networks are more complex than those on Web sites with banner ads. For many social networks, advertising and promotion are either banned or taboo. Some users create subtle promotion through what are essentially scripted conversations on the sites. These "undercover," deceptive marketing efforts are intended to appear as if they happened naturally and are referred to as **stealth marketing**.

Recent research by the Internet Advertising Bureau in the United Kingdom addressed the methods for maximizing results from social networking: "The IAB research found that exclusive content, which appeals to 28% of social networkers, and genuine interest in the message, which attracts 37%, are the keys to a positive response from consumers on social networks. And because only 5% say they actively dislike messages from brands, there are big opportunities for marketers who can hit the right notes."[9] In addition to online social networking, the option of **mobile social networking**, the updating of social-network sites via mobile handsets, is increasing. This means that users are accessing the information at all times and at any location.

stealth marketing undercover, or deceptive, marketing efforts that are intended to appear as if they happened naturally.

mobile social networking the updating of social-network sites via mobile handsets.

Consumer-Generated Advertising

This can include campaigns in which the company solicits advertisements from customers. You can ask them to create videos, stories, print advertisements, and the like—generally through a contest or promotion—to fuel your advertising programs. Such promotion creates authenticity and credibility in a way that company-generated advertising cannot. Consumer-generated media (CGM) also comes in a variety of forms that are not

---

[9]Emma Hall, "How to Get the Most Out of Social Networks and Not Annoy Users," *Advertising Age*, April 27, 2009, p. 30.

specifically solicited by companies, such as message-board posts, blogs, and forum commentary. Consumer-generated advertising can generate enthusiasm and engagement as well as increased loyalty.

Viral Marketing

viral marketing the process of promoting a brand, product, or service through an existing social network, where a message is passed from one individual to another—much as a virus spreads.

Interactive marketing options have been expanded through technology to include **viral marketing**, a term coined by Tim Draper of Draper Fisher Jurvetson. Viral marketing is defined as the process of promoting a brand, product, or service through an existing social network, typically an online version, such as Instagram or Facebook, in which a message is passed from one individual to another—much as a virus spreads. A viral campaign can be an e-mail or a video that may include hyperlinked promotions, advertisements, games, or online newsletters. There has to be a reason for people to tell others about the message or pass it along, such as entertainment value, uniqueness, or potential financial reward.

In August 2007, with a budget of $150,000, TuitionBids.com's agency, Fanscape, created a viral marketing campaign targeted at 16- to 24-year-old high school and college students and their parents, with the intention of creating buzz and awareness of the company and to drive sales leads.[10] The strategy used was to "surround and deliver [the] target audience with valuable information." They used a multifaceted approach that "fused online Content and Promotional Integration programs, Social Media techniques, dedicated emails from Fanscape's proprietary database, a pay-per-click (PPC) campaign, and display ad buys to create as many relevant touch points with the target audience as possible." This included an e-mail to 100,000 members of the Fanscape database. The results included "32 million branding impressions with over 40,000 clicks, 150 WOM placements, 26 editorial placements for over 2 million unique views, 8 contests, adding another 3 million unique views, a 25% open rate on the Fanscape email (well above industry averages)." Tuitionbids.com had a 6.4% conversion rate, which is about three times the industry average.

By creatively generating interest in and excitement about your story, or an aspect of your business, you can work to create a viral campaign. Kristen Smith, Executive Director of WOMMA, suggests the following six ways to keep people talking about your company and your products:[11]

1. Listen, speak, listen some more.
2. Be transparent and disclose.
3. Evaluate ROI continually.
4. Spread the word, not the manure.
5. Encourage an enterprise-wide WOMM.
6. Employ online and offline WOMM.

Publicity Potential

Generating Publicity

Learning Objective 9

Describe publicity and public relations.

Publicity, sometimes referred to as public relations (PR)—as discussed in Chapter 4—is defined by the Institute of Public Relations as "the planned and sustained effort to establish and maintain goodwill and mutual understanding between an organization and its public." Always save any

---

[10]WOMMA Web site http://www.womma.org, accessed May 18, 2009, http://www2.fanscape.com/tuitionbids/womma0808.html.

[11]Kristen Smith, "Six Ways to Leverage Word-of-Mouth," March 1, 2009, accessed May 17, 2009, http://www.womma.org.

publicity you receive. Frame and display articles prominently in your place of business, and make copies to send or hand out when appropriate. Each item of publicity has enormous value. Consumers give publicity credibility because it is not paid for.

Publicity is important for a small business, which often has a negligible advertising budget. To get publicity, you will need to mail or fax a pitch letter and a press release to the magazine, newspaper, TV station, or radio station you hope to interest.

A **pitch letter** sells the story. It tells the person reading it why he or she should be interested in your business. A **press release** is an announcement sent to the media to generate publicity and states the "who, what, when, where, and why" of a story. A pitch letter allows you to explain the story behind the press release and why it would be interesting and relevant to the media outlet's readers, listeners, or viewers.

> **pitch letter** correspondence designed to explain the story behind a press release, and why it would be interesting and relevant to the media outlet's readers, listeners, or viewers.

Before mailing or faxing a pitch letter and press release, call or e-mail the outlet and ask to whom you should direct the material. Say something like, "My name is Jason Hurley, and I'm a young entrepreneur with a downtown delivery/messenger service. I'd like to send WKTU a press release about the commitment we have just made to donate 10 hours of free delivery service per month to Meals on Wheels for seniors. To whom should I direct a press release?" Sometimes you can find this information on the Internet.

> **press release** an announcement sent to the media to generate publicity that explains the "who, what, when, where, why, and how" of a story.

Get to know the print, radio, and television journalists pertinent to your business, so you can get publicity. The most effective way to get notice for your venture is to contact the reporters yourself. You might be tempted to hire a professional publicist, but many reporters are bombarded by these people and would rather hear directly from you. Dedicate a block of time to send e-mails and make phone calls pitching your business and explaining why your story is worth covering. Be totally honest and build positive relationships. The type of reporting you want will develop most often because the writer comes to care about your story and sees it as interesting and important. Once you establish rapport and credibility with reporters, they are likely to call you for stories, insights, and comments.

Press releases can generate positive reports and stories about your business in newspapers and magazines and on radio stations. For newspapers, make sure you send the release about a month before the event you are promoting. Follow up with a phone call two weeks later and then one week after that (a week before the occasion). The precise timing will depend on the media outlet and its publication or broadcast schedule.

Telling the Story

Younger entrepreneurs can have an advantage here because relatively few young people start their own businesses. The print, radio, and television journalists in your area may want to hear about you.

Bear in mind, however, that reporters are looking for stories that will interest their readers. It is fine to send out a press release announcing the opening of your business, but be aware that it will not be a story until it is up and running. There is no point sending out a pitch letter and press release until you are actually in business and have a story to tell. The fact that your business is open, however, doesn't necessarily translate into a story of interest. You have to make the connection:

- Who are you and what has happened to you or what have you done that would make you and your business an interesting story?
- Did you have to overcome any obstacles to start your business?

- What about your product or service is unique? Is it something your community really needs?
- When is a specific event taking place that is newsworthy or of interest for a story?
- Where are you locating the business or where is the event or activity occurring?
- How has your business changed you and helped members of your community?

Always answer the basic questions of who, what, when, where, why, and how for reporters. Answers to these questions will help them determine whether your story might be of interest to their readers or viewers. Reporters are busy people, so keep your answers to these questions tight and concise. Try to find one focus or angle for your story. What's the "hook"?

Sample Press Release

As we have said, in order to tell your story in a press release or to a reporter, you will have to answer the six basic questions: who, what, when, where, why, and how. Who are you; what did you do; when, where, why, and how did you do it?

A press release must provide contact information (name, phone, e-mail, and Web site) and answer the six questions (see **Figure 9-6**).

Follow Up a Press Release

Follow up your press releases with phone calls and e-mail. Try to reach the journalists directly. Be polite but persistent. Do not wait for a newspaper or radio station to return your call; call again (but do not make a pest of yourself)—they receive many press releases every day.

We suggest saving all publicity you receive to show potential customers because it has enormous value. Simply put, it can attract more publicity and more customers. Remember, it has greater credibility for consumers than advertising, which you will have paid for.

Public Relations

In addition to publicity, you can build positive public relations for your company through involvement in the local community and in local, national, and international professional and business organizations that pertain to your business. Some ways of doing this are with special events, sponsorship, networking, and public speaking.

Special Events

Hold contests, throw parties, or put together unusual events to attract attention and customers. Contests and sweepstakes can gather valuable names for your mailing list. Or, participate in special events yourself to gain publicity for your business, through effective networking with other participants.

Sponsorships

Sponsoring a local sports team is a great way to involve your business in the community and meet potential customers. Sponsorships are a way of advertising. Just be certain that the audience for the event fits into your target market.

Networking

Networking, as discussed in Chapter 1 with respect to effective selling, is the exchange of information and contacts. When done efficiently and courteously, networking can serve as an excellent promotional vehicle.

Figure 9-6 *Sample Press Release*

Entrepreneurship Event demonstrates that Springfield Technical Community College students can create their own jobs

EET Contact: Laura MacMinn
Telephone: (800) 930-8021 x705
Cell Phone: (704) 252-1516
Email: laura@iempact.com

FOR IMMEDIATE RELEASE

The Extreme Entrepreneurship Tour features high-energy keynotes and informative workshops designed to provide prospective entrepreneurs with the inspiration they need to follow their dreams, pursue their passions and start their own businesses

Springfield, MA — With the economy continuing to struggle, job hunters - particularly high school and college students and recent college grads - are faced with limited options, often spending weeks or months looking for a job. Yet, what many job seekers don't realize is that creating their own job is within reach.

On Thursday, Sept. 26, the *Extreme Entrepreneurship Tour* will be returning to Springfield for a high-energy event, hosted by Springfield Technical Community College. The event will take place from 9:30 AM to 1:30 PM in the STCC Gymnasium located at One Armory Square in Springfield, MA. Some of the country's top young entrepreneurs, who have developed or sold successful companies before the age of 30, will be the event's keynote speakers.

Since 2006, the *Extreme Entrepreneurship Tour* has hosted more than 500 entrepreneurship events in 35 states, inspiring thousands of young people across the country to become entrepreneurs. Entrepreneur speakers showcase the many faces of entrepreneurship, showing the many opportunities for starting a business beyond the overnight success tech startups we always hear about.

Michael Simmons, co-founder of the Extreme Entrepreneurship Tour and Partner at Empact believes that prospective entrepreneurs should be inspired, not intimidated, by the current economic climate. "More than half the companies on the 2009 Fortune 500 list were launched during a recession or bear market." Simmons said, "Technology and globalization have made it very inexpensive to start a business. Now is the best time to become your own boss."

Laura Mac Minn, Director of Events for the Tour, agrees with Simmons that there is opportunity, and that opportunity can have a significant impact on the job market: "Today's students can be critical forces in the next 10 years to help create the 20 million jobs we need in this decade."

Registration for the Extreme Entrepreneurship Tour at Springfield Technical Community College is available at http://extremetour.org/stcc. On-site registration will begin at 8:30 AM. on Thursday, September 26.

About Empact

Empact's work focuses on facilitating a culture of entrepreneurship in communities across the globe through exposure, celebration and early stage startup support.

Empact has held more than 500 events exposing young people to the many faces of entrepreneurship through its Extreme Entrepreneurship Tour (www.extremetour.org); and annually celebrates the role of young entrepreneurs through the Empact Showcase and Empact100 list of top young entrepreneurs age 30 and under (www.empact100.com).

Each year, Empact brings together the top thought leaders from the entrepreneurship education ecosystem to share and act on the biggest ideas during the Empact Summit. For more information, please visit iempact.com

Source: Empact.

Public Speaking

Taking advantage of opportunities to address members of your target audience as a guest speaker or paid professional can build your credibility and attract recognition and customers. In addition, you will have the added weight of the sponsoring organization behind you.

Chapter Summary

Now that you have studied this chapter you can do the following:

1. Define integrated marketing.
   - Communications strategies, tactics, and other components should be integrated for maximum effectiveness.
   - Integrated communications can involve advertising, promotions, personal selling, database marketing, direct marketing, alternative marketing, e-active marketing, and public relations.
   - Your integrated communications should reinforce your brand and your unique selling proposition.
2. Conduct promotional planning and budgeting.
   - Promotional planning determines the best opportunities for quality and effective customer contact.
   - All parts of your organization should be involved.
   - Complete a promotions opportunity analysis to create a promotion strategy.
   - Establish communications objectives.
   - Create a promotional budget to accomplish the objectives.
3. Understand advertising and advertising management.
   - Advertising objectives include
     - Building brand and image
     - Providing information
     - Persuading
     - Stimulating action
     - Reinforcing a purchasing decision
   - Determine if and when to use an advertising agency or freelancer.
   - Take advantage of assistance from media companies, trade associations, and suppliers.
   - Decide which advertising will be institutional and which will be product advertising.
4. Identify and evaluate media options.
   - The customers' interests and benefits should be the focus of media decisions.
   - Develop a media strategy and schedule tied to an overall marketing strategy.
   - Work internally or with a media planner and buyer to assess your options based on an analysis of anticipated media effectiveness.
     - Broadcast media include television and radio.
     - Print media include newspapers, magazines, and directories.
     - Outdoor advertising primarily consists of billboards.
     - Internet advertising is a key part of e-active advertising.
   - Plan measurement into your media decisions.
   - Collateral materials should reinforce the company's competitive advantage.

5. Discuss sales promotion.
   - Encourage customers to buy more frequently through promotional tools.
   - It is best to use promotional tools for highly targeted, time-limited increases in response.
   - Advertising specialties will remind customers of your business or product.
   - Trade show exhibits can provide high engagement and impact.
   - Mall carts and kiosks may be effective for seasonal or start-up businesses or for product trials.
6. Explore alternative marketing options.
   - Guerilla marketing is unconventional, creative marketing that can get your message to your target market.
   - Buzz marketing gets the story of your business and/or products out through word of mouth.
   - Product placements and branded entertainment are more subtle ways to gain exposure.
   - Lifestyle marketing engages customers according to their needs, interests, desires, and values and takes into account their behaviors.
   - Samples and demonstrations, point-of-purchase materials, and shelf placement are forms of in-store marketing.
   - Other, often spur-of-the-moment and unexpected, media venues can also have an impact.
7. Analyze database and direct-response marketing opportunities.
   - Use databases to create highly targeted, customized communications.
   - Design and implement the data-collection plan to maximize value.
   - Code and analyze the data to extract information and target it.
   - Create communications based on the databases.
8. Incorporate e-active marketing.
   - Keep in mind that e-commerce options can increase sales.
   - Use interactive marketing to collect customers' information and then communicate with them via the Internet.
   - Include online advertising—typically banner ads—on Web pages to reach targeted customers.
   - Employ brand spiraling to integrate your offline and online branding strategies.
   - Maintain blogs as journals for public reading on the Internet.
   - Take advantage of opportunities through online social networks such as Facebook, MySpace, and BlackPlanet to create targeted messages.
   - Support consumer-generated advertising and media to fuel your promotional programs.
   - Explore the use of viral marketing campaigns to spread the word about a company, product, or service rapidly and effectively.
9. Describe when and how to use publicity and public relations.
   - Use press releases and pitch letters to generate publicity for your business.
   - Ensure that your pitch letter tells the reader why he or she should be interested in your business, product, service, or event.
   - Organize your press release to tell the who, what, when, where, why, and how of your story.
   - Build customer relations through special events, sponsorships, networking, and public speaking.

Key Terms

blog, 295

blogosphere, 295

brand spiraling, 294

buzz marketing, 289

cost per rating point (CPRP), 284

cost per thousand (CPM), 284

data mining, 292

e-active marketing, 293

edutainment, 290

frequency, 278

gross ratings points (GRP), 279

guerilla marketing, 289

institutional advertising, 277

lifetime value, 291

media buyer, 279

media planner, 279

media schedule, 278

media strategy, 278

mobile social networking, 295

opportunities to see (OTS), 279

pitch letter, 297

press release, 297

product advertising, 277

promotions opportunity
  analysis, 272

rating, 284

reach, 278

RFM analysis, 291

stealth marketing, 295

viral marketing, 296

Entrepreneurship Portfolio

Critical Thinking Exercises

9-1. Identify a well-known public figure and discuss his or her brand. How has this individual enhanced the brand? How has he or she damaged it?

9-2. Brainstorm five creative ways for a small business with a low budget to advertise and promote its products or services using the latest developments in communications and Internet technology.

9-3. Why does viral marketing have such success potential? How can a viral marketing campaign work against a company?

9-4. Word of mouth or "word of mouse"; which is more impactful in advertising?

Key Concept Questions

9-5. Name four common marketing objectives. Explain why they are important.

9-6. What are the types of communications budgets? What is the best method of budgeting?

9-7. Identify the parts of promotions opportunity analysis planning.

9-8. The examples provided in the Entrepreneurial Wisdom section of this chapter include several sites targeted to specific ethnic, demographic, or lifestyle groups. Select three of the Web sites listed there and answer the following:
   a. What types of marketing messages can you find on the site?
   b. How do the messages differ from one another?
   c. How are the messages the same?
   d. How might you use the information on these Web sites to assist in creating integrated marketing communications plans?

9-9. How can entrepreneurs stretch their advertising budgets? Name at least five ways.

9-10. What are some benefits of using marketing databases for small businesses?

Application Exercises

9-11. Answer the questions that follow and use them to write a press release for your business.
   a. What was your life like before you began to learn about entrepreneurship?
   b. Were you having any problems in school or at home?
   c. What have you learned about business that you did not know before?
   d. What is the best thing about running your own business? What obstacles have you had to overcome to get your business going?
   e. Has running your own business changed how you are doing in school? Has it changed how you get along with your family?
   f. Are you more involved in your community since you started your business?

g. How has your business changed your life? What would you be doing if you were not an entrepreneur?

h. If you could give one piece of advice to students who were thinking about starting a business, what would it be?

i. What are your goals for the future?

9-12. Use your press release to write a pitch letter for the opening of your business.

9-13. Create a chart like the one below to describe your marketing plan in detail. If you do not have a business concept, create a plan for a religious bookstore in a location that you specify. Include each media supplier, if possible, and delete the types that you are not expecting to use.

Company Name: _____

Media Type or Promotional Method	Name of Outlet(s) (list each separately)	Target Market	Budget ($)	Objective(s)
Newspaper				
Magazine				
Directory				
Television				
Radio				
Outdoor				
Internet				
Brochures				
Flyers				
Newsletters				
Business Cards				
Signs				
Sales Promos				
Advertising Specialties				
Trade Shows				
Carts/Kiosks				
Alternative Marketing				
Other Media				
Direct Response				

Exploring Your Community

9-14. Visit three independently owned businesses (not on the Internet) that are in the same industry. Identify the target market for each (demographic, geographic, psychographic, and behavioral). Note the various advertising and promotional methods in use at the business location. Search online for a company Web site. Ask the store owner or manager where they advertise and whether they create press releases. Report back on the results.

9-15. Obtain ad rates from two local radio stations, a local newspaper, and a cable television channel.

Media	Advertising Rates	Reach
Radio _____	_____	_____
Radio _____	_____	_____
Newspaper _____	_____	_____
Cable _____	_____	_____

Exploring Online

9-16. Select either your own company or an entrepreneurial venture that interests you. Find three similar businesses on the Internet and select the two best sites. What features make them attractive? Why did you think they were better than the third site? How would you distinguish your own site?

BizBuilder Business Plan Questions

After studying this chapter, you should be able to answer the following Business Plan Questions. The entire outline for the Business Plan is found in Appendix 2.

5.0 Marketing Strategy and Plan

5.3 *Promotion*

A. Identify the ways you plan to promote your product or service, including the message, the media, and the distribution channels. Describe why you have chosen these methods and why you think they will work. Include a table showing the methods and budgets.

B. Show examples of marketing materials you intend to use to sell.

C. What is your business slogan?

D. What is your business logo? How do you intend to protect it?

E. Where do you intend to advertise (be specific, including identifying reach and frequency)?

F. How do you plan to get publicity for your organization?

Dr. Farrah Gray: Young Millionaire, Entrepreneur, and Philanthropist

Dr. Farrah Gray
(© Everett Collection Inc./Alamy)

Most 6-year-olds have not begun to dream of entrepreneurship. Most 14-year-olds only dream about being millionaires. Most 21-year-olds are in the early stages of their work lives or in college. None of this was true for Dr. Farrah Gray.

At age 6, young Farrah (who was born in 1984) was selling products door-to-door from his home on the South Side of Chicago, one of the toughest areas of the city. He was a self-made millionaire by age 14. He received an honorary doctorate at the age of 21.

Gray is a master of promotion, inspiration, and entrepreneurship. He achieved more before the age of 30 than most people do in their entire lives. The National Urban League named him one of the most influential black men in America. He has been a syndicated columnist, writing for the National Newspaper Publishers Association, reaching 15 million readers in 200 weekly newspapers. He serves as an AOL money coach and has been featured on the Dream Team of Financial Experts in *O, The Oprah Magazine*. He is a professional speaker on topics that include financial management, creativity, personal development, and leadership. He has been many times in print and on broadcast media.

Dr. Gray has created numerous business ventures, fulfilling his dream of becoming a 21st-century CEO. These include a mail-box franchise, prepaid phone cards, an interactive teen talk show, and Farr-Out Foods. As a 12-year-old, he was the inspirational cohost of Las Vegas-based *Backstage Live*, which was simulcast to 12 million people weekly. He is the author of three books—*Reallionaire: Nine Steps to Becoming Rich from the Inside Out*; *Get Real, Get Rich: Conquer the 7 Myths Blocking You from Success*; and *The Truth Shall Make You Rich*—and is the CEO of Farrah Gray Publishing. Most recently he partnered with rapper Flavor Flav in creating Flavor Flav's House of Flavor Take Out Restaurant in Las Vegas.

While enjoying this spectacular success, Dr. Gray's commitment to philanthropy also emerged early and continues to flourish. When he was 8, he cofounded the Urban Neighborhood Enterprise Economic Club (U.N.E.E.C.) on Chicago's South Side. He later created New Early Entrepreneur Wonders (NEEW) Student Venture Fund to engage and encourage at-risk young people to find legal sources of entrepreneurial income. This was followed by the establishment of the Farrah Gray Foundation, which supports scholarships for students at historically black colleges and universities (HBCUs) and promotes youth entrepreneurship. He is a spokesman for the National Marrow Donor Program and the National Coalition for the Homeless.

Dr. Farrah Gray is an extraordinary example of a successful young entrepreneur and philanthropist.

Case Study Analysis

9-17. Clearly, Farrah Gray is a master of integrated promotion. List the promotional methods he has used and why he may have selected each.

9-18. What is the most interesting part of his story for you? Why?

9-19. The Farrah Gray Foundation serves as a vital part of Gray's activities. Explain how it is important.

9-20. If you were going to meet with Farrah Gray, what would you want to discuss and why?

Case Source

Farrah Gray, accessed August 3, 2013, http:// www.farrahgray.com.

decide to import products or components to take advantage of the cost and/or quality factors discussed previously.

Because of intense price competition at the global level, you may have to import to remain competitive. Domestic costs may just be too high for business success in markets in which price outweighs other factors for customer advantage, making the import of less costly components, agricultural products, or finished goods a necessity. Whereas companies like Nicole Miller Ltd. may be able to continue production in New York City, many firms in the fashion industry have switched to importing goods, largely for cost reasons. Importing requires specific skills and knowledge to achieve planned quality levels and cost savings, so you may have to make considerable changes in your business model to succeed. However, small firms can be nimble and may be able to take advantage of import opportunities and secure a significant advantage in the market. Also, if you design your organization to be a global business from the start, importing may be a core strategy and skill that will bring success.

Importing is a highly regulated, complex process that requires research, commitment, and cultural competency. Clearly, the Internet has made searching for some suppliers easier, but many will not have an Internet presence or may not have English-language skills. You may have to put forth considerable effort to meet people where they are, rather than where you would like them to be, in terms of readiness and interest. For example, you may know about a remote village in the Andes where amazing craftswomen create beautiful, marketable textiles that no one is importing to the United States. However, the route from their looms to your customers may be treacherous, both literally and figuratively. You will need to do your research and establish your target costs. You also must become intimately familiar with and sensitive to cultural and ethnic traditions, so that you can be effective in your interactions with foreign businesses and their people. A keen understanding of your rights and responsibilities with respect to importing laws and regulations, combined with the right relationship with intermediaries, is essential to importing success.

There is a well-developed system of trading through international brokers and dealers that will manage almost every aspect of the importing process, but ultimately the importing company must pull together all of the components. Foreign embassies, consulates, and the National Customs Brokers and Forwarders Association of America (http://www.ncbfaa.org) are good sources of information on importing options and the companies that can facilitate the process. Whether you find the supplier at a U.S. trade show or an international trade fair, online, through a sales representative or a friend, or while on a vacation or buying trip, you will need to determine the fit of the foreign business with your markets and its capacity to deliver products and/or services of consistent quality in a timely fashion at a stable, profitable price.

Exporting

One of the most traditional methods of entering the global marketplace is through **exporting**—the sale of domestically made goods or services to foreign customers. The U.S. government is committed to supporting the export of goods and services around the globe. Entrepreneurial ventures can enter international trade with relatively low risk and low cost. For most businesses, it is not necessary to locate abroad or even open a satellite office, so the capital and human-resource investments are minimized. For some companies that take advantage of technology, the incremental costs of exporting

exporting the sale of goods or services produced domestically to foreign customers.

Step into the Shoes . . .

Zildjian Company

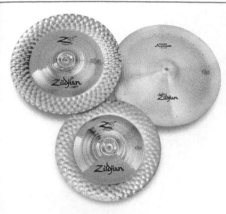

Rhythm Magazine/Getty images

Cymbals Heard Globally

The Avedis Zildjian Company Inc. is America's oldest family business, and its cymbals are familiar to musicians around the world. Founded in 1623 by Avedis Zildjian I in Istanbul, in the Ottoman Empire (present-day Turkey), the company has been recognized for the exceptional quality of its cymbals.

Zildjian is operated today by the fifteenth generation of family members from its location in Norwell, Massachusetts.

Avedis Zildjian III moved the company to the United States in 1929. The facility was relocated to its current space in 1973, on the 350th anniversary of the business. Today, his granddaughters, Craigie and Debbie Zildjian, manage the international brand and its museum.

Cymbals have had an evolving role in music around the world, and Zildjian has supplied musicians for over three centuries. For example, renowned nineteenth-century composers Hector Berlioz and Richard Wagner each requested that only Zildjian cymbals be used in performing their works. Family members still travel to exhibitions to spread the word about their company and the quality of their products.

Source: Zildjian, accessed August 6, 2013, http:www.zildjian.com/about/.

are primarily shipping and tariffs, so that they can profitably market abroad by charging higher prices to cover these expenses. If products, labeling, and packaging do not have to be modified, and if incremental costs can be covered, exporting can be a successful business strategy. **Exhibit 10-2** identifies some of the advantages and disadvantages of exporting.

Companies that are interested in exporting have many resources available for the exploration of their options, including World Trade Center

---

Exhibit 10-2 *Advantages and Disadvantages of Exporting*

Reasons to export (advantages) include:

- enhancing competitiveness,
- increasing sales and profits,
- gaining global market share,
- reducing dependence on existing markets,
- exploiting corporate technology and know-how,
- extending sales potential of existing products,
- stabilizing seasonal market fluctuations,
- enhancing potential for corporate expansion,
- selling excess production capacity, and
- gaining information about foreign competition.

A business may be required to (disadvantages):

- subordinate short-term profits to long-term gains,
- hire staff to launch the export expansion,
- modify products or packaging,
- develop new promotional material,
- incur added administrative costs,
- dedicate personnel for traveling,
- wait longer for payment,
- apply for additional financing, and
- obtain special export licenses.

Source: U.S. Small Business Administration, *Breaking into the Trade Game: A Small Business Guide to Exporting,* 4th ed., 2008.

affiliates, international trade-lead services, trade intermediaries, and trade missions. These can provide assistance tailored for exporters in their localities. International trade leads for potential exporters and importers consist of searchable international opportunities, company directories, electronic marketplaces, and the like. These lead sources may either be free or require paid membership. They may focus on a particular country or region—such as TradeIndia or Australia on Display—or they could be global in scope, such as the International Business Forum, Bidmix.com, or the World Bank FundLine. The Federation of International Trade Associations (http://www.fita.org) and the U.S. Commerce Service (http://www .export.gov) can provide extensive lead information.

Trade intermediaries serve as contract distributors of products between countries and have extensive trading networks and contacts. Such intermediaries simplify the exporting process so that the exporter can focus on making the product. They minimize the costs and risks of entry into world markets. **Exhibit 10-3** identifies several such intermediaries. Another excellent preliminary way to find global market opportunities is to participate in a **trade mission**, an international trip taken by government officials and businesspeople to promote exports or to attract investment. Such a mission might be sponsored by a state government (economic development office), trade group, federal agency, or foreign government. A trade mission will generally require that each participating business pay its own costs, plus a share of the overall mission costs.

trade intermediary organization that serves as a contract distributor of products traded between countries.

trade mission an international trip by government officials and businesspeople organized to promote exports or to attract investment.

U.S. companies that are successful exporters span a multitude of industries and come from across the nation. The Pampered Chef, Ltd., founded in 1980 by Doris Christopher with $3,000 borrowed against her husband's life insurance policy, markets in the United States, Canada, the United Kingdom, Germany, and Mexico through a direct sales force of over

Exhibit 10-3 *Selected Trade Intermediaries*	
Confirming House (Buying Agent)	These companies are agents of foreign firms that are paid a commission to locate U.S. products at the lowest possible price. They may include government agencies or quasi-governmental companies and can be involved in purchasing missions to the United States.
Export Agents, Merchants, or Remarketers	These commissioned sales representatives carry multiple noncompeting product lines for manufacturers in international markets. These agents operate under their own names and maintain their identities. They do not offer all of the services of EMCs (see below), including financial and advertising support. The export agent is most effective when you are not planning to establish your own export department, are entering a new foreign market, or are introducing a new product. You give up marketing and promotional control of your products and carry the risk that your future sales will be adversely affected.
Export Management Company (EMC)	It provides global sales expertise and serves as the exclusive export department for noncompeting companies, often in a particular industry or sector. Most operate on buy-and-sell agreements with domestic companies, so that small businesses can acquire a global presence and international exposure at relatively low cost and with limited resources. EMCs can work as your global marketing department with proven, established access to markets and in-depth knowledge of foreign trade. Expect to pay them on either a commission basis (approximately 15 percent on industrial goods and 10 percent on consumer goods) or via a discount on goods they buy from you.
Export Trading Company (ETC)	EMCs and ETCs are similar in their capacity to act as your global marketing department for the export of goods and services. They can take title to the products, as well. Some ETCs are operated by producers and may include competitors. The U.S. Office of Export Trading Company Affairs (OETCA) in the Department of Commerce promotes the creation and success of export intermediaries and issues them trade certificates of review.
Piggyback Marketing	Rather than entering a foreign market on your own, you may be able to work with another manufacturer or service company that will distribute your product or service. Such a situation can occur when a U.S. company needs to supply a variety of products and must secure them from multiple vendors.

Source: U.S. Department of Commerce, *A Basic Guide to Exporting,* 2012, accessed August 7, 2013, http://export.gov/basicguide/eg_main_017244.asp.

60,000 independent consultants and serves 12 million customers.[9] The Pampered Chef markets to customers through home parties that include demonstrations of some of the 300 or so high-quality kitchen tools offered in a cooking-show format that is tailored to individual locations.

Numerous small business exporters are recognized by the U.S. Small Business Administration, and in business and trade publications. A sampling of such recognition is exemplified by the 2013 *Commercial News USA* Exporter of the Year awardees, which are shown in **Exhibit 10-4**.

It is worthwhile to note that exports need not be limited to products or agricultural goods. Exports also include services that can be provided to customers abroad. As shown in **Exhibit 10-5**, the types of services demanded have expanded from traditional service exports to include technical and business expertise.

Exporting may well present excellent potential for entrepreneurs, but it also has significant challenges and costs. Finding the right trading partners;

Exhibit 10-4 *Exporters of the Year, 2013*

Company Name	Location	Brief Description
Bay Ru LLC	Chicago, IL	Online store sells goods from the United States to Russian consumers.
Complete Inspection Systems Inc.	Indiatlantic, FL	Creates custom solutions for packaging, medical device, and pharmaceutical industries.
Defibtech LLC	Guilford, CT	Manufactures Automated External Defibrillators.
Diesel Specialists LLC	Baton Rouge, LA	Sells Caterpillar, Cummins, Detroit Diesel, and Perkins parts and engines.
Fluidmesh Networks Inc.	Buffalo Grove, IL	Sells wireless systems for security, industrial, and mission-critical applications.
FoodTools Inc.	Santa Barbara, CA	Focuses on advancements in the food portioning industry.
GAME Equipment LLC	Napoleonville, LA	Specializes in tractors, sugar cane planters, vegetable sprayers, and other types of agricultural equipment.
KMI Group Inc.	Newport Beach, CA	Global manufacturer and distributor of plastic resins for molders, extruders, compounders, and manufacturers serving almost every major industry.
Neo-Turf Systems Inc.	Dalton, GA	Designs and manufactures durable turf for landscape and sport turf applications.
Phoenix Process Equipment Company	Louisville, KY	Serves the aggregate mining, municipal, industrial, and water-recycling industries through liquid/solids separation, residuals dewatering, and water reuse technologies.
Physicians Care Alliance LLC (PCA SKIN)	Scottsdale, AZ	Develops professional medical-care products that are sold in more than 70 countries.
Red Devil Inc.	Tulsa, OK	Produces several types of glass cutters.
Viking Spas Inc.	Wyoming, MI	Manufactures portable spas made exclusively in the United States.

Source: "The 2013 Exporter of the Year Awards," *Commercial News USA,* accessed August 6, 2013, http://www.thinkglobal.us/ exporteroftheyear.

---

[9]The Pampered Chef, Ltd., accessed August 5, 2013, http://www.pamperedchef.com.

Exhibit 10-5 *Service Exports*

Most Common Service Exports	More Recent Service Exports Demanded
Travel	Business, Technical, and Accounting
Transportation	Advertising
Financial	Engineering
Entertainment	Franchising
Health Care	Consulting
Telecommunications	Public Relations
	Testing
	Training

Source: U.S. Small Business Administration, *Breaking into the Trade Game: A Small Business Guide to Exporting,* 4th ed., 2008.

Exhibit 10-6 *Exporting Costs: Above and Beyond Material and Labor*

Export Packaging	Bunker Surcharge	Bank Collection
Container Loading	Courier Mail	Cargo Insurance
Inland Freight	Tariffs	Telex
Truck/Rail Unloading	Forwarding	Demurrage
Wharfage	Export Documentation	Import Duties
Handling	Consular Legalization	Ocean Freight
Terminal Charges	Bank Documentation	Dispatch

Source: U.S. Small Business Administration, *Breaking into the Trade Game: A Small Business Guide to Exporting,* 4th ed., 2008.

overcoming information, language, cultural, financial, and governmental barriers; and coping with volatile political and economic conditions require persistence and research. Grasping the complex cost structures to determine profitable pricing means considering a multitude of variables that are unique to international markets. **Exhibit 10-6** identifies a number of exporting costs above and beyond labor and materials. In addition, the requisite product changes and disclosures that involve financial costs and loss of intellectual property advantages may be obstacles to address. The good news is that many small businesses have found success through exporting. According to the SBA, "70% of all U.S. exporters have 20 or fewer employees."[10]

You too can succeed as an exporter with excellent planning and superior execution.

Strategic Alliances

Perhaps a strategic alliance involving two or more firms, in which each partner provides a particular set of skills or resources, is the best way for an entrepreneur to reach the global market. Such alliances may be technology-based, production-based, or distribution-based. International strategic alliances involve partners from at least two countries, one of which is a local partner in the targeted geographic location—for example, the various alliances formed by domestic and foreign airlines, such as the Star Alliance, established in 1997 as the first of its kind. With 28 members, including U.S. Airways, Lufthansa, Singapore Airlines, South African

---

[10]U.S. Small Business Administration, accessed August 5, 2013, http://www.sba.gov/services/.

Digital Vision/Thinkstock

royalties fees paid to a licensor by a licensee based on the production or sales of a licensed product.

Airways, and THAI, Star Alliance permits each to have more efficient in-country transit. By combining the foreign company's language, cultural, sociopolitical, and market knowledge with the capacity and skills of other alliance partners, all companies can reduce their risks and improve their potential rewards. The shared risks and rewards foster greater collaboration and trust than is normally achieved in a conventional supplier-customer relationship, thereby creating increased opportunities for success.

International Licensing

When importing and exporting are not viable options, international licensing may create a valuable revenue stream by selling the rights to use patents, copyrights, trademarks, products, processes, or technology. Licensing is a way to secure rights to a product or process that you want to develop and market domestically. Or, on the other hand, you can grant a license (as the licensor) to a foreign company (the licensee) and earn royalties. **Royalties** are fees paid to a licensor by a licensee based on production or sales of the licensed product. An example of international licensing is Peter Paul Mounds and Almond Joy candy bars, which are brand names owned by Cadbury Schweppes, a British food and beverage company, but are manufactured and marketed in the United States by Hershey Foods. Disney and Coca-Cola products are licensed globally.

If you own intellectual property, proprietary products, specialized technology, or substantial brand recognition, international licensing may be a good fit. There may be greater potential value in licensing technology or intellectual property than in exporting or direct foreign investment, especially when the competitive nature of the international market is unfavorable or unfamiliar. With foreign licensing, market entry is faster, simpler, and less costly. Also, where import quotas or tariffs might make

Global Impact . . .

Finding Foreign Partners

Large corporations often maintain foreign operations or have relocated because of lower costs or other market advantages. Changes in technology have made it easier than ever for small companies to benefit from such cost savings, too. UPS, FedEx, and others are all competing for your international shipping business. You can also ship larger products by boat. Ocean freight is slower but much less expensive.

The World Wide Web, electronic mail, and teleconferencing have made the world smaller, so that entrepreneurs can find global opportunities. For example, locating an overseas manufacturing partner could turn your idea into a profitable business.

The following resources can help you find foreign partners:

1. The CIA's *World Factbook* at https://www.cia.gov/library/publications/the-world-factbook/ includes such information as
   • How much a particular country's average worker earns per year

   • How much education the citizens have
   • What languages are spoken
2. Locate foreign companies on foreign search engines. Find "International Search Engines," or "[your country of interest] Search Engines," to get connected.
3. Foreign countries have embassies in Washington, D.C., and consulates in the larger cities. They can be good starting points for making international business connections.

a market too restricted, a license can help to avoid both. Licensing can also reduce transportation costs and avoid restrictive laws and practices. Cosmederm Technologies Inc. (http://www.cosmederm.com), a California company, has secured worldwide patent and trademark protection for its COSMEDERM-7 and Cosmederm products for dermatologists and other skin care industry providers; it is working with Britain's pharmalicensing.com to access foreign markets.

wendy connett/Alamy

Licensing is a relatively straightforward way to enter global markets, although, as with any contractual relationship, the licensing agreement must be carefully constructed. If licensing requires disclosure of too much proprietary product or competitive information, the licensee may act in bad faith and become a competitor. Another risk is that of the licensee not producing to company standards or otherwise damaging the brand.

International Franchising

As noted in Chapter 2, international franchising can be an excellent option for those who want to become franchisors or franchisees. Established franchisors have been making franchises available internationally for over 30 years, to the point where it is a major American export industry, typically by country or region. Usually, some legal relationship with local owners is required, and the laws vary widely from place to place. As domestic markets become cluttered, with limited room for growth, international franchising presents an opportunity to increase sales and profits for U.S. franchise operations.

International franchises vary with respect to consistency of products and services relative to the United States-based franchisor. Just as there are regional variations on the menus of domestic restaurant franchises, products and services may be adapted to suit customers in international markets. Foreign consumers may want to purchase food from McDonald's, but they expect to see traditional American fare along with products specifically created for their palates and in accordance with local custom. Franchisors often offer products and services that are identical with their flagship brand offerings, in addition to those tailored to consumers in a given market.

International Facilities

You may not want to establish a new venture or a franchise in an international location; rather, you may find significant value in creating a branch abroad for an existing business. Whether you establish such a facility to more efficiently and effectively serve customers in a specified geographic area or to produce goods or components more cost-effectively, international operations can present significant opportunities. For many entrepreneurial ventures, establishing a foreign sales office or production facility may be frustrating, too expensive, and overly complex. In countries with weak infrastructure or corrupt bureaucracies, the process can be difficult to navigate, even with assistance. At the same time, if you plan to grow in the global marketplace, locating a physical office or plant in a target market can be lucrative.

Step into the Shoes . . .

Signature Systems Europe, Ltd.

Arnon Rosan created Signature Fencing in the United States when he purchased SportPanel and Signature Panels from Tensar Poly Technologies in 1998. Five years later, the company became Signature Fence and Flooring, with the addition of portable flooring products. Over the following years, additional product lines and divisions were added. While initially serving the domestic market, the company began expanding into international ones.

In 2010, this New York-based company opened a sales and distribution facility in Darlington, England, to serve customers in Europe, the Middle East, and Asia. This facility is operated as Signature Systems Europe and is one of the divisions of the U.S.-based company. Products of the European division include: flooring, fencing, staging, temporary roadways, and turf-protection systems. Signature Systems Europe provided the 2012 London Olympics with temporary flooring and roadways, the largest project in the company's history.

Signature Systems has been sold twice since Arnon Rosan purchased the company, and he has remained at its helm. First, it was bought by a small, private equity firm, Dubin Clark & Company, in 2007. In 2013, it was purchased by a mid-market private equity firm, Linsalata Capital Partners. In the interim, Signature Systems has grown through acquisitions, in addition to exports. During 2008, the company acquired both Portable Dance Floors and American Turf & Carpet. Thus, Signature Systems has grown internally and through acquisitions to become a major international force.

Source: Signature Systems Group, accessed August 7, 2013, http://www.signaturesystemsgroup.com/history.php; http://www.signaturesystemsgroup.com/our-brands-by-division.php#SSE.

The initial impetus for locating a sales office or plant abroad is often cost savings. This can be because costs in the United States are prohibitive and those in the other country are significantly lower, or because an established international customer base warrants a sales office, distribution center, or production center close to the customers. Establishing such an operation should be a strategic decision, based on a realistic assessment of the costs and benefits of locating abroad. It is important to fully understand the business and political environment before moving forward, so that the full potential can be realized.

Challenges to International Trade

Learning Objective 3

Explore the challenges to international trade.

Entering and succeeding in international trade is not without its challenges, but overcoming those challenges can lead to global entrepreneurial success. Recognizing sources of potential difficulties and planning to meet and overcome them is the key to success. Global marketing has inherent risks from external factors—such as economic or political changes in individual countries—as well as the internal factors of organizational capacity. Successful global marketers are well informed about trade conditions and geopolitical affairs. They also make the internal preparations required to manage an international customer and/or supplier base.

Economic Risk

economic risk the possibility that changes in the economy of a country where it does business will cause financial or other harm.

When a company begins to trade outside its home country, it assumes **economic risk**, which is the possibility that changes in the economy of the country where it does business will cause financial or other harm. Factors such as the inflation rate, availability of financial resources, and the like can work in favor of a global company, or against it.

Prudent international entrepreneurs learn all that they can about the economy of the countries where they intend to do business and stay current with respect to changes where they are active. They also work with merchants and agents that can help to minimize economic risk, due to their knowledge and experience in the local markets. In addition, the

U.S. Export-Import Bank (Ex-Im Bank) provides information about the economic and political risks in a given country and has an export credit insurance program to protect against failure—for economic or commercial reasons—of repayment by foreign customers.

A particular risk facing global entrepreneurs is the foreign exchange rate (FX). The rate of exchange between any two currencies can shift favorably or unfavorably for one of the trading partners in the interval between ordering and payment, sometimes radically altering profitability. For a firm located abroad and operating in terms of the local currency, this can pose particularly serious problems. You can insulate imports or exports being affected by rate changes by trading in U.S. dollars and by using financing strategies known as *currency hedging*. By making the transaction in U.S. dollars, the business shifts exchange-rate risk to your trading partner.

Political Risk

As you might expect, there is also **political risk** inherent in global marketing, the possibility of a country's political instability reaching a breaking point or a government's new policies negatively impacting foreign companies doing business inside its borders. To minimize these risks, it is critical that you carefully assess the political environment of a potential host country and understand its laws and leadership. The relative stability of the government will largely define the political risk. While researching potential trade areas, it is critical to understand the overall sociopolitical environment, as well as specific laws and regulations as they pertain to your business field. Aspects to evaluate include:

political risk the possibility of a country's political structure and policies impacting a foreign company transacting business in its geopolitical borders.

- The attitude of the government toward foreign companies/foreign investment, including direct investment. Is it welcome or unwelcome?
- The political structure of the host nation and its stability. Is the current leadership solidly entrenched or might a regime change be imminent?
- Anticipated reactions from the host government. How, if at all, will it support, challenge, or prevent your operations?
- Any potential points of conflict, or friction between the planned venture and the national interests of the host country. What are the potential problems?

Examples of political challenges would be for a country to ban all exchange of goods with the United States, the prohibition of direct foreign investment, or a government seizure of foreign assets. More subtle, but equally disastrous, would be regulations requiring a full disclosure of product information that stripped away the intellectual property protection enjoyed in the United States, thus revealing trade secrets.

Organizational Capacity

Any overseas marketing effort will always be more complex than operating in your home market. It will require a serious commitment of time and effort and could stretch organizational capacity to the limit. **Exhibit 10-7** shows specific issues to be considered during the decision to export that may apply to global marketing in general.

Effective communication will be critical to global marketing success. Communication with customers must be effective linguistically and culturally. In order to drive such contact successfully, internal teams must communicate well, often across languages and cultures. As a global competitor, you will have to be highly responsive to inquiries, so that prospective customers are not lost because of lack of diligence.

Exhibit 10-7 *Management Issues in the Decision to Export*

Management Objectives

- What are the company's reasons for pursuing export markets? Are they solid (e.g., increasing sales volume or developing a broader, more stable customer base) or are they frivolous (e.g., the owner wants an excuse to travel)?
- How committed is top management to an export effort? Is exporting viewed as a quick fix for a slump in domestic sales? Will the company neglect its export customers if domestic sales pick up?
- What are management's expectations for the export effort? How quickly does management expect export operations to become self-sustaining? What level of return on investment is expected from the export program?

Experience

- With what countries has business already been conducted, or from what countries have inquiries already been received?
- Which product lines are mentioned most often?
- Are any domestic customers buying the product for sale or shipment overseas? If so, to which countries?
- Is the trend of sales and inquiries up or down?
- Who are the main domestic and foreign competitors?
- What general and specific lessons have been learned from past export attempts or experiences?

Management and Personnel

- What in-house international expertise does the firm have (international sales experience, language capabilities, etc.)?
- Who will be responsible for the export department's organization and staff?
- How much senior management time should be allocated and could be allocated?
- What organizational structure is required to ensure that export sales are adequately serviced?
- Who will follow through after the planning is done?

Production Capacity

- How is the present capacity being used?
- Will filling export orders hurt domestic sales?
- What will be the cost of additional production?
- Are there fluctuations in the annual work load? When? Why?
- What minimum-order quantity is required?
- What would be required to design and package products specifically for export?

Financial Capacity

- What amount of capital can be committed to export production and marketing?
- What level of export-department operating costs can be supported?
- How are the initial expenses of export efforts to be allocated?
- What other new domestic development plans are in the works that may compete with export plans?
- By what date must an export effort pay for itself?

Source: "Management Issues Involved in the Export Decision," Export.gov, accessed August 6, 2013, http://export.gov/exportbasics/eg_main_017455.asp.

Cultural and linguistic dissimilarities between employees of different countries can be a source of inspiration and learning, as well as possible friction and miscues. Flexibility, tolerance, and acceptance become particularly important. Management approaches that are effective in a home market may be ineffective elsewhere, and hiring practices, compensation, hours, holidays, and benefits may be radically different.

In addition to human-capital stresses, financial-capital issues abound. Of particular concern is the financial impact of currency fluctuations and the company's capacity to manage them. Another set of concerns centers on the movement of funds out of foreign countries, and maintaining adequate cash flows. Organizational capacity may be strained because of financial requirements and constraints.

All areas of a small company will be tested by global expansion, so that the marketing, accounting, operations, and legal spheres are also affected. The marketing aspects—research and analysis, market adaptation, product modification, pricing, distribution channels, and promotion—will all demand attention. International accounting standards and practices vary widely, with any foreign operation needing to comply and integrate with that country's standards and practices. Even for businesses that export or import, addressing currency conversion can be problematic. Operating issues include the ability to understand and interpret international rules and regulations and to successfully implement production and distribution. Finally, global marketing exponentially increases the legal issues facing the business, including customs, tariffs, and taxes domestically, and intellectual property, local laws and regulations, and trade barriers abroad.

Global marketing may test the limits of any entrepreneurial venture. However, entrepreneurs need not go it alone. There are numerous free and fee-based services to supplement their internal capacity. For many, going global can be a key to success.

Legal and Regulatory Barriers

The number of laws and regulations facing global marketers eclipses that of purely domestic companies, because each country or region has its own unique set of laws and regulations. Barriers to trade include tariffs, quotas, embargoes, and dumping, as well as political and business barriers. Understanding and navigating these obstructions can be a significant challenge for many small companies.

Tariffs

Governments impose **tariffs**, which are taxes or duties on goods and services imported into a country, thereby increasing the cost of the imports to consumers. Tariffs are intended as *protectionist* measures, to weaken competition for comparable domestic products and services. The United States imposes tariffs on thousands of goods, and U.S. Immigration and Customs Enforcement is responsible for implementing more than 400 statutes and has personnel in 47 offices overseas.[11] When importing, you will need to include tariffs in your cost calculations. When exploring export markets, remember to account for any tariffs levied by those countries to determine your potential price competitiveness.

tariffs taxes or duties on goods and services imported into a country.

Quotas

As an alternative to tariffs, some countries create limits on the amounts of specific products (such as cheese or wine or automobiles) that can be imported. Such limits, called **quotas**, effectively ration imported goods and thus protect domestic producers from foreign competition. Countries may impose and lift quotas at will, and it is critical for small firms to be mindful of changes.

quotas limits created by countries on the amounts of products that can be imported.

---

[11]United States Immigration and Customs Enforcement, accessed August 5, 2013, http://www.ice.gov/about/overview.

Embargoes

embargo the total prohibition on imports of all or specific products from one or more nations.

Taken to the extreme, quotas become *embargoes*. An **embargo** is the total prohibition of specific products or of all imports from a particular nation. Embargoes may have purposes above and beyond economic ones, such as political, health, environmental, or other motives. Political embargoes are commonly used by the United States government to express dissatisfaction with the political policies of other nations. Health reasons for embargoes may include restricting agricultural imports to prevent the spread of disease. The United States has placed embargoes on all goods from Cuba and North Korea, among other countries, for political reasons, and has banned imports of certain produce, plants, and animals for health reasons.

Dumping

dumping when companies price products below cost and sell large quantities in foreign markets.

Some companies price products below cost and then sell large quantities in foreign markets through a process called **dumping**. Domestic firms can be harmed because their prices are undercut. As a protectionist measure, many countries have enacted antidumping laws. In the United States, such a statute is the U.S. Antidumping Act. Companies that file complaints under this law must prove that they suffered direct harm and that the prices being charged in the United States are lower than those in the dumping company's home country.

In addition to the previously mentioned rules, countries have various regulations regarding such things as labeling, packaging, and certification. For example, France requires GMO-free certification, warranting that a food product is free from genetically modified ingredients. Ingredient disclosures and nutrition information on foods will vary radically from country to country. Product warnings and other information will also be different. All of these factors should be researched, assessed, addressed, and taken into account to avoid costly errors.

© JJM Stock Photography/Alamy

Cultural and Ethnic Considerations

Much has been written about the importance of understanding the cultural norms in global markets and adapting to them in order to successfully conduct international trade. The values, perspectives, beliefs, and norms shared by a group of people constitute its *culture*.

What is an acceptable business practice in one country can be considered rude and inappropriate in another. For example, the Japanese have a different sense of personal distance from that of Americans; some Americans may feel uncomfortable when Japanese colleagues seem to invade their personal space. By the same token, in many countries, including Japan, business is transacted through personal relationships first, often with the bulk of interaction time spent on seemingly irrelevant social chatter. In other cultures, the business interaction is a more formal process, with protocols for exchanging business cards, greeting one another appropriately, and only then discussing business.

Business considerations also extend to marketing promotions, quality expectations, and the importance of personal relationships. Marketing approaches that work in the United States may be ineffective or even offensive elsewhere, so that it is important to work with experienced, successful marketers when exporting. Also, your Web site may need to be available in multiple languages and be translated not just literally, but with any necessary idiomatic adjustments. Each culture also has its standards for personal relationships and face-to-face meetings. Whether you can rely on telephone and electronic media or will have to meet personally will depend on the culture. You should be aware of the protocol around hierarchy as well, so that you do not offend a customer or supplier by having someone they perceive to be of lesser rank working with them. Finally, expectations of quality need to be made clear so that no misunderstanding has been caused through faulty communications.

Becoming sensitive to cultural norms and being careful to avoid violating them is important for engaging in international trade. A good way to guarantee failure is to ignore cultural customs. The path to success includes understanding and honoring the background of those with whom you do business.

Support for Global Ventures

Entering the global marketplace is not for the faint of heart, but it also doesn't have to be a solo expedition.

There are a wide variety of resources available to support entrepreneurial ventures with global interests. Services include

◀ **Learning Objective 4**
Learn about the types of support that are available for global ventures.

- readiness assessment,
- market research, analysis, and planning,
- consulting/counseling,
- training and education programs,
- publications,
- databases,
- trade missions,
- trade shows,
- partner search, and
- financing.

Resources are offered both online and in person through a range of federal, state, and local agencies, as well as trade associations and other not-for-profits, and commercial organizations.

Market Research, Analysis, Planning, and Readiness

As with any business start-up or expansion, market analysis, readiness assessment, and planning are critical steps to entering worldwide markets. Of particular concern to small firms preparing to go global is finding the right markets and creating a marketing plan. Numerous organizations and agencies will help with finding existing data on markets, laws, and regulations. Some information sources are listed in **Exhibit 10-8**, and others are distributed throughout this chapter.

Before entering a market at all, you should either rely on the expertise of the trade intermediary that you have carefully identified and researched, visit the country in question, or both. If you cannot make a personal visit, learn as much as you can from both official and unofficial sources—such as from Americans who currently do business in the country—as well as directly from its citizens. Also, keep up with markets through publications such as

---

Exhibit 10-8 *Information Resources for International Trade*

United States Department of Commerce

- International Trade Administration (ITA): advice and information.
- Export portal (http://www.export.gov): information about federal export programs, services and staff.
- United States and Foreign Commercial Services (US&FCS or the Commercial Service)—trade specialists available through e-mail in 69 cities with Export Assistance centers, and in 70 countries:
  - access through export assistance centers or at http://www.buyusa.gov;
  - specialists organized by industry;
  - information regarding foreign markets, agent/distributor services, and trade leads;
  - counseling on business opportunities, trade barriers, and overseas prospects.

Small Business Development Centers and SCORE

- Services are supported by the U.S. Small Business Administration (SBDCs) and state, local, and private resources, and are affiliated with colleges and universities.
- Counseling, training, and research assistance.
- Programs on international business development.

United States Export Assistance Centers (USEACs)

- Designed as a single point of contact to exporters for federal export promotion and finance programs.
- Readiness-assessment services.
- Referral to how-to-export programs.
- Market-entry programs:
  - Industry and country profiles,
  - Help with finding distributors,
  - Identifying tariffs and regulatory requirements,
  - Assistance with financing, and
  - How to get paid.

District Export Councils (DECs)

- Sponsored by ITA, with 51 councils and 1,800 volunteers.
- Volunteers assist small businesses in entering the global marketplace.
- Often found through local Commercial Service or Export Assistance Centers.

Source: U.S. Small Business Administration, *Breaking into the Trade Game: A Small Business Guide to Exporting,* 4th ed., 2008.

International Trade Update (http://trade.gov/publications/ita-newsletter/index .asp) and *International Trade Forum* (http://www.tradeforum.org).

Some organizations that assist small businesses also provide readiness-assessment services. These sources of assistance can help you determine what you need to do to be prepared for global marketing. For example, you may have a product that is viable from a market perspective, but you may need to address packaging and compliance issues before exporting it. By assessing readiness, you can avoid costly mistakes and position your company for international success.

Customer and Partner Identification and Relationship Building

Once target markets are identified through the market-analysis and planning process, specific leads need to be generated, customer contacts initiated, and customer relationships built. The number of Web sites that

Exhibit 10-9	*Selected No-Fee International Trade-Lead Web Sites*	
Name of Service	**Web Site URL**	**Description**
B2B Manufactures	http://www.manufacture.com.tw	Trade lead listings for Taiwan and China.
eMarket Services	http://www.emarketservices.com	Not-for-profit project funded by the trade promotion organizations of Australia, Denmark, Holland, Iceland, Italy, New Zealand, Norway, Portugal, Spain, and Sweden.
FITA/Alibaba Marketplace	http://www.fita.alibaba.com	Partnership between FITA and Alibaba.com featuring exporters from China.
Foreign Trade Online	http://www.foreign-trade.com	Trade leads and other resources.
Global Trade and Technology Network	http://www.usgtn.net	GTN is a U.S. Agency for International Development (USAID)-sponsored/U.S. Department of Commerce-sponsored marketplace for the transfer of technology and services.
Importers.com	http://www.importers.com	Trade-lead listings.
U.S. Commercial Service	http://export.gov	Trade leads and international market reports of U.S. exporters in selected industries.
United Nations World Trade Point Federation ETO System	http://www.tradepoint.org	Trade leads from the World Trade Point Federation.
USDA Foreign Agricultural Services	http://www.fas.usda.gov/agx/	Trade leads for import and export with the U.S. agricultural trade information.

are designed to assist in identifying trade leads is large and growing. The Federation of International Trade Associations' list of no-fee (free) sites alone contains 89 names. A selection of free Web sources from that list appears in **Exhibit 10-9**. These organizations offer leads for importers and exporters, with some geared toward specific regions or nations. In addition to the free leads, fee-based services are available to develop leads for you.

In addition to the lead sources, the various providers of counseling and assistance can offer contacts, and you can pursue your own networking to identify prospective customers and/or partners. As noted previously, trade missions put together by governmental and nongovernmental organizations also offer opportunities for travel to countries of interest, to explore international options. Plus, trade intermediaries can handle much of the initial marketing and communications for you and will work with their networks of contacts.

Once you establish these relationships, it will need to be a high priority for you to maintain and grow them. It will be much more difficult to sustain a relationship with a firm that is literally halfway around the world than with one that is a mile away. You can work with the advisors and build a network with other global marketers to establish a plan for supporting customer relationships.

Financing

For many small businesses, a significant barrier to global marketing is not being able to access financial resources. The usual sources of business financing, including customer-based, are not available for exporting and other international trade endeavors. However, commercial banks, alone or in cooperation with the U.S. Small Business Administration, as well as the Export-Import Bank and trade intermediaries, have financing products available to support international trade. These forms of assistance include letters of credit, export loan programs, and international trade loans. **Figure 10-2** provides an overview of the payment

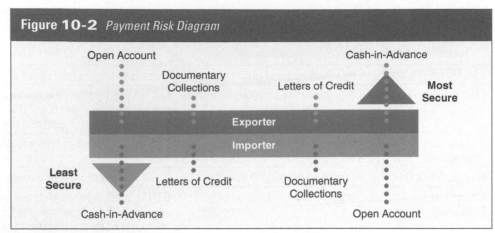

Figure 10-2 *Payment Risk Diagram*

Open Account — Documentary Collections — Letters of Credit — Cash-in-Advance — **Most Secure**

Exporter

Importer

Least Secure — Cash-in-Advance — Letters of Credit — Documentary Collections — Open Account

Source: U.S. Department of International Trade Administration, Trade Finance Guide 2008, accessed August 24, 2010, http://www.export.gov.

risk associated with various financing options from the importer and exporter perspectives.

Letters of Credit

letter of credit a financing instrument that is usually issued by a bank on behalf of a customer that promises to pay a certain amount of money once specific conditions are met.

A commercial **letter of credit** is a financing instrument that is issued by (usually) a bank on behalf of a customer and serves as a promise to pay a certain sum of money once specific conditions are met. It is used for financing the movement of goods internationally. The letter of credit adds the reputation and resources of the financial institution to that of the customer. Letters of credit are only as good as the bank that issues them.

Each letter of credit is customized for the particular circumstances and is valid for a single transaction. Such letters are particularly valuable for exporters because they know that they will be paid, as long as the letter-of-credit terms are met.

A *standby* letter of credit provides credit from the issuing bank for a transaction not involving the movement of goods. Standby letters of credit are irrevocable once issued, making it much like a bank guaranty.

Working Capital Loan Program (EWCP)

The EWCP is a loan-guaranty program offered to commercial banks by the SBA to encourage lending to businesses that generate export sales and need working capital.[12] Banks can make loans of up to $2 million for working-capital purposes to companies exporting goods from the United States, and the SBA will provide a 90-percent guaranty as a credit enhancement, up to $1.5 million. It has the same 90-percent guaranty for amounts over $1.5 million through a co-guaranty program with the Export-Import Bank of the United States. Loans are typically made for 12 months, and interest rates are set by the lenders. EWCP borrowers must have been in business for a minimum of one year (waivers are possible) and meet SBA eligibility and size

[12]U.S. Small Business Administration, accessed August 5, 2013, http://www.sba.gov.

requirements. There is not a content requirement from the government, but exports must be shipped and titled from the United States. Shipments to embargoed nations are excluded. Collateral requirements include the receivable generated by the sale and the export-related inventory. EWCP loans can be reissued annually.

Export Express Loan Program

In this SBA guaranty program, lenders use their own credit underwriting and documentation and receive expedited review and response (24 hours or fewer) from the SBA. The program is for loans and lines of credit up to $250,000 that are available for "manufacturers, wholesalers, export trading companies and service exporters."[13] Lenders obtain an 85-percent guaranty for loans of up to $150,000, and loans from $150,000 to $250,000 get a 75-percent guaranty. Interest rates are set by the lenders, as are collateral requirements. Loans are set with differing maturities, depending upon their purposes. The SBA Web site's list of permitted export development activities includes

- standby letters of credit,
- foreign trade-show participation,
- translation of marketing materials,
- general lines of credit,
- transaction-specific needs for export orders, and
- real estate and equipment to produce exports.

Export Express loans come with technical assistance for exporters from the SBA's Export Assistance Centers and other agency resources, such as Small Business Development Centers (SBDCs) and the Service Corps of Retired Executives (SCORE).

International Trade Loans

The International Trade Loan program from the SBA is for exporters and for companies that have been adversely affected by imports; it is intended to improve the borrower's competitive position. The program operates through SBA lenders and permits a higher SBA-guaranteed portion ($1.75 million versus $1.5 million) than with a regular "SBA 7(A)" loan. The maximum gross loan amount is $2 million, and the interest rate is determined by the lender. Collateral requirements for SBA International Trade Loans include a first-lien position or first mortgage on the property or equipment being financed, with additional collateral used to reach the full value of the loan, if possible. This loan is designed for financing long-term fixed assets, and working capital cannot be part of the loan. Maturities vary from 10 to 25 years.

Ex-Im Bank's Export Working Capital Guarantee Program

This program is designed to facilitate exports by providing pre-export financing through commercial lenders with a guarantee from the Export-Import Bank.[14] Exporters must have at least one year of operating history and a positive net worth and must be located in the United States. The goods to be exported must have a minimum of 50 percent U.S. content and must be shipped from the United States, and any services sold need to be performed by U.S.-based personnel. The Ex-Im Bank normally provides a

[13]Ibid.

[14]Export-Import Bank of the United States, accessed August 7, 2013, http://www.exim.gov/products/workingcapital/index.cfm.

90-percent guaranty and has no minimum or maximum amount, but the portion of the contract to be borrowed depends on the nature of the loan or the collateral offered. Loans are generally for one year but can extend up to three years. According to the Ex-Im Bank Web site,

Exporters may use the guaranteed financing to

- purchase finished products for export;
- pay for raw materials, equipment, supplies, labor and overhead to produce goods and/or provide services for export;
- cover standby letters of credit serving as bid bonds, performance bonds, or payment guarantees; and
- finance foreign receivables.

In addition, the Ex-Im Bank has short-term, multibuyer export-credit insurance, which U.S. exporters that have working capital loans can purchase at a discount.

Export Medium-Term Delegated Authority Program

This program provides guarantees to commercial banks for the foreign buyers of U.S. exports, to reduce the risks for U.S. banks and to allow U.S. companies to compete globally. Selected commercial banks can offer 180-day to five-year loans, with guarantees given without prior federal approval (as of 2009). These loans are made to foreign purchasers of U.S. capital goods, and the lender shares the risk with the Ex-Im Bank by retaining 10 percent of the risk. Transactions benefitting a small business exporter or supplier require lower commercial bank risk.[15]

Ex-Im Bank's Loan Guarantee

The Loan Guarantee program enhances export capacity by guaranteeing financing to creditworthy international buyers of U.S. exports and covers 100 percent of political and commercial risks, without limit to transaction size. The financing is primarily intended for the purchase of U.S. capital equipment and services, but can also be available for software and certain other fees and expenses of the business, as detailed by the Ex-Im Bank. The level of Ex-Im Bank support depends on the value of the goods or the portion of U.S. content, and the buyer must make a 15-percent cash payment to the exporter. Repayment terms are generally 5 to 10 years.

Trade Agreements Influence Global Marketing

Learning Objective 5

Describe regional trade agreements that influence global trade.

Many countries and regions have established trade agreements, laws, and tariffs that affect global trade. As noted previously, tariffs, quotas, and embargoes are various forms of trade barriers erected by individual countries. There are also trade agreements among and between countries that establish the rules of the game. Depending on where you want to trade, these agreements may have a direct impact on your international efforts. Even if you are not planning to become a global marketer, you may find that these and other agreements will affect your domestic competitive environment.

---

[15]Export-Import Bank of the United States, "Pennsylvania Small Business Is First to Benefit from Ex-Im Medium-Term Delegated Authority Program," March 6, 2009, accessed August 5, 2013, http://www.exim.gov/pressrelease.cfm/.

Regional Trade Agreements (RTAs) focus on removing barriers at the border by reducing tariffs to increase market access between signatory nations. RTAs are designed to facilitate trade on a regional basis, generally including tariff cutting and often including complex regulations regarding trade between participating countries. Among the more sophisticated RTAs, there are rules on competition, labor, investment, and the environment. A total of some 575 notifications of RTAs were received (as of July 31, 2013) with Regional Free Trade Agreements (RFTAs) and partial-scope agreements.[16] RFTAs go a step further by simplifying commercial regulations and reducing tariffs to zero (or very low levels) to eliminate trade barriers between them, without establishing a common trade policy for nonmembers. The WTO provides cautionary comments with respect to RTAs because such agreements are inherently discriminatory, and the ultimate net impact may not be positive. Of particular concern is the membership of countries in multiple RTAs. Descriptions of some of the most noteworthy RTAs follow.

Regional Trade Agreements (RTAs) are designed to facilitate trade on a regional basis, generally including tariff cutting and trade regulations between signatory nations.

Regional Free Trade Agreements (RFTAs) Regional Trade Agreements that simplify commercial regulations and bring tariffs toward zero for member states.

European Union (EU or EC)

The European Union (or European Community) is a political and economic confederation formed in 1993 that has addressed foreign and security policy, created a central bank, and adopted a common currency (the euro). The member nations of the EU are Austria, Belgium, Bulgaria, Croatia, Cyprus, Czech Republic, Denmark, Estonia, Finland, France, Germany, Greece, Hungary, Ireland, Italy, Latvia, Lithuania, Luxembourg, Malta, the Netherlands, Poland, Portugal, Romania, Slovakia, Slovenia, Spain, Sweden, and the United Kingdom.

European Free Trade Association (EFTA)

The European Free Trade Association was founded in 1960 with its stated premise as "free trade as a means of achieving growth and prosperity amongst its Member States as well as promoting closer economic cooperation between the Western European Countries."[17] The member states are Iceland, Liechtenstein, Norway, and Switzerland.

North American Free Trade Agreement (NAFTA)

The North American Free Trade Agreement is a trilateral accord established in 1994 to support free trade between Canada, Mexico, and the United States. This agreement created the world's largest free trade area. Much has been written and debated about the positive and negative impacts on labor costs, markets, and the like, and you may find that NAFTA directly or indirectly affects your competitive circumstances and opportunities.

Southern Common Market (Mercosur)

Mercosur, a regional association formed in 1991, has Argentina, Brazil, Paraguay (suspended in 2013), Uruguay, and Venezuela as members and permits free transit of goods and services between them, eliminating customs rights and nontariff transit restrictions and setting a common external tariff and trade policy regarding nonmember states.[18] Mercosur moved from free trade to a common market, which permits the free movement of labor and capital across borders.

[16]World Trade Organization, accessed August 5, 2013, http://www.wto.org/english/tratop_e/region_e/region_e.htm.

[17]European Free Trade Association, accessed August 5, 2013, http://www.efta.int.

[18]Guido Nejamkis and Ana Flor, "Mercosur Welcomes Venezuela, Suspends Paraguay," Reuters, June 29, 2012, accessed August 5, 2013, http://www.reuters.com/article/2012/06/30/us-mercosur-idUSBRE85S1JT20120630.

Association of Southeast Asian Nations (ASEAN) Free Trade Area (AFTA)

AFTA has member countries progressing in lowering intra-regional tariffs in accordance with the Common Effective Preferential Tariff (CEPT).[19] Most tariffs on CEPT products have been lowered to between zero and 5 percent, and the members have agreed to work on nontariff barriers. The member states are Brunei, Darussalam, Cambodia, Indonesia, Laos, Malaysia, Myanmar, the Philippines, Singapore, Thailand, and Vietnam.

Common Market of Eastern and Southern Africa (COMESA)

This agreement defines its role as "economic prosperity through regional integration."[20] COMESA's mission is to "endeavor to achieve sustainable economic and social progress in all member states through increased cooperation and integration in all fields of development particularly in trade, customs and monetary affairs, transport, communication and information technology, industry and energy, gender, agriculture, environment and natural resources."[21] The formation of a free trade area through the removal of tariff and nontariff barriers, including coordination of trade statistics, customs procedures, and management systems, was COMESA's first goal. A free trade area was established with 14 members. Formation of a Customs Union with a common external tariff was the first goal achieved. A full monetary union with a common currency and central bank is the next priority. The member states of COMESA are Burundi, Comoros, Democratic Republic of the Congo, Djibouti, Egypt, Eritrea, Ethiopia, Kenya, Libya, Madagascar, Malawi, Mauritius, Rwanda, Seychelles, Sudan, Swaziland, Uganda, Zambia, and Zimbabwe.

One topic in particular to analyze when considering global marketing is whether any U.S. trade agreement provides you with a competitive advantage or whether a country with which you want to trade is a member of an RTA. The Office of the U.S. Trade Representative, in the Executive Office of the President, has an online resource center (http://www.ustr.gov/countries-regions/) that will provide information on RTAs, including primary imports and exports and RFTA status. This analysis could dramatically alter your cost structure and present a greater opportunity for global marketing success.

BizFacts

Duties are assessed under many agreements, including

- North American Free Trade Agreement (NAFTA),
- Generalized System of Preferences (GSP),
- Caribbean Basin Initiative (CBI),
- Andean Trade Preference Act (ATPA),
- U.S.–Israel Free Trade Area Agreement,
- U.S.–Jordan Free Trade Area Agreement,
- Compact of the Free Association (FAS),
- African Growth and Opportunity Act (AGOA), and
- U.S. Caribbean Basin Trade Partnership Act (CBTPA).

---

[19]Association of Southeast Asian Nations, accessed August 5, 2013, http://www.asean.org.

[20]Common Market of Eastern and Southern Africa, accessed August 5, 2013, http://www.comesa.int.

[21]Ibid.

Chapter Summary

Now that you have studied this chapter you can do the following:

1. Understand the reasons to market globally.
   - Expanding market opportunities
   - Acquiring access to resources that are scarce or more competitive
   - Reducing materials, labor, and other costs
   - Taking advantage of resources specific to a location
2. Articulate the primary strategic options for global ventures.
   - Importing goods and services to the home market
   - Exporting goods and services to global markets
   - Creating and managing strategic alliances with global partners to improve performance
   - Licensing products and processes to attain the maximum benefits of intellectual property
   - Franchising on an international scale to increase business opportunities and enter new, profitable markets
   - Operating international facilities to supply regional customers or provide parts or inventory to other operations
3. Recognize the factors that challenge and impede global marketing.
   - Economic risk threatens financial stability and success.
   - Political risk poses threats to global ventures as regime changes, changes in laws, and cultural norms may have profound negative impact.
   - Organizational capacity for global marketing, in the form of human and financial capital, may limit success.
4. Explain the types of support available to global firms.
   - Assistance with market analysis and planning is offered to provide advantages in the global economy.
   - Customer relationship building is fostered through networks of support services.
   - Financing for exporting can be obtained through credit guarantees.
5. Describe regional trade agreements that influence global trade.
   - Regional Trade Agreements and Regional Free Trade Agreements are designed to facilitate trade between signatory nations.
   - The United States has agreements with many nations that facilitate trade.

Key Terms

dumping, 328
economic risk, 324
embargo, 328
exporting, 317
importing, 316
international outsourcing, 314
letter of credit, 332
offshoring, 314
political risk, 325

quota, 327
Regional Free Trade Agreement (RFTA), 335
Regional Trade Agreement (RTA), 335
royalties, 322
tariff, 327
trade intermediary, 319
trade mission, 319

Entrepreneurship Portfolio

Critical Thinking Exercises

10-1. How do trade agreements affect trade barriers? What can this mean to small business?

10-2. Why are cultural competency and sensitivity important for participants in the global marketplace?

10-3. How can emerging markets provide opportunities for entrepreneurial ventures? Threats?

10-4. What contributions can trade intermediaries make for small firms?

Key Concept Questions

10-5. Why is "going global" essential for businesses today? Illustrate with suitable examples.

10-6. Are there other ways of globalizing your business other than import and export? Illustrate with real-world examples.

10-7. Why do companies export their goods to foreign markets? Discuss the advantages and disadvantages of exporting in detail.

Application Exercise

10-8. Identify two ways that globalization may affect your business or a business with which you are familiar. What are the positive and negative aspects of each?

Exploring Online

10-9. At the U.S. Department of Commerce's export Web site (http://www.export.gov), find the Trade Events category and click on it. Using the menus and search tool, find trade missions and trade events in biotechnology or hotel/restaurant equipment that are scheduled over the next 12 months. Select one trade event and note its location and date. Indicate the price for registration and any special requirements. How would you decide whether this is a worthwhile event for a company?

10-10. Visit the *World Fact Book* (https://www.cia.gov/library/publications/the-world-factbook) and find a profile of one of the countries in Top 10 Emerging Markets. Identify two products or services to import from that country or to export to it, and answer the following:

   a. Why would these products or services be suited to this country?

   b. What steps would you take to import or export them?

   c. What sources of support might you access? Why?

   d. What challenges would you expect to encounter?

BizBuilder Business Plan Questions

After studying this chapter, you should be able to answer the following Business Plan Questions. The entire outline for the Business Plan is found in Appendix 2.

3.0 Company Description

1. Where will you physically operate the organization?
2. What is the geographic reach of the organization?

4.0 Opportunity Analysis and Research

4.2 Environmental Analysis

1. What external/environmental factors are likely to impact your business? How likely are they?
2. Are there customers for your business in other countries? How do you plan to reach them?

5.0 Marketing Strategy and Plan

5.4 Place

A. Where do you intend to sell your product? Describe the advantages and disadvantages of your location(s). If you have a specific site, provide detailed information about it.

Case Study | Luggage Concierge

Every year, millions of bags are mishandled by U.S. airline companies. Luggage Concierge alleviates this problem by shipping luggage to and/or from customers' travel destinations. Customers benefit from faster and easier airport check-ins, fewer worries about late or lost luggage, and the freedom from hauling their bags around. This is especially helpful when traveling with odd-shaped or oversized luggage, such as skis or golf bags.

Luggage Concierge's shipping service is initiated by visiting its Web site or calling its toll-free telephone number. The customer provides the addresses where the luggage is to be picked up and where it is going. The number of pieces, as well as their sizes and shapes, are also given. This information, the type of service (one-way or round trip), and the delivery speed determines the price.

Next, Luggage Concierge sends the customer a Welcome Packet with instructions and shipping labels. One of the company's Luggage Coordinators schedules pick-up times for the luggage and tracks the shipment to ensure proper arrival and return. To add to customers' peace of mind, complimentary insurance covering each bag's contents is included in the price.

Luggage Concierge has many strategic business partners, including credit card companies (such as MasterCard and American Express), resorts and hotels (such as Caesars Palace and Marston Hotels), cruise and travel businesses (such as Crystal Cruises and CouTour Travel), shipping companies (such as UPS and DHL), and more. For example, as part of the alliance with Crystal Cruises, Luggage Concierge provides a dedicated, 24/7 telephone line for passengers. Crystal's repeat customers also get a 20 percent discount on luggage shipments to and from the cruise ships.

When it formed an alliance with UPS International in 2009, Luggage Concierge was able to expand its shipping services to 220 worldwide destinations, more than any of its competitors. The "Wheels Up Customs Clearance" that this partnership provides allows Luggage Concierge's customers to have their luggage delivered to most countries within eight business days. Customers can also know where their luggage is at all times, thanks to real-time tracking capability.

Creatas/Thinkstock

Case Study Analysis

10-11. What reason to market globally (as noted in the chapter) does the Luggage Concierge and UPS alliance serve? Explain.

10-12. Luggage Concierge has created a number of strategic alliances with domestic and global partners.
   a. What is the rationale for Luggage Concierge's decision to create alliances rather than expanding on its own?
   b. Identify three of these partnerships and the value of global alliance for each party.

10-13. How do customers benefit from the alliance between UPS International and Luggage Concierge?

10-14. What are some of the challenges that Luggage Concierge would have likely faced in becoming a global marketer that UPS can handle?

Case Sources

"Cruise Travel: Take the LUG Out of Luggage," October 8, 2007, accessed August 6, 2013, http://cruisediva.blogspot.com/2007/10/cruise-travel-take-lug-out-of-luggage.html.

Luggage Concierge, accessed August 6, 2013, http://www.luggageconcierge.com.

"Luggage Shipping Companies Allow Travelers to Fly Light," August 1, 2007, accessed August 6, 2013, http://voices.yahoo.com/luggage-shipping-companies-allow-travelers-fly-473235.html.

Lourdes "Chingling" Tanco, MIDA Trade Ventures, Inc.

A Global Seafood Legacy

Chingling Tanco has traveled the world to bring success to her companies, MIDA Trade Ventures Inc. and MIDA Food Distributors Inc. Started in the Philippines, these sister companies are in the seafood trade business. MIDA Trade acts as the buying agent, whereas MIDA Food focuses on the distribution of frozen seafood at home and abroad.

MIDA Trade was the first company to export seafood from Indonesia to the United States. The strong, international business network that Chingling and her team have built over the past 20 years has helped to keep MIDA at the top of its industry. Many market segments are served, including restaurants, cafeterias, hotels, resorts, and even private households.

MIDA has offices across Southeast Asia—the Philippines, Indonesia, Vietnam, and Singapore. As many as 200 different kinds of seafood are stocked by MIDA Food, including a wide variety of fish, mollusks (clams, oysters, mussels, and scallops), crustaceans (shrimp, lobsters, and crabs), and cephalopods (squid, cuttlefish, and octopus).

MIDA Food also distributes value-added products, in which the seafood has been prepared in some manner. This category includes portioned entrees and appetizers, which are created in marinated, breaded, smoked, and sauced versions. In addition, MIDA has a division for canned seafood.

In the Beginning

Before she became an entrepreneur, Chingling earned an economics degree from Bryn Mawr College in Pennsylvania. After graduating, she worked for a business that traded feed and fertilizers in the United States and Asia. When that company was bought by ConAgra Foods in 1985, Chingling stayed on and became involved in shrimp trading. At that time, ConAgra owned Singleton Seafood, the largest shrimp processor in the United States. The following year, ConAgra sent Chingling to Indonesia to manage a joint-venture trading company.

In 1990, Chingling was reassigned to the Philippines. Very soon afterward, she decided to

MIDA distributes seafood internationally
(Jaimie Duplass/Shutterstock)

create her own company. MIDA Trade Ventures was founded to be a global buyer for ConAgra and Singleton Seafood. MIDA continued to grow, adding new clients in the United States as well as in Europe, Australia, and northern Asia.

In the late 1990s, an economic crisis caused seafood prices in the Philippines to skyrocket. Seafood stock was also becoming harder to find in the Philippines. Chingling found a way to turn those problems into an opportunity, by importing tuna from Indonesia and selling it directly to Filipino restaurants. The initial cargo sold fast, and MIDA Trade made a profit. As a result, Chingling launched MIDA Food Distributors in 1997, with its own trucks and cold-storage. MIDA Food was soon distributing frozen seafood to more than 1,000 local hotels and restaurants.

Today, MIDA Trade and MIDA Food continue to work as a successful team, supplying seafood to both local and international markets. Chingling's vision enabled her to turn her background knowledge and experience into an entrepreneurial success story.

Keys to Global Success

The MIDA companies pride themselves on being seafood specialists. With Chingling's leadership, the following strategies have helped create and maintain a thriving business.

Hire the Right People for the Job, and Train them Well. MIDA employs a multicultural group of people with degrees in many areas, including economics, custom brokerage, microbiology, industrial engineering, fisheries, food technology, and more. MIDA also provides on-the-job training and continuing education to ensure its employees excel at their positions. MIDA Food's staff has been certified by the Aquaculture Certification Council. The term *aquaculture* refers to the cultivation or farming of marine and fresh-water animals and plants.

Know Your Customers/Markets. MIDA recognizes that knowing its clients means understanding their laws and culture, as well as their product needs and expectations. MIDA staff travel extensively to develop and maintain customer relationships. This includes attending international trade shows and conferences to stay on top of market trends. MIDA is also a member of multiple professional seafood associations, and it subscribes to many seafood-related publications.

Provide High-Quality Products Consistently. Supplier assessment and quality control are two main areas to which MIDA pays a lot of attention. For example, MIDA buys only from seafood producers who can provide high-quality products in adequate volumes, maintain strict food-safety standards, and use ethical practices. A seller's financial stability and capacity to provide products in a timely and efficient manner are also important. MIDA freezes fresh seafood only in plants, which are certified for export to the United States, Japan, or Europe. Deliveries are made promptly, and products must be kept at a certain temperature.

Be Actively Responsible. MIDA regularly inspects processing plants to assess how well its suppliers are complying with environmental and social responsibilities. Environmental issues include proper water disposal, mangrove destruction/replanting, and sustainable aquaculture practices. Social responsibilities include preventing child labor and meeting minimum wage standards. In addition, Chingling serves on the Fisheries and Aquaculture Board of the Philippines.

Provide Excellent Service From Beginning to End. MIDA's customer service starts with supplier negotiations, in an effort to obtain the best prices and highest-quality products for its clients. MIDA also handles all logistical issues. This means monitoring customer deadlines, taking care of all contractual and shipment paperwork, following various countries' packaging and labeling requirements, using only reputable shipping companies, and overseeing the loading of all cargo. Customer service is concluded by confirming that the cargo has been received, with follow-up to ensure the customer was satisfied.

Case Study Analysis

10-15. How has Chingling used her education and prior work experience to support the success of MIDA?

10-16. MIDA is based in the Philippines, a country that is a member of a Regional Trade Agreement (RTA). Which RTA is it? How might this affect the business dealings of the company?

10-17. What are MIDA's marketing advantages?

Step into the Shoes . . .

Positively Outrageous Service

T. Scott Gross is a motivational speaker and management training consultant who has operated in both the entrepreneurial and corporate worlds. He was the national director of training for the Church's Chicken chain and became a Church's franchisee in 1985. Gross was fortunate to be able to use his earnings from speaking and consulting to keep the restaurant in business. He and his staff quickly learned that running the restaurant by the book simply was not sufficient. That led to the concept of Positively Outrageous Service (POS).

How much service is enough? How good does it need to be? For Gross and his team, it was not enough just to satisfy customers. Businesses should delight and astound them.[7] He describes POS as, "[T]he story you can't wait to tell . . . unexpected service delivered at random. . . . It is a memorable event and is so unusual that the customer is compelled to tell others."[8]

Gross tells the following story:

> In the borderline bizarre category is our now-famous drive-through wind-shield-washing service. It was my response to a suggestion by my brother, Steve, our manager, that we should do 'something outrageous.' Now, while a Church's employee wielding a spray bottle attacks their windshields, I handle the microphone and the other half of the fun: "Good afternoon. Thanks for choosing Church's. As soon as that tubby guy gets out from in front of your car, pull up to the window for the best lunch you've had all day. No, on second thought, when he gets in front of your car, pull on up!" If a woman customer jokes that we should clean the car's interior, too, I might say: "Oh, madam, we aren't going to do insides. But if you come through tomorrow, we're going to try our hand at hair styling, and on Saturday, we're going to take a shot at dentistry!" The result is almost always a customer who is laughing when he or she reaches the pickup window. Doing the unexpected for our customers has earned us a reputation as a fun place to do business, where you can count on getting treated well.[9]

T. Scott Gross

Positively Outrageous Service

- is random and unexpected: the element of surprise is part of its power;
- is out of proportion: it's an extravagant gesture that catches attention;
- involves the customer personally: it's an invitation to play that personalizes the service; and
- creates positive word of mouth: more powerful than advertising, POS generates its own buzz.[10]

Could providing Positively Outrageous Service fit into your business?

Use your self-control to stay polite, even when a customer is getting angry. Do your best to find a solution that will send him or her away satisfied and diffuse any lingering ill will. Your effort will protect your business and may even earn you a customer for life. Often, if you simply ask, "What will it take to make you a satisfied customer?" you will find that the customer will pause and suggest a reasonable solution to the situation.

Customer Complaints Are Valuable

You may not enjoy hearing a customer complain about your product or service, but a complaint is full of valuable information that probably no one else will tell you, and you do not have to pay for it! Listen closely to learn what your customers need and want:

- Always acknowledge complaints and criticism and deal with them. Never pretend that you did not hear a negative comment. If the customer *perceives* a problem, it *is* a problem.

---

[7] T. Scott Gross, *Positively Outrageous Service: How to Delight and Astound Your Customers and Win Them for Life*, 2nd ed., Chicago: Dearborn Trade Publishing, 2004, p. 5.

[8] Ibid.

[9] Gross, *Positively Outrageous Service*, p. 6.

[10] T. Scott Gross, accessed August 31, 2010, http://www.tscottgross.com.

interactions with customers to generate maximum customer satisfaction and optimal profitability. CRM is a purposeful program of guidelines to ensure excellence in customer service and relationship management. Carried out properly, the designed positive interactions will encourage repeat purchases and referrals. All of the sales and customer-service skills and best practices introduced in this chapter can be components of a CRM system. Implementation can be simple, such as methods for greeting and treating customers, to sophisticated, such as using state-of-the-art technology to provide highly targeted customer information and analytics.

CRM affirms that customer service is an aspect of marketing. Marketing brings a customer to your business, but it does not stop there. Once the customer is inside your door or you are speaking to him or her on the phone, the treatment should be consistent with your marketing. If your competitive advantage is speedy service, make sure your employees move quickly. If your advantage is a cozy, easygoing environment, make sure each customer is warmly welcomed and made to feel at home. Your customer service must reinforce your overall marketing plan. Through a well-designed and executed CRM system, you are reinforcing and building marketing effectiveness.

> **customer relationship management (CRM)** company-wide policies, practices, and processes that a business uses with its customers to generate maximum customer satisfaction and optimal profitability.

Why Does CRM Matter?

Customer relationship management can be the component of your business that makes it a sustainable entity. The costs of securing new customers are invariably significantly higher than the costs of keeping a repeat customer. According to the Customer Service Institute, 65 percent of a company's business comes from existing customers, and it costs five times as much to attract a new customer as it does to keep an existing one satisfied.[12] *Losing* a customer is even more expensive. TARP Worldwide's (Technical Assistance Research Programs Institute) recent word-of-mouth (WOM) survey found that

> 42% of consumers who hear about a positive product experience will buy that product for the first time and another 21% of those consumers will buy more. The effects of positive WOM mirror those of negative WOM as 42% of consumers who hear of a negative WOM stop buying that product and 14% buy less. However, consumers with negative experiences provide more detailed explanations through more channels than those who have positive experiences.[13]

When you know the purchasing patterns and interests of a customer, you can make informed decisions about the products, services, and promotional offers that will be of interest and result in additional sales. With CRM, you can focus on optimal interactions with customers during all types of transactions (i.e., purchases, returns, ordering, inquiries, and complaints), as well as building on and using data regarding customer behavior to foster positive transactions.

Because customer service is also a valuable source of market research, CRM supports market research for companies that employ it. Market research should not end once you open your business. Each customer can be a valuable source of information. Some easy ways to collect market research as part of your customer service for retail businesses include:

- Providing a short survey on a stamped postcard listing every item purchased, or directions to a Web site with a survey and reward printed on every receipt. Or include a survey at the point of purchase that can be redeemed for a discount on the next item bought.

---

[12]Customer Service Institute of America, accessed August 7, 2013, http://www.serviceinstitute.com/CCSM.htm.

[13]"Consumer Word of Mouth Changes Buying Habits 60% of the Time, TARP Worldwide Poll Finds: Men and Senior Citizens Most Likely to Complain," Press release. TARP Worldwide, February 12, 2008, accessed June 23, 2009, http://www.tarp.com/news_wom_poll.html.

- Asking selected customers to fill out a longer survey—again, offering a discount or prize drawing as an incentive.
- Always asking standard questions when completing a sale, such as "Do you have any suggestions on how we could improve our product?" or "Were you satisfied with the service you received today?" or "Were you able to find everything you wanted?"

Components of CRM for the Small Business

CRM has consistent components that may be incorporated across business types and sizes. It encompasses aspects of the marketing, sales, and service functions of a business to create positive customer experiences. **Exhibit 11-2** shows the Solution Map of CRM as described by SAP, the top seller of CRM systems. In the case of businesses that purchase highly sophisticated software, these components are part of the software solution, but for companies with less complex operations and fewer resources, many of these functions can be carried out without software applications beyond basic record keeping with simple databases, contact-management software, and industry-specific systems.

The SBA Web site (http://www.sba.gov) offers a perspective on customer service, and customer relationship management in general, relating it to the axiom inherent in the Golden Rule, "Do unto others as you would have them do unto you," and stating, "Companies of all sizes are realizing that their strongest selling point can sometimes boil down to treating customers as they would like to be treated—or better."[14] The message is getting through. According to John Goodman, president of TARP, "In the past few years, companies began to realize that service was really a competitive factor, and began to view it as an integral part of their product."[15] It is often in the area of service and CRM that a small business can outclass its larger competitors, so that customers may spend more to buy from them because of the service differential. The SBA offers three Golden Rules for small businesses with respect to CRM.

- Golden Rule 1: Put the customer first.
- Golden Rule 2: Stay close to your customers.
- Golden Rule 3: Pay attention to the details.

Exhibit 11-2 *SAP Solution Map for CRM*

Marketing	Sales	Service
Marketing Resource Management	Sales Planning and Forecasting	Service Sales and Marketing
Segmentation and List Management	Sales Performance Management	Service Contracts and Agreements
Campaign Management	Territory Management	Installations and Management
Real-Time Offer Management	Accounts and Contacts	Customer Service Support
Lead Management	Opportunity Management	Field Service Management
Loyalty Management	Quotation and Order Management	Returns and Depot Repair
Communication Promotion	Pricing and Contracts	Warranty and Claims Management
	Incentive and Commission Management	Service Logistics and Finance
	Time and Travel	Service Collaboration, Analytics, Optimization

Source: SAP Web site, http://www.sap.com/solutions/business-suite/CRM/businessmaps.epx, accessed June 20, 2009 (as submitted). SAP Solution Map for CRM courtesy of SAP AG.

---

[14]U.S. Small Business Administration Web site, accessed June 29, 2009, http://www.sba.gov.
[15]Ibid.

The SBA offers further advice on the components of customer care that they translate into five rules. These imperatives are part of the essential components of successful CRM.

1. ***Conduct your own survey.*** Profit from the ideas, suggestions, and complaints of your present and former customers. Talk and meet with your customers. Ask questions. Learn how they feel, what they want, and what they dislike.

2. ***Check employees' telephone manners periodically.*** This notion is particularly important for small businesses because bad telephone handling can undermine other constructive efforts to build a profitable enterprise.

3. ***Emphasize the importance of rules such as prompt answering and a cheerful attitude of helpfulness.*** Have someone whose voice is unfamiliar play the role of a customer or prospective customer, preferably a difficult one.

4. ***Make customer service a team effort.*** Use group meetings, memos, posters, and in-house publications to build customer consciousness throughout the organization. Continually drive home the crucial rule that getting and holding customers requires team play, and invite employees' suggestions.

5. ***Extend your efforts after hours.*** It's the friendly feelings people have that draw them to you and your business. Take advantage of the relaxed atmosphere of social occasions, or a neighborly chat over the back fence, to turn friends into customers or to reinforce the loyalty of existing ones.[16]

How Technology Supports CRM

The general conception of CRM is that it is technology used to build and maintain customer relationships. Certainly, as noted, the use of computer technology can have a significant role in CRM, but the system should be inclusive of all forms of relationship management, from greeting a customer on the phone, in-person, or even on the home page of your Web site, to the use of sophisticated software systems. With CRM, customer interactions with all parts of the company are unified and customer information is tracked, analyzed, and used to improve customer satisfaction and business profitability. Specialized CRM software is available to companies large and small. **Exhibit 11-3** shows the top vendors of CRM software.

Exhibit 11-3 *Worldwide Vendor Revenue Estimates for Total CRM Software (Millions of U.S. Dollars)*

Company	2012 Revenue	2012 Market Share (%)
SalesForce.com	$2,525.6	14.0
SAP	$2,327.1	12.9
Oracle	$2,015.2	11.1
Microsoft	$1,135.3	6.3
IBM	$649.1	3.6
Others	$9,437.7	52.1
Total	$18,090.0	100.0

Source: Rob van der Meulen, "Gartner Says Worldwide Customer Relationship Management Software Market Grew 12.5 Percent in 2012," Gartner, Inc., Press Release, accessed August 7, 2013, http://www.gartner.com/newsroom/id/2459015.

[16]Ibid.

database a collection of information that is generally stored on a computer and organized for sorting and searching.

It truly is not necessary to invest in a sophisticated CRM software system to use technology to benefit your customer relationships. You can purchase a database package to create significant gains. A **database** is a collection of information that is generally stored on a computer and organized for sorting and searching. Create a database on your computer to collect any information you obtain from customers, either by using a package such as Microsoft Access or with a specialized customer software system for your industry. Your database should include every customer you have ever had, as well as potential ones: friends, family, and other contacts. The database should include contact information (name, e-mail address, phone and fax numbers, and mailing address); any preferences or pertinent personal information (e.g., sizes, birthdays, family, hobbies, memberships); and purchase and payment history. Also, include any contact information, such as when the contact was made, who was involved, what type of contact it was (in person, telephone, text, social network, or e-mail), and a note about the topics of discussion and any appropriate follow-up. Design the database and start collecting this information from the beginning, and you will be ahead of the game when you are ready to make sales calls or send out marketing material.

As your database grows, you can make it more sophisticated by organizing it by region, customer interest, or any number of other variables, so you can send out targeted e-mails. If you sell gourmet sauces, for example, your notes could tell you whether a customer is interested in hot sauces or dessert sauces. When you add a new hot sauce to your product line, you will know whom to target with an e-mail announcement introducing it, possibly with a special offer. Use the resources available to you to maximize your culture of focus on the customer and strong customer-relationship management.

Chapter Summary

Now that you have studied this chapter, you can do the following:

1. Explain the importance of selling based on benefits.
   - Features are the qualities of a product or service.
   - Benefits are what the product or service can do to fill customer needs.
   - Customers purchase based on perceived benefits.
2. Use the principles of selling to make effective sales calls.
   - Make a good personal impression.
   - Know your product or service.
   - Believe in your product or service.
   - Know your field.
   - Know your customers.
   - Prepare your sales presentation.
   - Think positively.
   - Keep good records.
   - Make an appointment.
   - Treat your customers like gold.
3. Know how to make a successful sales call.
   - Use technology to assist you.
   - Prequalify your leads, so that you are making the best use of your time and theirs.

- Focus on the customer, not on the product or service.
- Incorporate the eight-step sales call.

4. Analyze and improve your sales calls.
   - Was I able to get the customer to open up to me? Why, or why not? Did I do or say anything that turned the customer off?
   - Which of my questions did the best job of helping the customer zero in on his or her problem?
   - Was I able to make an honest case for my product/service being the one that could solve the customer's problem?
   - Did I improve my relationship with this individual during the call?

5. Provide excellent customer service.
   - Customer service is everything you do to keep your customers happy, especially after the sale. It includes maintaining and repairing the product or service once it has been sold, and dealing with customer complaints.
   - A successful business is built on repeat customers.

6. Define customer relationship management and understand its value.
   - Identify the key components of CRM.
   - Recognize that CRM can be simple or complex and that you can incorporate technology to obtain higher value.
   - Use CRM to tailor your products, services, and promotions to customers to yield increased profitability.

Key Terms

customer relationship
  management (CRM), 357
customer service, 354
database, 360

lurk, 349
prospect, 349
spam, 349

Entrepreneurship Portfolio

Critical Thinking Exercises

11-1. Describe the features of each product listed below and then create a benefit statement for each that you would use as selling points.
   a. wristwatch with daily-events calendar
   b. milk-free chocolate
   c. vegetarian dog food
   d. personal lie detector

11-2. It has been said that selling is an art and the essence of selling is in teaching customers about one's product or service. Do you agree? Why or why not?

11-3. Describe a business that you deal with as a customer. Describe the customer service you receive there. What do you like (or dislike) about it? How could it be improved?

11-4. Why is it more important to listen rather than talk while initiating a sales call? Illustrate with an example.

11-5. Identify five specific sales-call prospects for your business. Prequalify them using these questions: (a) Is the prospect in my market? (b) Does he or she need my product/service? (c) Will my product/service remove a problem or source of "pain" or improve the individual's life? (d) Can he or she afford it?

11-6. Assume you were trying to sell a program on event management to a prospective client. You are unsure if your call was successful. How will you analyze your sales call and hone your skills further? Enumerate the questions which will help you analyze your call and then answer them.

Key Concept Questions

11-7. Explain Joe Girard's Law of 250 in your own words, and give examples of it from your own life.

11-8. Why is customer service an extension of marketing?

11-9. Give three reasons why you think it is important to keep collecting market research even after you have opened your business.

11-10. What do you expect your "personal look" to be when you start selling your product/service, and why?

11-11. What sources of information can you use to develop a customer profile?

11-12. List three ways you intend to provide superior customer service.

11-13. Create a company signature for your business e-mail. Keep it under eight words.

Application Exercises

11-14. Develop a brief sales pitch for three items you are wearing. Try out the pitch for each on a partner. Have your partner help you time the pitches to one minute. Do the same for your partner.

11-15. Write a memo to your partner discussing his or her sales calls and how they could be improved. When analyzing your partner's efforts, use the eight steps of a sales call in the text as your guide.

11-16. Arrange to receive a sales pitch from a competitor in the business field you intend to enter. After the presentation, write down your objections to purchasing the product/service. Use Brian Tracy's method to categorize your objections and then phrase them in a single question composed of 25 words or less. Be conscious of arranging the sales pitch non-deceptively.

Exploring Your Community

11-17. Visit three businesses in your community and take notes on your experience as a shopper. Write a memo comparing the customer service at each. Include such information as the following: Were you greeted when you came in? Did anyone offer to help you? If you bought something, were you given a survey? What differentiates the best of the three from the worst in terms of customer service?

11-18. Interview an entrepreneur about the type of CRM she uses. Discuss customer service and complaint handling in particular. Summarize the interview in a short paper.

BizBuilder Business Plan Questions

After studying this chapter, you should be able to answer the following Business Plan Questions. The entire outline for the Business Plan is found in Appendix 2.

5.0 Marketing Strategy and Plan

5.1 Products/Services

D. Describe the features and benefits of the product/service your business will focus on selling.

5.3 Promotion

G. List ways you intend to provide superior customer service.

H. How will you keep your customer database? What essential questions will you ask every customer for your database?

Case Study | BNI—Building Businesses through Networking

Dr. Ivan Misner, known as "The Father of Modern Networking," is the ultimate business networking professional. He founded the world's largest business networking organization, Business Networks International, in 1985 and is a *New York Times* best-selling author. His blog (http://www .BusinessNetworking.com) provides insights into building a successful business-referral network.

As of 2013, BNI had over 6,440 chapters throughout every populated continent of the world. BNI reports that it generated 7.1 million referrals resulting in over $3.3 billion worth of business for its members in 2012.[17] According to the organization's Web site, "The mission of BNI is to help members increase their business through a structured, positive, and professional 'word-of-mouth' program that enables them to develop long-term, meaningful relationships with quality business professionals."

BNI members join chapters in their local areas that consist of prescreened individuals with a limit of one member per classification. For example, there can be only one general contractor and one mortgage banker. These groups meet weekly at designated locations to share business opportunities and network with one another. The idea behind BNI is to create "VCP," or *visibility, credibility,* and *profitability* for its members. This is done with the underlying philosophy of Givers Gain®, meaning that, by referring others, the members will build their own businesses.

Members are expected to provide referrals for one another on both a formal and informal basis. For example, they are asked to share information at the regular meetings. They are also expected to carry business cards and distribute them to one another when the opportunity for a referral arises. There are webinars for members that support creation of effective member profiles and provide guidance on maximizing the benefits of referrals.

Dr. Misner suggests, "You have to be an active, responsible, professional, accountable participant and show your fellow networkers the respect, attention, and support that you want them to give you."[18] BNI is clear that "The most successful chapters of BNI are comprised of participants who are sincerely committed to helping one another through networking. They are a team."

BNI suggests that there are numerous benefits of being a member, including:

- Increased exposure to many other people and businesses
- Building solid business relationships that will last for the rest of your life
- Tools to network more effectively, including educational workshops and mentoring
- Visibility, credibility, and profitability for each member

While members can find participation beneficial, it is important to understand that referral networks work when members trust and respect one another. Joining a networking organization such as BNI is a step toward gaining referrals. However, successful members nurture relationships with other members over time and through their actions. Dr. Misner writes, "Remember, if you start putting together your network when the need arises, you're too late. The better way is to begin developing relationships now with the people whose help you will need in the future."[19]

Case Study Analysis

11-19. How does BNI reinforce the importance of selling based on benefits?

11-20. List three things that BNI does that you could adopt to help build business relationships.

---

[17]BNI, accessed August 15, 2013, http://www.bni.com.

[18]Ivan Misner, "10 Ways to Waste Your Time in a Networking Group," *Professional PerformanceMagazine.com*, July 2013, vol. 21, no. 3, p. 33, accessed August 15, 2013, http://successnet.czcommunity.com/tag/professional-performance-magazine/.

[19]Ibid., p. 33.

11-21. What type of referral network might support your proposed venture? Find such a group and write a paragraph about it and why it could be of value.

11-22. Visit the BNI site at http://www.bni.com and find the chapter closest to your home.

   a. What is the name of the chapter?

   b. When does it meet?

   c. Who is the executive director of the chapter?

   d. How many members are in the chapter?

   e. What are the professional classifications of three of the members?

Case Sources

BNI, accessed August 15, 2013, http://www.bni.com.

Ivan Misner, "10 Ways to Waste Your Time in a Networking Group," *Professional PerformanceMagazine.com*, July 2013, vol. 21, no. 3, p. 33, accessed August 15, 2013, http://successnet.czcommunity.com/tag/professional-performance-magazine/.

Amazing Customer Service Propels Amazon

During the 2013 holiday season, some of Amazon's deliveries were late. The company's customer promise of two-day delivery was not met. While UPS and FedEx, the delivery companies involved, offered excuses and essentially blamed customers for complaining about the situation, Amazon worked to restore customer satisfaction.[20] Not only did it issue shipping refunds, but it distributed $20 gift cards and apologized profusely and meant it. Customer service is critical for Amazon, and lapses are not tolerated.

A Culture of Service

Founder Jeff Bezos has focused the organization on excellence in customer service since its founding as a pure-play Internet retailer in 1995. Amazon was named the top customer service company by MSN Money/Zogby Analytics four years in a row.[21] As an MSN Money business writer notes, "Amazon's user-friendly website, along with low prices, one-click shopping, no-hassle returns, free-shipping options and even the sense of community it fosters, has welcomed some 180 million happy buyers into the fold. Combined, those contented clickers buy an average of 9.6 million items a day."[22] The National Retail Federation Foundation also ranked Amazon as a top retailer in its Customers' Choice Awards.[23]

Amazon is known for its culture of customer service. Bezos has said, "We see our customers as invited guests to a party, and we are the hosts. It's our job every day to make every important aspect of the customer experience a little bit better."[24] This focus drives the company.

Swimming Against the Current

The company has been innovative and willing to defy the popular wisdom with its customers. When the bookselling industry relied on brick-and-mortar stores, Amazon was created as an Internet-only retailer. Today, many companies have

Jeff Bezos, Amazon.com
(Justin Lane/Newscom)

both online and physical stores. Often, the stores are considered "showrooms" for additional online sales. Greeting and directly serving customers face-to-face is seen as critical. Amazon has steered away from these practices and seen both traditional booksellers and large chains such as Borders go out of business.

Whereas other online retailers tend to specialize in narrow niches for products, Amazon has expanded its offerings to include everything from Kindle books to candy to clothing to cookery. It has become a one-stop shop for millions of consumers, who keep coming back for more.

Using Technology to Sell

The Amazon team is highly skilled in using the available technology to increase sales. Amazon user purchases are tracked and the resulting data is used for multiple purposes. Registered users each have their own custom shopping areas, such as "Caroline's Amazon.com." When they visit, customers are greeted with customized advertising, a visual list of "Related to Items You've Viewed," "More Items to Consider," "New for You," and "Recommendations" to visit. They also have access to account information and wish lists among multiple other choices. While shopping on the site, they are prompted to add

[20]Jeff Macke, "Amazon proves it's the customer service champ yet again," Yahoo Finance, January 13, 2014, http://finance.yahoo.com/blogs/breakout/amazon-proves-it-s-the-customer-service-champ-yet-again-151657935.html, accessed January 31, 2014.

[21]Karen Aho, "2013 Customer Service Hall of Fame," MSN Money, (n.d.), http://money.msn.com/investing/2013-customer-service-hall-of-fame, accessed January 31, 2014.

[22]Ibid.

[23]National Retail Federation Foundation, Customers' Choice Awards, January 12, 2012, http://www.nrffoundation.com/content/customers-choice-awards, accessed February 2, 2014.

[24]Brainy Quote, http://www.brainyquote.com/quotes/quotes/j/jeffbezos173311.html#8bvMf76imSRezkoa.99, accessed January 31, 2014.

© Alex Segre/Alamy

purchases by displays of related products, opportunities to earn free shipping, and advertisements for Amazon Prime. Also, customer reviews and ratings are readily visible to shoppers.

Away from the site itself, customers receive emails from Amazon. When they make a purchase, a confirmation email is sent with a thank you. When their orders ship, shipping and tracking information is sent to customers. Customers receive opt-in, customized promotional emails for categories of goods purchased, such as Kindle mysteries and business books. These emails are based on purchase data and are tailored to customer groups rather than generic messages.

Actively Seeking Customer Feedback

Customer input is more than just lip service at Amazon. The total experience is wrapped around the customer to build customer satisfaction, sales, and repeat purchases. While some companies seek customer feedback periodically or more subtly, Amazon has multiple points of contact for responses. One direct method is through soliciting feedback on purchases via email. The company sends out emails asking for reviews on the products (physical and Kindle) and the packaging. Kindle readers are prompted to provide reviews at the end of each book, and they are offered reviews and ratings on the front end. While on the site, customers can comment on products and indicate their interest in or satisfaction with them.

The Total Customer Experience

With all of the various sophisticated uses of customer tracking data, customer feedback, and other options, Amazon has worked relentlessly to attain its ranking as a leading retailer for customer service and top sales leader.

Case Study Analysis

11-23. Why would Amazon accept responsibility for the shipping problems of its vendors, UPS and FedEx? How would you feel about the company's response if you were among the customers who did not receive two-day shipping as promised?

11-24. List the pros and cons of Amazon's customer relationship management system from the company and customer perspective.

11-25. How has Amazon compensated for the lack of brick-and-mortar stores?

11-26. Go to the Amazon.com site and search for *The Lean Startup* by Eric Reis.

    a. What formats are available?

    b. What other categories of information are provided, and how might they boost sales for the company?

    c. What ordering options are offered? Are any more convenient than others? Why?

Case Sources

Karen Aho, "2013 Customer Service Hall of Fame," MSN Money, (n.d.), http://money.msn.com/investing/2013-customer-service-hall-of-fame, accessed January 31, 2014.

Amazon.com web site, accessed January 31, 2014, https://www.amazon.com.

Jeff Macke, "Amazon proves it's the customer service champ yet again," Yahoo Finance, January 13, 2014, http://finance.yahoo.com/blogs/breakout/amazon-proves-it-s-the-customer-service-champ-yet-again-151657935.html, accessed January 31, 2014.

National Retail Federation Foundation, Customers' Choice Awards, January 12, 2012, http://www.nrffoundation.com/content/customers-choice-awards, accessed February 2, 2014.

Empact: Making an Impact for Entrepreneurs

Michael Simmons and Sheena Lindahl
(Courtesy of Sheena Lindahl)

Michael Simmons and Sheena Lindahl founded Extreme Entrepreneurship Education LLC (now Empact) just upon graduating from New York University. The company was started as a for-profit organization, although it centers on a social mission: to facilitate a culture of entrepreneurship in communities around the world through exposure and celebration of young entrepreneur stories.

MAKING A STRATEGIC PIVOT

Michael and Sheena originally intended to be publishers of entrepreneurial content. They launched the company by publishing a book about the entrepreneurial mindset written by Michael, *The Student Success Manifesto*. The profit per book unit was good, but they needed to sell a lot of units in order to make publishing profitable enough to support them.

To sell more books, Michael and Sheena began seeking bulk purchases from schools and other youth organizations. One marketing strategy included talking to groups of students when the schools purchased books. This tactic helped Michael and Sheena to realize that people would pay them to speak, whether books were purchased or not, and their impact as speakers was strong. They started charging for their speaking services.

One thing led to another. They explored ways to also include the stories of other young, successful entrepreneurs and the Extreme Entrepreneurship Tour (EET) was launched in 2006.

The EET is the first national entrepreneurship tour in which community members and students from all academic disciplines participate in half-day events featuring young entrepreneurs who share the ups and downs of their experiences in entrepreneurship. The high-energy events are designed to get attendees excited about entrepreneurship and ready to take action and then connect and feed them into the programs and resources available on their campus and in their community that can help them. In addition to delivering great amounts of inspiration to participants, Tour events have boosted the number of students taking part in entrepreneurship courses and participating in business plan competitions, and these events have also helped to gain awareness for new offerings. Tour events are customized depending on the audience and goals of a host institution.

The standard four-hour tour event includes two successful young entrepreneurs who serve as keynote speakers and panelists; a moderator who facilitates the day's events and delivers a workshop; exhibits; speed networking; and a panel discussion with local entrepreneurs. Empact also has shorter two- and three-hour tour events for hosts with smaller budgets and will even simply connect organizations with vetted, high-energy, successful entrepreneurs to speak apart from the tour event.

MARKETING FOR THE TOUR

Extreme Entrepreneurship event organizers can visit a resource Web site to find templates for promotional posters and flyers, marketing best practice reports and checklists, and logistical checklists. An Empact Director of

Events supports hosts with marketing and logistics, and Empact offers the complimentary services of a public relations firm to help get local media coverage of the event. The host is responsible for the promotion, event venue, refreshments, and audio-visual. On the day of the event, two Empact staff facilitate registration, hand out materials (including an event program/workbook, a copy of *Inc.* magazine, and other giveaways), and make sure all runs smoothly.

Extreme Entrepreneurship Tour Bus
(Courtesy of Sheena Lindahl)

Since the EET was started in 2006, more than 500 events have been held, and that number keeps growing. The core team consists of Michael and Sheena, Chief Operating Officer Sarah Green, and a Director of Events. A key element of delivering successful events is having a large network of quality entrepreneur speakers to choose from. In fact, Empact has found that this focus on building networks based on authentic relationships and connecting individuals from within those networks has led to its success.

EMPACT SHOWCASES: BUILDING RECOGNITION, MARKET, AND A SUPPLY OF SPEAKERS

Empact achieves its mission to celebrate the many faces of entrepreneurship (and keeps its network of young entrepreneurs fresh) by facilitating a nationwide showcase and annual celebration of young entrepreneurs called the Empact Showcase. Since the Empact Showcase launched in 2011, celebration events have taken place at the White House, U.S. Chamber of Commerce, and the United Nations headquarters. Empact then sources its speakers for the Extreme Entrepreneurship Tour and other events through those the company comes to know from these recognition events.

In order to qualify for the Showcase, entrepreneurs must be age 35 or under and have made at least $100,000 in annual revenue. The average revenue of a Showcase company is $3.2 million; in combination, the 2013 Showcase companies employed more than 8,000 individuals.

Each year at the celebration event, special honor is given to the Empact100 (top 100 companies in the Showcase) as well as category honorees in categories such as most disruptive, largest potential, best social company, best female company, and more. The Empact100 and category honorees are selected by an Academy of high-level entrepreneurs, including people like Tony Hsieh (President of Zappos), Gene Landrum (founder of Chuck E Cheese), and Kay Koplovitz (founder of USA Networks).

EMPACT SUMMITS

Another network that Empact has rooted itself in is the entrepreneurship ecosystem at large. Also in 2011, Empact launched the first Empact Summit on the Future of Entrepreneurship Education, created to bring together high-level thought leaders from all parts of the entrepreneurship ecosystem. With a carefully curated invite-only guest list, the Summit bridged connections between the various elements of the entrepreneurship ecosystem in the United States that don't often communicate with each other, including sectors such as government, investors, foundations, education, corporations, media, entrepreneur support organizations, and entrepreneurs.

The mission of the Summit is to spark conversations that facilitate relationship building in order to forge and strengthen bonds in both local and global entrepreneurship ecosystems, thus making entrepreneurship a viable career option. The Summit provides a forum for the most influential leaders to share ideas, highlights influential leaders and innovative programs in the "entrepreneurship ecosystem," and demonstrate the importance of the entrepreneurship ecosystem to major societal leaders.

In addition to helping Empact further its social mission, the Summit contributes to Empact's thought leadership, builds goodwill, and helps programs gain financial support that could allow them to host events.

GUEST AUTHOR: BUILDING CREDIBILITY AND BROADENING REACH

In 2013, Michael began writing a guest column for *Forbes* magazine, and Sheena began writing one for *Entrepreneur* magazine. Their articles focus on building networks and connections and work-life balance—key concepts they've come to master in growing their company. The columns provide a forum to share insights and build thought leadership on topic areas the duo find interesting, as well as a way to maintain credibility and offer resources to their markets.

SOCIAL MEDIA

Through its social media, Empact has focused on finding a voice that reflects its internal culture and values to deliver wow, pursue growth and learning, and be positive and authentic. All communications are intended to deliver a message that fits these characteristics.

RECOGNITION

The Extreme Entrepreneurship Tour has won recognition for its excellence by receiving Northern Michigan University's 2007–2008 Program of the Year Award and the 2008 Innovation Award from the National Association of Development Organizations. Michael and Sheena have been named to *Inc.* Magazine's 30 under 30 list and *BusinessWeek's* 25 under 25; they have been recognized on AOL's homepage and featured in many other media outlets.

Case Study Analysis

U3-1. How do Michael Simmons and Sheena Lindahl incorporate the Four Ps into a creative, effective, integrated marketing effort?

U3-2. What is the product mix that Empact's enterprises have developed?

U3-3. How are its services delivered (through what channels)?

U3-4. Discuss the company's global marketing (check its Web sites, if necessary).

U3-5. What was Empact's first marketing effort?

U3-6. What was the result of this effort?

U3-7. How does Empact extend its brand?

Case Sources

Empact, http://www.iempact.com

Empact Showcase, http://www.empactshowcase.com

Empact Summit, http://www.empactsummit.com

Extreme Entrepreneurship Tour, accessed August 4, 2010, http://www.extremetour.org

Used by permission of Extreme Entrepreneurship Education LLC.

SHOW ME THE MONEY: FINDING, SECURING, AND MANAGING IT

Chapter 12
UNDERSTANDING AND MANAGING START-UP, FIXED, AND VARIABLE COSTS

Chapter 13
USING FINANCIAL STATEMENTS TO GUIDE A BUSINESS

Chapter 14
CASH FLOW AND TAXES

Chapter 15
FINANCING STRATEGY: DEBT, EQUITY, OR BOTH?

© sarapulsar38/Fotolia

UNDERSTANDING AND MANAGING START-UP, FIXED, AND VARIABLE COSTS

Learning Objectives

1. Identify the investment required for business start-up.

2. Describe the variable costs of starting a business.

3. Analyze your fixed operating costs and calculate gross profit.

4. Set up financial record keeping for your business.

Jupiter Images

Seeking out optimal medical services has become global, due to advances in technology, ease of travel, and variety of cost structures. Aravind Eye Care System (AECS), a social enterprise, is based in Madurai, India, and claims it is "the largest and most productive eye care facility in the world." Aravind provides eye surgery and outpatient care at each of its five hospitals. AECS was founded in 1976 by Dr. Govindappa Venkataswamy ("Dr. V") with the goal of eliminating blindness. In 2008, Dr. P. Namperumalsamy, Chairman of AECS, was awarded the Ernst & Young Entrepreneur of the Year for Health Care in Mumbai.

In addition to the facilities at its 41 primary, 5 secondary, 5 tertiary, and 6 outpatient eye care centers, AECS provides award-winning telemedicine services in rural areas of the country. It has become an international training center (Lions Aravind Institute of Community Ophthalmology) and AECS treats patients from around the world. The program has focused on creating cost efficiencies in the delivery of care to enable outreach to a broader base of patients. In addition, AECS manufactures optical products (specifically, intraocular lenses for cataract patients) through its Aurolab

© Picture Partners/Alamy

division for use in its hospitals and for outside sale to raise funds to serve more patients in poverty. Funding for AECS comes from many countries, and a good number of ophthalmology interns are Americans.

The efficiencies achieved by AECS allow it to provide well over half of its surgical care at no cost or reduced fees. By creating what is essentially an assembly-line layout and procedure for cataract surgeries and working in small, specialized teams, the time necessary for each surgery is minimized; and the surgeons complete a maximum number of operations per day. Also, because Indian laws differ from those in the United States, more than one patient can be in an operating room at a time, so that surgeons can rapidly move from one patient to the next with minimal down time.

Between April 2012 and March 2013, some 371,000 people underwent surgeries at one of the Aravind Eye facilities, and 3.1 million obtained care on an outpatient basis. Approximately half of the surgeries were under its free-care programs for the poor.

What Does It Cost to Operate a Business?

To run a successful business, you will need to keep track of your costs and have more cash coming in than going out. The bedrock principle of business is that it earns a profit by selling products or services for more than they cost.

A business can make a profit only if the selling price per unit is greater than the cost per unit. A litmus test for profitability is the *economics of one unit* (EOU), as discussed in prior chapters. It tells an entrepreneur if the business is earning a profit on each individual unit. Knowing your EOU will be helpful as you determine your venture's viability.

Many costs are associated with the establishment and growth of a small business. These include start-up purchases, fixed and variable costs, and cash reserves. Each will be discussed in turn. All are components of your accounting records, the documents that are used to classify, analyze, and interpret the financial transactions of an organization.

Start-Up Investment

There is another critical cost to discuss before establishing accounting records for your business. We have talked about the costs of operating a business, but what about the money required to *start* the business? Start-up investment, or **seed capital**, is the one-time expense of opening a business. In a restaurant, for example, start-up expenses would include stoves, refrigeration, food processors, tables, chairs, utensils, and other items that would not be replaced very often. Also included might be the one-time cost of buying land and constructing a building or the cost of renovating an existing space. Some entrepreneurs also choose to consider the time they put into getting their businesses off the ground as part of the start-up investment. To do so, place a value on your time per hour and multiply by the number of hours you think you will need to put in to get your business going. You might be shocked at how big that number is.

For a hot dog stand, the start-up investment list might look like this:

Beginning inventory (hot dogs, mustard, buns, etc.)	$50
Business cards and flyers	150
Business licenses (city and state)	200
Hot dog cart	2,500
Cash box and other	100
Total start-up investment without contingency	$3,000
Contingency @ 10% of start-up investment	300
Total start-up investment with contingency	$3,300

A fitness center is an example of a complex business (Jupiterimages/Thinkstock)

For a more complex business, like a 24-hour franchise fitness center opening in leased space, the summary start-up sheet could be as shown in **Exhibit 12-1**. The items would be broken down into greater detail in order to secure quotations on prices. For example, each piece of equipment would be identified and a quote secured, assuming the franchisor does not have a preset package of equipment that a franchisee must purchase.

For a manufacturing business, developing a prototype for the item being manufactured may be a major start-up cost, perhaps totaling in the millions. A **prototype** is a model or pattern that serves as an example of how a product would look and operate if it were manufactured. Companies that specialize in creating prototypes can be found in the *Thomas Register of American Manufacturers.*

Brainstorm to Avoid Start-Up Surprises

Before starting your business, try to anticipate every possible cost by analyzing all components and possibilities. Talk to others in your industry and ask them what start-up costs they failed to anticipate. Research industry information and obtain quotations from potential suppliers. Use **Exhibit 12-2** to estimate your start-up investment.

Once you have created a list, take it to your advisors and have them review it. They will probably find costs you have overlooked. You might not have realized that the electric company requires a $1,000 deposit to turn on service, for example.

Exhibit **12-1** *Seed Capital Estimate for a 24-Hour Fitness Center*		
Item/Category	**Cost**	**Estimate or Quote?**
Start-Up Expenses		
Debt service (interest on $130,000 at 10%)	$2,167	Estimate
Employee wages, salaries, and benefits	$3,100	Estimate
Financing costs and fees (2% of $130,000)	$2,600	Estimate
Franchise fees	$40,000	Quote
Insurance	$1,000	Quote
Licenses and permits	$300	Quote
Memberships (trade associations, chambers of commerce, and the like)	$900	Mixed
Owner time (valued at $25 per hour)*	$5,000	Estimate
Professional services (attorney, accountant, architect, engineers, and the like)	$3,000	Estimate
Promotions and advertising	$1,800	Mixed
Rent on location identified	$2,000	Quote
Supplies	$400	Estimate
Taxes (wage and other)	$500	Estimate
Training, conventions, and seminars	$1,000	Quote
Utilities	$400	Estimate
Total Start-Up Expenses	$64,167	
Start-Up Assets		
Computers and other technology	$5,000	Quote
Deposits on rent and utilities	$5,600	Quote
Equipment, furniture, and fixtures	$105,000	Quote
Installation of equipment and fixtures	$2,800	Quote
Inventory	$200	Estimate
Leasehold improvements	$3,200	Quote
Petty cash	$300	Quote
Total Start-Up Assets	$122,100	
Total Pre-Opening Investment	$186,267	
Contingency Funds (10%)	$18,626	
Start-Up with Contingency**	**$204,893**	

* If no wage or salary is being paid to the owners, this is a "soft" cost and can be considered an optional item on the list. However, including it makes the list more comprehensive and more reflective of the total.

** This figure does not include cash reserves or cash requirements for initial cash shortfall during operations. Both should be added to reflect total financing needed.

Or you may need licenses and insurance you did not expect. Tack on an additional 10 percent to your estimates for contingencies and emergencies.

Keep a Reserve Equal to One-Half the Start-Up Investment

Start-up investment should include one more thing: a **cash reserve**—that is, emergency funds and a pool of cash resources, which should equal at least half your start-up costs. For the previously mentioned hot dog cart example, therefore, the reserve would be half of $3,300, or $1,650, making the total required $4,950.

    Entrepreneurs must be prepared for the unexpected; the only good surprise is no surprise. The reserve will provide a moderate cushion of

cash reserve emergency funds and a pool of cash resources.

Exhibit **12-2** *Start-Up Investment Checklist*		
Item/Category	**Cost**	**Explanation/Note**
Land and building (if constructing or purchasing)		
Equipment and machinery		
Furniture and fixtures		
Leasehold improvements (if renting)		
Installation of equipment and fixtures		
Computers and other technology		
Employee wages, salaries, and benefits		
Owner time (valued at $ _____ per hour)*		
Professional services (attorney, accountant, architect, engineers, and the like)		
Promotions and advertising		
Licenses and permits		
Deposits on rent and utilities		
Rent		
Utilities		
Insurance		
Debt service (normally interest only)		
Taxes (wage and other)		
Memberships (trade associations, chambers of commerce, and the like)		
Registration fees		
Training, conventions, and seminars		
Licensing or franchising fees		
Financing costs and fees		
Supplies		
Inventory		
Petty cash		
Total pre-opening investment		
Allowance for contingencies/emergencies (10%)		
Initial Investment**		

* If no wage or salary is paid to the owners, this is a "soft" cost and can be considered an optional item on the list. However, including it is more comprehensive and more reflective of total costs.

** This figure does not include cash reserves, or cash requirements for initial cash shortfall during operations. Both should be added to reflect total financing needed.

protection if you need it. When your computer goes down or an important supplier raises prices, you will be glad you had this money on hand.

Having a cash reserve will also allow you to take advantage of opportunities. Say you own a vintage clothing store and you hear from a friend whose great-aunt died and left him a great deal of authentic vintage clothing and jewelry. He is willing to sell you the whole lot for $500, which you figure you can resell in your shop for at least $2,000. If you have the cash on hand, you can take advantage of this profitable opportunity.

Predict the Payback Period

payback period estimated time required to earn sufficient net cash flow to cover the start-up investment.

When compiling and analyzing start-up costs, one consideration will be how long it will take for you to earn back your start-up investment. The **payback period** is an estimate of how long it will take your business to bring in enough cash to cover the start-up costs. It is measured in months.

$$\text{Payback} = \frac{\text{Start-Up Investment}}{\text{Net Cash Flow per Month}}$$

Example: Ashley's business requires a start-up investment of $1,000. The business is projecting a net cash flow per month of $400. How many months will it take to make back her start-up investment?

$$\text{Payback} = \frac{\$1,000}{\$400} = 2.5 \text{ Months}$$

Knowing the payback period is important for a firm, so that the time horizon is known and timing of funds availability is clear. However, the payback period does not take into consideration future earnings, opportunities for alternative investments, or the overall value of the company. It is based on net cash and is a good indicator of the time needed to earn back initial disbursements.

Estimate Value

Financial managers use several tools to determine the current value of proposed investments, of which *net present value* (NPV) is widely accepted as the most theoretically sound. Entrepreneurs can use such a technique to consider the financial returns on their initial investment. If the NPV calculation yields a positive value, the investment will result in a positive return based on the owner's (and investors') required rate of return.

Ryan McVay/Thinkstock

There are multiple methods of calculating NPV, including using a formula, tables, a spreadsheet program, or a financial calculator. You can calculate NPV with the following information: required rate of return (%), annual net cash flows, initial investment, and number of years of cash flows. **Exhibit 12-3** shows an NPV calculation for a business with an initial investment of $1.5 million.

Exhibit **12-3** *Calculating Net Present Value with Excel*		
Description	**Data**	**Notes**
Initial investment	$1,500,000	Seed capital needed to start the business
Required rate of return	0.12	Return required by investors (owners)
Net Cash Year 1	$0	First year of operations, yielding no net cash
Net Cash Year 2	$100,000	Second year of operations with earnings
Net Cash Year 3	$200,000	Subsequent year
Net Cash Year 4	$500,000	Subsequent year
Net Cash Year 5	$850,000	Subsequent year
Net Cash Year 6	$1,200,000	Subsequent year
Net Cash Year 7	$600,000	Results show declining market
Net Cash Year 8	$400,000	Further decline
Net Cash Year 9	$0	Company closed
Calculated Present Value	$2,063,067.47	Use NPV formula
Net Present Value	**$563,067.47**	Value above initial investment
NPV > $0?	Yes	NPV is positive, so it is a "go"

Exhibit **12-4** *Manufacturing Business: Unit = 1 Hand-Painted T-Shirt*			
Economics of One Unit (EOU) Analysis			
(Define the Unit of Sale)			
Selling Price (per Unit)			$35.00
COGS (Cost of Goods Sold)			
Materials per Unit		$7.00	
Labor per hour	$10.00		
# of Hours per Unit	0.75		
Total Labor per Unit	7.50	7.50	
Total COGS (per Unit)		$14.50	$14.50	14.50
Gross Profit (per Unit)			$20.50
Other Variable Costs			
Commission (10%)		3.50	
Packaging		0.50	
Total Other Variable Costs		$4.00	4.00	4.00
Total Variable Costs (per Unit)			$18.50
Contribution Margin			$16.50

Fixed and Variable Costs: Essential Building Blocks

variable costs expenses that vary directly with changes in the production or sales volume.

fixed costs expenses that must be paid regardless of whether sales are being generated.

Small business owners divide their costs into two categories. **Variable costs** change based on the volume of units sold or produced. **Fixed costs** are expenses that must be paid regardless of whether or not sales are being generated.

Variable costs change with production and sales. They fall into two subcategories:

1. Cost of goods sold (COGS) or cost of services sold (COSS). Each is associated specifically with a single unit of sale, including:
   - The cost of materials used to make the product (or deliver the service)
   - The cost of labor used to make the product (or deliver the service)
2. Other variable costs, including:
   - Commissions or other compensation based on sales volume
   - Shipping and handling charges

Fixed costs stay constant over a range of productions, whether you sell many units or very few. Examples of fixed costs include rent, salaries, insurance, equipment, and manufacturing facilities.

Henry Ford spent money on efficient manufacturing equipment (a fixed cost) but saved a fortune on labor (COGS) by doing so. This reduced his total costs because labor was used in each of the millions of cars Ford produced, but he only had to pay for the plant and equipment once.

For any product, you can study its economics of one unit (EOU) to figure out what it cost to make that sale. **Exhibit 12-4** shows an example from a business that sells hand-painted T-shirts.

Calculating Critical Costs

To determine the most important factors with respect to costs in your business, you can calculate *critical* costs. This will help you to determine profitability and the factors that can and cannot be easily changed to impact your profits and cash flow.

Calculating Total Gross Profit (Contribution Margin)

You can use EOU to calculate whether and by how much you will come out ahead on your per-unit costs for each sale. By using the EOU, you can figure the gross profit per unit (**contribution margin** per unit sold, which is the selling price minus all variable costs).

contribution margin gross profit per unit—the selling price minus total variable costs plus other variable costs.

Calculating EOU When You Sell Multiple Products

Most businesses sell more than a single product, and they can also use EOU as a value measure of product profitability. A business selling a variety of products has to create a separate EOU for each item to determine whether each is profitable. When there are many similar products with comparable prices and cost structures, a "typical" EOU can be used.

Example: Jamaal sells four kinds of candy bars at school. He sells each bar for $1, but he pays a different wholesale price for each:

Chocolate Delight	$0.36 each
Almond Euphoria	$0.38 each
Fruit Envy	$0.42 each
Junior Crunch Bar	$0.44 each

Rather than make separate EOUs, Jamaal uses the average cost of his four candy bars (see **Exhibit 12-5**).

Costs of the four candy bars = ($0.36+$0.38+$0.42+$0.44) ÷ 4
Average cost of the four candy bars = $1.60 ÷ 4
Average cost of each bar = $0.40

Using a simple average works as long as Jamaal sells roughly the same number of each brand of bar. If he can no longer get Chocolate Delight and Almond Euphoria at some point, for example, he should then change his EOU to reflect the higher price of the other two bars.

What if each unit of sale is made up of a complex mix of materials and labor? The EOU can still help you figure the COGS, other variable costs, and gross profit for the product, although the process will be more complex.

inventory costs expenses associated with materials and direct labor for production until the product is sold.

Example: Denise sells sandwiches from her deli cart downtown on Saturdays. She sells each for $5. The materials and labor that go directly into making one sandwich are the COGS. The costs of the materials and direct labor for production are called **inventory costs** until the product is sold. There will also be some other variable costs, such as napkins, a paper wrapping for each sandwich, and plastic bags.

First, make a list of the COGS and any other variable costs:

COGS

a. Turkey costs $2.60 per lb. Each sandwich uses 4 ounces of turkey meat (1/4 of a pound).

b. Large rolls cost $1.92 per dozen. One roll is used per sandwich.

c. A 32-ounce jar of mayonnaise costs $1.60. One ounce of mayonnaise is used per sandwich.

Many small businesses have inventory costs
(JoeFox/Radharc Images/Alamy)

Exhibit **12-5** *Retail Business: Unit = 1 Candy Bar*		
Economics of One Unit (EOU) Analysis		
One Unit of Sale = One Candy Bar		
Selling Price		$1.00
COGS (direct cost of the product or service)		
Average Cost of Candy Bars (COGS)	0.40	
Average Shipping Cost per Unit	0.06	
Total COGS	**0.46**	0.46
Gross Profit		0.54
Other Variable Costs (none)	—	—
Contribution Margin		**$0.54**

d. Lettuce costs 80 cents per pound. One ounce (1/16 of a pound) is used on each sandwich.
e. Tomatoes cost $1.16 each. Each uses one-fourth.
f. Pickles cost 5 cents each. Each sandwich comes with two pickles.
g. Employees are paid $8 per hour and can make 10 sandwiches per hour (we are assuming no down time and no payroll costs).

Other Variable Costs

a. Napkins cost $3 per pack of 100. One napkin is included with each sale.
b. Paper wrapping costs 20 cents per foot (cut from a roll). Each sandwich uses two feet of paper.
c. Plastic carryout bags cost $7 per roll of 100. Each sandwich sold uses one plastic carryout bag.

The EOU for the turkey sandwich is shown in **Exhibit 12-6**.

Exhibit **12-6** *Retail Business: Unit = 1 Turkey Sandwich*					
Selling Price per Unit:					$5.00
Cost of Goods Sold	**Price**	**Units**	**Quantity Used**	**Cost Each**	
Turkey (4 oz.):	$2.60	Per lb.	¼ lb.	$0.65	
Bread (roll):	$1.92	Per dozen	¹⁄₁₂ dozen	$0.16	
Mayonnaise (1 oz.):	$1.60	Per 32-oz. jar	¹⁄₃₂ jar	$0.05	
Lettuce (1 oz.):	$0.80	Per lb.	¹⁄₁₆ lb.	$0.05	
Tomato (¼ lb.)	$1.16	Each	¼ each	$0.29	
Pickles (2):	$0.05	Each	2 each	$0.10	
Direct Labor (6 min.):	$8.00	Per hr.	¹⁄₁₀ hr.	$0.80	
Total Cost of Goods Sold per Unit:				**$2.10**	2.10
Gross Profit					**$2.90**
Other Variable Costs					
Napkin:	$3.00	Per 100-pack	¹⁄₁₀₀ pack	$0.03	
Paper Wrapping:	$0.20	Per foot	2 feet	$0.40	
Plastic Bag:	$7.00	Per roll (100)	¹⁄₁₀₀ roll	$0.07	
Total Other Variable Costs per Unit:				**$0.50**	
Total Variable Costs per Unit:					0.50
Contribution Margin per Unit:					$2.40

Fixed Operating Costs

Costs, such as rent or the Internet bill, which do not vary per unit of production or service, are called **fixed operating costs**. Total fixed costs do not change based on volume (an advertising cost of $1,000 will be the same whether it generates 50 sales or 500). Fixed cost per unit decreases as the number of units increases ($20 per unit above versus $2).

Fixed operating costs do not change based on sales activity levels; therefore, they are not included in the EOU. A sandwich shop has to pay the same rent each month whether it sells one turkey sandwich or a hundred. However, the owner of the shop can change the cost of the rent by moving or can increase or decrease the advertising budget, for example. These changes are not calculated on a per-unit basis.

It is easier to remember several of the most common categories of fixed expenses by remembering the phrase:

fixed operating costs
expenses that do not vary with changes in the volume of production or sales.

◀ **Learning Objective 3**
Analyze your fixed operating costs and calculate gross profit.

I SAID U R · "Other FXs"

Insurance
Salaries (indirect labor—managers, office staff, sales force)
Advertising
Interest
Depreciation
Utilities (gas, electric, telephone, Internet access)
Rent
Other **F**ixed e**X**penses

Most of these categories are self-explanatory, but *depreciation* may need clarification. **Depreciation** is the percentage of value of an asset subtracted each year until the value becomes zero—to reflect wear and tear on the asset. It is a method used to *expense* (list as an expense on the income statement) costly pieces of equipment. Some items, such as a computer server, are expected to last for a number of years. A business could choose to expense the server during the year it was bought, but that would not be accurate. The server that will be used for four years will have been only 25 percent "used up" during the year it was purchased. Expensing the entire cost during that year would make the accounting records and financial statements inaccurate. If more than 25 percent of the server's cost is expensed in the first year, the income statement will show a lower profit than it should. Meanwhile, profits in subsequent years will appear to be higher than they should.

depreciation the percentage of value of an asset subtracted periodically to reflect the declining value.

Depreciation spreads the cost of an item purchased by a business over the time. If the computer server is expected to have a useful life of more than one year, the full price should be shown as an asset and then expensed according to federal tax law and accounting practice.

Fixed Operating Costs Can Change Over Time

If you pay your restaurant manager $3,600 per month in salary, you will have to pay that amount whether the restaurant sells one meal or a thousand. The cost is fixed.

Fixed operating costs do change over time; at some point you may give your restaurant manager a raise. Or you might hire a new manager at a higher salary. The word *fixed* does not mean the cost *never* changes, just that it does not change in response to units of production or sales over a relevant range of production. For instance:

- *Advertising.* The cost of advertising will change based on decisions the entrepreneur makes about how much to spend to reach the consumer, not because of current sales.

Case Study | Damon White Party Promotions[5]

The Problem

The telephone rang. Damon White put on his headset and answered, "Good evening, Seattle Teen Hotline. My name is Damon. How can I help you?" The year was 2009. Damon had been working as a hotline counselor at the Mayor's Youth Committee for three years. Every night, from 6 to 11 p.m., he took calls from teenagers in the Seattle area, advising them on many different issues: relationships, family problems, school, and more. Damon had a natural talent for being a good listener. In fact, he listened so well that over time he started noticing similarities in the types of problems that young people were discussing on the hotline. Specifically, Damon observed that younger teens in the Cedar Park and Eastlake neighborhoods did not feel safe going out on the weekends. Parents were also worried about the safety of their children and sometimes called to ask whether the Youth Committee ever sponsored teen parties or other gatherings. Damon always felt bad telling parents that the Committee did not have the funds to organize these types of events. Damon liked helping people, but this was the kind of problem he did not feel he could solve.

Thinkstock

Problems Can Lead to Opportunities

But then, one day in October, Damon came up with an idea:

> Everybody was asking, "Is there going to be a Halloween party?" But there was not anyone who was throwing a party, so I said; I'll throw my own party. I did not know how to DJ, but I had friends who worked as professional DJs. I just contacted everyone I knew who could help out and then made it happen.

Damon decided to use all $700 of his personal savings to purchase services and supplies for the party. His intention was to earn this money back and also generate a profit, by charging a $10 admission fee. He thought that $10 was a reasonable price, because it was about the same amount that teens would typically spend on a weekend night to go out to a movie or play video games at the arcade. Damon knew that he had to be careful about how he allocated his resources, because a $700 start-up investment was not going to get him very far.

Getting Organized

Damon's first step in planning his party was to brainstorm a list of all the things he would need to purchase and arrange. The list he created was as follows:

Item	Cost
Space Rental	
DJ	
Security	
Insurance	
Flyers	
Food	
Party Decorations	

He thought this was a pretty good list; the only problem was that he did not know how much each item would cost. Could he pay for these goods and services with his limited funds? He was not certain. First, he needed to do some research.

Damon Investigates His Costs

Damon called his friend Janae, who worked as a professional DJ, to find out how much she would charge to spin records at the party. Janae normally got $500 as a DJ at Seattle's hottest clubs, but she agreed to reduce her fee to $100, because she saw that Damon was trying to do something positive for the community.

Damon then spoke with another friend, who worked as a security guard, to ask if he could organize a security squad for the event. The friend agreed to find four coworkers who could staff the party for $50 each.

[5] This case is based on a real-life example, but selected details have been fictionalized. Thanks to Stephen Spinelli and Alex Hardy for granting permission to adapt this case from its original version.

Damon needed a large, centrally located venue where he could host the party. He remembered that his friend Quinetta had once rented a dance studio in an old, converted factory. The studio would be perfect because it was located in the heart of downtown Seattle, near the highway. He contacted the studio's owner and negotiated a deal to rent the space for $200 for four hours. This rental fee included insurance, in case there was an accident.

Throughout the planning process, Damon leveraged his personal network to assemble the necessary components for the party. He explained:

> *If I had to go out and hire professionals, I wouldn't know them. And the fact that I did not have the money right then to pay full market prices for people's services—but these people trusted me and said, "We believe in what you're doing, so we'll provide our services at a discount."*

Damon's final step was to get the word out about the party to teens and parents. He called his friend John, who freelanced as a graphic designer, and offered to pay him $50 to design and print 300 flyers. By this point, Damon had already committed $600 of his savings toward entertainment, space rental, security, and promotional costs. With his remaining $100, he decided to purchase chips, soda, cups, and napkins. He figured that he could recoup his investment by selling these snacks at a modest profit.

After making these arrangements Damon filled in the actual cost of each item on the list.

Item	Cost
Space Rental and Insurance	$200
DJ	100
Security	250
Graphic Design and Flyer Production	50
Food, Decorations, and Misc. Supplies	100
TOTAL	$700

Damon felt satisfied that he had managed his limited resources effectively. He was finally ready for the party. All he had left to do was decide on what costume to wear.

The Party

On the night of the party, Damon arrived early to set up. Despite weeks of planning, he still felt nervous. He had never done anything like this before. What if no one showed up and he lost all his money? The doors opened at 9 p.m., and by the end of the first hour only 20 people had arrived. Damon realized that, at $10 apiece, that was only $200. The room looked empty, no one was on the dance floor, and Damon's nerves were on overdrive. Suddenly, at 10:30, the party filled up quickly and, by 11, Damon was amazed to see that a line of kids had formed outside the door. The studio had a fire-hazard limit of 300, and by 11:30 the party was filled to capacity.

Keeping Good Records

In the end, Damon's party was a great success, personal and financial. When he sat down to calculate his revenue, he discovered that the party had generated $3,750. Damon tabulated his receipts and created the chart below, so that he could see how he had accomplished this.

Item	Selling Price per Unit	Number of Units Sold	Revenue Generated
Admission Tickets	$10.00	300	$3,000.00
Chips	$0.50	300	$150.00
Soda	$1.00	600	$600.00
TOTAL SALES REVENUE			$3,750.00

It had taken Damon three long years of careful saving to put away $700 from his part-time job at the hotline, so he was amazed that so much money could be generated in a single evening. As he reflected on the experience, Damon realized:

> *Even if not many people had come to the Halloween party, it would have been a success because I put something together, and I profited from it. Not only profited financially, but profited as an individual. It was something deeper than just the money. You've got to go into business because it is something you love to do and you want to create that independence. If you do something that you love, you always do your best.*

Future Possibilities

As he drove home after the party, Damon's mind was reeling. He was thinking about the future and what he wanted to accomplish. Maybe he would use some of the profit he earned to throw an even bigger party or perhaps start a party-planning business. He was not sure. After all, organizing the party had caused him a lot of stress. Or maybe he would put the money in his bank account so that he could save up for school. He had several possibilities to consider. Damon drove home and parked his car. As he got ready for bed, he resolved to think further about future plans in the morning.

Case Study Analysis

12-21. Assume that Damon decides to start a party-planning business:

a. Identify two ways he could assess the cost of goods or services sold for this business.

b. Which costs, described in the case, would become part of Damon's operating-cost structure?

c. Make a list of additional items Damon will need to purchase to get his business off the ground. Research the cost of these items.

12-22. One of the reasons why Damon earned a substantial profit is because he convinced his personal contacts to provide their services at a discounted rate. If he decides to grow his party-planning business, do you think he can continue to use this strategy? Why or why not? What would his costs have been if he had paid full price for everything?

12-23. Brainstorm three things Damon might have done differently in planning his party to increase sales revenue.

12-24. At the end of the case, Damon describes how he profited as an individual from the experience of throwing the Halloween party. What did he mean by this? Is it possible to profit from something on a personal level, even if you do not necessarily earn a financial profit? Can you think of an example from your own life where this happened? Explain.

Chapter 13

USING FINANCIAL STATEMENTS TO GUIDE A BUSINESS

Learning Objectives

1. Understand an income statement.

2. Examine a balance sheet to determine a business's financing strategy.

3. Use the balance sheet equation for analysis.

4. Perform a financial ratio analysis on an income statement.

5. Calculate return on investment (ROI).

6. Perform same-size analysis of an income statement.

7. Use quick, current, and debt ratios to analyze a balance sheet.

Jack Hollingsworth/Thinkstock

The allure of an ice cream truck is undeniable, as it travels through a neighborhood where children and adults eagerly gather for frozen treats. For Dylan Bauer, a Temple University entrepreneurship graduate and founder of Chilly Dilly's Ice Cream Company in York, Pennsylvania, the allure was far greater.[1] However, Dylan learned early that it was not enough to have a "cool" business. This young entrepreneur learned the importance of detailed and accurate financial statements early, so that he knew the financial condition of Chilly Dilly's at all times.

Each year, Dylan created the next season's cash budget in order to plan major expenditures. The majority of Chilly Dilly's sales occurred between June and September, so Dylan reported, "Each October I am sitting on a ton of cash, but it gets used up over the winter months paying bills and planning for the next season." After five years of operations, he had achieved a 105.7 percent increase in profits—and the fifth year saw a rise of more than 250 percent in revenues over the fourth year. However, as he evaluated future options, Dylan recognized that such growth would likely be unsustainable and financing would be a challenge. Fortunately, Dylan understood his financial circumstances and relied on his financial savvy, marketing expertise, and the input of trusted advisors.

Rose Horridge, Lucy Claxton/DK Images Ltd

Scorecards for the Entrepreneur: What Do Financial Statements Show?

In this chapter you will learn how to prepare and use the income statement and balance sheet to guide your business and keep it strong. Entrepreneurs use three basic financial documents to track their businesses:

- an income statement
- a balance sheet
- a cash flow statement

Together, they show the health of a business at a glance.

Best practice for entrepreneurs is to use their financial records to prepare monthly income statements and balance sheets and then finalize these at the end of the fiscal year. Cash flow statements (as will be discussed in Chapter 14) should be prepared at least monthly. These statements will provide a concise, easily read and understood company financial picture. Whereas transaction records—such as those kept in a journal or check register—will show the cash balance on hand, the income statement and balance sheet give an overview of the organization. By performing financial-statement analysis, you can gain a comprehensive understanding of how any enterprise is doing.

---

[1]Based on a case prepared by Dr. Jay Azriel and Dr. Andrew Sumutka, of York College of Pennsylvania.

Income Statements: Showing Profit and Loss Over Time

Learning Objective 1

Understand an income statement.

The income statement shows whether the difference between revenue (sales) and expenses (costs) is a profit or a loss over a given period. If revenues are greater than expenses, the income statement balance will be positive, showing that the business is profitable. If costs are greater than sales, the income statement balance will show that the business is operating at a loss—that it is unprofitable.

The income statement is a scorecard for the entrepreneur. If the business is not making a profit, examining the statement can reveal what may be causing the problem. Steps can then be taken to correct it and prevent insolvency. *Profit* is a reward for making the right business choices. The income statement will enable you to determine whether your decisions have kept you on the right track.

Parts of an Income Statement

The income statement is composed of the following:

1. *Revenue.* Income from sales of the company's products or services. For companies using the cash method of accounting, sales are recorded when payment is received.
2. *COGS (Cost of goods sold)/COSS (Cost of services sold).* These are the costs of materials used to make the product (or deliver the service) plus the costs of the direct labor used to make the product (or deliver the service). An income statement reports total COGS for a period.
3. *Gross profit.* The result of revenues minus COGS.
4. *Other variable costs (VC).* Costs that vary with sales and are not included in COGS.
5. *Contribution margin.* Equals revenues minus COGS and other variable costs, or gross profit minus other variable costs.
6. *Fixed operating costs.* Costs of operating a business that do not vary with sales over a relevant range. Common fixed operating costs are rent, salaries, utilities, advertising, insurance, depreciation, and interest.
7. *Earnings before interest and taxes (EBIT).* The result of gross profit minus other variable costs minus fixed costs, except interest and taxes.
8. *Pre-tax profit.* EBIT minus interest costs. This is a business's profit after all costs have been deducted, but before taxes have been paid. Pretax profit is used to calculate how much tax the business owes.
9. *Taxes.* A business must pay taxes on the income it earns as a separate entity from the owners' personal taxes, depending on its legal form (e.g., a corporation). It may have to make monthly or quarterly estimated tax payments.
10. *Net profit/(loss).* This is the business's profit or loss after any taxes have been paid.

Entrepreneurial Wisdom . . .

Whenever a number in a financial statement is enclosed in parentheses, it is negative. If you see ($142,938) at the bottom of an income statement, it means the business had a net loss of $142,938.

A Basic Income Statement

The power of the income statement is that it will tell you whether you are fulfilling the formula of buying low, selling high, and meeting customer needs. See **Exhibit 13-1** for an example of an income statement for a relatively simple business. It illustrates how an income statement functions.

David buys 100 handbags at $10 each and sells them all at $25 each at a flea market, for revenue of $2,500. He gives each customer a petite charm (at a cost of 50 cents) to attach to the handbag. He also spends $25 on flyers to advertise that he will be selling on Saturday at the flea market, and $500 to rent the booth. The income statement in **Exhibit 13-2** quickly shows whether or not he made a profit. The income statement not only shows that David's business is profitable but also illustrates exactly *how* profitable.

Exhibit 13-1 *Basic Income Statement*

A Basic Company, Inc.
Income Statement for the Month Ended June 30, 2013

Sales/Revenue			$ 24,681
COGS (Cost of Goods Sold)			
Total Materials	$ 2,468		
Total Labor	3,579		
Total COGS	$ 6,047	$ 6,047	$ 6,047
Gross Profit			$ 18,634
Other Variable Costs			
Commissions	$ 1,234		
Packaging	236		
Total Other Variable Costs	$ 1,470	$ 1,470	1,470
Contribution Margin			$ 17,164
Fixed Operating Costs (USAIIRD)			
Utilities	$ 200		
Salaries	3,000		
Advertising	600		
Insurance	300		
Interest	300		
Rent	1,000		
Depreciation	50		
Other	50		
Total Fixed Operating Costs:	$ 5,500		$ 5,500
Pre-Tax Profit			$ 11,164
Taxes (0.34%)			3,796
Net Profit			$ 7,368

Total Sales/Revenue = Units Sold × Unit Selling Price
Total Cost of Goods or Services Sold = Units Sold × Cost of Goods or Services Sold per Unit
Gross Profit = Sales − COGS
Total Other Variable Costs = Units Sold × Other Variable Costs per Unit
Total Variable Costs = Total Cost of Goods or Services Sold + Total Other Variable Costs
Contribution Margin = Total Sales − Total Variable Costs
Total Fixed Costs = Total of USAIDIRO
Pre-Tax Profit/(Loss) = Contribution Margin − Total Fixed Costs
Taxes = Profit × .34 (Estimated)
Net Profit = Pre-Tax Profit − Taxes

Exhibit **13-2** *Handbag Store Income Statement*			
David's Income Statement			
Handbag sales at flea market (one time) — for one month			
Sales:	100 handbags × $25/bag		$2,500
Less COGS	100 handbags × $10/bag	$1,000	1,000
Gross Profit			$1,500
Other Variable Costs	100 charms × $0.50/charm	50	50
Total Variable Costs		$1,050	
Contribution Margin			$1,450
Fixed Costs			
Rent ($500 to rent booth)		$500	
Advertising ($25 for flyers)		25	
Total Fixed Costs		$525	525
Pre-Tax Profit			$925
Taxes (25%)			231
Net Profit			$694

The Double Bottom Line

The expression, "What's the bottom line?" refers to the last line on an income statement, which shows whether a business has made a profit.

Another bottom line can be considered, though, aside from whether the organization (either for-profit or not-for-profit) is making money. Is your business achieving its mission? If your dream was to have your venture fill a need in the community, is this goal being realized? Are you able to make a profit and operate the business in a way that makes you feel satisfied and fulfilled? Goals that go beyond profit might include:

- being a good citizen by doing business in a way that respects the environment—recycling, minimizing waste, looking for energy sources that do not pollute;
- encouraging local people to invest in the business and become equity owners;
- always dealing honestly with customers and suppliers, and treating everyone you do business with the way you would like to be treated;
  - treating employees with respect regarding their health and safety; and
  - setting up profit-sharing plans, so that employees can share in the success they help create.

Ideally, you want to have a positive *double* bottom line: You are making a profit so you can stay in business *and* achieve your mission. Not-for-profit organizations all have a double bottom line to measure. They must achieve successful financial results in order to continue operations and work toward their mission. Not-for-profits explicitly strive to attain successful double bottom lines.

An Income Statement for a More Complex Business

The income statement in **Exhibit 13-3** follows the same format as the previous one and its goal is still the same—to show how profitable the business is. However, this statement includes the category of depreciation.

Working on a financial statement
(Shutterstock)

Exhibit 13-3 *Income Statement for a Manufacturer*		
Lola's Custom Draperies, Inc. **Income Statement for the Month Ended March 31, 2014**		
Sales:		$85,456
Cost of Goods Sold:		
Materials	$11,550	
Labor	17,810	
Total COGS:		29,360
Gross Profit:		$56,096
Other Variable Costs:		
Sales Commissions	8,000	8,000
Contribution Margin:		$48,096
Fixed Operating Costs:		
Factory Rent and Utilities	$8,000	
Salaries and Administrative	12,000	
Depreciation	2,000	
Total Fixed Operating Costs:		22,000
Profit Before Taxes:		$26,096
Taxes (25%):		6,524
Net Profit/(Loss):		$19,572

Publicly traded companies have the same essential format as shown in **Exhibit 13-3**. Their statements are available to shareholders and other members of the public through their quarterly and annual filings with the U.S. Securities and Exchange Commission (10Q and 10K reports), and annual reports to shareholders. If you are not familiar with financial statements, it may help to look at the annual report of a large public company in a peer industry. The reports are generally available in the investor- or shareholder-relations section of corporate Web sites.

Global Impact . . .

By the Numbers—Quintiles Transnational Corporation

As the leader in the $20 billion industry of outsourcing clinical trials, with 27,000 employees in some 100 countries, Quintiles Transnational relies on data collection and analysis as its core business. Dennis Gillings, CBE, PhD, a British statistician and former professor at the University of North Carolina at Chapel Hill, is the founder and 24-percent owner of the company that provides clinical, commercial, capital, and consulting solutions in biologic and pharmaceutical services.

However, clinical data is not all that Quintiles tracks. Financial information is essential to guiding company performance. Although privately held until May 2013, the company did report sales of $3.7 billion in 2012. In 2011, Quintiles reported, "$500 million in earnings before interest, taxes, depreciation, and amortization, and $400 million in free cash flow" on revenues of $3.0 billion.[2]

Quintiles recognized the opportunity to improve its financial performance by restructuring its debt financing. In a press release dated March 8, 2011, it announced the start of the refinancing of $2.425 billion in credit facilities to take advantage of better debt terms.[3] Subsequently, its parent holding company has gone public on the New York Stock Exchange.

Understanding and using financial data is critical for this global leader. Financial savvy helped Dennis Gillings grow his entrepreneurial venture from its humble beginnings in a trailer on the UNC campus.

---

[2]Matthew Herper, "Money, Math and Medicine," *Forbes*, November 22, 2010, p. 142.
[3]Quintiles Transnational Corporation, accessed August 18, 2013, http://www.quintiles.com.

The Balance Sheet: A Snapshot of Assets, Liabilities, and Equity at a Point in Time

Learning Objective 2

Examine a balance sheet to determine a business's financing strategy.

net worth (owner's equity) the difference between assets and liabilities.

owner's equity (net worth) the difference between assets and liabilities.

fiscal year the financial reporting year for a company.

You can quickly see a company's financing strategy by looking at its *balance sheet* (see **Exhibits 13-4** and **13-5**). A balance sheet is a financial statement that shows the assets (what the business owns), liabilities (debts), and **net worth** of a business. The net worth is the difference between assets and liabilities and is also called **owner's equity**.

1. *Assets.* Items (tangible and intangible) a company owns that have monetary value.
2. *Liabilities.* Debts a company has that must be paid, including unpaid bills.
3. *Owner's equity (OE).* Also called net worth, the difference between assets and liabilities. It shows the amount of capital in the business. It consists of common equity, preferred equity, paid-in capital, and retained earnings.

The balance sheet for a large business is typically prepared quarterly and at the end of the fiscal year, unlike cash flow and income statements, which are prepared monthly. The **fiscal year** is the 12-month accounting period chosen by the business. A fiscal year may differ from the calendar year (January 1 through December 31). A business that uses the calendar year as its fiscal year would prepare its balance sheet for the annual time frame ending December 31.

Exhibit 13-4 *Balance Sheet (Horizontal)*

A Basic Company, Inc.
Balance Sheet
December 31, 2013

Assets			Liabilities		
Current Assets			**Current Liabilities**		
Cash		$75,000	Accounts payable		$475,000
Accounts receivable		250,000	Notes payable		175,000
Inventory		500,000	Accrued wages payable		75,000
Supplies		80,000	Accrued taxes payable		20,000
Prepaid expenses		15,000	Accrued interest payable		25,000
Total Current Assets		**$920,000**	**Total Current Liabilities**		**$770,000**
Long-Term (Fixed) Assets			**Long-Term Liabilities**		
Land		$500,000	Mortgage		$900,000
Buildings	$700,000		Notes payable		500,000
Less accum. depreciation	70,000	630,000	**Total Long-Term Liabilities**		**$1,400,000**
Vehicles	$200,000				
Less accum. depreciation	60,000	140,000	**Owner's Equity**		
Equipment	$250,000		Prime Owner, paid in capital		$197,500
Less accum. depreciation	12,500	237,500	Common stock		100,000
Furniture and fixtures	$50,000		**Total Owner's Equity**		**$297,500**
Less accum. depreciation	10,000	40,000			
Total Fixed Assets		**$1,547,500**			
Total Assets		**$2,467,500**	**Total Liabilities and Owner's Equity**		**$2,467,500**

Exhibit 13-5 *Balance Sheet (Vertical)*

A Basic Company, Inc.
Balance Sheet
December 31, 2013

Assets

Current Assets

Cash		$75,000
Accounts receivable		250,000
Inventory		500,000
Supplies		80,000
Prepaid expenses		15,000
Total Current Assets		**$920,000**

Long-Term (Fixed) Assets

Land		500,000
Buildings	$700,000	
Less accum. depreciation	70,000	630,000
Vehicles	$200,000	
Less accum. depreciation	60,000	140,000
Equipment	$250,000	
Less accum. depreciation	12,500	237,500
Furniture and fixtures	$50,000	
Less accum. depreciation	10,000	40,000
Total Fixed Assets		**$1,547,500**
Total Assets		**$2,467,500**

Liabilities

Current Liabilities

Accounts payable		$475,000
Notes payable		175,000
Accrued wages payable		75,000
Accrued taxes payable		20,000
Accrued interest payable		25,000
Total Current Liabilities		**$770,000**

Long-Term Liabilities

Mortgage		$900,000
Notes payable		500,000
Total Long-Term Liabilities		**$1,400,000**

Owner's Equity

Prime Owner, paid in capital		$197,500
Common stock		100,000
Total Owner's Equity		**$297,500**
Total Liabilities and Owner's Equity		**$2,467,500**

Many entrepreneurs, however, also prepare a balance sheet monthly. To keep the business on track, business owners use these three financial tools: the balance sheet, the income statement, and the cash flow statement.

Short- and Long-Term Assets

Assets are all items of worth owned by the business—cash, inventory, buildings, vehicles, furniture, machinery, and the like. Assets are divided into short-term (current) and long-term (fixed).

current assets cash or items that can be quickly converted to cash or will be used within one year.

long-term assets those that will take more than one year to use.

- **Current assets** are cash itself or items that could be quickly turned into cash *(liquidated)*, or that will be used by the business within one year. Current assets include accounts receivable, inventory, and supplies.
- **Long-term assets** are those that would take more than one year for the business to use, or could not be quickly liquidated. Equipment, furniture, machinery, and real estate are examples of long-term assets.

Current and Long-Term Liabilities

Liabilities are all debts owed by the business, such as bank loans, mortgages, lines of credit, and loans from family or friends.

current liabilities debts that are scheduled for payment within one year.

long-term liabilities debts that are due in over one year.

- **Current liabilities** are debts that are scheduled for payment within one year. These include the portion of long-term debt due within that year.
- **Long-term liabilities** are debts to be paid over a period of more than one year.

The Balance Sheet Equation

Learning Objective 3

Use the balance sheet equation for analysis.

The terms *owner's equity, capital,* and *net worth* all mean the same thing: what's left over after liabilities are subtracted from assets. Owner's equity is the value of the business on the balance sheet to the owner. The equation for calculating owner's equity is the *balance sheet equation.* As the name suggests, the balance sheet must always be in balance, with assets equal to the sum of liabilities plus equity. A sure sign of a calculation or record-keeping error is to have an imbalance.

$$\text{Assets} = \text{Liabilities} + \text{Owner's Equity or}$$

$$\text{Assets} - \text{Liabilities} = \text{Owner's Equity or}$$

$$\text{Assets} - \text{Owner's Equity} = \text{Liabilities}$$

- If assets are greater than liabilities, net worth is positive.
- If liabilities are greater than assets, net worth is negative.

For example, if the Dos Compadres Restaurant has $10,000 in cash on hand, owns $8,000 in equipment, and owes $5,000 in long-term liabilities, what is the restaurant owner's equity (net worth)?

$$\$18,000 \text{ (Assets)} - \$5,000 \text{ (Liabilities)} = \$13,000 \text{ (Net Worth)}$$

The Balance Sheet Shows Assets and Liabilities Obtained through Financing

Every item a business owns was obtained through either debt or equity. That is why the total of all assets must equal the total of all liabilities and owner's equity.

- If an item was financed with *debt,* the loan is a liability.
- If an item was purchased with the owner's own money (including that of shareholders), it was financed with *equity* (or from the net worth).

Exhibit **13-6** *Balance Sheet*			
The Greasy Spoon, LLC **Balance Sheet** **December 31, 2013**			
Assets		**Liabilities**	
Cash	$10,000	Short-Term Liabilities	$ 0
Inventory	4,000	Long-Term Liabilities	5,000
Capital Equipment	8,000		
Other Assets	0	**Owner's Equity**	17,000
Total Assets	**$22,000**	**Total Liabilities · Owner's Equity**	**$22,000**

The Greasy Spoon Diner owns its tables and chairs (worth $3,000) and its stove (worth $5,000); has $10,000 in cash; and holds $4,000 in inventory; in other words, the business has a capital equipment investment of $3,000 + $5,000 = $8,000, and $4,000 in inventory plus the $10,000 in cash. The restaurant also has a $5,000 long-term loan, which was used to buy the stove. Its total assets are $22,000 ($8,000 + $4,000 + $10,000). It has $5,000 in liabilities (the loan for the stove), which leaves $17,000 in owner's equity (OE).

Assuming the restaurant has no other assets and liabilities, **Exhibit 13-6** shows how its balance sheet would look.

Again, on a balance sheet, assets must equal the total of liabilities and owner's equity.

Total Assets = Total Liabilities + Owners Equity (OE)

The OE is $17,000. It is equal to the total of the cash ($10,000); the stove, tables, and chairs ($8,000); plus $4,000 in inventory; minus the $5,000 in liabilities.

The stove is financed with a ($5,000) loan (debt financing). This is a long-term liability. Together, the liabilities and the owner's equity have paid for the assets of the business. When reviewing a side-by-side balance sheet, remember that the assets (what you own) on the left are funded by the liabilities (what you owe), plus equity (your owners' stake) on the right.

The Balance Sheet Shows How a Business Is Financed

The balance sheet is an especially effective tool for looking at how a business is financed. It clearly shows the relationship between debt and equity financing. Sometimes businesses make the mistake of relying too heavily on either debt or equity. The appropriate mix depends on the industry and the individual firm.

- An entrepreneur who relies too much on equity financing from outside owners can lose control of the company. If the other owners control a large percentage of the business, they may insist on making the decisions or may impede decision making and create inefficiency and confusion.
- An entrepreneur who takes on too much debt and is unable to make loan payments can lose the business, and possibly personal assets as well, to banks or other creditors.

All the information you need to analyze a company's financing strategy—total debt, equity, and assets—is in its balance sheet. People who invest in businesses use *ratios* to grasp a company's financial situation quickly. As an entrepreneur, you will want to understand these ratios so you will be

Entrepreneurship Portfolio

Critical Thinking Exercises

13-1. Repeat the exercise from Key Concept Questions for this chapter using accounting software. Then run the following what-if scenarios and create graphs or other visuals showing how each would affect the business's monthly and yearly financial picture:

- What if the restaurant finds a supplier that is willing to provide paper for only $8,000 in June and $96,000 for the year?
- What if sales for June were $250,000 and sales for the year were $2,000,000? (Do not forget the taxes, assumed at 25 percent.)
- What if the owner of this franchise faced start-up costs of $400,000 instead of $300,000? How would that affect the ROI?

13-2. If you were to open a clothing store, what do you think would be a reasonable operating ratio for the rent, and why?

13-3. Which items in your business would you depreciate, and why?

13-4. Using **Exhibit 13-12**, the balance sheet of Angelina's Jewelry Company at the end of July that follows, calculate all four financial ratios (quick, current, debt, and debt-to-equity) for the business.

13-5. Write a memo analyzing the financial strengths and weaknesses of Angelina's venture. Use the common-size statement information in **Exhibit 13-13**. Would you invest in her business? Why or why not?

13-6. Using The Greasy Spoon Diner balance sheet in **Exhibits 13-7** and **13-8**, answer the following:

a. What are the debt-to-equity ratios at the beginning and end of the 2013 fiscal (business) year? Has it improved? If so, by how much?

b. The restaurant has less cash at the end of the year than it had at the beginning. Is this a bad thing or not? Explain.

c. Does the restaurant have enough cash to pay its expenses going into 2014? Why or why not?

d. If the restaurant grew its owner's equity by 31 percent during the 2013 fiscal year, at that rate, how much will the business have in owner's equity after one more year (on December 31, 2014)?

e. The restaurant added some capital equipment during the year. Did it take out another loan for that equipment, or did it pay cash? Explain your thinking.

Exhibit 13-12 *Balance Sheet for Angelina's Jewelry Company*

Angelina's Jewelry Company Balance Sheet As of July 30, 2014			
Assets		**Liabilities**	
Current Assets		**Short-Term Liabilities**	
Cash	$ 1,000	Accounts Payable	$ 1,000
Inventory	1,000	Short-Term Loans	500
Securities	1,000	**Total Short-Term Liabilities**	**$ 1,500**
Total Current Assets	**$ 3,000**	**Total Long-Term Liabilities**	1,500
Long-Term Assets	7,000	**Owner's Equity**	**$ 7,000**
Total Assets	**$10,000**	**Total Liabilities · Owner's Equity**	**$10,000**

Exhibit 13-13 *Comparative Balance Sheet for Angelina's Jewelry Company*

Angelina's Jewelry Company Balance Sheet	Aug. 30, 2013	July 30, 2013	% Change
Assets			
Current Assets			
Cash	$ 500	$ 1,000	(50)%
Inventory	2,000	1,000	100%
Securities	1,500	1,000	50%
Total Current Assets	**$ 4,000**	**$ 3,000**	33%
Long-Term Assets	**7,000**	**7,000**	0%
Total Assets	**$11,000**	**$10,000**	10%
Liabilities			
Short-Term Liabilities			
Accounts Payable	$ 1,500	$ 1,000	50%
Short-Term Loans	—	500	(100)%
Total Short-Term Liabilities	**$ 1,500**	**$ 1,500**	0%
Total Long-Term Liabilities	**500**	**1,500**	(67)%
Owner's Equity	**$ 9,000**	**$ 7,000**	29%
Total Liabilities · Owners' Equity	**$11,000**	**$10,000**	10%

13-7. On a separate sheet of paper or using a spreadsheet, create a balance sheet for Tropical Aquaculture—a shrimp farm—using the information below. Calculate and analyze the quick, debt, and debt-to-equity ratios.

Cash	$45,000
Accounts receivable	$12,000
Shrimp feed	$8,400
Accounts payable	$9,700
Equipment	$75,000
Bank loan	$20,000
Property and ponds	$124,000

13-8. Use the following balance sheet to answer the following questions:

a. What is the year-to-year percentage change in the value of the following:
- inventory
- accounts payable
- land
- taxes payable
- liabilities and owner's equity

b. What is the ratio of the following:
- Cash equivalent to inventory in 2014? How did it change from 2013?
- Owner's equity to total assets in 2014? How did it change from 2013?

Jean M's Florida-Style Subs, Inc. Balance Sheet December 31, 2013 and 2014		
	2014	**2013**
Assets		
Current Assets		
Cash and cash equivalents	$10,000	$10,000
Accounts receivable	2,000	7,000
Inventory	20,000	25,000
Total Current Assets	**$32,000**	**$42,000**
Fixed Assets		
Plant and machinery	$5,000	$9,000
Land	9,000	8,000
TOTAL ASSETS	**$46,000**	**$59,000**
Liabilities		
Accounts payable	$10,000	$15,000
Taxes payable	6,000	5,000
Total Liabilities	**$16,000**	**$20,000**
OWNER'S EQUITY	**$30,000**	**$39,000**
LIABILITIES and OWNER'S EQUITY	**$46,000**	**$59,000**

    c. Investors and buyers like to put their money into companies that have a low ratio of liabilities to assets. Has that ratio become more or less appealing from 2013 to 2014?

13-9. Create a projected balance sheet for your business for one year.

    a. Create a pie chart showing your current assets, long-term assets, current liabilities, and long-term liabilities.

    b. What is your debt ratio?

    c. What is your debt-to-equity ratio?

Key Concept Questions

13-10. Given the following data, create monthly and yearly income statements for Quick Meals to Go, LLC in New York City.

    a. Sales for the month of June were $300,000. Sales for the year were $2,600,000.

    b. The sum of $66,000 was spent on food in June ($792,000 for the year). The store spent $9,000 on paper to wrap food items in June and $108,000 for the year.

    c. Taxes for June were $15,000. For the year, they were $233,000.

    d. Fixed operating costs for June were $175,000. For the year, they were $1,000,000.

    e. Use Excel or other software to create a graph showing the monthly and yearly income statements for this business.

13-11. If the owner of Quick Meals to Go invested $300,000 in start-up costs, what was his ROI for the year? (Assume June as average.)

13-12. Calculate the financial ratios (ROI and ROS) for the monthly and yearly income statement you created in 13-10. What do the financial ratios tell you about this business?

13-13. What would the profit before taxes be if the owner above found a paper supplier who only charged $100,000 for the year?

13-14. What would the profit margin for the year be based on 13-13?

13-15. Suppose the owner of Quick Meals on the Go wanted to raise profits by $5,000 a month. What would you recommend he do, and why?

13-16. State the financial equation for the balance sheet in three different ways.

13-17. How is depreciation treated on the balance sheet, and what is the logic behind this treatment?

Application Exercise

13-18. Below is a real estate investor's balance sheet (in millions) as of December 31, 2013. All the businesses in her real estate empire were separately incorporated for liability reasons, and many of them were heavily *leveraged*, or debt-financed. Calculate the debt ratios for each of the properties, then answer the questions.

Asset	Estimated Worth	Debt	Net Worth	Debt Ratio
The Pyramids of Gaza	$820	$820	$0	1.0
East Side Yards	450	175	30	_____
Phoenix Casino	640	275	345	_____
Mogul's Lair Casino	600	415	6	_____
Serena's Shuttle	400	400	0	_____
Stefania's Tower	200	100	0	_____
Cash	130	160	−30	_____
Igor's Condos	115	5	45	_____
Marketable Securities	90	75	15	_____
Serena's Palace	80	80	0	_____
Stefania's Plaza	70	50	3	_____
Grand Brand Hotel (50%)	70	30	40	_____
Igor Regency	65	85	−20	_____
Igor Plaza Coops	45	0	25	_____
Mogul Air	40	0	30	_____
Personal Transportation	40	0	30	_____
Personal Housing	30	40	−9	_____
Total (in millions)	$ _____	$ _____	$ _____	_____

13-19. What was the mogul's highest-priced asset?

13-20. What was mogul's net worth for the Serena's Shuttle? Why?

13-21. On which asset was the mogul's net worth the greatest?

13-22. Which asset carried the most debt?

13-23. Which properties did the mogul own free of debt?

13-24. On which properties did the mogul owe one dollar of debt for each dollar of the asset?

Exploring Online

Use the Internet (try the Edgar site at http://www.sec.gov/edgar/searchedgar/companysearch.html for public companies) to find the balance sheets of two companies with which you are familiar. Use percentages to analyze these balance sheets, and compare how well each is doing compared to The Greasy Spoon Diner example from this chapter. Then compare them to each other. Consider choosing either two similar companies, such as Pfizer Inc. and Johnson & Johnson, or two different industries, such as an airline and a car manufacturer.

13-25. Create common-size balance sheets for each.

13-26. Calculate their balance sheet ratios.

13-27. How do the companies compare in growing owner's equity?

13-28. How do the companies compare in reducing debt?

13-29. Describe how you think market conditions (such as gas prices, for example) are affecting each company's growth.

13-30. How, if at all, do the ratios of these companies relate to that of The Greasy Spoon Diner?

BizBuilder Business Plan Questions

After studying this chapter, you should be able to answer the following Business Plan Questions. The entire outline for the Business Plan is found in Appendix 2.

7.0 Financial Analysis and Projections

7.3 *Balance Sheet Projections*

   A. Create a projected balance sheet for your business for the first four quarters and the second and third years of operation.

   B. Create a pie chart showing your current assets, long-term assets, current liabilities, and long-term liabilities.

7.4 *Income Statement Projections*

   A. Create a projected income statement for your business for the first four quarters and the second and third years of operation.

   B. Create a bar chart showing your gross revenues, gross profit, and net income.

7.5 *Breakeven Analysis*

   A. Use Excel or another spreadsheet program to create a spreadsheet projecting the fixed and variable expenses for your business. Use this data to perform a breakeven analysis.

7.6 *Ratio Analysis*

   A. Use your projected financial statements to calculate all your key ratios.

   B. Compare these ratios to your industry using publicly available data.

7.7 *Risks and Assumptions*

   A. List the risks and assumptions that underlie your financial projections.

   B. Identify any external factors that you feel should be disclosed as substantial risks.

Gentle Rest Slumber, LLC: Using Financials to Build Employee Performance[4]

Sean O'Neal decided that he wanted to be his own boss after working for several years making mattresses with a small, custom mattress shop in Santa Fe, New Mexico. He knew that the retail market was dominated by several licensed brands such as Sealy, Serta, Restonic, and Simmons. He also believed he could create products with clear customer value propositions at a profit for himself. When Sean started Gentle Rest Slumber with his meager savings, he promised himself to treat his employees differently from the way he had been treated in the custom shop. Part of this promise was to be honest with his team about the company's financial condition.

© MBI/Alamy

When he brought in employees, Sean took the time to help them understand the company's key performance indicators and to work with them on setting goals. His team consisted of sewers, warehouse staff, truck drivers, and other unskilled and semi-skilled workers. Sean didn't intend to make them all accountants, nor did he wish to become one. However, he was familiar with the critical financial statement ratios for his industry and saw clearly his vision for the company.

At first, the team was uncomfortable with the idea of reviewing financial performance and setting goals for the company. They understood piece-work programs, where they were paid according to the number of quality items they completed per shift, but they weren't so sure about being responsible for more than that. However, by the third year of this "open-book" system, employees were fully engaged and motivated to participate.

Among the key financial data Sean presented to them was the following:

	2013	2012	% Change	Industry 2013
Revenue	$2,200,000	$2,000,000	10%	−5%
Material	14%	10%	4%	11%
Labor	23%	20%	3%	18%
Gross Profit	63%	70%	−7%	72%
ROS	3%	10%	−7%	6%
ROI	6.6%	20%	−13.4%	22%
Current Ratio	0.9	1.1	−18.2%	1.2
Debt-to-Equity	1.5	1.0	50%	1.2
Collection Period	60 days	45 days	−33%	50 days

The employees were excited to see that revenues had increased, but they were concerned about the other results. This led to intense discussions about the concerns and how to best move forward.

Case Study Analysis

13-31. What are the positive aspects the employees could glean from the financial data?

13-32. What concerns should they have?

13-33. What additional information would you want to know?

13-34. What would you recommend if you were an employee? Why?

---

[4]This is a fictional case.

Portland Freelancers' Café: Amy and Steve's Business Idea[5]

In 2003, Amy Chan and Steve Lee formed a partnership to start an Internet café in Portland, Oregon. For many years, Amy and Steve had worked as freelance writers. They enjoyed bringing their laptops to local coffeehouses to complete their writing projects. Having an endless supply of good strong coffee at their disposal helped them to stay focused on their work.

Ryan McVay/Getty Images

Over time, they began to daydream about owning their own café. Although Portland already had many great coffeehouses, Amy and Steve felt that none of them catered well to freelancers like themselves. More and more, people in Portland seemed to be doing their work in informal settings. Everywhere they turned, twenty- and thirty-somethings were sipping lattes while conducting business deals on cell phones. Amy and Steve sometimes wondered if anyone worked in a traditional office anymore.

We Can Do Better

As much as they enjoyed Portland's café culture, they felt that a fatal flaw compromised each of their favorite coffee spots. One was too loud. Another had uncomfortable chairs and tables that weren't well suited for laptop users. Their particular favorite, The Magic Bean, only had three outlets, which meant that only a few laptops could be plugged in at one time. Just a handful of the coffeehouses in downtown Portland offered high-speed Internet access at that time.

Amy and Steve felt they could do a better job of running a café that catered to the needs of freelancers. They made a list of everything they

would want in a café and then asked their freelance friends for additional feedback. The two partners resolved that, in their café, customers would be able to enjoy high-speed Internet access; laser printers; a soundproof, quiet room; and comfortable, up-to-date work stations. To attract their target market, Amy and Steve decided to name their business the Portland Freelancers' Café.

Deluxe Purchases

They spent $10,000 up front installing super-fast T1 Internet lines. They imported a $7,000, top-of-the-line espresso machine from Italy. To make the café look sleek and modern, all of the furniture was custom-designed for the space, as were the curved metallic ceiling and wall panels. Installing the soundproof interior room was more costly than they had anticipated. Their equipment costs totaled $25,000. At $500 per month, they had negotiated a good deal on their rent, so they figured that they could afford to splurge on these other features.

Financing

The café's start-up investment totaled $100,000. This included a $10,000 cash reserve. Amy and Steve contributed a combined $20,000 of their personal savings. Steve's brother invested another $20,000, in exchange for a 20-percent equity stake. Amy's mother wrote a check for $10,000, which she gave to the partners as a gift. Also, Amy and Steve received a $50,000 loan from Amy's uncle. The partners agreed to pay back the loan with interest at an annual rate of 12 percent.

Funding Source	Equity	Debt	Gift
Personal Savings (80% equity)	$20,000		
Steve's Brother (20% equity)	$20,000		
Amy's Uncle (12% interest)		$50,000	
Amy's Mother			$10,000
Subtotal	$40,000	$50,000	$10,000
Total Start-Up Investment	$100,000		

[5]Note: This is a fictional case.

Computer Glitch

Because so much money was needed for start-up, Amy and Steve tried to cut costs by hiring a local high school student, who agreed to work 100 hours per month at an hourly wage of $10. It soon became apparent to frustrated customers, however, that none of the staff, including Amy and Steve, knew how to solve the technical problems customers encountered with the computers and printers. Amy and Steve tried to find a permanent technical support person, but computer experts were in high demand at the time, and the partners felt they couldn't afford to pay a competitive salary.

Business Troubles Brew

Before starting their business, Amy and Steve assumed that revenue would come from two primary sources, food and beverage sales and computer/Internet services. Together they had calculated two economics-of-one-unit analyses, one for each of the two sources.

Amy and Steve's EOU

The partners originally assumed that the average customer would spend $6 at the café and that $2 of this revenue would be generated by food and beverage sales. The remaining $4 would come from the sale of computer and Internet services. They believed the business could be very successful if they did well selling computer services. After all, they could charge customers $4 for an hour of service that would only cost them 45 cents to provide. In comparison, food and beverage sales would not be nearly as profitable. For every $2 of lattes and muffins sold, they would pay $1 in direct costs.

Amy and Steve built a 5 percent manager's commission into their EOU, even though they did not yet have the funds to hire a manager. They wanted to account for this cost because they did plan to hire a manager at some point in the future, and the commission would be a real cost of doing business.

The café's EOU based on Amy and Steve's analysis of both revenue streams together follows.

In Hot Water

When the Portland Freelancers' Café first opened, Amy and Steve were encouraged by how busy things seemed. The café was buzzing with customers and they received some positive reviews in the local papers. They expected to lose money at first but figured that, in a few months' time, the business would become profitable. After three months, they had a major shock when they realized this was not happening. What went wrong?

EOU for Food and Beverage Sales	
Average Sale per Customer	
• Food/Beverage Sales	$2.00
Variable Costs per Unit	
COGS per Unit	
• Food/Beverage Costs	$1.00
TOTAL COGS per Unit	$1.00
Other Variable Costs per Unit	
Manager's Commission @ 5%	$0.10
Total Variable Cost per Unit	$1.10
Contribution Margin per Unit	$0.90

EOU for Computer/Internet Services	
Average Sale per Customer	
• Computer Services	$4.00
Variable Costs per Unit	
COGS per Unit	
• Paper, Toner	$0.25
TOTAL COGS per Unit	$0.25
Other Variable Costs per Unit	
Manager's Commission @5%	$0.20
Total Variable Cost per Unit	$0.45
Contribution Margin per Unit	$3.55

Changes in the Environment

Initially, Amy and Steve's customers willingly paid $4 an hour to use the computers and high-speed Internet connection. However, soon after the grand opening, wireless Internet service became available throughout the Portland area. Within two months, the café's customers no longer wanted to pay to go online. They put pressure on Amy and Steve to become a wireless hot spot. This meant that Amy and Steve would have to foot the bill of providing free Internet service.

The partners carried out some research and learned that it would cost $300 to purchase the basic equipment for wireless Internet connectivity, plus an additional $30 per month in service fees. They had counted on charging their customers for Internet access, and now it looked like *they* would have to pick up the tab. They wondered how they could pay for this unexpected cost and also make up the lost revenue they *weren't* selling. On the other hand, they feared that the Portland Freelancers' Café would not be able to compete unless they adapted to changes in the market.

EOU: Average Sale per Customer	
Average Sale per Customer	
• Computer Services	$4.00
• Food and Beverage Sales	$2.00
Variable Costs per Unit	
COGS per Unit	
• Paper, Toner	$0.25
• Food/Beverage Costs	$1.00
TOTAL COGS per Unit	$1.25
Other Variable Costs per Unit	
Manager's Commission—Computer Services @5%	$0.20
Manager's Commission—Food and Beverage @5%	$0.10
TOTAL Commission Costs	$0.30
Total Variable Cost per Unit	$1.55
Contribution Margin per Unit	$3.20

Amy and Steve's EOU Revisited

Three months after they opened the café, Amy and Steve discovered that their monthly unit sales of computer services had been cut by more than half. In their first month, they had sold 1,500 units, but by month three they were only averaging 600. They worried that this number would only continue to decline.

The café was holding steady with its food and beverage sales—in fact, the monthly units sold had climbed steadily from 4,500 units in month one to 5,000 in month three. Customers were enjoying the café's free wireless service. This feature created a situation where people would stay longer and order more coffee. But even with increased sales of cappuccino, the overall finances of the operation were not improving. In looking at their EOU analysis of food and beverage sales, the partners could see that their gross profit per unit for food and beverage sales was only 90 cents. Even if they sold 5,000 food and beverage units per month, they would still only be earning $4,500 in gross profit. In the scheme of things, this was not very much money—not nearly enough to cover the monthly fixed costs of $8,332.

An Uncertain Future

One year into their venture, Amy and Steve began to seriously doubt their decision to start the Portland Freelancers' Café. In hindsight, they realized they knew a lot about being customers, but running a state-of-the-art coffeehouse was a lot harder than they had imagined. By the end of the year, the Portland Freelancers' Café was on the verge of going out of business. Take a look at the café's financial statements in **Exhibits 13-14** through **13-17** and then analyze how this happened.

Case Study Analysis

13-35. Evaluate the economics-of-one-unit analysis that Amy and Steve conducted, and then answer the following:

a. Amy and Steve assumed that, for every $6 in sales, $4 would come from selling computer-related services. Calculate what percentage of their total sales revenue per unit this $4 represents.

b. For every $2 in food and beverage sales, Amy and Steve assumed that their COGS per unit would be $1. Calculate the markup percentage.

c. For every $4 in computer services sales, Amy and Steve assumed that their COGS per unit would be 25 cents. Calculate the markup percentage.

13-36. List three things that Amy and Steve should have considered doing to adapt to the changes in the environment when their customers no longer wanted to pay for Internet services and expected the café to provide free wireless connections.

13-37. Evaluate Amy and Steve's income statement for their first month of operations:

a. Is the café operating at a profit or a loss?

b. How many units above or below breakeven were sold?

13-38. Amy and Steve decided to take on a $50,000 loan to finance their start-up investment. Each month they are paying $1,469 in interest charges. Look at their total monthly fixed costs. What percentage of their total monthly fixed costs does this $1,469 represent?

13-39. What is the debt-to-equity ratio of the Portland Freelancers' Café?

13-40. Look at each section of the café's cash flow statement. Write a memo highlighting three insights you have about why this business is not succeeding, based on what you see in its cash flow statement.

13-41. Review the café's balance sheet. Explain why the net value of the café's property and equipment has decreased from $80,000 in month one to $64,000 at year's end.

Exhibit 13-14 *Start-Up Investment and Economics of One Unit*

Start-Up Investment		
Start-up Costs		
Soundproof Room	$15,000	
Espresso Machine	7,000	
High-Speed Internet Access Setup	10,000	
Workstations	20,000	
Supplies/Equipment	25,000	
Furniture	8,000	
Fixtures	5,000	
Cash Reserves	10,000	
Total Start-up Investments	**$100,000**	

Economics of One Unit (EOU) Unit of Sale: Computer/Internet Services (Average per Customer)			
Average Sale Total (Revenue)			**$4.00**
Less COGS			
Computer time	–		
Printer materials	0.25		
Total COGS	0.25	0.25	0.25
Gross Profit			**$3.75**
Less Other Variable Costs			
Commission 5% to manager	0.20		
Total Other Variable Costs	0.20	0.20	0.20
Total Variable Costs (COGS + Other VC)		0.45	
Contribution Margin			**$3.55**

Economics of One Unit (EOU) Unit of Sale: Food and Beverage Sales (Average per Customer)			
Average Sale Total (Revenue)			**$2.00**
Less COGS			
Food	0.80		
Beverage	0.20		
Total COGS	1.00	1.00	1.00
Gross Profit			**$1.00**
Less Other Variable Costs			
Commission 5% to manager	0.10		
Total Other Variable Costs	0.10	0.10	0.10
Total Variable Costs (COGS + Other VC)		1.10	
Contribution Margin			**$0.90**

Exhibit 13-15 *Income Statement*

The Portland Freelancers' Café INCOME STATEMENT *for the Year Ending 12/31/2003*

		Jan	Feb	Mar	Apr	May	Jun	Jul	Aug	Sep	Oct	Nov	Dec	Year
No. Units Sold—Computer Services		1,500	1,000	600	550	550	500	500	450	450	450	400	400	7,350
No. Units Sold—Food and Beverage		4,500	4,750	5,000	5,100	5,200	5,300	5,400	5,500	5,600	5,700	5,800	6,000	63,850
Revenue														
Computer Service Fees		$ 6,000	$ 4,000	$ 2,400	$ 2,200	$ 2,200	$ 2,000	$ 2,000	$ 1,800	$ 1,800	$ 1,800	$ 1,600	$ 1,600	$ 29,400
Food and Beverage Sales		9,000	9,500	10,000	10,200	10,400	10,600	10,800	11,000	11,200	11,400	11,600	12,000	127,700
Total Revenue		**$15,000**	**$13,500**	**$12,400**	**$12,400**	**$12,600**	**$12,600**	**$12,800**	**$12,800**	**$13,000**	**$13,200**	**$13,200**	**$13,600**	**$157,100**
Less COGS														
Printer Mat'ls (paper, ink)		375	250	150	138	138	125	125	113	113	113	100	100	1,838
Food		3,600	3,800	4,000	4,080	4,160	4,240	4,320	4,400	4,480	4,560	4,640	4,800	51,080
Beverages		900	950	1,000	1,020	1,040	1,060	1,080	1,100	1,120	1,140	1,160	1,200	12,770
Total COGS		$ 4,875	$ 5,000	$ 5,150	$ 5,238	$ 5,338	$ 5,425	$ 5,525	$ 5,613	$ 5,713	$ 5,813	$ 5,900	$ 6,100	$ 65,688
Gross Profit		**$10,125**	**$ 8,500**	**$ 7,250**	**$ 7,163**	**$ 7,263**	**$ 7,175**	**$ 7,275**	**$ 7,188**	**$ 7,288**	**$ 7,388**	**$ 7,300**	**$ 7,500**	**$ 91,413**
Less Other Variable Costs														
Commission, Computer	(5%)	300	200	120	110	110	100	100	90	90	90	80	80	1,470
Commission, Food/Bev.	(5%)	450	475	500	510	520	530	540	550	560	570	580	600	6,385
Total Other Variable Costs		$ 750	$ 675	$ 620	$ 620	$ 630	$ 630	$ 640	$ 640	$ 650	$ 660	$ 660	$ 680	$ 7,855
Total Var. Costs (COGS + Other VC)		5,625	5,675	5,770	5,858	5,968	6,055	6,165	6,253	6,363	6,473	6,560	6,780	73,543
Contribution Margin*		**$ 9,375**	**$ 7,825**	**$ 6,630**	**$ 6,543**	**$ 6,633**	**$ 6,545**	**$ 6,635**	**$ 6,548**	**$ 6,638**	**$ 6,728**	**$ 6,640**	**$ 6,820**	**$ 83,558**

*Remember: Revenue − COGS = Gross Profit − Other Variable Costs = Contribution Margin.

(Continued)

Exhibit 13-15 *(continued)*

The Portland Freelancers' Café INCOME STATEMENT *for the Year Ending 12/31/2003*

		Jan	Feb	Mar	Apr	May	Jun	Jul	Aug	Sep	Oct	Nov	Dec	Year
Less Fixed Costs														
Utilities														
Electricity		150	150	150	150	150	150	150	150	150	150	150	150	1,800
Gas		250	250	250	250	250	250	250	250	250	250	250	250	3,000
Water		100	100	100	100	100	100	100	100	100	100	100	100	1,200
Telephone		75	75	75	75	75	75	75	75	75	75	75	75	900
High-Speed Internet		425	425	425	425	425	425	425	425	425	425	425	425	5,100
Wireless Internet Service		30	30	30	30	30	30	30	30	30	30	30	30	360
Total Utilities		$ 1,030	$ 1,030	$ 1,030	$ 1,030	$ 1,030	$ 1,030	$ 1,030	$ 1,030	$ 1,030	$ 1,030	$ 1,030	$ 1,030	$ 12,360
Salaries														
Amy & Steve Salary		1,000	1,000	1,000	1,000	1,000	1,000	1,000	1,000	1,000	1,000	1,000	1,000	12,000
Tech Support (Part time)		1,000	1,000	1,000	1,000	1,000	1,000	1,000	1,000	1,000	1,000	1,000	1,000	12,000
Total Salaries		$ 2,000	$ 2,000	$ 2,000	$ 2,000	$ 2,000	$ 2,000	$ 2,000	$ 2,000	$ 2,000	$ 2,000	$ 2,000	$ 2,000	$ 24,000
Advertising		1,000	1,000	1,000	1,000	1,000	1,000	1,000	1,000	1,000	1,000	1,000	1,000	12,000
Insurance		500	500	500	500	500	500	500	500	500	500	500	500	6,000
Interest		1,469	1,469	1,469	1,469	1,469	1,469	1,469	1,469	1,469	1,469	1,469	1,469	17,628
Rent		1,000	1,000	1,000	1,000	1,000	1,000	1,000	1,000	1,000	1,000	1,000	1,000	12,000
Depreciation		1,333	1,333	1,333	1,333	1,333	1,333	1,333	1,333	1,333	1,333	1,333	1,333	15,996
Total Fixed Costs		$ 8,332	$ 8,332	$ 8,332	$ 8,332	$ 8,332	$ 8,332	$ 8,332	$ 8,332	$ 8,332	$ 8,332	$ 8,332	$ 8,332	$ 99,984
Pre-Tax Profit		$ 1,043	($ 507)	($ 1,702)	($ 1,790)	($ 1,700)	($ 1,787)	($ 1,697)	($ 1,785)	($ 1,695)	($ 1,605)	($ 1,692)	($ .512)	($ 16,427)
Taxes	(20%)	209	($ 07)	($ 1,702)	($ 1,790)	($ 1,700)	($ 1,787)	($ 1,697)	($ 1,785)	($ 1,695)	($ 1,605)	($ 1,692)	($ 1,512)	($ 16,427)
Net Profit		$ 834	($ 07)	($ 1,702)	($ 1,790)	($ 1,700)	($ 1,787)	($ 1,697)	($ 1,785)	($ 1,695)	($ 1,605)	($ 1,692)	($ 1,512)	($ 16,427)

Exhibit 13-16 *Cash Flow Statement*

The Portland Freelancers' Café CASH FLOW STATEMENT for the Year Ending 12/31/2003

	Jan	Feb	Mar	Apr	May	Jun	Jul	Aug	Sep	Oct	Nov	Dec	Year
Number of Units—Computer Services	**1,500**	**1,000**	**600**	**550**	**550**	**500**	**500**	**450**	**450**	**450**	**400**	**400**	**7,350**
Number of Units—Food & Beverage Sales	**4,500**	**4,750**	**5,000**	**5,100**	**5,200**	**5,300**	**5,400**	**5,500**	**5,600**	**5,700**	**5,800**	**6,000**	**63,850**
Cash Flow from Operating:													
Cash Inflows:													
Computer Usage Fees	$ 6,000	$ 4,000	$ 2,400	$ 2,200	$ 2,200	$ 2,000	$ 2,000	$ 1,800	$ 1,800	$ 1,800	$ 1,600	$ 1,600	$ 29,400
Food and Beverage Sales	9,000	9,500	10,000	10,200	10,400	10,600	10,800	11,000	11,200	11,400	11,600	12,000	127,700
Total Cash Inflows	$ 15,000	$ 13,500	$ 12,400	$ 12,400	$ 12,600	$ 12,600	$ 12,800	$ 12,800	$ 13,000	$ 13,200	$ 13,200	$ 13,600	$157,100
Cash Outflows:													
Variable Costs													
COGS	$ 4,875	$ 5,000	$ 5,150	$ 5,238	$ 5,338	$ 5,425	$ 5,525	$ 5,613	$ 5,713	$ 5,813	$ 5,900	$ 6,100	$ 65,688
Other Variable Costs	$ 750	$ 675	$ 620	$ 620	$ 630	$ 630	$ 640	$ 640	$ 650	$ 660	$ 660	$ 680	$ 7,855
Utilities													
Electricity, Gas, Water, Telephone	$ 500	$ 500	$ 500	$ 500	$ 500	$ 500	$ 500	$ 500	$ 500	$ 500	$ 500	$ 500	$ 6,000
High-Speed Internet Access	425	425	425	425	425	425	425	425	425	425	425	425	5,100
Wireless Internet	30	30	30	30	30	30	30	30	30	30	30	30	360
Salaries													
Part-Time Tech Support Salary	$ 1,000	$ 1,000	$ 1,000	$ 1,000	$ 1,000	$ 1,000	$ 1,000	$ 1,000	$ 1,000	$ 1,000	$ 1,000	$ 1,000	$ 12,000
Amy and Steve's Salary	$ 1,000	$ 1,000	$ 1,000	$ 1,000	$ 1,000	$ 1,000	$ 1,000	$ 1,000	$ 1,000	$ 1,000	$ 1,000	$ 1,000	$ 12,000
Advertising	$ 1,000	$ 1,000	$ 1,000	$ 1,000	$ 1,000	$ 1,000	$ 1,000	$ 1,000	$ 1,000	$ 1,000	$ 1,000	$ 1,000	$ 12,000
Insurance	$ 500	$ 500	$ 500	$ 500	$ 500	$ 500	$ 500	$ 500	$ 500	$ 500	$ 500	$ 500	$ 6,000
Interest Expense	$ 1,469	$ 1,469	$ 1,469	$ 1,469	$ 1,469	$ 1,469	$ 1,469	$ 1,469	$ 1,469	$ 1,469	$ 1,469	$ 1,469	$ 17,623
Rent	$ 1,000	$ 1,001	$ 1,002	$ 1,003	$ 1,004	$ 1,005	$ 1,006	$ 1,007	$ 1,008	$ 1,009	$ 1,010	$ 1,011	$ 12,000
Total Cash Used in Operating Activities	$ 12,549	$ 12,600	$ 12,696	$ 12,784	$ 12,895	$ 12,983	$ 13,095	$ 13,183	$ 13,294	$ 13,405	$ 13,494	$ 13,715	$156,626
Net Cash Flow from Operating	$ 2,451	$ 900	($ 296)	($ 384)	($ 295)	($ 84)	($ 295)	($ 383)	($ 294)	($ 205)	($ 294)	($ 115)	($ 474)

(Continued)

Exhibit 13-16 (continued)

The Portland Freelancers' Café CASH FLOW STATEMENT for the Year Ending 12/31/2003

	Jan	Feb	Mar	Apr	May	Jun	Jul	Aug	Sep	Oct	Nov	Dec	Year
Cash Flow Out from Investing:													
Soundproof Room	$ 15,000	$ 0	$ 0	$ 0	$0	$ 0	$ 0	$ 0	$ 0	$ 0	$ 0	$ 0	$ 15,000
Espresso Machine	7,000	0	0	0	0	0	0	0	0	0	0	0	7,000
High-Speed Internet Access Setup	10,000	0	0	0	0	0	0	0	0	0	0	0	10,000
Workstations	20,000	0	0	0	0	0	0	0	0	0	0	0	20,000
Supplies/Equipment	25,000	0	0	0	0	0	0	0	0	0	0	0	25,000
Furniture	8,000	0	0	0	0	0	0	0	0	0	0	0	8,000
Fixtures	5,000	0	0	0	0	0	0	0	0	0	0	0	5,000
Net Cash Flow Out from Investing	$ 90,000	$ 0	$ 0	$ 0	$ 0	$ 0	$ 0	$ 0	$ 0	$ 0	$ 0	$ 0	$ 90,000
Financing:													
Cash Received from Uncle (12% APR)	$ 50,000	$ 0	$0	$ 0	$ 0	$ 0	$ 0	$ 0	$ 0	$ 0	$ 0	$ 0	$ 50,000
Cash Received from Brother	20,000	0	0	0	0	0	0	0	0	0	0	0	20,000
Cash Received from Mother	10,000	0	0	0	0	0	0	0	0	0	0	0	10,000
Cash Received from Personal Savings	20,000	0	0	0	0	0	0	0	0	0	0	0	20,000
Net Cash Flow In from Financing	$100,000	$ 0	$ 0	$ 0	$ 0	$ 0	$ 0	$ 0	$ 0	$ 0	$ 0	$ 0	$100,000
Net Increase (Decrease) in Cash	$ 12,451	$ 900	($ 296)	($ 384)	($ 295)	($ 384)	($ 295)	($ 383)	($ 294)	($ 205)	($ 294)	($ 115)	$ 10,474
Cash, Beginning:	$ 10,000	$ 22,451	$ 23,351	$ 22,055	$ 22,671	$ 22,376	$ 21,992	$ 21,697	$ 20,314	$ 20,020	$ 20,815	$ 20,521	$ 10,000
Cash, End:	$ 22,451	$ 23,351	$ 22,055	$ 22,671	$ 22,376	$ 21,992	$ 21,697	$ 20,314	$ 20,020	$ 20,815	$ 20,521	$ 20,406	$ 20,474

Exhibit 13-17 *Balance Sheet*

Portland Freelancers' Café
BALANCE SHEET
for the Year Ending 12/31/2003

	Opening	Closing
ASSETS		
Current Assets:		
Cash	$110,000	$20,474
Accounts Receivable	0	0
Total Current Assets	$110,000	$20,474
Fixed Assets (Property and Equipment):		
Soundproof Room	$ 15,000	$15,000
Espresso Machine	2,000	2,000
Workstations	30,000	30,000
Supplies/Equipment	25,000	25,000
Furniture	3,000	3,000
Fixtures	5,000	5,000
Total Property and Equipment	$ 80,000	$80,000
Less Accumulated Depreciation	$ 0	$15,996
Total Property and Equipment (Net)	$ 80,000	$64,004
Total Assets	$190,000	$84,478
LIABILITIES AND OWNER'S EQUITY		
Current Liabilities:		
Accounts Payable	$ 0	$ 0
Total Current Liabilities	$ 0	$ 0
Long-Term Liability (Uncle's Loan)	$ 50,000	$32,377
Total Liabilities	$ 50,000	$32,377
Owner's Equity	$140,000	$52,101
Amy	40%	40%
Steve	40%	40%
Steve's Brother	20%	20%
Total Liabilities and Owner's Equity	$190,000	$84,478

Chapter 14

CASH FLOW AND TAXES

Learning Objectives

1. Understand the importance of cash flow management.

2. Know the difference between cash and profits.

3. Read a cash flow statement.

4. Create a cash budget.

5. File appropriate tax returns for your business.

UpperCut Images/Superstock

Jessica Mah and Andy Suh cofounded inDinero Inc. as 19-year-old computer science majors at the University of California at Berkeley. Their company provides a Web-based, real-time financial "dashboard" for small businesses. In addition to receiving seed funding from Y Combinator in 2010, they are backed by angels—including Jeremy Stoppelman (Yelp), Dave McClure (500 Startups), Fritz Lanman (Microsoft), David Wu (Intuit), Jawed Karim (YouTube), and Keith Rabois (Slide).[1] These investors recognize that inDinero fills a need for small businesses in an innovative, compelling, and highly efficient manner.

inDinero users benefit from a simple visual system to keep track of the key financial aspects of their businesses. The dashboard displays such information as revenues, budgets, bank balance, credit card balance, and a cash balance graph. Users enter information from their financial accounts and submit receipts to manage their transactions. For many entrepreneurs, maintaining detailed records is a challenge, and bringing a box of receipts to an accountant at the end of the year can be costly (in the accountant's time) and inaccurate. inDinero.com is designed to make organizing and understanding simpler, so that companies can avoid cash-flow surprises and perform better.[2]

Cash Flow: The Lifeblood of a Business

Learning Objective 1

Understand the importance of cash flow management.

Cash is the energy that keeps your business flowing, the way electricity powers a lamp. Run out of cash, and your business will soon go out like a light. Without cash on hand, you will not be able to pay essential expenses, even while the income statement says you are earning a profit. If your phone is cut off, it will not matter what the income statement says. The success of your business will depend on cash, from start-up through its entire existence. Cash is essential for the initial investment, ongoing operations, and growth. Managing cash is more critical than managing sales, because sales without cash receipts are a recipe for disaster. Cash truly is the lifeblood of a business.

The income statement shows you what the situation is with sales and profits over a period of time. It tells you how much revenue has come in and how it relates to the cost of goods sold and operating costs. The balance sheet is a snapshot of your business. It shows your assets and liabilities and net worth at one moment in time. Each of these statements and the associated ratios is important, but without a firm handle on the cash situation, business success will be elusive.

The Income Statement Does Not Show Available Cash

Once you start a business using the accrual method of accounting, you may notice that sometimes when the income statement says you are making a profit, you have no cash. There is often a time lag between making a sale and getting paid. With the accrual method, if you make a sale and the customer promises to pay you in a week, the sale is recognized on

[1] Rip Empson, "inDinero Now Lets Small Businesses Track Their Financial Transactions and Receipts on One Platform," *TechCrunch*, October 6, 2011, accessed August 26, 2013, http://techcrunch.com/2011/10/06/indinero-now-lets-small-businesses-track-their-financial-transactions-and-receipts-on-one-platform/.

[2] inDinero, accessed August 26, 2013, http://www.inDinero.com.

Name	Vendor Number	Not Due (in discount)	Not Due (no disc.)	15 Days Past Due	30 Days Past Due	60 Days Past Due
Ace Supply	51-09238		$5,000			
Big Guys	62-78749				$1,000	
Champions	10-83297			$4,000		$2,000
Youth Style	23-83940	$7,500				
Zoo Pals	51-10239	$1,000			$2,000	
Total		$8,500	$5,000	$4,000	$3,000	$2,000
Percent		37.8%	22.2%	17.8%	13.3%	8.9%

Exhibit 14-5 *Aging Schedule for Accounts Payable—As of June 30, 2014*

price negotiation. The leverage you have to negotiate will depend on the balance of power in the relationship. Often, new accounts have less favorable terms with vendors until they establish a solid track record. Other times, a company may offer extended payment terms as part of a new-customer incentive or other promotional program. Once you have been a customer for a while and have demonstrated that you are desirable in terms of purchase volume and timely payment, you can revisit your payment terms to secure additional time. As you become an increasingly significant customer for your vendor, you can renegotiate prices, including payment terms.

You also may be able to negotiate payment terms when you are experiencing difficulty with cash flow. This is not something you should do routinely. However, if you can see that your cash flow will not permit you to pay part or all of the balance due on time, you should notify your supplier/vendor/creditor and negotiate realistic payment terms. This should be handled deftly, so that they understand you genuinely need their cooperation; they should not become alarmed and retrench on future supplies or credit terms. It can be a delicate transaction.

Timing Payables

Just as you should establish an accounts receivable aging schedule, you should also create an accounts *payable* aging schedule (see **Exhibit 14-5**). In addition to noting where you are in terms of days outstanding, be certain to indicate terms received and variances. Recognize that you may have to start out with prepayment or payment on delivery, which will be difficult for cash flow because you will have to disburse money before you sell anything. Depending on the business you are in, this could be a long interval.

The aging schedule for accounts payable will make your cash requirements clear. You can see what is coming due, where you can benefit from discounts, and where there are problems. This simple approach can be invaluable to your cash management.

Capital Budgeting and Cash Flow

Cash management is not only for operating cash and financing. It also includes the planning for *capital assets* (fixed assets or earning assets). The purchase of machinery, equipment and its installation, and the like requires initial cash outflows for assets and incremental working capital for new projects, the inflow of cash from operations as a result of purchases, and terminal cash flows from liquidation of old, outdated, or replaced equipment.

Capital budgeting will help you understand the cash flow required for investments and the expected impact on operating cash flows. Budgeting will lead you to calculate the depreciation associated with capital investment, so that you can anticipate the tax effects. (Remember, increased depreciation means decreased taxes.) Finally, as you budget for the terminal values, you will see cash flow effects from disposal of assets and the related tax consequences. Making a capital budget can shed considerable light on cash-flow expectations. **Exhibit 14-6** shows a capital budget for NRG Savers Inc., as the company considers the purchase and installation of equipment for a new line of environmentally friendly products.

We can see that the components of the capital budget fit into the full cash-flow budget of a company, once the project is accepted or rejected. By creating and analyzing each capital project separately, you can apply your decision criteria and determine which to accept and which to reject. You can plan for your financing needs well in advance and be prepared to justify your repayment plans.

The Burn Rate

When you start your business, it will be normal to have a negative cash flow from operations for at least the first few months. You are likely to spend more than you earn in the beginning stages. Some businesses, such as biotechnology companies that spend a great deal on research and development (R&D), can have a negative cash flow of as much as $1 million per month. You will need to build these initial cash deficits into your business plan so that they can be covered in start-up costs.

Exhibit 14-6 *NRG Savers, Inc.—Capital Budget 2013*

	Year 1	Year 2	Year 3	Year 4	Year 5
Initial Investment					
Machinery and Equipment	$82,000				
Installation	18,000				
Working Capital	10,000				
Total Initial Investment	**$110,000**				
Operating Cash Flows					
Operating Cash Inflow	$200,000	$300,000	$400,000	$500,000	$550,000
Depreciation	20,000	32,000	19,000	12,000	12,000
Net Change in Income	$180,000	$268,000	$381,000	$488,000	$538,000
Tax Effect (@ 30%)	48,000	80,400	114,300	146,400	161,400
Net Operating Cash Flow	**$132,000**	**$187,600**	**$266,700**	**$341,600**	**$376,600**
Terminal Cash Flow					
Sale of Equipment					$40,000
Tax on Income (sale)					10,500
Net on Sale of Equipment					$29,500
Recovery—Working Capital					10,000
Total Terminal Cash Flow					**$39,500**
Project Cash Flow	**$22,000**	**$187,600**	**$266,700**	**$341,600**	**$416,100**

Because a new company will probably spend more money than it earns while it is getting off the ground, the question will be: how long can you afford to lose money? The answer will depend on the amount of capital invested and the amount of revenue being earned.

The pace at which your company will need to spend capital to cover overhead costs before generating a positive cash flow is called the **burn rate**. The burn rate is typically expressed in terms of cash spent per month. A burn rate of $10,000 per month means that the company is spending that amount monthly to cover rent and other operating expenses. If the company has $20,000 in cash and is making $2,000 a month in sales, how long could it hold out?

burn rate the pace at which a company must spend capital before generating positive cash flow.

$$\text{Number of Months before Cash Runs Out} = \frac{(\text{Cash Available} + \text{Revenue})}{\text{Negative Cash Outflow per Month}}$$

The Value of Money Changes Over Time

When considering cash and cash flow, it is also important to evaluate the changing value of money over time. A dollar today available for investment is worth more than a dollar tomorrow. Cash goes up or down in terms of buying power depending on several factors. For example, the value of a dollar changes depending on inflation rates and variations in exchange-rate strength relative to foreign currencies. Finally, it can grow as the money earned previously gathers interest.

The Future Value of Money

Interest-earning funds grow fastest in investments that offer a *compound* rate of return—that is, those that are calculated on interest that has already accumulated. The younger you are when you start saving for a goal, such as retirement, the more compounding will help your money grow. Suppose you put $100 into an investment that pays 10 percent compounded annually. At the end of a year, you will have $110 ($100, plus $10 interest). At the end of the next year, you will have $121 ($110, plus $11 interest). Your money will grow faster each year because you are earning interest on the interest. The formula for this is

$$FV = PV \, (1 + i)^n$$

Where **FV** is the future value of the investment; **PV** is the present value, or amount invested today; *i* equals the interest rate per compounding period in decimal form, and *n* equals the number of compounding periods. For example, $1,200 invested at 5 percent per year for 10 years will yield

$$FV = \$1{,}200 \, (1 + 0.05)^{10} = \$1{,}200 \times 1.63 = \$1{,}956$$

Figure 14-4 shows the effect of compounding $1,000 at 0 percent, 5 percent, 10 percent, and 20 percent for five years.

The **future value** of money is the amount it will *accrue* (gain) over time through investment. For a single investment at a constant interest rate, you can use the formula provided, or you can determine this easily using a future value chart such as the one in **Exhibit 14-7**. Look up 10 periods at 10 percent on the chart, and you will find that $100 invested at 10 percent will grow to $259 in 10 years. Note that these values can also be figured on a financial calculator and via spreadsheet software, such as Excel. If there are multiple amounts, variable interest rates, and the like,

future value the amount an asset will gain over time.

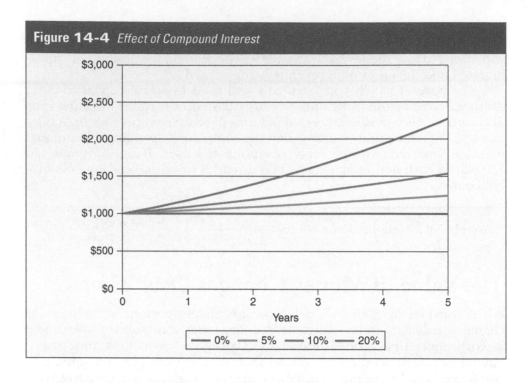

Figure 14-4 *Effect of Compound Interest*

Exhibit 14-7 *Future Value of $1 Today in n Periods in the Future*

Periods	1%	3%	5%	8%	10%
1	1.0100	1.0300	1.0500	1.0800	1.1000
2	1.0201	1.0609	1.1025	1.1664	1.2100
3	1.0303	1.0927	1.1576	1.2597	1.3310
4	1.0406	1.1255	1.2155	1.3605	1.4641
5	1.0510	1.1593	1.2763	1.4693	1.6105
6	1.0615	1.1941	1.3401	1.5869	1.7716
7	1.0721	1.2299	1.4071	1.7138	1.9487
8	1.0829	1.2668	1.4775	1.8509	2.1436
9	1.0937	1.3048	1.5513	1.9990	2.3580
10	1.1046	1.3439	1.6209	2.1589	2.5937
15	1.1610	1.5580	2.0789	3.1722	4.1773

compound interest used with interest or rate of return and applied when earnings also accumulate interest or other returns, in addition to earnings on principal.

you can consult a basic financial management book or the Internet for appropriate calculation techniques. Remember, **compound interest**, money making money, is the essence of investment.

The Present Value of Money

Another way to look at investing is illustrated by the old saying, "A bird in the hand is worth two in the bush." You always prefer to have your money *now*. If you cannot have it immediately, you want to be compensated with a return. Your money is worth more to you when it is in your hand for three reasons:

1. ***Inflation.*** When prices rise, a dollar tomorrow will buy less than a dollar does today.

Periods	1%	3%	5%	8%	10%
Exhibit 14-8 *Present Value of $1 to be Received n Periods in the Future*					
1	0.990	0.971	0.952	0.926	0.909
2	0.980	0.943	0.907	0.857	0.826
3	0.971	0.915	0.864	0.794	0.751
4	0.961	0.886	0.823	0.735	0.683
5	0.951	0.863	0.784	0.681	0.621
6	0.942	0.837	0.746	0.630	0.584
7	0.933	0.813	0.711	0.583	0.513
8	0.923	0.789	0.677	0.540	0.467
9	0.914	0.766	0.645	0.500	0.424
10	0.905	0.744	0.614	0.463	0.386
15	0.861	0.642	0.481	0.315	0.239

2. **Risk.** When you put money into an investment, there is always some risk of losing it.
3. **Opportunity.** When you put money into an investment, you are giving up the opportunity to use it for what might be a better investment.

Say a customer promises to pay you $10,000 three years from now for designing a Web site. Your next-best opportunity for investment has an ROI of 10 percent.

Present value is the amount an investment is worth discounted back to the present. Look at the present value chart (see **Exhibit 14-8**) under period three (for three years) and 10 percent. The present value of $1 at three years and 10 percent is $0.751. The present value of the promise of $10,000 in three years, therefore, is $7,510 ($10,000 × 0.751 = $7,510). Your client's promise is worth only $7,510 in the present. If you accept this arrangement, you should charge interest because you are essentially providing a $10,000 loan for three years. Anytime you are asked to wait for payment, you should be compensated, because money in your hand now is worth significantly more than money promised for the future. If you want to calculate this using a mathematical formula, you can use the inverse of the future value formula.

present value what the future amount of an asset or other investment is worth at face value discounted back to the present.

$$PV = FV(1/(1 + i)^n)$$

So, the prior example would be

$$PV = \$10,000(1/(1 + 0.10)^3) = \$7,510.$$

Understanding the time value of money permits managers to compare investment options and other opportunities based on their real values so that they can better manage cash flows.

BizFacts

When you sell a business, the price reflects more than the nuts and bolts of the operation. You are also selling the future stream of income the business will be expected to generate. This income is reflected in the price of the business, which is its *present value*. This is why businesses typically sell for several times their annual net income.

Taxes

Another factor that affects cash flow for a business is taxes. Like other creditors, tax-levying bodies expect payment in a timely fashion. More importantly, tax payments must be kept current, because some delinquencies can result in business closure and substantial personal penalties.

Cash Flow and Taxes

Once your business begins making a profit, you will have to pay taxes on those profits either through your corporation or directly through personal resources, whether or not you have a positive cash flow. In addition, self-employed people such as sole proprietors must pay their own **self-employment tax** on any owner's draws paid to themselves. This is the Social Security tax obligation for those who are self-employed and is the equivalent of the combination of the employee and employer taxes paid for employees. These taxes must be paid quarterly, so cash should be put aside in order to make the payments on the due dates.

self-employment tax federal tax that business owners are assessed on wages paid to themselves.

As an employer, you will collect and pay all employment taxes to the appropriate government entities. These taxes are particularly important to report accurately and pay on time. Federal penalties for tax-code violations with respect to wages are especially harsh. The government may "sweep" your company bank accounts (take out any available funds), assess significant fines, and secure your personal assets. Using withheld wage taxes as a source of cash flow and/or failing to pay these taxes could be a disastrous decision.

sales tax an assessment levied by governments on purchases and collected by merchants.

The federal government is financed largely by personal and corporate income taxes. States usually raise money from **sales taxes** on goods. Most states also levy an income tax. City and other local governments are supported primarily by taxes on property.

Filing Tax Returns

Corporate, partnership, and individual income tax and self-employment tax returns must be filed (mailed or submitted online) to the U.S. Internal Revenue Service (IRS) by specific dates each year. Corporate returns are due earlier than the deadline for individual returns. If you file late, you may have to pay penalties and interest. You can check the IRS Web site at http://www.irs.gov for deadlines, instructions, and forms.

The tax code is extremely complex. Check the aforementioned IRS Web site for information, but if you are still not certain which tax forms to file and when to do so, the IRS also offers booklets and telephone service to help answer questions. Alternatively, you can go to your local IRS office and meet with an agent who will guide you through the forms for free. It can be worth investing the time and money to ensure your own correct tax filings (rates and forms can change from year to year). As soon as you do so, you will probably want to seek the services of a tax professional (an accountant or CPA). Remember, in addition to federal taxes, businesses are

File appropriate tax returns for your business (moodboard/Superstock)

subject to state and local taxes. Check with state and local revenue departments for details.

Collecting Sales Tax

If you sell products or services to the public, you will have to charge state sales tax in most states and then turn over the collected money, monthly or quarterly, to the proper agency. Apply to your state's department of taxation for the necessary forms. In New York State, for example, entrepreneurs use the New York State and Local Sales and Use form to report quarterly sales taxes. Some states only charge tax on products; some charge tax on products and services, whereas a very few do not have a sales tax.

Tax Issues for Different Legal Structures

The legal structure best suited to a business depends on a number of variables, which will be discussed later in this text. Each legal structure has tax advantages and disadvantages.

- *Sole proprietorship.* All profit earned by a sole proprietorship belongs to the owner and affects his or her tax liability. The business does not pay taxes on profits separately.
- *Partnership.* The tax issues are basically the same as for the sole proprietorship, except that profits and losses are shared among the partners, who report them on their respective personal income tax returns.
- *Limited partnership.* This is treated the same way as a partnership, except that a limited partner can use losses as a tax shelter without being exposed to personal liability. This can be an incentive for potential investors.
- *C corporation.* A corporation's profits are taxed whether or not a portion of them is distributed to the owners. Owners must also pay personal income tax on any profit distribution they receive. This so-called double taxation is considered a disadvantage of C corporations.
- *S corporation.* Small companies can use this structure to avoid the double taxation mentioned above. The S corporation does not pay tax on profits. Profit is taxed only once, as owner income on personal tax returns. This structure requires all owners to take profits and losses in proportion to their ownership (thus it does not offer the tax-shelter advantages of the limited partnership).
- *Limited liability company (LLC).* This structure separates the members (owners) from personal liability and provides a more flexible allocation of profits and losses.

Finally, note that dividends paid by a business to stockholders are not tax deductible to the business, but interest payments made to creditors are. This can be an incentive to raise capital via borrowing, depending on the tax issues your business faces.

Make Tax Time Easier by Keeping Good Records

You and your tax preparer will have an easier time if you keep accurate records throughout the year. Together, you will determine your net income and many other financial values. If you have kept accurate and timely accounting records, this should not be difficult.

Organization is critical!
(Thomas Northcut/Thinkstock)

Mistakes on your tax return, or just the luck of the draw, could cause the IRS to *audit* you. The IRS will send an agent (auditor) to your business to examine your books and records to make sure your taxes were filed correctly. An audit can be a time-consuming and stressful process. This is another excellent reason to keep good records and file all invoices and receipts, whether or not you use an accountant for tax preparation.

Do not confuse accounting with taxation. Your accounting software generates financial records, but you will still need tax-preparation assistance and/or tax software, to get your returns ready to file. Some accounting software will allow you to export your financial information into your tax program.

If you prepare your own tax returns on a computer, it will still be a good idea to have a tax professional review them. An accountant will be familiar with changes to the tax code and can offer valuable advice. Accountants often will not charge for questions asked throughout the year, if they have been hired to prepare a business's annual tax return.

One of the best investments you can make is to hire a top-notch small-business tax accountant or attorney as a consultant. Maximize the amount of professional advice and you will minimize the chances of problems with the IRS.

Chapter Summary

Now that you have studied this chapter, you can do the following:

1. Understand the importance of cash flow management.
   - Cash flow is the difference between the money you take in and the money you disburse.
   - Without cash on hand, you can find yourself unable to pay essential bills, even while the income statement says you are earning a profit.
2. Know the difference between cash and profits.
   - Profits are based on accrued revenues and expenses, for most businesses.
   - It is possible to be profitable and to be out of cash.
3. Read a cash flow statement.
   - The first section of the cash flow statement records all sources of cash income that come into the business.
   - The next section reports cash outflows (disbursements).
   - The last section shows the net change in cash flow.

4. Create a cash budget.
   - Project your cash receipts from all possible sources.
   - Subtract the expenses you expect to have from these projected cash receipts.
   - Understand the future value of money.
   - Calculate the present value of money.
5. Calculate working capital.
   - The formula for working capital is: current assets minus current liabilities.
   - It tells you how much cash is left over after paying all your short-term debt.
   - Working capital should be considered when creating cash flow projections.
6. File appropriate tax returns for your business.
   - Both income tax and self-employment tax returns must be filed by specific dates (corporate returns are due earlier than individual returns).
   - Tax returns must be filed on time and accurately.
   - Collect sales tax. If you sell products or services to the public, in most states, you will have to charge your customers applicable sales tax and then turn it in to the state periodically.
   - Apply to your state's department of taxation for the necessary forms.

Key Terms

burn rate, 447
cash flow statement, 434
compound interest, 448
credit, 444
factoring, 444
future value, 447

noncash expenses, 435
pilferage, 441
present value, 449
sales tax, 450
self-employment tax, 450
working capital, 435

Entrepreneurship Portfolio

Critical Thinking Exercises

14-1. Describe what you think the seasonality scenario would be for one year for a business you can imagine starting. Explain how you think the cash flow will be affected over the course of the year.

14-2. Imagine you are the owner of an upscale clothing store, like Barneys in Manhattan, which was driven out of business by a 7-percent pilferage rate. What creative solutions could you identify to reduce pilferage?

14-3. Give three rules for managing your cash.

14-4. Calculate the projected burn rate for your planned business.

14-5. Figure out how much income tax each of the following individuals owes. The marginal tax rates are structured as follows:
- $0 to $8,925 = 10% rate
- $8,926 to $36,250 = 15%
- $36,251 to $87,850 = 25%
- $87,851 to $183,250 = 28%
- $183,251 to $398,350 = 33%
- $398,351 to $400,000 = 35%
- $400,001 and above = 39.6%

The different rates apply to different portions of one's income.

Name	Taxable Income	Tax Due
Jamie	$42,000	_____
Miguel	$98,750	_____
Suzette	$24,000	_____
Kimu	$100,520	_____

Key Concept Questions

14-6. Create a cumulative cash flow graph for a business with the following monthly cash balances:

January	$40,000
February	$25,000
March	$13,000
April	$5,000
May	$12,000
June	$2,000
July	0
August	0
September	$1,500
October	$8,500
November	$12,000
December	$21,000

14-7. Fill in the following table, using the future value chart in this chapter, to show the amounts of one invested dollar's growth at the interest rates and time periods given.

Periods	Interest Rate (%)	Future Value of $10
2	5	$11.03
5	8	_____
10	10	_____
1	1	_____
7	3	_____

14-8. Fill in the following table, using the present value chart, to show the amounts of the net present value of $100 at the interest rates and time periods given.

Periods	Interest Rate (%)	Present Value of $100
2	5	$90.79
5	8	
10	10	
1	1	
7	3	

14-9. Calculate working capital for Angelina's company. Describe how her level of working capital might affect her business decisions.

Angelina's Jewelry Company Balance Sheet July 30, 2014		
ASSETS		
Current Assets		
Cash	$10,000	
Inventory	10,000	
Other Current Assets (Securities)	10,000	
Total Current Assets		$30,000
Long-Term Assets		70,000
TOTAL ASSETS		$100,000
LIABILITIES		
Short-Term Liabilities		
Accounts Payable (AP)	$10,000	
Short-Term Loans	5,000	
Total Short-Term Liabilities		$15,000
Total Long-Term Liabilities		15,000
OWNER'S EQUITY		70,000
TOTAL LIABILITIES + OWNER'S EQUITY		$100,000

Application Exercise

14-10. Create a projected cash flow statement for your business for one year.

Exploring Online

14-11. Print the tax documents list available at http://www.ideacafe.com/tax_center/index.php and highlight the forms that a C corporation producing glass bottles would need.

14-12. Visit Business Owners Idea Café online (http://www.businessowners ideacafe.com) and use the tool provided under Financing to figure out how much capital you would need to get your business off the ground.

BizBuilder Business Plan Questions

After studying this chapter, you should be able to answer the following Business Plan Questions. The entire outline for the Business Plan is found in Appendix 2.

7.0 Financial Analysis and Projections

7.2 Cash Flow Projections

A. List and describe your monthly fixed costs and add a cash reserve that covers three months of fixed costs.

B. Create a projected cash flow statement for your business for the first four quarters and the second and third years of operation.

C. Calculate the burn rate for your business.

7.7 Risks and Assumptions

A. List the risks and assumptions that underlie your financial projections.

B. Identify any external factors that you feel should be disclosed as substantial risks.

Case Study | Holterholm Farms—Radical Change for Maximum Impact

Ron Holter is a fifth-generation farmer in Jefferson, Maryland (in the Middletown Valley). He has learned to innovate the management of his farm to create a desirable quality of life for his family, while keeping profits and cash coming in. Holterholm Farms was purchased by William Holter in 1889, and it has been a dairy farm ever since.

Having grown up on this small family farm, Ron saw at first hand the challenges and opportunities inherent in running it. After returning home to the farm to work full time in 1981, Ron realized that the prevalent industrial system of agriculture demanded an incredible amount of labor on his part, for few tangible results. He was not going to be able to spend time with his children as they were growing up. By the 1990s, Ron saw that he would need to make changes if the farm was going to remain viable. But small producers were barely able to eke out a living. He knew that there had to be a way to keep the farm successful and maintain a reliable cash flow.

In 1995, Ron planted the farm's entire 207 acres in permanent vegetative cover (grass) and put the whole herd of cows out to pasture the following year. This grazing system not only provided the animals with a grass-based diet, it also allowed Ron to work fewer hours at a lower intensity to take care of the same acreage and the same number of cows, while simultaneously improving his profitability. Because of the switch to a grazing system, Ron saw a precipitous drop in expenses. Veterinary bills were almost nonexistent, because the grazing animals were healthier on a grass diet than a confinement herd could ever be. Seed purchases ended, because the entire farm was planted in permanent grasses.

Due to the cows' all-grass diet, Holterholm produced nearly a third less milk. But, because of the minimalization of costs, it became one of the most profitable farms in Maryland, netting $1,199.90 per cow in 1996, in comparison to the state average for confinement farms of $471.00 per cow.

Ron took this low-input system of agriculture on Holterholm one step further, by making the decision to operate as a seasonal enterprise. This switch to seasonal production meant a further decline in milk totals. Despite that, Holterholm Farm's profitability stayed roughly the same, and the seasonal system meant less year-round labor to support new calves. Now, all cows born in a given year were about two months' apart in age

Holterholm Farms is a member of the Organic Valley Coop
(© ZUMA Press, Inc./Alamy)

and thus could be fed and cared for together; labor and feeding costs fell even lower.

Starting in 2000, Ron began to operate the farm organically. He did not use drugs or artificial hormones on the cows, nor did he treat the soil with artificial fertilizers or pesticides. When both Horizon and Organic Valley Cooperatives moved into Maryland in 2005, looking for organic producers, Holterholm Farms was able immediately to certify its acreage as "organic"; it took only three months to certify the cows.

In the short term, securing a contract with Organic Valley meant that Ron was paid roughly twice as much for his milk than what he was getting previously. It also meant that Ron had to switch to feeding his cows organic grain, to

© Mexrix/Fotolia

supplement the grass cover. With organic grain prices as high as they were, he soon realized it was not profitable to feed the cows grain. His cash flow was being adversely impacted. He was losing money, despite producing more milk. So, in October 2007, Ron fed the last of the grain to his herd. Milk production dropped, as expected, but the financial results were astounding. In 2008, the farm made $858 per cow—this with no grain feed and less milk production. In 2009, the farm returned to the $1,000 mark, netting $1,004 per cow—again, with no grain-feed expenses.

Holterholm Farms began producing less milk than ever, compared with its days as a confinement operation. In 2009, two years into the no-grain-feed policy, the farm was producing only 22 pounds of milk per cow per day, yet earned as much as in 1996. This was significantly more than could ever have been earned prior to grazing.

Having adapted the dairy portion of Holterholm Farms to become more profitable with fewer inputs, Ron explored and adopted additional sources of revenue. He added beef, eggs, and produce to the mix. These were relatively small revenue generators, but required comparatively few cash outlays and added reliably positive cash flows.

Ron's son, Adam, is making his imprint on the farm's operations by creating a Community Supported Agriculture (CSA) venture that requires an upfront investment in used equipment and marketing that can be recouped quickly. The CSA has the particular benefit of collecting "shares" in advance, to the maximum available,

while incurring only the costs of growing and distributing produce from the fertile Holterholm Farms' land. Customers buy shares of the season's produce based on a weekly allocation of the total production. Adam might sell 50 shares in total to collect $25,000 at the beginning of the year and then provide each shareholder with 2-percent of the production each week. The payments are up front, with the expenditures at the back end.

The Holter family is managing the land to sustain it for generations to come.

Case Study Analysis

14-13. Why did switching the cows' feed entirely to grass improve Holterholm Farms' cash flow?

14-14. How could adding beef, eggs, and produce be beneficial from a cash flow perspective?

14-15. Search for Community Supported Agriculture (CSA) on the Internet. Why might it be good for Holterholm Farms to have a CSA? What are the risks involved? Why would consumers be willing to pay for their produce up front?

14-16. What would you ask the Holter family about the cash management of Holterholm Farms?

Case Sources

Adam Holter, "A Study in Efficiency: Holterholm Farms," unpublished manuscript, Shepherd University, December 2010.

Case Study | Managing Cash: CakeLove and Love Café

How does a lawyer with a master's degree in public health from George Washington University become a cake magnate? Warren Brown was a 28-year-old attorney in Washington, D.C., who, in 1999, made a New Year's resolution to learn how to bake. This led to his leaving his position at the U.S. Department of Health and Social Services in 2000 to become a full-time baker. Warren opened his first CakeLove bakery in Washington on U Street, N.W., in March of 2002 and the Love Café 17 months later.

Warren Brown, CakeLove
(Cake Love)

He eventually became the owner of five more CakeLove bakeries in the D.C. area, as well as the Love Café. CakeLove pound cakes, brownies, scones, and cookies are available via the Internet for delivery nationwide (http://www.cakelove .com). Warren's first cookbook, *CakeLove*, arrived on bookstore shelves in the spring of 2008, and his second book, *United Cakes of America*, highlights his favorite recipes from every state. To top it off, he hosted the Food Network's *Sugar Rush*. Warren was named U.S. Small Business Administration Entrepreneur of the Year in 2006, and CakeLove was selected top bakery in the *Washington Post Best Bets* readers' poll in 2005 and 2006 and in the *Washington Post Express* in 2009.

This meteoric rise in recognition required a number of essential ingredients. In addition to the all-natural components used in Cake-Love's products, the business aspects had to be properly balanced and mixed. Such rapid change demanded a lot of hard work, passion, determination—and cash flow. When Warren stepped away from his secure, full-time government job into full-time entrepreneurship, he had $10,000 of personal resources, including his credit card. In order to open his first storefront, Warren needed $125,000. Fortunately, he was able to secure a commercial loan from his community bank, CityFirst Bank of DC. Commercial lenders at larger, mainstream financial institutions were not convinced that a self-taught baker who had abandoned a promising legal career was a particularly good credit risk. Warren still maintained 100 percent ownership of CakeLove after the acquisition of start-up capital, and he continues as the sole owner after significant growth.

Within a couple of months of opening CakeLove, Warren decided to open Love Café—directly across the street from the bakery. The space popped up as an opportunity, and he wanted to take advantage of it. This required an additional infusion of capital for leasehold improvements, equipment, furnishings, and other start-up costs. There were few expenses from CakeLove that Love Café could leverage for this start-up, to attain economies of scale. Aside from being able to sell bakery-direct to consumers, he had little obvious financial advantage. However, CakeLove was strictly a take-out facility, housing production and sales areas, whereas Love Café would be a full-service establishment with a menu of baked goods, sandwiches, and coffee, in what Warren described as a "laid back, relaxed atmosphere incorporating natural elements and including WiFi, sofas, large windows." Because CakeLove was new and had little positive cash flow, Warren could not finance the second location with the cash flow of the first. So, he turned again to CityFirst Bank. Ultimately, due to increased rent and competition, Warren closed Love Café in 2012.

Between September 2007 and July 2008, CakeLove opened three additional retail bakeries. Each successive expansion created a need for additional cash. Warren managed to avoid selling shares of the company by leveraging resources and partnering with a community lender. His banking partner, CityFirst, financed each location—to supplement earnings generated from existing operations.

Growth in the number of retail bakery storefronts has carried the business to new heights. Warren continues to serve as the primary manager of cash flow and human resources for his organization. Inventory theft has not been a significant issue because of well-planned store layouts and careful procedures; CakeLove has established cash-handling policies (cash-counting systems) to prevent pilferage from the cash drawers. Because CakeLove sells baked goods and other perishable items, spoilage and unsold product can become significant contributors to cash flow problems. Warren and his team have instituted a waste-tracking system and have been able to keep a "pretty good eye on the way inventory is moving."

The growth of the organization has not been the greatest challenge to cash flow for Cake-Love. Warren notes that diets have been more of a detriment to the business than expansion or an abysmal economy. CakeLove experienced its most significant cash-tightness at the height of popularity for the Atkins Diet, when counting carbohydrates led dieters to cutting out sweets and bakery treats. During times of reduced cash inflow, Warren and his team have to look to cut expenses, particularly by monitoring labor costs more closely than usual. When Warren opened his first CakeLove bakery, he had three employees, including himself. As of July 2008, he had 105. This has meant meeting the cash flow requirements of a large payroll and its associated expenses for the various locations, including being responsible for the support of numerous families.

Warren Brown has the following advice for aspiring entrepreneurs, "Do the homework. Know the industry you want to enter cold, so that you absolutely know how to make or do whatever it is that you want to make or do. Don't rush in. See it well and don't be afraid to get messy and to keep an open mind. There is always a way to improve. Know the product very well and have good confidence in what you are selling. People will always have unsolicited advice for you. If you don't have that confidence, you will get little chinks in your armor that can make your business less enjoyable and even miserable. Confidence is critical." Warren's recipe for growth has produced sweet rewards.

Case Study Analysis

14-17. How has Warren Brown been able to finance the growth of his company?

14-18. What methods has CakeLove used to manage cash flow? What others might it adopt?

14-19. What types of cash flow management issues would you expect CakeLove to encounter if it continues to grow at a rate of three bakeries per year or more?

14-20. How do Warren Brown's recommendations to aspiring entrepreneurs pertain to cash flow?

Case Sources

CakeLove, accessed August 31, 2013, http://www.cakelove.com.

"Lawyer Turned Entrepreneur of the Year, Warren Brown of CakeLove," *The Africana-Connect*, accessed January 12, 2008, http://www.theculturalconnect.com/new/2007/11/23/warren-brown-africana.

Warren Brown, *CakeLove: How to Bake Cakes from Scratch*, New York: Stewart, Tabori and Chang, 2008.

Chapter 15

FINANCING STRATEGY: DEBT, EQUITY, OR BOTH?

Learning Objectives

1. Explore your financing preferences.

2. Identify the types of business financing.

3. Compare the pros and cons of debt and equity financing.

4. Identify sources of capital for your business.

5. Understand stocks and bonds as investment alternatives.

Superstock

E tsy, Inc., was founded in 2005 by Robert Kalin, Chris Maguire, and Haim Schoppik in an environment that Kalin describes like this: "Early on it was a little bit like the Wild West where it starts with what you have on hand."[1] Frustrated by his inability to find online distribution for his handcrafted wood products, Kalin created a Web site that connected creators of handmade items and sellers of vintage goods and craft supplies with buyers through e-commerce. With reported gross merchandise sales of $895.1 million in 2012 and over 30 million registered users, Etsy has grown from a bootstrap company to a business that, after five rounds of venture investment, was worth almost $300 million.[2]

Kalin went to people he knew for his earliest financing. He had installed a bar for Spencer Ain and helped restaurateur Sean Meenan with a technology installation, before they became his first (2005) and second (2006) round investors.[3] Next, working through his networks, Kalin got Caterina Fake and Stewart Butterfield, founders of Flckr, along with Delicious founder Joshua Schachter, Albert Wenger, and Union Square Ventures to invest $1 million—also in 2006.[4] Union Square Ventures invested again in Series B (January 2007) and C (July 2007) with $3.25 million each time.

The next financing round for Etsy raised $27 million, with the word on the street being that "Etsy was valued a $90 million pre money."[5] Accel Partners was a significant investor in the Series D financing. The fifth—$20 million (Series E)—round saw Index Ventures as a new lead investor, joined by Accel Partners and Burda Media.[6] The company's subsequent valuation rose to nearly $300 million.

© Web Pix/Alamy

Going It Alone versus Securing Financing

To start or expand a business, you will need to have money, either on hand or through **financing**, which is the act of providing or raising funds (capital) for a purpose. For entrepreneurs, that means obtaining the money to start and operate a successful business.

There are three ways to finance a business venture, assuming you do not have enough funds in your savings:

1. obtain gifts and grants,
2. borrow money (debt),
3. exchange a share of the business for money (equity).

For many (or even most) people who want to start a business, there will be a need for financing. Whether that requirement is for $500 or $5 million,

[1]Evelyn Ruslie Visits Etsy in New York: Robert Kalin video interview, 2011, accessed April 21, 2011, http://techcrunch.tv/interviews-and-profiles/watch?id=NubDNrMToBvPOXXVnACzktftfSHzFljz.

[2]Etsy, accessed September 1, 2013, http://www.etsy.com.

[3]Op cit., Evelyn Ruslie Visits Etsy.

[4]PrivCo, "Etsy, Inc. Receives $1 million Series A Investment from Caterina Fake, Stewart Butterfield, Joshua Schachter, and Others," accessed April 21, 2011, http://www.privco.com/private-company/etsy.

[5]Erick Schonfeld, "Etsy Raises $27 Million: Accel's Jim Breyer Joins Board," *TechCrunch*, January 30, 2008, accessed April 11, 2011, http://techcrunch.com/2008/01/30/etsy-raises-27-million-jim-breyer-joins-board/.

[6]Erick Schonfeld, "Index Ventures Buys Into Etsy, Triples Valuation to Nearly $300 Million," *TechCrunch*, August 26, 2010, accessed April 21, 2011, http://techcrunch.com/2010/8/26/etsy-300-million-valuation.

the entrepreneur will have to bridge the gap between what he or she has and what the business's cash flows and prudent reserves require. Sometimes an entrepreneur can use home equity, credit cards, or funds from friends or family to make up this shortfall. In other cases, these resources are not available, are not sufficient, or would not make sense for the business. In those situations, debt or equity financing becomes a necessity.

How Often Do Small Businesses Really Fail?

Before you search for financing, you may want to know more about success and failure rates for start-ups. It is a popular misperception that four out of five small firms fail in the first five years of operation. You are likely to hear this from well-meaning friends, family, and potential investors. According to *The Portable MBA in Entrepreneurship*, however, "This claim has no basis in fact. Actually, there is good evidence that more than half— rather than one-fifth—of new small firms survive for eight or more years."[7]

creditor person or organization that is owed money.

Business failure is defined by Dun & Bradstreet (D&B)—which operates the largest and oldest commercial credit-rating service in the United States—as "business termination with losses to creditors." A **creditor** is an organization or individual from which you have borrowed money that must be repaid. D&B, which followed 814,000 small firms formed in 1977–1978 for eight years, reported that only 20 to 25 percent of those small ventures that were recorded as terminated during their first eight years of operation actually closed because of bankruptcy. The other 75 to 80 percent reported as terminations were:

- businesses that were sold to new owners;
- businesses that changed—for example, from a flower shop to a general nursery; or
- businesses that were closed because the owners retired or moved on to other businesses.

More than half of all new small companies can expect to survive for at least eight years.[8]

For many, a small business is considered a high-risk, high-return investment—although in truth entrepreneurs are generally calculated risk takers and only pursue opportunities after they have weighed the chances of success. For the investor willing to accept the risk, a small business can be a great opportunity. The return on investment (ROI) of a successful small business can be thousands of percent, but the possibility of business failure is also definitely present. If your business fails, you and your investors will lose money. Your task, when you write your business plan and do your research, will be to demonstrate how your venture will succeed and that your investors can look forward to appropriate returns for the risk they are assuming.

What Is the Best Type of Financing for You and Your Business?

Learning Objective 2
Identify the types of business financing.

Financing is not a one-size-fits-all proposition. Each venture has unique requirements and circumstances, along with the structure and challenges of the selected industry. For some, such as the restaurant business, standard

---

[7]William D. Bygrave and Andrew Zacharkis, eds., *The Portable MBA in Entrepreneurship*, New York: John Wiley & Sons, 1997, p. 199.

[8]E. Lewis Bryan, "Financial Management and Capital Formation in Small Business," *Journal of Small Business Management*, July 1, 1984.

commercial loans may not be an option because traditional lenders will not be willing to make them. For others, such as research-based technology firms, equity will be needed. Regardless of your preferences and the types of financing available, you will invariably have to be the first investor in your own business. Lenders and investors alike will insist that entrepreneurs have their personal resources involved before they put in additional funding. It is easier to persist and work hard when you have a personal financial stake in success. If putting your personal assets at risk is not something you (or your family) are willing to do, expect to be rejected by investors and lenders.

Your **risk tolerance**, the amount of risk (threat of loss) you are willing to sustain, will also help to define possible financing options. For example, if you own a home and are seeking a commercial loan, you will likely have to put it up as security, in case you cannot repay the debt. Or, if you are relinquishing ownership through equity, you may have to give up control of the company you founded to obtain needed financial resources. Be prepared to face these types of decisions as you seek financing that works.

risk tolerance the amount of risk or threat of loss that an individual is willing to sustain.

There are three ways for a business to raise the capital it needs to grow.

1. *Finance with earnings.* If a company is profitable and has positive cash flow, it can use some of its profits to finance expansion. This will help ensure that the company does not take on too much debt or grow more quickly than its finances can handle.

2. *Finance with equity.* If a company is incorporated, it can sell stock (privately or through the stock market) to raise capital. People who purchase shares of stock are getting *equity* (part ownership). Other types of businesses may also have equity investors.

3. *Finance with debt.* Any type of business, depending on its *creditworthiness* and that of its owner(s), can borrow money. An incorporated company can also sell *bonds*, although it is difficult and cost-prohibitive for small businesses to do so. People who purchase bonds will receive interest on the loan they are making to the company, with repayment of principal in a lump sum at maturity.

Both stocks and bonds are heavily regulated by the federal government. Issuing either one requires considerable technical guidance and monetary outlay. This is not a do-it-yourself procedure. Rather, the counsel of investment bankers, accountants, and attorneys will be needed.

Gifts and Grants

Businesses have opportunities to receive gifts and grants. However, these opportunities must be pursued with caution because gifts may come with strings attached and grants often have requirements. Informal gifts include such items as cash, free use of facilities and equipment, unpaid labor by friends and family, and forgiveness or deferral of debts. Official gifts—grants—are furnished primarily by the federal government and include specific types of investments to stimulate designated geographic areas or to support particular populations. These may be in the form of **tax abatements** (legal reductions in taxes), and **tax credits** (direct reduction of taxes). Business grants are primarily made for research and commercialization efforts and are difficult for start-up, low-technology companies to acquire. Because gifts and grants do not require repayment or incur financing costs, they are often at the top of the entrepreneur's list of desired resources. They are also among the hardest to obtain. The most readily available form of gifts for entrepreneurs are those found through "crowdfunding" sites, which are discussed in the accompanying BizFacts feature.

tax abatement legal reduction in taxes.

tax credit direct reduction of taxes.

BizFacts

Recently, a number of Internet sites have been created to link entrepreneurs in need of funds with investors. These are often called crowdfunding or person-to-person (P2P) lending sites. Businesses and investors can find sites tailored to their industries and funding requirements. Funds may be gifts or donations, investments, or loans. The sites may screen potential participants and may only offer money to a company after its funding goal is reached. Others may issue partial funding. In some cases, rewards are used to attract repeat investor participation. Some popular crowdfunding sites are shown below.

Crowdfunder Web Sites

Kiva	Microenterprise	www.kiva.org
Profounder	Small business	www.profounder.com
Microfundo	Music	www.microfundo.org
Kickstarter	Creative projects	www.kickstarter.com
Rockethub	Creative arts	www.rockethub.com
Cat Walk Genius	Fashion	www.catwalkgenius.com
IndieGoGo	Creative art	www.indiegogo.com
Grow VC	Mobile & Web 2.0	www.growvc.com

Debt Financing

Many businesses have some combination of debt and equity financing. The variety of possible loans and investments is quite large and growing. One challenge that you may face is determining what type of debt financing to pursue, based on your business type and life-cycle stage; your personal finances, wealth, and preferences; and the options available to you. Before pursuing debt for your business, calculate your personal *net worth* by tallying your assets (i.e., cash, investment accounts, personal property, real estate, and intangibles) and subtracting your debts (such as credit card balances, vehicle loans, student loans, and mortgages). Your lenders will want to know what you own, what you owe, and what your business finances are. The percentage of small firms using credit by credit type is shown in **Exhibit 15-1**.

Debt financing comes in many forms, with widely varying repayment and qualification terms. Different types of lenders will have various rates and fees, so it is worthwhile to compare the total package costs. Some debt options are discussed in **Exhibit 15-2**.

Debt Financing: Pros and Cons

Learning Objective 3

Compare the pros and cons of debt and equity financing.

promissory note a loan document that is a written promise to pay a specific sum of money on or before a particular date.

principal the amount of debt or loan before interest and fees are added.

To finance through debt, the entrepreneur applies to and contracts with a person or an institution that has money, and borrows it, signing a **promissory note**, a document agreeing to repay a certain sum of money (with interest) by a specified date.

Interest is determined as a percentage (interest rate) of the loan principal. The **principal** is the amount of the loan or outstanding balance on the loan amount, not including interest. If $1,200 is borrowed at 10 percent to be paid back over one year, the interest on the loan is $120 ($1,200 × 0.10). Typically, the borrower makes monthly payments until the loan is fully paid. The term, or length, of the loan generally depends on what is being financed, with working capital having the shortest term and real estate the longest.

The beginning entrepreneur should consider carefully the costs and terms of debt, because it often takes time for a new business to generate cash for repayment. One risk of debt is that failure to make loan payments can destroy a company before it can generate positive cash flow.

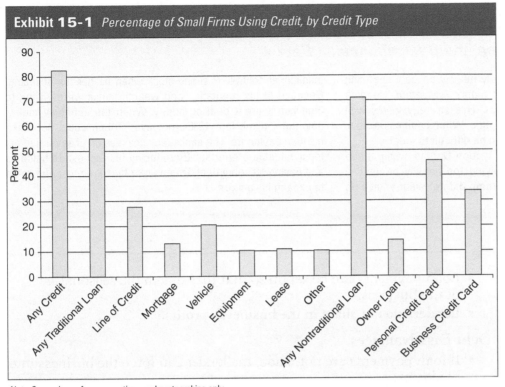

Exhibit 15-1 *Percentage of Small Firms Using Credit, by Credit Type*

Note: Owner loans for corporations and partnerships only.
Source: U.S. Small Business Administration, Office of Advocacy, "Financing Patterns of Small Firms: Finding from the 1998 Survey of Small Business Finance," September 2003.

Exhibit 15-2 *Debt Financing Options*

Debt Category	Description	Common Types	Terms
Commercial Loans	Business loans typically provided by a bank or other financial institution.	• Real estate • Equipment and improvements • Working capital • Asset based • Accounts-receivable factoring	Up to 20 years Up to 7 years 1 year or less Depends on the type of asset pledged Often 30 days
Personal Loans	Loans taken out on your personal credit and used for the business. May have a fixed term (length) or "revolving" term.	• *Credit cards* • *Home equity loans* • *Title loan* • *Payday loan*	Revolving Variable terms; some are lines of credit Short-term, fixed repayment Short-term, fixed repayment
Leases	Debts incurred for the rights to use specific property, such as automobiles, trucks, or equipment.	• *Vehicle lease* • *Equipment leases*	Often for 2 or 3 years with a purchase option at the end of the term Varies widely depending on the nature of equipment leased
Bonds	Long-term debt instruments used by corporations to raise large sums of money.	See Bonds section later in the chapter	

Debt Advantages

- A lender has no say in the management or direction of the business, as long as the loan payments are made and contracts are not violated.
- Loan payments are predictable; they do not change with the fortunes of the business.

Step into the Shoes . . .

Donald Trump and Overreliance on Debt

Companies that rely heavily on debt financing are described as highly *leveraged*, meaning financed with debt. This strategy works well when business is good. When business is slow, debt payments can be difficult to meet.

Real estate tycoon Donald Trump made the mistake of relying too heavily on debt in the early 1980s. Trump did not want to give up managerial control by selling stock when he needed financing. Because of his reputation and wealth, banks were willing to lend him a great deal of money. When the economy took a downturn in the late 1980s, however, Trump could not make his loan payments. The banks took possession of several of his most valuable properties. By reducing his real estate holdings and paying off some debt, Trump was able to recover and go on to expand his empire.

---

leveraged financed by debt, as opposed to equity.

- Loan payments can be set up so that they match the seasonal sales of the business.
- Lenders do not share in the business's profits.

Debt Disadvantages

- If loan payments are not made, the lender can force the business into bankruptcy.

default the results of a borrower failing to meet the repayment agreement on a debt.

- The lender can take the home and possessions of the owner(s) to settle a debt in case of **default**—when the borrower fails to meet the repayment agreement.
- Debt payments increase a business's fixed costs, thereby lowering profits.
- Repayment reduces available cash.
- Lenders expect regular financial reporting and compliance with the loan contracts.

Equity Financing

Equity means that, in return for money, an investor will receive a percentage of ownership in a company. For the $1,200 investment discussed previously, an equity investor might want 10 percent ownership of the company, which would mean 10 percent of the business's profits. (This would indicate that the business was valued at $12,000.) The investor is hoping that 10 percent of the profits will provide a high rate of return, over time, on the initial investment of $1,200.

Equity Financing: Pros and Cons

The equity investor assumes greater risk than the debt lender. If the business does not make a profit, neither does the investor. The equity investor cannot force the business into bankruptcy to get back the investment. If creditors force a business into bankruptcy, equity investors have a claim on whatever is left over only after the debt lenders have been paid. However, the potential for return is also higher. The equity investor should make an investment back many times over if the business prospers.

Money raised via equity does not have to be paid back unless the business is successful. Equity investors may offer helpful advice and provide valuable contacts. However, if the entrepreneur gives up more than 50 percent ownership, control of the business passes to the equity holders. Even with less than half the ownership, investors may assert managerial influence.

Step into the Shoes . . .

Apple's Steve Jobs

Relying too heavily on equity can also be the downfall of a founding entrepreneur, as the story of Steve Jobs, cofounder of Apple Computer, illustrates. Because Jobs and his partner, Stephen Wozniak, were young men with very little money, debt financing was not an option. To raise money, they sold pieces of the company.

By the late 1980s, Apple had become so successful that Jobs hired a prominent PepsiCo executive, John Sculley, as Apple's chief executive officer. Sculley gradually convinced Apple's board of directors that Jobs was a disruptive influence in the company. Eventually a vote was taken of Apple shareholders, and Jobs did not own enough equity to fend off Sculley's effort to fire him. He was voted out of the highly successful company he started.

Jobs was invited back to lead Apple as interim CEO in 1997, however, and was elected permanent CEO by the shareholders in 2000. He remained a leader at Apple until his death in 2011.

Bloomberg/Getty Images

Equity Advantages

- If the business does not make a profit, the investor does not get paid.
- There are no required regular payments in the form of principal or interest, and dividends for common stockholders are distributed at the discretion of the board of directors.
- The equity investor cannot force the business into bankruptcy in order to recoup the investment.
- The equity investor has an interest in seeing the business succeed and may therefore offer helpful advice and provide valuable contacts.

Equity Disadvantages

- Through giving up too much ownership, the founding entrepreneur could lose control of the business to the equity holders.
- Even with small amounts of equity, investors may interfere with the business via unsolicited advice and/or continuous inquiries.
- Equity financing is riskier for investors, so they frequently want both to be able to influence how the company is run and to receive a higher rate of return than a lender.
- The entrepreneur must share profits with other equity investors.

Where and How to Find Capital That Works for You

The decision of where to seek capital is complex, and the options that are available will depend on both personal and business factors. Your preferences should weigh heavily in the decision. However, it is a rare business owner that wants to pledge all family assets, pay high interest rates and fees, or give up majority ownership. Yet, many start-up and experienced entrepreneurs must do just that in order to secure the funds they need. Identifying and securing financing often involves exploring multiple potential options and creating a complex, multilayered financing mix. The optimal resources for a business may not be the obvious ones. Therefore, it is valuable to be aware of the range of sources.

There are many potential sources of capital, and it may take you numerous attempts to find what works. Some are identified in **Exhibit 15-3**.

◀ Learning Objective 4
Identify sources of capital for your business.

Exhibit 15-3 *Selected Sources of Business Financing*

Financing Source	Category of Financing	Type(s) of Financing	Uses of Funds	Notes
Entrepreneur/Self	Debt or Equity	Loan or Owner's Equity	Any	Debt terms to be established at borrowing. Earnings through dividends and/or sale of company.
Friends or Family	Debt or Equity	Loan or Stock	Any	Negotiable on debt. Earnings through dividends and/or sale of stock.
Small Business Investment Companies (SBICs), Minority Enterprise SBICs (MESBICs), Rural Business Investment Companies (RBICs), New Markets Venture Capital funds (NMVC) *http://www.sba.gov/inv/index.html*	Debt or Equity	Loan or Stock	Varies according to licenses with the SBA and the types of entities served. Funds are to be used as requested by the businesses.	Generally installment loans for debt. Earnings through dividends and/or sale of stock.
Small Business Innovation Research (SBIR) or Small Business Technology Transfer (STTR) *http://www.sba.gov/aboutsba/sbaprograms*	Grant	Research Grant	Specific research as defined in grant application.	Must complete requirements of grant funding.
Community Development Corporations *http://www.opportunityfinance.net*	Linked Deposits and Savings	Gift	According to program guidelines.	Savings and financial literacy requirements.
Venture Capitalists	Equity	Stock	Start-up or growth	IPO, buy-out, dividends, royalties
Community Development Venture Capital Funds *http://www.cdvca.org*	Equity	Stock	Start-up or growth	IPO, buy-out, dividends, royalties
Angel Investors	Equity	Stock	Start-up or growth	IPO, buy-out, dividends, royalties
Investment Banks	Equity	Stock	Private or public placements (IPOs)	Paid in fee income.
Economic Development Agencies *http://www.eda.gov*	Debt	Varies	Varies	Varies broadly from state to state and other localities.
Leasing Companies	Debt	Vehicles or Equipment	To acquire use of vehicles and/or equipment.	Monthly payments of fees. Purchase option generally available at end of term.
Banks/Financial Institutions	Debt	Real Estate Loans	Real estate	Mortgage—long term with installment payments.
		Equipment, Vehicle, or Other Working Capital	Equipment and other capital as specified in the loan request. Supplies, materials, cash flow.	Promissory note—medium term with installment payments. Lines of credit usually with a maximum of 1-year term. Must be paid to $0 annually.
		Home Equity	Personal loan for any purpose secured against a home.	Many variations; often a monthly payment.
		Credit Card	Unsecured loan for business or consumer use.	Revolving credit with minimum monthly payments.

Financing Source	Category of Financing	Type(s) of Financing	Uses of Funds	Notes
Mortgage Companies	Debt	Real Estate Loans	Real estate	Mortgage—long term with installment payments.
		Home Equity	Personal loan for any purpose secured against a home.	Many variations; often a monthly payment.
Insurance Companies	Debt	Policy Loan	Any	Reduces cash surrender value. Varies.
Community Development Banks *http://www.opportunityfinance.net*	Debt	Similar to Banks	Capital to rebuild communities through targeted lending.	Terms vary according to mission and community need.
Community Development Credit Unions *http://www.natfed.org*	Debt	Loans to Members	Per community ownership	Varies depending on type of loan.
Community Development Loan Funds *http://www.opportunityfinance.net*	Debt	Equipment, Leasehold, or Other Working Capital	Purchase of essential equipment and improvement for start-up and growth operation.	Primarily term loans. Some lines of credit. Typically for nontraditional credit. May include microloans, lending to not-for-profits, and to developers of affordable housing.
Microenterprise Development Loan Funds *http://www.microenterpriseworks.org* *http://www.opportunityfinance.net*	Debt	Primarily Working Capital and Start-Up	Relatively small loans ($35,000 maximum) for purpose detailed in applications and/or business plans.	Installment loans. Designed for nontraditional customers.
Receivable Factors	Debt	Accounts Receivable	Any	Factor is repaid by entrepreneur's customers. Receivables discounted and funds held back until they are paid.
Title Lenders	Debt	Title Loans	Any	Short terms with high interest rates.
Pay Day Lenders	Debt	Pay Day Loans	Any	Short terms with high interest rates.
Vendors	Debt	Trade Credit	Any	Entrepreneur delays payment of invoices.

Having an Excellent Business Plan Goes a Long Way

When you seek financing for your business, the quality of your business plan could make the difference between success and failure. Lenders and investors will need to recover their principal plus interest or investment plus a rate of return. If your business plan realistically, clearly, and convincingly demonstrates that you can and will achieve your goals, your chances of obtaining financing will greatly increase.

How Capital Sources Read Your Business Plan

People read business plans in different ways, but rarely are they read through from front to back as written. For example, a lender may look at the cash flow projections first. But one thing is for certain: You will need to capture the reader's attention in the Executive Summary or the plan is unlikely to be read.

Family and Friends

Family and friends are obvious sources for loans. But what about offering them equity instead? Explain that if they *loan* you money, they will only earn back the amount of the loan plus interest. If they invest capital in exchange for *equity*, on the other hand, they could get back much more than the original amount. Acknowledge that equity is more risky than debt, but explain that the potential for reward is much higher. Be careful not to take money from friends and family members who could not afford to lose it if the business failed.

Also, be sure that any financial agreements are properly documented and signed, so that there is no misunderstanding later. There are online services that create formal business agreements between family members, and attorneys can make the agreements legal. Nothing ruins a good relationship more quickly than a dispute over money. As Shakespeare's Polonius advises in *Hamlet*, "Neither a borrower nor a lender be; for loan oft loses itself and friends." Whereas borrowing may be unavoidable, the cautionary note on borrowing from friends is well directed.

Financial Institutions and Dimensions of Credit

It can be difficult for new entrepreneurs to get loans from banks and other financial institutions, partly because bankers tend to be conservative lenders. Start-ups are riskier than established businesses, because their performance is necessarily based on projections rather than historical data. Banks are in the business of lending money they are confident will be repaid, with interest. Bankers operate on the principles of the five Cs of credit (see **Figure 15-1**):

1. *Collateral.* Property or other assets pledged against the loan that the lender can take and sell if the loan is not repaid. Examples of such assets are business real estate, equipment, inventory, an owner's home, certificates of deposit, money market accounts, stock certificates, and bonds. Commercial lenders never want to have to take such assets, but they need collateral so that they can be confident of some level of repayment.

2. *Character.* Typically analyzed in the form of the owner's *personal credit* (ability to borrow money) for a small business. Before a financial services company will lend you money, it will want to know your **credit history**, which is the record of how reliably and punctually

credit history a record of credit extended and the repayment thereof.

Figure 15-1 *The Five Cs of Credit*

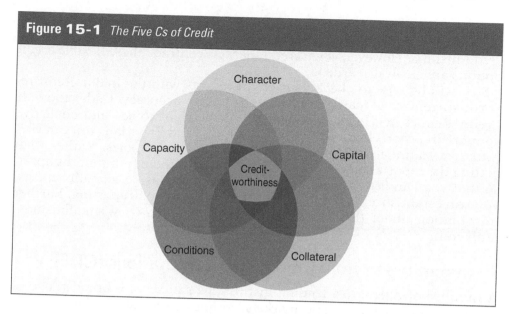

you or your company has paid past loans. The lender will obtain your credit report from a **credit reporting agency (CRA)**. These companies—primarily TransUnion, Equifax, and Experian—collect and analyze information supplied by financial institutions and others that extend credit.

3. *Capacity.* The business cash flow must be sufficient to cover the regular loan payments and expenses. You will have to report your projected cash flow, so the lender can determine whether you will be able to repay the loan. Your **debt service** is the amount you will have to pay over a given period of time, until the loan is repaid.

4. *Capital.* How much of your own money have you invested in your business? Have you gotten friends or family to invest? As we have noted, bankers want to see that you are risking your own resources before they risk the bank's.

5. *Conditions.* This is the state of the industry and economic climate at the time the loan is made and during its anticipated term. If inflation is on the rise, for example, the bank may be concerned that your earnings will not keep pace with it, thus reducing your capacity to repay the loan.

Lenders will expect you to sign a **personal guarantee**, which states that you will be responsible for paying off the loan in the event that the business cannot do so. In other words, in the case of default, the lender will have the right to take business *and* personal assets.

What constitutes good credit may not be objectively apparent. It is not merely the absence of bad credit. You may think that you have good credit because you have never borrowed money or used a credit card. You are wrong. What you have is *no* credit. To establish credit, you must prove that you are capable of making regular payments on debts. Typically, most banks will not lend to anyone without a credit history, but many stores will, through revolving **charge accounts**, which are credit accounts that have a set borrowing limit and may be used and repaid on a repeated cycle. One way to begin a good credit history is to open one of these store accounts, charge a few small purchases, and never miss a payment or pay later than the due date. This record of on-time payment will become a part of your credit report.

credit reporting agency (CRA) an organization that collects, analyzes, and resells information supplied by financial institutions and others who extend credit.

debt service the amount a borrower is obligated to pay in a given period until a loan is repaid.

personal guarantee the promise to pay issued by an individual.

charge account credit extended by a company allowing qualified customers to make purchases up to a specified limit, without paying cash at the time of purchase.

There have been efforts to encourage the acceptance of regular savings deposits and/or timely payments of rent and utilities in lieu of a traditional credit history.[9] However, when credit markets contract, these flexible credit options are easily discarded.

It will be wise to check your credit reports with the major credit reporting agencies at least once a year, to ensure accuracy. Under the Fair Credit Report Act, federal law gives you the right to see and challenge your credit reports from TransUnion, Equifax, and Experian. You can visit http://www.annualcreditreport.com to obtain your reports. Rather than getting the reports all at once, it is better to space them four months apart, so that you can better check for errors. For your business credit reports, you can establish a history at Dun & Bradstreet by self-reporting. Further information about this option is available at http://www.smallbusiness.dnb.com.

Community Development Financial Institutions (CDFIs)[10]

A number of alternative lending institutions can serve a broad range of needs in emerging domestic markets. Although they share the common vision of expanding economic opportunity, and improving the quality of life for low-income people and communities, the four CDFI sectors—banks, credit unions, loan funds, and venture capital (VC) funds—are characterized by different business models and legal structures.

Community Development Banks

Community development banks (CDBs) provide capital to rebuild economically distressed communities through targeted lending and investing. They are for-profit corporations with community representation on their boards of directors. Depending on the individual charter, such banks are regulated by some combination of the Federal Deposit Insurance Corporation (FDIC), the Federal Reserve, the Office of the Comptroller of the Currency, the Office of Thrift Supervision, and state banking agencies. Their deposits are insured by the FDIC.

Community Development Credit Unions

Community development credit unions (CDCUs) promote ownership of assets and savings and provide affordable credit and retail financial services to low-income individuals, often with special outreach to minority communities. They are nonprofit financial cooperatives owned by their members. Credit unions are regulated by the National Credit Union Administration (NCUA)—an independent federal agency—by state agencies, or both. In most institutions, deposits are also insured by the NCUA.

Community Development Loan Funds

Community development loan funds (CDLFs) provide financing and development services to businesses, organizations, and individuals in low-income communities. There are four main types of loan funds: microenterprise, small business, housing, and community service organization. Each is defined by the type of client served, although many loan funds serve more than one type of client in a single institution. CDLFs tend to be nonprofit and governed by boards of directors with community representation.

[9]C. Glackin and E. Mahoney, "Savings and Credit for U.S. Microenterprises: Integrating Individual Development Accounts and Loans for Microenterprise," *Journal of Microfinance*, Volume 4, Number 2, 2002, pp. 93–125.

[10]Opportunity Finance Network Web site, accessed September 4, 2013, http://www.opportunityfinance.net.

Case Sources

Darren Fishell, "Newsmakers 2011: Josh Davis," *The Times Record*, December 28, 2011, accessed September 1, 2013, http://www.timesrecord.com/news/2011-12-28/Front_Page/Newsmakers_2011_Josh_Davis.html.

James McCarthy, "Seed capital tax credit program hits its cap," *MaineBiz*, March 4, 2013, accessed September 1, 2013, http://www.mainebiz.biz/apps/pbcs.dll/article?AID=/20130304/CURRENTEDITION/302289994/1088.

The Gelato Fiasco, accessed September 1, 2013, http://www.gelatofiasco.com/our-story.

"Thanks Starbucks! Now I'm your competitor," *CNN Money* interview, n.d., accessed September 1, 2013, http://money.cnn.com/video/smallbusiness/2012/02/16/sbiz_starbucks_loan_gelato.cnnmoney/?fb_ref=fbLike&fb_source=profile_oneline.

Chilly Dilly's Ice Cream Company: Financing Growth

Case prepared by Dr. Jay Azriel and Dr. Andrew Sumutka of York College of Pennsylvania.

Dylan sat at his parents' kitchen table going over the season's revenues. He smiled as he checked over his figures for a second time. He could hardly believe that his earnings had increased more than 250 percent over the previous year, despite the tough economic times. His hard work, careful planning, and creative ideas were responsible, at least in part, for a 105.7-percent increase in profits as well. His smile widened as he thought about the role that his entrepreneurship courses and professors at Temple University had played in his success. He had certainly come a long way from that night when he was stranded on the side of a highway with little cash, a dead cell-phone battery, sitting in an ice cream truck that he had used almost all his savings—$5,000— to buy. However, his smile quickly faded as he got back to work on his strategic plan.

Dylan looked up from the numbers and thought about what he should do next. He knew that growing his business by triple digits the next year would not be as easy as it was during the first two. He had maxed out his line of credit with the only bank in town that would loan his business money, so it would be a great risk to put even one additional truck on the road. He was glad that he resisted the temptation to pay back his loan early and instead conserved the cash for investing in the growth of his business. However, the cash balance fell short of what was necessary to finance his growth plan. Although Dylan had already booked several after-season sales at area companies, these would not generate enough profit to fund his expansion plan for the following year. He knew that putting three additional trucks on the road would extend his operations beyond the area of his hometown of York, Pennsylvania, into some of northern Maryland's wealthier suburbs that had been overlooked by the few ice cream truck operators still in business. He hoped that he would not have to seriously consider his father's suggestion of inviting a partner into the business. He had heard too many stories of failed partnerships in his entrepreneurship classes. However, what choices did he really have?

Dylan thought hard about what his next steps should be. He knew his business was at one of those important "crossroads" his professors mentioned. The business he was building was more than just a fleet of ice cream trucks. He wanted to bring back something big, like the ubiquitous "Good Humor man" of the past. He just needed to figure out how to finance this growth. His family broke his concentration, as they piled into the kitchen to get dinner ready. He put his paperwork aside and joined them.

Old fashioned ice cream truck
(© David R. Frazier/Alamy)

Dylan's Dream

Dylan had always been entrepreneurial. He got his first taste of the world of high finance at the age of nine, when he started a paper route he ran for five years. Although his $2,500 annual earnings were good for a kid, Dylan always dreamed of something bigger. After the paper route, he started a lawn-mowing business and, in high school, a concert-promotion company. While Dylan had learned a great deal from these ventures, "It was always a dream of mine to start an ice cream business." When he was a senior in high school, Dylan began plans to start his dream business to help pay for college. His first idea was to serve hand-scooped ice cream from a truck. However, this plan was short lived. "After researching this I realized that novelty ice cream is easier and more profitable."

Dylan kept thinking about his ice cream business while studying entrepreneurship at Temple University in Philadelphia. In fact, during his freshman year, Dylan investigated the ice cream industry for one of his courses and recognized an opportunity for starting such a venture in York. He learned that the ice cream vendor industry was fairly fragmented, mostly run by operators who owned one or two trucks. Thus, he would not have to contend with any large players in his market. During winter break, he began to seriously investigate purchasing his first ice cream truck. Dylan scoured a number of Web sites and found a truck on eBay that he thought might work. The vehicle he had set his sights on was a Good Humor truck from 1970. Dylan took several train rides to a small community on Long Island, New York, to take a look at the truck. Excited that he would actually be starting a business, he decided to hand over $5,000—virtually all his savings—without making more than a cursory inspection of the old GMC P30 Step Van.

On the long drive back to York, an excited Dylan made phone call after phone call on his cell phone to tell family and friends about his newly purchased truck. Then, right outside of Philadelphia his truck just stopped running and coasted to a stop on the side of the interstate—more than two hours from home. Dylan called his local mechanic and had his crippled truck towed back to York. The mechanic's diagnosis was that only the freezer was worth saving. The rest of the truck went to the scrap yard. Dylan lost his truck and the $5,000.

However, he did not let this setback extinguish his dream of becoming York's ice cream king. Armed with more information, Dylan carefully checked out a 1971 Ford Good Humor truck. However, he did not have the $15,000 asking price. "After losing everything, I was forced to ask for money from the bank." Dylan secured a $20,000 loan, which was enough to pay for the truck with an additional $5,000 for start-up costs, including his initial inventory. The loan did not come easily, even with a carefully written business plan; the bank would not make the loan unless he had a qualified cosigner. His father cosigned his loan, and Dylan was in business. His business venture was finally on its way!

Revenue Streams

Food vendors often seek out high-pedestrian-traffic areas, such as parks and beaches. Often, special permits are needed to operate in these areas, which cuts down on competition. Dylan knew vendors who made a good living setting up near Temple and selling to the students. However, there were few areas in York that would lend themselves to a one-location setup.

Instead, like most ice cream truck operators, Dylan's Chilly Dilly trucks traveled from neighborhood to neighborhood to sell their products. Chilly Dilly drivers developed their own local routes, which they followed on a weekly cycle. The strategy behind weekly—instead of daily—visits was to create a loyal parental following by not "over-visiting" neighborhoods, while at the same time covering a broader geographic area with the same number of trucks. However, Chilly Dilly's trucks did visit parks and popular recreational areas on a daily basis to serve the constantly changing clientele.

Dylan also recognized that greater-York-area companies were another outlet for his products and would provide revenues beyond September. Dylan offered these businesses two affordable but profitable group-package rates:

Standard: $3.00 per person

Premium: $4.00 per person

Both had dozens of delicious choices, including sugar-free and all-natural items. A delivery charge was added to cover the cost of gas.

In his first year of operation, 20 companies hired Dylan to provide their employees with cold treats. This more than doubled to 45 during his second year. In addition to these corporate outlets, Dylan adapted this "package" model to the catering of private parties, such as barbecues, church picnics, and weddings. Dylan added a third option for these customers: $2.00 for cones and slushies. He made sure he covered his costs by requiring a minimum order of fifty.

Business Expansion

In May 2008, Dylan graduated with a degree in Entrepreneurship from Temple. Then he was able to focus on his business full time. He purchased three used trucks at $6,500 each. He financed this expansion with a $25,000 loan from a local bank, at a rate of 6.5 percent (prime plus two). The season was profitable; however, the recession and fuel prices squeezed his margins.

In 2009, Chilly Dilly's, as Dylan named his company, had grown to eight additional employees. The company had six trucks on the road. Two of them sold soft-serve ice cream products—including coffee shakes—which were popular with adults. The first of these he purchased for $36,500, fully outfitted. This truck was on the road seven days per week and was the most profitable of the six, as soft-serve products had a higher profit margin. In addition, Dylan found that creating his own high-profit ice cream novelties further boosted the company's bottom line.

Dylan's hard work in developing relationships with local companies had also paid off. Despite route sales being down, his overall sales were up, due to new and repeat business from corporate customers. "My website is paying off, as I am getting more leads from there than from the mailing lists," Dylan noted. However, the recession had put pressure on his business catering, as customers began cancelling bookings as a cost-saving measure: "A number of customers who gave me firm bookings cancelled at the last minute due to trying to cut costs. I was quite surprised by this, as we have a package to fit every budget, and this just did not happen last year after someone made a commitment."

By the end of the 2009 season, Dylan had grown the business to the point where each truck averaged $30,000 in gross revenue. However, his trucks had been expensive to get into working order and could be expensive to keep on the road. Still, Dylan observed that "We will be spending between $4,000 and $5,000 a year on each truck, since we are now keeping up rather than catching up with maintenance costs."

Dylan's business had started to take off. Grownups and kids alike were excited when one of his trucks rolled into the neighborhood. Parents liked to see the Chilly Dilly's trucks, because they did not have to see them every day. The Chilly Dilly's man offered a variety of products at different prices. The coffee-flavored drinks and soft-serve items also proved to be a hit with parents. Dylan's success was due in part to creating Chilly Dilly's as a local brand name, but he needed to figure out a way to expand the business beyond York County.

Funding Chilly Dilly's Growth

Dylan had grown his business from a single truck to eight in less than five years. However, his dream was to create a brand that spanned South Central Pennsylvania and Northern Maryland. Dylan also wanted to expand east, into the wealthier areas of Lancaster, and establish a facility there so that his drivers could save 90 minutes a day in travel time. Dylan knew from his entrepreneurship courses that he would have to plan this expansion carefully. He could only manage so many employees on his own, and he was hesitant to increase his overhead and risk by hiring managers.

Thus, financing the company's growth was a critical issue for the young company. Dylan was able to pay for his business's start-up through a local bank loan. However, this bank was not in

a position to give him another. The economic conditions were such that banks in general were unwilling to extend loans to small businesses without significant collateral, even with an SBA-loan guarantee. Dylan wanted to avoid asking his parents to cosign another loan for him. Thus, he needed to look for other sources to fund Chilly Dilly's growth.

Organic Growth Through Bootstrapping. The first option Dylan looked into was internally funding his business's expansion. He thought about new, higher-margin products that he could manufacture that would provide some additional capital. He had found that his customers were willing to purchase high-margin soft-serve products. But outfitting another truck with this equipment would require a higher investment. Then Dylan thought about new ways to increase revenues with the equipment he already owned or could purchase more cheaply. He also knew he could grow the demand for his products through low-cost guerilla marketing techniques. He just needed to sit down and think of some new strategies.

Loans from Friends, Family, and Strangers. A second option for Dylan was to approach friends and family for some additional capital. The availability of such funding lay in the liquidity of his family and friends and the level of risk they would be willing to take. In addition, private investors were another potential group he could tap for growth capital. However, the interest rate could well be higher, and angel investors might be more interested in owning a piece of his business than lending money. An investor with some business savvy might be a smarter move, despite the potential cost. These "smart money" investors are often willing to mentor young entrepreneurs.

Dylan could have also applied for additional credit through a credit card company; however, the interest rate might have exceeded 20 percent. A fairly new option would have been to apply for a loan through a peer-to-peer lending Web site, which would provide between $8,000 and $25,000. Peer-to-peer companies, such as Prosper or Lending Club, act as intermediaries—much like eBay—by matching potential investors with people who are seeking personal or business loans. Generally speaking, these borrowers have problems getting loans from traditional sources, such as commercial banks, due to their credit history, debt-to-equity ratio, or a lack of collateral. The lenders seek a higher return than some banks do, but interest rates can turn out to be lower than what an entrepreneur could obtain from a local bank, because investors bid against one another; often a loan ends up with a dozen or more individuals who each have a small part of the loan. Thus, the risk is spread.

Equity Investors or Partners. Another option for financing Chilly Dilly's growth would have been to attract either equity investors or business partners. His dad, a chiropractor, was partnered with several other doctors in a professional corporation. This partnership not only allowed the doctors to see more patients and generate higher revenues, but also helped to spread fixed business expenses over a larger patient base. Dylan had given a great deal of thought to finding a partner. However, he did not know anyone with whom he would be willing to share his business. Dylan realized that entering into a partnership was like getting married. His professor and several guest speakers in his entrepreneurship courses had related stories of partnerships gone sour. Dylan was thus hesitant to take a partner.

Conclusion

Dylan spoke with his family about his growth plans over dinner. He explained the opportunity to rent space in the local indoor farmers market, which "will not only allow me to sell my products year round, but also give me manufacturing space to produce my novelties and lower my product costs and boost my profits." An earnest Dylan turned to his father and asked, "What should I do to make this happen?"

Case Study Analysis

15-18. What are the advantages and disadvantages for each of Dylan's funding options?

15-19. Are there options to fund Chilly Dilly's growth that Dylan has not considered?

15-20. Which option(s) would you suggest Dylan implement?

Table 15-1 Dylan's Timeline for Each Summer Season

2004	2005	2006	2007	2008	2009
Started Chilly Dilly's with the purchase of first truck.	First full season.	Focused on business catering.	Hired first employee.	Graduated from Temple University. Purchased three additional trucks and hired new employees.	Purchased two additional trucks. Started selling coffee drinks.

Lee's Ice Cream

As the bell rang and the clock struck three, South High School social studies teacher Jimmie Lee raced to the parking lot. It was a sunny afternoon in May, a perfect day to sell ice cream. Four years before, Jimmie had begun selling frozen treats in the spring and summer to children on Cleveland's east side. He had always wanted to be his own boss, and driving an ice cream truck seemed like a great idea, because he could operate his business in the afternoons and during the summer months, when school was not in session. It helped that he was one of the most popular teachers at South High. All of Jimmie's students and their parents ignored the other ice cream trucks and waited for Mr. Lee to drive down the block.

GETTING STARTED: JIMMIE DOES HIS RESEARCH

To get Lee's Ice Cream off the ground, Jimmie had to learn to be creative, resourceful, and patient. When he first decided to bring his idea to reality, Jimmie called his friend Joy Greaves, who had worked in the ice cream business for over 15 years. He wanted to know how much Joy thought it would cost to start his business. Joy estimated that Jimmie would need about $25,000 to purchase the necessary supplies and equipment, which would include the list below.

Joy's Start-Up Investment Estimates	
Item	**Estimated Cost**
Ice cream truck	$18,000
Freezer	3,000
Soft-serve ice cream machine	2,200
300 portions of soft-serve ice cream, napkins, toppings, and ice cream cones	200
Insurance, first quarterly payment	500
Commercial vendor's permit	100
Electric generator	1,000
Total estimated start-up investment	**$25,000**

CAN JIMMIE REDUCE HIS START-UP INVESTMENT?

As a public school teacher, Jimmie did not earn a large salary. He had $7,000 in savings, but based on Joy's projections, this was not going to go very far. Initially, Jimmie was discouraged, but then he started to brainstorm. Perhaps he could lower his start-up investment by purchasing used equipment. He understood there was a risk of used equipment needing costly repairs or replacement parts that were no longer available. He scoured the local classifieds for used trucks, generators, and freezers, to see how much he could save. Based on this research, Jimmie calculated a revised start-up investment budget.

Jimmie's Start-Up Investment Estimates	
Item	**Estimated Cost**
Used ice cream truck (including freezer)	$10,000
Used soft-serve ice cream machine	1,500
300 servings of soft-serve ice cream, napkins, toppings, and ice cream cones	200
Insurance, first quarterly payment	500
Commercial vendor's permit	100
Service fees for refurbishing used equipment	1,000
Used electric generator	700
Total estimated start-up investment	**$14,000**
Difference between Joy's total start-up investment estimate and Jimmie's estimate	$11,000

If Jimmie purchased the equipment he researched, he would save $11,000. This was a lot of money. He decided it was worth the risk. He hoped that, if he ever did have to pay for repairs, it would cost less than $11,000, in which case he would still come out ahead.

Financing Strategy

Jimmie felt better knowing that he would only need $14,000 to get his business off the ground. He already had $7,000, which covered half of the projected costs. He wondered how he could raise the rest of the money. A friend suggested that he apply for a bank loan, but when he inquired at his bank, he was told that the chances of obtaining a loan were slim. Jimmie had never run a business before and the loan was small, so the bank was hesitant to invest in him. What other options did he have?

Jimmie decided to pitch his idea for Lee's Ice Cream to his friends and family. Perhaps they would be willing to loan him money if he agreed to pay them back with interest. He asked his brothers and sisters, but they turned him down. They did not think Jimmie was truly serious about his business. Then he called his best friend, Greg Allen, who worked as an auto shop teacher at South High, to see if he had any ideas. Greg said that he had an old electric generator he would be willing to repair and donate. He even agreed to install it free of charge. Jimmie had planned to pay $700 for a used generator, so this was a great savings. Jimmie was one step closer to achieving his dream.

After hanging up the phone with Greg, Jimmie decided to visit his mother, to see if she would be willing to give him a loan. At first Jimmie's mother was resistant, but he took the time to walk her through the business plan he had created. His mother was still not totally convinced, but she liked the fact that Jimmie

Stephen Wilkes/Getty Images

had thoroughly researched what he would need. She decided to loan him $3,000. Jimmie promised that he would pay her back, at 8 percent interest, within a year.

WHERE IS THE MONEY COMING FROM?

At this point, Jimmie was close to having his funding in place. He created a chart to get a clearer picture of his start-up progress.

Jimmie was so close to having all his start-up investment capital in place, he could practically taste it. He only needed $3,300. That evening, Greg called to say that he had finished repairing the electric generator and could install it as soon as Jimmie was ready. Jimmie explained that he did not feel comfortable purchasing a truck until he had secured his total start-up investment. "How much do you still have left to raise?" Greg asked. "Only $3,300," Jimmie replied. "Well, if you will sell me an equity stake in your company," Greg said, "I'll write you a check for $3,300."

TO SELL OR NOT TO SELL?

Jimmie was not sure how he felt about this. He really liked the idea of owning his business outright. Did he want to share ownership with someone else, even if it was Greg, his best friend? Also, Jimmie was not sure what percentage of his total equity he should offer Greg in exchange for $3,300. How could he figure out what Lee's Ice Cream was worth if his business had not yet earned a dime? Jimmie thanked Greg for his offer and explained that he needed to think about it overnight. He promised to call him back first thing in the morning.

Funding Source	Equity	Debt	Gift
Personal Savings	$7,000		
Relatives		$3,000 loan from his mother (to be paid back at 8% interest within one year)	
Friends			
Grants or Gifts			Electric generator ($700 value)
Other			
Subtotal	$7,000	$3,000	$700
Total Equity + Total Debt + Total Gift = Total Financing: $10,700			
Difference between Total Start-Up Investment and Total Financing = $14,000 − $10,700 = $3,300			

Case Study Analysis

U4-1. If you were in Jimmie's shoes, would you sell Greg an equity stake in Lee's Ice Cream? Explain. If Jimmie does sell equity to Greg for $3,300, what percentage of the business should he offer?

U4-2. Assume that Jimmie rejects Greg's offer. Brainstorm and list three other financing strategies for Jimmie to investigate.

U4-3. Jimmie's mother agreed to loan him $3,000 at 8 percent interest. Calculate the total amount Jimmie will owe his mother.

U4-4. Jimmie will sell his ice cream cones for $2 each. Assume the following about Jimmie's cost of goods sold for one ice cream cone:

Soft-serve ice cream:	$0.20
Ice cream cone:	$0.05
Napkin:	$0.02
Topping:	$0.03

    a. What is the total COGS for one ice cream cone?

    b. What is Jimmie's gross profit per unit?

U4-5. Jimmie believes he can sell an average of 150 ice cream cones per day at $2 per cone. Jimmie operates his business 7 days per week between May and August, for a total of 123 days. Calculate the following:

    a. How many ice cream cones would Jimmie sell in total?

    b. What would Jimmie's total revenue be?

    c. What would be Jimmie's total COGS?

    d. Calculate Jimmie's gross profit.

    e. Assume that Jimmie's total monthly operating costs are $1,500. His business operates for four months of the year. Calculate his total net profit for one year of business operations.

    f. Create a projected income statement for the period from May 1 until August 31, 2012. Remember to include the interest to his mother for the four months and taxes at 25%. Assume that there is no depreciation or operating costs other than those described in the case study.

U4-6. Examine Jimmie's projected income statement you developed for the previous question. Assume that Jimmie does decide to sell Greg partial ownership in Lee's Ice Cream. Using the projected income statement as a guide, determine what percentage of his total equity Jimmie should offer Greg in exchange for $3,300. Is this a different percentage from the answer you gave in Question U4-1? Explain.

OPERATING A SMALL BUSINESS EFFECTIVELY

Chapter 16
ADDRESSING LEGAL ISSUES AND MANAGING RISK

Chapter 17
OPERATING FOR SUCCESS

Chapter 18
LOCATION, FACILITIES, AND LAYOUT

Chapter 19
HUMAN RESOURCES AND MANAGEMENT

© Kruwt/Fotolia

ADDRESSING LEGAL ISSUES AND MANAGING RISK

Learning Objectives

1. Choose a legal structure for your business.

2. Understand the importance of contracts.

3. Recognize key components of commercial law.

4. Protect your intellectual property.

5. Protect your tangible assets and manage risk.

Corbis Images

On May 8, 1886, Dr. John Stith Pemberton, an Atlanta pharmacist, produced the syrup for Coca-Cola and brought a jug of it to Jacobs' Pharmacy, where it was mixed and sold as a soda fountain drink. The beverage was proclaimed to be "delicious and refreshing," a theme that Coca-Cola reinforces today.

Dr. Pemberton's partner and bookkeeper, Frank Robinson, thought that "Two C's would look well in advertising," recommended the name *Coca-Cola,* and created the famous trademark in his own script.

Over time, businessman Asa Candler bought into the company and eventually acquired complete control of it. According to the company's Web site, in May 1889, Candler published a full-page advertisement in *The Atlanta Journal* that proclaimed his wholesale and retail drug business as "Sole proprietors of Coca-Cola. . . . Delicious. Refreshing. Exhilarating. Invigorating." By 1892, Candler's flair for marketing had boosted sales of Coca-Cola syrup nearly tenfold. With his brother John, Frank Robinson, and two other associates, Candler formed the Coca-Cola Company as a corporation. The trademark *Coca-Cola,* which had been used since 1886, was registered in the United States Patent Office in 1893 and has been renewed periodically.[1]

Dr. John Stith Pemberton
(Corbis Images)

Learning Objective 1 ▷

Choose a legal structure for your business.

Business Legal Structures

Most businesses, no matter how humble their beginnings, have the potential to grow into much larger ventures, so it is important that founders think through every step of the company's development as they form it. How the entrepreneur organizes the company—such as the legal structure chosen, the relationships developed with suppliers, the managers hired—will have vital impact on its ability to grow.

After you pick the kind of business and industry you want to be in, you will know where you fit in the production-distribution chain; you will be able to research markups, markdowns, and discounts in your industry in order to be competitive. You will also have to choose one of the three basic legal structures:

1. sole proprietorship,
2. partnership,
3. corporation.

Sole Proprietorship

sole proprietorship
a business owned by one person who has unlimited liability and unlimited rights to profits.

A **sole proprietorship** is a business owned by one individual, often with no other employees. This owner earns all the profits from the business and is also responsible for all losses. Most U.S. businesses are sole proprietorships.

The sole proprietor is personally liable for any lawsuits that arise from accidents, faulty merchandise, unpaid bills, or other business setbacks.

---

[1]Information from Coca-Cola Web site, http://www.Coke.com.

This means a sole proprietor could lose not only business assets in a lawsuit, but could be forced to sell private possessions to satisfy a court judgment. He or she could lose a house or a car, for example.

Advantages of a Sole Proprietorship

- It is relatively easy to start. A person becomes a sole proprietor— albeit not a registered, legal one—simply by selling something to someone else.
- Proper registration does not require much paperwork, and registration is relatively inexpensive.
- There are fewer government regulations than for the other forms of business.
- Sole proprietors can make quick decisions and act without interference from others.
- A sole proprietor is entitled to all the profits from the business.

Disadvantages of a Sole Proprietorship

- It can be difficult to raise enough money by oneself to start or expand a business.
- A sole proprietor must often put in long hours, working six or even seven days a week, with no one to share the responsibilities.
- There is no way to limit personal legal liability from lawsuits related to the business.
- There is often no one to offer encouragement or feedback.
- All profits earned are taxed personally, whether or not the funds are withdrawn from the business or cash is left in it.

How to Register a Sole Proprietorship

In most states and localities, it is easy and relatively inexpensive to register a sole proprietorship. When you do, you will have a legal business.

- If you operate a business without registering it, you may be liable to civil or even criminal penalties.
- Registered sole proprietorships can use the court system and bring lawsuits.
- Banks want to see legal business ownership the way employers like to see that employees have had previous work experience. If your business is not registered, banks will not even *consider* loaning you money, although some alternative lenders might do so. The time that you operated without registration will be discounted. Lack of registration can be perceived as a lack of integrity.

Steps to Registering

The registration process varies from state to state and by locality, but there will be a few common steps:

- Choose a name for your business.
- Fill out a registration form, which sometimes requires a *doing business as* (DBA) document that will show the name of the business and your name, so the state will know who will be responsible for tax payments.
- An official may then conduct a name search to make sure the name you have chosen is not already being used in that jurisdiction. You may even be asked to help research the records yourself.

- Once your registration is completed satisfactorily, you will pay the required fee. This fee can range from under $100 to significantly more, depending on the type of business and state and municipal laws and regulations. Professional firm (e.g., doctor, lawyer) registrations, in particular, can become quite expensive.
- You may be asked to take the form to a **notary**—an individual who has been given the authority by the state to witness the signing of documents—to have it *notarized* and then brought back to the registration office. You will have to show the notary valid identification to prove who is signing the form. There is usually a modest charge for this service.

notary a person who has been authorized by the state to witness the signing of documents.

Partnership

A **partnership** consists of two or more owners, who make the decisions for the business together and share the profits, losses, assets, and liabilities. As in a sole proprietorship, partners face unlimited liability in any lawsuits. This means that *each* partner can be held responsible for paying debts or judgments, even those incurred by other partners without their knowledge or agreement.

The exception to this is the **limited partnership**. The limited partners have no official say in the daily operation of the business and have, as a result, liability limited to the amount of their respective investments. One or more *general* partners manage the company and assume legal liability. There must be at least one general partner who will be liable for all partnership debts.

Ideally, partners bring different strengths and skills to a business. This can help the venture grow and succeed. In addition, partners can support and advise each other. On the other hand, disagreements can become intolerable and destroy the partnership, friendship, and business.

Despite the advantages of partnerships, caution is the watchword. You should be extremely careful and thorough about entering into a partnership, particularly with a good friend or relative. A lawyer should be consulted and a partnership agreement drawn up that carefully defines the roles and

partnership a business with two or more owners that make decisions for the business together and share the profits, losses, assets, and liabilities.

limited partnership business partnership owned by a general partner with unlimited liability and one or more limited partners with no official input in daily operations and limited liability.

PhotoAlto/Superstock

responsibilities of each partner. A partnership agreement is absolutely critical, regardless of how well or poorly the company ultimately performs.

Corporation

corporation a legal entity composed of stockholders under a common name.

There are several types of **corporations**, but each is considered a "legal person," or *entity*, composed of stockholders under a common name. A corporation has rights and responsibilities under the law; it can buy and sell property, enter into leases and contracts, and be prosecuted. Corporations issue stock that is divided among the founders and sold to investors. These *shareholders* then elect a board of directors that is responsible for representing their interests in the management of the company. The shareholders who own the stock own the corporation in proportion to the number of their shares.

The corporate legal structure offers three key advantages:

1. Corporations may issue stock to raise money. Essentially, the company sells pieces of itself in the form of equity to stockholders.

2. The corporation offers limited personal liability to its owners. Unlike sole proprietorships and partnerships, the owners of a corporation are protected from having their personal assets taken to pay business lawsuit settlements or debts. Only the assets of the corporation can be used to pay corporate debts. However, most lenders will not loan money to a small, closely held corporation unless the owners personally guarantee the debt, in which case the owners do become personally liable. In addition, it is possible to "pierce the corporate veil" if the business affairs of the corporation and its shareholders are tightly entwined, so that shareholders may be held personally liable in a lawsuit. This is a strong argument for keeping business and personal finances separate.

3. Corporations can exist indefinitely, so they do not cease when an owner dies or otherwise leaves the business.

As we have already noted, a disadvantage of corporations is that corporate income is "taxed twice." A corporation must pay corporate income tax on its earnings because it is a legal entity. Then, the corporation may distribute earnings as dividends to stockholders. The stockholders must include those dividends as personal income on their tax returns. For example, a corporation with taxable income of $100,000 that distributed $10,000 in dividends would have a tax bill of $34,000 (34-percent corporate tax rate), and its shareholders would owe $2,800 (assuming a 28-percent personal tax rate) more, for a total tax of $36,800. The total tax on $100,000 for a sole proprietor could be $28,000 (28-percent personal tax rate), reflecting no dividends—for an $8,800 difference.

If corporate stock is privately held, the shares are typically owned by only a few investors and are not *traded* (bought and sold) publicly, such as on the New York Stock Exchange or that of London or Tokyo. In a public corporation, such as Ford or IBM, the company's stock is offered for sale to the general public; anyone with sufficient resources may purchase it at the market price. Stockholders may be paid dividends when the company's management considers they are warranted by profits or other considerations. Dividends are part of the stockholders' return on their investment in the company.

There are several types of corporations:

- *C corporation.* Most large companies and many smaller ones are C corporations. They sell ownership as shares of stock. Stockholders have the right to vote on important company decisions at the annual meeting or to vote by proxy. To raise capital, the C corporation can sell more stock, issue bonds, or secure other types of loans.

Thinkstock

- *Subchapter S corporation.* This type of corporation has a limit of 100 stockholders. It offers most of the limited-liability protection of the C corporation, but Subchapter S corporate income is only taxed once, as the personal income of the owners. It is a "pass-through" entity for tax purposes. The net profits of an S corporation are taxed at the personal income-tax rates of the individual shareholders, whether or not the profits are distributed.

- *Professional corporation (PC).* Medical practices, engineering firms, law firms, accounting firms, and certain other professions can form professional corporations. The initials PC after a doctor's or lawyer's name mean that the individual has incorporated the practice or belongs to a group of practitioners that has incorporated. Each state designates which professions can form such corporations. Professional corporations are subject to special rules, such as meeting

BizFacts

Advantages of Corporations

- Shareholders have limited personal legal liability.
- Funds can be raised through the issuance of stock.
- Ownership can be transferred easily.
- The legal entity survives beyond the life span or participation of individuals.

Disadvantages of Corporations

- Corporations are often more heavily taxed than sole proprietorships or partnerships. Their profits are taxed twice: first, as the income of the corporation (except S corporations) and again as personal income, when dividends are distributed to stockholders.
- The founder of a corporation may lose control to the stockholders if he no longer owns more than half the stock.
- It is more expensive to start a corporation than a sole proprietorship.
- Corporations are subject to many government regulations.

the licensing requirements of bar associations or medical societies. Professional corporations cannot protect individual members from malpractice liability, but the other members of a PC are protected from liability arising from the negligence of one of the group.

- *Nonprofit corporation.* A nonprofit corporation is not set up for the purposes of shareholder financial gain, but rather with a specific mission to improve society. Churches, museums, charitable foundations, and trade associations are examples of nonprofit corporations (also called not-for-profits). Nonprofits are tax-exempt. Nonprofits may not sell stock or pay dividends. There are no individual shareholders for a not-for-profit corporation, and any net profits that are earned must go toward the advancement of the mission, so there are no dividends issued and income taxes are not paid. Not-for-profits may have members rather than shareholders. Such organizations must be careful to follow applicable laws, rules, and regulations in order to maintain their tax-exempt status.

- *Public benefit corporation (B-corporation).* This form of company explicitly includes a civic or environmental benefit into its charter, in addition to including profitability as a goal. The priority level is meant to be the same. B-corporations must report on social and environmental impact as well as financial performance.

- *Limited liability company (LLC).* The LLC combines the best features of partnerships and corporations and can be an excellent choice for small businesses with a small number of owners. In an LLC, profits are taxed only as the personal income of the members, whose personal assets are protected from lawsuits as in a C corporation. In addition, many of the restrictions regarding the number and type of shareholders that apply to the Subchapter S corporation do not apply to LLCs, making them even more attractive. An LLC has a variety of options that make it a flexible type of legal entity. The advice of legal counsel is vital in establishing an LLC, because each state has different laws, and the creation and maintenance of LLC status requires continued compliance.

- *Series limited liability company (SLLC).* The SLLC is a form of LLC that provides liability protection across "multiple series" (akin to divisions or subsidiaries) while protecting each from the liability of the others. It is a relatively new form and is available in a few states. The SLLC is like a master corporation with subsidiaries and may be useful when multiple acquisitions are involved.

To compare these legal structures, see **Exhibit 16-1**.

Tips for Entrepreneurs Who Want to Start a Nonprofit Organization

There are huge needs in society for food, shelter, education, and more; and there are many people who cannot access these fundamental necessities and requirements. In the United States, the 501(c)(3) nonprofit corporation is designed to help address this situation (this designation refers to the relevant section in the tax code). A 501(c)(3) is a tax-exempt legal structure that can receive charitable donations from individuals, businesses, the government, and philanthropic foundations. Examples of well-known nonprofit corporations include the Boys and Girls Clubs, the YMCA, and the Sierra Club. People who donate money to not-for-profits benefit from their generosity by knowing that they are making a gift to a cause in which they believe. Also, they are able to deduct these contributions from their taxable income.

Exhibit 16-1 *Comparison of Common Legal Structures*

	Sole Proprietorship	General or Limited Partnership	C Corporation	Subchapter S Corporation	Nonprofit Corporation	Limited Liability Company
Ownership	The proprietor	The partners	The stockholders	The stockholders	No one	The members
Liability	Unlimited	Limited in most cases	Limited	Limited	Limited	Limited
Taxation Issues	Individual* (lowest rate)	Individual* (lowest rate)	Corporate rate; "double taxation"	Individual* (lowest rate)	None	Individual* (lowest rate)
How Profits Are Distributed	Proprietor receives all	Partners receive profits according to partnership agreement	Earnings paid to stockholders as dividends in proportion to the number of shares owned	Earnings attributed to stockholders as in proportion to the number of shares owned	Surplus cannot be distributed	Same as partnership
Voting on Policy	Not necessary	The partners	Common voting stockholders	Common voting stockholders	The board of directors/trustees	Per agreed-on operating procedure
Life of Legal Structure	Terminates on death of owner	Terminates on death of partner	Unlimited	Unlimited	Unlimited	Variable
Capitalization	Difficult	Easier than sole proprietorship	Excellent—ownership is sold as shares of stock	Good—same as partnership	Difficult because there is no ownership to sell as stock	Same as partnership

*When the double taxation of corporations is taken into account.

In the United States, close to 1 million organizations were registered with the IRS as public charities in 2007, compared with 600,000 in 1993.[2] Charitable donations rose from $148 billion to $308 billion in the same period, accounting for about 22 percent of total revenues in 2007.[3] Whereas competition for financial resources has increased, more technical and educational resources are now available to support the management and growth of organizations that choose to incorporate as nonprofits.

Like any business, a not-for-profit will need to generate revenue to cover its expenses. Failure to meet cash requirements will mean a failure to survive. A not-for-profit needs to identify a target market (constituency) and determine how it will deliver its products and services. Some key differences and considerations exist, however, and you should be aware of them before you apply to the IRS for approval:

- *No individual can own a not-for-profit organization.* A nonprofit cannot be bought and sold like other businesses. You would not be able to dissolve the company and sell it for financial gain. Nor could you issue stock to raise money. These organizations are meant to improve society, not create wealth for the founder, shareholders, or employees.

- *Nonprofits are mission-driven.* Before you can operate as a nonprofit, you will need to be crystal clear about your organization's mission. What problem(s) are you trying to solve? The IRS will not grant tax-exempt status without such a stated mission and considerable additional information. Also, ask yourself if there is another organization that is working toward the same goal. Could you work together rather than creating a new entity and duplicating services and costs? Is there a large enough donor base and grant supply to combine with earned income for sustainability? Also, do you expect the organization to accomplish its mission in the foreseeable future and thus cease to need resources?

- *Define your unit of change.* In a for-profit business, the return on investment is calculated by looking at the corporation's financial records. Not-for-profit entrepreneurs think about returns a little differently. Not-for-profits do not exist to make money, so the ultimate measure of success will not be financial, although financial goals and measures are part of the equation. Your ROI will be based on how much it will cost you to provide your services, as compared with the level of change that was brought about as a result of this investment.

- *Determine how you will evaluate your success.* As a not-for-profit entrepreneur, you will need to set goals regarding the changes you wish to effect. How many homeless people will you feed? How many students will graduate as a result of your dropout-prevention program? What changes in knowledge, skills, or attitudes will result from the efforts of your organization? The output and outcome goals you establish must tie back into your financial and human-resource inputs. How much does it cost to provide these services? Given the costs, how many "units of change" did your organization achieve? How can you document that your organization brought about these changes?

- *Analyze your financing strategy.* Nonprofit corporations borrow money and earn it. They also have access to a revenue stream that other business structures cannot tap. Nonprofits generate revenue through grants and gifts (donations) from individuals and organizations, but they cannot sell stock to raise equity.

[2]The Urban Institute, National Center for Charitable Statistics, Business Master File 12/08, accessed November 12, 2009, http://nccs.urban.org/statistics.

[3]The Urban Institute, National Center for Charitable Statistics, Business Master File 12/08, accessed November 12, 2009, http://nccs.urban.org/statistics; and Jessica Stannard-Friel, *MBAs at the Crossroads of Corporate and Nonprofit America*, from On Philanthropy Web site, accessed December 3, 2004, http://www.onphilanthropy.com.

Contracts: The Building Blocks of Business

Regardless of the type of legal entity you elect to establish, you will need to enter into a variety of legal contracts. A **contract** is a formal agreement between two or more parties to perform or refrain from performing particular actions. When you sign up for mobile telephone service with a provider, such as Verizon or AT&T, you are signing a contract. You agree to pay for the service at a specified price per month, and in return the company agrees to provide you with access to telephone service, voice mail, data services, text messaging, and the like. Remember that rental leases, promissory notes or mortgages, and advertising or partnership agreements are all contracts. How they are written can often make or break your business.

Contracts are the building blocks of business. The relationships between the links in a production-distribution chain are defined by contracts. For example, if a department store wants to sell your hammered-silver necklaces, you might create a six-month contract specifying how many necklaces you will supply at what price and how and when the store will pay you.

With that contract in hand, you can call your wholesaler. Because you have a large order, you will want to get your supplies in bulk. With the contract as written proof of your relationship with the store, wholesalers may give you credit. You can arrange to buy the silver you need now to fill the order and pay for it after you sell the necklaces to the store. You can also plan ahead with your advertisers, or work out an advertising plan with the store as part of the contract. Or, you may be able to secure bank financing for the contract production.

The power of a contract is that, once the individuals or other entities involved have signed it, they are obligated to comply with its terms and conditions or risk being sued and penalized according to the contract terms or in a court of law. If the store fails to buy your necklaces as agreed, you can go to court to force payment. Because of the contract, you will be able to honor your contract with your supplier. At the same time, the contract obligates you to produce what you have promised and deliver it when you said you would.

Working with an Attorney

There are certain times in the life of an organization when investing in the expense of professional services is essential, even though the out-of-pocket cost may seem high at the time. Contract drafting and review is one of them.

- Never sign a contract without having an attorney examine it for you.
- Never sign a contract that you have not read completely and carefully, even if your lawyer tells you it is all right. Ultimately, you are responsible for what you sign.

If you are ever taken to court and argue, "I didn't understand that part of the contract," it will not satisfy the judge. Your signature at the bottom tells the court that you read, understood, and agreed to every word.

Attorneys typically charge by the hour, so be as prepared and organized as possible before visiting one. Many issues can be resolved efficiently and effectively through e-mail and telephone calls, so that billable hours are minimized. Always read the contract ahead of time and make a copy of it. Mark sections that you do not agree to or understand. Indicate your suggestions for changes. This will help your attorney advise you effectively.

◀ **Learning Objective 2**
Understand the importance of contracts.

contract an agreement between two or more parties that is enforceable by law.

Drafting a Contract

Consult an attorney if you need to *draft*—write—a first version of a contract or agreement, with the understanding that it will need to be developed and rewritten. Be certain that you identify and make a list of the key points in advance. Attorneys often have standard formats for types of legal agreements, sometimes called **boilerplate language**, which can make the process quicker and less costly.

boilerplate language a standard format for a specific type of legal agreement.

A Successful Contract Should Achieve the Four A's

1. **Avoid** misunderstanding,
2. **Assure** work,
3. **Assure** payment, and
4. **Avoid** liability.

Avoid Misunderstanding

When putting together a contract, clearly state everything that will be performed by all parties, even what is obvious. Go into full detail (not just how many shirts you will supply to the store and when, but which types, colors, and sizes). If you do not cover all the details, the person with whom you are contracting may add provisions or find loopholes you will not like. At the same time, leave enough flexibility to accomplish what will need to be done successfully.

Assure Work

For a contract to be legally binding, all parties will be required to do one of the following:

- perform an action or exchange something of value, or
- agree *not* to do something the party was legally entitled to do.

Sometimes $1 is exchanged, as a token payment to legalize a contract. The contract should assure that each party fulfills some kind of obligation. The exact nature of the obligation, and the time frame for accomplishing it, should be specified fully.

Assure Payment

A good contract specifies how payment will be made, when, and for what. It should leave no room for misinterpretation.

Avoid Liability

Because this world is full of surprises, your contract should spell out **contingencies**, events beyond your control that could cause delay or failure to fulfill contractual responsibilities. The contract should list contingencies for which you would not be liable. Common contingencies are "acts of God" (earthquake, hurricane, etc.) or illness.

contingency a condition that must be met in order for something else to occur.

When you share the draft or a list of key topics of your contract with an attorney, ask these two basic questions:

1. Will this agreement fully protect my interests?
2. What would you add, drop, or change?

Letter of Agreement

Sometimes you will not need a full, formal contract, because the relationship will be brief or the work and money involved are relatively minor. In such cases, a **letter of agreement** that puts an oral understanding in writing, in the form of a business letter, may be enough. The other party must respond to it in writing, either approving it or suggesting changes, until an agreement is reached. However, use this option with care and with legal advice.

letter of agreement a document that puts an oral understanding in writing, in the form of a business letter.

Breach of Contract

A contract is broken, or *breached*, when a **signatory** (an individual that signed the contract) fails to fulfill it. The person injured by the signatory's failure to comply with the contract may then sue for **breach of contract**.

For a contract to be breached, it must first be legally binding. Most states require that all signatories be at least 18 years of age and that the contract represent an exchange of value. If a contract is breached, legal action must be brought by the injured party within the state's **statute of limitations**, the time period within which legal action may be taken.

A lawsuit is an attempt to recover a right or claim through legal action. Because attorney's fees are expensive and court cases time-consuming, lawsuits should be avoided whenever possible. Other options are **small claims court** and **arbitration**.

signatory an individual who signs a contract.

breach of contract the failure of a signatory to perform as agreed.

statute of limitations the time period in which legal action may be taken.

small claims court a legal option for solving conflicts involving less than a certain sum of money.

arbitration a method of dispute resolution using an arbitrator to act as the decision maker rather than going to court.

Small Claims Court

Conflicts involving less than a certain sum of money, which varies by state law, can usually be resolved in a small claims court. In Delaware, for example, claims for $15,000 or less (excluding interest) can be settled through civil action in the Justice of the Peace Court. In small claims court, people are allowed to represent themselves before a court official. This individual hears the respective arguments and makes a decision that is legally binding.

Arbitration

Sometimes contracts specify that conflicts may be settled through *arbitration* instead of in court. An *arbitrator*, someone both sides trust, is chosen to act as the decision maker to resolve the conflict. The parties agree to abide by the arbitrator's decision.

A Contract Is No Substitute for Trust

A contract is not a substitute for understanding and communication. If you do not trust someone, having a contract will not improve the relationship, but it will address your concerns in writing. However, entering into a business contract with a party you do not trust could lead to a lawsuit. Avoid signing a contract with someone you do not trust.

A good reason never to sign a contract with such a person is that you might need to renegotiate the terms at some point, and this could be unpleasant and difficult. Running a small business is challenging and unpredictable. In the jewelry example mentioned previously, how would you pay back the silver supplier if the store decided not to buy the necklaces after all? If you had a friendly relationship, you would be able to discuss your situation and possibly renegotiate or cancel the contract.

Entrepreneurial Wisdom . . .

Lying about the Risks of Your Product Is Fraud

Failure to inform a customer of potential danger from your product or service, or misrepresenting it in any way for commercial benefit, is a type of fraud. If a customer proves you knew your product or service was dangerous but sold it anyway, you could be directed by a court to pay damages. Your insurance company will not be expected to pay for costs in the case of fraud.

The entrepreneur has a moral duty to inform customers of possible danger. It is best not to sell a product or service that could cause harm when in normal use. Even if you are selling something as "safe" as neckties, make sure they are not made of highly flammable material!

Before you decide to sell a product or offer a service, try to imagine how it might possibly cause injury to someone. If you think it might harm a customer when used according to directions, do not sell it.

A company that specializes in fire insurance will have information about fires in restaurants that goes back many years. Analysts at the company study this information and determine the frequency with which fires tend to occur and the value of what is destroyed. Even if some fires do take place, the cost of insurance paid out to a few policyholders has been covered by the premiums paid by many others.

Protect Your Computer and Data

Data are critical to any business. Important business information on your computer might include mailing lists, invoices, letters, and financial records. The risk of the loss of this information is very real, and you will need to address it proactively. Because your computer is an electronic device, you should protect it from the three primary occurrences that can easily wipe out your data:

1. *Power surges or outages:* A power blackout can destroy data. You can purchase an "uninterruptible power supply" (UPS) that will keep your computer running for a certain amount of time after the power goes out. A power surge can damage your computer and destroy the data stored on it. Plug all your computer equipment into a multi-outlet surge protector, which can be bought at any hardware store. Or, better yet, invest in a surge protector UPS unit for each computer.

2. *Computer viruses:* Viruses are malicious computer software that can attach themselves to your software or files and ruin them. Protect your computer with virus-protection software like Norton or McAfee. Remember to set the software to automatically scan your computer frequently.

3. *Disk failure:* Hard drives can crash (fail), destroying valuable data. To prevent this, save everything you do to back-up media, such as external drives, cloud-based storage services, CDs, or jump drives. Periodically back up your entire drive and store it in another location.

Disaster Recovery Plans

What would you do in the case of fire or other catastrophe that would make carrying on your business difficult or impossible? Insurance policies may cover many things, but they do not ensure smooth business operations in times of disaster. Whether you operate a small, home-based business or a large, multinational enterprise, you should have a disaster-recovery plan appropriate to the scale and complexity of your organization. Be sure to write it down and share it with your employees. Practice it once or twice a

Maxim Tupikov/Shutterstock

year with the whole team; the investment of time and money is worthwhile. Include critical information that team members keep securely off-site. Some issues to address are:

- **Communications:** Who will contact each person in the company and critical vendors and customers? How will they reach them? Include names, titles, telephone numbers, e-mail addresses, and street addresses. Update the contact information regularly. Also, know what the message will be.
- **Base of operations:** Where will people go if the normal place of business is inaccessible? This could be someone's home, another company site, or another location entirely.
- **Priority activities:** Which business activities are most essential/ time-sensitive? Which activities could be postponed? What is the time frame for reactivation?
- **Return to facilities:** Define a process for regrouping and planning, and designate a leader.

This is a partial and hypothetical list for a disaster recovery plan. Whereas it may seem to be more than might be needed, a straightforward plan put in place before disaster strikes can make the difference between business failure and survival.

Licenses, Permits, and Certificates

There is more to creating a legal business than naming and registering it. Once registered, you will need to comply with any federal, state, and local regulations that apply to your business. You should research these regulations before deciding to start your business, because they may affect what you can do, how you can do it, where you can operate, and when. Such regulations can completely change your potential business operations.

Zoning regulations often prohibit certain types of businesses from operating in specified areas. There may be other regulations, too, such as restrictions on obtaining a liquor license for a bar or restaurant. If your business involves food, you will need to comply with safety and health regulations, conduct food safety training, and obtain certain permissions and certificates.

Contact local, county, and state government offices, or your chamber of commerce, to find out which licenses and permits will be necessary.

- **Permit** An official document that gives you the right to engage in a specific activity, such as holding an outdoor concert.
- **License** An official document that gives you the right to engage in an activity for as long as the license is valid. A driver's license, until it expires, gives you the right to operate a motor vehicle. A child-care license permits you to operate a particular size and type of child-care facility.
- **Certificate** Official document that verifies something. A certificate of occupancy proves that a building is safe and ready for use.

If you hire people to work for you, you will also need to comply with any federal, state, and local regulations regarding employees.

permit an official document that gives a party the right to hold a specific event.

license an official document that grants the right to engage in an activity for a specified period of time.

certificate an official document that verifies something.

Chapter Summary

Now that you have studied this chapter, you can do the following:

1. Choose a legal structure for your business.
   - A sole proprietorship is owned by one person who also may be the sole employee.
   - A partnership consists of two or more owners who make the decisions for the business together and share the profits and losses.
   - A corporation is a legal entity composed of stockholders under a common name.
   - A Subchapter S corporation limits the number of stockholders to 100. It offers most of the limited liability protection of the more common C corporation, but Subchapter S corporate income is only taxed once—as the personal income of the owners.
   - A nonprofit (or not-for-profit) corporation is set up with a specific mission to improve society. Churches, museums, charitable foundations, and trade associations are examples of nonprofit corporations. Nonprofit corporations are tax-exempt.
   - A limited liability company (LLC) combines the best features of partnerships and corporations and is an excellent choice for many small businesses.
2. Understand the importance of contracts.
   - A contract is a formal agreement between two or more parties.
   - The relationships between the links in a production-distribution chain are defined by contracts.
   - Never sign a contract without having an attorney examine it.
   - Never sign a contract that you have not read yourself from top to bottom.
   - A successful contract should:
     - Avoid misunderstanding
     - Assure work
     - Assure payment
     - Avoid liability

3. Recognize key components of commercial law.
   - The Uniform Commercial Code is a collection of business laws adopted by most states that covers a broad spectrum of transactions.
   - The law of agency addresses principal-agent relationships.
   - The bankruptcy code concerns the inability or impaired ability to pay debts as they come due.
4. Protect your intellectual property.
   - Your ideas and creations are your intellectual property.
   - Trademarks and service marks protect your brand identity.
   - Copyrights protect works of authorship.
   - Patents protect invented products and processes.
5. Protect your tangible assets and manage risk.
   - Insurance protects people and businesses from the risk of having property or wealth stolen, lost, or destroyed.
   - When buying insurance, choose the policy with the highest deductible you can afford. This will give you the lowest possible premium.
   - Consider the normal and customary types of business insurance:
     - workers' compensation,
     - disability,
     - commercial fleet,
     - property,
     - liability,
     - business income,
     - errors and omissions, and
     - life.
   - Create and practice a disaster recovery plan.

Key Terms

arbitration, 509
bankruptcy, 511
boilerplate language, 508
breach of contract, 509
certificate, 521
contingency, 508
contract, 507
corporation, 502
deductible, 517
electronic rights, 515
insurance, 517
letter of agreement, 509
license, 521

limited partnership, 501
notary, 501
partnership, 501
patent, 516
permit, 521
premium, 517
public domain, 516
service mark, 513
signatory, 509
small claims court, 509
sole proprietorship, 499
statute of limitations, 509

Entrepreneurship Portfolio

Critical Thinking Exercises

16-1. What can happen to an entrepreneur who is personally liable for a business? How can an entrepreneur protect herself from personal liability? Say your friend wants to start a business making custom skateboards. Write a memo to your friend, explaining the risks involved and suggestions for limiting liability.

16-2. With a partner, make a list of the technological tools each of you could personally access. Brainstorm how you might combine your resources to create a successful business. Describe in detail how the partnership would work. For example, would the partner contributing more technology have a larger share of the business, or would profits and expenses be split equally? Write a partnership agreement that specifies each partner's duties and how much money and time each will invest.

16-3. Which legal structure will you choose for your business?
   a. Why did you choose this structure?
   b. Who will the partners or stockholders of your company be?
   c. Describe the steps you will take to register your business.

16-4. If your business will be incorporated, what percentage of the company would be represented by one share of stock? Will your corporation's stock be publicly or privately held?

16-5. Use computer software to create a logo for your business. Do you intend to trademark your logo? Explain.

16-6. Describe any intellectual property you are developing (without improperly disclosing a potential patent).

16-7. How do you plan to protect your intellectual property? Explain why it would qualify for protection.

16-8. Give an example of a business in your community that you think may be infringing on someone else's intellectual property.

16-9. What types of insurance will your business need and why? What is the highest deductible you feel you can afford? Pick one type of insurance you want to have for your business and find a company online that sells it. List the premium, deductible, and payout.

Key Concept Questions

16-10. What is the most important contract you will need to operate your business? Describe any additional contracts you have or plan to secure.

16-11. Negotiate and write a letter of agreement between you and a fellow student. You could agree to become business partners, for example, or to supply a product or service for the other student's business.

16-12. Find a lawyer who might be willing to help you with your business. Ask your parents/guardians who are in business or store owners in your community for referrals. The Small Business Administration or Community Legal Aid Society sometimes offers free or low-cost legal services to entrepreneurs.

16-13. What is the purpose of having a form notarized?

16-14. What does your signature at the bottom of a contract mean in a court of law? Which two things should you do before signing a contract?

16-15. Suki is buying an old van from her brother to start her flower-basket delivery service. She planned to buy auto insurance that would pay all her expenses in case she ever got into an accident. She finds that such insurance would cost $3,000 per year, which, according to her business-plan projections, is more than she can afford. What do you think Suki should do? Why?

16-16. Some businesses sell products and services that can injure customers. List three examples and explain how these companies probably use insurance.

Application Exercise

16-17. Carry out a search online for the name you intend to use for your business. What did you find? Will you still use this name? Why or why not? How do you plan to protect the name of your business?

Exploring Your Community

16-18. For the business you plan to start, research licensing regulations in your area and describe how they will affect your operation.
   a. Have you applied for a sales tax ID number?
   b. What are the zoning laws in your location? Would your business comply?

16-19. What nonprofit business could you start in your community? Answer the following questions to describe it:
   a. What is the name of your nonprofit?
   b. What societal problem(s) are you trying to solve?
   c. Describe the mission of your organization.
   d. Describe the programs and services you plan to create.
   e. How will your organization achieve the changes you intend to bring about?
   f. What is the unit of change (per person, animal, house, etc.)?
   g. How will you measure these changes?
   h. Who are your competitors?
   i. How much will it cost to deliver one unit of service?
   j. What sources of funding will you seek?

16-20. Interview an entrepreneur about insurance policies. Ask how he decided what kind of insurance to carry and whether to have high or low deductibles. Present a report on your entrepreneur's insurance plan to the class.

BizBuilder Business Plan Questions

After studying this chapter, you should be able to answer the following Business Plan Questions. The entire outline for the Business Plan is found in Appendix 2.

3.0 Company Description
   D. What is your organization's legal structure (sole proprietorship, partnership, LLC, C corporation, etc.)?
   E. Why did you choose this legal structure?

   F. In what state are you registered or do you intend to register?

   G. Where will you physically operate the organization?

   H. What is the geographic reach of the organization?

   I. Who will be the owner(s), partners, or stockholders for your company?

   J. If your business is incorporated, describe what percentage of the company is owned by each shareholder.

6.0 Management and Operations

6.2 Research and Development

   A. What type of research are you doing? What do you intend to do?

   B. What are others in the industry doing?

   C. How will you protect your intellectual property?

6.3 Physical Location

   A. Describe the actual physical place in greater detail than above.

   B. What are the zoning laws in your area? Does your business comply?

6.5 Inventory, Production, and Quality Assurance

   J. What methods will you use to ensure that you comply with federal, state, and local tax laws?

   K. What laws—such as minimum wage and age requirements, health and safety regulations, or antidiscrimation laws—will affect your business?

The Bun Companies—Rising through Time

Cordia Harrington, known as "The Bun Lady," founded the Tennessee Bun Company in 1996—with the funds from the sale of her McDonald's franchises and her bank savings—to become a supplier for McDonald's. Since then, her company has grown into The Bun Companies, including the baking facilities in Dickson and Nashville, Cold Storage of Nashville, and Cornerstone Baking Company. The companies supply fresh and frozen buns, biscuits, and English muffins for chains, including McDonald's, Chili's, and Pepperidge Farm, primarily in the South.

Mandel Ngan/Getty Images

Over the years, Cordia has purchased and sold businesses and worked with numerous suppliers and vendors. From her career in real estate to becoming a McDonald's franchisee and owning a Greyhound bus station to creating the Tennessee Bun Company, Cordia has navigated many legal, regulatory, and risk factors. She added cold storage and delivery capacity to her bakery business when the risk of missed deliveries arose.

In 2011, The Bun Companies expanded during a down economy because of customer demand and added biscuit production to its facility in Nashville. This 30,000-square-foot addition is highly efficient, with the capacity to produce 1,800 biscuits per minute.[11] The company used a Decision Matrix (Pugh Matrix) approach for the project and fast-tracked it to meet customer requirements. By using the matrix, managers evaluated their options and prioritized the factors that would matter most in the process. They also used competitive bids and tested the new equipment multiple times.

Case Study Analysis

16-21. What legal issues has Cordia needed to address?

16-22. What kinds of regulations would you expect her baking, transportation, and storage companies to encounter?

16-23. With whom would you expect Cordia to have contracts? Why?

Case Sources

Laurie Gorton, "Tennessee Bun Company: Revs up biscuit line at Nashville," *Baking & Snack*, September 1, 2011, pp. 36–42, accessed September 7, 2013, http://www.nxtbook.com/sosland/bs/2011_09_01/index.php#/36.

Tennessee Bun Company, About, accessed September 7, 2013, http://www.buncompany.com/about-us/.

---

[11]Laurie Gorton, "Tennessee Bun Company: Revs up biscuit line at Nashville," *Baking & Snack*, September 1, 2011, pp. 36–42, accessed September 7, 2013, http://www.nxtbook.com/sosland/bs/2011_09_01/index.php#/36.

Airbnb—Navigating the Sharing Economy

Travelers frequently stay with friends and family as they visit various places. Some stay with alumni from their colleges through alumni networking sites, others stay with friends of friends. The concept of "couch surfing" is not new. However, Airbnb has taken the concept global.

Airbnb, founded in 2008 and headquartered in San Francisco, is a pure play Internet business that connects travelers with accommodations in private homes or properties worldwide. The company has offices in San Francisco, London, Paris, Barcelona, Sao Paulo, Copenhagen, Moscow, Hamburg, Berlin, Milan, and Singapore. As of September 2013, Airbnb had accumulated over 300,000 listings in more than 34,000 cities and 192 countries.[12] This amounted to over 10 million nights booked and some 600 million social connections.

Chris Weeks/Getty Images

The Process

Individuals offer rooms in their homes, entire homes, condominiums, or other accommodations or shared spaces on the Airbnb site. They set prices and terms and provide photos and descriptions, as well as house rules to be posted on Airbnb. The company's job is to list a site, respond to prospective guest inquiries, accept bookings, and act as a host for the guests.

Guests can visit featured locations or search for places they might like to visit. Through the Airbnb search function, they can find accommodations that match their criteria. They can then view photos, descriptions, rules, available dates, and guest reviews for the situations that interest

them. If they are willing to share a home with a host, they can search for sharing opportunities. If guests have questions, they can send an inquiry through Airbnb and expect a response directly from the prospective host. The site tracks the speed and frequency of responses for each host, and this is posted for site visitors to see.

Once a guest decides on a place to stay, he or she requests a reservation through the Airbnb site and provides credit card information. Airbnb then requests a booking confirmation from the host. When the host accepts the booking, Airbnb charges the guest's credit card according to its policy. The host is paid one day after the guest checks in at the property.

Legal Guidelines from Airbnb

Airbnb has specific legal language on its Web site defining its role in the transaction and those of the hosts and guests. When hosts register their listings on Airbnb, they agree to certain terms and conditions. Specifically, the site states, "You understand and agree that Airbnb is not a party to any agreements entered into between hosts and guests, nor is Airbnb a real estate broker, agent or insurer. Airbnb has no control over the conduct of hosts, guests and other users of the site, application and services or any accommodations, and disclaims all liability in this regard."[13] It further elucidates:

> You acknowledge and agree that you are responsible for any and all Listings you post. Accordingly, you represent and warrant that any Listing you post and the booking of, or Guest stay at, an Accommodation in a Listing you post (i) will not breach any agreements you have entered into with any third parties and (ii) will (a) be in compliance with all applicable laws, Tax requirements, and rules and regulations that may apply to any Accommodation included in a Listing you post, including, but not limited to, zoning laws and laws governing rentals of residential and other properties and (b) not conflict with the rights of third parties. Please note that Airbnb assumes no responsibility for a Host's compliance with any

[12]Airbnb, accessed September 8, 2013, https://www.airbnb.com/about.

[13]Airbnb, accessed September 14, 2013, http://www.airbnb.com.

the customer. For the product to succeed, it has to be designed so that it can be produced at a profit when manufactured in moderate volume. You cannot design a luxury product using expensive components and expect to sell it at an economy price.

Cost factors will arise in all aspects of a product, from design and patenting costs to tooling, prototypes, equipment, and facilities, to raw materials, components, production, assembly, quality assurance, packaging, and delivery. The primary delineation of costs lies between the *functional* design (the product itself) and the *production* design (how it is made). Each aspect needs to be considered in determining which product(s) to bring to market.

Making versus Buying

Every business that sells a product has to determine how much of it to produce and how much to buy. The question may be one of the degrees of **vertical integration**—going forward or backward on the idea-to-market continuum—that it wants to incorporate. This is analogous to the difference between having bread delivered to your retail store and selling it to consumers, or growing and milling the grain and other ingredients, mixing and preparing the dough, baking it, packaging it, and then selling consumers the finished product. What you will choose in your business will depend on many factors. Critical issues include: capacity for production at each phase of the process, cost effectiveness, and customer requirements and preferences.

vertical integration the process of going forward or backward on the idea-to-market continuum.

Global Impact . . .

Paper Wealth

Zhang Yin (Cheung Yan) of Nine Dragons Paper (Holdings) Limited, in China, is the richest self-made woman in the world. Her personal wealth is estimated at $4.7 billion.[5] Her company recycles scrap paper, often from the United States, and produces cardboard. The cardboard is used to make boxes for Chinese goods, many of which find their way back to the United States.

Zhang Yin, originally an accountant from Guangdong Province, has moved between China and the United States, first opening a paper company in Hong Kong (1985) with $3,800 in cash, and then a paper-export company in the United States (1990). American Chung Namp Inc. became the largest exporter of waste paper from U.S. sources. Working with her Taiwanese-born and Brazilian-raised husband and her brother, she co-founded Nine Dragons in Hong Kong in 1995. The company raised almost $500 million through its initial public offering on the Hong Kong Stock Exchange in 2006.

American Chung Namp and Nine Dragons are able to maintain low overhead by hauling away unwanted scrap and by creatively exploiting shipping opportunities.[6] Rates to China are particularly attractive because of excess capacity on ships returning to China from the United States.

As of 2007, Nine Dragons had 5,300 employees, 11 huge papermaking machines, and reported profits of $175 million on $1 billion in annual revenues.[7] It expanded into a third manufacturing plant, located near Shanghai, in August 2008 and a fourth facility opened in Tianjin in September 2009.[8] By using the latest in machinery and less costly labor and fuel, the company has significant production advantages. Nine Dragons met ISO (International Organization for Standardization, discussed later in chapter) quality and environmental standards and obtained Occu-

Zhang Yin of Nine Dragons Paper (Mike Clarke/Getty Images)

pational Health and Safety management system certification to support its continuous improvement. In addition to paper production, according to its Web site, the company has facilities to provide, ". . . power, steam, water treatment and excellent logistical support. The integration of these facilities provides and increases the Group's operational flexibility and control, while enabling the Group to facilitate best practices in terms of environmental protection."

The Nine Dragons Web site clearly states the company's goal: "The Group aims to become the world's leading containerboard product manufacturer in capacity, profitability and efficiency."

[5]Allen Cheng, "Cardboard Puts Woman at Top of China's Rich List," *The Standard*, January 17, 2007, accessed November 14, 2009, http://www.thestandard.com.hk/.
[6]Ibid.
[7]David Barboza, "Blazing a Paper Trail in China," *New York Times*, January 16, 2007, accessed November 13, 2009, http://nytimes.com/2007/01/16/business/.
[8]Nine Dragons Paper (Holdings) Limited, accessed November 13, 2009, http://www.ndpaper.com.

Facilities Location and Design

Regarding retail business, you have no doubt heard the cliché about the importance of "location, location, location." It is true. For all businesses, location and layout are critical. Where you locate your business will have considerable impact on your access to supplies and customers. For example, you may want to be near critical suppliers or customers or somewhere with ready access to a major highway, rail service, or airport. You may want to be in a retail location, an office building, or an industrial park. Your business must be located where zoning laws permit its operation. In fact, you may have a *virtual* business with no physical storefront, manufacturing facility, or warehouse. More information regarding site selection is included in Chapter 18.

Defining Quality: It Is a Matter of Market Positioning

Learning Objective 5
Ensure product quality.

quality degrees of excellence; conformance to specifications or standards.

The concept of **quality** is used broadly and has multiple definitions, including how to determine degrees of excellence and conformance to specifications or standards. As a business owner, quality products or services will be largely defined by your market-positioning strategy. For example, a meal at a five-star restaurant will be vastly different from one at a local diner. In either case, excellence is a matter of consistently performing to the standards that have been established to meet or exceed customer expectations. However you position your organization, your quality and the viability of the business will depend on the match between the expectations you create through market positioning and the experience of your customers.

Profits Follow Quality

For many years, American companies had focused less on quality than on short-term profits. In the early 1950s, however, American economist W. Edwards Deming argued that business should focus on making quality products instead of on maximizing profits and that profit would follow from that focus. His revolutionary concept was ignored by American corporations, so he went to Japan, which was rebuilding its economy after the devastation of World War II.

In those days, Japan was notorious for the poor quality of its manufactured goods. The phrase "Made in Japan" was jokingly used to refer to anything poorly fabricated. Deming gave a series of lectures in Japan, though, that the Japanese took to heart. They began focusing on quality and soon proved that Deming's theory—profits follow quality—was correct. The subsequent quality of Japanese cars and stereos, among other products, became famous and won customers worldwide.

American entrepreneurs and corporate executives traveled to Japan to study why the Japanese had become so successful. They brought Deming's ideas back home, where they finally began to be adopted.

As you develop your business, it will be the consistent quality of your product or service that will lead to profits. If you can develop a way to deliver quality consistently, you will have a business model that can be profitable, with the potential for generating even greater revenues in the future.

Organization-Wide Quality Initiatives

Quality management and quality assurance is not solely the job of the production team. As organizations have evolved in our rapidly changing technology- and service-driven environment, quality has come to require

Step into the Shoes . . .

Positioning Stone Hill Winery through Quality

Jim and Betty Held took over the Stone Hill Winery in 1965, with four young children and a vision of restoring the historic Hermann, Missouri, winery to its pre-Prohibition glory days.[9] They succeeded until the 1970s, when high interest rates combined with escalating costs. The winery grew slowly during the 1980s and into the 1990s, and then more rapidly from the later years of that decade.

Sweet and semi-sweet wines have always been the most popular items that Stone Hill Winery produced. Jon Held states, "We have provided a wide spectrum of wine styles to satisfy all consumers rather than only the tastes of a select few wine elite. Most importantly, we have listened to our customers rather than to the wine pundits." The Helds analyzed consumer loyalty to wine brands and discovered that one significant factor was first-time consumption of the product, specifically the atmosphere in which it was consumed. They changed their advertising message accordingly, inviting the public to, "Come out to the winery and have a great time."

The Helds knew that if they could invest in new vineyards and equipment, they could attain economies of scale.[10] As recently as 2008, the winery expanded through the addition of new fermentation and storage capacity, totaling 99,000 gallons. They needed to apply the latest grape-and-wine production technology so that the winery could consistently produce a range of wine styles of high quality and value. To raise money for this

technology, they had to grow significantly. The marketing approach with the application of technology worked.

Stone Hill Winery is a three-location tourist destination. It now produces more than 260,000 gallons of wine annually with gross revenues exceeding $9 million per year, while employing the Helds, two of their adult children, and more than 100 other people. Stone Hill has 190 acres of vineyards under cultivation and uses grapes from other Missouri vineyards to supplement production.

Jim and Betty Held and their family combined market research, determination, state-of-the-art production equipment and techniques, and quality assurance to create an award-winning enterprise.

Stone Hill Winery (Lucinda Huskey/ Stone Hill Winery)

---

[9]Stone Hill Winery, accessed September 21, 2013, http://www.stonehillwinery.com/ourWinery/.

[10]"Stone Hill Winery: New Tastes, New Approach," *Insights and Inspiration: How Businesses Succeed, The 1995 Blue Chip Enterprise Initiative®*. Published by *Nation's Business* magazine on behalf of Connecticut Mutual Life Insurance Company and the U.S. Chamber of Commerce, in association with the Blue Chip Enterprise Initiative, 1995, p. 27. Courtesy of Stone Hill Winery.

---

the active involvement of the entire company. A number of initiatives and methods have been formed to help businesses ensure quality. Among these are lean manufacturing, *benchmarking, ISO 9000, Six Sigma, Total Quality Management*, and *The Malcolm Baldrige Award*. Each of these can assist your company in providing the quality that your customers should expect.

Benchmarking

One the most basic organization-wide approaches that you can pursue is the use of **benchmarking**, which is the comparison of your company's performance against that of other companies in your industry—or against best practices, standards, or certification criteria. Benchmarking is what you are doing when you create a competitive comparison for marketing purposes or when you compare your projected or actual financial ratios to industry levels. In addition to standard performance measures, such as return on investment, profitability, market share, and the like, individual industries have benchmarks. For example, retail stores measure sales per square foot, and restaurants evaluate by number of customers per labor hour. By using benchmarking, you can identify opportunities for improvement.

A simple method of benchmarking is to create a list of measures that are important to your customers (using primary market research) or to customers in your industry (using secondary research, such as trade-journal reports) and then to compare outcomes. You can then compare other statistics, if it is helpful. **Exhibit 17-1** illustrates a portion of such a table for a restaurant.

benchmarking the comparison of a company's performance against that of companies in the same industry, or against best practices, standards, or certification criteria.

Exhibit **17-1** *Quality Measures for the Country Diner*					
Measure of Quality	**Rating (1 Is Poor, 5 Is Excellent— Based on Industry and Customer Data)**				
Customers per labor hour	1	2	3	④	5
Average customer wait time for seating	1	2	3	4	⑤
Satisfactory inspection ratings	1	②	3	4	5
Number of meals returned to the kitchen	1	2	③	4	5
Customer satisfaction ratings	1	2	3	④	5
Amount of food wasted	1	2	3	4	5
Return on sales	①	2	3	④	5

ISO 9000

The family of standards for quality management systems established by the International Organization for Standardization (ISO) is ISO 9000. These standards are certified by independent companies to document that consistent business procedures are being used and that the organization has been independently audited for compliance. Initially, ISO standards were applied solely to manufacturing. However, service firms have become the predominant recipients of certificates. Organizations will sometimes market their ISO certification as a mark of excellence, although it is rather a guarantee of compliance with standards.

process management
the measurement, monitoring, and optimization of tasks.

Numerous standards have been employed under varying numbers. Beginning with the ISO 9001:2000 version, **process management** (measuring, monitoring, and optimizing tasks), upper management involvement, continuous improvement, recording customer satisfaction, and using numeric measures of effectiveness all became critical to the process. Industry-specific variations may apply to your business. There are eight quality-management principles for organizational improvement:

1. customer focus
2. leadership
3. involvement of people
4. process approach
5. system approach to management
6. continual improvement
7. factual approach to decision making
8. mutually beneficial supplier relationships

Regardless of the size of your firm, you can find considerable information on the ISO standards and build them into your organization from the start. Assistance is available through the American Society for Quality (ASQ) at http://www.asq.org, the American National Standards Institute at http://www.ansi.org, and ISO at http://www.iso.ch.

Six Sigma

Six Sigma is a measurement of quality that was originated in the 1980s by Motorola engineers. It is the use of statistical methods to eliminate defects to a failure rate of 3.4 defects per 1 million opportunities, or a 99.9997-percent success rate. This is a rigorous process-improvement program that aims to achieve near-perfection. The two sub-methodologies employed are DMAIC and DMADV.[11] The DMAIC (define, measure, analyze, improve, and control) system is intended to enhance existing production. The DMADV (define, measure, analyze, design, and verify) process is meant to support new procedures and products.

For most enterprises, this is an intense program, maybe more so than is practical in the early stages of a business. However, it may be worthwhile to learn about it and consider whether you can include such methods as you start your business. Further information is available at:

SSA & Company	*http://ssaandco.com*
The Quality Portal	*http://www.thequalityportal.com*
iSixSigma LLC	*http://www.isixsigma.com*
Motorola	*http://www.motorola.com/motorolauniversity.jsp*

Total Quality Management

The quality-assurance methodology of striving for strategic advantage through quality concepts inspired by Deming is called **total quality management (TQM)**. Developed in the 1950s, as described earlier, many of the principles of TQM are still valid and valued. **Continuous improvement**, or always identifying and implementing changes throughout the organization to focus on requirements of internal and external customers—is valid for any business. TQM involves constant improvement of processes, typically using specific measures of quality, such as compliance with product specifications and operating standards, volume of production, on-time delivery, and repeat rates.

TQM's success depends on the commitment of all employees to treat one another as customers and to work together to ensure that standards are met at all stages. Each employee accepts responsibility for a role in the production of the products and services.

total quality management (TQM) the quality-assurance methodology of striving for strategic advantage through quality.

continuous improvement always identifying and implementing changes throughout an organization to focus on the requirements of internal and external customers.

Malcolm Baldrige Award

Whereas the previous concepts have focused on quality-management methodologies, the Malcolm Baldrige Award is a competitive process established by the United States Congress in 1987 to recognize quality management. The Baldrige Award is given to businesses and educational and nonprofit organizations by the president of the United States and is administered by the National Institute of Standards and Technology (NIST).[12] Organizations apply for the award and are judged in the areas of:

- leadership: organizational leadership and social responsibility;
- strategic planning: strategy development and deployment;
- customer and market focus: market and customer knowledge and customer relationships and satisfaction;
- measurement, analysis, knowledge management: measurement and analysis of organizational performance and management of information and knowledge;
- human resources focus: work systems, employee learning and motivation, and employee well-being and satisfaction;
- process management: value-creation and support processes;
- business results, including customer-focus, product and service, financial and market, human resources, organizational effectiveness, governance, and social responsibility.

---

[11]Available at http://www.isixsigma.com.

[12]Available at http://www.nist.gov/public_affairs/factsheet/.

Thousands of organizations use the Baldrige criteria for self-assessment, training, and the creation of business processes. You can obtain a list of these Baldrige standards and incorporate them into your business at any time. They are more comprehensive than many of the specific production and process measures identified previously in this chapter.

Using Technology to Your Advantage

Learning Objective 6
Use technology to benefit your business.

Regardless of the size or nature of your business, technology can work to your advantage. Even if your business is not technological, you can apply technology to make your operations more efficient and effective. The technology could be as simple and common as a telephone or as complex as a specialized piece of medical equipment. What *is* important is that you are aware of the technology available to you and how it might benefit your business. At the same time, you should be wary of adopting new technology just for the "wow" factor. A cost/benefit analysis for technology implementation is as important as for any other substantial investment.

Computer Access Is Essential

Advances in technology that ordinary people can use have been an important part of the entrepreneurial scenario for at least 15 years. With this in mind:

- Every entrepreneur should have access to a computer.
- Every business should have a Web site and electronic mail.
- Every business should hire employees who are conversant and comfortable with technology.
- Every entrepreneur should be aware of the specialized computer software and equipment that is designed for his or her industry.

hyperlink word(s) that, when clicked on, transfer the computer user to another Web page.

uniform resource locator (URL) a Web-page address.

hypertext Web-based documents that combine text and graphics.

The Internet came into being in 1989, when an Englishman named Tim Berners-Lee invented **hyperlinks**, words that, when clicked on, transferred the reader to a new document page somewhere else on the Internet. Today, pictures, or even video, can be links as well. Every Web page has an "address," called a **URL (uniform resource locator)**, and you can surf from one URL to another using hyperlinks. Web pages are **hypertext** documents, meaning they combine text with graphics, video, or sound.

One of the best early investments you can make for your business is a computer. You do not need to have the latest model or even a new one; refurbished computers can be purchased quite inexpensively. Even the most basic model can be used to:

- access the Internet;
- create stationery and business cards (although professional designs are preferable);
- produce professional letters and check spelling, grammar, and syntax;
- keep financial records; and
- maintain an updated mailing list of customers and print mailing labels.

Cultura/Corbis Images

Capture the Potential of the Telephone

Do not forget, however, that technology does not have to be new to be useful. The telephone is still one of the businessperson's most important technological tools.

You can turn your phone into an answering service for your business by using a voice-mail system, or you can hire an answering service to provide a more personal touch. Either approach is acceptable until you have the staff to answer customer inquiries—although some companies use automated telephone-answering systems, even if they have hundreds, or thousands, of employees.

Whether you use voice mail or an answering service, make sure the message that callers hear represents your desired business image and is clear and professional. Change your message periodically to advertise specials and sales and to keep customers listening. Use mobile phones to stay in touch with customers, employees, and suppliers.

A separate telephone line for your business will provide a number of advantages. Business telephones can be listed under your business name in directories, and you will know to always answer with your business name when that phone rings. Also, if you have a home-based business and children, it will be easier to have them resist answering the phone when it is clearly the business line. With text messaging and e-mail sent over mobile phones, the versatility and importance of telephones to today's businesses cannot be overstated.

Identify Market-Specific Software and Technology

To increase efficiency and effectiveness in operations, businesses use software and technology designed for their industry or type of business. For example, retail stores often use point-of-sales (POS) systems that are tailored to their products, and restaurants use ordering systems customized to their menus. Not-for-profits have specialized fund-raising and accounting software. Sports stadiums, concert venues, and movie theaters have ticketing systems. Manufacturing plants have materials-planning and inventory systems.

Typically, trade journals feature advertisements for software specific to an industry. Software companies commonly exhibit at trade shows and conferences. Evaluations and comparisons of hardware and software solutions can be found in trade publications and on the Internet.

An investment in industry-specific technology is often many times greater than in generic business equipment and software. However, the upfront investment may lead to both considerable efficiency and savings over the short and/or long term.

Electronic Storefront (Web Site)

No matter what type of business you have, opening an **electronic storefront** will make it more accessible to local customers and can introduce it to potential customers all over the world. An electronic storefront is an online site that customers can visit to view your catalog, price lists, and other information. Today, it is relatively easy to add the option of purchasing your products online, either directly, through a credit-card merchant account, or through a service such as PayPal or Bill Me Later.

You will need to decide if you want to put your store up with an online service or by yourself. An online service would typically build your storefront for you and include promotion and advertisements as part of the deal to help make its subscribers aware of your store. On the other hand, if you put a site up yourself, you would have more control over what it looked like and where it was located; and your potential customers would not be limited to the subscribers to a particular online service. One of the most cost-efficient ways to set up an electronic storefront is to hire a competent consultant to help you design it and choose which server to use.

electronic storefront an online site that customers can visit to view a company's catalog, price lists, and documentation.

Chapter Summary

Now that you have studied this chapter, you can do the following:

1. Understand the significance of operations in a business.
   - Operations is delivering on promises.
   - What is required depends on the specific industry and business.
   - Inputs are transformed or converted into outputs through operations.

2. Develop a production-distribution chain for your business.
   - Manufacturers make products in large quantities.
   - Wholesalers buy smaller quantities in bulk from manufacturers.
   - Retailers buy from wholesalers (and sometimes manufacturers).
   - Consumers buy from retailers.

3. Manage suppliers and inventory.
   - Supply-chain management is used to create and maintain efficient flow of materials between supply partners.
   - Suppliers may be found in a variety of ways and may be located worldwide.
   - Inventory can be managed to minimize cost and maximize customer satisfaction.

4. Explore the idea-to-product process.
   - Different people are interested in and skilled at fulfilling specific stages of a business.
   - Ideas may evolve into patentable product designs with drawings and specifications.
   - Product designs can be made to test and improve prototypes.
   - Parts and materials lists are needed for sourcing and production.
   - Manufacturing can be done directly, with part and/or subassembly suppliers, and through job shops.
   - Manufacturing methodologies, location, and purchasing all have important roles.

5. Ensure product quality.
   - Quality is determined by meeting and exceeding standards, including customer satisfaction.
   - Profits follow quality.
   - Organization-wide approaches to quality include
     - ISO 9000 certification,
     - Six Sigma certification,
     - total quality management (TQM), and
     - Malcolm Baldrige Awards.

6. Use technology to benefit your business.
   - Technology can provide competitive advantage.
   - Computers are a necessity in today's business world.
   - The telephone continues to be a major asset.
   - Industry-specific software and equipment are frequently beneficial.
   - Electronic storefronts (Web sites) provide additional distribution opportunities.

Key Terms

benchmarking, 543
continuous improvement, 545
economic order quantity
  (EOQ), 535
electronic storefront, 547
hyperlink, 546
hypertext, 546
job shop, 538
just-in-time manufacturing
  (JIT), 539
operations, 532
process management, 544
prototype, 539
quality, 542

reorder point (ROP), 534
safety stock, 534
setup cost, 539
supply chain management
  (SCM), 533
tolerance, 538
tooling cost, 539
total quality management
  (TQM), 545
uniform resource locator
  (URL), 546
value-engineer, 539
vertical integration, 541
visual control, 534

Entrepreneurship Portfolio

Critical Thinking Exercises

17-1. Production-distribution chain

    a. How do you plan to distribute your product to your target market?

    b. What is the estimated delivery time between when you place an order with your supplier and when the product will be available for your customers?

17-2. A manufacturer makes a line of women's handbags. The company offers 600 different styles of handbags in its catalog. It sells almost 25,000 handbags per year, but it is not known which style is going to sell from one week to the next.

    The company has both a JIT system and a mass-production system to make the same line of handbags. Both manufacturing systems work well, and both cost about the same to operate. The JIT system can make up to 100 handbags a day; however, it is very flexible. If necessary, it can produce 100 different styles in a single day of operation.

    The mass production system takes half a day to set up and can make 1,000 handbags—all the same style—in the second half of the day. It is 10 times as fast as the JIT system.

    Raw materials cost $4 per handbag and are the same whichever system is used to do the work. The company likes to order enough materials to make 2,000 handbags, which is usually enough to cover a month of orders.

    The company has discovered a trick to run more than one style of handbag with the mass-production system. If it sets up in the morning and runs just one handbag until noon, it can use the afternoon to change over to a different style and still have time to run another handbag before closing at 5:00. This gives it two handbags produced in one day, if necessary.

The Average Day: 100 Handbags, Each of a Different Style, Are Ordered	Mass-Production System, Using the Regular Method	Mass-Production System, Using the Two Setups Trick	JIT System
Units shipped	1	2	100
Percentage of orders for the day filled	1%	2%	100%
Amount of unsold inventory created	999	0	0
Raw materials available for future work	1,000 units / $4,000 value	1,998 units / $7,992 value	1,900 units / $7,600 value

    a. Which system is more efficient? Why?

    b. If the company could only keep one of these manufacturing systems, which do you think it should keep? Explain.

17-3. Give an example of a business that is known internationally for the quality of its products; what defines quality for this company?

17-4. How does the design of a facility affect product quality and production efficiency?

17-5. Choose a partner in class and make a list of the technology each of you can personally access. Brainstorm how you might combine your technological resources to create a successful business. Describe in detail how the partnership would work. For example, would the person contributing more technology have a larger share of the business, or would profits and expenses be split equally? Draw up a partnership agreement that specifies each partner's duties and how much money and time each will invest in the business.

17-6. Examine a label on either the shoes or a piece of clothing you are wearing today. Which items were made in foreign countries? How many dollars per hour do you think the people earned who made these articles of clothing? Why do you think the company that manufactured these items had them made abroad?

Key Concept Questions

17-7. Use your local telephone company's business-to-business directory or *The American Wholesalers and Distributors Directory* to locate wholesalers you could visit, or from whom you could order products for resale.

17-8. Choose one of the quality-assurance methodologies described in this chapter and explain how it might apply to your educational institution.

Application Exercises

17-9. What might the supply chain look like for one of the following:
   a. manufacturer of custom tire rims for automobiles
   b. car dealership
   c. building materials wholesaler

17-10. Suggest at least three quality-assurance measures for the following businesses:
   a. bank
   b. residential cleaning service
   c. commercial HVAC (heating, ventilation, and air conditioning) contractor
   d. computer manufacturer

Exploring Your Community

17-11. Identify two businesses in your community with which you are familiar. Suggest four measures of quality for each. Rate each business on these quality dimensions. Then, answer the questions below.

Measure of Quality	Rating (1 is poor, 5 is excellent)				
Company Number 1					
Measure 1	1	2	3	4	5
Measure 2	1	2	3	4	5
Measure 3	1	2	3	4	5
Measure 4	1	2	3	4	5
Company Number 2					
Measure 1	1	2	3	4	5
Measure 2	1	2	3	4	5
Measure 3	1	2	3	4	5
Measure 4	1	2	3	4	5

a. What do these measures tell you about the respective businesses?

b. How might they improve on one of the indicators?

c. Does each business have a customer feedback mechanism? If so, what is it? If not, what would you recommend?

Biz Builder Business Plan Questions

After studying this chapter, you should be able to answer the following Business Plan Questions. The entire outline for the Business Plan is found in Appendix 2.

6.0 Management and Operations

6.5 Inventory, Production, and Quality Assurance

A. Where are you purchasing the products you plan to sell or the parts you will use to manufacture those products? Illustrate your supply chain.

B. Do you intend to manufacture your product? If so, describe the manufacturing processes you will use. If not, describe how your product will be made.

C. Are there any economies of scale to be attained for your business? At what point do you anticipate attaining them?

D. Have you developed and/or adopted any innovations in production, inventory management, or distribution that are significant? What are they and why are they meaningful?

E. How do you plan to distribute your product to your target market?

F. Show the production-distribution channel for your business and the markups along the chain.

G. What is the estimated delivery time between when you place an order with your supplier and when you will have the product available for your customers?

H. What method(s) will you use to define and ensure the quality of your products/services?

Producing Quality American Made Furniture: Gat Creek Furniture

In 1996, Gat Caperton decided that his future lay in purchasing and operating a manufacturing venture. At the time, he was a graduate student in Chicago and a full time consultant specializing in manufacturing. Caperton envisioned that he would benefit from increasing production efficiency and revenues in an existing business rather than through starting his own venture.

During his acquisition search, Caperton found Tom Seely Furniture in Berkeley Springs, West Virginia, saw value in the acquisition, and purchased the company. Tom Seely created the company to produce reproductions of antique furniture some 40 years earlier after his experience as an antiques dealer taught him that he could manufacture and sell reproductions for greater profit and have more satisfied customers.

Caperton recognized the market value of hand-made Appalachian cherry wood antique reproductions and worked to create a production facility that would create the products for his target market. After some years of operating as Tom Seely Furniture, the company became Gat Creek Furniture and Caperton Furniture Works for its wholesale and private label markets respectively. Each furniture piece is hand-crafted and signed by one of Caperton's 120 plus employees or made by a local subcontractor (often individual craftspeople) using the company's specifications. Materials are sourced locally with 95 percent of raw materials originating within 350 miles of the factory.

While the furniture is assembled by the local workforce in a traditional way, the company makes use of modern technology to ensure quality and minimal environmental impact. For example, Gat Creek monitors all materials entering and leaving its facility to reduce waste, pollution, and emissions. Gat Creek uses a state-of-the-art renewable biomass boiler system so that scrap materials become fuel for heating. The company has an innovative storm water management system and has received recognition for its efforts.

A core value for Caperton is sustainability, and he has implemented a manufacturing process that emphasizes care for the environment throughout its processes. As Caperton states, "Over the past five years we have won a number of design, environmental and workplace safety awards. The award we cherish most is our customers' trust. We hold home sacred and hope to have the opportunity to share some of our craft with you and your home."[13]

---

[13]Gat Creek Furniture, accessed September 19, 2013, http://www.gatcreek.com/index.php/about-us/our-story.

Gat Creek Furniture

Case Study Analysis

17-12. How has Gat Creek brought modern technology to the traditional processes of building furniture?

17-13. What is the source of production inputs for Gat Creek?

17-14. How might Gat Creek assure quality? Why?

17-15. What types of regulations are particularly important to Gat Creek and its employees, given the nature of the business?

Case Sources

Gat Creek Furniture, accessed September 20, 2013, http://www.gatcreek.com.

"Gat Creek Takes Sage Environmental Award," *Home Furnishings Business*, October 15, 2012, accessed September 24, 2013, http://furniturecore .com/Default.aspx?tabid=732&articleid=5484& gat-creek-takes-sage-environmental-award.

Case Study | Sewing Up Business in New Ways—Sew What? Inc.

Question: What do Maroon 5, Slip Knot, Green Day, Rod Stewart, Elton John, Madonna, and schools near you have in common?

Answer: They are customers of Sew What? Inc., a manufacturer of custom draperies and curtains for theaters, concert tours, exhibitions, and special events.

Sew What? founder Megan Duckett has been passionate about theater and concert production since high school. She started her career as a part-time employee at the Arts Centre in Melbourne, Australia, before she graduated from a Church of England girls' grammar school (high school). The Arts Centre, the heart of theater in Melbourne, provided an opportunity to apprentice as a lighting technician with a master theater electrician, Jim Paine. There, Megan was exposed to the businesses that serve the theater industry; she discovered that working in this industry was what she was born to do.

Not long after that, 18-year-old Megan moved into the rock-and-roll marketplace and continued to work as a lighting technician and on other backstage aspects of the business. A critical turning point in her life came unexpectedly one year later. She was assigned to drive Billy Joel's band around while they were in Melbourne. They had an instant rapport and the crew invited her to visit the United States. Much to their surprise, Megan showed up on their doorstep shortly thereafter—and soon got a job at a staging company for rock concerts. Megan knew she needed to find her niche and stand out from everyone else. As she has noted, "I needed to be invaluable and irreplaceable." Little did she know that sewing would be her ticket to success.

The opportunity to make her mark through sewing essentially came out of nowhere. However, Megan quickly realized it was the opportunity she sought. Her first sewing job was to reupholster 10 coffins for a Haunted Halloween show. She had neither the equipment nor the materials to do the job when she accepted it. Undeterred, Megan rented a sewing machine and went to a local fabric store, where she bought the necessary supplies (at full retail price) and did the work at her kitchen table. The customer could see that it was wonderfully done and called two weeks later with more work. That customer referred others and the business took off. That was in 1992.

Megan Duckett
(Sew What Inc.)

For five years, Megan says, "The phone kept ringing with orders."

As Megan was preparing her tax return in 1997, she realized that the earnings from the custom projects sewn at her kitchen table matched the pay from her 40-hour-a-week job. She and her husband, Adam, had just purchased a home and transformed the garage into a sewing room. After considerable discussion, Megan left her steady, full-time employment, incorporated Sew What? a few weeks later, and rented an 800-square-foot space a few miles from their house. She had no formal advisors and no written plan, but she did have a strong customer base, determination, and an understanding of the business. Just six weeks later, Megan landed a contract big enough so that she had to hire her first employee—a stitcher named Maria—who continues as part of the Sew What? family to this day. In 2002, Adam quit his own job and joined Sew What?

Megan relates, "The soft-goods industry is traditionally very much a cottage industry and is not known for embracing technology. We didn't like the way that felt." From the beginning, the

Ducketts incorporated technology into the business. The company team recognized that, as the quality of the clientele and the size of the contracts increased, customers would expect excellence. Sew What? began deliberately streamlining and fine-tuning the product and service aspects of the business.

Advances in technology were instituted throughout the operation. The office equipment was upgraded to include a network setup, faster computers, and multiple servers to increase speed, in order to function in real time with customers. Sew What? is currently on its third inventory-management system. The first was an Excel-based configuration developed in house. The second method was part of the automated accounting program. The most recent arrangement is a sophisticated manufacturing system called VISTA, from Epicor. Sew What? has moved into lean manufacturing procedures, and every function is timed, scanned, and measured to reduce waste and maximize use of resources. In addition, some patterns are cut using computer-guided tools, although many are still cut by hand—because runs of fabric can be so long and the tolerances so tight that hand cutting makes the most sense.

The company's Web site is a particularly important sales tool. Megan lost a substantial job early on because, without one, her business lacked credibility with the prospective customer. Megan resisted the idea of putting up a Web site, but she came to realize that she needed it, so she built one over a weekend using clip art—a far cry from the professional site Sew What? has today. Megan notes, "Generation Y will be the purchasing agents of the future. They expect a Web site. They need the visual communication." A Web site is particularly helpful for Sew What?, which has clients across the country and around the world (the company is headquartered in Rancho Dominguez, California). The site includes e-swatches, so that visitors can look at fabric samples online.

The sales force and production team also benefit from the use of technology, through a custom software program. By means of a series of drop-down menus, such variables as fabric, color, and production method can be selected. To that can be added dimensions and other specifications. The system calculates a "bid window" of the high and low price that can be offered. It determines the minutes of labor and the yards of materials. Once the job is sold and a contract secured, the file is digitally editable, and the Sew What? team can make final adjustments. It is then sent to a report generator (Crystal Reports) and translated into Spanish for the team of stitchers. This system permits Sew What? to sell more effectively, quote more accurately, replicate the work more easily, and make fewer mistakes. Sew What? has used its technological infrastructure to maximize productivity.

The company won the Dell/NFIB (National Federation of Independent Business) 2006 Small Business Excellence Award, and was featured on

The Sew What? team
(Sew What Inc.)

the Dell Web site for the Integration of Technology into a business. With a 15,000-square-foot building and a staff of more than 30, finding ways to maximize technology is essential.

The sales and order cycles for Sew What? are largely dependent on the type of customer. For example, rock-and-roll touring curtains might take anywhere from three days to four weeks from inquiry to order. These customers may also recycle or replace their curtains after a tour. (They may even donate them to charity.) Often, quick delivery is important for the touring customers, and because Sew What? generally uses only U.S.-milled products, the production cycle can be relatively quick after the order is placed.

For a school or church group buying or replacing stage curtains, the cycle is often three to six months. The process generally includes multiple steps, including when a group realizes the drapes don't open/close properly or it needs new ones. A student or PTA parent researches available vendors and calls Sew What? The sales team helps by focusing first on making sure the individual knows what is needed and what will be provided. The customer is directed to samples and possible solutions, often through the Web site. Sew What? submits a price, the gatherer compares prices, and the school or church group raises funds. With money in hand, they finalize the order, and Megan's team speaks with the person who will install the drapes. Sew What? makes and ships the drapes, the customer receives and installs them, and Megan reaches out to see that they are satisfied.

In July 2008, Megan Duckett launched a second company, Rent What? Inc. with partner Marce Forrester. Offering rental stage curtains (manufactured by Sew What?) and theatrical equipment to the concert and special event market, Rent What? gives customers the means to rent the same high-quality products that are available through Sew What? Rent What? has provided rental drapery and equipment to diverse clients, including Journey, Lady Antebellum, and the television show *Glee*. In the summer of 2010, Rent What? began its third year of operation with the launch of a new customer-focused redesign of its Web site (http://www.rentwhatinc.com).

Megan was thrilled to have her products on the cover of the 1,000th issue of *Rolling Stone*. She won a 2007 Stevie Award for Most Innovative Company of the Year (up to 100 employees) and was a finalist for the 2008 Enterprising Woman of the Year. Sew What? was named to Diversity Business.com's 2008 list of the top 500 small businesses in the United States. In her feature as a young millionaire in *Entrepreneur* magazine, Megan stated, "The secret [to success] is hard work, dedication, and being able to take a blow and get up and move forward again. Be willing to accept criticism and comments, find mentors and learn from others. Try to be inspired by other people's success." With sales of about $5 million annually, the answer to *Sew What?* is "sewing up business." Or, as the company's Web site declares: *Sew What? Inc. It's not a question, it's the answer.*

Case Study Analysis

17-16. How does technology sustain Megan Duckett's business?

17-17. Why does Megan credit computer technology and the Web for a significant portion of her company's growth?

17-18. What have been some critical steps in the growth of the company?

17-19. What is (are) the sales cycle(s) for Sew What?

17-20. What channels of distribution would you expect the company to use?

Case Sources

Dell Case Studies, at http://www.dell.com/html/us/segments/bsd/case_studies/sew/index.html.

Sew What? Inc., accessed November 15, 2009, http://www.sewwhatinc.com.

"Young Millionaires Say More," http://www.entrepreneur.com/slideshow/184476.html.

Chapter 18

LOCATION, FACILITIES, AND LAYOUT

Learning Objectives

1. Understand the importance of the physical location of a business.

2. Know the key factors to consider in the location decision.

3. Learn how location needs differ by business type.

4. Determine business location preferences via multiple methods.

5. Explore the design of facilities and their layouts.

6. Recognize the special considerations for home-based businesses.

7. Describe location factors for Web-based businesses.

Blend Images/Alamy

Frederick W. Smith wrote a paper about air-freight shipping in the "coming computer age" while an undergraduate at Yale in 1965.[1] Just a few years later (1971), after three years in the Marine Corps, Smith purchased controlling interest in an Arkansas-based aviation company. As he was developing the ideas from his term paper, Smith explored locations for his venture. Though incorporated as Federal Express in 1971, Smith's company began actual operations in Memphis, Tennessee (rather than Arkansas), in 1973.

Smith selected Memphis for a number of reasons. It was centrally located for the original target market. The weather in Memphis is such that airport closures are rare. And the Memphis International Airport had hangar space for the 14 Federal Express Dassault Falcon jets Smith was going to start with and was willing to adapt its facilities to accommodate his venture.

Since then, FedEx has expanded its operations to global proportions and is the largest airline in the world, based on number of aircraft and tons of freight flown. The 660 planes in today's FedEx fleet fly to 375 airports in 220 countries. FedEx continues to maintain its headquarters and "super hub" at Memphis. However, there are now seven other domestic hubs: Anchorage, Fort Worth, Indianapolis, Miami, Newark (New Jersey), and Oakland. International hubs are located in Paris, Toronto, Guangzhou-Baiyun in Southern China, and Cologne-Bonn in Germany.

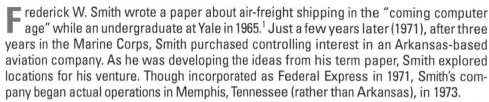

Kim Karpeles/Alamy

With its 150,000 team members and average daily movement of 4 million packages and 12 million pounds of freight, FedEx has demonstrated expertise in identifying locations that will support the logistical requirements of the business.

The Importance of Physical Location

The choice of location for your business can make the difference between success and failure. The oft-quoted business mantra, "location, location, location," is broadly accepted as a crucial factor for retail stores. However, the choice of site is a pivotal strategic decision for manufacturing, wholesale, and Internet businesses as well, albeit for different reasons. The location decision may be a one-time scenario, or it may arise multiple times during the life of a business. Location strategy impacts revenues, customer satisfaction, costs, and the overall levels of risk and profitability.

Your business may need to generate customer floor traffic, to provide conveniently located services, or to have ready access to highways, a port, a railroad line, or an airport, or it may be able to operate virtually anywhere. In any case, the location decision will affect your access to markets and essential aspects of your cost structure. For a brick-and-mortar retailer, the marketing expenditures required to generate potential customers in a low-traffic location will probably be significantly higher than in a high-traffic area. For businesses with high transportation costs, a poor location choice can translate into prohibitive expenses. On the other hand, distribution-cost efficiencies can save money and offer a competitive advantage.

Learning Objective 1 ▶

Understand the importance of the physical location of a business.

---

[1]FedEx, accessed September 21, 2013, http://about.van.fedex.com/company-information.

Key Factors in Deciding on a Location

Learning Objective 2

Know the key factors to consider in the location decision.

The important factors in deciding on a location will depend on the nature of the business and its customers. Common considerations include:

- access for customers
- access to suppliers
- climate and geography
- convenience
- cost of facilities (rent, construction, and the like)
- demographics
- economic conditions and business incentives
- governmental regulations and laws, including environmental impact
- labor pool
- proximity to competitors
- visibility

Figure 18-1 shows the factors affecting location decisions at the country, regional/community, and site levels.

Figure 18-1 *Some Considerations and Factors That Affect Location Decisions*	
	Critical Success Factors
National Decision	1. Political risks, governmental regulations, national attitudes, and incentives
	2. Cultural and economic issues
	3. Location of markets
	4. Labor talent, attitude of labor pool, productivity, costs
	5. Availability of supplies, communications, energy
	6. Exchange rates and currency risk
Regional/Community Decision	1. Corporate desires
	2. Attractiveness of region (culture, taxes, climate, etc.)
	3. Labor availability, costs, attitudes toward unions
	4. Cost and availability of utilities
	5. Environmental regulations
	6. Government incentives and fiscal policies
	7. Proximity to raw materials and customers
	8. Land/construction costs
Site Decision	1. Site size and cost
	2. Air, rail, highway, waterway systems
	3. Zoning restrictions
	4. Proximity of services/supplies needed
	5. Environmental-impact issues

Source: Jay Heizer and Barry Render, *Operations Management,* 8th ed. (Upper Saddle River, NJ: Pearson Prentice Hall, 2007), p. 249.

Different Types of Businesses Have Different Location Needs

Every business venture will have a unique set of location criteria and priorities. Trade publications and industry research will provide insight into industry-specific location issues. What's important to a specialty retailer at a brick-and-mortar location might be meaningless for a service business. The challenge is to identify the critical success factors for your business, tempered by the realities of budget and other constraints, to find your best available option.

◄ Learning Objective 3
Learn how location needs differ by business type.

Options and Criteria for Manufacturing Facilities

Manufacturing businesses have multiple location-criteria considerations that are primarily centered on customer service and costs. Manufacturers need to meet, or exceed, customer delivery and quality goals. That means locating within ready access for distribution (perhaps near warehousing and/or transportation routes) and having a labor pool of sufficient size and skill to meet quality standards. Also, labor wage rates and productivity should be considered. For example, a producer of organic fertilizer may locate close to its farming customers. A machine shop may be best served by locating in a community with trained CAD/CAM operators and machinists. In addition, some manufactured goods cannot be moved over long distances without transportation costs becoming prohibitive (mattresses, for example), so that they can serve only local markets effectively and must locate in relatively close proximity to potential customers. For others, global options are available.

Other factors for manufacturers to consider include access to suppliers, cost of facilities, and laws and regulations. When product freshness or speed of delivery of supplies is essential to business success, producers need to consider their proximity to suppliers. This is also true for heavy, bulky, fragile, or expensive finished goods and their delivery. Bakeries and bottlers often locate near customers for this reason. If delivery can be made on a timely basis without nearby suppliers, this factor loses its significance.

Maintaining facilities will be a significant fixed cost for a manufacturer, with considerable impact on its operating breakeven point, operating leverage, and overall business viability. The cost of manufacturing facilities

Step into the Shoes . . .
Finding the Location That Fits

When José Echeverri left Merrill Lynch to start his own financial planning firm, he chose a location in a small city near his home on a well-traveled road and furnished it like an executive office at a major brokerage house. He invested precious start-up funds in leasehold improvements and in quality furniture and décor. A couple of years later, José determined that he could find opportunities in a small but rapidly growing community 20 miles away. He opened a second office in that town and hired a colleague to operate it.

After a year, José found that the majority of his business was coming from the second office, which had been chosen based on demographics rather than proximity. He moved his primary location to that town, expanded the office slightly, and

closed his initial location. As it turned out, he needed a modest office in a community with stronger demographics rather than a "fancy" space in a less-well-chosen location. José explains, "One of my biggest mistakes in starting this business was trying to create a mini-Merrill rather than finding my own niche from the beginning. Now that we are in the right place and doing the right things, the business is stronger than ever."

Jose Echeverri, Echeverri Financial Services

Source: Courtesy of José Echeverri.

varies widely. It is important to consider current and future needs and to carefully assess them to select a location that balances these issues with costs. The costs will probably include rent or mortgage payments, leasehold improvements, renovation or construction, maintenance, energy and utility charges, and property taxes.

Finally, manufacturing laws and regulations can make a difference between operating efficiently and being fined, temporarily shut down, or permanently closed. Compliance with zoning regulations is critical. Zoning laws define the types of businesses that can operate in a given area. For example, a heavy manufacturing plant cannot be set up in a district zoned for light manufacturing. Zoning laws may prohibit specific types of manufacturing, or all manufacturing, in residential neighborhoods. State and local environmental regulations vary from place to place and must be taken into consideration in making a location decision for a manufacturing business. There could be a financial incentive to support selection of one site over another. For example, low-cost financing or tax breaks might be associated with a particular location.

Options and Criteria for Wholesale Businesses

Wholesale businesses face many of the same options and criteria as manufacturers, usually with fewer constraints. For wholesalers, the ability to distribute goods efficiently to customers is the primary consideration. Proximity to customers and/or suppliers is important, as is the availability of a well-developed transportation network. Costs such as rent or mortgage, utilities, taxes, labor, and transportation are paramount. As with manufacturers, government regulations and incentives contribute to the decision-making process.

Options and Criteria for Retail Businesses

Retail businesses with brick-and-mortar sites focus heavily on the revenue-generating aspects of locations, as opposed to the cost focus of manufacturers and wholesalers. Retailers concentrate on the drawing power of

Rihardzz/Shutterstock

a site—the alignment between target markets and the demographics of customer-attracting areas with the competitive environment. The ability to draw paying customers in sufficient numbers and adequate frequency is essential to success. Demographic data from the U.S. Census (http://www .census.gov), the U.S. Economic Development Administration (http://www .eda.gov), state and local economic-development offices, and chambers of commerce will provide considerable insight into local demographics.

Customer convenience and company image is vital. Also, the proximity to **traffic generators**, which are complementary businesses that attract customer traffic to the retailer's area, can significantly increase revenues. For example, a child-care center and a nearby toy store will almost certainly be a factor in drawing business to a children's clothing boutique. Be sure that the value gained from traffic generators will be greater than the incremental cost. For example, a mall location next to a supermarket may be worth higher rental fees. Sometimes, proximity to direct competitors as traffic generators, **clustering**, may be a viable strategy. In commercial areas there might be clusters of antique dealers, jewelers, or automobile dealerships.

> **traffic generators** complementary businesses that attract customer traffic to the retailers' area.

> **clustering** the strategy of similar businesses locating near each other.

Researching the average sales per square foot in your industry can help you determine a good location by permitting comparison of your anticipated performance to that of others in the vicinity. If there is a great difference, you may need to reconsider your site selection. The sources of such statistics include trade associations for your industry and the International Council of Shopping Centers (ICSC, at http://www.icsc.org); the public library reference section; annual reports of publicly traded companies; the U.S. Census Bureau; the U.S. Economic Development Administration; state and local economic development offices; and chambers of commerce, which provide considerable insight into local demographics.

Another reason to research sales per square foot is to determine the amount of space you will need for your retail location. Until you know how much **selling space**—actual retail floor space, excluding storage and warehousing, administrative, and utility areas—you need, it will be impossible to determine which sites will be appropriate for your business. To calculate the selling space, you will need the industry data on sales per square foot and the estimate of your annual sales volume. That formula is

> **selling space** the retail floor space available for actually selling to customers, excluding storage and warehousing, administrative, and utility areas.

Selling Space = Sales Volume/Sales per Square Foot

If you expect your New Age boutique to generate $300,000 in annual sales, with average sales per square foot of $200, you would need about 1,500 square feet of selling space. Then, add sufficient area for storage, offices, and restrooms.

Cost factors are important, but will be relatively stable once you select a location. Generally, retail stores incur rental costs and salaries and wages as major factors. Rent will be determined by the location of the property and should be weighed against the revenue-generating potential.

Options and Criteria for Service and Professional Businesses

Service and professional businesses face divergent requirements. The choice of location for service and professional firms will depend on many of the factors discussed previously, as well as customer convenience. Some businesses, such as cleaning companies, temporary staffing firms, home health care, and delivery services go to their customers to provide the service and need to have efficient access to their customer base. Physicians, dentists, and other health-care providers—where people come to them—often locate in areas where

RTimages/Alamy

the population fits the service's target demographics and frequently near other health-care providers. Attorneys often locate where there is convenient access to the local courthouse and other legal practices. With the advent of the electronic filing of legal documents, this need for geographic proximity is diminishing.

Another factor to be considered in the location decision for service and professional firms is *image*, or positioning. A firm wishing to convey an upscale, high-end image will be much better served by locating in an elegant suite in a prestigious office building than in a downscale strip mall outside of town. By the same token, a firm providing telemarketing services could be located anywhere where the technology and labor force meets its requirements. That explains why such businesses are often located outside of metropolitan areas, where facility and labor costs are lower. The success of call centers in Bangalore, India, for U.S.-based companies is one example of this phenomenon. For health care professionals, accessibility for their patients and proximity to other providers is often more important than top-of-the-line space, but patients also expect a certain level of cleanliness and a respectable appearance. The recent emergence of medical travel to other parts of the globe (such as Brazil, Mexico, Germany, and India from the United States) for treatment has redefined the meaning of accessibility in some areas of health care. In all cases where customers travel to a service or professional firm, access from highways/streets and/or public transportation, as well as safety and security, matter.

Evaluating Location Alternatives

Learning Objective 4

Determine business location preferences via multiple methods.

The selection of a location—a critical business success factor—is often a one-time event and is generally expensive to change. Therefore, familiarizing yourself with some of the methods for evaluating location alternatives is good practice. These methods range from simple and inexpensive to highly sophisticated and costly. The expense of selecting the profit-maximizing location for your business is an investment in its future success.

New business owners commonly opt for the simplest method of site selection: *Go with the one you know.* Although this is a more intuitive method than the others, it can be effective. For a lifestyle business, one that draws from a limited local area or one where physical location is less critical, such an approach may produce solid results. When you live and/or work in an area, you become familiar with the demographics, traffic patterns, and existing businesses through daily observation. However, it is risky to assume that your perceptions will be entirely accurate. This method is best used as one consideration, to be paired up with objective research.

factor-rating method
location-selection approach whereby decision criteria are prioritized and weighted to eliminate subjectivity.

Another common technique for location analysis is the **factor-rating method**, whereby decision criteria are prioritized and weighted to eliminate subjective features. This method incorporates quantitative and qualitative considerations. The factor-rating method can be employed for any type of business and can include as many or as few factors as desired, in six basic steps:

1. Develop a list of critical success factors.
2. Determine the weight of each factor according to its relative importance.
3. Create a measurement scale for the factors.
4. Score each proposed location for each factor (best if done by a team) according to the scale.

Global Impact . . .

Disney Selects a European Site[2]

Site selection can create magic when done well. It can also ruin dreams when done poorly. Walt Disney planned to add a European property when he looked to the future of his company. In the 1980s, the Disney organization began a search with approximately 1,200 potential locations for its proposed Euro Disney Resort. Ultimately the list was reduced to two sites in Spain and two in France. The governments offered incentives for locating in each, and Disney executives decided on one in France. The Euro Disney Resort opened to much fanfare in 1992 in a location about 20 miles from Paris in Marne-la-Vallée.

The initial reception for the French location was disappointing for Disney, which expected a resounding success from the opening day. However, some Europeans thought of Disneyland as an American cultural intrusion, and the term "euro" is associated primarily with money and business. Yet, in the years since EuroDisney was renamed Disneyland Paris Resort and repositioned, it has gained considerable ground.

[2]Adapted from Andrew Lainsbury, *Once Upon an American Dream: The Story of Euro Disneyland*, University Press of Kansas, 2000.

© Photoshot Holdings Ltd/ Alamy

5. Multiply the factor weight by the factor score for each factor in each location.
6. Use the sum of these weighted factors for the locations, to compare them and make a location recommendation/decision.[3]

Exhibit 18-1 shows factor rating for a proposed electric car manufacturing plant. In 2009, an innovative, federally funded, and venture-backed company faced a location decision that included the entire country. After management decided to consider only locations where automotive plants had recently closed, the decision alternatives rapidly narrowed. Although the factor-rating criteria shown are highly speculative, the firm made a commitment to a location in Delaware rather than in the heart of car country in the Midwest.

One tool that is available to entrepreneurs at all stages is geographic information systems (GIS). These include demographic data; extensive maps and topographic information; and major transportation routes, health care facilities, and the like. After you have identified the factors that are important to your business, you can use a GIS system to discover potential profit-maximizing locations.

Exhibit 18-1 *Factor Ratings for a Hybrid Automobile Manufacturing Plant*					
Critical Success Factors	**Weight**	**Scores (out of 10)**		**Weighted Scores**	
		Michigan	**Delaware**	**Michigan**	**Delaware**
Labor (United Auto Workers Union)/Management Relations	0.25	5	10	1.25	2.50
Readiness of Facility	0.20	7	9	1.40	1.80
Proximity to Customers	0.20	7	7	1.40	1.40
Tax and Financial Incentives	0.20	10	6	2.00	1.20
Proximity to an Atlantic Port	0.15	3	10	0.45	1.50
Total	1.00			6.50	**8.40**

[3]Jay Heizer and Barry Render, *Operations Management*, 10th ed., Upper Saddle River, NJ: Prentice Hall, 2011, p. 253.

Larger companies often develop customized GIS systems tailored to their particular location requirements. Franchisors such as Dunkin' Donuts can use GIS to target areas for new stores. For entrepreneurs with fewer resources, Microsoft MapPoint software may be well suited. MapPoint includes demographics and maps that can be combined with firm-specific or industry data. **Figure 18-2** shows a GIS map for Prince William County, Virginia.

A decidedly more low-tech approach to assessing locations is to gather demographic, psychographic, and geographic data and information on competitors in order to create lists of location options. The U.S. Census Bureau can provide substantial data to inform your decision. Maps and traffic data can be added to the mix, as can trade-association information. For example, if the jewelers' trade association reports that customers will travel two miles to purchase jewelry, you can identify possible locations with sufficient people to sustain your business. Then, you can narrow your choice by assessing the competitive environment (both clustering in "jewelers' row" and stand-alone should be considered), weighing personal preferences, site availability in the potential location, traffic counts, and other factors that would contribute to success.

Figure 18-3 shows a drawing of the population of the United States. If you would like a business location within 10 miles of a population area of 200,000 or greater, this drawing will provide an excellent visual guide. **Figure 18-4** shows a census map of Santa Fe, New Mexico, with concentric circles drawn from the heart of its highest-income census tract, to show

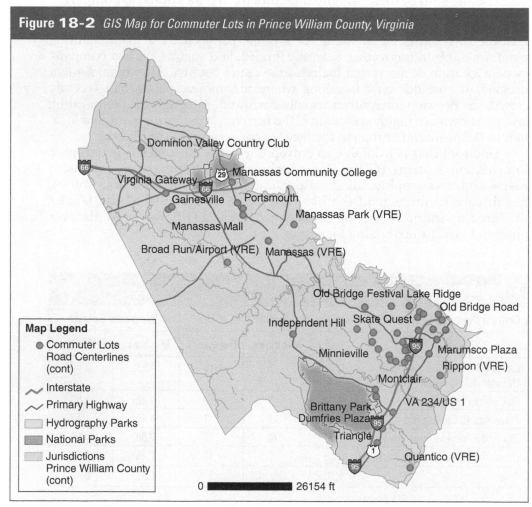

Figure 18-2 *GIS Map for Commuter Lots in Prince William County, Virginia*

Dominion Valley Country Club

66

Manassas Community College

29

Virginia Gateway
Gainesville
66
Portsmouth

Manassas Park (VRE)

Manassas Mall

Broad Run/Airport (VRE)   Manassas (VRE)

Old Bridge Festival Lake Ridge

Old Bridge Road

Independent Hill   Skate Quest

Minnieville

95

Marumsco Plaza

Rippon (VRE)

Montclair

VA 234/US 1

Brittany Park
Dumfries Plaza
95
Triangle
1

Quantico (VRE)

95

Map Legend
- Commuter Lots
  Road Centerlines (cont)
- Interstate
- Primary Highway
- Hydrography Parks
- National Parks
- Jurisdictions
  Prince William County (cont)

0 ▬▬▬▬▬▬▬ 26154 ft

Source: © 2010 Prince William County; aerial imagery © 2009 Commonwealth of Virginia.

Figure 18-3 *Population of the United States*

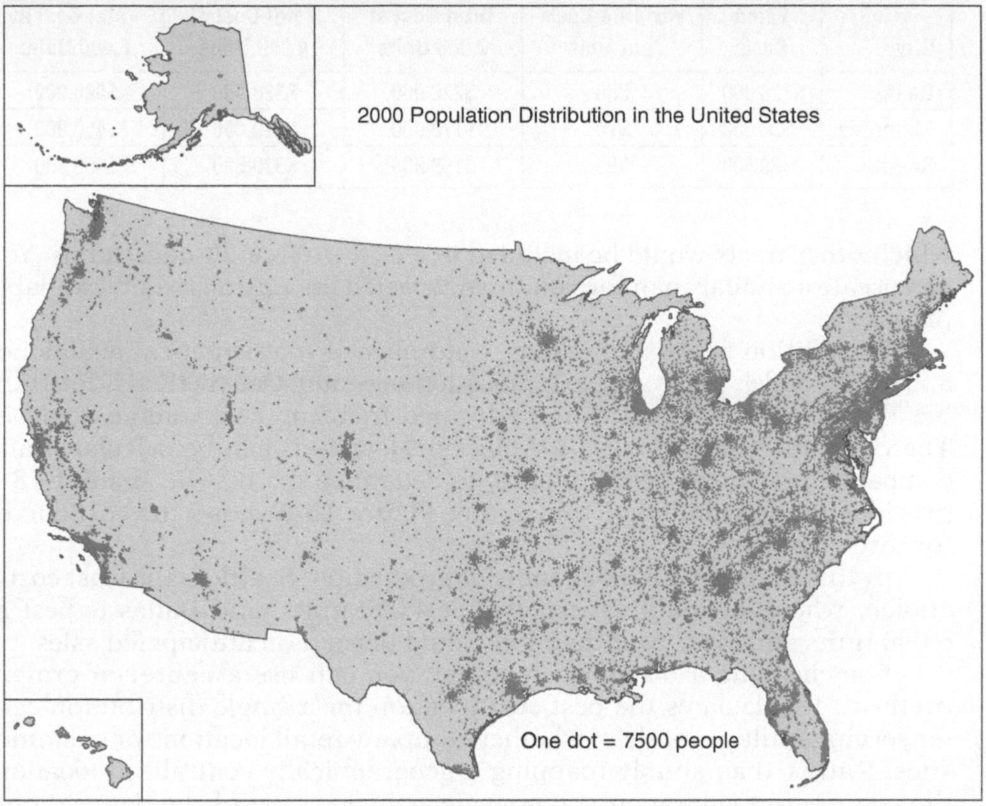

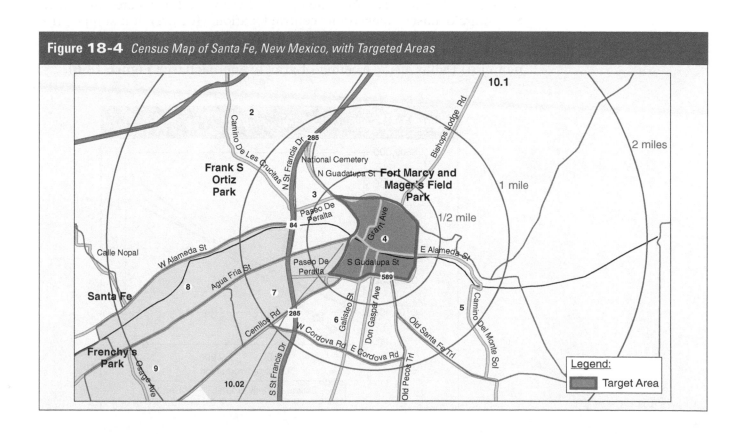

2000 Population Distribution in the United States

One dot = 7500 people

Source: From the U.S. Census at http://www.census.gov.

Figure 18-4 *Census Map of Santa Fe, New Mexico, with Targeted Areas*

Exhibit 18-2 *Location Breakeven Analysis*

City	Fixed Costs	Variable Costs per Unit	Total Cost at 2,000 Units	Total Cost at 4,000 Units	Total Cost at 6,000 Units
Dallas	$120,000	$50	$220,000	$320,000	**$420,000**
Memphis	$30,000	$70	$170,000	**$310,000**	$450,000
Seattle	$9,500	$80	**$169,500**	$329,500	$489,500

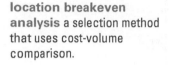

location breakeven analysis a selection method that uses cost-volume comparison.

which other tracts would be included in a 2-, 5-, 10-, or 20-mile radius. You can create a similar map for your own targeted area using readily available programs.

In addition to these methods, a number of mathematical techniques and other models are available for location selection. One method is **location breakeven analysis**, which is performed by using cost-volume analysis. The fixed and variable costs for different locations can be calculated and compared, particularly using graphs, to determine the best fit. **Exhibit 18-2** provides the calculation of values, and **Figure 18-5** shows the cost curves for three locations.

In this example, for 2,000 units of production, Seattle is the least costly choice, whereas Memphis is better at 4,000 units, and Dallas is best at 6,000 units and over. Your decision would depend on anticipated sales.

center-of-gravity method an approach that calculates the best cost location for a distribution center serving multiple sites.

For choosing a distribution center, you can use a **center-of-gravity method**. It calculates the best cost location for a single distribution center serving multiple outlets, whether company retail locations or customer sites. Rather than simply mapping a geographically centralized location, the center-of-gravity approach considers the location of the destinations, quantities of product to be shipped to each, the frequency of delivery, and cost of delivery. For example, a distributor in Texas selling to customers in Dallas, Houston, San Antonio, and El Paso would be located in or near San Angelo, based solely on its central location. However, if it shipped five times as much product to Dallas as to any of the other areas and very low volumes at infrequent intervals to El Paso, the company should be located nearer to Dallas, using a center-of-gravity approach (see **Figure 18-6**).

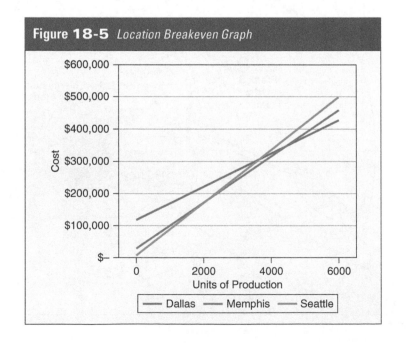

Figure 18-5 *Location Breakeven Graph*

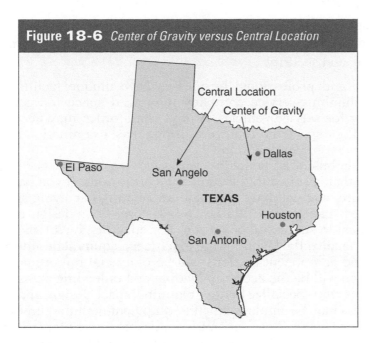

Figure 18-6 *Center of Gravity versus Central Location*

Facilities Design and Layout

The geographic location and suitability of business facilities matter greatly. You may have seen signs from real estate companies stating, "Will build to suit." This means that they will put up a structure for your particular business. A purpose-built edifice is necessary for certain businesses, such as restaurants or hotels. Other buildings may be constructed for general purposes and outfitted for a specific business through supplemental work. If a building is leased, these changes to adapt an existing structure are called **leasehold improvements**.

The type and size of facility, as well as other physical requirements, will depend on the type of business you are operating. For manufacturing, warehousing, and distribution firms, key considerations include:

- capacity for efficient movement of materials, equipment, and people (floor space and ceiling height will matter);
- flexibility to adapt to changing business requirements;
- loading docks and vehicle access for deliveries and outbound shipments;
- an environment conducive to work requirements (natural light, appearance, and the like);
- the ability to include requisite controls, such as regulation of temperature and humidity and cleaning rooms;
- parking for commercial and employee vehicles, as well as spaces for visitors (including those with special accessibility needs);
- adequate utility services to the building (including power, water, and telecommunications); and
- security and safety.

Retail facilities must meet such business requirements as:

- appropriate selling area and configuration of that space;
- permission to complete necessary leasehold improvements or improvements to be made by landlord;
- space for offices, storage, restrooms, deliveries, and other special needs;

◀ **Learning Objective 5**
Explore the design of facilities and their layouts.

leasehold improvements
changes made to adapt a rented property for a particular business.

- signage for rules/regulations;
- parking that is adequate for the anticipated customer volume; and
- lighting and security.

Service and professional businesses have unique facilities requirements. A plumbing-service company may need space for parts storage and parking for service vehicles. A physician's office may need the same amount of floor space but require waiting areas, examination rooms, and safe, convenient patient parking.

Whatever business and facility you decide on, you will need to create a work space that is suited to the company's operations. If you have a home-based venture, you will have to create an area in your living space where your business can operate. With a retail store, floor design and storage will be critical to successful operation. For a factory, repair shop, or other production facility, the layout of the machinery, equipment, inventory, raw material, and component sections will be of crucial importance. Another consideration will be the access to loading and unloading areas. There are professionals who specialize in floor planning, space design, and work flow. Some of these may be employed by the equipment manufacturers and landlords who want you as a customer. Do not hesitate to ask for free services in these matters. **Figure 18-7** shows the layout of a mattress factory.

Manufacturing layouts can be categorized as **product layouts**, **process layouts**, and **fixed-position layouts**. If a product is made through a continuous process, a mass-production or product layout is likely to be best. For example, an automobile assembly line is a product layout. When common processes are used on varied products, a process, or "functional, layout may work well. For example, a layout with departments (or shops), such as a faucet-manufacturing plant, with casting, grinding, polishing, plating, packaging, and other divisions, is a process layout. A fixed-position layout is appropriate for the production of very large items that are either difficult to move or are designed to stay in place. In this case, the materials and production teams are brought to a single location. Commercial and residential construction and yacht building are examples of fixed-position layouts, as is some hand-made furniture production, like that which is accomplished at Gat Creek Furniture, a case study from Chapter 17.

Store layout is a particularly important part of a retail business's marketing and revenue-generation operations. The exterior of the store, including window displays and signage, can attract or repel customers. Even the cleanliness of the windows sends a message.

In-store layout should be designed to entice customers to make purchases, preferably spending more than they had initially planned. Retail stores often place new items or signature products at the front, with sale

product layout mass-production design appropriate for continuous fabrication processes.

process layout functional arrangement that works well where there are common processes.

fixed-position layout used for the production of large objects, where materials and teams are brought to a single location, as in manufactured housing.

JG Photography/Alamy Images

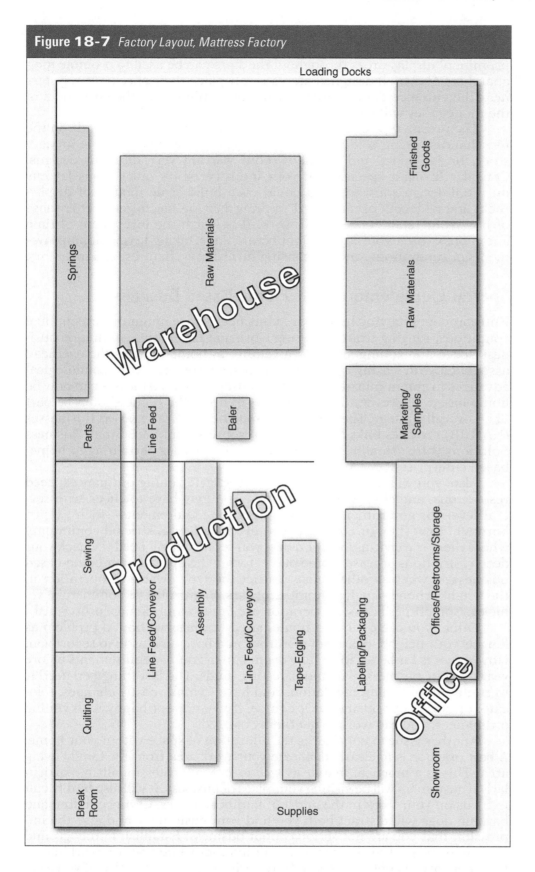

Figure 18-7 *Factory Layout, Mattress Factory*

goods toward the rear or against the walls, thereby compelling customers to pass by a variety of potentially enticing items. "End-caps" and other prominent display areas throughout the store can be used to promote merchandise. Also, well-designed stores rarely place their check-out registers near the entrance doors, thereby avoiding reminders to the customers of the money they will be spending.

The precise type of layout that is best for a retail store depends on the merchandise being sold and the shopping experience desired. A grocery store, bridal salon, and car showroom warrant very different designs. Consider hiring a specialist in your industry, or try out various layouts on retail-design software. You could even build scale models of display racks and tables out of cardboard, or draw them online, to get a better sense of how your retail concept will work. It is worth the investment of time and money to get your layout right before undertaking leasehold improvements or renovations, and purchasing furnishings, fixtures, and inventory.

Special Considerations for Home-Based Businesses

Learning Objective 6

Recognize the special considerations for home-based businesses.

Entrepreneurs starting home-based businesses face numerous exceptional conditions, ranging from allocating work and family time to unique business space and zoning. Starting a venture at home reduces the overhead associated with leasing or purchasing a separate site. With technological advances in communications and computing, many businesses can now be home-based. However, the decision to set up in the home should be part of an overall strategy. The National Association of Home Based Businesses (NAHBB) provides links to numerous resources, and D&B Small Business Solutions (http://smallbusiness.dnb.com) has articles pertaining to home-based enterprises.

Also, you will need to thoroughly investigate zoning ordinances, deed restrictions, and civic association rules. You may have to check with several levels of government zoning offices for requirements—such as city, borough, township, or county. If you live in a deed-restricted community where there is a civic association or if you rent, you will need to check your deed restrictions or lease. Some places forbid the operation of home-based businesses, whereas others may restrict the type or size of operation in the neighborhood—such as number of cars, foot traffic, or commercial vehicles. Sometimes hours of operation are limited and signage proscribed.

Often, you can operate a home-based business without a problem as long as your neighbors are not disturbed and have no reason to report you. However, it is far better to be fully cognizant of zoning requirements before writing your business plan and investing funds. The last thing you need is to run afoul of zoning regulations and have to make costly changes, relocate, or close your business. Of course, if you are not happy with zoning ordinances, you can work to get them changed.

Another issue to consider is the allocation of space within your home. A best practice is to clearly delineate your work area from the family living area. This is a practical matter as well as one of professionalism, particularly if customers will be visiting your place of business. It will also be difficult to focus on your work in the midst of family activities. Crying children and barking dogs will distract both you and your customers, and give the impression that you are not serious about business. Establish family ground rules with respect to the way you will interact while you are working, so that there aren't conflicts caused by differing expectations. Also, if you elect to have a home-based business, furnish it appropriately, and get a separate telephone line. A separate entrance for customers is also desirable.

space percentage the portion of the home used for business versus living space.

Another consideration is **space percentage**, the portion of your home used for business, versus your living area. This can affect the type of zoning

There are specific steps in the recruiting process:

1. ***Defining the job.*** First, think about what you need this employee to do and what kinds of skills are needed to create a job profile, and then develop a position description. The **job profile** identifies the knowledge, skills, and abilities required to perform the specific tasks of the job. The **position description** includes the knowledge, skills, and abilities from the job profile, as well as what the reporting and working relationships and goals and objectives of the position will be. It should also contain a description of the physical requirements and special working conditions of the position (for example: lifting, bending, walking, etc.). Prioritize the list of key requirements that you will develop with those who will work with the new hire. Be certain to designate specific experience, qualifications, characteristics, and traits that will be required. Also, decide on the wage or salary range that fits your budget before recruiting.

2. ***Posting and advertising the job.*** Determine how people will find out about the position. Are there potential internal candidates? Will you place an ad in a newspaper, run online ads, or solicit employee referrals? Finding good employees has become much easier with the advent of online job-listing services such as Indeed (*http://www.indeed.com*) and Monster.com (*http://www.monster.com*), as well as industry-specific sites, which are often managed by trade and professional associations.

3. ***Screening resumes and/or applications.*** A resume is a summary of an individual's education and work experience. Ask interested parties to send their resumes. Some online services permit you to screen resumes using keywords that are important to your search. Other times, you might have an individual or committee review applicants against basic requirements. You may have a secondary review to narrow the search to the top three to five candidates, whom you will then interview.

4. ***Assessing skills.*** Identify pertinent skills and determine ways to assess them. For example, if a new employee is supposed to write grants, create a brief scenario and ask the applicant to create a document according to your specifications. For an administrative

job profile identification of the knowledge, skills, and abilities required to perform the specific tasks of an employment position.

position description the explanation of the knowledge, skills, and abilities of a job profile, as well as the position's reporting and working relationships, plus its goals and objectives.

Managers conducting a panel interview
(Cathy Yeulet/Thinkstock)

staff member, typing proficiency and skills in written communications and editing may be required and can be tested. If a job requires measurement and math skills, both can be evaluated easily. It is far better to eliminate unqualified applicants early in the process rather than waste their time and yours. The time to find out if a candidate is capable is before hiring.

It is critical to use the same process (such as a typing test) at the same stage in the interview for all applicants to guard against the appearance of discrimination, especially vis-à-vis "protected classes." For example, if a typing test is given to administrative job applicants, it should be given to all applicants at the same point in the process (usually prior to the job interview). It is also important to ensure that the assessment-instrument design could not be perceived as discriminatory. It is best to use instruments that have already been validated. Instruments that are not already tested are potentially dangerous because a protected-class applicant that is not hired because of a test score might have a legitimate case for legal action.

5. *Interviewing candidates.* Based on the resumes you receive, select several individuals to interview. Prepare an **interview guide**, a document to assist in developing questions regarding an applicant's knowledge, skills, abilities, and interests. Determine who will interview the candidates and whether the interviews will be performed one-on-one or by a panel. Many books, articles, and online resources can guide you in creating a **behavioral interview**, which is designed to determine the fit of a prospective employee with the requirements of the position, using prior-experience examples. Remember, the candidate should be provided with the interview schedule in advance. **Exhibit 19-1** suggests the topics to cover in an interview. **Exhibit 19-2** provides some sample interview questions.

6. *Checking references.* Ask the candidates who interest you to provide at least three references from previous employers or others who could tell you about their character and work performance. Check the references. Create a few questions that are pertinent to the job being filled and related career paths. Include questions about how the candidate and his or her references know each other. One question that often provides critical insight from former coworkers, managers/supervisors, and others is, "Would you rehire this person?" Some employers will only provide confirmation of former employees' dates of employment, so you might need to request additional references. Reference-check forms should be consistent and ask the same questions for each candidate being considered for a position.

Some search firms and employers request an extensive list of references. For example, Diversified Search, a top executive search

interview guide a document to assist in question development regarding an individual's knowledge, skills, abilities, and interests.

behavioral interview dialogue designed to determine the fit of a prospective employee with the requirements of a position, using prior-experience examples.

Exhibit 19-1 *Examples of Competencies that May Be Included in Job Interviews*

- General questions on skills and interests
- Teamwork
- Problem solving
- Communications
- Productivity/time management
- Customer service (internal or external customers)
- Interpersonal

Exhibit 19-2 *Sample Interview Questions*

General

- Could you share with us a recent accomplishment of which you are proud?
- What are your qualifications in this area of expertise; i.e., what skills do you have that make you the best candidate for this position? Discuss any special training you have had (on-the-job, at college, continuing education, seminars, reading, etc.) and related work experience.
- Tell us about a personal or career goal that you have accomplished and why it was important to you.
- Why should we hire *you*?
- If you were offered this position, when would you be available to start?
- Tell us anything else you would like us to know about you that will aid us in making our decision.
- What questions would you like to ask us?

Teamwork

- How do you think the people you work with would describe you?
- Tell us about the most effective contribution you have made as part of a task group or special-project team.
- When groups work together, conflicts often emerge. Tell us about a time that conflict occurred in one of your work groups and what you did about it.

Problem Solving

- What was one of the toughest problems you ever solved? What steps did you take to solve it?
- How do you analyze the different options to determine which is the best alternative? Give an example of when you have done this.

Communications

- Describe a time when you were able to overcome a communication barrier.
- Give an example of how you consider your audience prior to communicating. What factors influence your communication style?

Productivity/Time Management

- When you have a lot of work to do, how do you get it all done? Give us an example.
- Describe a time you identified a barrier to your (and/or others') productivity and what you did about it.
- How do you determine what amount of time is reasonable to complete a task? Please give an example.

Customer Service

- We all have customers or clients. Who are your clients and how do you identify them?
- Tell us about a time when you went out of your way to give great service to a customer.
- Tell us about a time when you had trouble dealing with a difficult or demanding customer. How did you handle this?

Interpersonal

- Describe what you see as your strengths related to this job/position. Describe what you see as your weaknesses related to this job/position.
- Describe how you prefer to be managed, and the best relationship you've had with a previous boss/supervisor.
- What kind of people do you find most difficult to work with? Give an example of a situation where you had difficulties dealing with someone different from yourself. How did you handle it?
- What do you do when you know you are right and your manager disagrees with you? Give an example of this happening in your career.
- Describe a difficult time you have had dealing with an employee, customer, client, or coworker. Why was it difficult? How did you handle it? What was the outcome?
- Describe a situation you wish that you had handled differently, based on the outcome. What would you change if faced with a similar situation?

Source: Adapted from the Society for Human Resource Management, http://www.shrm.org (accessed January 2, 2010).

firm in Philadelphia, routinely requests 10 references and completes 30-minute or longer interviews with each of them. By the time the recruiter completes the reference-checking process, a comprehensive picture of the candidate has emerged. Such an extensive process is reserved for the finalists in top-executive-level quests, but could be applied to whatever level you might deem it helpful. Requesting so many references offers information in and of itself. Some candidates can send the complete list virtually immediately, whereas others simply vanish at that point. One human resources professional tells the story of calling several references provided by a candidate, who looked excellent on paper and interviewed like a dream. Each and every reference directly told her to avoid hiring him at all costs. This reinforces the importance of checking references.

You also may want to call previous employers and interview each supervisor (be sure to have a release signed by the applicant). By the time this process is complete, you will have a better picture of the candidate. This vetting process is time-consuming, but it can prevent considerable issues later. Consider the case of a small business that had found an ideal marketing manager, until it made reference checks and was repeatedly told to stay away from that individual for both legal and ethical reasons.

Whether you request a few or many references, be sure to contact them and ask sound, well-thought-out questions.

7. *Negotiating compensation.* You and the candidate you choose will negotiate how much you will pay as well as any benefits the job includes, such as paid vacation, sick leave, and health insurance. You should have a clearly defined pay range for each position and stay within it. Don't fall in love with a candidate you just cannot afford. However, you also should be realistic about the compensation package you are offering. Benchmark your total package against that of other potential employers.

Recently, an executive found himself in an untenable position. He had begun a search to fill a critical leadership role, formed a search committee, advertised in professional journals and at conferences, had extensive two-day interview schedules for five finalists, received two recommendations from the committee, and threw out the search. He decided he needed a more experienced candidate and insisted on a second search. Committee members were outraged. They had found fully qualified candidates based on the position description, the charge given to them, and the salary available. Some of the committee members participated in a second-round search, eventually making an offer to a candidate satisfactory to their manager. The candidate declined the offer. Again, the committee members conducted a search, with particular weight placed on meeting individuals at an annual professional conference. Round three also fell flat because the salary to be offered was $25,000 to $35,000, too low to attract ideal candidates. The position remained vacant for almost two years while the search dragged on; the compensation issue stood in the way, the search committee was frustrated, and the responsibilities of the job went unfulfilled.

job offer letter a formal written invitation extended by an employer to a candidate selected for hiring that states basic employment terms—such as the position offered, starting date, salary, and so forth.

8. *Hiring.* After negotiating compensation, you will have additional work to complete before the new employee's start date. These undertakings include background checks, drug testing, offer letters, and physicals. The **job offer letter** is a formal, written invitation extended by an employer to a candidate that states basic employment

terms—the position offered, the start date, the salary, the benefits start date, and other pertinent informa- tion. Employers typically have the candidate sign and return the letter to indicate acceptance and an under- standing of what is being offered. A physical examina- tion may be required; this must be performed after the offer has been accepted but prior to the start date.

The nature and extent of a background check (including reference checking) will depend on the spe- cific position. A basic background check, a criminal background check, and drug testing is good practice. The $50 or so investment in a criminal background check could save thousands of dollars. Don't be guilty of negligent hiring because you ignore this precau- tion. A rural taxi service recently went out of business after the bad publicity generated by the arrest of one of its drivers on charges of assaulting an elderly pas- senger. The driver had a history of assaulting older women, and the company was held liable for putting him in a position in which he had the opportunity to commit another crime. In addition to criminal back- ground checks, you may also want to examine official copies of college transcripts or high school diplomas, and be sure to check previous employment history— the positions held and dates of employment. If the job requires driving, a check with the Department of Motor Vehicles will also be appropriate.

Creatas/Thinkstock

Comply with all employment laws in carrying out these checks and investigations, getting signed release forms as required. Drug- test authorization and background-check release forms are typically provided as part of an employment-application package and should be completed prior to interviewing the candidate. Once you decide to hire someone, you will also have to complete an I-9 and tax and payroll forms. The I-9 form must be completed on the first day of hire, to ensure that the employee is legally authorized to work in the United States.

9. *Orientation.* This is the process of introducing the employee into the company, including its mission and its culture, and teaching him or her about the position. An employee manual that has passed legal review can save you a great deal of money and heartache. Orientation should be more than a brief talk about employee benefits, instructions to complete necessary forms, and a review of the employee handbook. Ideally, orientation is an extensive process of helping a new employee understand the structure of the organi- zation and its mission, getting to know other employees, and even circulating through various departments. Some companies require that all new hires spend some time in customer service as part of orientation. Retail organizations may have all employees work on the floor for a while, or as a cashier, to experience customer contact.

More on Interviews

Interviews should be carefully planned, so that they provide the data needed to assess accurately the quality of fit between the company's needs and the candidate's qualifications and suitability. A poorly planned inter- view can easily result in a bad fit and unhappiness for both the employer and employee. Interviews should consist of several components, which may be adapted according to the company culture. These could include:

- a welcome and icebreaker,
- formal interview, and
- informal interview.

Welcome and Icebreaker. Candidates are often nervous and self-conscious when they arrive for an in-person interview. Companies can create a welcoming environment by greeting the candidate warmly and professionally, offering to validate parking and/or reimburse expenses as appropriate, asking whether the candidate would like refreshments, and asking whether he or she might need to freshen up before the interview. If the candidate is early, offer a seat and some company information as reading material. The interviewer should not start later than expected. It is inconsiderate and will create an unfavorable impression of the company.

Once in the interview room, preferably a quiet conference room that is free of distractions rather than an individual office, the interviewer starts the process by making small talk to put the candidate at ease and then briefly provides an overview of the company and position.

Formal Interview. The interview itself should be thoughtfully prepared, to elicit the best information to assess a candidate. The inclusion of consistent core questions that address experiences and behaviors will help to increase objectivity and ease of comparison. This question bank should include formulations that:

- assess capacity for and interest in the requirements of the position.
- ask behavioral interview questions that include job-related situations and open-ended questions to better understand the candidate's prior performance; these can be an excellent indicator of future performance. The questions should elicit the situation, the action taken, and the results achieved through each inquiry.
- bring out valuable information about the candidate's character and traits by using questions such as, "How do you . . .?" or "What would you . . .?"or "How do you feel when . . .?"
- encourage candidates to discuss their successes and failures. You will frequently learn more from the answers to how they acted in difficult situations than from those where they easily succeeded.
- give an opportunity for the candidate to express reasons for interest in the company and position.
- discuss geographic fit in terms of relocation, commuting distance, and the like.
- leave an opening for questions from the candidate.

During an interview, what a candidate doesn't say can be as important as what she says. As you take notes, pay attention to when the candidate avoids answering a question directly; these are clues to probe further.

Informal Interview. Whereas the formal interview (or series of interviews) is generally conducted in an office or conference room and may include executives, managers, and peers, informal interviews are typically peer-to-peer and conducted in a less "official" setting. For example, a casual lunch or coffee break with a few team members could reveal a lot about a candidate. Attention to the personal interaction, manners, and interest of a candidate can be illuminating. For example, the candidate may not show interest in what his prospective peers have to say or may be rude to wait staff in a restaurant.

Exhibit 19-3 *Interview Questions to Avoid*

Question(s)	Reason It Is Inappropriate
Where were you born? Are you a U.S. citizen?	Immigration Reform and Control Act prohibits discrimination on the basis of national origin.
How old are you?	Age Discrimination in Employment Act (ADEA) prohibits discrimination on the basis of age. If there is a minimum age, it is okay to ask whether the candidate is above it.
How much alcohol do you drink each day? Week? Month?	Okay to ask whether drugs or alcohol are used but not what sort or how often.
Have you ever been arrested?	Asking about convictions is legal, but an arrest is not a conviction; thus, this question is not acceptable.
Are you married?	Implied discrimination against a particular group (married or single people) is inappropriate.
Do you presently have children or plan to have them?	This is discrimination against women (sex discrimination) and violates Title VII.
Have you ever filed a lawsuit against an employer?	Multiple federal laws protect workers who file claims against their employers.
Do you have any physical disabilities or chronic illnesses that would prevent you from doing any part of your job?	Violates the Americans with Disabilities Act. However, you may ask, "Are you able to fulfill the physical requirements of this position with or without accommodation?"
Do you have mental health issues?	Violates the Americans with Disabilities Act (ADA).
What is your religion?	Violates Title VII of the Civil Rights Act of 1964.

As a cautionary note, you and your team must avoid asking questions that are overly personal or discriminatory. The easiest way to avoid problems with the Equal Employment Opportunity Commission (EEOC)—or equivalent departments in state governments—with respect to hiring practices is to focus on the knowledge, skills, abilities, and traits pertinent to the job. By concentrating on such questions, you will likely avoid peripheral ones that could get you in trouble. **Exhibit 19-3** provides some examples of questions to avoid and a brief explanation of why.

As you conduct the interview, recognize that it is somewhat like a date; both parties are trying to be attractive, while deciding whether they want to see each other again. As an entrepreneur, you want a candidate to be interested in pursuing the employment opportunity, and he or she wants you to make a job offer. Deciding to move forward should be a mutual decision based on a realistic assessment of fit and potential.

Conclude the interview process with a brief wrap-up that includes discussing the candidate's final questions and shoring up interest. Thank the candidate and apprise him or her of the time line and path forward. Once the candidate has departed, interviewers should compare notes. After all candidates have been seen, the interview team should convene and make a selection.

Growing Your Team

Once you decide to add employees to your company, it could take considerable time and effort to identify and hire the right talent. Even in times when the economy is weak and unemployment is high, qualified candidate pools may be thin. You may have to find individuals to bring into your organization, rather than waiting for them to come to you. The less known your company is or the more remote its location, the more likely will be the need to actively recruit candidates.

◀ **Learning Objective 3**
Know where and how to find qualified job candidates.

Companies plan and hire according to staffing requirements and budgets and typically use a combination of internal recruiters (employees), outside recruiters (retained search firms or contingency search firms), and Internet job-board postings. Certainly, advertising and online postings may uncover a strong candidate pool and eliminate the need for internal or external recruiters. However, from time to time, you may need to use either or both of them. If you are growing rapidly and are looking for a skilled, educated workforce or if you are hiring executives, recruitment may be the key to successful hiring. Some ways to find the employees that will fit your company include the following:

- *Campus recruiting.* Established companies visit college campuses to meet and scout students who are about to graduate. Firms in banking, consulting, accounting, consumer products, technology, health care, and other segments of the economy are major recruiters on campuses. Smaller employers may participate in job fairs and other recruitment events. Contact the career service offices of the colleges and universities to find out about recruitment and internship possibilities.

- *Executive or retained searches.* When companies need to hire a senior executive, they often engage in an executive, or retained, search. These top job openings are commonly not advertised; the process is frequently managed by a retained search firm (sometimes called "headhunters"). Executive search firms perform a full range of recruitment, screening, interviewing, and reference services. They work with clients to develop a detailed job profile and position description, and create a profile of the ideal candidate. In the end, though, companies will decide which candidates to hire. Retained search firms are paid for searches regardless of whether they fill the position. Contingency searches are much like retained searches, but compensation is based on finding a successful applicant.

Creating and Managing Organizational Culture

Learning Objective 4

Develop your organizational culture.

A primary role of the founding entrepreneur is to convey the vision for the company and to foster its culture. The *culture* of an organization is the shared beliefs, values, and attitudes—informally referred to as "how things

Step into the Shoes . . .

CEO Resources

Linda Resnick, founder and president of CEO Resources Inc., has built her firm on comprehensive, retained executive-search services—from the initial assessment of hiring needs to the integration of qualified executive talent into the new company.[2] CEO Resources, founded in 1990, fills a broad range of executive, general management, and top technological/scientific positions at an annual compensation level of more than $150,000. However, the firm also offers "a la carte services," such as creating hiring and recruiting strategies, defining executive positions, assessing team capabilities and candidate qualifications, completing

candidate due-diligence and 360° reference checks, and succession planning.

CEO Resources broke new ground as a retained executive search firm with a focus on entrepreneurial companies. Its primary markets are in technology, life sciences, and other innovative sectors. The geographic reach is centered on the mid-Atlantic region.

---

[2]CEO Resources Inc., accessed October 4, 2013, http://ceoresourcesinc.com.

are done around here." The culture of an entrepreneurial firm can be its competitive advantage. As a company grows and adds employees, one challenge for an entrepreneur is to maintain the culture or to guide its evolution strategically. When culture is explicit and strategic, it is more readily shared through orientation and storytelling. Hewlett-Packard was famously recognized for stories told about its cofounder, David Packard, that reinforced "the Hewlett-Packard way."

The culture you create for your business should be a strategic translation of your vision and mission into norms, values, and behaviors. It should combine the best practices in business with the type of work environment you want. Your business will reflect the messages you send. Consciously or not, employees take their cues from their managers. What you say and do (or don't say or do) telegraphs messages to your team.

Culture is not an isolated aspect of your business, rather a combination of its parts. Company culture incorporates qualities of integrity; diversity; concern for society, community, employees, and customers; quality of products and/or services; and mission. For many companies today, this includes a focus on a balance between work and family life and the need for a positive, enjoyable environment.

Organizational culture is sometimes located in the continuum between the entrepreneurial and the administrative. Firms of most any size can be placed somewhere within these parameters, although it becomes increasingly difficult to operate effectively in an informal, entrepreneurial style as a firm adds employees. A company's culture is made clear through a multitude of words and actions. The type of culture you create is a choice you make, reinforce, and revise on a continuous basis. **Exhibit 19-4** identifies cultural clues, large and small. Consider the messages they send, and which of them you would want to incorporate into your business's culture.

Determining Organizational Structure

As you create and grow your company, you will change its organizational structure for your evolving requirements. Initially, you may be a one-person band, handling all responsibilities yourself. Or you may have a founding team that is a centralized locus of control, with team members serving in multiple roles. With growth will come a need for specialization, delegation, supervision, and management. A relatively "flat" organization may work with few employees and ready communications; as the number of employees changes, so must the organizational structure. One of the most difficult transitions for founding entrepreneurs is often from entrepreneur to entrepreneurial manager—a critical success factor for company growth.

A number of organizational structures may be viable for emerging firms. The evolutionary process for a business involves moving from one stage of maturity and structure to another. This process is not defined by time. It is not strictly defined by the number of employees, either. However, communications, control, and coordination are primary drivers. With emerging structural changes, companies often evolve from simple **line organizations**, in which each person reports to one supervisor, to **line and staff organizations** that also include specialists such as attorneys who assist in the management. Managerial **spans of control**, or the number of direct reports, become more defined, and the **chain of command**, or hierarchy of reporting and communications, is more distinct.

◄ **Learning Objective 5**
Determine your organizational structure.

line organization a business structure in which each person reports to a single supervisor.

line and staff organization a business structure that includes the line organization, plus staff specialists (such as attorneys) who assist management.

span of control the number of direct reports for a manager or supervisor.

chain of command hierarchy of reporting and communications.

Exhibit 19-4 *Selected Aspects of Organizational Culture Communications*

Structure and Hierarchy	
Positive, upbeat, affirming	Doom-and-gloom, mean-spirited, sarcastic, teasing, cursing
Information-sharing, including financial performance	Information held closely, with sharing on a need-to-know basis
Employees contribute ideas and input, which is valued	Employees may be heard but not listened to
Employees address one another as peers	Hierarchy reinforced through the use of formal titles and forms of address (i.e., Mr., Mrs., Dr.), or formal address for managers and informal address for others
Customers spoken about with respect and value	Customers ridiculed or spoken about as an inconvenience
Storytelling used as a way to share history and culture	History and culture communicated through orientation and indoctrination
Telephones answered promptly and in a polite and friendly manner	Telephones answered slowly or not at all and in a grudging or unfriendly manner
Face-to-face communication valued highly	Formal written communications valued and face-to-face communications avoided or discounted

Structure and Hierarchy	
Flat organization with few levels of supervision	Hierarchical organization with multiple layers and clear distinctions between them (i.e., everyone communicates with only those one level above or below, and their peers)
Individual and communal	Paternalistic
Quick discussion and task-focused decisions	Meetings, meetings, meetings
Empowerment	Single locus of control
Flexible work schedules	Punching a time clock or closely observed comings and goings
Telecommuting	Anchored to the office/plant
No offices or little distinction in work environments	Office or workspace laid out by rank
Common eating area/cafeteria	Executive dining room
Shared parking area—first come, first served	Reserved parking for select individuals
All employees initially trained in a common customer-contact role, such as customer service or point of sales	No common training experience
Employee input in performance review and goal setting	Manager or supervisor prepares performance reviews and sets goals
Shared dress code, as appropriate to work conditions	Executives, the "suits," dress distinctly differently from others

Other	
Egalitarian	Elitist
Equal treatment	Preferential treatment with respect to such things as punctuality, extended meals, family
Individual and team recognition	Individual performance valued most highly
Environmental concerns practiced (e.g., reducing carbon footprint, recycling, energy efficiency)	Lack of environmental concern, or active damage to the environment
Community involvement encouraged (e.g., paid volunteer time, United Way corporate campaign, charitable contributions, or product tie-ins)	Community involvement discouraged (i.e., charitable contributions and work-time volunteerism avoided)
Ethics, or the focus on doing the right things	Focus on profitability over ethics
Quality, or the focus on doing things right; meeting and exceeding standards	Focus on profitability over quality
Personal space, if any, reflects the employee	Sterile personal space
Fun, playful, positive work environment	Dour, dull, negative environment
Opportunities to fail as a positive	Failure is not an option
Trust	Distrust
Shared glory	Blame game
Clean, well-maintained physical environment	Poor maintenance and dirty physical environment
Family friendly—such as photos in offices, child care on site, maternity and parental leave, referral services for child and/or eldercare, children welcome at work in emergencies, telecommuting, sick days available for child illness	Unfriendly to families; parents act as if their families don't exist during working hours

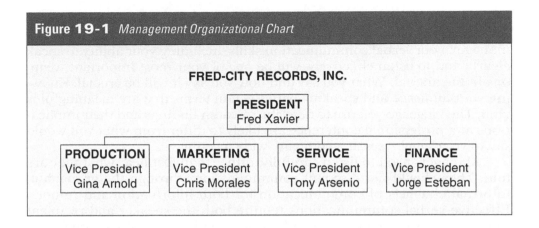

Figure 19-1 *Management Organizational Chart*

A management organizational chart for a typical small business might look like the example in **Figure 19-1**.

Whatever organizational structure you choose for your company at each stage of growth, it should be a strategic decision. Be careful not to create a hodgepodge of positions in a convoluted structure in order to keep people who do not fit.

Getting the Best Out of Your Employees

When you hire people, treat them fairly and with respect. Respect for individuals, diversity, and a balance of work and family will create a culture that affirms the value of employees. Employees who are valued are likely to want to go the extra mile for their employers. In addition to creating a strong, positive culture, many companies make their employees owners by giving them shares of corporate stock, thereby entitling them to a portion of the company profits, or offer them various incentives for positive performance.

Follow these basic guidelines to be a good to excellent employer:

- Get the right people. Taking the time and effort to fill positions with personnel who fit is at least half the battle. Know each employee's knowledge, skills, abilities, interests, and character traits.
- Provide a competitive salary and superior working conditions.
- Share your vision for the company and create an environment that encourages buy-in to your goals.
- Give employees incentives to work effectively. Ensure that the incentives match the company's goals and objectives and do not skew results.
- Empower employees by giving them control over their work.
- Provide career opportunities and training and development.
- Communicate expectations and goals clearly, and provide ongoing feedback and recognition.

Communicating Effectively

Much of the success of a manager depends on communications effectiveness. The same message may be interpreted in many ways, if not delivered clearly and understood as intended. As a manager, you will use written, verbal, and nonverbal communication. Which form is best will depend on individual circumstances.

Face-to-face communication is often optimal for individual discussion. The addition of nonverbal signs will add meaning and reinforcement. As a manager, your verbal communication skills, including your ability to speak clearly and to listen effectively, will be one of your most important weapons in the arsenal. What you say and how you say it will be crucial. Knowing your audience and speaking with them in terms that are meaningful is vital. The language you use to describe research findings and their implications at a professional conference are likely to differ from what you would say to your employees at a company-wide meeting.

grapevine an informal communications channel that transmits information and rumors.

Managers need to listen carefully, rather than just hear what they are told. They should not discount communications through the **grapevine**, informal channels of communication for both information and rumors. Effective verbal communications require both the speaker and recipient to be active participants. "It can be stated, with practically no qualification, that people in general do not know how to listen. They have ears that hear very well, but seldom have they acquired the necessary aural skills which would allow those ears to be used effectively for what is called *listening*."[3] Using **active listening** skills—focusing solely on what the other person is saying in a conversation and then validating understanding of the content and meaning—will significantly improve your verbal-communication effectiveness.

active listening the focus solely on what the other person is saying in a conversation and the subsequent validation of understanding the message's content and meaning.

Formal written communications, in the form of letters, faxes, memoranda, policies, plans, e-mails, and the like, will be particularly useful when a topic needs to be recorded, whether as a prelude to or follow-up of a conversation. Written communications can be used to clearly and concisely provide information, often to multiple individuals at once. With respect to human resources, written communications can be used to extend job offers, provide performance and disciplinary data, commend superior performance, or terminate employment—among many other topics.

Anything put into writing, including e-mail, should be something you would be willing to have examined in a court of law, so be careful what you write. Also, recognize that lack of clarity can cause problems in employee relations. More significant on a day-to-day basis is the fact that, with written communications, nonverbal signals are missing, so that the intended emotional import and underlying message may be open to misinterpretation.

With respect to what might be called informal written communications, such as quick e-mails to relay an anecdote or bit of information, electronic invitations, and tweets on Twitter.com, it is important to note that no communication is truly informal. Be careful to consider both clarity and potential secondary audiences. Don't write anything that you would not want the world to see—because it just might.

Human Resources Fundamentals

Learning Objective 6

Understand the functions of human resources management.

human resources the segment of a business that hires, trains, and develops a company's employees.

Human resources is the branch of a company that is responsible for staffing, training and development, compensation and benefits, employee relations, and organizational development. Human resources is commonly referred to as HR, human capital, casting (Disney's term), or personnel.

For a business just starting out, it may not be practical to have a director of human resources, and the founding entrepreneur will handle these tasks. A company will probably not need a full-time human resources professional until it has 20 or more employees.

---

[3]Ralph G. Nichols and Leonard A. Stevens, "Listening to People," *Harvard Business Review*, September–October 1957.

Step into the Shoes . . .
Matching Employers and Employees—Indeed

With over 100 million unique visitors per month, Indeed, a subsidiary of Recruit Holdings Co., Ltd., claims the top spot among job sites on the Internet.[4] Founded in 2004 by Rony Kahan and Paul Forster, Indeed has offices in four U.S. cities and London and Dublin. The service covers some 50 nations and a multitude of languages.

Indeed is a pay-for-performance recruitment advertising network that provides free access to jobs from company Web sites and job boards. It consolidates available openings into a single meta-search for job seekers. Employers pay for the service when job seekers click on job openings.

Prior to founding Indeed, Kahan and Forster were successful cofounders of jobsinthemoney.com, a site for financial professionals. They sold it to Financial News in 2003 and founded Indeed a year later.

---

[4]Indeed.com, accessed October 4, 2013, http://www.indeed.com/intl/en/ourcompany.html.

Regardless of how many, once you have any employees, there will be human resources functions to be managed. For companies of sufficient size, each of the following areas might represent one or more full-time jobs in the HR department.

Compensation and Payroll

The compensation and payroll area addresses such issues as the level of wages and base salary, bonuses, sales commissions, stock grants, stock options, other forms of compensation, and the issuance of payroll and associated taxes (although payroll is often a finance department function). Along with the entrepreneur and top management, compensation and payroll addresses which employees will receive stock in the company, in what amounts, and under what terms. It analyzes how compensation ties into the overall strategy and finances of the business and how the company's compensation program compares to that of competitors. Human resources executives work closely with finance managers to answer questions about compensation and to set company policy.

Benefits

Full-time employees expect to be provided an array of paid benefits and opportunities to purchase discounted benefits, as part of their compensation package. Basics may include health insurance, life and accidental death and dismemberment insurance, paid holidays, vacation and sick time, and retirement savings plans. Other options may be tuition reimbursement, disability, and insurance discounts such as automobile, long-term care, and even pet health insurance. HR usually leads the process of selecting the benefits programs that the company will make available. It is common practice to provide employees with benefit options and to have them share in the cost of their benefits, particularly for insurance.

Organizational Development

The HR team plays a pivotal role in organizational development. The key components are

- *Organizational structure.* The HR department will help the founder, CEO, management team, and board of directors identify and analyze the pros and cons of different options, establish the appropriate organizational structure, and help manage transitions from one framework to another.

BizFacts

Many companies staff their human resources units using a ratio of one HR executive per 50 to 200 employees.

- *Employee retention.* Sometimes compensation alone is not sufficient to prevent an individual from being lured away to work for a competitor. Human resources develops employee-retention programs that help build morale, create mentoring opportunities, and provide professional development and other benefits to keep employees excited about staying. The cost of losing a skilled, valued employee is high in terms of impact on the company and coworkers and in terms of the cost of recruiting, hiring, and training a replacement.
- *Succession planning.* As employees are promoted, retire, or resign, it is important to have plans in place to fill their positions. This is particularly true for individuals in key leadership roles that are not easily replaced. When you promote your sales manager to vice president of sales, who will fill the vacancy? The HR department works with managers to find the best successor and makes succession plans for key executives, so that sudden changes are not devastating.

Education and Development

Even senior executives require professional-development education from time to time. Human resources managers develop employee training in-house and may use outside training providers. There are businesses that help companies train their sales teams. Leading institutions, such as the Wharton School and Harvard Business School, offer executive-education curricula.

Labor Law and HR Compliance

The United States has well-developed laws to protect the rights of employees. Everyone involved in hiring, firing, and managing people needs to be aware of the letter and the spirit of these laws, which are typically translated into policies by the HR and legal teams at a company. For example, laws forbid businesses from failing to hire or promote on the basis of age or race. It is illegal for employers to ask job candidates how old they are, whether they are married and/or have children, or where they are from. Companies can expose themselves to significant liability if they do not properly manage the process of hiring, rewarding, and terminating employees.

As the business grows and you hire employees, you will have to become familiar with the laws and tax issues affecting employment. You may choose to contact attorneys who specialize in labor law regarding the legality of your hiring process—including your job application and interview questions; employee manual; performance-appraisal process; compliance with antidiscrimination, fair labor, and other such laws; and firing and termination procedures. Some of the laws and tax issues of concern include:

payroll tax a deduction employers must make from their employees' pay and forward to the appropriate governmental entity.

- **Payroll tax** is a series of wage taxes based on earnings that are deducted from employees' pay. Your accountant can advise you in more detail when you get to this point, and you can find information on the IRS Web site (http://www.irs.gov), as well as those of state and local revenue departments. You will be responsible for contributing to Social Security, unemployment compensation, and other programs. Of particular importance are the withholding taxes that must be paid in a timely fashion, because the penalties for not doing so can be devastating.

- The **Equal Pay Act of 1963** requires employers to pay men and women the same amount for substantially equal work.

- The **Fair Labor Standards Act**, passed in 1938, requires that employees receive at least the federally mandated minimum wage. It also prohibits hiring anyone under the age of 16 full time. Also, minimum-wage information must be posted where it is visible.

- **Title VII of the Civil Rights Act of 1964** prohibits discrimination against applicants and employees on the basis of race or color, religion, sex, pregnancy, or national origin, including membership in a Native American tribe. It also prohibits harassment based on any of these protected characteristics and employer retaliation against those who assert their rights under the Act. This Act is enforced by the U.S. Equal Employment Opportunity Commission (EEOC).

- The **Age Discrimination in Employment Act (ADEA)** prohibits discrimination against and harassment of employees aged 40 or older. Employers may not retaliate against those who assert their rights under the Act. This Act is also enforced by the EEOC.

- The **Americans with Disabilities Act (ADA)** prohibits employers from discriminating against a person who has a disability or who is perceived to have a disability in any aspect of employment. It also prohibits refusal to hire or discrimination against someone related to or an associate of someone with a disability. ADA prohibits harassment and retaliation in these cases. This Act is enforced by the EEOC and the U.S. Department of Justice.

- The **Immigration Reform and Control Act of 1986 (IRCA)** prohibits employers from discriminating against applicants or employees on the basis of their citizenship or national origin. In addition, it affirms that it is illegal for employers to knowingly hire or retain in employment individuals who are not authorized to work in the United States. Employers must keep records that verify that all employees are authorized to work here.

Performance Management

You can maintain and build your team through appraisal and thorough follow-up. Although often dreaded, a **performance appraisal**, the formal process used to evaluate and support employee performance, can be valuable for both employees and employers. It is an opportunity to set goals, assess progress, identify opportunities for improvement, plan for individual growth and development, and provide performance feedback. Done poorly, the process is a waste of time and energy at best, and counterproductive at worst.

performance appraisal the formal process used to evaluate and support employees' work performance.

The keys to valuable performance appraisals are planning and consistency. Be clear about the purpose of appraisal and create a system for it. Nothing in the appraisal process should come as a surprise for anyone involved, if performance feedback is discussed routinely and course corrections are made throughout the year. Good channels of communication make the performance-appraisal process work more fluidly.

Performance appraisal is an opportunity to communicate goals, establish training and development needs, and provide feedback to increase productivity and employee retention. An effective process will also link performance to pay, which will help create a high-accomplishment culture in which superior performers earn higher pay increases than inferior ones. It also can help to protect a company against lawsuits by employees who have been fired, demoted, or not given a pay raise. Appraisals provide formal documentation for discussions on performance.

There are multiple methods of implementing performance appraisal, and these often vary according to the size and culture of an organization. Some companies have managers and supervisors review direct reports and provide feedback. Others have employees complete a self-appraisal and then have managers and supervisors put together reviews for discussion. Still others use feedback including impressions from the entire spectrum of staff—such as peers, direct reports, customers, and others—concerning a particular employee.

For some organizations, performance is broken down into key aspects of the job, typically based on the position description as well as annual goals and rated on a scale. A subset of these organizations provides descriptions of the meaning of each numeric value to create greater consistency in ratings. Generally, a brief statement of examples to support the rating is required. A condensed version of the supervisor/manager portion of a performance review form appears in **Exhibit 19-5**. If the employee does a self-appraisal, it will be similar. There are numerous variations on the forms used and the style of presentation. Consulting any of the many books on human resources or visiting the Society for Human Resource Management (http://www.shrm.org) should provide ample information.

The performance-review meeting should be structured to create an environment for discussion and support rather than debate and contention. It should be scheduled in advance and held in neutral territory, rather than in the office or workspace of either participant. The environment should be free of distractions and interruptions. The manager can begin with a brief overview of the purpose of the appraisal and its objectives. Then, the employee should provide a statement of his or her own performance, not a step-by-step reading of the self-appraisal, but a verbal synopsis. The next portion will be the planned performance appraisal from the manager. It should stay focused on the performance and avoid dilution. It should provide feedback and not be an item-by-item review of the form. An item-by-item review tends to lead to negotiation and/or confrontation. If there are performance problems, they should be discussed in terms of the gap between the actual performance and the goal. Remember, be careful to measure as per the agreed-upon goal, not some other standard. Once performance has been reviewed, a new action plan with goals and development objectives can be created. Wrap up with a summary of the positives, remarks on the next steps, and a thank-you.

development plan a document stating how an employee will attain specific performance goals.

If there are specific issues to be worked on to improve performance because of deficiencies noted during the review period, an additional plan may be needed. The manager and employee can create a **development plan**, which is a document stating how the employee will attain specific performance outcomes. The development plan includes action steps, such as any educational and professional development, milestones with dates, and any feedback that is required. This document is meant to be agreed on by both parties and should be signed.

Once the performance-appraisal process is complete, the manager or supervisor will continue to monitor employee progress. In addition, managers should evaluate their approach and methods of performance appraisal, identifying opportunities for improvement.

Exhibit 19-5 *Sample Performance Review Form—Supervisor/Manager Portion*

Name: _____   Date of Review: _____

Period Under Review: _____   Department: _____

Part A. Success Factors

Factors	Rating					Comments
I. KEY RESPONSIBILITIES FOR THIS POSITION						
Performs key responsibilities as articulated in the job description. *(insert each essential function from the position description)*	1	2	3	4	5	
II. CORE COMPETENCIES						
1. Inclusiveness (defined in greater detail)	1	2	3	4	5	
2. Problem solving / decision making	1	2	3	4	5	
3. Planning and organizing	1	2	3	4	5	
4. Communication	1	2	3	4	5	
5. Quality focus	1	2	3	4	5	
6. Leadership	1	2	3	4	5	
7. Teamwork	1	2	3	4	5	
8. Department-specific competency	1	2	3	4	5	

Part B. Last Period's Goals

Rate the progress made on each of the goals established at the beginning of the period and any new goals. Note any modifications to the original goals.

Goal	Rating					Comments
1. (specify as many goals as are appropriate for the employee)	1	2	3	4	5	
2.	1	2	3	4	5	
3.	1	2	3	4	5	

OVERALL RATING (based on Parts A and B)	1	2	3	4	5	

Part C. Next Period's Goals

Enter the performance goals for the next period to be evaluated.

1. Measure of success:
2. Measure of success:
3. Measure of success:

Progress toward meeting these goals will be reviewed at the time of the next evaluation.

Part D. Professional Development Plan

Signatures:

Employee: _____   Date: _____

My signature indicates that I have received a copy of this evaluation.
  _____ I would like to include comments from my self-assessment.

Manager/Supervisor Name:_____

Signature: _____   Date: _____

Department Manager Name: _____

Signature: _____   Date: _____

Human Resources Strategy

Strategic human resources departments will also identify ways to maximize the productivity and effectiveness of the overall organization through its HR practices.

- *Diversity.* Many leading companies—for example, Avon Products—have found that they better represent and understand their customer base by creating a more diverse workforce in terms of gender and ethnicity. This translates into increased sales and greater customer loyalty. Avon is known for having a diverse workforce, from the CEO to the sales-representative level, and uses the tagline, "The Company for Women."
- *Benchmarking.* For companies to be competitive, they must understand their own employee base and the skills and motivations of the employees of the companies with which they compete. Benchmarking is a process that lets companies compare themselves with their competitors. As an entrepreneur, ensure that your employees' skills keep pace with or are ahead of those of your competitors.
- *Retention.* It is paramount for companies to keep the employees who drive the business. HR strategy focuses on programs and benefits that keep employees engaged and motivated, to fulfill the company's mission.

Firing and Laying Off Employees

Sometimes you hire someone and it just does not work out, even after repeated attempts to fix the problems. If you have to let someone go, you should document the reasons as they occur. You can be sued for wrongful termination, or breach of contract, if an employee believes he or she was fired for no good reason. The rules for termination vary from state to state, so it is essential to know your state's laws.

- Protect your company from wrongful-termination claims by conducting regular employee-performance reviews. Use performance-improvement or development plans to give the employee an opportunity to fix those aspects of performance that are subpar.
- If an employee is violating rules, give notification in writing (and keep a copy for your records) and work on corrections as the problems arise, rather than waiting for a performance review. If performance continues to be unsatisfactory, and you have to let the employee go, you will have documentation that there were problems with his or her performance. Be very careful to document the problem, not to editorialize or speculate about the employee.

Sometimes you might have to lay off employees. They may have performed their jobs well, but you either no longer need their skills or cannot

Global Impact . . .

Human Resources Service Firms

Many companies, large and small, are dedicated to providing human resources services to corporate clients around the globe. Here is how some leading firms got started: Adecco was founded in 1957, when Henri-Ferdinand Lavanchy, an accountant at the time, was asked by a client to help him fill a position. Today, Adecco provides staffing services to 250,000 clients around the world. In 1969, Lester Korn and Richard Ferry started a recruitment firm with a $10,000 investment. Today, with over $650 million in revenue, Korn/Ferry International specializes in helping clients hire top executives, including CEOs. When companies have thousands of employees, the task of getting paychecks out twice a month can be daunting. Payroll provider Automatic Data Processing Inc. (ADP) cuts checks for over 50 million employees on behalf of its clients. ADP was started by Henry Taub in 1949, when he was 22. The company had eight clients and $2,000 in revenue in its first year.

afford to continue employing them. To minimize complications, if you can do so, offer employees **severance**, pay that is continued for a limited time as compensation for being let go, and make serious efforts to help them find new employment.

severance pay that is continued for a limited time to an employee who has left a company.

Chapter Summary

Now that you have studied this chapter, you can do the following:

1. Describe the basic tasks handled by managers.
   - Planning: strategic, tactical, and operational
   - Organizing
   - Leading
   - Controlling
2. Recruit your employees.
   - Define the job.
   - Post the job.
   - Screen resumes and/or applications.
   - Assess required skills.
   - Interview candidates.
   - Check references and other background information.
   - Negotiate compensation.
   - Hire a candidate.
   - Orient the new employee.
3. Know where and how to find qualified job candidates.
   - Advertising (internal and external)
   - Online postings
   - Campus recruiting
   - Executive search firms
4. Develop your organizational culture.
   - The culture of a company is the shared beliefs, values, and attitudes among employees.
   - The entrepreneur can strategically determine the culture.
   - Cultures vary, from entrepreneurial to administrative.
   - A multitude of cultural components are conveyed through words, actions, and structures.
5. Determine your organizational structure.
   - Structure evolves as the company grows and changes.
   - The transition from entrepreneur to entrepreneurial manager is often difficult.
   - Different organizational stages are related to the maturation of the company.
6. Understand the functions of human resources management.
   - Compensation and payroll
   - Benefits administration
   - Organizational development
   - Education and development
   - Labor law and HR compliance
   - Performance of appraisal and review
   - Human resources strategy
   - Firing and laying off employees

Key Terms

active listening, 596

behavioral interview, 586

chain of command, 593

development plan, 600

grapevine, 596

human resources, 596

interview guide, 586

job offer letter, 588

job profile, 585

line organization, 593

line and staff organization, 593

operational plan, 583

payroll tax, 598

performance appraisal, 599

position description, 585

recruitment, 584

severance, 603

span of control, 593

strategic plan, 583

tactical plan, 583

Entrepreneurship Portfolio

Critical Thinking Exercises

19-1. Will you be hiring employees during your first year of operations? If so, name their positions and describe the required qualifications, anticipated compensation, and their role in helping your business.

19-2. Would you prefer campus recruitment or executive searches for your business? Why? Explain with examples.

19-3. What kind of organizational structure would you prefer in your envisioned business? Why?

19-4. Is human resources management important for your organization? What training and development methods would you employ to make your people a source of sustained competitive advantage?

19-5. Why is establishing job profiles and position descriptions before recruiting important?

19-6. What are the benefits of a well-executed performance-appraisal process?

19-7. Describe the components of an organizational culture that you would find appealing.

19-8. What are the characteristics of an organizational culture that you would find unappealing?

Key Concept Questions

19-9. How old does someone have to be before he or she can work full time in the United States?

19-10. What is one kind of tax employers have to pay for employees?

19-11. Can you legally fire an employee if you have an argument about religion?

19-12. What is nonverbal communication? How can it impact overall communications? How can the loss of nonverbal cues affect e-mail, instant messaging, and other written communications?

19-13. What is an interview guide? What are the critical components of an interview guide?

19-14. What are the functions of management? Describe each briefly.

19-15. What are antidiscrimination laws? What protections do they include?

Application Exercises

19-16. What qualities and qualifications would you look for in employees for your business? List five and explain why they are the most important to you.

19-17. What would push you to fire an employee? List five reasons you believe would justify termination. Describe how you would handle the firing.

19-18. Visit a local bricks-and-mortar business (not a Web site) where you buy products or services. Go through your shopping experience as you normally would. Once you have left the place of business, describe its culture. Use the information in **Exhibit 19-4** to assist you.

Exploring Online

19-19. Visit the Web site for a U.S. state, or use another reliable source, to identify the antidiscrimination laws in that state. What form(s) of discrimination do they prohibit? When were they enacted? To which organizations (type and size) do they apply?

19-20. Search the Internet for two position descriptions from different businesses. Make a chart identifying which of the following are included: job title, job summary, duties to be performed, nature of supervision, and the job's relation to others in the company. How might each description be improved?

In Your Opinion

19-21. Discuss with a group: Should an employer be able to fire an employee if the latter is often ill? Before the discussion, prepare by searching the Internet to determine the legal issues that may be involved.

BizBuilder Business Plan Questions

After studying this chapter, you should be able to answer the following Business Plan Questions. The entire outline for the Business Plan is found in Appendix 2.

6.0 Management and Operations

6.1 Management Team

A. Create an organizational chart for your business.

B. Will you be hiring employees? If so, describe what their qualifications should be, what you intend to pay them, and how they will help your business.

C. How do you intend to pay yourself? Explain.

D. What will your policies toward employees be? How will you make your organization a positive and rewarding place to work?

If at First You Don't Succeed . . . Enablemart Learns a Valuable Lesson

Nick Tostenrude and Dennis Moulton founded Enablemart when they were freshmen at the University of Portland to bring rehabilitation software—developed by Dennis's father—to market. Founded in 1999, as Mindnautilus.com, and incorporated in 2000, Nick and Dennis soon discovered that their original business concept was not viable and switched to making computers that were accessible to people with disabilities. This became a niche market to be served by Enablemart, which began marketing assistive technologies in 2001. Enablemart (http://enablemart.com) grew to become the world leader in assistive technology, with 14 employees and $9 million in annual sales in the United States and a subsidiary in the United Kingdom (TechReady.co.uk), at the time of its acquisition by Manufacturers Resource Network in 2007.

The path from the dorm room to the boardroom was not always smooth. Creating an advisory board with numerous industry pioneers

Meeyoung Son/Alamy Images

went relatively well. However, Enablemart needed someone with credibility and access to capital. For Nick and Dennis, local entrepreneurial events provided networking opportunities and led to finding a candidate that Nick described: "We couldn't have asked for a better person to have in our corner." They found someone who was older, appeared to have experienced success as an entrepreneur, and had a passion for the work.

The next step was to secure an employment contract. The founders were pleased that the candidate offered to provide a contract he had used previously. The contract was daunting, but Nick and Dennis trusted their new colleague. Nick later wrote, "We were a bit thrown back, but this individual seemed trustworthy because, after all, he believed in our idea. So we signed the contract and celebrated hiring our new chairperson."

This new chairperson was active for a couple of months, helping to find an excellent CFO, and then he gradually stopped working and communicating with Nick and Dennis. Lawyers reviewed the employment contract and, after they stopped laughing at how ludicrous it was, they explained that the best thing to do was to avoid accomplishing the things that would trigger payouts to the chairman. The contract included giving him a percentage of stock with a nondilution clause and an option that permitted him to sell it to anyone he wanted at any time. Whenever they raised capital, he would receive substantial compensation. There was no way to hold the chairman accountable for poor performance because his job duties were so unclear. On top of all of these issues, rather than signing the agreement on behalf of the corporation, the founders had signed it personally.

Instead of continuing to pursue the high-growth strategy and raising significant capital as they had planned, Nick and Dennis again revised their game plan. They knew that investors would avoid them as long as the chairman's contract hung over them. After two years of a slow-growth strategy, fueled primarily with funds from friends and family, Enablemart bought out the contract for $20,000 and terminated the chairman's employment, ending the protracted agony of their first executive hiring experience.

Case Study Analysis

19-22. Enablemart's founders created a board of advisors early in the life of the company. How might they have taken advantage of the advisors' counsel when hiring their chairman?

19-23. Name at least three steps that Nick and Dennis could have taken to avoid the dreadful experience they had with their first executive hire.

19-24. What are the implications of signing an employment contract personally, rather than as a representative of a corporation?

19-25. Nick and Dennis sought legal counsel when their chairman simply stopped working, and they had to slow down their growth plans. Comment on how you think this affected them and the company.

Case Sources

Nick Tostenrude, "Turning 25¢ into $1: The Unique Advantages and Disadvantages of Being Young Entrepreneurs," in *Student Entrepreneurs: 14 Undergraduate All-Stars Tell Their Stories*, compiled by Michael McMyne and edited by Nicole Amare, Nashville: Premium Press America 2003.

In the early afternoon of June 20, 1992, as Roger Parks, the reservation manager of Casino Grande was packing his briefcase to go out of town to a hospitality association conference, Randolph Jackson, the general manager, called him into his office and the following conversation ensued.

Don Hammond/Alamy Images

Jackson: Damn it, Roger, didn't I tell you to talk to those two girls about getting to work on time? All they do around here is drink coffee. I guess I'm going to have to install martial law around here. They both recently got raises, too; who do they think they are, anyhow? You tell them in no uncertain terms that if they don't shape up, we'll give them the sack. We can still hire people who follow the rules.

Parks: Whoa, back! What's going on? What in the heck are you talking about?

Jackson: Don't pretend with me. You know just what I'm talking about. It's those two girls, Kane and Palumbo. I saw them come into the employee cafeteria this morning at 8:00 and they were still there when I left at 8:20 to come upstairs. They couldn't have gotten to their desks until 8:30 or later! Then, at 10:30 they were back down there for coffee; I saw them with my own eyes! They're just going to have to shape up. Other people have noticed as well. Why, Cooperider (housekeeping assistant manager) mentioned it just the other day. Why on earth didn't you talk with them like I told you to do?

Parks: Cool it, Randy. I did talk the whole thing over with Marshall, and she talked with the two women. She told me later that she had, and said the women had agreed to do better from then on.

Jackson: Posh, they aren't doing it! We just gave them salary increases, too. We gave them increases, and that's how they're showing their appreciation. I say, if they don't shape up we fire their butts. That Kane's a pain. She says she wants more responsibility, we give it to her, and a raise; and then she comes in late every morning and drinks coffee all day long.

Parks: Simmer down, Randy. You'll have to admit we don't set much of an example. It seems there is always a gang of supervisors in the coffee line at all times, and your secretary and her friend stand around the cigarette machine way after 8:00 a.m.

Jackson: That's not relevant. You can't get cigarettes unless you stand in that line. Cripes, we can't go clear out to the lobby stand, can we? Oh, it's all right to grab a cup of coffee on occasion, but those two girls are always out together. They're abusing the privileges. They drive to work together every day; I've seen them, and then they go into the cafeteria at 8:00 and have breakfast. It's got to end.

Parks: Okay, okay. We'll have another chat with them. The offices and the whole back-of-the-house are pretty lax in regard to timeliness. I agree we don't want reservations standing out as the worst offenders. Part of it is that they go out together, and that makes it conspicuous alright. I'm leaving town this afternoon, but I'll talk with them personally today and let you know before I take off.

Jackson: Okay. Just make it good. We've got to stop abuses, or we'll just have to crack down on everyone. It's always a few who make it hard on everyone.

On the way back to his own office, Mr. Parks detoured into reservations and found Ms. Jean Marshall, talking on the telephone. When she hung up, Mr. Parks related his conversations with

[5]Craig C. Lundberg and Cheri A. Young, *The Hospitality Case Manual: Developing Competencies in Critical Thinking and Practical Action*, Upper Saddle River, N.J.: Pearson Education, Inc., 2009, pp. 152–156.

Mr. Jackson. This was the second time in two months that Mr. Jackson had called the behavior of Kane and Palumbo to his attention. After a brief discussion, they decided that the proper thing to do was to call the two women into the departmental conference room and talk with them. When Mr. Parks, Ms. Marshall, Mrs. Kane, and Mrs. Palumbo had assembled, the following conversation took place.

Parks: While I sure don't like to bring up a complaint a few hours before I go out of town, I've just come from Mr. Jackson's office. He has complained again about you two getting to work late and about you taking so much time away from your desks for coffee. He rather emphatically stated that he has seen you in the cafeteria after 8:00 several times and that you both seem to be there having coffee together every time he stops by. I believe Jean spoke with you about this several weeks ago. What do you think we ought to do about it?

Kane: Yes, Ms. Marshall talked to us before about it. We've been trying to watch it since then. I believe we've been doing a lot better. You know how hard it is to get to work winter mornings, and we do go down once in a while for a cup of coffee. The new cafeteria is so nice now. Everybody is using it more. Why shouldn't we?

Parks: Yes, you're right, of course. More people are using the cafeteria. You'll agree with me, I'm sure, that this property has a pretty relaxed attitude about getting to work on time occasionally and about getting out of the office for coffee or Coke or a smoke. But let's face it. Mr. Jackson is riled. If we abuse the privileges we have, it will be necessary for Jackson to create some rules that constrict us. We'll all suffer then. There must be some way you can work it out so you'll not be so conspicuous when you take a break once in a while? Isn't it possible for you two to get to work on time so when you take a break it won't be so objectionable?

Kane: All the other reservations women do it. All the office force does it. The smokers go out all the time. Most use the lavs, but it's always so crowded there we prefer to go down to the cafeteria.

Parks: Part of the problem, of course, is that you two are always seen together. That makes you stand out. Why can't you split up, or go some other place? Mrs. Kane, you've indicated more than once that you want more responsibility in reservations. Let's face it; we can't get it for you if the GM thinks you're abusing the situation.

Kane: Of course that makes sense. What do you want us to do? Stop taking breaks altogether?

Parks: Mrs. Palumbo, what do you think you should do?

Palumbo: Gee, I don't know. We don't do anything that the others don't do. But we don't want to get into trouble. The Casino has been generous enough.

Parks: The way things stand now, well, you can see how things are. Both Mr. Jackson and Cooperider have commented on you. Jackson's the GM, remember, he approves all job changes and all recommendations for raises. It's just not smart to have him on your case.

Kane: We want to do what's right, of course. I sure wouldn't want to do anything that would hinder my next promotion. I suppose we could go somewhere else and maybe not take so many breaks—at least not together. Suppose we lay low for a while until the top brass forgets about it?

Parks: And, get to work a little more promptly in the morning. Sure, all of us are a touch lax sometimes about getting in on time, but the finger is pointing at you, so how about doing a bit better than you've been doing of late?

Kane: Okay, but as you know, I've three kids to get off to school every day. What with car problems, the storms tying traffic up, it's awfully hard to get here on time.

Parks: I'll leave it up to you. I know you're both good workers, and I know you're both trying to get ahead here. You must realize that if old Jackson doesn't see an immediate turnaround, well, I'm not sure what he'll do. You've been talked to twice now. We wouldn't want our GM to do something that would hurt all of the staff, now, would we? (Pause) Jean, what do you think is the best thing to do?

Marshall: You've outlined the situation very well, Mr. Parks. I think these women are attracting undue attention by going out together all the time. The whole staff has been lax about starting promptly. I'll certainly work with reservations to see that we put a drive on to get us to work on time. I think they shouldn't take quite so many breaks, and not together. That way they won't cause so many negative comments.

Parks: Well, it's up to these women. I'm about to leave for a conference, tonight, in fact. I'll be away, so I won't hear anything. If Jackson gets in a twit, he'll no doubt call you down, Jean, and I know you'll do whatever he says. See if you two ladies can't stay out of trouble, please. I'll be back in five days. Good luck.

Roger Parks returned to his own office and telephoned Mr. Jackson. He told Jackson that he and Ms. Marshall had talked to Kane and Palumbo and that he believed that Jackson would see an immediate improvement. Parks asked Jackson to call Ms. Marshall if there are any further complaints. Jackson replied, "You're darn right I will."

About Casino Grande

Casino Grande was an older, mid-sized casino hotel, employing approximately 2,000 people, on the boardwalk section of a mid-Atlantic city. Mr. Randolph Jackson was the general manager of Casino Grande and, as such, had the ultimate authority over all departments and functions at the property. He took unusual interest in the human resource activities of the casino/hotel, establishing both personnel policies and office procedure personally. The ordinary interpretation of these policies and procedures, however, was handled by the department managers and section supervisors with consultation available from the employee relations department.

Roger Parks was the manager of Casino Grande's reservations department. He had begun his employment with the casino in 1982 as a night programmer in the accounting department, while he was finishing his B.S. in hotel administration from a prominent eastern university. After graduation, Roger continued to work in accounting for two years; then he requested a transfer to the newly established computer system group, where he worked for another two years before he replaced a section head and, thus, acquired his

first truly supervisory experience. In late 1987, Roger obtained an interview for a section manager's position in the front desk department, and for which he was hired. In 1990, Casino Grande significantly upgraded its computer facilities, including a sophisticated reservations system. Roger was transferred to the reservations unit to take charge of it. When he began to organize this function, he hired Ms. Marshall and two clerks. About a year later, when an opening occurred, Mrs. Kane was hired. In Mr. Parks's opinion, Ms. Marshall was a technical whiz who got along fairly well with her people. She had a reputation within the reservations group of sometimes being impatient; she kidded her workers a lot and usually got a lot of high-quality work from them, but was considered somewhat lax in enforcing discipline.

Mrs. Kane, about 39 years old, had three children of ages 11, 8, and 6. Her husband was a sales trainer with a major manufacturing company and was away from home for extended periods. Mrs. Kane's mother lived with them, taking care of the children so that Mrs. Kane could work. She was made senior reservations clerk on January 1, 1992, receiving a substantial raise. At that time, Mrs. Kane was told she was doing excellent work but had a quick temper that sometimes disturbed her fellow employees. She was also told that she often disrupted the office by talking too loudly and too often. The position of senior reservationist provided a wage differential over the others and required her coworkers to bring their questions about procedures and assignments to her. All other matters, such as salary and training questions as well as performance appraisals, were handled by Ms. Marshall. Mrs. Kane took her work seriously and expressed resentment toward the indifferent attitude of the younger reservation clerks. She was trying to get ahead financially. She did not like housekeeping or childcare and planned to continue working as long as her mother could look after her children.

Mrs. Palumbo was about 28 years old and a college graduate. Her husband was in the Army and had been in the Middle East for two tours after Operation Desert Storm. Mrs. Palumbo lived alone in a small apartment and planned on working only until her husband was posted in the United States. Mrs. Palumbo did a good job as a reservation clerk and got along well with everyone in the department. She also got a raise on January 1, 1992.

The office rules at Casino Grande did not permit smoking on the job but allowed personnel to leave the office to do so, although there were no designated smoking spaces.

On Monday, August 15, 1992, the following notice was posted on the bulletin board just inside the employees' entrance to the property:

TO: All Casino Grande Office Personnel

Some employees have been taking advantage of our company's coffee break privilege. In order to be fair to those who are being reasonable about going to the cafeteria for coffee, we do not wish to rescind this privilege altogether. We do expect all office employees to start work at 8:00 in the morning, meaning come ready to work, already having had breakfast. There is no excuse for having coffee, therefore, after 8:00 a.m.

From now on the following rules will apply to coffee breaks:

1. No one should visit the cafeteria for coffee before 9:30 a.m.

2. Groups from the same department should not take breaks together, since this would disrupt the service provided.

3. No one should stay away from his/her workstation for longer than 15 minutes.

4. It is unnecessary to leave one's office for coffee or any other beverage more than once a day.

These simple rules should be clear to everyone. If, in the future, these rules are ignored, the coffee break privilege will be canceled altogether. Your wholehearted cooperation is expected.

R. L. Jackson
General Manager

Case Study Analysis

19-26. List the pros and cons of Mr. Jackson's decision to post the coffee-break notice. Was it a good management decision? Why or why not?

19-27. Imagine a scenario where you are Mr. Parks. What do you think you would have done after the conversation with Mr. Jackson? Write a paragraph describing your action plan.

19-28. Write a paragraph describing Mr. Jackson's philosophy of human-resources management.

19-29. List some examples of why the ladies might see the reprimands as unfair or unjust.

19-30. What is Jackson's leadership style?

ONLC Training Centers: Virtual IT Training in a Classroom

ONLC Training Centers has used its many locations to drive significant sales growth and become one of the leaders in the information technology (IT) training industry, an industry that was in rapid decline from 2000 through 2009. Today, ONLC has some 300 locations from coast to coast; but as recently as 2004 it only had offices in Philadelphia; Wilmington, Delaware; and Princeton, New Jersey. In 2009, ONLC Training Centers was named the eighth fastest-growing education company on *Inc.* magazine's list of fastest-growing companies. How did it achieve such remarkable growth in a declining industry during the worst economic downturn in 70 years?

RIDING THE TIDE AND BATTLING THE CURRENTS

Bucking industry and economic trends, ONLC realized multiple new revenue streams by rapidly expanding its geographic distribution of classroom training. In 2009, approximately 50 percent of ONLC's revenues came from sites that had not been open a year earlier. Two of the key drivers to the success were the strategic use of locations to accelerate sales and the redefinition of classroom training.

Jim Palic and Andy Williamson, ONLC
(ONLC Training Centers)

613

Andy Williamson and Jim Palic left the DuPont Company to cofound ONLC in 1983, and they were at the leading edge of the PC revolutions when they began offering classroom training to individuals using personal computers in the workplace. Throughout the rest of the 1980s and the 1990s, their original facilities were IT classrooms designed for face-to-face instruction. However, as corporate training and travel funds dried up after 2000, the demand for these services dropped precipitously and the industry consolidated rapidly. Many companies with large computer-training facilities closed or switched to other lines of business, such as IT consulting.

PIVOTING THE BUSINESS

Andy and Jim recognized that, although the demand for training had significantly declined, it had not disappeared. To serve the small market demand for public IT training (classes not held by companies on their own sites), they needed to transform their business model.

They considered offering virtual training, where people would join ONLC's classes from their homes or offices, which would certainly reduce costs. However, their years of industry experience taught them that people preferred formal classroom training for many good reasons. A classroom provides an interruption-free environment in which to learn. There are fewer technical issues when training is conducted in a classroom. And last, but not least important, going to an offsite location elevates the importance of the event and helps people focus on the job of learning.

The founders thought they could design a training offering that would include the classroom as an important part of the mix. Adding an actual classroom to virtual training would significantly increase ONLC costs but provide a better learning experience. In addition, they saw that their competitors were beginning to offer virtual training. If hundreds of other companies started to offer training virtually, how would ONLC be able to differentiate itself?

DIFFERENTIATION THROUGH REMOTE CLASSROOM INSTRUCTION

Instead of abandoning bricks-and-mortar classroom-based training, Andy and Jim decided to go deeper into that strategy. They designed a virtual training solution that keeps the classroom as part of the solution and called it "remote classroom instruction" (RCI). Their clients obtain a higher-quality learning solution, and ONLC achieves a more defensible market position.

Challenges Facing Classroom IT Training after 2000

Their solution was this: A single national training schedule is promoted on the ONLC Web site (http://www.onlc.com). If people see a class that they want to take that is running on January 15, for example, they can register for that class in any one of over 300 locations around the country. These locations contain small classrooms that can seat two to four people at a time. The class running on January 15 might be taught in a traditional classroom in Philadelphia, with an instructor teaching three students face-to-face in that room. In addition, as many as nine other people could be joining the class from up to nine other physical locations around the country.

"It is our ability to easily aggregate low demand for public training that makes our model successful," Andy explained. By combining the enrollments from hundreds of locations, they are able to have fewer classes cancelled because of low enrollments. In any given city, there might only be one or two people interested in an event. Whereas competitors who needed a large number of students in a room with an instructor would have had to cancel the class, ONLC is able to run it with one attendee.

SYSTEMATIC SITE SELECTION

ONLC management has carefully studied potential opportunities and identified strategic roll-out priorities, by looking at U.S. Census data by metropolitan statistical areas (MSAs). Unlike its old business model, in which leases were secured for multiple years and each site had to be staffed, the new model relies on a network of executive-suite locations. The company can sign short-term, six-month leases for only the needed space. It can start by renting a single classroom in any city. If demand becomes strong enough, it can rent additional rooms; if demand is low, it can cancel the lease at the end of the term and redeploy its computer hardware to a new, more productive location.

Training sites in areas with greater population densities have survived because there were more people. However, some rural areas are also successful. While those areas have lower demand, there are typically no

ONLC Training Sites—2013
(Courtesy of ONLC Training Centers)

direct competitors. Whereas the total demand in the area might be relatively low, the demand facing the firm is higher, because ONLC can capture a larger share of the market. In addition, the small-site strategy is more cost effective.

ONLC estimates that over 80 percent of the U.S. population is within an hour's drive from one of its training sites. Andy explains how ONLC has overcome the tyranny of geography that author Chris Anderson defines as an audience being spread so thinly that it is the same as no audience at all.[6] Andy observes, "People wanting training in remote locations have been suffering from the tyranny of geography where no classroom training is available to them because demand is so low. When demand for a particular class drops below a certain point, a traditional face-to-face class is taken off the schedule of the local training company. When demand for IT training in general drops below a certain point, the traditional training company closes its doors."

THE BUSINESS OF ONLC IS LOGISTICS

By creating hundreds of small, efficient training facilities and aggregating the demand for training across the country through its remote-classroom-instruction model, ONLC cost-effectively captures the demand for public IT classes. The staff schedules more than 100 events and registers more than 700 students weekly. Then, they ensure that each class has an instructor and that books are shipped to hundreds of locations each week. Student and instructor connections are established for each class and phone bridges are managed. In fact, ONLC is a logistics company that delivers training.

Through rapidly expanding the number of training facilities to provide nationwide coverage and by redefining classroom training with its RCI model, ONLC cost-effectively delivers classroom training where its competitors can't. As Andy says, "Lowering the cost of delivery has radically changed the economics of providing training, and has democratized distribution. It has also positioned ONLC for a successful future delivering virtual training in a classroom."

Case Study Analysis

U5-1. What does ONLC do to determine where to offer training? What are the critical location factors?

U5-2. How does this business model democratize distribution?

U5-3. How can ONLC have over 300 locations and maintain an efficient cost structure at low volumes in each?

U5-4. What is the level of importance of the location of the ONLC headquarters? Why?

U5-5. What were the main differentiating characteristics of ONLC's remote-classroom-instruction offering, compared to its competitors who were also offering virtual training?

U5-6. What is the ONLC business model?

Case Source

Courtesy of ONLC Inc.

---

[6]Chris Anderson, *The Long Tail: Why the Future of Business is Selling Less of More*, New York: Hyperion, 2006.

LEADERSHIP, ETHICS, AND EXITS

Chapter 20
LEADERSHIP AND ETHICAL PRACTICES

Chapter 21
FRANCHISING, LICENSING, AND HARVESTING:
CASHING IN YOUR BRAND

© WavebreakMediaMicro/Fotolia

Chapter 20

LEADERSHIP AND ETHICAL PRACTICES

Learning Objectives

1. Identify leadership styles.

2. Organize for effective time management.

3. Pursue ethical leadership to build an ethical organization.

4. Make sure your business is run in an ethical manner.

5. Maintain your integrity.

6. Incorporate social responsibility into your company.

Ciaran Griffin/Thinkstock

In 1906, a Hungarian immigrant named Henry Feuerstein built a textile mill, Malden Mills Industries Inc., outside of Boston. The business was passed down to Henry's grandson, Aaron. Malden Mills invented and marketed a unique fabric, called Polartec; it was a lightweight, warm, and durable fleece made from recycled plastics. Malden Mills used Polartec to manufacture jackets, vests, and other outerwear garments. In 1999, *Time* recognized Polartec as one of the top inventions of the century.

In the meantime, many manufacturing businesses had relocated to Mexico or overseas, where labor and production costs were lower. But Malden Mills kept its operations firmly planted in Massachusetts. Aaron Feuerstein had been raised by his father and grandfather to value his workers and to treat them with respect. As Feuerstein explained, "We have a mission of responsibility to both shareholders and our top asset: our employees. We're not prepared to skip town for cost savings."

Late in 1995, a devastating fire broke out at the Malden Mills plant, and most of the factory burned to the ground. The 3,000 employees feared that their jobs had been destroyed. But Feuerstein announced that he would rebuild the factory buildings and vowed to use the insurance money to continue paying his employees, with full benefits, until the plant was back in business.

It took Feuerstein months to rebuild, and it cost millions of dollars to fulfill the promise he had made to his employees. "I consider our workers an asset, not an expense," he explained. "I have a responsibility to the workers, both blue-collar and white-collar. I have an equal responsibility to the community. It would have been unconscionable to put 3,000 people on the streets and deliver a deathblow to the cities of Lawrence and Methuen. Maybe on paper our company is worth less to Wall Street, but I can tell you it is worth more."[1]

© Ed Quinn/CORBIS

The Entrepreneur as Leader

No matter who you hire to manage your company, *you* will set the tone for how the business operates. Are you disorganized and chaotic? Chances are your company will be, too. Are you honest and straightforward? Your managers and employees are likely to behave similarly.

leader a person who gets things done through influence, by guiding or inspiring others to voluntarily participate in a cause or project.

A **leader** is someone who gets things done through influence, by guiding or inspiring others to voluntarily participate in a cause or project. *Leadership* comes from self-esteem applied to knowledge, skills, and abilities. If you believe in yourself and know what you are doing, you can accomplish things confidently and inspire others. Develop a positive attitude, and you can become a leader. Great leaders are optimists; they have trained themselves to think positively. Running a successful business requires leadership.

Leadership Styles That Work

Learning Objective 1 ▶
Identify leadership styles.

As your business grows, the type of leader you are will be reflected throughout your company. Some leadership styles are more conducive to internal competition, whereas others foster teamwork and a collaborative

---

[1] Articles and press releases featured on the former Malden Mills Web site. See http://www.polartec.com/about/corporate.php.

Iromaya/Thinkstock

environment. You may find that you have to blend leadership styles, or shift from one to another to some extent, as circumstances change.

Companies like Wal-Mart and Home Depot invest significant sums to create a work environment that inspires and motivates their employees. You may not have the sort of funds that they do, but you can model a positive leadership style. How you or your managers treat one another and the employees will determine the company culture. Adopt the best leadership style for your company, maintain it consistently, and learn to adapt it as needed. According to researcher Daniel Goleman, the principal styles and their advantages and drawbacks are:[2]

- *Coercive.* To *coerce* means to pressure someone into doing what you want. This commanding approach can be effective in a disaster scenario or with problem employees who need a forceful manager. In most situations, however, a coercive leadership style damages employee morale and diminishes the flexibility and effectiveness of the company. Employees stop thinking and acting for themselves.

- *Authoritative.* An authoritative leader takes a "come with me" approach, stating the overall goals but giving employees freedom to figure out how best to achieve them. This can work well if the leader is an expert, but may not be so effective if the scenario is one of a nominal leader heading up a group of individuals who have more expertise in the field than he or she does (a team of scientists, for example).

- *Affiliative.* This is a "people come first" method that is effective when the business is in the team-building stage. It can fail when employees are lost and need direction.

- *Democratic.* This style gives employees a strong voice in how the company is run. It can build morale and work if employees are prepared to handle responsibility, but it could result in endless meetings and a sense of leaderlessness and drifting.

- *Pacesetting.* This type of leader sets high personal performance standards and challenges employees to meet them, too. This can be very good when employees are also self-motivated and devoted, but can overwhelm those who are not so committed.

- *Coaching.* This style focuses on helping each employee to grow, through training and support. This can be a good approach for starting and growing a business, but may not work with employees who have been with the company for a while and are resistant to change.

How Entrepreneurs Pay Themselves

Before you hire employees, figure out how to pay your first employee—yourself. Once your business is breaking even, decide how you will distribute the profit on a cash-available basis. The decision you make will affect your financial record keeping and your taxes, so think it through. But remember, you can change it to fit circumstances, too. The choices are

- *Commission.* A set percentage of every sale. It is treated as a variable operating cost because it fluctuates with sales.

---

[2]Daniel Goleman, "Leadership That Gets Results," *Harvard Business Review*, March–April 2000.

- *Salary.* A fixed amount of money paid at set intervals. You could choose to receive your salary once a week or once a month. A salary is a fixed operating cost because it is not connected to fluctuating sales.
- *Wages.* If you have a service or manufacturing business, you could pay yourself an hourly wage. Wages are considered a cost of goods sold, because they are factored into the cost of the product or service.
- *Dividend.* Usually a share of a company's profits issued to shareholders, based on what remains after investments. As a small business owner, you could use this method to pay yourself; your compensation would depend on how the business was doing.

Entrepreneurs who do not pay themselves regularly tend to overstate their return on investment; they have not taken their compensation as a cost of the business. Recognize that you can only pay yourself (or anyone else) when you have sufficient cash to do so.

Another reason to pay yourself is that it enables you to be honest about whether the business is really worth your time. Could you be making more money in a different business or working for someone else? What are your opportunity costs? Is the best choice to keep working for yourself? Thinking entrepreneurially includes a realistic consideration of whether you would be happier *not* running a business, at least for a while.

Manage Your Time Wisely

Leaders learn how to manage their time, so that they can accomplish more with less. One of the most important things you can do is to learn how to manage your time efficiently. Getting more done in less time can contribute to success.

◀ Learning Objective 2
Organize for effective time management.

Even if you do not have employees to manage, you could probably use your own time better. **Exhibit 20-1** is an example of a valuable tool called a Gantt chart that you can use to organize the many things you need to do. This one is related to business start-up tasks. As your venture grows, you can use the Gantt concept to manage more complex operations. You

Exhibit 20-1 *Sample Gantt Chart*						
Task	**Week 1**	**Week 2**	**Week 3**	**Week 4**	**Week 5**	**Week 6**
Build banking relationship						
Order letterhead						
Select location						
Register business						
Obtain bulk mail permit						
Select ad agency						
Meet with attorney						
Meet with accountant						
Create vendor statement						
Pay utility deposits						
Order marketing material						
Install phone system						
Have Web site designed						
Set up database						
Network computers						

can also create charts using software, such as Microsoft Project, and share them among team members. The best method to select is the one that you will actually use.

Leaders perpetually have more tasks to complete than time to complete them, even when using project-management tools. It is easy to get sucked into unexpected meetings and conversations. For founders, this is compounded by being the locus of more company and product expertise than others, because of being a "one-person band"—or at least a high percentage of a small founding team. This means being called in as the "fire-fighter," or problem solver. The balancing act between being accessible—and creating a positive environment—and being inaccessible can be intricate. Time-management issues are also more difficult for leaders who cannot let go of decision making and involvement in every aspect of the company, even when they can and should delegate responsibilities.

There is a seemingly endless variety of books and articles on time management and on managerial and organizational effectiveness. Some tips that can assist in increasing such effectiveness include:

- Prioritize. Know what is important.
- Set realistic daily goals, allowing for customer contact, meetings, and some flexibility for surprises.
- Don't spend too much time on e-mail. It is easy to become distracted by nonessential correspondence. If you check at the beginning, middle, and end of the day, you will be able to focus better on other tasks.
- Avoid letting your attention get caught up in portable electronic devices. Whereas multitasking and constant availability may seem to increase efficiency, each interruption is a diversion from the work in progress and may cause you to lose your train of thought. These disruptions may also distract your coworkers, decreasing productivity even more.
- Schedule sit-down meetings only when they will be more efficient than other less time-consuming methods of communication. Try stand-up meetings. Also, consider going to other staff members' offices, so that you can end the meetings more easily.
- Only accept meeting invitations where your presence is required in order for progress to occur. As the firm grows, many of the operational meetings should disappear from your schedule. If you don't know why you have been invited to a meeting, don't attend it.
- Delegate responsibility and authority and trust your team; hire the best people for the job and support them in their success. There is little that is more wasteful and counterproductive than a manager who does not delegate or who nominally delegates and then undermines the team's work.
- Remember to allow yourself downtime, play time, and creative-thinking time. One of the reasons people become entrepreneurs is to gain control over their time. And one positive characteristic of entrepreneurs is their creativity. By allowing time to think and relax, your company will benefit.

ethics a system of moral conduct and judgment that helps determine right and wrong.

Learning Objective 3
Pursue ethical leadership to build an ethical organization.

Ethical Leadership and Ethical Organizations

True leadership comprises all of the actions and attributes that have been noted, plus the personal values underlying them. **Ethics** are a system of principles that define a code of behavior to distinguish between good and bad or right and wrong. The Golden Rule, "Do unto others as you would have others do unto you," is a well-known and widely accepted ethic. A behavior may be legal and still not be ethical.

Step into the Shoes . . .

Charles Schwab Does Well by Doing Good

Charles "Chuck" Schwab opened his own brokerage firm in the early 1970s when he was 34. Like Jacoby & Meyers with legal services, Schwab uncovered a market niche when he began offering discount pricing for informed investors who were tired of paying sizable commissions to stockbrokers. These investors did not need anyone else to do their research and make their decisions, and they flocked to take advantage of the lower rates.

By 1981, Charles Schwab & Company's earnings were $5 million. In 1983, Bank of America bought the company for $55 million but left Schwab in place as CEO.[3] Just four years later, management repurchased the company and took it public as Charles Schwab Corporation. In the 1990s, Schwab became the leading online discount broker and the fastest-growing American company of the decade.

Chuck Schwab expressed his attitude toward employees as, "I have yet to find the man, however exalted his station, who did not do better work and put forth greater effort under a spirit of approval than criticism." As of the end of the third quarter of 2013, Schwab had $2.08 trillion in assets under management, 9 million active brokerage accounts, 1.3 million corporate retirement plans, and 926,000 banking accounts.[4]

Charles Schwab
(John Todd/AP Images)

[3]Charles Schwab Corporation, accessed October 5, 2013, http://www.aboutschab.com.
[4]Schwab Corporation, accessed October 5, 2013, http://www.schwab.com/investor_relations.

Ethical business behavior is not only moral, but it makes good business sense. Have you ever bought something from a store and felt you were cheated? How did you react? Did you want to go back? Probably not. You may have even told your friends about the experience. The store lost more than just one customer.

An Ethical Perspective

For a business, ethics are individual and organizational moral principles applied to actions and issues within the company context. In order to create an organization that is ethical, the values and standards of conduct must be clearly and broadly understood and accepted. Each substantive decision has an ethical component, although sometimes the right thing to do is so evident that many choices are virtually automatic.

However, the right thing to do is not always easy to determine. Often the choice is not between right and wrong, but rather between partially right and partially wrong, so that making a choice is difficult at best. There is sometimes a gray area in a scenario that cannot be clarified by relying on individuals to simply "know what's right."

Establishing Ethical Standards

One of the best ways to create an ethical business is to codify the fundamental rules of the game. Underlying values provide a basis for ethical behavior; clear, written guidelines can create a firmer foundation and more consistent implementation. Many companies create a code of ethics, a code of business conduct, or a combined code of ethics and business conduct. A **code of ethics** is the statement of the values of a company. A **code of conduct** is a set of official standards of employee behavior. A **code of ethics and business conduct** combines the two. By creating, disseminating, and establishing employee buy-in, a business will *empower* employees, meaning they will be free to make decisions and take action on their own, around a core set of ethical norms and rules for action.

A code of conduct can help to eliminate the problem of **ethical relativism**, which arises when ethical standards are believed to be subject to interpretation. It can also help to prevent or resolve **ethical dilemmas**, which are situations in which employees do not have a clear choice. By clarifying

code of ethics a statement of the values of a company.

code of conduct a set of official standards of employee behavior for a company.

code of ethics and business conduct a combination of a written statement of values with official standards of employee behavior.

ethical relativism situation where ethical standards are believed to be subject to interpretation.

ethical dilemma a circumstance in which there is a conflict of ethical values, which thus muddy decision making.

Exhibit 20-2	*Six Pillars of Character: Ethical Values*
Value	**Actualized Form**
Trustworthiness	Honesty, integrity, reliability (promise-keeping), loyalty
Respect	Civility, courtesy, decency, dignity, autonomy, tolerance, acceptance
Responsibility	Accountability, pursuit of excellence, self-restraint
Caring	Concern for others, compassion, benevolence, altruism
Fairness	Process (open), impartiality, equity
Citizenship	Law abiding, volunteerism, environmental awareness, action

Source: Six Pillars of Character® adapted from the Josephson Institute of Ethics, http://josephsoninstitute.org (accessed January 25, 2010). Six Pillars of Character is a registered trademark of the Josephson Institute. Used by permission.

which actions should and should not be taken, many of the gray areas that invite confusion are eliminated. One general recommendation is that organizations put into place a procedural guide for dealing with ethical challenges. This document will contain a basic method, with a multistep process of asking key questions, to get at the best answer with regard to an ethical consideration. A company will include in the guide actual scenarios that have arisen or that could be expected to occur.

A comprehensive list of potential ethical values would be quite long, but they are neatly summarized in the Six Pillars of Character, as described in **Exhibit 20-2**.

By selecting 6 to 10 of these actualized concepts, you can develop a core value set and create a code of conduct that specifies the actions that are in alignment with those values. For example, if *impartiality* is critical, the code of ethics might require that employees refrain from accepting personal gifts from stakeholders, such as vendors.

As with any standards, a code of ethics and business conduct is only as good as its practice. Appropriate rewards for compliance and consequences for breaches of ethics are needed to have a viable code of ethics. What will happen to an employee who takes company funds? What if an employee consistently takes extra-long lunches, comes in later than scheduled, or leaves early? What if he takes home pens and paper? What if she goes on Facebook or eHarmony during working hours?

Step into the Shoes . . .

Publishing Concepts Inc. (PCI) Establishes Values

As a third-generation, family-owned business, PCI developed and defined its corporate culture and values. Advertising themselves as "notthebigcompany," PCI refers to its employees as "associates." PCI's Seven Driving Values are:

1. **Excellence.** If it's worth doing, it's worth doing right.
2. **People.** We believe people have potential. We believe people have the capacity for greatness.
3. **Integrity.** We require complete honesty and integrity in everything we do. We are trustworthy. We keep our promises.
4. **Service.** We see each day as an opportunity to serve our clients and each other. We embrace the principles of servant leadership.
5. **Fun.** Work is an important part of life and it should be fun.
6. **Profitability.** To meet our personal and professional goals, we must make money and generate cash.
7. **Change.** Like the samurai warrior, our motto is "Act Fearlessly."

All of this information for associates was sent out to customers and prospects in lieu of a holiday greeting in December 2009. An enclosed note from Drew Clancy, president of PCI, states, "The booklet outlines the promises and commitments we make to ourselves, to each other, and to our clients—not only at this special time of year, but each and every day."

Source: PCI's Seven Driving Values and Seven Promises from PCI Holiday Mailing 2009. Courtesy of Publishing Concepts Inc. and PCI Web site, accessed October 5, 2013.

Corporate Ethical Scandals

The issue of business ethics exploded in 2002 when several large corporations were found to have published inaccurate financial statements. These fictitious numbers made the companies look so good that they were some of the most highly recommended stock picks on Wall Street.

Top executives at Enron, WorldCom-MCI, Tyco, Global Crossing, and other well-known firms had inflated corporate earnings so that they would receive huge bonuses, while misleading shareholders and employees. When the truth came out, public confidence in the stock market plummeted along with stock prices. Investors lost millions.

> Report Ethical Concerns and/or
> Violations at Ethos Company.
> Calls are toll-free and confidential.
> **1-800-ETHICAL**

One of the companies, the energy giant Enron, had strongly encouraged its own employees to invest their retirement funds in company stock, even while top executives knew the worth of that stock was based on false numbers. These employees had their life savings wiped out by the unethical behavior of the executives.

Enron collapsed and thousands of employees lost their jobs and saw their pensions reduced to nothing; Tyco was split into four different companies. Tyco's CEO was forced to resign because he used company money to buy an $18 million apartment in Manhattan and furnish it with expensive artwork—among other egregious abuses.

The scandals of 2002 were a failure of **corporate governance**, meaning that these companies did not have rules and safeguards in place to ensure that executives behaved legally and ethically. Even early in developing your business, think about how you will guarantee that your company remains both ethical and legal as it grows.

◀ **Learning Objective 4**
Make sure your business is run in an ethical manner.

corporate governance
rules and safeguards to ensure that executives behave legally and ethically.

- *Do not treat company profits as personal funds.* Haphazardly taking business profits for your own use is a bad habit. Decide on a wage or salary you will pay yourself and always document this, as well as your business expenses. You should enjoy the rewards of a successful venture, but be careful to do it ethically and legally. In particular, **tax evasion**, which is trying to avoid paying taxes through illegal or deceptive means, is to be avoided.

- *Keep accurate records.* Have your business records checked once a year by a professional accountant. By the time your company becomes a multimillion-dollar corporation, you will have established a reputation for honest financial reporting.

- *Use financial controls.* This will help to eliminate the potential for embezzlement, which is the crime of stealing money from a company. Once you have employees, use such simple financial controls as
  - Always have two people open the mail, so no one is tempted to take company checks.
  - Arrange for yourself and one other person to be required to sign all checks sent out by the business. Using a double signature will assure that no one can use the company money for personal expenses.
  - Implement a cash-counting and control system, if employees will be handling cash.

- *Create an advisory board.* Ask selected businesspeople and other community leaders you respect to be on your **advisory board or advisory council**. This group of people will provide you with sound, ethical business advice without having the responsibilities of a board of directors. Choose the members carefully, and listen to what they have to say.

tax evasion the deliberate avoidance of an obligation to pay taxes; may lead to penalties or imprisonment.

advisory board or council a group that provides advice and counsel but does not have the responsibilities of a board of directors.

An advisory board can provide valuable guidance
(Nick White/Thinkstock)

Integrity and Entrepreneurial Opportunities

Stated company values are significant and will contribute to entrepreneurial opportunities—to the extent that they are implemented in day-to-day actions. The consistency and demonstrated commitment to the espoused values system can create further opportunities. For example, in the early 1980s, Johnson & Johnson earned the respect and acceptance of its many stakeholders when the company withdrew millions of bottles of potentially contaminated Tylenol from store shelves. Johnson & Johnson did not issue the recall because they were ordered to do so but because it was the right thing to do. Its executives put their money where their mouth was, acknowledged the problem, and took swift and decisive action. Although the company has not been a small, entrepreneurial venture for a very long time, Johnson & Johnson provides an excellent example of values in action.

What Is Integrity?

Integrity is upholding behavioral standards on the level of the ethical principles that an individual espouses. All codes of ethics and conduct are worthless without the integrity to put those words into action. That means that acting ethically is not something to be done only when it is convenient or when it will not be costly. It is a daily, decision-by-decision process.

Doing the Right Thing in Addition to Doing Things Right

Learning Objective 5

Maintain your integrity.

As a business, ethical practices involve doing the right things and doing them ethically. There is a potential conflict between strategic priorities and ethical behavior. Profit maximization is one of the most common challenges to ethical behavior. By harming the environment, using substandard components, or cutting corners, a company can maximize its short-term profitability. A clearly defined and commonly shared code of ethics and business conduct can go a long way toward incorporating ethical decision making into strategic priorities. This will facilitate incorporating "doing the right thing" into company strategy from the start, thereby avoiding ethical conflicts.

Balancing the Needs of Owners, Customers, and Employees

Although it may seem simple and straightforward to retain your integrity, it can become more complex as you add partners, customers, and employees to the equation. People's moral compasses do not always point in the same direction. What seems just, right, and fair to one person may seem unjust, unfair, and wrong to another. Often, this is caused by the conflicting needs of owners, customers, and employees.

Owners face multiple pressures, such as the need to have their businesses survive, the repayment of debts, and the welfare of employees. Customers need products and services that meet expectations. Employees need to earn a living wage and experience job satisfaction. On the surface, fulfilling these aims should not pose ethical challenges.

However, as each constituency strives to meet its needs, ethical dilemmas may arise. As a business owner, for example, you may have to make a choice between paying a vendor in accordance with the credit terms, or as otherwise promised, and having sufficient cash to cover the employee payroll. Or, you might have to choose between paying a vendor for critical production materials or paying withholding taxes to the federal government. Making a choice between the two would certainly be an ethical dilemma. Who would you make wait for the money? Or, imagine yourself as an employee that has to make a choice between reporting illegal pollution by your employer, which could close down the company and result in your unemployment, or turning a blind eye to the situation to keep your family housed and fed. The short-term interest of both the company and the employee in these examples would be to act unethically.

Or, envision the customer that benefits from a company's mistake and has to decide what to do. Have you ever been given too much change for a purchase or had an item left off a bill? You gain and the business loses. On the flip side, a company may overcharge, double-bill, or somehow provide less than promised. Then you lose and the company gains. The relationship between a company and its customers is fraught with potential ethical challenges.

Complying with the Law

One of the most difficult aspects of maintaining integrity for any entrepreneur is complying with the multitude of laws that apply to business. The number of laws and regulations from federal, state, local, and other authorities is seemingly endless and can be mind-boggling. In certain cases, small firms are exempt from regulations that lawmakers consider unduly burdensome. However, for the most part, entrepreneurial firms must comply with the same laws as their larger brethren.

Ethics would dictate that companies avoid discrimination, harassment, and tax evasion. Providing a safe workplace and living wages also seem obvious. So do the avoidance of pollution or paying taxes on time. Problems can arise when complying with the law is more costly and/or less convenient than not doing so. Many of the safeguards for employees and the environment add costs for employers. In some cases, businesses have to choose between compliance and profitability, or even continued existence. In a perfect world, entrepreneurs would never face a trade-off between doing what is legal vis-à-vis what is best for the business and themselves.

Because of the large number of laws and regulations, you may find it nearly impossible to know every one of these that applies to your business. Whether you are aware of them or not, you are responsible for compliance. The good news is that, if you act ethically, you are likely to be in compliance. If you have any questions regarding the law, check with your attorney. Don't rely upon hearsay or "logic." Also, make your best efforts to stay informed with respect to changes in the law. State and local chambers of commerce can be excellent sources of information and advocacy.

Many activities are unethical but still legal. For example, adjusting budget numbers or telling your employees to do so to ensure specific results, withholding vital decision-making information, or complaining about others are not typically illegal behaviors but are unethical.

Social Responsibility and Ethics

Learning Objective 6

Incorporate social responsibility into your company.

corporate social responsibility the ethical obligation of a company to its community.

social entrepreneurship the sale of products or services on a for-profit basis to benefit a social purpose.

in-kind donation a contribution of products or services that may include time or goods rather than cash.

Ethics, corporate social responsibility, and social entrepreneurship are three related topics that are often conflated. **Corporate social responsibility** is the ethical obligation of a company to its community. **Social entrepreneurship** is the sale of products and/or services on a for-profit basis to benefit a social purpose. Both have ethical components and can be of value to entrepreneurial firms.

Companies exhibit their commitment to the communities they serve through a variety of means and with varying motivations. Some examples are financial contributions to not-for-profit community organizations, supporting volunteerism, and in-kind donations. An **in-kind donation** is a contribution of products or services—including employee time—rather than cash. Companies also show this commitment through paying livable wages and providing safe and sanitary working conditions. Another aspect of corporate social responsibility is to make any financial investment in only ethical and legal ventures, and in countries with human rights values in alignment with the company's ethics. Environmental friendliness is another way of demonstrating community care. For example, Peninsula Regional Medical Center, on the Eastern Shore of Maryland, is working toward becoming eco-friendly and energy efficient throughout the organization.

Leading with Integrity and Examples

Leading by example is the best way to command the attention and respect of others. If you refuse to accept inferior goods, your employees will, too. If you give voice and form to company values and demonstrate integrity, the workplace will become and remain a community of stakeholders that values integrity, honesty, and open communication. Modeling the behavior you desire is an excellent route to attaining the desired results.

Encourage Your Employees to Be Socially Responsible

As you have read, early in the twentieth century, Madam C. J. Walker motivated her employees by encouraging them to get involved in helping their communities, and in the process she became the first African-American millionaire. There are many ways that entrepreneurs can use their businesses to contribute to society. By being an entrepreneur, you have already made an important contribution by providing goods or services to consumers in your area who need them. You can also use your business to support social issues that are important to you. By running your company in a way that is consistent with your ethics and core values, you will develop a socially responsible business.

Global Impact . . .

Mohammad Yunus and Grameen Bank: Banker to the Poor

Mohammad Yunus, Nobel Peace Prize winner, social entrepreneur, and "banker to the poor," has used his enterprising spirit to foster entrepreneurship and lift literally millions of people out of poverty. He describes his activities: "I did something that challenged the banking world. Conventional banks look for the rich; we look for the absolutely poor. All people are entrepreneurs, but many don't have the opportunity to find out."

Grameen Bank, founded in Bangladesh in 1976, is largely owned by its borrowers. As of December 2012, Grameen Bank had disbursed $1,437 billion (cumulative), and had $997 million in loans outstanding, from 6.71 million active borrowers, served by 2,914 branches, with a staff of 22,610. Over 96 percent of the borrowers are women.[5]

The basis of Grameen Bank's relationship with its borrowers is a core set of values explicitly stated in its Sixteen Decisions. Grameen has found a way to flip conventional banking knowledge on its head. For Grameen Bank, credit is perceived as a human right, not a benefit for the wealthy. Its branches are distributed across rural areas, bringing the bank to the people.

In 2002, Grameen created its Struggling Members Programme, targeted at beggars. This initiative has encouraged people to give up begging and make a living as door-to-door salespeople. As of 2012, 19,678 of the 111,296 who joined the program had left begging. About 10 percent of the program members became members of mainstream Grameen groups, and 80 percent of the funds disbursed have been repaid.

Mohammad Yunus
(Vittorio Zunino Celotto/
Getty Images)

Source: Grameen Bank Web, accessed October 5, 2013, http://www.grameen-info .org/.

[5]Grameen Bank, accessed October 6, 2013, http://www.grameen-info.org.

Ways to make your business socially responsible include:

- recycling paper, glass, and plastic;
- donating a portion of your profits to a charity;
- refusing to use animal testing on products;
- offering employees incentives to volunteer in the community; and
- establishing a safe and healthy workplace.

You can also emphasize being a **sustainable** business, as you ensure meeting the Earth's current needs while preserving resources for future generations.

sustainable referring to a scenario in which current needs are met while preserving future resources.

Chapter Summary

Now that you have studied this chapter, you can do the following:

1. Identify leadership styles.
   - A leader is someone who has the confidence and energy to do things on her own.
   - Leadership comes from self-esteem. If you believe in yourself, you can do things with confidence and inspire confidence in others.
   - Leaders learn how to manage their time so they can get more done.
2. Pursue ethical leadership to build an ethical organization.
   - View decisions through an ethical lens.
   - Establish ethical standards.
   - Build ethical employer/employee relationships.
3. Incorporate social responsibility into your company.
   - Encourage environmentalism.
   - Support charitable efforts.
   - Maintain a safe and healthy workplace.
   - Consider sustainability throughout the organization.

Key Terms

advisory board or council, 625

code of conduct, 623

code of ethics, 623

code of ethics and business
    conduct, 623

corporate governance, 625

corporate social responsibility, 628

ethical dilemma, 623

ethical relativism, 623

ethics, 622

in-kind donation, 628

leader, 619

social entrepreneurship, 628

sustainable, 629

tax evasion, 625

Entrepreneurship Portfolio

Critical Thinking Exercises

20-1. Describe three leaders you admire. What characteristics do you most respect about them and why?

20-2. Consider ways that you might find 10 additional hours in your weekly schedule to manage your business. Create a weekly time-management schedule for yourself reflecting this activity.

20-3. Fill out a Gantt chart for your business or one that you can imagine, or use Microsoft Project or another software package to do the same thing.

20-4. Describe the corporate governance plan for your company. It should include five policies (rules) that will be the backbone of your company's ethics.

20-5. Thinnow Corporation, an entrepreneurial venture, has developed a weight-loss drug, Fatgo. After an intense FDA review and approval process, Thinnow has received permission to market Fatgo. Testing had shown that there may be serious (even deadly) side effects to consumers of Fatgo. A warning label is being provided. Identify the legal and ethical issues in this case.

Key Concept Questions

20-6. What is your entrepreneurial leadership style and which style is suitable for your business? Give reasons for your answer.

20-7. What is a code of conduct? What are its potential benefits?

20-8. What is the relationship between social responsibility and ethics?

20-9. What is insider trading? Why is it unethical? If you owned a company and knew that it was about to report increased earnings and thus drive its stock price up, why would it be unethical to tell this to family members?

Application Exercises

20-10. Identify a business leader, preferably an entrepreneur. Describe his or her leadership style based on at least two public sources (excluding any *wikis*, such as Wikipedia) and give examples to support your conclusion.

20-11. Keep track of the direct opportunities to decide whether to act ethically/unethically and/or legally/illegally that arise during a 48-hour period. What, if anything, surprises you about the list?

20-12. Choose three things you would plan to do to run a socially responsible business. Explain why you made the selections you did.

Exploring Online

20-13. Choose a corporation that has been involved in an ethical scandal and research it online. (Enter *corporate* and *scandal* into a search engine.) Present its story to the class. Describe the lessons you learned from researching this company.

20-14. Using an online search engine, find a company that practices corporate social responsibility and answer the following:

a. Which values are important?

b. How are these values translated into action?

c. Are the values shared broadly within the company, or are they primarily those of the president/CEO?

BizBuilder Business Plan Questions

After studying this chapter, you should be able to answer the following Business Plan Questions. The entire outline for the Business Plan is found in Appendix 2.

6.0 Management and Operations

6.1 Management Team

D. What will your policies toward employees be? How will you make your organization a positive and rewarding place to work?

E. Describe the corporate governance plan for your organization. It should include five policies (rules) that will be the backbone of your organization's ethics.

F. Provide information for each of your mentors or advisors. If there is a board of advisors, list each member and describe his/her commitment to the board.

Agritechno geneticist Dr. Lev Andropov is working in his laboratory with his colleague, Dr. Tamika Brown (also a geneticist), and his two lab assistants, André and Bonita. As the four are conducting their work, Donna Holbrook from Marketing, Stefan Girard from Accounting, and Jaylen Castillo from Product Development enter the lab with some discouraging news. They have been getting early reports from growers in the South that some of the caterpillar-resistant transgenic corn developed by Agritechno and planted this year is failing in areas that are having higher than normal rainfall. The group must decide how, if at all, they should report the information to growers and investors.

© Blend Images/Alamy

Dr. Andropov led the team that developed the caterpillar-resistant transgenic corn, in addition to having come up with numerous other strains of insect- and disease-resistant hybrids and varieties of this plant. Dr. Brown has worked alongside Dr. Andropov for many years and is hoping to be promoted to head her own lab for the development of transgenic fruits. The success of the caterpillar-resistant corn would be essential to her being promoted this year. Doctors Andropov and Brown are disappointed to hear of the crop failures and would like to investigate the cause. They do not want to commit to time lines or solutions without proper scientific inquiry.

Stefan Girard is focused on shareholder value and the potential damage to stock prices if these problems leak out to investors. He wants to send a letter to shareholders immediately, stating that the few incidents of crop failure are flukes.

At the same time, Donna insists on sending a letter to the growers, alerting them to an overwatering problem. Donna, Stefan, and Jaylen all agree that the letters have to be sent right away because heavy rains are expected in Nebraska, where 40 percent of the seeds have been sold.

Dr. Andropov is frustrated and nearing anger at these suggestions. He asks, "How can we do this? We don't even know that our product is flawed. We cannot send out conflicting messages." Also, he asks, what they should tell people who are both growers *and* investors. Dr. Brown adds that they do not know that the problem is in the seeds, and they cannot say with certainty when an analysis will be completed and a solution found. She does not want to promise what the company cannot deliver.

Jaylen is more anxious about getting a letter out to investors immediately. She suggests telling them that Agritechno's scientists have figured out the problem and found a solution. The scientists bristle at the suggestion.

Donna then attempts to find a satisfactory approach for all participants by reframing the situation to focus on yields for the coming year. Dr. Andropov is not satisfied with this option, noting that Agritechno won't know how many bushels of the transgenic corn have been produced for another four or five months, and they won't be able to fully identify the problem until then. He suggests sending out a letter stating that a few crops have failed and Agritechno is investigating.

Stefan grumbles that he hates to report problems to investors because it scares them away.

Case Study Analysis

20-15. Why are Drs. Andropov and Brown frustrated and angry about the suggestions from Holbrook, Girard, and Castillo?

20-16. What are the arguments for and against notifying Agritechno's investors? What is the basis for each argument?

20-17. What are the arguments for and against notifying Agritechno's growers? What is the basis for each argument?

20-18. What method of communication, if any, would you recommend for investors? Growers?

20-19. What should Agritechno tell its investors and growers, if anything, about the crop failures and proposed solutions?

AYZH Inc.—Seeing Opportunities to Improve Women's Health

"We exist as a commitment to save lives and change lives, one product at a time, making one happy woman at a time."

—Zubaida Bai

Zubaida Bai is an accomplished professional woman who has chosen a path that incorporates her skills and passions. She is a leading entrepreneur in the delivery of health care to impoverished women. Her role reflects the confluence of a number of facets of her life.

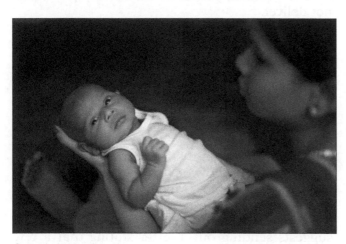

© Pakistan Images/Alamy

Zubaida grew up in India and completed her initial education there, earning a degree from Madras University. She studied development of modular products at Sweden's Darlana University en route to a master's degree in engineering. She later moved to the United States and earned an MBA in social sustainability enterprise at Colorado State University.

This entrepreneur and engineer gained several years of work experience in the social development space. One role was as a Project Officer at the Lemelson Foundation Initiative, collaborating with Impoverished Innovations Network and the Indian Institute of Technology Madras. She also knows five languages: English, Hindi, Tamil, Gujarati, and Teluga. Among the terms she uses to describe herself are: "brainstormer, business mentor, change agent . . . social entrepreneur."[6]

Zubaida has earned a number of awards and fellowships, including:

- Echoing Green Fellow—Echoing Green, 2012
- One of 60 Designs to Improve Life Globally—INDEX Awards, 2011
- Affordable Health Innovation Award—World Health Care Congress, 2011
- Young Champion of Maternal Health—Ashoka and Engender Health, 2010
- Outstanding Commitment Award—Clinton Global Initiative University, 2010
- TEDIndia Fellow—TED Ideas Worth Spreading, 2009
- International Presidential Fellow—Colorado State University, 2008[7]

Addressing Social Issues

As a child and young woman in India, Zubaida saw her own mother, and numerous other women, burdened by health and financial struggles. She wanted to find a way to relieve these problems. This purpose became even more personal when Zubaida's first child was born. She contracted an infection at childbirth that left her suffering. Her doctors said more children were out of the question. Zubaida was determined to take action and moved to the United States to add business skills to her engineering know-how.

She founded AYZH Inc. in 2010, with Habib Anwar and Kellen McMartin. Today, Zubaida is a recognized leader in engineering design of economical health products for developing areas.

As Zubaida states, "AYZH aims to be the leading global provider of life-saving, life-changing health products for underprivileged women worldwide. Our goals are to reduce maternal and infant mortality through improved quality of care at time of birth."[8]

[6]Zubaida Bai, "TED Community: Zubaida Bai," accessed October 6, 2013, http://www.ted.com/profiles/254505.

[7]Changemakers, "About Zubaida Bai: AYZH, Founder and Chief Executive," accessed October 6, 2013, http://www.changemakers.com/users/zubaida-bai.

[8]Karen Eng, "Women and children first: Fellow Friday with Zubaida Bai, who creates lifesaving kits for maternal health," *TED Blog*, August 16, 2013, accessed October 6, 2013, http://blog.ted.com/2013/08/16/women-and-children-first-fellows-friday-with-zubaida-bai-who-creates-lifesaving-kits-for-maternal-health/.

Operating as a For-Profit Business with a Social Mission

AYZH's first product is the JANMA (Sanskrit for "birth") Clean Birth Kit. It consists of a biodegradable "purse" with six items that are used to reduce maternal and infant infections and mortality in underprivileged areas of the world. The tools can ensure safe and sterile conditions. The "purse" can be used after the delivery. As of August 2013, AYZH sold 38,000 Clean Birth Kits, primarily in India and Africa.[9] In India, the kits are assembled by local women.

Additional types of kits are planned to meet other needs in related health problems. In addition, the company plans to extend its reach to disadvantaged populations on a global scale. AYZH is focused on connecting its products to the Safe Birth Checklist Initiative of the World Health Organization.

AYZH launched an Indiegogo campaign in August 2013, which raised $14,711 from 114 funders (on a $50,000 goal). The company planned to use the funds for "impact" research and to train healthcare workers.

As a relatively new company, AYZH has a small core team, as well as interns and contract employees. Zubaida serves as Chief Executive. One of her cofounders, Habib Anwar, is responsible for operations and finance. There also are team members responsible for communications and public relations, fundraising, social media, and sales and partnership building. The third cofounder, Kellen McMartin, serves as an advisor. As noted above, assembly of the JANMA Clean Birth Kits is done by contracted women in India.

Growing the Organization's Outreach through Partnerships

AYZH relies on both for-profit and not-for-profit customers and partners to distribute its products to developing areas and for support. For-profit institutions, such as clinics and rural health centers, sell the kits. JANMA Clean Birth Kits are also distributed by nongovernmental aid organizations. Scholars at Harvard University are working to conduct an analysis of Clean Birth Kits' effectiveness in improving health outcomes. In addition, AYZH is partnering with the Rural Technology Business Incubator in India. Rural healthcare workers will receive pertinent information via voice messages through the groundbreaking Mobile Phone Training Program.

If Zubaida Bai has her way, women's health will improve around the world.

Case Study Analysis

20-20. What type of leader do you think Zubaida is, according to Goleman's typology?

20-21. What motivates Zubaida in her company?

20-22. How do her education and experience relate to her role as founder and CEO of AYZH?

20-23. What is the role of ethics at AYZH? How might the company's integrity be challenged?

Case Sources

Akosha Changemakers, "About Zubaida Bai: AYZH, Founder and Chief Executive," accessed October 6, 2013, http://www.changemakers.com/users/zubaida-bai.

Karen Eng, "Women and children first: Fellow Friday with Zubaida Bai, who creates lifesaving kits for maternal health," *TED Blog*, August 16, 2013, accessed October 6, 2013, http://blog.ted.com/2013/08/16/women-and-children-first-fellows-friday-with-zubaida-bai-who-creates-lifesaving-kits-for-maternal-health/.

Zubaida Bai, "Small purse BIG CHANGE," Indiegogo.com., August 21, 2013, accessed October 6, 2013, http://www.indiegogo.com/projects/small-purse-big-change.

Zubaida Bai, "TED Community: Zubaida Bai," accessed October 6, 2013, http://www.ted.com/profiles/254505.

---

[9]Zubaida Bai, "Small purse BIG CHANGE," Indiegogo.com, August 21, 2013, accessed October 6, 2013, http://www.indiegogo.com/projects/small-purse-big-change.

Investors Will Care about Your Exit Strategy

We have emphasized that your exit strategy will be important to your investors. Your business plan should spell out in how many years you expect them to be able to cash out, and the financial data in your plan must show this. Again, it will not be enough to mention that someday the company will go public and their share of the business will be worth "a lot" of money. Of the thousands of new ventures launched every year in the United States, only a small percentage will ever be listed on a stock exchange. Yet, according to David Newton, on Entrepreneur.com (January 15, 2001), over 70 percent of formal business plans presented to angel investors and venture capitalists cite going public as the primary exit strategy. Most estimate that going public will happen within just four years from the business's launch date. Be more realistic.

Chapter Summary

Now that you have studied this chapter, you can do the following:

1. Determine how you want to grow your business and then exit from it.
   - Decide what your ultimate goals and objectives are.
   - Consider creating a business that will provide employment and wealth for your family.
   - Identify options to broaden product and service offerings through diversification.
   - Evaluate replication strategies.
2. Describe how businesses use licensing to profit from their brands.
   - A brand is a name, term, sign, logo, design, or combination of these that identifies the products or services of a company and differentiates them from those of competitors.
   - The licensee pays a fee for the license and will probably also pay the licensor a royalty (share of the profits).
   - Licensing is only effective when the licensor is confident that his or her company name will not be tarnished by how the licensee uses it.
3. Explain how a business can be franchised.
   - A franchise is a business that markets a product or service in the exact manner prescribed by the founder or successors of the parent company.
   - As an entrepreneur, you could develop a concept and business operation that can be reproduced and sold to other entrepreneurs. They would pay you a fee for the right to run the business exactly the way that you direct and pay you a royalty as well.
4. Learn methods of valuing a business.
   - Book value (net worth = assets – liabilities)
   - Future earnings
   - Market-based (value = P/E × estimated future net earnings)
5. Discuss five ways to harvest a business.
   - Increase the free cash flows. Once you are ready to exit, you can begin reducing reinvestment and collecting revenue as cash.
   - Management buyout. The entrepreneur sells the firm to the managers, who raise the money to buy it via personal savings and debt.

- Employee stock ownership plan (ESOP). This provides an employee retirement plan and allows the entrepreneur and partners, as they exit the company, to sell their stock to the employees.
- Merging or being acquired. Joining together with another company or being bought by one.
- Initial public offering (IPO). Going public is getting your company listed on the stock exchange to be traded on the open market.

Key Terms

book value, 643
diversification, 638
fair market value, 642
harvesting, 641
licensing, 638

line extension, 639
liquidation, 641
merger, 645
replication strategy, 639

Entrepreneurship Portfolio

Critical Thinking Exercises

21-1. Describe the differences between a licensing and a franchising agreement.

21-2. Give an example of a business that could lead to licensing agreements and a business that could be franchised.

21-3. Do you plan to franchise your business or license any of your products? Explain.

21-4. Describe the exit strategy you plan to use to harvest your business. Why do you think this exit strategy will be attractive to potential investors?

Key Concept Questions

21-5. Identify two companies that merged during the past three years. Describe the structure of the merger and what has happened to the resulting organization since then.

21-6. Choose one of the harvesting strategies described in the chapter and research it in depth. Write a report per instructor guidelines.

Application Exercise

21-7. Look around your local community and select a popular business that is an independent company—not a franchise or part of a major corporation. Identify the possible harvesting strategies that the owners(s) could employ. What would you recommend and why?

21-8. Select five companies that are profiled in this text from the Step into the Shoes and Global Impact features in other chapters. Indicate whether each has been harvested (you may need to do an Internet search). If so, what strategy did the owner(s) employ? If not, what would you recommend?

Exploring Online

21-9. The American Association of Franchisees and Dealers (AAFD) is a national trade association that represents the rights and interests of franchisees and independent dealers across the country. Visit this association online at http://www.aafd.org to learn more about franchises and the resources available. As a potential franchisor, you should know what your prospective customers are reading.

Search the site for the article, "AAFD Road Map to Selecting a Franchise." Read the section called "8 Things to Look for in a Franchise." For each of the tips in the article, write a one-sentence summary and note how it might apply to your business as a franchisor.

21-10. Find a franchise online like the one you might want to create. Answer the following:

a. What is the franchise? What does it sell?

b. Why are you interested in it?

c. What is the franchise fee?

        d. What are the start-up costs?

        e. What is the royalty fee?

        f. Describe the training the franchisor offers to franchisees.

        g. Describe the marketing the franchisor provides for franchisees.

21-11. Find a company online that is similar to the type of business you would like to launch. Assume you would want to sell it. Describe how much you would expect from a buyer and explain your valuation method.

Bizbuilder Business Plan Questions

After studying this chapter, you should be able to answer the following Business Plan Questions. The entire outline for the Business Plan is found in Appendix 2.

8.0 Funding Request and Exit Strategy

8.2 Exit Plan

    A. How will investors get paid back/out? Public offering? Employee buyout? Merger or acquisition? Liquidation? Stock buyback?

    B. When will this happen?

    C. Do you plan to franchise your business or license any of your products? Explain.

8.3 Milestones

    A. Create a Gantt chart for your organization to make your plans clear to potential investors.

Case Study | Anago Cleaning Systems— Growth through Franchising

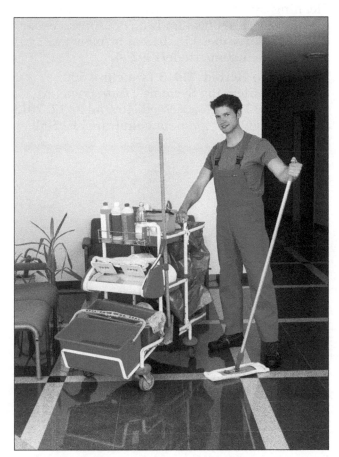
Andrey_Popov/Shutterstock

Anago Cleaning Systems, based in Pompano Beach, Florida, is a company created for growth through franchising. As a 15-year veteran of owning a cleaning business, David R. Povlitz exited his Florida retirement to start Anago. His original cleaning business, Imperial Professional Building Maintenance, was in Michigan, and he owned it with his three brothers. When they sold the company, Povlitz retired and relocated. A short while later, he took a job at leading janitorial franchisor Jani-King and learned more about its franchising system. Anago was born in 1989 and started franchising in 1991.

Anago Cleaning Services focuses on commercial rather than residential cleaning. It takes advantage of the cost cutting methods developed over years of experience and knowledge of competitors.

Franchising from the Start
Growth has been through increasing the number of franchises. According to Anago's Web site, the

number of "unit" franchises is 2012 was 2,427, compared with 732 in 2005 and 73 in the 1990s. The number of "master" franchises has reached 30 and continues to grow. The company was ranked as *Entrepreneur* magazine's 10th Fastest Growing Franchise in 2013 and was 5th in 2010 and 2011.

Master Franchises
The company focuses largely on the acquisition of master franchises to grow. Anago master franchises, called Regional Franchises, have the exclusive rights to the company's system in their contractual territories. Each contractual region has a population base of at least 500,000 people and at least 5,000 businesses. It is the master franchise's job to recruit unit franchises within its territories. As the Anago site explains, "As a Master Franchise Owner, you are not in the cleaning business, you are in the franchising business."

Master franchises pay for assistance in site selection, live and computer training, computer software, and various support options. Fees are about $39,000 for the regional franchise rights with an additional $75,000 to $100,000 in working capital. Plovitz reduced the price in 2011 citing the weak economy, and challenged other top franchise companies to reduce their fees.

Unit Franchises
Anago's unit franchises, or Janitorial Franchises, are responsible for cleaning the commercial properties that master franchises get under contract. The bulk of marketing and administrative tasks are handled by master franchises through regional offices. Unit franchises do not have to identify clients, prepare estimates, or set up cleaning contracts. They also are not responsible for billing and collections. The regional office provides them with orientation and ongoing support.

Unit franchises pay a franchise fee of $4,590 to $32,348 with an investment of $11,185 to $66,853. There is a 10 percent discount for veterans. The ongoing royalty fees are 10 percent of gross revenues, and franchise contracts are for 10 years and are renewable. Franchisees do not need prior business or janitorial experience and are expected to be owner-operators.

Continued Opportunities for Growth
The company continues to actively recruit master franchises with a list of 66 available territories.

Povlitz has successfully leveraged his knowledge, experience, and resources to grow Anago Cleaning Systems.

Case Study Analysis

21-12. What benefits did Anago Cleaning Systems gain from franchising?

21-13. What benefits do Anago's master franchises get from the company that they would not have independently?

21-14. What are the demographic requirements for selecting a master franchise region?

21-15. Who is most likely to be interested in an Anago unit franchise? Why?

21-16. Visit the Anago Cleaning Systems Web site at http://www.anagousa.com and find information about obtaining a master franchise.

    a. What are the competitive advantages that Anago identifies?

    b. What proprietary systems and services are noted?

    c. How are master franchisees incorporated into the site?

Case Sources

Anago Cleaning Systems, http://www.anagousa.com.

Dennis Romero, December 22, 2008, "Anago Cleaning Systems: Meet a franchisor with a willingness to get his hands dirty," *Entrepreneur*, accessed November 11, 2013 at http://www.entrepreneur.com/article/199294.

Tracy Stapp Herold, "2013 Franchise 500: #39 Anago Cleaning Systems," *Entrepreneur*, December 12, 2012, accessed November 12, 2013 at http://www.entrepreneur.com/franchise500/index.html.

When iContact cofounders Ryan Allis and Aaron Houghton decided to exit from their company, they sold it to Vocus Inc. for $169 million. They founded Raleigh, North Carolina-based iContact in 2003 and sold it in February 2012.[7] At the time of the sale, iContact had some 300 employees, $50 million in annual sales, and 70,000 customers.[8]

iContact

The company offers e-mail marketing software for small and medium-sized businesses and not-for-profits. The iContact products automate the creation, delivery, and tracking of e-mail communications. The software permits its users to determine the effectiveness of e-mail marketing campaigns through the analysis of critical data, such as how many e-mails are opened, customer "likes," follows, click-throughs, and so forth. One feature that provides a competitive advantage for iContact is the ability to integrate with Facebook and Twitter for campaigns that will use social networks to build word-of-mouth support. According to the iContact website, the platform has some one million registered users.

iContact, as operated by its founders, describes itself in press releases as "a purpose driven company that makes social media and email marketing easy, so that small and midsized companies and causes can grow and succeed . . . the company maintains B Corporation status, a certification awarded to companies meeting comprehensive and transparent social and environmental performance standards. As part of its ongoing social mission, iContact applies the 4-1s Corporate Social Responsibility Model, donating one percent from each of its payroll, equity, product, and employee time to local and global communities."

Vocus Inc.

Vocus, based in Beltsville, Maryland, is a publicly traded company (NASDAQ: VOCS) that already had search marketing, social marketing, and publicity applications in its operations. According to the Vocus Web site, "our software sends real-time marketing opportunities directly to marketers in the form of leads, prospects, social media conversations, curated content and inbound media inquiries. With our marketing consulting and services team ready to help, our software solution delivers marketing success." As a provider of cloud-based public relations and marketing software, the addition of e-mail marketing capabilities will broaden its range of products and strengthen its marketing suite.

Vocus was founded in 1992 by Rick Rudman and Bob Lentz, primarily as a political public relations firm. The firm expanded and went public in 2005, raising $45 million in its initial public offering. Starting in 2006, the company acquired PRWeb, Help a Reporter Out (HARO), and North Social. Vocus reported revenues of $170.8 million in 2012, with customers that included British Airways, Farmers Insurance, Make-A-Wish Foundation, and Wyndham Worldwide.

iContact's Founders

Both Ryan Allis and Aaron Houghton are serial entrepreneurs. Ryan was born in Pittsburgh in 1984. He created Virante, a Web-design business, while in high school. He received his undergraduate degree in economics from the University of North Carolina at Chapel Hill and then completed the EO/MIT Entrepreneurial Masters Program. After a year in the Harvard MBA program, Ryan went to San Francisco to start Connect.

Ryan has many interests and talents. He has authored *Zero to One Million* (McGraw-Hill, 2008) and *The Startup Guide: Building a Better World Through Entrepreneurship* (http://www.startupguide .com). He is a philanthropist and agent of social change through his roles as a member of the United Nations Foundation Global Entrepreneur Council, Board Chairman of Nourish International, and Founder of the Humanity Fund. He has invested in such companies as EvoApp, Ark, and Close and served as the National Co-Chairperson for Technology for President Obama. Ryan is the recipient of numerous awards for his humanitarian work.

Aaron Houghton is currently running his fifteenth startup, the Raleigh-Durham-based BoostSuite, where he is a cofounder and the CEO. He received his undergraduate degree in computer science from the University of North Carolina at Chapel Hill (2003), where he and Ryan met. He also completed the Entrepreneurial Masters Program at MIT (2012).

Aaron was the President and CEO of Preation, both before and during his tenure as Chairman

---

[7]Leena Rao, "Vocus Acquires iContact for $169 Million," *TechCrunch*, February 28, 2012, accessed October 7, 2013, http://techcrunch.com/2012/02/28/vocus-buys-email-marketing-company-icontact-for-169-million.

[8]"Ryan Allis," CrunchBase profile, accessed October 13, 2013, http://www.crunchbase .com/person/ryan-allis.

University Parent, Inc.

Executive Summary

University Parent, Inc.
University Parent (UPI) produces institution-specific guides and comprehensive websites for parents of college students. Revenues are generated through the sale of advertising in the local guides and on the websites.

Today, there are 32 million parents of college students
According to surveys and interviews conducted by UPI, parents do not receive the information they need from colleges. They want to know where to have a nice dinner in their student's college town, where to stay, and fun activities to do while visiting. They also want to know how to parent their college student and need to understand the issues their child is facing such as managing money, avoiding credit card debt, and balancing school, a part-time job, and extra-curricular activities.

UPI can help
UPI will produce three free guides per year for each college that will be distributed during summer orientation and August move-in, Fall Parent's Weekend, and in the Spring to prospective parents through the Admissions Office and Campus Tour Office. At the University of Colorado, over 25,000 prospective parents tour the campus. The magazines will be distributed through the university, hotels, and restaurants. The magazine content will include: restaurant reviews, a lodging directory, a shopping guide, calendar of events, graduation requirement Information, map of the city, and a Q&A section.

Proven track record
The first issue of the *Parent's Guide to Boulder* was published in October 2003 and immediately profited from advertising sales. The second edition will be published June 2004, and due to advance advertising sales, will also be profitable. Demand for these first guides have proved that advertisers are committed to purchasing space in the guide and that parents are interested in reading the guide.

Experienced, enthusiastic management team
Sarah Schupp is the founder, CEO, and Chairman of the UPI Board of Directors. She published the initial *Parent's Guide to Boulder* in 2003. A graduate of the University of Colorado with degrees in Business Administration and English Literature, Sarah is capable of expanding the vision of UPI to Colorado and Texas. In Year 3, UPI plans to hire a CEO with national rollout experience.

Other UPI employees include VP Marketing Michelle Dorenkamp, CFO Kara Grinnell, and CTO Ryan Roth. In addition to an excellent management team,

3

University Parent, Inc.

UPI is in the process of developing a board of twelve directors that bring experience in advertising, magazine writing, start-ups, and venture capital.

Plan for expansion

Because of the initial success of the *Parent's Guide to Boulder*, UPI is currently expanding its marketing base to Colorado State University and the University of Denver. A regional office in Boulder will handle advertising sales for the three guides. UPI plans to broaden its base beginning in Year 2, with a goal of being in 44 schools by Year 5.

The offering

UPI is offering 35% of the company for $500,000. This will provide investors with a 60% rate of return, translating to $4.3 million in Year 5 when UPI plans to sell to Hearst Publishing or Conde Nast Publishing. UPI breaks-even in Year 2, generating revenues of $1.8 million. In Year 5, UPI will have revenues of $12 million and a net profit of $4.1 million.

Company Overview

With two successful publications for the University of Colorado and established relationships with over 35 advertisers, UPI is positioned for nation-wide expansion. In October of 2004, UPI plans to produce a total of 9 publications and 3 websites for the University of Colorado, the University of Denver, and Colorado State University. We project UPI will produce 132 publications and high-traffic websites for 44 colleges and universities by Year 5. This will result in net revenues of $12.3 million, net profits of $4.1 million, and a valuation of $70 million. Also in Year 5, UPI plans to market the company to suitable buyers such as Hearst Publishing or Conde Nast Publishing.

University Parent, Inc.

Product/Service Description

Introduction

You arrive on campus to drop off your freshman student. This is always one of the hardest times of the year for you. Leaving your child miles from home, millions of questions are running through your head. How do they register for classes? How many credits will they need to graduate? What issues will they face being away from home? As you are signing in for orientation, you receive a magazine that specifically answers these questions. Not only does it answer campus life questions, it also offers restaurant reviews, lodging suggestions, and a detailed map of the city. The magazine directs you to a website where you can talk to other parents who have your same concerns. Suddenly you have a sense of relief. Now you have a source of information at your fingertips.

As a Boulder business, you have always wondered how you can directly advertise to CU parents who visit often and spend thousands of dollars while visiting. One day a packet arrives at your business with the first *Parent's Guide to Boulder* from the 2003 Parent's Weekend and a rate card. You are excited that there is now a reasonably priced and direct way to contact CU parents and inform them of your business. You know that purchasing advertising will be well worth every dollar. (Boulder, Colorado served as UPI's test market.)

Description

University Parent produces a comprehensive local guide as well as a website for parents of college students. Through its compilation of articles, pictures, maps, current events, and advertisements, it provides a convenient, thorough source of information for CU parents.

Parent

Guide Feature	Benefit
Distribution through the university, hotels, and restaurants	Convenience
Provides useful information about their student's environment and community	Comfort, Sense of Security
Makes navigating Boulder easier and allows for advance planning	Saves Time
Free! Gives information and coupons for good values in: lodging, eating, shopping, and having a good time	Saves Money

University Parent, Inc.

Advertiser

Guide Feature	Benefit
Targets specific niche	Targeted ROI
Mid-ranged priced advertising	Saves Money
Effective distribution channels	Reaches Target Market, Generates Revenue

Market Comparison

Unlike other publications in college towns, UPI offers its readers focused, relevant information that is unavailable through local newspapers and magazines. It also offers advertisers a targeted, identifiable market.

Stage of Development

UPI produced its first guide in Boulder for Parent's Weekend '03. The profitability of the first guide demonstrated UPI's ability to sell advertising and to produce a useful product. UPI is currently marketing and creating articles for its Summer '04 publication. Our CTO, Ryan Roth, launched the Guide to Boulder's website in April of '04, http://www.guidetoboulder.com. Advertising sales for the website are scheduled to begin in May '04.

Client Base

UPI currently has over 35 clients for the *Parent's Guide to Boulder*. These advertisers include: Wells Fargo, Walnut Realty, McGuckin Hardware, the CU Book Store, the CU Foundation, Greenbriar Inn, Boulder Broker Inn, Boulder Outlook Hotel & Suites, Boulder Express Shuttle, and many more. Of the initial advertisers in the Fall '03 guide, 100% of advertisers solicited purchased advertising for the Summer '04 guide.

Potential Readership Base

Demographic
> 32 million U.S. parents of college students, growing at an annual rate of 6%
> We expect 20% of each college's parent population to read our magazines

Family Income
> Most families sending children to college have a combined household income ranging from $80,000 to $150,000

Cost of Education
> A college education is likely the biggest investment they will make in their student
> A college education costs anywhere from $30,000 to $200,000
> Parents typically provide for their children while in college, paying for expenses such as transportation (car, bike), car insurance, textbooks, clothing, computers and software, food, rent, etc.

2890 Shadow Creek – Boulder, Colorado – 303.579.9871 – info@upi.com

University Parent, Inc.

These expenses average between $800—$1,500 per month.

Potential Advertisers

Independent marketing firms that handle national accounts
Local business owners and/or Marketing Managers representing hotels, restaurants, retail stores, travel agencies that must make buying decisions based on distribution and cost.

Industry and Marketplace Analysis

The publication industry has over 17,000 magazines that gross $24 billion in revenue each year. Historically, this industry has grown at a rate of 7 percent, and is expected to grow 6 percent in the future. There is little demand for new titles with the exception of demand for specialty, niche magazines that enable advertisers to reach a well-defined market. Our primary, unexplored niche consists of parents of college students. According to surveys, virtually all CU parents (95%) are uninformed about campus activities, news, and pertinent issues. Currently no other publications are addressing these needs and concerns of CU parents.

In recent years, there has been an increase in online magazines and online versions of print magazines. Major threats in the periodical industry include other advertising mediums such as television, radio, and print. The most competition for publications is in print advertising, which ranges from daily newspapers to monthly magazines. Another threat to the publication industry is the rising cost of paper, which is driving down profits. Some of the internal market changes revolve around a concern over rising paper costs because of deforestation.

Leading advertisers in the magazine industry include: automobile manufacturers, consumer goods companies, entertainment conglomerates, and tobacco firms. Some of the internal market changes revolve around a concern over rising paper costs because of deforestation.

Leading advertisers in the magazine industry include: automobile manufacturers, consumer goods companies, entertainment conglomerates, and tobacco firms. The publication industry is affected by changes in economic conditions since revenue is advertising-dependant.

2890 Shadow Creek – Boulder, Colorado – 303.579.9871 – info@upi.com

University Parent, Inc.

Marketing Strategy

Introduction

UPI's target readership market will include students, parents of present and future students, university faculty and staff, and high school counselors. Aggressive distribution will insure that all sectors of our target market will receive our free guide as well as website information. Our target market for advertising is businesses that want to make parents of college students aware of their products and/or services. We provide these businesses an opportunity to reach a specific, identifiable market at a reasonable cost.

Target Market Advertising Strategy

We will position ourselves as the only publication offering information specifically for parents of CU students and as the only publication offering businesses the opportunity to advertise to these parents.

In Boulder, the primary advertising media are the *Colorado Daily*, *Daily Camera*, *The Onion*, and *Boulder Magazine*. UPI's targeted, niche market strategy offers businesses a superior, more cost-effective media product at a lower cost than these publications. UPI will produce a quarterly mailing to businesses in Boulder that offer a product/service that CU parents may be interested in purchasing. The mailing will be directed to the "businesses' owners" and will include a previous *Parent's Guide to Boulder*, a cover letter specifying why advertising with UPI is effective, testimonials from current advertisers, and a rate card.

As UPI moves into additional markets, this strategy will be replicated and customized as needed.

Pricing Strategy

University Parent will generate revenue from two sources: print advertising in our guides and online advertising on our website.

Print advertising prices (per guide):

Size	Full Color
Eighth Page	$250
Quarter Page	$400
Half Page	$600
Full Page	$800
Back Cover, Inside Cover, Back Inside	$1000

8

University Parent, Inc.

Website advertising prices (per month):

Size	Full Color
2" x 1"	$400
2" x 2"	$500
Banner, 1" x 7"	$700
Pop Up	$1000
Ad in email newsletter	$500

Businesses can purchase yearlong magazine and website advertising at a10% discount. The website advertising prices are likely to change based on our website's traffic. The higher the traffic, the higher the price we can charge.

Distribution Strategy

UPI will distribute guides to parents through the university admissions office, parent relations office, and campus tour office. The guide will also be distributed in hotels, restaurants, businesses, and through the Chamber of Commerce. There will be an option on the website to download the guide or have it mailed for a small fee (postage).

Advertising, Sales & Promotion Strategy

UPI will be promoted to advertisers through local networking at Boulder Chamber of Commerce events, press releases in local papers, direct mailings, and referral incentives for current clients. In addition, the website will serve as an effective tool to inform both businesses and parents of our services.

Marketing & Sales Forecasts

UPI's revenue is generated through print and website advertising sales. We project revenues from print advertising at 54% and website advertising sales at 46% of total revenues.

Advertising revenues are calculated by using the print advertising rates multiplied by expected sales for three guides. UPI projects sales of 25 print advertisements per issue at an average cost of $1,000 and 72 website sales per year per institution at an average cost of $750.

Revenue (In thousands $)

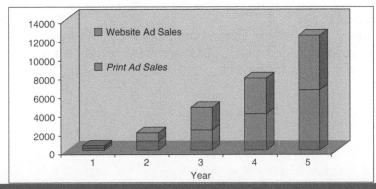

2890 Shadow Creek – Boulder, Colorado – 303.579.9871 – info@upi.com

University Parent, Inc.

Revenue Projections

	Year 1	Year 2	Year 3	Year 4	Year 5
Product A—Magazine					
Number of Schools	3	9	22	32	44
Total Issues/Year	9	36	66	96	132
Magazines Printed/Year	90,000	360,000	660,000	960,000	1,320,000
Printing Cost/Per Magazine	0.25	0.23	0.21	0.19	0.17
Number of Units/Ad	225	900	1,800	2,925	4,425
Avg. Price/Ad Page	$1,000	$1,100	$1,210	$1,331	$1,464
Print Adv Total	$225,000	$990,000	$2,178,000	$3,893,175	$6,478,643
Product B—Website					
Advertisements Sold/Yr	360	1,080	2,640	3,840	5,280
Price per unit	$750	$825	$908	$998	$1,098
Web Adv Total	$270,000	$891,000	$2,395,800	$3,833,280	$5,797,836
Net Revenue	$495,000	$1,881,000	$4,573,800	$7,726,455	$12,276,479

Operations Plan

Operations Strategy

Our strategy is to establish a reputation with readers and advertisers that UPI consistently delivers well-received, well-designed, informative magazines and websites. We will develop this reputation by providing products that are professionally designed, error-free, and exceed the expectations of both our readers and our advertisers. We will measure our success through in-person as well as online surveys of our customers.

Our goal is to have highly satisfied customers—our parent readers and our advertisers. To that end, UPI will provide training for all employees that stresses the necessity of exceeding the expectations of our customers in ways such as delivering advertising proofs early or following up with a parent's question promptly and thoroughly.

Scope of Operations

At UPI headquarters, there will be 15 full-time employees. In Year 1, this office will handle advertising sales for the CU, DU, and CSU guides, as well as negotiate next year's Texas expansion.

2890 Shadow Creek – Boulder, Colorado – 303.579.9871 – info@upi.com

University Parent, Inc.

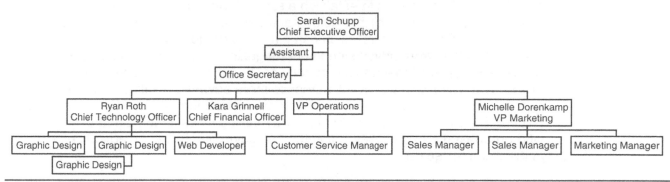

Headquarters Office Personnel
Boulder, Colorado

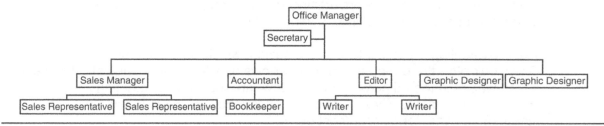

Regional Office Personnel
Locations: Dallas, Atlanta, Boston, Kansas City

Ongoing Operations

UPI headquarters will coordinate with the regional offices to produce a website and three magazines annually for each college. Issues will be published every summer, fall, and spring. The website will be updated as needed, daily if necessary. Advertising sales as well as contact with parents and university faculty and staff will be continuous throughout the year

Operating Expenses

	Year 1	Year 2	Year 3	Year 4	Year 5
Total Operating Expenses	$854,967	$1,547,676	$2,588,328	$3,611,938	$5,083,166
% of Revenue	172.7%	82.3%	56.6%	46.7%	41.4%

11

University Parent, Inc.

Development Plan

Development Strategy

The first priority for UPI is to establish a strong brand and reputation within each new market. UPI will publish a guide approximately every four months. Our relationship with advertisers will become much stronger with each issue as they realize the value from advertising in our magazine. After three issues (one year), we believe our relationships with advertisers will significantly increase revenues. In year two, returning clients will purchase more advertisements and clients who watched their competitors gain revenue from advertising with us. For the second issue of the *Parent's Guide to Boulder,* advertising sales doubled and every client who purchased an advertisement in the Fall guide purchased an advertisement in the Summer guide.

During the publication cycle for each issue, the first order of business is to brainstorm new ideas and themes. Once the themes are decided, we make those themes available to the advertisers. We then give advertisers a three-month window to purchase advertising space. Contact is made with potential advertiser through "cold-selling," a variant of cold calling.

The "cold-selling" begins with a mass mailing, which is followed up with an e-mail. One week after the e-mailing, our staff follows up with a telephone call. The next seven weeks in the ad purchasing "window" are reserved for meetings with potential advertisers. Through our past experience, we have found that such meetings are vital for closing most deals.

The artwork acceptance window is open from the moment an advertising contract is signed until the artwork acceptance deadline, one week after the close of advertising sales. The first payment for the advertisement is due on the last day of advertisement sales. The second payment is due one week before we send the magazine to the printer.

While ad sales are in full swing, the design of the magazine is developed. Concurrently, article research and story writing for the magazine are performed. Immediately after the design and story writing are finalized, we finalize the layout and update the website; both of these occur over a two-week period.

As soon as the layout is finished, the final copy is sent to the printer. Within 5 days, the printer overnights a digital proof for UPI's approval. Once approved, printing takes approximately one week. Once the copies are received, the magazine is ready for distribution. Distribution takes place over a two-week period. Most magazines are mailed directly from the printer to the distribution point. These distribution points include: the university, hotels, restaurants, and other local businesses.

2890 Shadow Creek – Boulder, Colorado – 303.579.9871 – info@upi.com

University Parent, Inc.

Roll-Out Plan

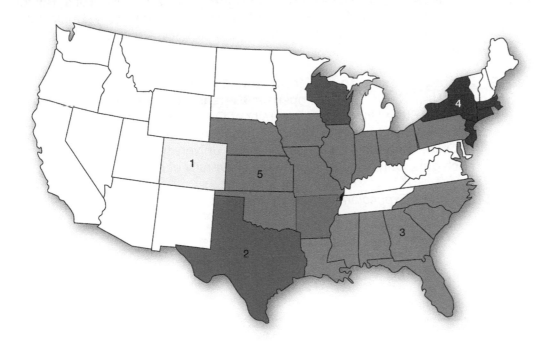

Year 1: Colorado
3 Schools: CU, University of Denver, and Colorado State University

Year 2: Colorado and Texas
9 Schools: *New Regional Office opens in <u>Dallas</u>: Southern Methodist University, University of Texas at Austin, A&M, Trinity University, Baylor University, Rice University

Year 3: Colorado, Texas, South
22 Schools: *New Regional Office opens in <u>Atlanta</u>: University of Georgia, University of the South, University of North Carolina, University of South Carolina, Duke University, University of Florida, Rollins College, University of Virginia, University of Richmond, University of Louisiana, Louisiana State University

13

University Parent, Inc.

Year 4: Colorado, Texas, South, Northeast
32 Schools: *New Regional Office opens in **Boston**: Harvard, MIT, Tufts, Boston University, Boston College, Princeton, New York University, Columbia University, Barnard College, Villanova University, University of Connecticut

Year 5: Colorado, Texas, South, Northeast, Midwest
44 Schools: *New Regional Office opens in **Kansas City**: University of Kansas, Kansas State University, University of Oklahoma, Oklahoma State University, University of Missouri, Missouri State University, University of Ohio, Ohio State University, Purdue University, University of Michigan, University of Wisconsin, University of Illinois

Year 6: *Continued Expansion*: Northeast, Midwest, West

14

University Parent, Inc.

Management

Sarah Schupp, Chief Executive Officer

Sarah founded *The Parent's Guide to Boulder* in June of 2003. A graduate of the University of Colorado with degrees in Business Administration and English Literature, Sarah is capable of expanding the vision of UPI across the U.S. In addition, she has developed relationships with the University of Colorado through her 2004 position as the Senior Class President and member of the President's Leadership Class.

Ryan Roth, Chief Technology Officer

Ryan comes to UPI with an extensive background in high-level web technology and information system deployment strategies. As team leader of numerous successful system development projects, Ryan is a valuable addition to UPI as Chief Technology Officer. He joined our team in early 2004 to provide in-depth, focused research on technology issues and solutions to provide University Parent with customized solutions unmatched by any other magazine publisher today. Ryan graduated from the Leeds School of Business at the University of Colorado with a B.S. in Business Administration and an emphasis in Information Systems.

Kara Grinnell, Chief Financial Officer

Kara is equipped with the financial knowledge needed to accomplish all the tasks included in the job of Chief Financial Officer. With a degree in Finance from the University of Colorado, Kara has the appropriate background to help UPI meet its financial goals. Kara has firsthand field experience with financial measurements and is prepared to help UPI become a $100 million venture.

Michelle Dorenkamp, VP Marketing

Michelle will graduate with a Bachelor of Science Degree in Business from the University of Colorado in May 2004. For the past three summers, she has worked in marketing and advertising for a real estate company. She has successfully worked with companies doing a direct mail campaign similar to the one that will be used to attract advertisers for the local guides.

University Parent, Inc.

Business Risks

Another company will copy our idea.
Because of a magazine's low start-up costs, it is likely that people will copy our concept. However, we can mitigate this risk by negotiating with national advertisers for annual contracts and with universities for distribution rights. Another way we can mitigate this risk is through strategic growth. By identifying the best regions for expansion, we will capture a new region each year. We are targeting geographically central locations with a high concentration of colleges and universities.

Universities will not cooperate to help us distribute the guide.
When selling advertisements to businesses, our greatest strength is that universities allow us to distribute the guide on campus. This distribution point makes advertisers believe their ROI will be greater because parents pay close attention to materials given to them by the university. However, our guide is an effective public relations tool for universities to give to parents and by maintaining appropriate content, we eliminate this obstacle.

Businesses will not buy advertising.
Our revenue projections are based on selling 25 or more print advertisements per issue and 10 Web ads per month per location. If businesses do not believe that our magazine will serve as an effective marketing tool, they will not purchase advertising. We must prove to advertisers that parents do and will read our magazine and will make buying decisions based on our information.

Each university has a different environment with different demographics.
Because we are producing guides with location-specific information, we must insure that the information we publish is accurate and appropriate for the area. If we miss the target demographic or culture of the area, parents will not read the guide and advertisers will not purchase advertising. To make sure we understand the area, representatives from our regional office will be familiar with every location in their region and will have student interns at each school that will help UPI understand the area and its parent population. In addition, we will use our website to collect marketing data. Weblogs, an online parent chat room, will allow us to track parents' comments and their geographic location, which will enable us to understand the issues at each university.

2890 Shadow Creek – Boulder, Colorado – 303.579.9871 – info@upi.com

University Parent, Inc.

Financial Plan

Financial Summary
Revenue for UPI is derived from magazine and website advertising sales. UPI plans to sell advertising to both national and local advertisers. As more people read our magazine and visit our website, the prices we can charge advertisers will increase.

The following table summarizes five years of pro forma financial statements. Assumptions for the financial statements are located in Section G of the Appendix.

	Year 1	Year 2	Year 3	Year 4	Year 5
Operating Revenue	$495,000	$1,881,000	$4,573,800	$7,726,455	$12,276,479
Operating Expenses					
Salaries, Wages, & Benefits	$323,000	$692,230	$1,152,524	$1,526,238	$1,907,539
Depreciation	$6,667	$20,000	$40,000	$60,000	$80,000
Rent & Utilities	$40,000	$85,600	$131,592	$180,803	$233,460
Total Operating Expenses	$854,967	$1,547,676	$2,588,328	$3,611,938	$5,083,166
Income Taxes	$0	$0	-$550,989	-$1,542,198	-$2,749,048
Net Income (Loss)	($401,329)	$197,583	$1,227,012	$2,313,297	$4,123,572

17

University Parent, Inc.

Balance Sheet
Years 0–5 ($)

	Begin	Year 1	Year 2	Year 3	Year 4	Year 5
ASSETS						
CURRENT ASSETS						
Cash	530,000	117,763	281,640	1,616,578	4,006,443	8,252,410
Accounts Receivable		0	0	0	0	0
Inventories		0	0	0	0	0
Other Current Assets		113	3,947	50,228	63,484	75,729
Total Current Assets	530,000	117,875	285,588	1,666,806	4,069,927	8,328,139
PROPERTY & EQUIPMENT	0	16,533	50,133	81,733	109,333	136,133
TOTAL ASSETS	530,000	134,409	335,721	1,748,539	4,179,261	8,464,272
LIABILITIES & SHAREHOLDERS' EQUITY						
CURRENT LIABILITIES						
Short-Term Debt	0	0	0	0	0	0
Accounts Payable & Accrued Expen		5,625	9,281	191,445	306,567	464,840
Other Current Liabilities		113	186	3,829	6,131	9,297
Current Portion of Long-term Debt	0	0	0	0	0	0
Total Current Liabilities	0	5,738	9,467	195,274	312,698	474,137
LONG-TERM DEBT (less current portion)	0	0	0	0	0	0
STOCKHOLDERS' EQUITY						
Common Stock	30,000	30,000	30,000	30,000	30,000	30,000
Preferred Stock	500,000	500,000	500,000	500,000	500,000	500,000
Retained Earnings		(401,329)	(203,746)	1,023,266	3,336,563	7,460,135
Total Equity	530,000	128,671	326,254	1,553,266	3,866,563	7,990,135
TOTAL LIABILITIES & EQUITY	530,000	134,409	335,721	1,748,539	4,179,261	8,464,272

18

University Parent, Inc.

Offering

Investment Requirements
UPI initially requires $500,000 in seed funding for the first year of operations. This amount will fund the expansion to the University of Denver and Colorado State University as well as funding new employee salaries and the opening of a Colorado regional office in Boulder. Investors will own 35% of the venture.

Valuation
Using the venture capital method, in Year 5, assuming net earnings of $4.1 million, and an industry P/E ratio of 17.3, UPI will have a market value of $70 million.

Financing
UPI seeks $500,000 in seed funding in Year 0. This round will provide the investor with a 35% stake in the venture at a 60% annual rate of return.

Exit Strategy
In Year 5, UPI we be marketed to Hearst Publishing and Condé Nast Publishing. These are logical acquirers because both companies own over 30 niche magazines.

University Parent, Inc.

Appendices

Income Statement...A

Balance Sheet ....B

Cash Flow Statement..C

Monthly and Quarterly Cash Flow Statements..D

Break-Even Analysis...E

Capital Expenditure Detail..F

Financial Assumptions ....G

Development Timeline ....H

Summary of Customer Surveys...I

Management Team Resumes ....J

    Sarah Schupp, CEO

    Kara Grinnell, CFO

    Ryan Roth, CTO

    Michelle Dorenkamp, VP Marketing

University Parent, Inc.

Appendix A, Income Statement, Years 1–5 ($)

	Year 1	Year 2	Year 3	Year 4	Year 5
NET REVENUES	495,000	1,881,000	4,573,800	7,726,455	12,276,479
COST OF REVENUE	26,362	90,741	152,471	204,023	255,692
% of Revenues	5.3%	4.8%	3.3%	2.6%	2.1%
GROSS PROFIT	468,638	1,790,259	4,421,329	7,522,432	12,020,787
% of Revenues	94.7%	95.2%	96.7%	97.4%	97.9%
OPERATING EXPENSES					
Sales & Marketing	240,750	364,610	674,953	1,023,764	1,734,098
Research & Development	219,800	291,186	360,569	434,809	514,245
General and Administration	394,417	891,880	1,552,806	2,153,364	2,834,823
Total Operating Expenses	854,967	1,547,676	2,588,328	3,611,938	5,083,166
% of Revenues	173%	82%	57%	47%	41%
EARNINGS FROM OPERATIONS	(386,329)	242,583	1,833,001	3,910,495	6,937,620
EXTRAORDINARY INCOME/ (EXPENSE)	(15,000)	(45,000)	(55,000)	(55,000)	(65,000)
EARNINGS BEFORE INTEREST & TAXES	(401,329)	197,583	1,778,001	3,855,495	6,872,620
INTEREST INCOME/(EXPENSE)	0	0	0	0	0
NET EARNINGS BEFORE TAXES	(401,329)	197,583	1,778,001	3,855,495	6,872,620
TAXES	0	0	(550,989)	(1,542,198)	(2,749,048)
NET EARNINGS	(401,329)	197,583	1,227,012	2,313,297	4,123,572
% of Revenues	-81.1%	10.5%	26.8%	29.9%	33.6%

21

University Parent, Inc.

Appendix B, Balance Sheet, Years 0–5 ($)

	Begin	Year 1	Year 2	Year 3	Year 4	Year 5
ASSETS						
CURRENT ASSETS						
Cash	530,000	117,763	281,640	1,616,578	4,006,443	8,252,410
Accounts Receivable		0	0	0	0	0
Inventories		0	0	0	0	0
Other Current Assets		113	3,947	50,228	63,484	75,729
Total Current Assets	530,000	117,875	285,588	1,666,806	4,069,927	8,328,139
PROPERTY & EQUIPMENT	0	16,533	50,133	81,733	109,333	136,133
TOTAL ASSETS	530,000	134,409	335,721	1,748,539	4,179,261	8,464,272
LIABILITIES & SHAREHOLDERS' EQUITY						
CURRENT LIABILITIES						
Short-Term Debt	0	0	0	0	0	0
Accounts Payable & Accrued Expen		5,625	9,281	191,445	306,567	464,840
Other Current Liabilities		113	186	3,829	6,131	9,297
Current Portion of Long-Term Debt	0	0	0	0	0	0
Total Current Liabilities	0	5,738	9,467	195,274	312,698	474,137
LONG-TERM DEBT (less current portion)	0	0	0	0	0	0
STOCKHOLDERS' EQUITY						
Common Stock	30,000	30,000	30,000	30,000	30,000	30,000
Preferred Stock	500,000	500,000	500,000	500,000	500,000	500,000
Retained Earnings		(401,329)	(203,746)	1,023,266	3,336,563	7,460,135
Total Equity	530,000	128,671	326,254	1,553,266	3,866,563	7,990,135
TOTAL LIABILITIES & EQUITY	530,000	134,409	335,721	1,748,539	4,179,261	8,464,272

22

University Parent, Inc.

Appendix C, Cash Flow Statement, Years 1–5 ($)

	Year 1	Year 2	Year 3	Year 4	Year 5
OPERATING ACTIVITIES					
Net Earnings	(401,329)	197,583	1,227,012	2,313,297	4,123,572
Depreciation	7,467	24,400	48,400	72,400	97,200
Working Capital Changes					
(Inc.)/Dec. Accts. Rec.	0	0	0	0	0
(Inc.)/Dec. Inventories	0	0	0	0	0
(Inc.)/Dec. Other CA	(113)	(3,835)	(46,281)	(13,256)	(12,245)
(Inc.)/Dec. Accts Pay Expenses	5,625	3,656	182,163	115,122	158,274
(Inc.)/Dec. Other CL	113	73	3,643	2,302	3,165
Net Cash Provided/(Used) Operating Activities	(388,237)	221,878	1,414,937	2,489,865	4,369,967
INVESTING ACTIVITIES					
Property & Equipment	(24,000)	(58,000)	(80,000)	(100,000)	(124,000)
Other					
Net Cash Used in Investing	(24,000)	(58,000)	(80,000)	(100,000)	(124,000)
FINANCING ACTIVITIES					
(Inc.)/Dec. Short-Term Debt	0	0	0	0	0
(Inc.)/Dec. Curr. Portion LTD	0	0	0	0	0
(Inc.)/Dec. Long-Term Debt	0	0	0	0	0
(Inc.)/Dec. Common Stock	0	0	0	0	0
(Inc.)/Dec. Preferred Stock	0	0	0	0	0
Dividends Declared	0	0	0	0	0
Net Cash Provided/ (Used) by Financing	0	0	0	0	0
INCREASE/(DECREASE) IN CASH	(412,237)	163,878	1,334,937	2,389,865	4,245,967
CASH AT BEGINNING OF YEAR		530,000	117,763	281,640	1,616,578	4,006,443
CASH AT END OF YEAR	530,000	117,763	281,640	1,616,578	4,006,443	8,252,410

23

University Parent, Inc.

Appendix D, Monthly and Quarterly Cash Flow Statements, Years 1–5 ($)

	Year 1	Year 2	Year 3	Year 4	Year 5
OPERATING ACTIVITIES					
Net Earnings	(401,329)	197,583	1,227,012	2,313,297	4,123,572
Depreciation	7,467	24,400	48,400	72,400	97,200
Working Capital Changes					
(Inc.)/Dec. Accts. Rec.	0	0	0	0	0
(Inc.)/Dec. Inventories	0	0	0	0	0
(Inc.)/Dec. Other CA	(113)	(3,835)	(46,281)	(13,256)	(12,245)
(Inc.)/Dec. Accts Pay Expenses	5,625	3,656	182,163	115,122	158,274
(Inc.)/Dec. Other CL	113	73	3,643	2,302	3,165
Net Cash Provided/(Used) Operating Activities	(388,237)	221,878	1,414,937	2,489,865	4,369,967
INVESTING ACTIVITIES					
Property & Equipment	(24,000)	(58,000)	(80,000)	(100,000)	(124,000)
Other					
Net Cash Used in Investing	(24,000)	(58,000)	(80,000)	(100,000)	(124,000)
FINANCING ACTIVITIES					
(Inc.)/Dec. Short-Term Debt	0	0	0	0	0
(Inc.)/Dec. Curr. Portion LTD	0	0	0	0	0
(Inc.)/Dec. Long-Term Debt	0	0	0	0	0
(Inc.)/Dec. Common Stock	0	0	0	0	0
(Inc.)/Dec. Preferred Stock	0	0	0	0	0
Dividends Declared	0	0	0	0	0
Net Cash Provided/ (Used) by Financing	0	0	0	0	0
INCREASE/(DECREASE) IN CASH	(412,237)	163,878	1,334,937	2,389,865	4,245,967
CASH AT BEGINNING OF YEAR	530,000	117,763	281,640	1,616,578	4,006,443
CASH AT END OF YEAR	117,763	281,640	1,616,578	4,006,443	8,252,410

530,000

2890 Shadow Creek – Boulder, Colorado – 303.579.9871 – info@upi.com

University Parent, Inc.

Appendix E, Break-Even Analysis, Years 1–5 ($)

	Year 1	Year 2	Year 3	Year 4	Year 5
Revenue	495,000	1,881,000	4,573,800	7,726,455	12,276,479
Cost of Revenue					
Variable	24,562	85,341	141,671	186,023	228,692
Fixed	1,800	5,400	10,800	18,000	27,000
Total	26,362	90,741	152,471	204,023	255,692
Operating Expenses					
Variable	49,500	188,100	457,380	772,646	1,227,648
Fixed	805,467	1,359,576	2,130,948	2,839,292	3,855,519
Total	854,967	1,547,676	2,588,328	3,611,938	5,083,166
Total Costs & Expenses					
Variable	74,062	273,441	599,051	958,668	1,456,340
Fixed	807,267	1,364,976	2,141,748	2,857,292	3,882,519
Total	881,329	1,638,417	2,740,799	3,815,960	5,338,858
Variable Costs/Revenue Ratio	0.15	0.15	0.13	0.12	0.12
Break-Even Point Revenues	949,301	1,597,154	2,464,540	3,262,032	4,405,087

Appendix F, Capital Expenditure Detail

	Year 1	Year 2	Year 3	Year 4	Year 5
Net Revenues	495,000	1,881,000	4,573,800	7,726,455	12,276,479
Capital Expenditures					
Computers, Software, & Office Equipment	20,000	40,000	60,000	80,000	100,000
Plant & Equipment	0	0	0	0	0
Other	4,000	18,000	20,000	20,000	24,000
Total Capital Expenditures	24,000	58,000	80,000	100,000	124,000

University Parent, Inc.

Appendix G, Financial Assumptions

General Assumptions

First Month of Operations	June 2004
Estimated Inflation	2.5%
Corporate Tax Rate	38%

Annual Projections

	Year 1	Year 2	Year 3	Year 4	Year 5
Product A—Magazine					
Number of Schools	3	9	22	32	44
Total Issues/Year	9	36	66	96	132
Number of Units/Ad	225	900	1,800	2,925	4,425
Avg. Price/Ad Page	$1,000	$1,100	$1,210	$1,331	$1,464
Print Advertising Sales	$225,000	$990,000	$2,178,000	$3,893,175	$6,478,643
Product B—Website					
Advertisements Sold/Year	360	1,080	2,640	3,840	5,280
Price per Unit	$750	$825	$908	$998	$1,098
Web Advertising Sales	$270,000	$891,000	$2,395,800	$3,833,280	$5,797,836

Printing Costs

	Year 1	Year 2	Year 3	Year 4	Year 5
Magazines Printed/Year	90,000	360,000	660,000	960,000	1,320,000
Printing Cost/Magazine	0.25	0.23	0.21	0.19	0.17
Total Costs	22,500	82,800	138,600	182,400	224,400

Funding

Total Shares Outstanding	2,000,000
Preferred Shares (Investors)	700,000 (35%)
Common Shares (Founders/Employees)	130,000 (65%)
Expected Investor IRR	60%
Total Funding Required	$500,000
Founders' Contribution	$30,000

26

University Parent, Inc.

Appendix H, Development Timeline, Year 1

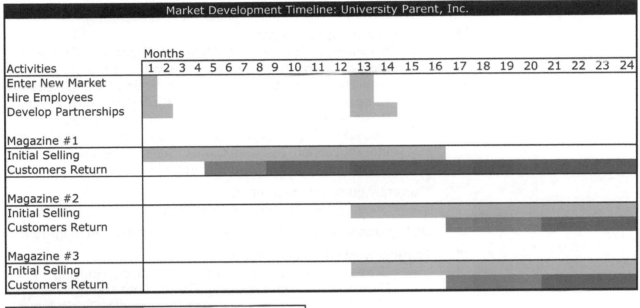

Market Development Timeline: University Parent, Inc.

	Performed by Staff
	Min Return Customers
	Med Return Customers
	Max Return Customers

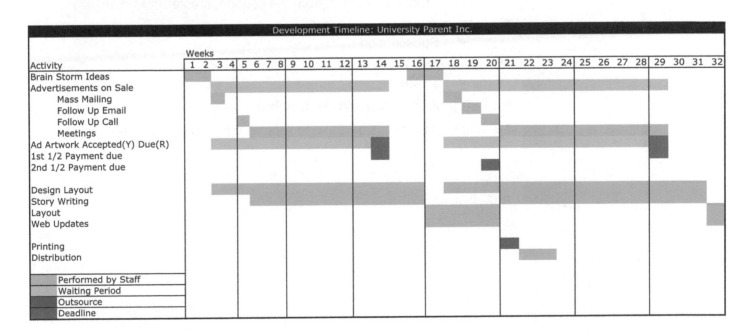

Development Timeline: University Parent Inc.

	Performed by Staff
	Waiting Period
	Outsource
	Deadline

2890 Shadow Creek – Boulder, Colorado – 303.579.9871 – info@upi.com

University Parent, Inc.

Appendix I, Customer Survey Results

40 Parents were interviewed about the UPI concept.

- Parents currently purchase:
  - ✓ Newsweek, Time, Weekly Standard, Economist, Forbes, Money, Sports Illustrated, AAE Journal, Martha Stewart Living, Real Simple, Family Circle, People, Young Riders, Redbook, Budget Traveler, Business Week, Kiplingers, Smithsonian, Business World, Outside, New Yorker, More, Good Housekeeping, In Style, Cosmopolitan, Allure, Fast Company, Inc, Prevention, Readers Digest, Sunset, Tennis, Golf, Consumer Reports, Veranda, Scientific American

- Currently purchase magazines:
  - ✓ Subscription, Airport, Grocery Store

- 90% percent of parents surveyed would purchase the magazine

- Parents want information about:
  - ✓ Grades, Scholarships, Travel Opportunities, Housing Expenses, Activities in College Town, Time Management, Social Life, Programs, Internships, Job Placements, Curriculum, Student Safety, Speakers, Career Guidance, Graduation Requirements, Student Groups, Transportation

- Currently receive information:
  - ✓ From the student, from the college, media

- Would like to purchase UP:
  - ✓ Subscription

- Would be willing to pay:
  - ✓ $1–$5

- 60% of parents would like a website

- 70% of parents would like to receive a monthly newsletter

2890 Shadow Creek – Boulder, Colorado – 303.579.9871 – info@upi.com

Appendix 2

BizBuilder Business Plan

Congratulations! Since you have made it this far, you've given yourself a comprehensive, basic education in entrepreneurship, and you will have made progress toward writing a business plan that will work for your operations and impress potential investors and lenders. At this point, you will probably want to expand and enhance your business plan to reflect all that you have learned. A sample comprehensive outline follows.

BizBuilder Business Plan Worksheet Questions/Notes

Cover Page

A. Full legal name of your organization.
B. Contact information for the organization, including the names of majority owners.
C. Confidentiality/nondisclosure language.
D. Date of the plan.

Table of Contents (Can Be Placed Before or After the Executive Summary)

A. List the key sections of the plan and the page numbers.

1.0 Executive Summary

A. Name of your organization.
B. Description of your business idea and the nature of the target market.
C. Type of organization (e.g., C corporation, LLC, sole proprietorship).
D. Brief description of the products and/or services you will offer.
E. Description of your marketing and sales strategy. Explain how your business idea will satisfy a customer need.
F. Key success factors for the organization.
G. Short-term business goals (less than one year).
H. Long-term business goals (from one to five years).
I. Resources and skills that you and other owners and managers have that will help make your organization successful, plus other skills needed and how they will be obtained.
J. Plan to share ownership (if there will be more than one owner).
K. Sources and uses of funds.
L. Summary of financial projections.
M. Growth and exit strategy.

2.0 Mission, Vision, and Culture

A. Write a mission statement for your organization in 21 words or fewer that clearly states your competitive advantage, strategy, and tactics.
B. Create a vision statement for your organization.
C. Describe the core beliefs you will use to run your organization and how they will be reflected in its culture.
D. Identify the ways you plan to run a socially responsible organization.

3.0 Company Description

A. What industry are you in?
B. What type of organization is it (manufacturing, wholesale, service)?
C. What needs will this business satisfy?
D. What is your strategic advantage?
E. What is your organization's legal structure (sole proprietorship, partnership, LLC, C corporation, etc.)?
F. Why did you choose this legal structure?
G. In what state are you registered or do you intend to register?
H. Where will you physically operate the organization?
I. What is the geographic reach of the organization?
J. Who will be the owner(s), partners, or stockholders for your company?
K. If your business is incorporated, describe what percentage of the company is owned by each shareholder.

4.0 Opportunity Analysis and Research

A. Describe your target customer along as many dimensions as you have defined (demographic, geographic, needs, trends, and decision-making process).
B. Describe the research methods you used to develop this section (surveys, focus groups, general research, and statistical research).

4.1 Industry Analysis (Remember to Correctly Cite any Sources)

A. What is the industry or set of industries in which your organization operates (include the NAICS codes and/or SIC codes)?
B. What factors influence the demand for your product or service?
C. What factors influence the supply for your product or service?
D. How large is your industry (historic, current, projected size)?
E. What are the current and anticipated characteristics and trends in the industry?
F. What are the major customer groups for the industry (consumers, governments, businesses)? Describe them in detail.
G. How large is your target market (number of customers, size of purchases, frequency of purchases, trends)? Quantify it. Describe the entire potential market and the portion that you will address or target.

4.2 Environmental Analysis

A. Perform a SWOT (strengths, weaknesses, opportunities, and threats) analysis of your organization. Remember that strengths and weaknesses are internal to your organization, and opportunities and threats are external.

B. What external/environmental factors are likely to impact your business? How likely are they?

C. Are there customers for your business in other countries? How do you plan to reach them?

4.3 Competitive Analysis

A. How do you define/describe your competition, both direct and indirect?

B. Describe your competitive advantage(s) along the dimensions of quality, price, location, selection, service, and speed/turnaround as they apply.

C. Find three competitors and describe them. Use the comparative analysis tables in Chapter 5 to perform a qualitative and/or quantitative analysis.

D. Describe any international competitors who may be able to access your customers. How do you intend to compete against them?

E. Describe your strategy for outperforming the competition.

F. What tactics will you use to carry out this strategy?

G. What barriers to entry can you create to block out competitors? How will you do so?

5.0 Marketing Strategy and Plan

A. Explain how your marketing plan targets your market segment (geography, demographics, psychographics, behaviors). Be specific.

B. What percentage of the market do you need to capture for your business to be profitable? Explain this.

C. Write a positioning statement for your business using the format from Chapter 6.

D. How do you plan to grow the organization (self-generated, franchising, acquisition)?

5.1 Products/Services

A. What products/services do you intend to market?

B. Explain how your product will meet a customer need.

C. Where is your product/service (not your business) in the product life cycle?

D. Describe the features and benefits of the product/service your business will focus on selling.

E. What copyrights, trademarks, patents, or other intellectual property do you own or expect to own?

F. How will your organization help others? List all the organizations to which you plan to contribute. (Your contribution may be time, money, your product, or something else.)

G. Do you intend to publicize your philanthropy? Why or why not? If you do, explain how you will work your philanthropy into your marketing.

5.2 Pricing

A. Describe your pricing strategy (value, prestige, cost-plus, penetration, skimming, meet-or-beat, follow-the-leader, personalized, variable, or price lining), structure, and the gross margins you expect to generate.

B. What will your discount structure, if any, be? How will it impact your average price (your pocket price)?

C. Will you extend credit to customers? On what terms? If doing retail sales, what forms of payment will you accept?

5.3 Promotion

A. Identify the ways you plan to promote your product or service, including the message, the media, and the distribution channels. Describe why you have chosen these methods and why you think they will work. Include a table showing the methods and budgets.
B. Show examples of marketing materials you intend to use to sell.
C. What is your business slogan?
D. What is your business logo? How do you intend to protect it?
E. Where do you intend to advertise (be specific, including identifying reach and frequency)?
F. How do you plan to get publicity for your organization?
G. List ways you intend to provide superior customer service.
H. How will you keep your customer database? What essential questions will you ask every customer for your database?

5.4 Place

A. Where do you intend to sell your product (physical and/or virtual locations)? Describe the advantages and disadvantages of your location(s). If you have a specific site, provide detailed information.
B. What are the surrounding businesses? Access routes?
C. If vehicular traffic is important to your organization, what is the traffic count for this location?
D. What is the workforce availability in the area as it pertains to your needs? Use census or workforce data and cite it.

6.0 Management and Operations

6.1 Management Team

A. Create an organizational chart for your business, if it will have more employees than you at any point. You may want to create one for the start-up period and one for a future time period, such as year 3.
B. Will you be hiring employees? If so, describe what their qualifications should be, what you intend to pay them, and how they will help your business. Detailed position descriptions can be placed in the appendices.
C. Do you intend to pay yourself a salary, wage, dividend, or commission? Explain the method and the decision criteria regarding the level of compensation.
D. What will your most important policies toward employees be? How will you make your organization a positive and rewarding place to work?
E. Describe the corporate governance plan for your organization. It should include five policies (rules) that will be the backbone of your organization's ethics.
F. Provide information on each of your mentors or advisors. If there is a board of advisors, list each member and describe his/her commitment to the board.
G. Provide contact information for your accountant, attorney, banker, and insurance agent.

6.2 Research and Development

A. What type of research are you doing? What do you intend to do?
B. What are others in the industry doing?
C. How will you protect your intellectual property?

6.3 Physical Location

A. Describe the actual physical place in greater detail than above.

B. What zoning laws apply to your business? Does it comply? Are variances required?

6.4 Facilities

A. What type of building and equipment will you have?

B. Identify which technological tools you plan to use for your organization, and explain why.

C. How do you plan to get access to the technology you need?

6.5 Inventory, Production, and Quality Assurance

A. From what companies or individuals will you purchase the products you plan to sell or the parts you will use to manufacture those products? Illustrate your supply chain.

B. Do you intend to manufacture your product? If so, describe the manufacturing processes you will use. If not, describe how your product is manufactured.

C. Are there any economies of scale to be attained for your business? At what point do you anticipate attaining them?

D. Have you developed and/or adopted any innovations in production, inventory management, or distribution that are significant? What are they and why are they meaningful?

E. How do you plan to distribute your product to your target market?

F. Show the production-distribution channel for your business and the markups along the chain.

G. What is the estimated delivery time between when you place an order with your supplier and when you will have the product available for your customers?

H. What method(s) will you use to define and ensure the quality of your products/services?

I. What types of insurance will your business need, and why?

J. What methods will you use to ensure that you comply with federal, state, and local tax laws?

K. What laws—such as minimum wage and age requirements, health and safety regulations, or antidiscrimination laws—will affect your business?

7.0 Financial Analysis and Projections

A. Describe your recordkeeping system, including the software you will use and whether it is specific to your industry.

B. List the types of bank accounts you will open for your organization.

7.1 Sources and Uses of Capital

A. How much capital do you need? When? What type and on what terms?

B. How will you use the money you raise? Be specific.

C. List the items you will need to buy to start your business and add up the items to get your total start-up capital.

D. List the sources of financing for your start-up capital. Identify each source as equity, debt, or gift. Indicate the amount, type, and desired terms for each source.

E. What is your payback period? In other words, how long will it take you to earn enough profit to cover start-up capital?

F. Describe financing sources that might be willing to invest in your business in exchange for equity.

G. Describe any debt financing you intend to pursue. What is your debt ratio? What is your debt-to-equity ratio?

H. Do you plan to use bootstrap financing? Explain.

I. Do you plan to pursue venture capital? Why or why not? List potential sources of venture capital.

7.2   Cash Flow Projections

A. List and describe your monthly fixed costs.

B. Create a projected cash flow statement for your business for the first four quarters and the second and third years of operation.

C. Calculate the burn rate for your business.

7.3   Balance Sheet Projections

A. Create a projected balance sheet for your business for the first four quarters and the second and third years of operation.

B. Create a pie chart showing your current assets, long-term assets, current liabilities, and long-term liabilities.

7.4   Income Statement Projections

A. Create a projected income statement for your business for the first four quarters and the second and third years of operation.

B. Create a bar chart showing your gross revenues, gross profit, and net income.

7.5   Breakeven Analysis

A. Perform a breakeven analysis and report your breakeven volume.

7.6   Ratio Analysis

A. Use your projected financial statements to calculate all of your key ratios.

B. Compare these ratios to your industry using publicly available data.

7.7   Risks and Assumptions

A. List the risks and assumptions that underlie your financial projections.

B. Identify any external factors that may be substantial risks.

8.0   Funding Request and Exit Strategy

8.1   Amount and Type of Funds Requested

A. Clearly state how much money you are requesting and the terms under which you anticipate obtaining the funds.

B. Do you intend to use debt to finance your business? Explain.

C. If you are asking for equity, how have you valued your company?

8.2   Exit Plan

A. How will investors get paid back/out? Public offering? Employee buyout? Merger or acquisition? Liquidation? Stock buyback?

B. When will this happen?

C. Do you plan to franchise your business or license any of your products? Explain.

8.3 Milestones

A. Create a GANTT chart for your organization to make your plans clear to potential investors.

Appendices

Resumes and Position Descriptions

A. Include a resume for each key team member.

B. Add position descriptions for any vital start-up positions that are not yet filled.

Sample Promotional Materials

A. Include any sample logos, letterhead, advertisements, brochures, or other items that can be inserted into the plan.

B. Add photos of any promotional items, signage, or larger materials to provide examples.

Product Illustrations/Diagrams

A. If you have nonproprietary drawings or properly authorized proprietary drawings, illustrations, or diagrams of your product or service concept, insert them here.

B. Any floor plans, assembly layouts, or the like should be included.

Detailed Financial Projections

A. Financial projections that are in greaterdetail than the main business plan document might be provided here.

B. Include detailed assumptions and notes underlying the projections.

C. Include information about significant contracts.

If You Are Starting a Not-for-Profit Organization, Also Consider

1. What is the name of your nonprofit?
2. What problem(s) are you trying to reduce or eliminate?
3. What is the mission of your organization?
4. What programs and services do you plan to create?
5. How will your organization achieve the changes you intend to bring about?
6. What is the unit of change (per person, animal, house, etc.)?
7. How will you measure these changes?
8. Who are your competitors?
9. How much will it cost you to deliver a unit of service?
10. What are your proposed sources of funding (earned income and grants/gifts)?

Appendix 3

Resources for Entrepreneurs[1]

Books

On Starting a Business—and Succeeding

The $100 Startup: Reinvent the Way You Make a Living, Do What You Love, and Create a New Future, Chris Guillebeau (Random House, 2012).

The Art of the Start: The Time-Tested, Battle-Hardened Guide for Anyone Starting Anything, Guy Kawasaki (Portfolio, 2004).

Crush It: Why Now Is the Time to Cash In on Your Passion, Gary Vaynerchuk (Harper Studio, 2009).

Do More Faster: Tech Stars Lessons to Accelerate Your Startup, David Cohen and Brad Feld (Wiley, 2010).

The 4-Hour Workweek, Timothy Ferriss (Crown Archetype, 2009).

The Four Steps to the Epiphany: Successful Strategies for Products That Win, Steve Blank (K&S Ranch Publishing, 2013).

Good to Great: Why Some Companies Make the Leap . . . and Others Do Not, Jim Collins (Harper-Business, 2001).

In Search of Excellence: Lessons from America's Best-Run Companies, Thomas J. Peters and Robert H. Waterman (Harper, 2004).

The Innovator's Solution: Creating and Sustaining Successful Growth, Clayton M. Christensen and Michael E. Raynor (Harvard Business School Press, 2003).

The Lean Startup: How Today's Entrepreneurs Use Continuous Innovation to Create Radically Successful Businesses, Eric Ries (Crown Business, 2011).

Online Success Tactics: 101 Ways to Build Your Small Business, Jeanette S. Cates (Twin Towers Press, 2002).

Reality Check: The Irreverent Guide to Outsmarting, Outmanaging, and Outmarketing Your Competition, Guy Kawasaki (Portfolio Trade, 2011).

Resourcing the Start-Up Business, Oswald Jones, Allan MacPherson, and Dilani Jayawarna (Routledge, 2014).

Screw Business as Usual, Richard Branson (Portfolio, 2011).

Social Entrepreneurship: What Everyone Needs to Know, David Bornstein and Susan Davis (Oxford University Press USA, 2010).

Start Your Own Business, 5th ed., Rieva Lesonsky (Entrepreneur Press, 2010).

The Startup Owner's Manual, Steve Blank and Bob Dorf (K & S Ranch, 2012).

What No One Ever Tells You About Starting Your Own Business: Real-Life Start-Up Advice from 101 Successful Entrepreneurs, 2nd ed., Jan Norman (Kaplan Business, 2004).

The Young Entrepreneur's Guide to Starting and Running a Business: Find Out Where the Money Is . . . and How to Get It, Steve Mariotti (Crown Business, 2014).

---

[1]Please note that the publisher cannot guarantee that listed URLs will remain active and is not responsible for future changes to the content of the Web sites.

On Thinking Like an Entrepreneur

The 7 Habits of Highly Effective People, anniv. ed., Stephen Covey (Simon & Schuster, 2013).

Awakening the Entrepreneur Within: How Ordinary People Can Create Extraordinary Companies, Michael Gerber (Harper, 2009).

Delivering Happiness: A Path to Profits, Passion, and Purpose, Tony Hsieh (Business Plus, 2010).

Escape from Cubicle Nation: From Corporate Prisoner to Thriving Entrepreneur, Pamela Slim (Berkley Trade, 2010).

The Entrepreneurial Mindset: Strategies for Continuously Creating Opportunity in an Age of Uncertainty, Rita Gunther McGrath and Ian MacMillan (Harvard Business School Press, 2000).

Focus: The Future of Your Company Depends on It, Al Ries (Harper, 2005).

Heart, Smarts, Guts, and Luck: What It Takes to Be an Entrepreneur and Build a Great Business, Anthony K. Tjan, Richard J. Harrington, and Tsun-Yan Hsieh (Harvard Business Review Press, 2012).

The Innovator's DNA: Mastering the Five Skills of Disruptive Innovators, Clayton M. Christensen, Jeff Dyer, and Hal Gregersen (Harvard Business Review Press, 2011).

Never Get a "Real" Job: How to Dump Your Boss, Build a Business, and Not Go Broke, Scott Gerber (Wiley, 2010).

Oh, the Places You'll Go! Dr. Seuss (Random House, 1990).

Secrets of the Young & Successful: How to Get Everything You Want Without Waiting a Lifetime, 2nd ed., Jennifer Kushell and Scott M. Kaufman (Ys Media Corp., 2006).

The Student Success Manifesto: How to Create a Life of Passion, Purpose, and Prosperity, Michael Simmons (Extreme Entrepreneurship Education Co., 2003).

Think and Grow Rich: The Secret to Wealth Updated for the 21st Century, Napoleon Hill (CreateSpace, 2010).

A Whack on the Side of the Head: How You Can Be More Creative, 25th anniv. rev. ed., Roger Von Oech (Business Plus, 2008).

On How Other Entrepreneurs Succeeded

The Accidental Entrepreneur: The 50 Things I Wish Someone Had Told Me About Starting a Business, Susan Urquhart-Brown (AMACOM, 2008).

Brewing Up a Business: Adventures in Beer from the Founder of Dogfish Head Craft Brewery, 2nd ed., Sam Calagione (Wiley, 2011).

Built from Scratch: How a Couple of Regular Guys Grew The Home Depot from Nothing to $30 Billion, Arthur Blank and Bernie Marcus (Crown Business, 2001).

By Invitation Only: How We Built Gilt Groupe and Changed the Way Millions Shop, Alexis Maybank and Alexandra Wilkis Wilson (Penguin Group, 2012).

Display of Power: How FUBU Changed a World of Fashion, Branding and Lifestyle, Daymond John (Thomas Nelson Publishers, 2007).

Entrepreneurs in Profile: How 20 of the World's Greatest Entrepreneurs Built Their Business Empires . . . and How You Can Too, Steve Mariotti and Michael Caslin with Debra DeSalvo (The Career Press, Inc., 2002).

The Everything Store: Jeff Bezos and the Age of Amazon, Brad Stone (Little, Brown and Company, 2013).

Founders at Work: Stories of Startups' Early Days, Jessica Livingston (Apress, 2007).

The Idea Man, Paul Allen (Penguin Group, 2011).

Kitchen Table Entrepreneurs: How Eleven Women Escaped Poverty and Became Their Own Bosses, Martha Shirk, Anna Wadia, Marie Wilson, and Sara Gould (Westview Press, 2004).

Losing My Virginity: How I Survived, Had Fun, and Made a Fortune Doing Business My Way, Richard Branson (Crown Business, 2011).

The Men Behind Def Jam: The Radical Rise of Russell Simmons and Rick Rubin, Alex Ogg (Omnibus Press, 2009).

The Midas Touch: Why Some Entrepreneurs Get Rich—And Why Most Don't, Donald Trump and Robert Kiyosaki (Plata Publishing, 2011).

Shark Tales: How I Turned $1000 into a Billion Dollar Business, Barbara Corcoran with Bruce Littlefield (Penguin Group, 2011).

Start Something That Matters, Blake Mycoskie (Spiegel & Grau, 2011).

Steve Jobs, Walter Isaccson (Simon & Schuster, 2011).

Student Entrepreneurs: 14 Undergraduate All-Stars Tell Their Stories, Michael McMyne and Nicole Amare (Premium Press America, 2003).

Trump: The Way to the Top: The Best Business Advice I Ever Received, Donald Trump (Crown Business, 2004).

Wild Company: The Untold Story of Banana Republic, Mel and Patricia Ziegler (Simon & Schuster, 2012).

You Need to Be a Little Bit Crazy: The Truth About Starting and Growing Your Business, Barry J. Moltz (Authorhouse, 2008).

On Negotiating

The Art of Woo: Using Strategic Persuasion to Sell Your Idea, G. Richard Shell and Mario Moussa (Penguin Group, 2007).

Bargaining for Advantage: Negotiation Strategies for Reasonable People, G. Richard Shell (Penguin Group, 2006).

Getting to Yes: Negotiating Agreement Without Giving In, Roger Fisher, William L. Ury, and Bruce Patton (Penguin, 2011).

Winning, Jack Welch (HarperCollins, 2005).

On Accounting

The Accounting Game: Basic Accounting Fresh from the Lemonade Stand, 2nd ed., Judith Orloff and Darrell Millis (Sourcebooks, Inc., updated rev. ed., 2008).

Accounting Made Simple: Accounting Explained in 100 Pages or Less, Mike Piper (Simple Subjects, LLC, 2013).

Barron's Accounting Handbook, 5th ed., Joel G. Siegel and Jae K. Shim (Barron's Educational Series, 2010).

E-Z Accounting, 5th ed., Peter J. Eisen (Barron's Educational Series, 2009).

Financial Statements: A Step-by-Step Guide to Creating and Understanding Financial Reports, Thomas R. Ittelson (Career Press Inc., 2009).

On Investing, Money Management, and Personal Finance

The Entrepreneur's Guide to Finance and Business: Wealth Creation Techniques for Growing a Business, Steven Rogers (McGraw-Hill, 2002).

Irrational Exuberance, 2nd ed., Robert J. Shiller (Broadway Business, 2006).

The Laws of Money, The Lessons of Life: Keep What You Have and Create What You Deserve, Suze Orman (The Free Press, 2003).

Rich Dad, Poor Dad: What the Rich Teach Their Kids About Money—That the Poor and Middle Class Do Not! Robert T. Kiyosaki and Sharon L. Lechter (BusinessPlus, 2010).

Understanding Wall Street, 5th ed., Jeffrey B. Little (McGraw-Hill, 2009).

On Marketing

Anatomy of Buzz: How to Create Word of Mouth Marketing, Emanuel Rosen (Crown Business, 2002).

The Art of the Pitch: Persuasion and Presentation Skills That Win Business, Peter Coughter (Palgrave MacMillan, 2012).

Blue Ocean Strategy: How to Create Uncontested Market Space and Make Competition Irrelevant, W. Chan Kim and Renée Mauborgne (Harvard Business School Press, 2005).

Brand Sense, Martin Lindstrom (Free Press, 2010).

Buy-o-logy: Truth and Lies About Why We Buy, Martin Lindstrom (Crown Business, 2008).

Contagious: Why Things Catch On, Jonah Berger (Simon & Schuster, 2013).

Conversation on Networking: Finding, Developing, and Maintaining Relationships for Business and Life, Steven Smolinsky and Kay Keenan (Forever Talking Press, 2006).

Crossing the Chasm: Marketing and Selling High-Tech Products to Mainstream Customers, Geoffrey A. Moore (Harper Business, 2006).

The Dragonfly Effect: Quick, Effective, and Powerful Ways to Use Social Media to Drive Social Change, Jennifer Aker, Andy Smith, Dan Ariely, and Chip Heath (Jossey-Bass, 2010).

Duct Tape Marketing: The World's Most Practical Small Business Selling Guide, John Jantsch (Thomas Nelson, 2008).

Guerilla Marketing: Easy and Inexpensive Strategies for Making Big Profits from Your Small Business, 4th ed., Jay Conrad Levinson (Houghton Mifflin Harcourt, 2007).

Influence: The Psychology of Persuasion, Robert B. Cialdini (Harper Collins, 2009).

The Long Tail: Why the Future of Business Is Selling Less of More, Chris Anderson (Hyperion, 2006).

Made to Stick: Why Some Ideas Survive and Others Die, Chip Heath and Dan Heath (Random House, 2007).

Permission Marketing: Turning Strangers into Friends, and Friends into Customers, Seth Godin (Simon & Schuster, 1999).

Poke the Box, Seth Godin (The Domino Project, 2011).

Positioning: The Battle for Your Mind, 3rd ed., Al Ries and Jack Trout (McGraw Hill, 2000).

Purple Cow: Transform Your Business by Being Remarkable, Seth Godin (Portfolio, 2003).

The Sales Bible: The Ultimate Sales Resource, New Edition, Jeffrey Gitomer (HarperCollins, 2008).

Selling the Invisible: A Field Guide to Modern Marketing, Harry Beckwith (Business Plus, 1999).

Setting the Table: The Transforming Power of Hospitality in Business, Danny Meyer (Harper Paperbacks, 2008).

Smarter, Faster, Cheaper: Non-Boring, Fluff-Free Strategies for Marketing and Promoting Your Business, David Siteman Garland (Wiley, 2010).

The Tipping Point: How Little Things Can Make a Big Difference, Malcolm Gladwell (Back Bay Books, 2002).

Web Analytics 2.0: The Art of Online Accountability and Science of Customer Centricity, Avinash Kaushik (Sybex, 2009).

Web Sites

Association Directory: http://www.asaecenter.org/Communities/Directories/ associationsearch.cfm, from the American Society of Association Executives.

BizBuySell: http://www.bizbuysell.com—sends registered users who might want to buy your business e-mails, alerting them that you want to sell.

Business Owners Idea Café: http—a tool for figuring out how much capital you will need to get your business off the ground.

Census Data: http://www.census.gov.

Copyright Office: http://www.copyright.gov.

Currency Converter: http://finance.yahoo.com/currency-converter/.

Internal Revenue Service: http://www.irs.gov.

Internet Public Library: http://www.ipl.org—a good source for industry and market statistics.

InterNIC: http://www.internic.net—register the name of your Web site through the U.S. Department of Commerce.

Practical Money Skills: http://www.practicalmoneyskills.com.

Standards of Corporate Responsibility: http://www.svn.org/initiatives/standards .html—provides ideas on how to make your business socially responsible.

Surveys can be created using *http://www.surveymonkey.com.*

Additional Resources

The **Small Business Administration (SBA)** is a federal agency created to support and promote entrepreneurs. The SBA offers free and inexpensive pamphlets on a variety of business subjects. Some local offices offer counseling to small business owners.

Contact the SBA at: Small Business Administration, 409 Third Street, SW, Washington, DC 20416, (800) 827–5722, or visit *http://www.sba.gov.*

The **Minority Business Development Agency (MBDA)** is a federal bureau created to foster the establishment and growth of minority-owned businesses. MBDA provides funding for a network of Minority Business Development Centers (MBDCs), Native American Business Development Centers (NABDCs), and Business Resource Centers (BRCs). The centers provide minority entrepreneurs with one-on-one assistance in writing business plans, marketing, management and technical assistance, and financial planning to assure adequate financing for business ventures.

To find a Minority Business Development Center in your area, visit *http://www.mbda.gov.*

The **Service Corps of Retired Executives (SCORE)** is a group of retired businesspeople who volunteer as counselors and mentors to entrepreneurs. To locate an office near you, contact SCORE Association, 409 3rd Street, SW, 6th Floor, Washington, DC 20024, (800) 634-0245, *http://www.score.org.*

The **National Association of Women Business Owners** helps female entrepreneurs network. You can join a local chapter of female entrepreneurs in your area.

National Association of Women Business Owners, 601 Pennsylvania Avenue, NW, South Building, Suite 900, Washington, DC 20004, (800) 55-NAWBO, *http://www.nawbo.org.*

The **United States Department of Agriculture (USDA)** is a federal agency that provides financial and business support in rural communities through its Business and Community Development Programs. It also offers Cooperative Services Programs to promote the use of co-ops to distribute and market agricultural products. Much like the SBA-supported Small Business Development Centers, there are Rural Business Entrepreneurship Centers nationwide.

USDA, 1400 Independence Avenue, SW, Washington, DC 20250, (202) 720-2791, *http://www.usda.gov.*

The **Kauffman Foundation** is a private foundation dedicated to creating economic independence through education and entrepreneurship. It offers a variety of resources for entrepreneurs, including training, research, and videos.

The Kauffman Foundation, 4801 Rockhill Road, Kansas City, MO 64110, (816) 932-1000, *http://www.kauffman.org* and *http://www.entrepreneurship.org*.

Awards for Entrepreneurs

If you are an entrepreneur under age 25, you may qualify for awards that promote youth entrepreneurship and education. Check the Internet for new programs.

Ernst & Young Entrepreneur of the Year Award

http://www.ey.com
To qualify for the Ernst & Young award, you must be an owner/manager primarily responsible for the recent performance of a privately held or public company that is at least two years old.

National Association for the Self-Employed Future Entrepreneur of the Year Award

http://www.nase.org/Membership/Benefits/NASE_Scholarships_Program.aspx
This scholarship is given to a young man or woman who is a microbusiness owner and demonstrates leadership and academic excellence, ingenuity, and entrepreneurial spirit.

NFIB Young Entrepreneur Award

http://www.nfib.com/page/nfibYoungEntrepreneurAward.html
The NFIB Young Entrepreneur Foundation grants NFIB Young Entrepreneur Awards to high school seniors nationwide.

NFTE Global Young Entrepreneur of the Year

http://www.nfte.com
NFTE graduates can win an all-expenses-paid trip to New York City for NFTE's annual "Dare to Dream" Awards Dinner and a grant to be used in the awardee's business or applied toward college.

SBA Young Entrepreneur of the Year Award

http://www.sba.gov
At National Small Business Week, one outstanding entrepreneur is named to represent each state, the District of Columbia, Puerto Rico, and Guam as the state Small Business Person of the Year. From this group, the National Small Business Person of the Year is chosen.

Staples Youth Social Entrepreneurship Competition

http://www.changemakers.com/competition/staplesyv
For young people from 12 to 24 inclusive who are operating a youth-led social venture and are able to demonstrate impact. Hosted by Ashoka and Staples, Inc.

Appendix 4

Useful Formulas and Equations

Liquidity Ratios

$$\text{Current Ratio} = \frac{\text{Current Assets}}{\text{Current Liabilities}}$$

$$\text{Quick Ratio} = \frac{\text{Current Assests} - (\text{Inventory} + \text{Prepayments})}{\text{Current Liabilities}}$$

Activity Ratios (Efficiency Ratios)

$$\text{Accounts Receivable Turnover} = \frac{\text{Annual Net Credit Sales}}{\text{Average Accounts Receivable}}$$

$$\text{Average Collection Period} = \frac{\text{Accounts Receivable}}{\text{Average Daily Credit Sales}}$$

$$\text{Inventory Turnover} = \frac{\text{Cost of Goods Sold}}{\text{Average Inventory}}$$

$$\text{Days' Sales in Inventory} = \frac{\text{Ending Inventory}}{\text{Daily Cost of Goods Sold}}$$

Profitability Ratios

$$\text{Gross Profit Margin} = \frac{\text{Gross Profit}}{\text{Net Sales}}$$

$$\text{Return on Sales} = \frac{\text{Net Income}}{\text{Sales}}$$

$$\text{Return on Assets (ROA)} = \frac{\text{Net Income} + \text{Interest} + \text{Income Taxes}}{\text{Average Total Assets}}$$

$$\text{Return on Common Equity (ROE)} = \frac{\text{Net Income} - \text{Preferred Stock Dividends}}{\text{Average Common Stockholders' Equity}}$$

Market Ratios

$$\text{Earnings per Share (EPS)} = \frac{\text{Net Income} - \text{Preferred Stock Dividends}}{\text{Common Shares Outstanding}}$$

$$\text{Return on Investment (ROI)} = \frac{\text{Net Income}}{\text{Average Owners' Equity}}$$

Debt Ratios (Leverage Ratios)

$$\text{Debt Ratio} = \frac{\text{Total Liabilities}}{\text{Total Assets}}$$

$$\text{Debt-to-Equity Ratio} = \frac{\text{Total Debt} + \text{Value of Leases}}{\text{Total Equity}}$$

$$\text{Times Interest Earned or Interest Coverage} = \frac{\text{EBIT}}{\text{Interest Expense}}$$

Glossary

accrual method accounting method wherein transactions are recorded at the time of occurrence, regardless of the transfer of cash.

acquisition a business purchase.

active listening the focus solely on what the other person is saying in a conversation and the subsequent validation of understanding the message's content and meaning.

advertising paid promotion through media outlets.

advisory board or **council** a group that provides advice and counsel but does not have the responsibilities of a board of directors.

angel investor a wealthy individual who invests in businesses.

arbitration a method of dispute resolution using an arbitrator to act as the decision maker rather than going to court.

area franchise or **multiple-unit franchise** a type of franchise that gives the exclusive rights to open franchisee-operated units within specified areas.

asset valuation a method that analyzes the underlying value of the firm's assets as a basis for negotiating the price.

asset any item of value.

audit a review of financial and business records to ascertain integrity and compliance with standards and laws, particularly by the U.S. Internal Revenue Service.

balance sheet a financial statement summarizing the assets, liabilities, and net worth of a business.

bankruptcy the legal process in which an individual or business declares the inability or impaired ability to pay debts as they come due.

barriers to entry the factors that contribute to the ease or difficulty of a new competitor joining an established market.

behavioral interview dialogue designed to determine the fit of a prospective employee with the requirements of a position using prior-experience examples.

benchmarking the comparison of a company's performance against that of companies in the same industry, or against best practices, standards, or certification criteria.

blog a journal that appears on the Internet periodically and is intended for the public.

blogosphere the collective term used for all the blogs on the Internet.

boilerplate language a standard format for a specific type of legal agreement.

bond an interest-bearing certificate issued by a government or business that promises to pay the holder interest as well as the face value of the bond at maturity.

book value valuation of a company as assets minus liabilities according to its books and records.

bootstrap financing the creative stretching of existing capital as far as possible, including extensive use of the entrepreneur's time.

brand a name (sometimes with an accompanying symbol or trademark) that distinguishes a business from its competition and makes its competitive advantage instantly recognizable to the consumer.

brand spiraling integrating a company's conventional offline branding strategy with its Internet strategy by using conventional approaches to drive traffic to its online sites.

breach of contract the failure of a signatory to perform as agreed.

breakeven point when the volume of sales exactly covers the fixed costs.

budget a plan to spend money.

burn rate the pace at which a company must spend capital before generating positive cash flow.

business broker a company or individual that buys and sells businesses for a fee.

business model a company's plan to generate revenue and make a profit from operations.

business plan a document that thoroughly explains a business idea and how it will be carried out.

business-format franchising a form of franchising in which the franchisee secures the product and trade-name benefits but also the operating, quality assurance, accounting, marketing methods, and support of the franchisor.

buzz marketing another name for word-of-mouth marketing.

capital money or property owned or used in business.

capitalism the free-market system, characterized by individuals and companies competing for economic gains, ownership of private property and wealth, and price determination through free-market forces.

cash accounting method a system wherein transactions are recorded when cash is paid out or received.

cash flow statement a financial statement showing cash receipts less cash disbursements for a business over a period of time.

cash flow valuation   a method of calculating the worth of a business by using projected future cash flows and the time value of money.

cash reserve   emergency funds in a pool of cash resources.

cause-related marketing   promotional efforts inspired by a commitment to a social, environmental, or political cause.

center-of-gravity method   an approach that calculates the best cost location for a distribution center serving multiple sites.

certificate   an official document that verifies something.

chain of command   hierarchy of reporting and communications.

charge account   credit extended by a company allowing qualified customers to make purchases up to a specified limit, without paying cash at the time of purchase.

clustering   the strategy of similar businesses locating near each other.

code of conduct   a set of official standards of employee behavior for a company.

code of ethics and business conduct   a combination of a written statement of values with official standards of employee behavior.

code of ethics   a statement of the values of a company.

collateral   property or assets pledged by a borrower to a lender to secure a loan.

commission   a percentage of a sale paid to a salesperson.

competitive analysis   research that compares an organization with several direct and indirect competitors by name in a manner that is meaningful to targeted customers.

competitive strategy   the combination of the business definition with its competitive advantage.

compound interest   used with interest or rate of return and applied when earnings also accumulate interest or other returns, in addition to earnings on principal.

contingency   a condition that must be met in order for something else to occur.

continuous improvement   always identifying and implementing changes throughout an organization to focus on the requirements of internal and external customers.

contract   an agreement between two or more parties that is enforceable by law.

contribution margin   gross profit per unit—the selling price minus total variable costs plus other variable costs.

conversion franchising   a stand-alone business or local chain becoming part of a franchise operation.

cooperative advertising fee   a fee paid by franchisees to contribute to a shared advertising fund that is separate from royalty fees.

core values   the fundamental, ethical, and moral philosophy and beliefs that form the foundation of the organization and provide broad guidance for all decision making.

corporate governance   rules and safeguards to ensure that executives behave legally and ethically.

corporate social responsibility   the ethical obligation of a company to its community.

corporation   a legal entity composed of stockholders under a common name.

cost of goods sold (COGS)   the cost of selling one additional unit of a tangible item.

cost of services sold (COSS)   the cost of selling one additional unit of a service.

cost per rating point (CPRP)   a measure of the efficiency of a media vehicle in a company's target market, calculated by dividing the media buy's cost by the vehicle's rating.

cost per thousand (CPM)   the cost of reaching 1,000 of the media vehicle's audience.

cost-plus pricing   takes the organization's product cost and adds a desired markup.

cost/benefit analysis   a decision-making process in which the costs of taking an action are compared to the benefits.

credit   the ability to borrow money.

credit history   a record of credit extended and the repayment thereof.

credit reporting agency (CRA)   an organization that collects, analyzes, and resells information supplied by financial institutions and others who extend credit.

creditor   person or organization that is owed money.

culture   the beliefs, values, and behavioral norms of an organization.

currency   a term for money when it is exchanged internationally.

current assets   cash or items that can be quickly converted to cash or will be used within one year.

current liabilities   debts that are scheduled for payment within one year.

current ratio   liquidity ratio consisting of the total sum of cash plus marketable securities divided by current liabilities.

customer relationship management (CRM)   company-wide policies, practices, and processes that a business uses with its customers to generate maximum customer satisfaction and optimal profitability.

customer service   everything a business does to keep the customer happy.

data mining   a computer program that analyzes and sorts data, in order to identify a business's best existing customers and model those who might become even better.

database   a collection of information that is generally stored on a computer and organized for sorting and searching.

debt   an obligation to pay back a loan; a liability.

debt ratio   measures total debt versus total assets.

debt service   the amount a borrower is obligated to pay in a given period until a loan is repaid.

debt-to-equity ratio   compares total debt to total equity.

deductible the amount of loss or damage a policy-holder covers before the insurer pays on a claim.

default the results of a borrower failing to meet the repayment agreement on a debt.

demographics population statistics.

depreciation the percentage of value of an asset subtracted periodically to reflect the declining value.

development plan a document stating how an employee will attain specific performance goals.

direct labor employees that actively produce or deliver a product or service.

direct marketing includes telemarketing, direct mail, in-person selling, and other personalized promotional efforts.

discount (referring to bonds) the difference between a bond's trading price and its par value when the trading price is below par.

diversification the addition of product or service offerings beyond a business's core product or service.

dividend each stockholder's portion of the profit-per-share paid out by a corporation.

due diligence the exercise of reasonable care in the evaluation of a business opportunity.

dumping when companies price products below cost and sell large quantities in foreign markets.

e-active marketing when the two major components of Internet marketing—e-commerce and interactive marketing—combine.

earnings valuation a method that assesses the value of the firm based on a stream of earnings that is multiplied either by an agreed-upon factor (the capitalization factor) or by the Price/Earnings ratio (for a publicly traded company).

economic order quantity (EOQ) the amount of inventory to order that will equal the minimum total ordering and holding costs.

economic risk the possibility that changes in the economy of a country where it does business will cause financial or other harm.

economics of one unit of sale (EOU) the amount of gross profit that is earned on each unit of the product or service a business sells.

edutainment a promotion that combines education and entertainment to make a more lasting impression upon an audience.

elastic demand customer demand changes significantly upward or downward when the price of a product changes.

electronic rights the right to reproduce someone's work online.

electronic storefront an online site that customers can visit to view a company's catalog, price lists, and documentation.

elevator pitch a 15-second to 2-minute presentation that conveys what a business is proposing and why the listener should be interested.

embargo the total prohibition on imports of all or specific products from one or more nations.

employee a person hired by a business to work for hourly wages, salary or commission.

entrepreneur a person who recognizes an opportunity and organizes and manages a business, assuming the risk for the sake of potential return.

environmental analysis a review that addresses the roles of the community, region, nation, or the rest of the world, as they relate to a business.

ethical dilemma a circumstance in which there is a conflict of ethical values, which thus complicate decision making.

ethical relativism situation where ethical standards are believed to be subject to interpretation.

ethics a system of moral conduct and judgment that helps determine right and wrong.

exporting the sale of goods or services produced domestically to foreign customers.

face value the amount of a bond, also known as par, to be repaid by the corporation or government at its maturity date.

factor-rating method location-selection approach whereby decision criteria are prioritized and weighted to eliminate subjectivity.

factoring receivables financing, or accessing cash for a business in exchange for offering a company the rights to the cash that will be collected from your customers.

fair market value the price at which a property or business is valued by the marketplace; the price it would fetch on the open market.

family business a firm that has two or more members of the same family managing and/or working in it and that is owned and operated for the benefit of that family's members.

feasibility analysis a study to assist in making the go/no go decision based on a close examination of product/service, market, industry, and financial data in a sufficient degree of detail to ensure confidence in the results.

financing the act of providing or raising funds (capital) for a purpose.

fiscal year the financial reporting year for a company.

fixed operating costs expenses that do not vary with changes in the volume of production or sales.

fixed-position layout used for the production of large objects, where materials and teams are brought to a single location, as in manufactured housing.

float the time between a payment transaction and the date the cash is actually in the payee's account.

follow-the-leader pricing a pricing strategy that is similar to a meet-or-beat-the-competition method, but uses a particular competitor as the model for pricing.

foreign exchange (FX) rate the relative value of one currency to another.

foundation a not-for-profit organization that manages donated funds, which it distributes through grants to individuals or to other nonprofit organizations that help people and social causes.

franchise   a business that markets a product or service developed by a franchisor, typically in the manner specified by the franchisor.

franchise   is a legal and commercial relationship between the owner of a trademark, service mark, trade name or advertising symbol and an individual or group seeking to use that identification in a business.

franchise agreement   contract that determines the specific parameters of the relationship between the parties in a franchise.

franchise broker   an individual acting as an intermediary between the franchisor and prospective franchisee.

Franchise Disclosure Document (FDD)   the primary source of information for prospective franchisees regarding franchisors.

franchisee   the second party to the franchise agreement, the owner of the unit or territory rights.

franchising   the system of operating a franchise governed by a legal agreement between a franchisor and franchisee.

franchisor   the person who develops a franchise or a company that sells franchises and specifies the terms and particulars of the franchise agreement.

free-enterprise system   economic system in which businesses are privately owned and operate relatively free of government interference.

frequency   how often individuals will be exposed to an advertisement during a particular time frame.

future value   the amount an investment is worth in the future if invested at a specific rate of return.

gazelle   a company that achieves an annual growth rate of 20 percent or greater, typically measured by the increase of sales revenue.

goodwill   an intangible asset generated when a company does something positive that has value.

grapevine   an informal communications channel that transmits information and rumors.

green entrepreneurship   business activities that avoid harm to the environment or help to protect it in some way.

gross profit   total sales revenue minus total cost of goods sold.

gross ratings points (GRP)   calculated by multiplying the media vehicle's rating (reach) by the OTS, or number of insertions, to measure the intensity (impact) of a media plan.

guerilla marketing   original, unconventional, and inexpensive small-business promotional strategies.

harvesting   the act of selling, taking public, or merging a company to yield proceeds for the owner(s).

human resources   the segment of a business that hires, trains, and develops a company's employees.

hyperlink   word(s) that, when clicked on, transfer the computer user to another Web page.

importing   the sale of products produced in a foreign country to customers in your home country.

in-kind donation   a contribution of products or services that may include time or goods rather than cash.

income statement   a financial document that summarizes income and expense activity over a specified period and shows net profit or loss.

industry analysis   a critical view of industry definition, industry size and growth (or decline), product and industry life cycle, and any current or anticipated legal or regulatory concerns.

inelastic demand   the type of demand that does not change in a significant way when prices change.

initial public offering (IPO)   first offering of corporate stock to investors on the open (public) market.

installment credit   loans that are to be paid back in installments over time.

institutional advertising   provides information about an organization, rather than a specific product, and is intended to create awareness about a firm and enhance its image.

insurance   a system of protection for payment provided by insurance companies to reimburse individuals and organizations when their property or wealth has been damaged, destroyed, or lost.

interest   payment for using someone else's money; payment received for lending money.

international outsourcing   the process of contracting with individual companies to secure international labor for a domestic company.

Internet franchise   a type of franchise company that does not depend on physical location for the delivery of its products or services; rather, it is a "virtual" business.

interview guide   a document to assist in question development regarding an individual's knowledge, skills, abilities, and interests.

inventory costs   expenses associated with materials and direct labor for production until the product is sold.

investment   something a person or entity devotes resources to in hopes of future profits or satisfaction.

job offer letter   a formal written invitation extended by an employer to a candidate selected for hiring that states basic employment terms—such as the position offered, starting date, salary, and so forth.

job profile   identification of the knowledge, skills, and abilities required to perform the specific tasks of an employment position.

job shop   a subcontractor for a manufacturer.

just-in-time manufacturing (JIT)   an inventory strategy to increase efficiency by receiving goods only as they are needed in the production process.

leader   a person who gets things done through influence, by guiding or inspiring others to voluntarily participate in a cause or project.

leasehold improvements   changes made to adapt a rented property for a particular business.

letter of agreement   a document that puts an oral understanding in writing, in the form of a business letter.

letter of credit   a financing instrument that is usually issued by a bank on behalf of a customer that promises to pay a certain amount of money once specific conditions are met.

leveraged   financed by debt, as opposed to equity.

liability   a business debt.

license   an official document that grants the right to engage in an activity for a specified period of time.

licensing   renting your brand or other intellectual property to increase sales.

lifestyle business   a microenterprise that permits its owners to follow a desired pattern of living, such as supporting college costs or taking vacations.

lifetime value   the total profit earned from a particular customer or customer segment.

limited liability company (LLC)   a form of business ownership offering the tax advantages of a partnership as well as limited legal liability.

limited partnership   business partnership owned by a general partner with unlimited liability and one or more limited partners with no official input in daily operations and limited liability.

line extension   using an established brand to promote different kinds of products.

line organization   a business structure in which each person reports to a single supervisor.

line-and-staff organization   a business structure that includes the line organization, plus staff specialists (such as attorneys) who assist management.

liquidation   the sale of all assets of a business concurrent with its being closed.

liquidity   the ability to convert assets into cash.

location breakeven analysis   a selection method that uses cost-volume comparison.

logo   short for logotype, a company trademark or sign.

long-term assets   those that will take more than one year to use.

long-term liabilities   debts that are due in over one year.

lurk   reading messages and getting a feel for discussions on a Web site, newsgroup, or the like, without participating in the online conversation.

manufacturing   making or producing a tangible product.

market   a group of people or organizations that may be interested in buying a given product or service, has the resources to purchase it, and is permitted by law and regulation to do so.

market clearing price   the particular price at which the supply of products and/or services matches the demand for them.

market research   is the collection and analysis of data regarding target markets, industries, and competitors.

market segment   a group of consumers or businesses that have a similar response to a particular type of product or service.

marketable securities   investments that can be converted into cash within 24 hours.

marketing   the development and use of strategies for getting a product or service to customers and generating interest in it.

marketing mix   the combination of the four factors—product, price, place, and promotion—that communicates a marketing vision.

marketing plan   a statement of the marketing goals and objectives for a business and the intended strategies and tactics to attain them.

markup pricing   a cost-plus pricing strategy in which a predetermined percentage is applied to a product's cost to obtain its selling price.

master franchise   a specific type of franchise that allows individuals and organizations to buy the right to subfranchise within a delineated geographic territory.

maturity   the date at which a loan must be repaid, including when a bond must be redeemed by the issuer.

media buyer   an individual who purchases advertising time/space and negotiates pricing and scheduling details.

media planner   an individual who creates a media plan, including a detailed advertising schedule.

media schedule   spells out the media vehicles to be used, the volume of usage, and the timing.

media strategy   the identification of the media a business will make use of and the creative decisions involved.

meet-or-beat-the-competition pricing   constantly matching or undercutting the prices of the competition.

mentor   a trusted advisor with whom a person forms a developmental partnership through which information, insight, skills, and knowledge are shared to promote personal and/or professional growth.

merchant card services   financial systems that permit acceptance of major credit cards.

merger   the joining of two companies in order to share their respective strengths.

microenterprise   a firm with five or fewer employees, initial capitalization requirements of under $50,000, and the regular operational involvement of the owner.

mission   a concise communication of strategy, including a business definition and explanation of competitive advantage.

mission statement   a brief, written statement that informs customers and employees what an organization's goal is, and describes the strategy and tactics to meet it.

mobile social networking   the updating of social-network sites via mobile handsets.

net present value   the net amount an investment is worth discounted back to the present.

net profit   the remainder of revenues minus fixed and variable costs and taxes.

net worth (owner's equity)   the difference between assets and liabilities.

noncash expenses   adjustments to asset values not involving cash, such as depreciation.

nondisclosure agreement   a legal document enumerating the type of information that is to remain confidential.

not-for-profit organization   an entity formed with the intention of addressing social or other issues, with any profits going back into the organization to support its mission.

notary   a person who has been authorized by the state to witness the signing of documents.

offshoring   relocating company operations to foreign locations.

operating ratio   an expression of a value versus sales.

operational plan   the stated short-term methods for achieving tactical goals.

operations   a set of actions that produce goods and services.

opportunities to see (OTS)   the cumulative number of exposures in a given time period—usually four weeks.

opportunity cost   the value of what must be given up in order to obtain something else.

owner's equity (net worth)   the difference between assets and liabilities.

par   the face value of a bond (typically $1,000) or the stated value of a stock.

partnership   a business with two or more owners that make decisions for the business together and share the profits, losses, assets, and liabilities.

patent   an exclusive right, granted by the government, to produce, use, and sell an invention or process.

payback period   estimated time required to earn sufficient net cash flow to cover the start-up investment.

payroll tax   a deduction employers must make from their employees' pay and forward to the appropriate governmental entity.

penetration pricing   a pricing strategy that uses a low price during the early stages of a product's life cycle to gain market share.

performance appraisal   the formal process used to evaluate and support employees' work performance.

permit   an official document that gives a party the right to hold a specific event.

personal guarantee   the promise to pay issued by an individual.

personalized pricing   a dynamic pricing strategy in which the company charges a premium above the standard price for a product or service to certain customers, who will pay the extra cost.

philanthropy   a concern for human and social welfare that is expressed by giving money through charities and foundations.

piggybacking or co-branding   occurs when two franchises share locations and resources.

pilferage   theft of inventory.

pitch letter   correspondence designed to explain the story behind a press release and why it would be interesting and relevant to the media outlet's readers, listeners, or viewers.

pocket price   the portion of the total price that remains after all pricing factors are deducted.

policy loan   a loan made against an insurance policy with cash value.

political risk   the possibility of a country's political structure and policies impacting a foreign company transacting business in its geopolitical borders.

position description   the explanation of the knowledge, skills, and abilities of a job profile, as well as the position's reporting and working relationships, plus its goals and objectives.

positioning   distinguishing a product or service from similar products or services being offered to the same market.

premium   (regarding bonds) the amount above par for which a bond is trading in the market.

premium   the cost of insurance.

present value   what the future amount of an asset or other investment is worth at face value discounted back to the present.

press release   an announcement sent to the media to generate publicity that explains the "who, what, when, where, why, and how" of a story.

prestige pricing   the pricing strategy in which a firm sets high prices on its products or services to send a message of uniqueness or premium quality.

price   the amount a seller requires in exchange for the use or transference of ownership of a product or service.

price lining   the process of creating distinctive pricing levels.

primary research   is conducted directly on a subject or subjects.

principal   the amount of debt or loan before interest and fees are added.

process layout   functional arrangement that works well where there are common processes.

process management   the measurement, monitoring, and optimization of tasks.

product   something tangible that exists in nature or is made by people.

product advertising   is designed to create awareness, interest, purchasing behavior, and post-purchase satisfaction for specific products and services.

product and trade-name franchising   the licensing of the product or the production of the product and the use of the trademark, logo, or other identity of the franchise.

product layout   mass-production design appropriate for continuous fabrication processes.

product life cycle (PLC)   the four stages that a product or service goes through as it matures in the market—introduction, growth, maturity, and decline.

profit   amount of money remaining after all costs are deducted from the income of a business.

profit and loss statement (P&L)   an income statement.

profit margin (return on sales)   net income divided by sales (percentage).

promissory note   a loan document that is a written promise to pay a specific sum of money on or before a particular date.

promotions opportunity analysis   a process that includes research into target markets and the promotional strategies to reach them.

proof of market   an investigation that provides evidence of a market opportunity.

prospect   a person or organization that may be receptive to a sales pitch.

prototype   a model or pattern that serves as an example of how a product would look and operate if it were manufactured.

public domain   property rights available to the public rather than held by an individual.

public relations   community activities that are designed to enhance an organization's image.

publicity   free promotion.

quality   degrees of excellence; conformance to specifications or standards.

quick ratio   indicates adequacy of cash to cover current debt.

quotas   limits created by countries on the amounts of products that can be imported.

rating   the percentage of a company's target market exposed to a TV show or print ad.

reach   the number of components in a target audience (people, businesses, households) that will be exposed to the advertising during a given period.

recruitment   the act of finding and hiring employees.

Regional Free Trade Agreements (RFTAs)   Regional Trade Agreements that simplify commercial regulations and bring tariffs toward zero for member states.

Regional Trade Agreements (RTAs)   are designed to facilitate trade on a regional basis, generally including tariff cutting and trade regulations between signatory nations.

reorder point (ROP)   the level at which materials need to be ordered again.

replication strategy   a way for a business to obtain money by letting others copy its success formula for a fee.

retail   selling individual items to consumers.

return on investment (ROI)   the net profit of a business divided by its start-up investment (percentage).

return on sales (ROS)   net income divided by sales for a particular time period (percentage).

RFM analysis   the creation of a three-digit score for each customer based on recency, frequency, and monetary values.

risk tolerance   the amount of risk or threat of loss that an individual is willing to sustain.

royalties   fees paid to a licensor by a licensee based on the production or sales of a licensed product.

safety stock   the amount of inventory or raw materials or work-in-progress that is kept to guarantee service levels.

salary   fixed amount of money paid to an employee at regular intervals.

sales tax   an assessment levied by governments on purchases and collected by merchants.

secondary research   is carried out indirectly through existing resources.

security   an investment instrument representing ownership in an entity (stock) or debt (bond) held by an investor.

seed capital (start-up investment)   the one-time expense of opening a business.

self-employment tax   federal tax that business owners are assessed on wages paid to themselves.

selling space   the retail floor space available for actually selling to customers, excluding storage and warehousing, administrative, and utility areas.

service   intangible work that provides time, skills, or expertise in exchange for money.

service mark   a design that identifies and distinguishes the source of a service rather than a product.

setup cost   the expense of establishing a production run.

severance   pay that is continued for a limited time to an employee who has left a company.

share   a single unit of corporate stock.

signatory   an individual who signs a contract.

skimming price strategy   seeks to charge high prices during a product's introductory stage, to take early profits when the product is novel and has few competitors, and then to reduce prices to more competitive levels.

small claims court   a legal option for solving conflicts involving less than a certain sum of money.

social business   a company created to achieve a social objective while generating a modest profit to expand its reach, improve the product or service, and subsidize the social mission.

social entrepreneurship   the sale of products or services on a for-profit basis to benefit a social purpose.

sole proprietorship   a business owned by one person who has unlimited liability and unlimited rights to profits.

space percentage   the portion of the home used for business versus living space.

spam   unwanted Internet advertisements or e-mails.

span of control   the number of direct reports for a manager or supervisor.

statute of limitations   the time period in which legal action may be taken.

stealth marketing   undercover, or deceptive, marketing efforts that are intended to appear as if they happened naturally.

strategic plan   typically a three- to five-year overall design to achieve long-term growth, sales, and positioning goals for a business.

strategy   a plan for how an organization or individual plans to proceed with business operations and outperform that of its competitors.

supply chain management (SCM)   the management of sourcing, procuring, production, and logistics to go from raw materials to end customers across multiple intermediate steps.

sustainable   referring to a scenario in which current needs are met while preserving future resources.

SWOT analysis   consideration of the internal strengths and weaknesses of an organization and the external opportunities and threats which it may face.

tactical plan   a short-term (one year or less) implementation that has limited, specific objectives.

tactics   the specific ways in which a business carries out its strategy.

target market   groups defined by common factors such as demographics, psychographics, age, or geography that are of primary interest to a business.

tariff   tax or duty on goods and services imported into a country.

tax abatement   legal reduction in taxes.

tax credit   direct reduction of taxes.

tax evasion   the deliberate avoidance of an obligation to pay taxes; may lead to penalties or imprisonment.

tolerance   the range of acceptable variation in products from specifications.

tooling cost   the expense of creating the specialized equipment for manufacturing.

total quality management (TQM)   the quality-assurance methodology of striving for strategic advantage through quality.

trade intermediary   organization that serves as a contract distributor of products traded between countries.

trade mission   an international trip by government officials and businesspeople organized to promote exports or to attract investment.

trade-off   the act of giving up one thing for another.

trademark   any word, name, symbol, or device used by an organization to distinguish its product.

traffic generators   complementary businesses that attract customer traffic to the retailers' area.

uniform resource locator (URL)   a Web-page address.

unique selling proposition (USP)   the distinctive feature and benefit that sets a company apart from its competition.

unit of sale   the basic unit of the product or service sold by the business.

value pricing   "more for less" strategy that balances quality and price.

value-engineer   to reduce the cost in a product while maintaining quality standards.

variable costs   expenses that vary directly with changes in the production or sales volume.

variable pricing strategy   provides different prices for a single product or service.

venture capitalist   an investor or investment company whose specialty is financing new, high-potential entrepreneurial companies and second-stage companies.

venture philanthropy   a subset or segment of social entrepreneurship wherein financial and human capital is invested in not-for-profits by individuals and for-profit enterprises, with the intention of generating social rather than financial returns on their investments.

vertical integration   the process of going forward or backward on the idea-to-market continuum.

viral marketing   the process of promoting a brand, product, or service through an existing social network, where a message is passed from one individual to another—much as a virus spreads.

vision   a broader and more comprehensive perspective on an organization than its mission; built on the core values and belief systems of the organization.

visual control   inventory-management method in which an individual assesses the stock level on hand by visual inspection and reorders when the supply appears low.

voluntary exchange   a transaction between two parties who agree to trade money for a product or service.

wage   fixed payment per hour for work performed.

wealth   the value of assets owned versus the value of liabilities owed.

wholesale   buying in bulk from manufacturers and selling smaller quantities to retailers.

working capital   the value of current assets minus current liabilities.

Index

Abby, Katie, 642
Accel Partners, 463
Accounting
    definition of, 383
    differences between countries, 410
    methods, 386
    software, 384–385
Accounts payable, 444–445, 477
Accounts receivable, 259, 443–444
Accrual method, 386
ACE Capital, 185
ACE-Net, 476
Acquisition
    as exit strategy, 645, 646
    growth through, 79–81
    ownership through, 42
Active Capital, 476
Active listening, 596
Adecco, 602
Adjusted book value, 87
Adobe, 247
ADP (Automatic Data Processing) Inc., 602
Advertising, 275–296
    agencies, 276–277
    consumer-generated, 295–296
    cost of, 381
    definition of, 111, 271
    effective, 278–279
    expenditures, 276f, 278f
    franchise support for, 60
    Internet, 285f, 293–296
    measurement of, 284–285
    and media outlets, 277–279
    objectives of, 275–276
    versus promotion, 229
    types of, 277–296
    venues for, 290–291
Advisors, 33–34
Advisory boards/councils, 625
Affiliative leadership style, 620
Agarwal, Shradha, 227
Age Discrimination in Employment
    Act (ADEA), 599
Agency law, 510–511
Aging schedules, 443, 445
Ahluwalia, Jasbina, 513
Ain, Spencer, 463
Airbnb, 527–528
Alexander, Ben, 30
All rights, concept of, 516
Alliances and global markets, 321–322
Allis, Ryan, 653, 654
Amador, Brian, 186, 188
Amador, Rosemarie (Rosi) Straijer, 186,
    188, 189
Amador Bilingual Voice-Overs, 186, 188
Amazon.com, 161, 219, 220, 366–367
American Electrical, Inc., 214
American Military University, 200
Americans with Disabilities Act (ADA), 599
Anago Cleaning Systems, 652
Angel investors, 476

Answering services, 546–547
Anwar, Habib, 634, 635
Appendices, 695
Appendices, in business plans, 118
Apple, 162, 175, 469
Appointments, for sales calls, 348
Aravind Eye Care System (AECS), 373
Arbitration, 509
Area franchises, 58, 64
Armstrong, Ishmael, 93
ASEAN Free Trade Area (AFTA), 336
Ash, Mary Kay, 345
Asian Garden Mall, 97
Assets
    on the balance sheet, 402–406
    definition of, 115
    sale of, 88
    valuation of, 86
Attorneys, 507–508
Audits, 384, 452
Authoritative leadership style, 620
Avedis Zildjian Company Inc., 318
Avey, Linda, 241
Awards, for entrepreneurs, 701
AYZH Inc., 634–635
Azriel, Jay, 488

B corporations, 504
Baack, Donald, 272
Back of receipt marketing, 290
Background checks, 589
Bai, Zubaida, 634–635
Baker, Mari, 241
Balance sheet equation, 404
Balance sheets, 115, 402–408,
    411–414
Baldrige Award, 545–546
Balloon Distractions, Inc., 30
Bankruptcy, 511–513
Barnes & Noble, 219
Barriers to entry
    definition of, 169
    sources of, 100
Bauer, Dylan, 397
Beatrice Foods, 93–94
Behavioral interviews, 586
Benchmarking, 543, 544e, 602
Benefits, employee, 597
Berners-Lee, Tim, 546
Better Business Bureau (BBB), 83
Bezos, Jeff, 366
Big Green Egg, 185
Bill and Melinda Gates Foundation, 230
Billboards, 282–283
BizTech, 230
Black, Bruce, 43
Blakely, Sara, 154–157
Blank, Steve, 193
Blogosphere, 295
Blogs
    definition of, 295
    and prospective sales contacts, 348–349

BNI (Business Networks International), 364
Bo Med, 531
Bob's Discount Furniture, 384
Body Shop Foundation, 231
Body Shop International, The, 38,
    203–204, 231
Boilerplate language, 508
Bonds, 479–481
Book value, 86–87, 643
Books, as research sources, 195, 200
Books-A-Million, 219, 220
Bookstore industry, 219–220
Bootstrap financing, 478
Bottom line, 400
Brain-builders, 46
Brand
    building your, 192, 225–228
    focus on, 639
    recognition, 60
    spiraling, 294–295
Branson, Richard, 29–30, 157, 169, 249, 271
Breach of contract, 509
Breakeven point
    definition of, 116
    for marketing costs, 234–236
BRIC countries, 312
Bridgecreek Development, 97
Broadcast media, 279, 285f
Brochures, 286–287
Bronner, Michael, 231
Brouse, Mark, 642
Brown, Warren, 459–460
Budgets
    managing cash, 438–439, 440e
    setting promotional, 273–275
Bun Company, The, 526
Burda Media, 463
Burger King, 202
Burn rate, 446–447
Business brokers, 83
Business ideas
    feasibility analysis of, 97–102
    finding, 38
    qualities of good, 39
    SWOT analysis of, 40
Business Model Canvas, 102–105
Business models, 102
Business Plan Pro, 116
Business plans, 105–122
    components of, 107–118
    definition of, 105
    and financing, 472
    guidelines for, 118–119
    of Honest Tea, 127–153
    marketing plans as part of, 233
    outline for, 108, 689–695
    presentation of, 119–120
    purpose and function of, 106–107
    sample, 661–688
    software packages for, 106
    University Parent Plan, 661
    and venture competitions, 120–122

Business(es)
  buying into, 88
  defining your, 162, 173–174
  goals and objectives for, 44–45
  harvest strategies for, 641, 644–645
  legal structures of, 499–504, 505e
  purchasing existing, 79–81
  rules for successful, 46
  selling, 643
  start-up costs of, 373
Business-format franchising, 58, 59
Butterfield, Stewart, 463, 644
Buyer power, 101
Buying power, of money, 447
Buzz marketing, 289

C corporations, 451, 502
CakeLove, 459–460
Candler, Asa, 499
Capacity
  and credit, 473
  in global market expansion, 325–327
Caperton, Gat, 553
Capital
  definition of, 27
  as dimension of credit, 469–478
  finding, 107, 113, 117
  sources of, 469–478
  working, 435
Capital assets, 445
Capital budgeting, 445–446
Capital equipment, 386
Capitalism, 27
Casey, Jim, 311
Cash
  importance of, 433
  as liquid investment, 479
Cash accounting method, 386
Cash flow
  and accounts payable, 444–445
  and accounts receivables, 443
  and capital budgeting, 445–446
  cyclical nature of, 435–437
  forecasting, 438–439
  and inventory, 441–443
  management, 433–449
  rules to manage, 435
  sample assumptions, 441e
  and taxes, 450
Cash flow statements
  and budgeting, 439e–440e
  definition of, 114, 434
  reading, 438
  requirements in different countries for, 440
  sample, 439e
Cash flow valuation, 87
Cash receipts, 438
Cash reserve, 375–376
Catalogs, 292
Cause-related marketing, 237
Center-of-gravity method, 568, 569f
CEO Resources Inc., 592
Ceremonies, use of, 166
Certificates, 521
Chain of command, 593
Chambers of commerce, 195, 200
Channels (CN), for building a business, 103f, 104, 105f
Character, 472, 624e
Charge accounts, 473
Charles Schwab Corporation, 623
Checking accounts, 386
Checklists, for startup investment, 376e
Chilly Dilly's Ice Cream Company, 397, 488–491

Chinery-Hesse, Herman Kojo, 168
Civil Rights Act of 1964, 599
Clancy, Drew, 624
Clow, Kenneth, 272
Clustering, 563
Coaching leadership style, 620
Co-branding, 65
Coca-Cola Company, 499, 658
Code of conduct, 623
Code of ethics, 623
Code of ethics and business conduct, 623
Coercive leadership style, 620
Collateral, as dimension of credit, 472
Collection, of debts, 443
Collection-period ratio, 414
College Hunks Hauling Junk, 65
Collins, Jim, 584
Commercial law, 510
Commission
  as compensation, 29, 346, 620–621
  as variable cost, 378
Common Market of Eastern and Southern
  Africa (COMESA), 336
Common-sized analysis, 411
Communications
  with employees, 595
  in global market expansion, 325–327
  marketing, 271
Community development banks (CDBs), 474
Community development credit unions
  (CDCUs), 474
Community development financial institutions
  (CDFIs), 474–475
Community development loan funds (CDLFs), 474
Community development venture capital
  funds (CDVCs), 475
Community Supported Agriculture (CSA), 458
Company description, in business plans, 110
Compensation
  of employees, 588
  of entrepreneurs, 29, 620–621
  as function of human resources, 597
Competition
  business plan, 120–122
  direct and indirect, 167–168
  researching, 99–100, 170–171
Competitive advantage
  company culture as, 592–593
  evaluation of, 169–171
  factors of, 169
  identifying your, 167–169, 174
  and marketing materials, 286
Competitive analysis, 110–111
Competitive spending method, 274–275
Competitive strategy, 173
Complaints, customer, 355–356
Compound interest, 447–448
Computers, 519, 546
Conditions, as dimension of credit, 473
Confirming houses, 319e
Constraints, on franchisees, 62–64
Consumer credit, 256
ContextMedia, Inc., 227
Contingencies, 508
Continuous improvement, 545
Contracts, 67, 507–509
Contribution margin, 379, 382, 398
Conversation on Networking (Keenan
  and Smolinsky), 353
Conversion franchising, 65
Cooper, Aysha Treadwell, 73–74
Cooperative advertising fees, 60, 63
Copyright, 515, 517
Core competencies. *See* Competitive advantage

Core values, 163–164
Corporate governance, 625
Corporate social responsibility, 628–629, 657
Corporation for Enterprise Development
  (CFED), 36
Corporations
  definition of, 502
  tax issues for, 451
Cosmederm Technologies Inc., 323
Cost of goods sold (COGS), 175, 378, 398
Cost of services sold (COSS), 175, 378, 398
Cost per rating point (CPRP), 284–285
Cost per thousand (CPM), 284–285
Cost reduction, of overseas ventures, 315
Cost structure
  in building a business, 103f, 104, 105f
  compared to competition, 171
Cost/benefit analysis, 32–33
Cost-leadership strategy, 41–42
Cost-plus pricing, 249
Costs
  categories of, 386
  of exporting, 321e
  of franchises, 63–64
  operating, 379–383
  production, 540–541
  of purchasing existing business, 81, 82
  start-up, 113, 114, 373–378
Coupons, 292–293
Cover pages, of business plan, 108
Covey, Steven, 641, 642
Cramer, Chuck, 531
Cramer Products, Inc., 531
Creating a World without Poverty (Yunus), 36
Creative Entertainment Services, 289
Creativity
  respect for others, 43–44
  using your, 29, 38–39
Credit
  agencies, 259
  costs and benefits of, 255
  definition of, 444
  extending, 258–260
  five C's of, 472–473
  and pricing, 257–258
  regulations, 259
  types of, 255–257
  use of, by small firms, 467e
Credit history, 472–473
Credit reporting agency (CRA), 473
Credit reports, 474
Credit unions, 474
Creditors, 464
Critical costs, 378–379
Crowdfunding, 465, 466
Crowley, Dennis, 53–54
Cruz, Noel, 61
Culture
  company, 165–166, 592–593, 594e, 622–623
  definition of, 109
  in global market expansion, 328–329
Currency, 180
Current assets, 404
Current liabilities, 404
Current ratios, 411
Customer relationship management (CRM),
  356–360
Customer segments, 102, 103f, 104, 105f
Customer service
  complaints, 355
  CRM as part of, 356–360
  definition of, 354
  Positively Outrageous, 355
  word choices in, 356e

Customers
  buying process of, 201
  cost of losing, 354–355, 357
  determining needs of, 168–169
  and ethics, 627
  extending credit to, 258–260
  finding, 104
  focus on, 349
  fostering repeat, 354, 357
  identifying, 102
  researching your, 195, 197–203
  satisfaction of, 164–165

Data collection, 291
Data mining, 292
Data protection, 519
Database marketing, 291–292
Database searches, as secondary
    research source, 195
Databases, 360
Davis, Josh, 486
De Garis, Hugo, 46
De Luca, Fred, 57
Debt, collection of, 443
Debt financing. See also Loans
  advantages and disadvantages, 466–468
  on balance sheet, 405
  options, 467e
Debt ratio, 413, 702
Debt service, 473
Debt/equity exchange, 646
Debt-to-equity ratio, 413
Deductibles, 517–518
Deductions, tax, 384
Dees, Gregory, 35–36
Def Jam Records, 41, 215
Default, definition of, 468
Delivery, as competitive advantage, 169
Demand, pricing based on, 255
Deming, W. Edwards, 542, 545
Democratic leadership style, 620
Demographics, 198
Demonstrations, in-store marketing, 290
Depreciation, 381, 408
Design
  of facilities, 569
  of market research, 193
  of products, 540–541
Development plans, employee, 600
Differentiation strategy, 42
Direct foreign investments (DFI), 382
Direct labor, 176, 178
Direct mail, 292, 293f
Direct marketing, 111
Directories, 282
Disability insurance, 518
Disaster recovery plans, 519–520
Disbursements, 438
Discounts
  in bond trading, 481
  pricing, 260
Discrimination, 591, 627
Disney, Walt, 565
Disney International Program, 314
Disneyland Paris Resort, 565
Distribution, 532–533
Diversification, 638
Diversity, in the workforce, 602
Dividends, as form of self-payment, 29, 621
DMADV process, 544–545
Documentation, for franchises, 66–67
Dorf, Bob, 193
Dorsey, Jack, 273, 273f
Draper, Tim, 295–296

Drucker, Peter, 37
Duckett, Adam, 555–556
Duckett, Megan, 555–557
Due diligence, 84–86
Dumping, definition of, 328
Dun & Bradstreet (D&B), 464
Durant, William "Billy," 345, 346
Duties and trade agreements, 336

E-active marketing, 293–294
Earnings before interest and taxes (EBIT), 398
Earnings valuation, 87
Earn-out exit strategy, 646
Echeverri, José, 561
Echeverri Financial Services, 561
E-commerce, 293
Economic order quantity (EOQ), 535–536
Economic risk, 324
Economics, 26
Economics of one unit of sale (EOU)
  definition of, 175
  and profitability, 176–180, 373
  and total gross profit, 379–380
Economy, definition of, 26
Edutainment, definition of, 290
Efficiency
  in operations, 414
  ratios, 702
E-Harmony, 308
Elastic demand, 255
Electronic rights, 515–516
Electronic storefronts, 547
Elevator pitch, 120
E-mail
  marketing, 292
  and prospective sales contacts, 348–349
Embargoes, 328
Empact, 368–370
Empact Showcase, 369
Empact Summit, 369–370
Employee stock ownership plan (ESOP), 645
Employees
  communications with, 595–596
  compensation for, 588
  definition of, 25
  finding, 584–588
  hiring, 588–589, 591–592
  orientation of, 589
  performance management of, 599–601
  retention of, 598, 602
  termination of, 602–603
  training of, 598
  treatment of, 595
Enablemart, 607
Enron, 625
Entrepreneurs
  awards for, 701
  benefits versus costs of becoming, 31–32
  definition of, 25–26
  as leaders, 619–620
  resources for, 696–701
Entrepreneurship
  definitions of, 37
  and integrity, 626–627
  options for, 35–36
  rewards of, 28–30
  types of, 43–44
Environmental analysis, 110
Equal Employment Opportunity Commission
    (EEOC), 591e
Equal Pay Act of 1963, 599
Equipment, 112
Equity financing, 405, 468–469
Ethical dilemmas, 623, 627

Ethical relativism, 623
Ethics
  in business, 623–624
  corporate scandals involving, 625
  definition of, 622
  and social responsibility, 628–629
Etsy, Inc., 463
Euro Disney Resort, 565
European Free Trade Association (EFTA), 335
European Union (EU), 335
Evaluation
  of competitive advantage, 169–171
  of existing businesses, 83
  of locations, 564–569
EWCP (Working Capital Loan Program),
    332–333
Excess-funds method, 275
Executive searches, 592
Executive summary, in business plans, 108–109
Ex-Im Bank's Export Working Capital
    Guarantee program, 333
Ex-Im Bank's Loan Guarantee program, 334
Existing businesses
  benefits of buying, 79–81
  disadvantages of buying, 81–83
  reasons for selling, 85
Exit strategies, 117, 638e, 646–647, 694–695
Expenses
  fixed, 379–383
  noncash, 435
Export Express Loan program, 333
Export management company, 319e
Export Medium-Term Delegated Authority
    program, 334
Export trade company (ETC), 319e
Export-Import Bank, 333–334
Exporting businesses, 317–321
  advantages and disadvantages to, 318e
  business loan programs for, 332–333
  definition of, 317
  intermediaries' roles in, 319
  management issues for, 326e
  recognized, 320e
  types of service, 321e
Extreme Entrepreneurship Tour (EET),
    368–369, 370

Face value, 481
Facilities
  design and layout of, 569
  international, 323–324
  location of, 542, 573–574
Factoring, 444
Factor-rating method, 564–565
Fad products, 206f, 207
Fair Labor Standards Act, 599
Fair market value, 642
Fake, Caterina, 463, 644
Family businesses, 88–90, 637–638
Fanscape, 296
Farrah Gray Foundation, 306
Farrah Gray Publishing, 306
Feasibility analysis, 97–102
  definition of, 98
  financial, 101–102, 113–114
  market and industry, 98
  product and/or service, 98–99
  using economics of one unit of sale (EOU),
      174–180
Federal Trade Commission (FTC), 57, 59, 65
FedEx, 559
Ferris, Matt, 43
Ferry, Richard, 602
Feuerstein, Aaron, 619

Feuerstein, Henry, 619
Fields, Debbi, 26, 45
Financial analysis, business plan outline for, 693–694
Financial ratio analysis. *See* Ratio analysis
Financial records, 383–386
Financial statements. *See* Balance sheets; Cash flow statements; Income statements
Financing
    of accounts receivables, 444
    and balance sheets, 405–406
    debt, 405, 466–468
    definition of, 463
    equity, 468
    for global market expansion, 331–333
    methods of, 463–464
    potential sources of, 472–478
    types of, 464–465
Fiscal year, 402
Five forces model, 99–101
Five Ps, of marketing, 223–232, 233
Fixed costs, 234, 378, 386
Fixed operating costs, 379–383, 398
Fixed-position layouts, 570
Flickr, 644
Float, definition of, 477
Focus
    versus diversification, 638
    importance of, 224–225
Focus groups, 194, 198
Focus strategy, 42
Follow-the-leader pricing, 250
Ford, Henry, 378, 476
Ford Motor Company, 225–226
Foreign exchange (FX) rate, 180, 325, 382
Forgatch, Greg, 308
Forster, Paul, 597
Foundations, 229, 232
Four Ps, of marketing, 111, 223–232
Foursquare, 53–55
Franchise agreements, 67, 641
Franchise brokers, 68–69
Franchise Disclosure Document (FDD), 66
Franchise Registry, 58, 60
Franchisees, 57
Franchises
    advertising support for, 277
    benefits of, 59–62
    choosing, 67–69
    definition of, 57
    disadvantages of, 62–64
    information sources on, 68e
    investing in, 58
    as path to ownership, 42
    rules and regulations governing, 65–67
    types of, 57–58, 65
Franchising
    definition of, 57
    to grow a business, 638–641
    industry structure, 64–65
    international, 62, 69–70, 323
    standards, 64
Franchisors, 57, 639–640
Fraud, 519
Free trade, 27
Free-enterprise system, 26–27
Freelancers, for advertising campaigns, 276–277
Freemium pricing, 249, 253
Frequency, of media, 278
Friedman, Nick, 65
FTC. *See* Federal Trade Commission
Future earnings method, 87, 643
Future value, 447–448

Gambetta, Stephanie Pietsch, 75
GameShowPlacements.com, 289
Gantt charts, 117, 621
Garten, Jeffrey E., 312
Gat Creek Furniture, 553
Gates, Bill, 28, 168, 230
Gazelles, 44
Gelato Fiasco, The, 486–487
General Agreement on Tariffs and Trade (GATT), 27
General Motors, 256
Gentle Rest Slumber, LLC, 422
Geographic information systems (GIS), 565–566
Gerber, Scott, 439
Geron, Tomio, 54
Geschke, Chuck, 247
Gifts, 465
Gillette, King C., 345, 434
Gillings, Dennis, 401
Ginsberg, Bruce, 391
Girard, Joe, 348
Global markets
    and alliances, 321–322
    availability of resources in, 314
    challenges in, 324–329
    cost reduction benefits in, 316
    entrance strategies to, 316–324
    financing options for entering, 331–334
    influence of trade agreements on, 334–336
    location-specific advantages, 315–316
    quality standards in, 316
    reasons to enter, 311–312
    types of support for, 329–330
Goals, implementation of, 117
Goldman, Laurie Ann, 156
Goldman, Seth, 655, 657–658
Goleman, Daniel, 620
Gonzalez, Maritza, 61
Good to Great (Collins), 584
Goodman, John, 358
Goodwill, concept of, 230
GoPayment, 256
Grameen Bank, 629
Grants, 465
Grapevine, 596
Gray, Farrah, 306
Green entrepreneurship, 36
Griff, Merle, 73
Gross, T. Scott, 355
Gross profit
    calculating, 176e, 379
    definition of, 175, 382
    as part of income statement, 398
Gross ratings points (GRP), 279
Growth strategies, 79–81, 637–638
Guerilla marketing, 289

Hall, Dawn, 185
Hall, Terry, 185
Happy Belly Curbside Kitchen, 185
Harassment, 599, 627
Harley-Davidson Motorcycles, 284
Harold Import Company (HIC), 265–266
Harrington, Cordia, 526
Harvesting strategies, 638e, 641, 644–645
Hay, Louise, 584
Heating and cooling costs, 382
Hewlett-Packard, 161
Hirshberg, Gary, 658
Historical earnings, 87
Holter, Adam, 458
Holter, Ron, 457–458
Holterholm Farms, 457–458

Home Depot, 202
Home-based businesses, 572–573
Honest Tea, 127–153, 655–660
Horseneck Wines and Liquors, 82
Houghton, Aaron, 653
Hoverter, Haley, 516
Hsieh, Tony, 160f, 161
Human resources, 596–603
    benefits, 597
    compensation and payroll function, 597
    and compliance, 598–599
    education and development, 598
    role in organizational development, 597–598
    strategies in, 602
Human-capital resources, in global market expansion, 314–316, 325–326
Hyperlinks, 546
Hypertext, 546

iContact, 653
Idea-to-product process, 537
Image and choice of location, 564
Imagination, use of, 39
Immigration Reform and Control Act of 1986 (IRCA), 599
Importing businesses, 316–317
    business loan programs for, 333
    laws and regulatory barriers to, 327
Impressions, personal, 346
Incentives, 260
Income statements, 398–401
    and cash flow, 433–434
    definition of, 116
    ratio analysis of, 408–411
Income taxes, 450
Indeed.com, 597
Index Ventures, 463
InDinero Inc., 433
Industry analysis, 99–101, 110
Industry associations, 195
Industry research, 199–200
Inelastic demand, 255
Inflation and investment, 448
Infomercials, 293
Information resources
    on businesses for sale, 83–84
    for finding foreign partners, 322
    on franchises, 68
    for global market expansion, 329–331
    on importing and exporting, 315, 317, 318
Initial public offering (IPO), 117, 645
In-kind donations, 628
In-N-Out Burger, 533
Installment credit, 257
Institutional advertising, 277
In-store marketing, 290
Insurance
    definition of, 517
    types of, 517–518
Insurance companies, 477, 519–520
Intangible assets, 513–517
Integrity, 626–628
Intellectual property, 43, 313, 513–517
Interactive marketing, 294
International Business Brokers Association, Inc., 83
International Franchise Association, 64, 640–641
International Franchising Opportunities, 62
International Organization of Standardization (ISO), 544
International outsourcing, 314
International Trade Loan program, 333

Internet
    advertising, 285f, 293–296
    for business plan promotion, 106–107
    credit services on, 256
    due diligence using, 85
    franchises, 65
    research resources, 84e
Intersections Match, 513
Interview guides, 586
Interviews
    for industry research, 199
    planning, 589–590, 591e
    as primary research method, 193
    sample questions for, 587e
    topics for, 586e
Inventory
    and cash flow, 441–443
    costs, 379–380
    definition of, 386
    methods for managing, 534–536
Inventory control, 112, 443
Inventory turnover ratio, 414
Investment
    as category of cost, 386
    definition of, 409
    securities, 479
    and value of money, 447–449
Investors, 647
Invoices, 385
Isenberg, Daniel, 37
ISO 9000, 544

Jackson, Bo, 531
Jackson, Joe, 168
JackThreads, 113
Jagemann, Paula, 637
Jan-Pro, 64
Jao, Frank, 97
Job offer letters, 588–589
Job profiles, 585
Job shops, 538–539
Jobs, Steve, 161, 162, 174, 224, 469
Just-in-time manufacturing (JIT), 539–540

Kahan, Rony, 597
Kalin, Robert, 463
Kateman, Paul, 391
Kaufman, Bob, 384
Kawasaki, Guy, 247
Keenan, Kay, 353
Key activities (KA), 103f, 104, 105f
Key resources (KR), 103f, 104, 105f
Keystone pricing, 253
Khan, Salman, 578
Khan Academy, 578
Kiosks, 288
Kitchen Arts & Letters, Inc., 217–219
Kiva, 475
Kopp, Wendy, 231
Korn, Lester, 602
Korn/Ferry International, 602
Krispy Kreme Doughnuts, 93–95
Kroc, Ray, 191, 345, 640
Kumon Math and Reading Centers, 61

Labor
    cost of direct, 176, 178
    and economics of one unit of sale (EOU),
        178–180
    laws, 598–599
Lacy, Sarah, 54
Lam, Wing, 75
Laub, Harold, 265
Lauder, Estée, 413

Lavanchy, Henri-Ferdinand, 602
Leaders, definition of, 619
Leadership
    ethical, 622–623
    styles of, 619–620
    and time management, 621–622
Lean Launch Pad, 192
Leasehold improvements, 569
Lee, Ed, 75
Lee, Jimmie, 492–495
Lee, Mingo, 75
Lee's Ice Cream, 492–495
Legal issues, in global market expansion,
    327–328
Leggett and Platt, 277
Lending institutions, 474
Lentz, Bob, 653
Lerner, Ben, 113
Lerner, Sandy, 52
Letters of agreement, 509
Letters of credit, 332
Leveraged, definition of, 468
Levinson, Jay Conrad, 228, 289
Liabilities, 115, 402, 404–405, 406
Licenses, 521
Licensing
    brand, 639
    definition of, 638
    international, 322–323
    technology, 43
Lifestyle businesses, 44
Lifestyle marketing, 289–290
Lifetime value, 291
Limited liabilities company (LLC), 451, 504
Limited partnerships, 451, 501
Lindahl, Sheena, 368–370
Line extension, 639
Line organization, 593
Line-and-staff organization, 593
Liquidation, 87, 512, 641
Liquidity, 411, 702
Loans
    as category of cost, 386
    for global market expansion, 332–334
    types of financial institutions for, 474
Location
    breakeven analysis, 568
    in business plan description, 112
    choosing, 560
    as competitive advantage, 169
    evaluation methods for, 564–569
    of facilities, 542, 573–574
    importance of, 559
    selling, 111
Logos, 226–227
Long-term assets, 404
Long-term liabilities, 404
Love Café, 459–460
Luggage Concierge, 340
Lurking, definition of, 349

Magazines, 282
Maguire, Chris, 463
Mah, Jessica, 433
Mainstream businesses, 44–45
Malcolm Baldrige Award, 545–546
Malden Mills Industries Inc., 619, 637–638
Malia Mills Swimwear, 243–244
Mall carts, 288
Management buyout (MBO), 644
Management team, in business plan
    description, 112
Managers, 583–584
Manufacturing, definition of, 162

Manufacturing businesses, 538–541
    economics of one unit of sale (EOU) for, 177
    facility considerations for, 569
    location considerations for, 561–562
    pricing challenges for, 258
    pricing techniques for, 251–252
    types of layouts for, 570, 571f
    unit of sale for, 175
MapPoint, 566
Market analysis
    for global market expansion, 329–330
    in marketing plans, 233
    in product life cycle, 206
    by segmentation, 204–205
Market clearing prices, 255
Market research, 193–201
    and customer relationship
        management, 357
    definition of, 195
    designing, 193
    for global market expansion, 329–330
    goals of, 197
    methods of, 197–200
    selling as source of, 346
Market segments
    definition of, 203
    types of, 204–205
Marketable securities, 412
Market-based value method, 643
Marketing
    alternative types of, 289–290
    cause-related, 230
    communications, 271, 292–293
    cost of, 234
    and customer relationship management, 357
    definition of, 192
    direct response, 291
    e-active, 293–294
    global, 311
    in global market expansion, 327
    interactive, 294
    materials, 286
    piggyback, 319e
    viral, 296
Marketing mix, 111, 223–228
Marketing plans, 111, 691–692
    components of, 233e
    development of, 208–209, 232–234
Markets
    and competitive advantage, 169
    definition of, 161, 192
    emerging, 312, 313f
    positioning in, 207–208, 542
    saturation of, 207
Markkula, Mike, 162, 175
Markup pricing, 249, 251, 252
Marn, Michael, 260
Master franchises, 58, 64
Maturity, definition of, 481
McAleer, Joseph A., Sr., 94
McCormick, Tom, 214
McDonald's, 191, 201–202, 640
McMartin, Kellen, 634, 635
Media buyers, 279
Media outlets, for advertising, 277, 278–279
Media planners, 279
Media schedule, 278
Media strategy, 278
Meenan, Sean, 463
Meet-or-beat-the-competition pricing, 249
Mentors, 33
Mercedes-Benz, 223
Merchant card services, 256
Mercosur (Southern Common Market), 335

Mergers
    definition of, 645
    as exit strategy, 645, 646
Microenterprises, 44
Microsoft, 230
Microsoft MapPoint, 566
MIDA Food Distributors, Inc., 341–342
MIDA Trade Ventures Inc., 341–342
Milestones, 117
Mills, Malia, 243–244
Minority Enterprise Small Business Investment
    Companies (MESBICs), 477
Minority-owned businesses, 38, 202
Misner, Ivan, 364
Mission, of a business, 109, 163
Mission statements, 109, 164–165
Mobile social networking, 295
MooBella LLC, 391
Moulton, Dennis, 607
Multiple-unit franchises, 58
MusicAmador Productions, 186, 187
Mycoskie, Blake, 226

Naked Communications, 286
Nalebuff, Barry, 655, 658
Nanda, Gauri, 314
National Foundation for Teaching
    Entrepreneurship (NFTE), 230
Navigenics, 241
Negotiation
    of business purchase, 88
    of payment terms, 444–445
Net loss, 398
Net present value (NPV), 377, 641–642
Net profit, 382, 398
Net worth, 115, 402
Network for Teaching Entrepreneurship
    (NFTE), 230
Networking
    concept of, 478–479
    to find businesses for sale, 84e
    to grow a business, 47, 298
    international, 331
    tips for successful, 353
New Markets Venture Capital Companies
    (NMVCCs), 477
New Venture Creation (Timmons), 25–26, 169
Newspapers, 281
Newton, David, 647
Nike, 192
Nine Dragons Paper (Holdings) Ltd., 541
Ning, 253
Nomes, Christopher, 53
Noncash expenses, 435
Nondisclosure agreements, 85
Nonprofit corporations. See Not-for-profit
    organizations
North American Free Trade Agreement
    (NAFTA), 27, 335
North American Industry Classification
    System (NAICS), 199
Notary, 501
Not-for-profit organizations, 229, 231, 504,
    506, 695

Objective and task method, 275
Observation, as research method, 194, 199
Offers
    competitive, 170
    defining, 162
Offshoring, 314
Onassis, Aristotle, 345
O'Neal, Sean, 422
ONLC Training Centers, 613–616

Online advertising, 294
Online searches, 194–195
Operating costs, 379–382
Operating manuals, franchise, 61
Operating ratio, 411
Operational plans, 583, 584
Operations
    in business plans, 112
    definition of, 532
    importance of, 531–532
Opportunities
    identification of, 37–40, 166–167
    internal and external, 40–41
    and investment, 449
    promotional, 272–273
    qualities of good, 39
    roots of, 40
    SWOT analysis of, 40
Opportunities to see (OTS), 279
Opportunity costs, 33
Oregon Mattress Company, 89
Organic Valley, 458
Organizational charts, 112, 595f
Organizational culture, 165–166, 592–593, 594e,
    622–623
Organizational structure, 593–594, 597
Orientation, of new employees, 589
Osterwalder, Alexander, 102
Outdoor advertising, 282–283, 285f
Owner's equity, 115, 402
Ownership, 29, 42–43

Pacesetting leadership style, 620
Palic, Jim, 613
Pan Shiyi, 163
Panera Bread, 64
Par, definition of, 481
Partnerships
    advantages and disadvantages of, 501–502
    definition of, 501
    foreign, 322
    key, in building a business, 103f, 104, 105f
    tax issues for, 451
Patents, 516–517
Payback period, 376–377
PayPal, 256
Pay-per-click, 294
Payroll service, as function of human
    resources, 597
Payroll tax, 598–599
PCI (Publishing Concepts Inc.), 624
Pemberton, John Stith, 499
Penalties, for franchise non-compliance, 64
Penetration pricing, 249
Percentage of sales method, 274
Perception, owning a, 201–202
Performance appraisals, 599
Permits, 521
Personal guarantees, 473
Personalized pricing, 250
Petty, William, 641
Philanthropy, 229–232
Pietsch, Mike, 75
Piggybacking, 65, 319e
Pigman, Reed, Jr., 267–268
Pigneur, Yves, 102
Pilferage, 442
Pitch letters, 297
P'Kolino, 118
Place, as part of marketing mix, 111, 224,
    228–229
Planning, types of, 583–584
Pocket price, 260
Point-of-purchase promotion, 290

Policy loans, 477
Political risk, 325
Poore, Christopher, 65
Portable MBA in Entrepreneurship, The, 464
Porter, Michael, 41–42, 99, 100–101
Portland Freelancers' Café (fictional business),
    423–431
Position descriptions, 585
Positioning, 207–208, 564
Positively Outrageous Service (POS), 355
Povlitz, David R., 652
Premium
    bond trading, 481
    insurance, 517
Present value, 447, 448–450
Press releases, 297–298, 299f
Prestige pricing, 249
Price
    adjustments to, 260–261
    as competitive advantage, 169
    definition of, 247
    as part of marketing mix, 223, 228
    and quality, 248
    sensitivity to, 250
Price lining, 250
Pricing
    and credit, 257–258
    steps to better, 248e
    strategies, 247–250
Primary research, 193–194
Principal, definition of, 466
Print media advertising, 280–282
Process layouts, 570
Process management, 544
Product advertising, 277
Product and trade-name franchising, 58
Product businesses, types of, 162
Product life cycles (PLCs), 206–207, 312–313
    as part of marketing mix, 111
Product placement, 289
Production
    versus buying, 541
    defining your, 162
    distribution chain, 532–533
    just-in-time manufacturing and, 540
Products
    and competitive advantage, 170
    creating, 224
    definition of, 25, 224
    designing, 540–541
    features versus benefits, 202
    layouts for, 570
    lifecycle of, 206–207, 312–313
    as part of marketing mix, 111, 223, 224–228
    positioning, 207–208
Product-uniqueness strategy, 41
Professional associations, for franchises, 60–61
Professional businesses, 563–564, 570
Professional corporation (PC), 503–504
Profit. See also Gross profit
    versus cash, 434
    definition of, 45
    and income statements, 398
    and quality, 542
Profit and loss statements (P&L), 116, 169
Profit margin, 410–411
Profitability, calculating, 176–180, 702
Projections, 113
Promissory notes, 466–467
Promotional support, in franchising, 60
Promotion(s)
    budgeting for, 273–275
    methods of, 229
    as part of integrated marketing, 271

as part of marketing mix, 111, 224, 229
planning, 272–273
sales, 286
Promotions opportunity analysis, 272–273
Proof of market, 110
Prospects, sales call, 349
Prototypes, 98, 374, 539, 540
Public benefit corporations, 504
Public domain, 516
Public relations, 111, 296, 298, 300
Public speaking, 300
Publicity, 111, 229, 271, 296–300
Publicly traded companies, 401
Purchasing
    plans, 536
    power, 60
    versus production, 541
    restraints, 62

Quality
    as competitive advantage, 169
    concept of, 542
    methods to insure, 542–546
    and price, 248
    principles for improvement of, 544
Quick ratio, 411–412
Quigg, Vincent, 348
Quintiles Transnational Corporation, 401
Quotas, 327

Rackham, Neil, 351
Radio advertising, 280, 285f
Rainert, Alex, 53
Rating, 284
Ratio analysis, 116–117, 408–414
Ratios
    debt, 413
    formulas for, 702
    operating-efficiency, 414
    quick and current, 411–413
    use of, by investors, 405–406
Reach, of advertising, 278
Readiness assessment, 330
Real estate, 479
Receipts
    cash, 438
    for record keeping, 385
Receivable turnover ratio, 414
Record keeping, 347, 383–386, 451–452
Recruitment, 584, 592
Regional Free Trade Agreement (RFTA), 335
Regional Trade Agreement (RTA), 335
Regulations
    and compliance, 627–628
    in global market expansion, 327–328,
        334–336
Relativism, ethical, concept of, 623
Rent What? Inc., 557
Reorder points (ROPs), 534–535
Reorganization, 511–513
Replacement value, 87
Replication strategy, 639
Research
    industry, 199–200
    methods of, 193–195, 197–199
    presentation, in business plan, 109
    reports, 198
    types of, 193
Resnick, Linda, 592
Resources, access to international, 314
Retail businesses
    definition of, 162
    economics of one unit of sale (EOU), 177
    facility considerations for, 569–570

location considerations for, 562–563
pricing techniques for, 252–253
types of layouts for, 570, 572
unit of sale for, 175
Retention, 602
Return on investment (ROI), 409–410
Return on sales (ROS), 410–411
Revenue
    definition of, 386
    as part of income statement, 398
    streams, 103f, 104, 105f
RFM analysis, 291
Rich, Adam, 113
Rick, Ronald, III, 65
Ries, Al, 225, 639
Risk
    assessment of, in business plan, 116
    in global market expansion,
        324–325
    and investment, 449
    management, 517
    of purchasing existing business, 80–81
    tolerance, 465
Risk Management Association (RMA) Annual
    Statement Studies, 116
Rivalry, among competitors, 99–100
Robinson, Frank, 499
Rockefeller, John D., 385
Rockney, Merton, 573
Roddick, Anita, 38, 203, 231, 231f
Rogers, Theresa, 82
Rogge, Thomas, 531
Rosan, Arnon, 324
Rosiello, Robert, 260
Ross, Jason, 113
Royalties, 61, 63, 322
Rubin, Rick, 41, 46, 215
Rudman, Rick, 653
Rudolph, Plumie, 93
Rudolph, Vernon, 93
Rural Business Investment Companies
    (RBICs), 477
Rush Communications, 215, 216
Ryan, Claude, 311

S corporations, 451, 503
Safety stock levels, 534–535
Salary, as form of self-payment, 29, 621
Sales
    international, 180
    repeat, 354
Sales calls, 348–352
    analyzing, 352
    finding prospects for, 348–349
    reviewing, 351–352
    steps of, 350–351
    successful behaviors during, 351
Sales promotions, 287
Sales tax, 450, 451
Same-size analysis, 411
Samples, 290
SAP, 358
SARAH Adult Day Service, Inc., 73
Sarah Blakely Foundation, 157
SarahCare of Snellville, 73–74
Say, Jean-Baptiste, 26
Schachter, Joshua, 463
Scheibel, Arnold, 46
Schneider, J. B., 118
Schoppik, Haim, 463
Schumpeter, Joseph, 37
Schupp, Sara, 345
Schwab, Charles "Chuck," 623
Sculley, John, 469

Secondary research
    definition of, 193
    methods of, 194–195
Security, 481
Seed capital, 374
Segmentation methods, for markets, 204–205
Selection, as competitive advantage, 169
Self-employment tax, 450
Selling
    essence of, 346
    as market research, 346
    personal skills for, 345
    principles of, 346–348
    teaching as essence of, 346
Selling space, 563
Selvadurai, Naveen, 53–55
Series limited liabilities company (SLLC), 504
Service
    as competitive advantage, 169
    definition of, 25, 224
    as part of marketing mix, 111
Service businesses
    economics of one unit of sale (EOU), 177
    facility considerations for, 570
    location considerations for, 563–564
    pricing techniques for, 254
    unit of sale for, 175
Service marks, 513–514
Setup costs, 539
Severance, 603
Sew What? Inc., 555–557
Shah, Rishi, 227
Shares, 75–76
Shaw, Clarke, 642
Shaw, Noel Pietsch, 75–76
Shelf placement promotion, 290
Shipping and handling charges, 378
Signatories, 509
Signature Systems Group, 324
Simmons, Michael, 368, 369, 370
Simmons, Russell, 41, 46, 215–216
Site selection, 542, 564–565. See also
    Facilities; Location
Situation analysis, 233
Six Sigma, 544–545
Sizzle It!, 439
Skimming prices strategy, 249
Sloan, Alfred, 256
Small Business Administration (SBA), 332–333,
    358–359, 477
Small Business Investment Companies
    (SBICs), 477
Small businesses
    definition of, 28
    failure rate of, 464
    reasons to start, 30–31
Small claims court, 509
Small Parts Manufacturing Company, Inc., 573
Smith, Frederick W., 559
Smith, Kristen, 296
Smolinsky, Steven, 353
Snyder, Harry and Esther, 533
Social businesses, 36
Social entrepreneurships, 28, 35, 628
Social media, 370
Social networks
    online and mobile, 295
    and prospective sales contacts, 348–349
SOFTtribe, 168
Software
    accounting, 384–385
    for customer relationship management,
        359–360
    industry-specific, 547

SOHO China, 163
Sol y Canto, 186–189
Sole proprietorships, 451, 499–501
Soliman, Omar, 65
Southern Common Market (Mercosur), 335
Space percentage, in home-based businesses, 572–573
Spam, definition of, 349
Span of control, 593
Spanx, 154–157
Speakman Company, 315, 316
Special events, 298
Sponsorships, 298
Square, 256
Standards, franchising, 64
Star Alliance, 321–322
Startup Owner's Manual, The (Blank and Dorf), 193
Start-ups
    existing business, 80
    in foreign countries, 382
    franchise, 59–60
Statistics, 198–199
Statute of limitations, 509
Stealth marketing, 295
Stock exchanges, 479–480
Stocks, 479–480
Stone, Biz, 273
Stone, W. Clement, 345
Storage, inventory, 441
Strategic plans, 583
Strategy
    definition of, 41, 174
    establishment of, 40–41
    versus tactics, 174
Strengths, of a business idea, 40
Substitutes, threat of, 100
SUBWAY, 57
Success
    definitions of, 31–32
    and market research, 192
    records of franchises, 62
Suh, Andy, 433
Sumutka, Andrew, 488
Suppliers
    finding, 534
    management of, 532–533
    power of, 100–101
    selection of, 537
Supply chain management (SCM), 533–537
Surveys, 193–194, 197–198
Sustainability, importance of, 167, 173, 629
Sweet dis(Solve), 516
Swinmurn, Nick, 161
SWOT analysis, 40
Sydney, Robin, 194
Szaky, Tom, 24f, 25, 109

Table of contents, in business plan, 108
Tactical plans, 583, 584
Tactics, 174
Taj Mahal, Atlantic City, NJ, 442
Tanco, Lourdes "Chingling," 341
Tangible assets, 517
Target markets, 110, 162, 272
Tariffs, 327, 336
Taub, Henry, 602
Tax abatements, 465
Tax credits, 465
Tax evasion, 625, 627
Tax returns, 450–451
Taxes, 450–452
    and legal structure, 451
    as part of income statement, 398

Teach for America, 231
Teaching, as essence of selling, 346
Teams, 46–47, 583
Technology
    and customer relationship management, 359–360
    in global market expansion, 313–314
    keeping up with, 37
    licensing, 43
    and sales calls, 352–353
    using, 546–547
Tech-World, 348
Telemarketing, 293
Telephone surveys, 193–194
Telephones, 546–547
Television advertising, 279–280, 285f, 293
Tennessee Bun Company, 526
Termination, of franchises, 64
Terms
    of payment, 444–445
    of sale, 88
TerraCycle, Inc., 25, 36, 109
Texas Jet, 267–268
Thomas Register of American Manufacturers, 374, 540
Thompson, J. Randall (Randy), 84
ThompsonGas, 84
Threats, to a business idea, 40
Time management, 621–622
Timmons, Jeffry A., 25–26, 39, 169
Timmons Model, 25–26, 169
Title VII of Civil Rights Act of 1964, 599
Tolerance, 538
TOMS Shoes, 226
Tooling costs, 539
Torres, Lynsi, 533
Tostenrude, Nick, 607
Total gross profit. *See* Gross profit
Total quality management (TQM), 545
Toyota, 249
Tracking, as research method, 194, 200
Tracy, Brian, 352
Trade agreements, 334–336
Trade associations, 200
Trade barriers, 27
Trade credit, 256, 257, 477
Trade intermediaries, 319, 319e
Trade leads, 330–331
Trade missions, 319
Trade organizations, 277
Trade show exhibits, 288
Trademarks, 227, 513–514
Trade-offs, 45
Traffic generators, 563
Training
    of employees, 598
    franchise, 61
Tropeano, Bruno, 486
Trump, Donald, 442, 468
TuitionBids.com, 296
Turco-Rivas, Antonio, 118
Turnaround. *See* Delivery
23andMe, 241–242
Twitter, 273f
Tyco, 625

Uniform Commercial Code (UCC), 510
Uniform resource locators (URLs), 546
Union Square Ventures, 463
Unique selling proposition (USP), 170–171, 271
Unit of sale, 175, 176e, 178
University Parent Media, 345, 661–688
Upromise, 231
UPS (United Parcel Service), 311

Urban Decay, 52
U.S. Census Bureau, 566
U.S. Department of Agriculture (USDA), 477

Valuation
    of existing businesses, 86–87, 642–643
    methods of, 643
Value
    added, 26
    estimating, 377–378
    propositions, 103, 105f
Value pricing strategy, 249
Value-engineering, of products, 539
Variable costs, 378, 386, 398
Variable pricing strategy, 250
Vendor financing, 477
Vendors, selection of, 536–537
Venkataswamy, Govindappa, 373
Venture capital, 478
Venture capitalists, 475–476
Venture philanthropy, 36
Vertical integration, 541
Video tapes, 230
Viral marketing, 296
Virgin Atlantic Airways, 249
Virgin Group, 30, 169, 271
Vision
    for a business, 163
    definition of, 109
    statements, 165
VISTA Staffing Solutions, 642
Vistaprint, 646
Visual control, of inventory, 534
Visualization, 349
Vocus, 653
Voice mail, 546–547
Volume sales, 179–180
Voluntary exchange, definition of, 27
Volunteerism, 230

Wages, as form of self-payment, 29, 621
Wahoo's Fish Tacos, 75–77
Walgreen, Charles R., Sr., 79
Walgreen's, 79
Walker, C. J., 583, 628
Walker, David, 89
Walker, Tom, 89
Wal-Mart, 228
Warnock, John, 247
Warren, Neil Clark, 308
Watson, Thomas, 161
Waxman, Nach, 217–219
Weaknesses, of a business idea, 40
Wealth, 409, 643
Web-based businesses, 228, 573–574
Websites
    for Community Development Financial
        Institution Resources, 475
    competitors, 195, 200
    crowdfunder, 466
    for finding manufacturers and job shops, 540
    importance of company, 547
    for international resources, 315
    retail, 228
    as secondary research source, 194–195
Wenger, Albert, 463
White, Damon, 393–395
Whole business sale, 88
Wholesale businesses, 229
    definition of, 162
    economics of one unit of sale (EOU), 177
    location considerations for, 562
    pricing techniques for, 252
    unit of sale for, 175

Williams, Evan, 273
Williamson, Andy, 613, 616
Winfrey, Oprah, 225, 225f
Wojcicki, Anne, 241
Women-owned businesses, 38, 202
Word choices, in customer service, 356e
Word-of-mouth advertising, 289
Workers' compensation, 518
Working capital, 435
Working Capital Loan Program (EWCP), 332–333

Working conditions, for entrepreneurs, 29
Work-made-for-hire, 516
World Franchising, 62
World Trade Organization, 27
Wozniak, Steve, 161–162, 174, 224, 469
Write-offs, 384
Written communications, 596
Written surveys, as research method, 194
WuXi AppTec Company, Ltd., 314

Yunus, Mohammad, 36, 629

Zappos.com, 161
Zhang Xin, 163
Zhang Yin, 541
Zildjian, Avedis, 318
Zomnir, Wende, 52
Zoning regulations, 520–521
Zorbitz, Inc., 194